A Tidy Faith

A Tidy Faith

Systematic Theology
from a Reformed Baptist Perspective

JONATHAN F. BAYES

RESOURCE *Publications* · Eugene, Oregon

A TIDY FAITH
Systematic Theology from a Reformed Baptist Perspective

Resource Publications
An Imprint of Wipf and Stock Publishers
199 W. 8th Ave., Suite 3
Eugene, OR 97401

www.wipfandstock.com

PAPERBACK ISBN: 979-8-3852-2762-4
HARDCOVER ISBN: 979-8-3852-2763-1
EBOOK ISBN: 979-8-3852-2764-8
VERSION NUMBER 08/26/24

The first five chapters of this book are adapted from my earlier work, *Systematics for God's Glory*, published in 2012 by Carey Printing Press. I am grateful to be able to include the substance of those chapters, albeit with various modifications.

Contents

Contents

Introduction

SEVERAL FRIENDS ARE ENJOYING a meal together. On the table there's a big bowl which had contained a beef casserole—the meat and various vegetables. It's almost empty and there are plenty of splodges of gravy around it on the table. There are also two slightly smaller bowls. One's got a few boiled potatoes left in it, and the other holds a mixture of peas and sweetcorn. There are a few peas and bits of sweetcorn scattered about the table. There's an assortment of serving spoons, some in the bowls, and some plonked on the table beside the bowls. In front of each friend there's a plate with the various ingredients of the meal all mixed up together, and their knives and forks are in various places on their plates, on the table, or in their hands.

But now the meal's over. The table's cleared and cleaned. The things are washed up and put away. In one cupboard the two sizes of bowls are piled up side by side. In the next cupboard there's a neat pile of plates. Above this cupboard there's a drawer full of cutlery, with the knives, forks, and spoons carefully arranged in separate sections. On the other side of the kitchen there's another cupboard in which is a row of several jugs, including one that was on the table. They are lined up in increasing order of size. The vegetables are back in the fridge, each one in its own compartment. Everything's very tidy.

Systematic Theology is an attempt to have a tidy faith. While you are eating a meal there are bowls and plates, knives, forks, and spoons at various places on the table. After the meal everything is arranged neatly. The only source book for Systematic Theology is the Bible. But God didn't give us his Word all neat and packaged. In the Bible God has prepared for us a feast of good things. A feast requires variety. But sometimes it can be helpful to bring together all the Bible's teaching on a particular theme. The task of Systematic Theology is to arrange tidily the various doctrines taught in the Bible.

Of course, we must not try to make our theology too neat and tidy. We dare not iron out every mystery. God's thoughts are always greater than ours. In Isaiah 55:9 God challenges us to remember this: "As the heavens are higher than the earth, so are my ways higher than your ways, and my thoughts than your thoughts."

As long as we live, we are still just learners. We would be fools if we imagined that we can get our faith so neat and tidy that we know it all. Systematic Theology always has to be theology in the process of being arranged in a tidy system. This book can only be like dipping a toe in the water of the vast ocean of divine truth.

Something I said a moment ago deserves to be re-emphasized: the only source book for Systematic Theology is the Bible. In studying this subject it can be very helpful to look at how other Christians in other places and at other times have tried to arrange a tidy faith. But our only authority is God's Word itself. Every opinion about every Christian doctrine has to be tested by Scripture.

As we study each doctrine, we shall take a fourfold approach. This structure was suggested to me over 20 years ago as a method for teaching Systematic Theology to trainee pastors overseas, and I have found it an extremely fruitful approach, for which I am very grateful.

First, we shall do an exegesis of key relevant passages of the Bible. Where appropriate we shall look first at the Old Testament and then at the New Testament. This will help to keep at the forefront of our minds the foundational place of Scripture in sorting Christian doctrine into a tidy framework. We shall call this the "Biblical Foundation." Please keep your Bible handy to consult as you read this section of each chapter.

Second, we shall formulate the doctrine in a systematic way. Our label will be "Doctrinal Formulation." This is the heart of presenting the faith in a tidy format. In this section we shall look at how our predecessors in the Christian faith summarized the doctrines in their Statements of Faith. We shall look first at the creeds which the early church put together.

We shall focus in particular on the Apostles' Creed, the Nicene Creed, the Chalcedonian Definition, and the Athanasian Creed.

We shall then turn our attention to the confessions of faith and catechisms which were published by the various Reformed churches of Europe during the Reformation period.

I have made use of the following Confessions and Catechisms: the Sixty-Seven Articles of Zwingli (1523); the Augsburg Confession (1530); the Genevan Confession (1536); the First Helvetic Confession (1536); the Genevan Catechism (1542); the French Confession (1559); the Scottish Confession (1560); the Belgic Confession (1561); the Heidelberg Catechism (1563); the Thirty-Nine Articles (1563); the Second Helvetic Confession (1566); the Formula of Concord (1576); the Anglican Catechism (1604); the Irish Articles of Religion (1615); the Canons of Dort (1619); the Baptist Confession of Faith (1644); the Westminster Confession (1647); the Westminster Larger Catechism (1647); the Westminster Shorter Catechism (1647); the Savoy Declaration (1658); the London Baptist Confession (1689).

Sometimes I shall refer to specific confessions, but on the whole the approach will be to synthesize their teaching.

Finally, we shall look at some examples of modern non-western doctrinal documents. Speaking of the younger churches beyond the western cultural context, John Leith notes that, "as yet, these churches have produced few creeds."[1] However, I have used three which are available, and a brief word about each is in order.

The first is the Confession of Faith of the United Church of Northern India, which came into being in 1924 as the result of the amalgamation of Congregational and Presbyterian denominations.[2] This confession locates itself firmly in the Reformed tradition. In its preamble it commends the following doctrinal standards: the Westminster Confession, the Canons of Dort, the Heidelberg Catechism, and the Augsburg Confession.

Second, we shall consult the Confession of Faith of the Huria Kristen Batak Protestant, produced in Indonesia in 1951,[3] which defines itself as "the continuation" of the three ancient creeds, the Apostles', the Nicene, and the Athanasian Creeds. It contains many echoes of those documents.

1. Leith (ed.), *Creeds*, 555.
2. Reproduced in Oosthuizen, 302–4.
3. Reproduced in Leith (ed.), *Creeds*, 556–66.

Finally, the Confession of Faith of House Churches in China, published in 1998 by representatives of four House Church networks,[4] has aptly been called "a classic restatement of Protestant Christian Theology."[5]

Third, we shall look at how the tidy formulation of doctrine has developed in the course of the centuries. Our approach here will vary. Sometimes we will take one or two classic statements of a doctrine from different eras of Christian history. Sometimes we shall look at controversies which have arisen in the course of the centuries. Sometimes, when necessary, we shall address errors in our own day relating to particular doctrines. This section can be named "Historical Elaboration."

Fourth, we shall finish our study of each doctrine with a section entitled "Practical Application." I agree with Professor Berkouwer, who pointed out that Systematic Theology is not intended "for the exclusive enjoyment of professional theologians," and that "theology is not an excursion into the stratosphere."[6] It is the application of Biblical truth to everyday life in God's church and in God's world. So we shall seek to draw out those applications for each of the doctrines before us. We must never forget that the study of Biblical truth is designed to achieve this goal: "that the man of God may be complete, equipped for every good work" (2 Tim 3:17).

That means that every single doctrine in the whole of Systematic Theology is relevant to the way in which we live for God in his world today. If those of us who are preachers make use of it, we need to ask, how do I preach this doctrine in such a way that its relevance is clear, whether to unbelievers whom I long to see saved, or to those believers to whom I minister, whether from the pulpit or in personal counseling situations?

However, before we are ministers of the Word, we are ourselves Christian believers. We need to apply God's truth to our own hearts and lives before we can dare to preach it to others. Like the apostle, we want to steer well clear of the hypocrisy that would mean that "when I have preached to others, I myself should become disqualified" (1 Cor 9:27).

Although I hope that the practical relevance of the teaching will be permeating the whole of our studies, it is useful to draw together the practical application at the end of each section.

4. Reproduced in Aikman, 297–303.

5. Aikman, 93.

6. Berkouwer, *Faith and Justification*, 160.

One other thing of which I am aware is the constant danger, especially for those of us who are pastors and preachers, who have to study God's truth day in day out, that we become too familiar with these doctrinal truths. If we are not careful, we can become so familiar with them that we lose the ability to be astonished by them. We treat them as too "matter of fact." We fail to be stirred to the depths of our emotions at the stupendous mercy of a redeemer God who has acted so dramatically, who has demonstrated such unimaginable kindness towards despicable sinners.

My prayer is that reading this book will not merely stimulate our minds, but also touch our souls. My hope is that writer and reader alike will be led by pondering the sublime truths of our faith into a deeper love for the Lord Jesus, and into more appreciative and grateful praise to our tremendous God of sovereign grace.

1

The Doctrine of God

THERE ARE TWO ASPECTS to the doctrine of God. First, it is necessary to consider God's character: what is he like? Second, we must ponder the mystery of his trinitarian nature. This chapter will therefore fall into two parts, and we shall follow the fourfold approach for each part in turn.

PART ONE: GOD'S CHARACTER

This is a vast subject. God is very great. We have to be selective. Our aim will be limited. We shall seek to get to the heart of the doctrine of God as he has revealed himself in the Scriptures.

I think that it is fair to say that we get our doctrine of God largely from the Old Testament. The New Testament takes it for granted that God is as he has already revealed himself to be. So how does the Old Testament introduce God? The key quality which sums up the Old Testament teaching about God is that he is merciful. As he makes himself known in and to a fallen world, the LORD displays his mercy, and if our doctrine of God does not center on mercy and grace, then we are not talking about the God of the Bible.

BIBLICAL FOUNDATION

The Book of Exodus is our starting point. In Exodus 3 God addresses Moses out of the burning bush. Moses hears God promise to liberate his people, and receives his commission to go to Pharaoh and demand their release.

In verse 13 Moses asks God what he should say if the people of Israel ask him the name of the God he represents. In verse 14 God replies, "I am who I am," and tells him to say to the people, "I AM has sent me to you." In verse 15 he replaces the phrase "I am" with the name "the Lord." This name is derived from the verb "to be;" hence the connection with I AM. And the Lord says, "This is my name for ever."

But on its own the verb "to be" is incomplete. The way in which the Lord introduces himself to Moses leaves us asking, you are—what? What word or phrase will complete the sense?

It is only in Exodus 33 that we find the answer. In verse 18 Moses asks the Lord to show him his glory. The word translated "glory" is *kābôd*. Its basic meaning is something heavy.[1] Moses wants to know what is God's weightiest characteristic.

In reply the Lord says in verse 19, "I will make all my goodness pass before you." "Goodness" is the translation of the Hebrew word *ṭûb*. This can have two main shades of meaning. It can refer both to kindness and to that which is morally right.[2] The two come together in that God regards it as doing the right thing when he shows kindness. However, in verse 22 he indicates that this is the same as his glory passing by. The glory of God is found in his goodness. Goodness is God's most impressive attribute.

The Lord continues in verse 19, "I will proclaim the name of the Lord before you." God is now going to explain the meaning of his name. He is going to complete the sense of "I am."

And what his name means is: "I will be gracious to whom I will be gracious and I will have compassion on whom I will have compassion." The full meaning of "I am" is "I am gracious and compassionate." Mercy is at the heart of the divine character.

In chapter 33 the Lord has been speaking with Moses about what he will do. The event itself takes place in Exodus 34: The Lord descends

1. Tregelles (ed.), *Lexicon*, 216.
2. Bowling, "*ṭôb*," 793b.

in the cloud to proclaimed his name—that is, to declare its fundamental meaning. That proclamation takes place in verses 6–7:

> The LORD, the LORD God, merciful and gracious, longsuffering, and abounding in goodness and truth, keeping mercy for thousands, forgiving iniquity and transgression and sin, by no means clearing *the guilty*, visiting the iniquity of the fathers upon the children and the children's children to the third and the fourth generation.

The first word which the LORD uses as he explains the meaning of his name is "merciful." Here is the starting-point for the definition of the LORD's character. This translates the Hebrew word *raḥûm*. It speaks of a depth of love and tender affection. It is connected with the word for the womb. The LORD's feelings for his people are compared with the intensity of a woman's emotions as she carries her unborn child. A related term, *rāḥam*, is translated "I will have compassion" in Exodus 33:19. Whereas *raḥûm* speaks of the intense emotion of mercifulness, *rāḥam* draws attention to the fact that the LORD puts that deep emotion into practice.[3] God's mercy does not remain just a feeling. It springs into action. It comes to the aid of needy, suffering sinners.

"Merciful" is followed by a cluster of related terms in verse 6. Robert Gordon comments that "it is as if the light of the glory/goodness of God is passed through a prism to reveal the variegated attributes of deity."[4] Each attribute mentioned is worth a brief comment.

(1) The LORD is gracious. The word here is *ḥannûn*. It tells us that the LORD yearns with sympathy towards people in need, and that this sympathy drives him into action to help.[5] In 33:19 "I will be gracious" renders the related verb, *ḥānan*.

(2) The LORD is longsuffering. This phrase is made up of two words, *ʾārek*, which means "long," and *ʾap*, the word for nose. This is a vividly picturesque description of God. God says that he has got a long nose! It means that it takes ages for him to breathe in far enough to begin to smell the stink of sin. He does not flare up at the first whiff of wrong. He puts up with it for so long.

---

3. Butterworth, "*rḥm*," *passim*; Coppes, "*rāḥam*," 2146a, c.

4. R. P. Gordon, "*ṭôb*," 355.

5. Yamauchi, "*ḥānan*," 694.0, d.

(3) The LORD is abounding in goodness. "Goodness" translates *ḥesed*. This is a merciful love, a love which is totally undeserved.[6] The LORD has this quality in abundance. In verse 7 we hear that God keeps *ḥesed*: he is not fickle and changeable.

(4) The LORD abounds also in truth. This is a translation of *ᵉmet*. God is true to his Word, unchanging in his commitment to his people, loyal and reliable.

All this is summed up in the statement that God forgives sin. Here is the focus of his mercy. God's mercy comes to light against the dark background of human sinfulness. It is the LORD's constant delight to forgive. The Hebrew word here is *nāśā'*. Its literal meaning is to lift up.[7] To forgive sins is to lift the burden of guilt off the sinner, and consign the memory of his sins to oblivion.

We must make two comments on the rest of verse 7.

First, there are no Hebrew words corresponding to the words "the guilty." That is why they are printed in italics. The original simply says that the LORD by no means clears. "The guilty" is a guess made by the translators. They assumed that this phrase was talking about God's judgment. However, that does not seem to suit the context. It is perhaps better to insert the word "sin." God will by no means clear sin. These words are explaining how God forgives. He does not do it by clearing sin, by treating it as if it does not really matter, by sweeping it under the carpet, by ignoring it. The word translated "clear" is *nāqâ*. On a number of occasions this is translated "go unpunished" (e.g., Prov 11:21; Jer 49:12). This seems to be the sense here. The LORD does not forgive sin by leaving it unpunished, but rather by providing a substitute to bear the punishment. There is a hint here of the sacrificial system in which a victim dies in the place of the sinner, and so the sinner is forgiven. This points forward to Jesus Christ and him crucified.

Second, the reference to visiting the fathers' sins on the third and fourth generations does not mean that God punishes anyone for their great-grandfather's sins. Such an idea would conflict with Ezekiel 18:20, which says categorically that "the soul who sins shall die," and that one generation shall not bear the guilt of another (see also Deut 24:16). The word rendered "visiting" is *pāqad*. A better translation would be "observing," or "reviewing."[8] These words are emphasizing God's merciful

---

6. R. L. Harris, "*ḥsd*," 698a.

7. Hamilton, "*nś*'," 160–61

8. Cf. T. F. Williams, "*pqd*," 658.

patience. He does not jump in with judgment immediately. In fact, he waits three or four generations before inflicting punishment. He reviews the situation. He observes things to see whether the children and grandchildren will turn away from the wicked ways of earlier generations. He is patient, hoping that he will not have to judge.

The Bible reveals a God who is amazingly merciful. He is a God who judges most reluctantly. He is a God whose delight is to forgive sins because the necessary punishment has fallen on a substitute. John Piper describes the point of Exodus 34:6 as "the contrast between the sluggishness of his anger and the effusiveness of his love:" he comments vividly like this: "God loves to show mercy. He is not hesitant or indecisive in his desires to do good to his people. His anger must be released by a stiff safety lock, but his mercy has a hair trigger."[9]

This theme runs right through the Old Testament, which takes up the teaching of this key text constantly. This may be demonstrated by reference to a number of other Scriptures. We have examined the five terms used in Exodus 34:6. We have seen that this proclamation of the LORD's name reveals what Exodus 33:19 calls the glory of his goodness. We have seen also that God's mercy comes to practical expression in the forgiveness of sins. A glance at other texts which use terms from this cluster of words, and related terms, will demonstrate that this is a dominant emphasis in the biblical doctrine of God:

> the frequent use through the rest of the Old Testament of the formula in Exodus 34:6 by which the nature of God is portrayed is an eloquent testimony to the centrality of this understanding of God's person.[10]

We shall examine 13 passages which quote or echo Exodus 34:6. Each one includes a phrase like "The LORD is . . . ," or "God is . . . ," or "You, LORD, are . . . ," followed by a descriptive term or a series of terms connected with God's mercy.

It is worth noting in passing that such phrases are also sometimes followed by an adjective associated with God's justice. It seems that mercy and justice are the two main aspects of God's character. Indeed, the concept of mercy really only makes sense against the background of justice. It is undeserving sinners who are the objects of God's mercy, sinners whose only desert is the imposition of justice with all its dire

9. Piper, *Pleasures*, 190–91.
10. Childs, *Exodus*, 612.

consequences. God's saving mercy delivers us from his penal justice. The amazing truth which Exodus 34:6 flags up is that, in a fallen world, where sinners deserve nothing but God's punitive justice, mercy is nonetheless his defining attribute.

Here, then are the thirteen texts on which we shall focus in particular.

Numbers 14:11–20

Moses is at prayer. The people have rebelled against the LORD's command to enter the land. They have been intimidated by the unfavorable report from the unbelieving spies. The LORD has threatened to destroy them and to start afresh with Moses. However, Moses intercedes for the people. He does so by quoting back to the LORD part of his own description of his character in Exodus 34:6–7. He reminds the LORD how he said:

> The LORD is longsuffering and abundant in mercy, forgiving iniquity and transgression; but he by no means clears *the guilty*, visiting the iniquity of the fathers on the children to the third and fourth *generation*.

This leads on, in verse 19, to a prayer that the LORD will pardon his people's iniquity in line with the greatness of his mercy, repeating the word *ḥesed*. The LORD then responds with an assurance of pardon.

Verse 18 contains three of the terms found in Exodus 34:6. The LORD is defined as 'slow to anger (*'ārek 'ap*) and abounding in steadfast love (*ḥesed*).' These qualities come to expression in the forgiveness (*nāśā'*) of sins.

In verse 19 Moses also repeats the word *nāśā'* as he reminds the LORD how often he has 'forgiven this people from Egypt even until now.' But when he prays that the LORD will again "pardon the iniquity of this people" he uses a different word—*sālaḥ*. Unlike *nāśā'*, which could be used of one person forgiving another, this word is only ever used of God's forgiveness.[11] God's forgiveness is unique, because, unlike human beings, he never needs to be forgiven by another. This underlines the astonishing mercy involved in his forgiveness, Moses is appealing directly to the character of God. In verse 20 the LORD responds by using the same word. He hears Moses' prayer, and his anger is turned away.

---

11. Kaiser, "*sālaḥ*," 1505.0; Olivier, "*slḥ*," 260.

Verse 17 prefaces this passage by portraying this aspect of the LORD's character as an expression of his great power. The power of God is best seen, not in creation or in mighty miracles, but in the mercy by which he overcomes his own anger.

Deuteronomy 4:31

Moses now speaks of the LORD as "a merciful (*raḥûm*) God." He is anticipating a day when the people of Israel have suffered the consequences of falling into idolatry. Then they will seek the LORD again. They will be able to find him, just because he is merciful. The verse goes on to explain what that means: "he will not forsake you nor destroy you, nor forget the covenant of your fathers which he swore to them."

2 Chronicles 30:1–9

Hezekiah is summoning the people of Israel to join the people of Judah at Jerusalem to keep the Passover. He sends a letter to every part of the country. It urges the people to end their stubborn unfaithfulness, and to return to the LORD. Hezekiah backs up his appeal by reminding the people of the character of the LORD their God: he "*is* gracious (*ḥannûn*) and merciful (*raḥûm*)" [verse 9]. The word "compassion" is the related verb, *rāḥam*.

Nehemiah 9:5–31

The Levites are leading the people in a prayer of confession. They acknowledge the LORD's grace and power: he chose Abram; he liberated Israel from Egypt; he led them through the desert; he gave them the law. Yet Israel's history was marked by constant disobedience. However, their confident hope now is based on what is said in the second half of verse 17: "you *are* God, ready to pardon, gracious and merciful, slow to anger, abundant in kindness, and did not forsake them."

Here we find the familiar terms *ḥannûn*, *raḥûm*, *'ārek 'ap*, and *ḥesed*. We are beginning to see that this combination of descriptions is the regular portrait of the LORD which runs right through the Old Testament.

The phrase "ready to pardon" translates *seliḥâ*, a noun related to the verb *sālaḥ*, used by Moses and the LORD in Numbers 14. In this phrase the people recognize that the LORD is the God of forgiveness. It is his essential nature to be forgiving towards sinners.

The prayer continues by pointing to examples from history which confirm that this is the character of God. Even when they made the golden calf, they found themselves preserved by the LORD's "manifold mercies (*rāḥam*)" [verse 19]. He never withdrew his guidance. He fed them with the manna. They lacked nothing. He gave them the land as promised. He multiplied their numbers.

But still the people were disobedient and rebellious. As a result, they suffered at the hands of their enemies. However, when they cried out to the LORD, once again they were confronted by his "abundant mercies (*rāḥam*)" [verse 27]. He sent the judges to save them, only for their hearts to turn away yet again. The pattern of subjugation by enemies, crying to the LORD, and merciful deliverance was repeated time and again. Verse 31 sums Israel's experience up: "in your great mercy you did not utterly consume them nor forsake them; for you *are* God, gracious and merciful."

Once again, the terms *ḥannûn* and *raḥûm*, which so often come as a pair, are used together.

Psalm 86

David is crying to the LORD in a time of trouble. Aware of his poverty and need, he prays for his preservation and for the restoration of joy. The basis of his confidence in praying like this is seen in verse 5: "you, Lord, *are* good, and ready to forgive, and abundant in mercy to all those who call upon you."

Here we have the words *ṭôb*, related to *ṭûb*, the term which defined God's glory in Exodus 33, *sālaḥ*, and *ḥesed*. Already in verse 3, David has prayed, "be merciful to me, O Lord." "Merciful" renders *ḥānan*.

From verse 8 onwards the Psalm becomes more positive in tone. Because the LORD is such a God, he is incomparable. The greatness of his works is destined to be acknowledged universally. For the time being, David is being attacked by men who fail to recognize the glory of the LORD, but he expresses his confidence again in the words of verse 15: "you, O Lord, *are* a God full of compassion, and gracious, longsuffering and abundant in mercy and truth."

The same four familiar terms which came in Nehemiah 9 reoccur here: *raḥûm*, *ḥannûn*, *'ārek 'ap*, and *ḥesed*, along with *'ᵉmet*, another of the cluster from Exodus. In fact, these words are an exact quotation of the second half of Exodus 34:6. David has referred to God's *ḥesed* earlier—in verse 13, and he prays again that God will be gracious (*ḥānan*) in verse 16.

Psalm 100

This Psalm of joy and thankfulness comes to its climax in verse 5: "the LORD *is* good; his mercy *is* everlasting, and his truth *endures* to all generations."

Here are two words from the familiar collection: *ṭôb*, and *ḥesed*, and the word *ᵉmûnâ*, which is connected to *ᵉmet*. *ᵉmûnâ* is used in Exodus 17:12. It speaks of the steadiness of Moses' hands as Aaron and Hur held them up after Moses had grown weary. As long as Moses' hands were raised and steady, Israel prevailed in the battle with Amalek. To speak of the LORD as faithful is to say that he has a safe pair of hands. A sinner who casts himself on God's mercy will never be dropped.

Psalm 103:1–18

This Psalm begins by celebrating the many benefits the LORD gives to his people. Amongst these benefits are "lovingkindness (*ḥesed*) and tender mercies (*rāḥam*)" [verse 4]. Verse 8 states the basis of the LORD's kindness: he "is merciful and gracious, slow to anger and abounding in mercy."

Here are the four familiar terms, *raḥûm*, *ḥannûn*, *'ārek 'ap*, and *ḥesed*. Apart from the fact that the name the LORD is inserted after the word "gracious" in Hebrew, this again is a citation of Exodus 34:6. That verse stated what God really is like. And he is so intent that we should understand that mercy is his heart that he goes on repeating it.

The verses that follow draw out the implications of the fact that God is like this: he restrains his anger; he deals with us quite contrary to what we deserve; he removes our sins. Verse 11 tells of the greatness of his mercy (*ḥesed*), and verse 13 speaks of his pity (*rāḥam*). In the context of a world of uncertainty, "the mercy (*ḥesed*) of the LORD is from everlasting to everlasting" (verse 17).

Psalm 111

Here we are being led in praise to the LORD for his wonderful works. But the most wonderful of his works are those which display his kindness to people. In verse 4 we are reminded that 'the LORD is gracious (*raḥûm*) and full of compassion (*ḥannûn*).' Then we hear of the LORD's provision for his people. Twice (in verses 7 and 8) reference is made to the LORD's verity or truth (both translating *ᵉmet*).

Psalm 116:1–5

In this Psalm the singer's love for the LORD is declared. Our love for him is a response to his love for us. He has heard our cry for deliverance. Verse 5 says that the LORD is gracious and merciful. Here again are the words *ḥannûn* and *rāḥam*.

Psalm 145:1–9

David begins by extolling the LORD for his greatness. This is evident from his works. But, as verse 7 indicates, his greatest works are those which give us cause to utter the memory of his great goodness (*ṭûb*). The next verse makes this statement: "the LORD *is* gracious and full of compassion, slow to anger and great in mercy."

Yet again, the four major terms which sum up the doctrine of God occur together: *raḥûm*, *ḥannûn*, *ᵉārek ᵓap*, and *ḥesed*. The next verse tells us again that 'the LORD is good (*ṭôb*),' and speaks of his mercy (*rāḥam*).

The word 'abounding' in verse 8 translates a different Hebrew word from 'abounding' in Exodus 34:6, Numbers 14:18, Nehemiah 9:17, Psalm 86:5 and 15, and Psalm 103:8. In all those texts the word is *rab*. It simply emphasizes the vast quantity of mercy which God possesses.

The word here is *gādôl*. This word refers less to quantity than to quality. It is certainly true that the LORD has an abundant quantity of mercy. But it is equally true that every particle of that mercy is of the finest possible kind. There is a richness, a splendor to God's mercy, which moves us to wonder and to praise.

Joel 2:12–14

The first part of Joel's prophecy has spoken about the coming Day of the LORD. That day of darkness and gloom has been foreshadowed in the judgment which God's people are facing at the time of Joel's ministry. This passage is an invitation to them to return to the LORD. The second part of verse 13 supports this exhortation with another clear allusion to Exodus 34:6. God's character makes repentance a genuine option: "for he *is* gracious and merciful, slow to anger, and of great kindness; and he relents from doing harm."

Here again we have the four standard terms, *ḥannûn, raḥûm, 'ārek 'ap*, and *ḥesed*. In practice a God of such a character is one who is so reluctant to inflict disaster, that he is very eager to bless.

Jonah 3:6—4:2

Why was Jonah so reluctant to go to Nineveh to proclaim God's message there? It was because he knew his God so well. When Jonah finally came to Nineveh, after first running away, his preaching met with a response of general repentance, led by the king himself. As a result, the disaster which God had threatened through Jonah did not materialize. This was exactly what Jonah had expected, and it made him angry. In Jonah 4:2 he says this to the LORD: "Therefore I fled previously to Tarshish; for I know that you *are* a gracious and merciful God, slow to anger and abundant in lovingkindness, one who relents from doing harm."

Once again, the four regular terms appear, *ḥannûn, raḥûm, 'ārek 'ap*, and *ḥesed*. Jonah knows what his God is like because he knows the Word of God. He is able to quote Exodus 34:6.

However, Jonah wants the LORD's mercy to be Israel's exclusive prerogative. He resents the thought that the LORD might share his mercy with the Assyrian rabble! At the same time, Jonah knows the open-heartedness of God. He knows that the LORD is world-hearted, that his mercy extends to the ends of the earth. Such is the God of the Old Testament, the God of the Bible, and Jonah cannot change him.

Nahum 1:1–3

A generation after Jonah's time, the people of Nineveh had reverted to their old ways. This time the LORD called Nahum to prophesy against the wicked city. His prophecy begins with stern words of warning. But in the middle of this solemn passage we come across these words in verse 3: "the LORD is slow to anger." Here is the phrase *'ārek 'ap*. Here is a hint, even to people who have gone back on their earlier repentance, that mercy is still available, because the LORD's anger takes so long to ignite.

This, then, is the God of the Bible. Mercy is his lifeblood, his heartbeat, his smile, his embrace. As Micah says, in the closing passage of his prophecy (Mic 7:18–20):

> Who *is* a God like you, pardoning iniquity and passing over the transgression of the remnant of his heritage? He does not retain his anger forever, because he delights *in* mercy. He will again have compassion on us, and will subdue our iniquities. You will cast all our sins into the depths of the sea. You will give truth to Jacob *and* mercy to Abraham, which you have sworn to our fathers from days of old.

DOCTRINAL FORMULATION

The Early Creeds

The Apostles' Creed and the Nicene Creed begin in a similar way. They speak of God as the Father, the Almighty, and the Creator. The Nicene Creed also adds the word "one." Its opening words are, "I believe in one God."

God as Father

J. N. D. Kelly argues that "Father" and "Almighty" are two distinct statements about God. It is not simply that the Father is almighty, but that first of all God is Father, then he is Almighty. And Kelly finds it significant that God's Fatherhood is mentioned first.[12] Early Christian writers often associated God's Fatherhood with his goodness and love. For example,

---

12. J. N. D. Kelly, *Creeds*, 132–33.

Clement of Rome, writing in the second century, speaks of "our gracious and merciful Father."[13]

The Fatherhood of God was a special theme in Jesus' teaching. However, it was not new. The Old Testament speaks of God as Father 15 times. It is striking how closely this title for God is linked with his mercy. This is clearest in the covenant with David. God promises to be the Father of the son of David who will sit on his throne. And to be Father means to maintain steadfast love and mercy. This is clear from the LORD's statement of his covenant commitment in 1 Chronicles 17:13: "I will be his Father, and he shall be my son; and I will not take my mercy away from him, as I took *it* from *him* who was before you." "Mercy" here translates *hesed*.

Psalm 89 is a celebration of the Davidic covenant. Verse 24 reads as follows: "My faithfulness (*'mûnâ*) and my mercy (*hesed*) *shall be* with him, and in my name his horn shall be exalted." Verse 28 continues in similar vein: "My mercy (*hesed*) I will keep for him forever, and my covenant shall stand firm with him."

In stating first of all that God is Father, the early creeds demonstrated their sensitivity to the major scriptural emphasis.

God as Almighty

In the original Greek form of the creeds the word translated "almighty" is *pantokratōr*. This really means "all-ruling." It does not refer to God's unlimited ability. It emphasizes the fact that the Lord governs absolutely everything.

The word occurs many times in the Bible. In the Septuagint (the Greek translation of the Old Testament) *kurios pantokratōr* is the normal rendering of the phrase "LORD of hosts." In the New Testament, to take just one example, Revelation 19:6 says: "Alleluia! For the Lord God omnipotent reigns!" The Lord God is almighty in the sense that he is reigning over all. A second-century writer, Theophilos of Antioch explained the almightiness of God like this: "The heights of the heavens, and the depths of the abysses, and the limits of the world are in his hand."[14] It is this all-ruling sovereignty which enables God to carry through his great purpose of disseminating his mercy in Christ.

---

13. Clement of Rome, "Corinthians," 29.
14. Theophilos, "To Autolycus," 1.4.

God as Creator

The creeds describe God as "Creator of heaven and earth." This stresses the complete distinction between God and everything else. The universe is not an emanation of God. It is not as if the universe is the body of which God is the Spirit. God and his creation are completely different realities.

Equally, the creation is not the work of some other being than the God who is the Father Almighty. He alone is the source of absolutely everything that exists outside himself. We are not pawns in some inconclusive cosmic battle between rival gods. There are only two realities—God and his creation.

It is just because the creation is God's work that he rules over it. It is the stage on which he fulfils his purpose of enacting his mercy in Christ.

The Nicene Creed expands on the basic statement that God is the Creator of heaven and earth by adding the phrase, "of all things, visible and invisible." This addition serves to emphasize the fact that there are some things which we are unable to see—angels, and the spiritual heaven as distinct from the visible heavens, for example, as well as the institutional structures in human society. However, none of these have any existence apart from the fact that God brought them into being.

God as One

This means that he is the only God. This was an important statement in the polytheistic context of Roman religion. R. M. Grant has noted the encounters in the book of Acts between the early Christian mission and polytheism. Three are particularly significant.[15]

First, we read in Acts 14:8–18 of Paul and Barnabas at Lystra. In response to the healing of a crippled man, the crowds assumed that the missionaries were human likenesses of Zeus and Hermes. These were the chief gods of their region.

Next, in Acts 17:16–34 we find Paul in Athens. We learn that "the city was given over to idols" (verse 16). There was even an altar "to the unknown god" (verse 23). This was an insurance policy. This extra altar was there just in case they had missed some god by mistake.

Finally, we hear in Acts 19:23–41 of the riot in Ephesus. It was caused by the dip in income which the image-makers were suffering as

---

15. Grant, *Gods*, 25–28.

a result of the success of the apostles' evangelism. Ephesus housed "the temple of the great goddess Diana" (verse 27). Her temple had brought fame to Ephesus. It was reckoned to be the first of the seven wonders of the ancient world.

Grant also notes how Paul opposed idolatry.[16] He cites Paul's words in 1 Thessalonians 1:9, "you turned to God from idols to serve the living and true God." The implication of these words is that idols are lifeless and false. Grant refers also to 1 Corinthians 12:2–3, where he contrasts "the creative speech of the divine Spirit" with "dumb idols."

Paul's clearest statement against the polytheism of paganism comes in 1 Corinthians 8:4–6:

> we know that an idol *is* nothing in the world, and that *there is* no other God but one. For even if there are so-called gods, whether in heaven or on earth (as there are many gods and many lords), yet for us *there is* one God, the Father, of whom *are* all things, and we for him; and one Lord Jesus Christ, through whom *are* all things, and through whom we *live*.

So there is only one God. Idols are non-existent, imaginary gods.

Grant says, "the model for the New Testament view of idols was set in the Old Testament." The truth that the LORD of mercy is the only real God is stressed repeatedly in the Old Testament. For example, in Isaiah 46:9 we read, "I *am* God, and *there is* no other; *I am* God, and *there is* none like me."

The nearest thing to a Statement of Faith in the Old Testament is the *š⁽e⁾maʿ* (Deut 6:4): "Hear, O Israel: The LORD our God, the LORD *is* one." *Š⁽e⁾maʿ* is the Hebrew word translated "hear" at the beginning of the verse. In Jewish understanding hearing includes taking seriously what you hear. So this solemn declaration that the LORD is the only God is a challenge to remain true to him. Hence, the next verse reads: "You shall love the LORD your God with all your heart, with all your soul, and with all your strength."

In Mark 12:29–30 Jesus quotes Deuteronomy 6:4–5. He calls it "the most important'" of all the commandments. All-embracing love for the Lord is the consequence of believing in his uniqueness. Because he is the only God he has a claim on every aspect of our lives.

---

16. Grant, *Gods*, 45–49.

The Reformation Confessions

The teaching of the confessions may be summarized in seven common themes.

There is only one living and true God

This recognizes that other religions claim to have their gods. However, they have no life; they are false. The real God is unique. The Second Helvetic Confession backs this up with several Scriptures, including Deuteronomy 6:4: "Hear, O Israel: The LORD our God, the LORD *is* one," and Isaiah 45:5: "I *am* the LORD, and *there is* no other; *there is* no God besides me." In the light of these texts, this confession describes the idea of a plurality of gods as an abomination.

Some of the confessions stress that the source of God's life is in and of himself. He is not dependent on anything else. His existence is a matter of necessity.

This one living and true God is Spirit

Having said that God is Spirit, the Westminster Confession immediately explains what this means: he is "invisible, without body, parts, or passions."

The first three of these descriptions belong together. It is because he has no physical body that God cannot be seen. As John 1:18 says, "no one has seen God at any time." And having no body, God cannot be divided up into constituent parts. His essence is a unity. Everything that God does, he does with complete integrity. He has no conflicting intentions. Paul summarizes the distress of the person who desires to obey God's law but finds that his personality is divided: "What I will to do, that I do not practice; but what I hate, that I do" (Rom 7:15). However, it is never like that with God.

A body is always vulnerable. A limb has to be amputated because of a serious illness. The person is still alive, but now he is severely handicapped. But God has no handicaps. A high-speed car crash may result in the body being crushed. The person is killed. But God's life is never in danger.

The confession also says that God is "without passions." At this point the Reformers are taking up a doctrine much loved by early Christian thinkers. However, such a description of God has been criticized in more recent years. A God without passions sounds cold and remote. Yet the Scriptures portray God as passionate in his love. He is a God who burns with anger, who is excited to show mercy, who finds great joy in blessing his people, a God who is grieved by sin and thrilled to save. How, then, can God be "without passions"?

One way of explaining it is given by an Anglican writer, Bishop Burnet:

> Passion produces a vehemence of action; so when there is, in the providences of God, such a vehemence as, according to the manner of men, would import a passion, then that passion is ascribed to God. When he punishes men for sin, he is said to be angry; when he does that by severe and redoubled strokes, he is said to be full of fury and revenge; when he punishes for idolatry, or any dishonor done to himself, he is said to be jealous; when he changes the course of his proceedings, he is said to repent.[17]

It is striking how many times Burnet uses the words "said to." God is said to be angry, to be full of fury and revenge, to be jealous, to repent. By implication Burnet is saying, "but of course he is not really like that."

However, in my view this leads to a rather unsatisfactory and unsatisfying doctrine of God. Is God's anger just some automatic reaction without a surge of feeling? Does the idea of passionless love and mercy even make sense? Is it possible to grieve without feeling grief?

What is more, if the biblical language about God's anger, jealousy, mercy, love, and grief is not the language of reality, then the Bible is no longer a genuine revelation of God. It is more like a cartoon comic that actually tells us nothing about God.

We need to understand what the early Christian writers meant when they spoke of God as being without passions. Many of the early fathers were careful to define this doctrine very precisely. They did not mean that God has no feelings or that he is unable to suffer.

What they meant was that if God suffers, he does so voluntarily. He is never out of control. He is never at the mercy of circumstances which defeat him. He is always in charge, never the victim. Even when he reacts passionately, he remains in sovereign control. He never flares up and loses his temper. But when he is angry his anger does burn passionately. His

---

17. Quoted by Shaw, *Confession*, 26–27.

love is not an expression of mere sentimentality, but he does love with feeling. Otherwise he would be a God who does not care. Lactantius, writing around the year AD 300, is probably the earliest patristic writer to elaborate on these crucial nuances.[18]

A modern writer whose approach resembles that of Lactantius is the Japanese theologian, Kazoh Kitamori. He speaks of "the pain of God," but still implies that God is without passions, in that his pain derives from his own will to embrace the unlovely, not from external circumstances.[19]

This one living and true Spirit is sovereign

The confessions use many terms which may be gathered together under the heading of God's sovereignty. For example, they speak of his greatness, his blessedness, his infinity, his all-sufficiency.

God is not dependent on other things. He has no needs. He is the fount from which everything has come, and every day he is still guiding all things according to his own will and for his own glory.

In 1993 a commemoration of the 350th anniversary of the Westminster Assembly was held in London. The opening sermon was preached by James Montgomery Boice. His theme was the sovereignty of God. His text was Daniel 4, which includes these words in verses 34–35:

> his dominion is an everlasting dominion, and his kingdom *is* from generation to generation; all the inhabitants of the earth *are* reputed as nothing; he does according to his will in the army of heaven and among the inhabitants of the earth. No one can restrain his hand or say to him, "What have you done?"

Boice highlighted three blessings which we receive in recognizing God's sovereignty: (1) it deepens our worship of God; (2) it brings comfort in the midst of trials, temptation and sorrow; (3) it provides encouragement for evangelism.[20]

18. Lactantius, "Anger of God," 15–17.
19. Kitamori, *Pain of God, passim.*
20. Boice, "Sovereignty," *passim.*

God has all the equipment he needs for the exercise of his sovereignty

The confessions taught God's wisdom and total knowledge. There is never any risk that he might make a mistake in exercising his sovereignty.

The confessions speak of God's almighty power. Robert Reymond notes that God's omnipotence does not mean that he can do absolutely anything. The Scriptures tell us of four things which God cannot do: he cannot lie (Heb 6:17–18; Titus 1:2); he cannot break his promise (2 Cor 1:20); he cannot disown himself (2 Tim 2:13); he cannot change (Num 23:19; 1 Sam 15:29). These impossibilities are vital to God's perfection.[21] God's almighty power is his ability to carry out his will unfailingly as he rules over everything.

The confessions speak also of God's eternity. This extends in both directions. He never began to be. He will never cease to be. He endures throughout all time—and beyond—and yet is never vulnerable to the ageing process. As Psalm 90:2 puts it, he was God even "before the mountains were brought forth," in fact, before the entire world had been formed: "even from everlasting to everlasting, you are God."

This is vital to God's sovereignty. If anything had come before God it might compromise his unrivalled supremacy. But this is not so!

The confessions also teach God's omnipresence: everything and everyone exists every moment in the inescapable presence of God. David asks the question, "where can I go from your Spirit? Or where can I flee from your presence?" (Ps 139:7). The answer is nowhere! Consequently, everything and everyone is permanently under God's sovereignty.

The confessions mention God's glory. The Hebrew word normally rendered "glory" is *kābôd*. It has to do with a heavy weight. The Greek word is *doxa*: it can be translated "opinion."[22] Putting the two together, we may say that God is of weighty importance, and that our opinion ought to be that he is of all-surpassing significance. A heavyweight God must leave his mark as he exercises his sovereignty.

---

21. Reymond, *New Systematic Theology*, 192.
22. Liddell & Scott, *Lexicon*, 178.

God is the God of mercy

In addition to mercy itself the confessions mention 13 more divine characteristics which are related to the Lord's exercise of mercy.

Five of them form the dark background against which God's mercy stands out in all its brilliance: God is holy; he hates sin; he is just; he inflicts terrible judgments upon sin; he is unable simply to ignore guilt. It is God's holiness which makes his mercy so amazing.

The other eight characteristics are aspects or expressions of mercy: God is immutable, loving, gracious, longsuffering, abundant in goodness, abundant in truth, forgiving, and the rewarder of those that seek him. The echoes of the Old Testament revelation of God flowing from Exodus 34:6–7 are obvious here.

We do not know everything about the true and living God

Some of the confessions include the word "incomprehensible" in their description of God. We understand some things about God. We understand especially that he is merciful, because he has told us so. But there are depths in the being of God which he has seen fit to conceal. And even in those areas where we do know about God, we must never assume that we know all that there is to be known.

We must always retain that humility which admits the possibility that we have misunderstood. Even where the Bible has clearly revealed truth about God, our finite minds, further limited by sin, may have misread what God has said. So please do not just assume that what I have written in this book is right. Go to the Scriptures yourself and read them prayerfully. Be like the Bereans. Examine the Scriptures daily to find out whether these things are so. God describes such an approach as "noble" (Acts 17:11).

Practical consequences follow from confessing faith in such a God

One of the earliest of the Reformed Confessions, the Genevan Confession of 1536, says this: "We acknowledge that there is only one God, whom we are both to worship and serve, and in whom we are to put all our confidence and hope."

Modern Confessions of Faith

It will be helpful to look at the teaching on the character of God in each of these three confessions in turn.

Confession of Faith of the United Church of Northern India

This confession's article on God centers on the fact that he is a Spirit who is distinct, not only from material things, but also from all other spirits. A list of divine attributes reaches its climax in the word "love." This appears to be a deliberate emphasis. At this point the confession closely echoes the Westminster Shorter Catechism, which describes God as "unchangeable in his being, wisdom, power, holiness, justice, goodness, and truth." The Indian confession says that God is "unchangeable in his being, wisdom, power, holiness, justice, goodness, truth and love."

Evidently the theologians of North India thought that the British document had stopped short by failing to mention God's chief, defining quality.[23] They recognized that a reference to love must be included if their confession was to be fully in tune with the biblical emphasis on the divine mercy. The confession stresses the fact that God must be worshipped, and that he is the only legitimate object of worship.

Confession of Faith of the Huria Batak Protestant

The first article of this confession begins with a list of divine attributes. It proclaims that God is one, eternal, almighty, unchanging, faithful, all-knowing, inscrutable, a righteous Judge, gracious, and all-bountiful. This final attribute brings the list to a climax in a way which accords with the biblical emphasis on God's mercy. The next sentence, likewise, builds up to a climax with the statement that God is "full of love." His omnipresence, truth, and holiness have been mentioned, but his love completes the list.

Having said that, the Confession is careful to emphasize that God's character is not gracious only. He is also a God of holiness and justice, and to deny this would lead to an unbiblical distortion of the truth about God.

---

23. Cf. W. Stewart, *Faith We Confess*, 6.

Confession of Faith of House Churches in China

The Chinese confession proclaims that there is "only one true God," and that he is eternal and self-existent. He "created all things," and "is the Lord of human history." It is in the course of history that God "manifests his sovereignty." The Confession insists that this is true "in all of human history." Nothing at all lies outside the sphere of the divine Lordship.

The Confession offers the following list of divine attributes: "The almighty God is just, holy, faithful, and merciful. He is omniscient, omnipresent, and omnipotent." However, primacy of place is given, at least by implication to God's mercy. Referring to the three persons of the Trinity, the Confession speaks of the different role of each "in the work of redemption." Each makes his distinctive contribution to human salvation. The fact that this is stressed suggests that the Confession regards human redemption and salvation as the chief of the works of God. So all his various attributes combine to further his work of mercy.

HISTORICAL ELABORATION

In this section, I want to do two things. First, I shall outline the teaching of two representative theologians from different periods of Christian history, both of whom celebrate the divine mercy. Second, I shall consider the distinction which is often made between God's communicable and incommunicable attributes.

Two Representative Theologians

Cyprian of Carthage

Cyprian was born about the year 200 somewhere in Africa. His family were wealthy pagans, and he was not converted until he was in his forties, by which time he was living in Carthage, on the North African coast. Within three years of his conversion he had become the senior pastor in the Carthage area. A year later he had to flee for his life to escape the persecution initiated by the Emperor Decius. The following year, when the persecution had subsided, he returned. Six years later he was arrested during the persecution by Emperor Valerian. After a year in captivity he was executed on 14th September, AD 258. He was the first African pastor to be martyred for the faith.

About a year before his arrest Cyprian wrote a treatise entitled *On the Advantage of Patience*. At the time the African church was embroiled in a controversy about the rebaptism of converts from heretical churches. While Cyprian was very clear where he stood on that matter, he was also concerned to maintain Christian unity in a spirit of patience. This work was designed to promote patient acceptance of one another on the part of all true Christians.

But Cyprian points out early on in the treatise that we can only achieve patience ourselves if we have known the patience of God. This leads him into an exposition of God's patience.[24]

He starts by pointing to the evidence that God is patient. He notes that the earth is full of profane temples, images, and idolatrous worship. He observes that people in general treat God's majesty and honor with contempt. In spite of these things, God makes the sun rise daily and shine on all people. He makes the rain fall, and excludes no one from its benefits. God patiently sends the seasons, and provides food for all people.

Cyprian continues like this:

> while God is provoked with frequent, yes, continual offenses, he tempers his anger, and waits patiently for the day of retribution, which he has pre-determined. And even though he has revenge in his power, he prefers to be longsuffering in his patience. He prefers to wait, to bear with us in his mercy, to delay judgment, so that, if at all possible, the long career of evil might at some time be changed; so that man, however deeply he is involved in the contagion of error and crime, may be converted to God, even at a late hour. God himself warns us: he says, "I have no pleasure in the death of the wicked, but that the wicked turn from his way and live" (Ezek 33:11); and again, "'now, therefore,' says the LORD, 'turn to me'" (Joel 2:12). And again: "return to the LORD, your God, for he *is* gracious and merciful, slow to anger, and of great kindness; and he relents from doing harm" (Joel 2:13).

Cyprian quotes Paul's words in Romans 2:4, "the goodness of God leads you to repentance." Cyprian writes: "God's judgment is just, because it is delayed, because it is repeatedly deferred, and for a long time, so that by God's long-enduring patience man may be benefited for life eternal."

---

24. Cyprian, "Patience," 2–4.

John Calvin

Calvin was a Frenchman, although for most of his ministry he was based in Geneva. He lived from 1509 to 1564. He was the leading Reformed theologian of his day. John Hesselink finds "the key concepts in Calvin's portrayal of God" to be free mercy, goodness, and love.[25]

In the opening chapters of his *Institutes* Calvin addresses the issue of our knowledge of God. In the course of this discussion it becomes obvious how he perceives the character of God.[26]

He rejects mere speculation about God's "essence." What matters is "what kind of being God is," by which Calvin means "what things are agreeable to his nature." However, we may not devise for ourselves a God of any character we please. We must "have him in the character in which he manifests himself." Calvin notes that we do not have a clear understanding of God's nature unless we see him as "the origin and fountain of all goodness."

In his very first paragraph Calvin describes the "blessings which unceasingly distil to us from heaven," as evidence of "the infinitude of good which resides in God." A little later he writes: "in the Lord, and none but he, dwell the true light of wisdom, solid virtue, exuberant goodness."

In the following chapter Calvin says that we worship God, because we recognize him to be "the fountain of all goodness." We perceive "that God our Maker supports us by his power, rules us by his providence, fosters us by his goodness, and visits us with all kinds of blessings." Calvin then sums up his understanding of God in these words:

> we must be persuaded not only that as he once formed the world, so he sustains it by his boundless power, governs it by his wisdom, preserves it by his goodness, in particular, rules the human race with justice and judgment, bears with them in mercy, shields them by his protection; but also that not a particle of light, or wisdom, or justice, or power, or rectitude, or genuine truth, will anywhere be found, which does not flow from him, and of which he is not the cause; in this way we must learn to expect and ask all things from him, and thankfully ascribe to him whatever we receive.

These words confirm the truth of Hesselink's observation: Calvin does indeed give generous mercy first place in his portrait of God. Calvin

---

25. Hesselink, *Calvin's First Catechism*, 116.
26. Calvin, *Institutes*, 1.1—2.2.

sums up his doctrine of God in five phrases: he governs all things, he is the source of every blessing, he is good and merciful, he is our Father and Lord, and he is a just judge. Such a God is characterized by faithfulness and clemency. He is a God in whom we may contentedly confide.

Communicable and Incommunicable Attributes

By the beginning of the seventeenth century it had become customary for the attributes of God to be divided between "incommunicable" and "communicable" attributes. Incommunicable attributes are those which have no counterpart in human life, such as God's self-sufficiency or his infinity. Communicable attributes are those which are reflected to some extent, in human nature. These in turn are often subdivided into mental attributes, such as knowledge or wisdom, and moral attributes, such as patience or mercy.

Not everyone has been happy with this scheme. Both A. A. Hodge in the nineteenth century, and Donald Macleod in the twentieth century pointed out that even God's so-called "communicable" attributes have incommunicable properties.[27] For example, God's patience is infinite, in a way that ours never is. Consequently, Macleod finds these classifications "artificial and misleading."

What interests me is that even those theologians who use this scheme tend to give prominence to the moral branch of the communicable attributes. So Louis Berkhof writes: "The moral attributes of God are generally regarded as the most glorious of the divine perfections."[28] Similarly, Robert Lewis Dabney begins his consideration of God's moral attributes with these words:

> We have now reached that which is the most glorious, and at the same time, the most important class of God's attributes; those which qualify him as an infinitely perfect moral Being.

A few lines later Dabney continues:

> Blessed be his name, he is declared, by his works and Word, to be a God of complete moral perfections. And this is the ground on which the Scriptures base their most frequent and strongest claims to the praise and love of his creatures. His power, his

---

27. A. A. Hodge, *Outlines*, 137; Macleod, *Behold*, 20.
28. Berkhof, *Systematic Theology*, 70.

knowledge, his wisdom, his immutability are glorious; but the glory and loveliness of his moral attributes excels.[29]

It is my contention that to give this prominence to God's moral attributes is to keep in line with the Bible's main emphasis on God's mercy. Herman Bavinck goes further, and comes even closer to the biblical priority, when he says, "Among the ethical attributes first place should be assigned to God's goodness." Bavinck proceeds to analyze God's goodness into its component parts, including lovingkindness, compassion, patience, grace, and love.[30]

PRACTICAL APPLICATION

(1) Since God has revealed himself to be a God of mercy, our first response can only be that we cast ourselves upon that mercy. Apart from the mercy of God, we are hopelessly lost, forever condemned to hell. We must face up in all honesty to our sin and shame, and humble ourselves before the Lord, recognizing that only his undeserved mercy can save us from the judgment that we do deserve. David celebrates God's lovingkindness (*hesed*) and draws out its practical relevance in Psalm 36:7: "how precious *is* your lovingkindness, O God! Therefore the children of men put their trust under the shadow of your wings."

God's mercy is located in Jesus Christ. To him we must come. Having come, we discover that God's mercy is the ultimate source of true joy: "I have trusted in your mercy (*hesed*); my heart shall rejoice in your salvation" (Ps 13:5). To know in experience the mercy of God in Christ is a source of great relief and abounding celebration as we battle on against sin.

(2) Once we have come to know God's mercy in Christ we must praise him with gratitude for that mercy. The apostle Paul sees it as a major outcome of the gospel "that the Gentiles might glorify God for *his* mercy" (Rom 15:9). The Old Testament refrain exhorts us, "Oh, give thanks to the LORD, for *he is* good! For his mercy (*hesed*) *endures* forever" (1 Chr 16:34). Our response should match David's: "I will sing aloud of your mercy (*hesed*) in the morning" (Ps 59:16).

This praise and worship should be an expression of genuine amazement that God has dealt with us in such astonishing kindness. Let us

29. Dabney, *Systematic Theology*, 165.

30. Bavinck, *God*, 203, 206–9.

never take God's mercy for granted, but be overwhelmed with wonder at the realization that "he has not dealt with us according to our sins, nor punished us according to our iniquities" (Ps 103:10). In response, let us indeed love God, our gracious heavenly Father, with all our heart and soul and mind and strength.

(3) As God's people, we need his mercy every day. We are constantly challenged by the circumstances that surround us. We face many temptations and trials. We are dragged down by our own sins and weaknesses. We need, then, to heed the summons of Hebrews 4:16 every day, taking comfort from their implied promise: "let us therefore come boldly to the throne of grace, that we may obtain mercy and find grace to help in time of need."

Our prayer must always be the same as David's prayer in Psalm 51:1: "have mercy upon me, O God, according to your lovingkindness; according to the multitude of your tender mercies, blot out my transgressions."

The Lord's ongoing patience with us is a source of immense relief, for which we should be truly thankful. Moreover, in any situation of need, we can appeal again and again to the mercy of God to help us, to sustain us, and so we find encouragement and contentment whatever our circumstances may be, whatever trials we have to face.

(4) Knowing that our God of mercy is also the sovereign ruler of his entire creation should bring us deep comfort and give us great confidence. We live in a world of uncertainty, but God is reliable. Trusting in his mercy, we may live at peace.

(5) As those who have experienced the mercy of God, it is our privilege and our duty to proclaim that mercy to our fellow sinners. We need to avoid Jonah's mistake of wanting to keep God's mercy for ourselves. Let us be constantly prayerful that the sovereign, saving mercy of God in Christ may be extended to the ends of the earth. Because of his mercy, the LORD says, "I have no pleasure in the death of one who dies." He appeals to sinners, "turn and live" (Ezek 18:32). Our joy as preachers of the gospel is to pass on that invitation. It is God's mercy which makes the Christian proclamation good news. It is an exciting message to preach. We must preach it with joy!

(6) We must heed the injunction of the Lord Jesus, where he says, "be merciful, just as your Father also is merciful" (Luke 6:36). In the context, beginning at verse 27, his particular concern is that we should love even our enemies. After all, God loved us when we were his enemies, and that merciful love is the model which we are called to emulate. Jesus

includes in this concept of being merciful, and loving as God himself does, that we should seek God's blessing on those who mistreat us, and pray even for those who insult or deprecate us. Mercy is expressed in non-retaliation when we are wronged, and in a spirit of generosity, even to those who show us no gratitude. The impetus for showing such mercy comes from knowing that our heavenly reward will be great, even if we are overlooked for reward on earth. It is the mercy of God which sets the pattern for our behavior, "for he is kind to the unthankful and evil" (verse 35).

(7) We must steer well clear of idolatry in all its forms. There is only one true and living God, and he must be the exclusive object of our devotion. Even if there is no danger that we would ever fall into the trap of bowing down to physical images, we must still strive to overcome the temptation to succumb to the modern secular forms of idolatry. It is so easy to idolize money, success, family, leisure activities, to accord to such things a priority in our affections and our activities which rightly belongs to God alone. We must seek God's grace to enable us to maintain an outlook which gives him alone that first place in our lives.

(8) We must ever face up to the unavoidable limitations in our understanding of God. Let us beware of talking about God as if we know him through and through, as if we have got him all worked out. There are infinite depths and heights in the being of God which will for ever remain beyond our ability to penetrate. We need to remember how puny we are, and humbly acknowledge the all-surpassing mystery and majesty of a God who is way beyond our capacity to grasp.

PART TWO: GOD'S TRINITARIAN NATURE

In Titus 2:13 Paul speaks of Jesus Christ as "our great God and Savior." And yet we hear Jesus Christ addressing his Father in heaven as God, as he does in John 17:3: "this is eternal life, that they may know you the only true God." How can we hold these two facts together? That is the question which the doctrine of the Trinity answers.

The first Christians became convinced that the man whom they had known as Jesus of Nazareth was nothing less than divine. The formulation of the doctrine of the Trinity was an offshoot of that conviction. The truth of the Trinity in itself, of course, was not the result of that conviction. It is an eternal reality. But only in the light of Christ could it become clear.

The christological conclusions came first. It was then necessary to relate those conclusions back to the doctrine of the one God. And with the benefit of that hindsight, we can now put the doctrine of God as Trinity nearer to the front of our Systematic Theology.

So we now learn that the God who is sovereign mercy exists in three "persons." And that sublime character of mercy is at the heart of all three. We must be careful not to think that it is in God the Father that we find mercy, but the Son and the Holy Spirit have different characters. The three persons are one God. They all share the same heart.

Strictly speaking, the doctrine of God *is* the doctrine of the Trinity. The distinction between the first two parts of these studies is as follows. The doctrine of God concerns the attributes, the qualities, the character of the one God. The doctrine of the Trinity tells us of the nature of that one God's being: it has a threefold aspect.

BIBLICAL FOUNDATION

It is sometimes said that the doctrine of the Trinity is not taught in Scripture. That is true in the sense that the Bible does not contain a fully formulated declaration that the only God exists in three persons. However, the raw materials for the doctrine are present. They are so obviously present that, once we start to ponder the hints and clues, no other conclusion becomes possible than that God is triune. We must now trace some of the clues.

New Testament

We shall start with the New Testament, because, as a matter of fact, it was in the light of the historical manifestation of the Son of God in Jesus of Nazareth that the trinitarian nature of God became clear. As Warfield says, "The revelation itself was not made in word but in deed. It was made in the incarnation of God the Son and the outpouring of God the Holy Spirit.[31] So Robert Reymond can say, "When we turn to the pages of the

---

31. Warfield, "Trinity," 33.

New Testament we find the doctrine of the triune character of God everywhere *assumed*."[32]

Evidence for the doctrine of the Trinity may be found in various places in the New Testament. We shall highlight some of the most important examples, taking them in biblical order.

Matthew 3:16–17

As Jesus came up out of the water after being baptized "the heavens were opened" and the Spirit of God descended like a dove to alight upon him. Then a voice from heaven declared, "this is my beloved Son, in whom I am well pleased." The Father claims Jesus as his Son, and the Spirit authenticates the claim. Albert Barnes writes:

> It is impossible to explain this transaction consistently in any other way than by supposing that there are three equal persons in the Divine Nature or Essence, and that each of these sustains important parts in the work of redeeming men.[33]

Matthew 28:19

Entrusting his disciples with the great commission the risen Lord Jesus said: "Go therefore and make disciples of all the nations, baptizing them in the name of the Father and of the Son and of the Holy Spirit." What is particularly striking is the use of the singular word "name" followed by the three epithets, Father, Son and Holy Spirit. "Father, Son and Holy Spirit" forms one name. They are not three names. John Gill says: "Hence a confirmation of the doctrine of the Trinity, there are three persons, but one name, but one God."[34]

John 14–16

These chapters contain Jesus' farewell address to his disciples in the upper room. In this address, the truth of the trinity is strongly indicated. As Charles Hodge says;

32. Reymond, *New Systematic Theology*, 209.
33. Barnes, *New Testament*, Vol. 1, 31.
34. Gill, *Exposition*, on Matthew 28:19.

> In the discourse of Christ, recorded in the 14th, 15th, and 16th chapters of John's Gospel, our Lord speaks to and of the Father, and promises to send the Spirit to teach, guide, and comfort his disciples. In that discourse the personality and divinity of the Father, Son and Spirit are recognized with equal clearness.[35]

There are five places in this passage where the three persons of the Trinity are mentioned together.

The first is 14:16–18, where Jesus says that he will pray to the Father, who will give his people another helper, soon identified as "the Spirit of truth." The fact that the three are mentioned together in that single sentence is significant. Moreover, Jesus then continues by telling his disciples that they will know the Spirit, "for he dwells with you and will be in you." However, he continues, "I will not leave you orphans; I will come to you." This indicates that, in the coming of the Spirit, Jesus himself is present with his disciples.

Whereas in those verses we heard that Jesus comes in the Spirit, from the second relevant passage, 14:23–26, we learn further that, in this coming of Jesus by the Spirit, the Father also comes to live with his people. Jesus says of those who love and obey him, "my Father will love him, and we will come to him and make our home with him." He also makes a further point: the Father sends the Holy Spirit in the name of the Son. The inseparability of, and yet the distinctions between, the three divine persons is evident.

Back in John 14:16 Jesus had asked the Father to send the Spirit. In 14:26 he has said that the Father sends the Spirit in the name of the Son. In 15:26, thirdly, he describes the helper, the Spirit of truth, as the one "whom I shall send to you from the Father." These parallel forms of description emphasize the oneness of the Father and the Son. Moreover, Jesus adds the comment that the Spirit "proceeds from the Father." This underlines the fact that his essential nature is identical with the Father's.

The fourth set of verses which we need to mention is 16:5–7. Here Jesus teaches his followers that it is when he returns to the Father that the Spirit will come, and he adds, once again, that he himself will send the Spirit.

Finally, we note from 16:13–15 that the Spirit is not a lone agent. He speaks under the authority of the whole triune Godhead; verse 13 reads, "when he, the Spirit of truth, has come, he will guide you into all truth;

---

35. C. Hodge, *Systematic Theology*, Vol. 1, 448.

for he will not speak on his own *authority*, but whatever he hears he will speak; and he will tell you things to come." Verse 14 announces that the Spirit's task is to glorify Christ by taking what is of Christ and declaring it to the disciples. Jesus then adds that he possesses everything that the Father has: they share the same essential divine nature.

1 Corinthians 12:3–6

Verses 4–6 are structured in a poetically repetitive way: "there are diversities of gifts, but the same Spirit. There are differences of ministries, but the same Lord. And there are diversities of activities, but it is the same God who works all in all." We note the three parallel phrases, "the same Spirit," "the same Lord," and "the same God."

The word "Spirit" is defined by verse 3. It refers to the Holy Spirit, who is also called here "the Spirit of God," a phrase which indicates that there is a distinction in some sense between God and his Spirit. Nonetheless, the parallelism which follows equates them in another sense.

"Lord" is the New Testament's favorite title for Jesus Christ. Verse 3, indeed, identifies him as the person in view in the use of this title here. In the providence of God it is significant that in the Hebrew Old Testament the divine name, Jehovah, was replaced (out of deference and respect) by the title "Lord." (Although the current scholarly consensus is the rendering YHWH, I prefer to retain the traditional form, Jehovah, since it remains more familiar to the wider Christian public). This means that when the New Testament takes up that title and applies it to Jesus, there lies behind it the divine name. Jesus is Jehovah. In the move from Old Testament to New the way has been prepared for the recognition of the triune nature of the Godhead.

The word "God" is often used in the New Testament of the Father specifically, though in a way which by no means reduces the divine status of the Son and the Spirit.

These verses therefore locate Jesus as Lord with the Father and the Spirit in the unity of the triune God.

2 Corinthians 13:14

This verse, which reads: "the grace of the Lord Jesus Christ, and the love of God, and the communion of the Holy Spirit *be* with you all," has been described by Murray Harris as an "embryonic trinitarian formula."[36] It has often been pointed out that to see Jesus Christ and the Holy Spirit as anything less than fully and truly divine would render such a blessing absurd.

Charles Hodge suggests that this apostolic benediction, along with the baptismal formula of Matthew 28:19, has a vital role to play in connection with the doctrine of the Trinity. In these liturgical forms, he writes, "provision was made to keep this doctrine constantly before the minds of the people, as a cardinal article of the Christian faith."[37]

1 Peter 1:2

Peter's opening greeting describes the believers to whom he is writing as "elect according to the foreknowledge of God the Father, in sanctification of the Spirit, for obedience and sprinkling of the blood of Jesus Christ." Edwin Blum comments that here Peter

> reminds his readers of their triune faith and of the triune work of God. While Peter does not go into the developed theological form of the trinitarian faith, the triadic pattern of the Christian faith is already evident in his words.[38]

1 John 5:7–8

In the New King James Version these verses read as follows:

> There are three that bear witness in heaven: the Father, the Word, and the Holy Spirit; and these three are one. And there are three that bear witness on earth: the Spirit, the water, and the blood; and these three agree as one.

However, there are those who would question whether John is here referring to the Trinity. The English Standard Version, for example, reads like this: "There are three that testify: the Spirit and the water and the blood; and these three agree." Such a translation completely omits any trinitarian implication.

The difference results from a discrepancy between different ancient Greek manuscripts. The majority of manuscripts do not have the words

36. M. J. Harris, "2 Corinthians," 406.

37. C. Hodge, *Systematic Theology*, Vol. 1, 447.

38. Blum, "1 & 2 Peter," 220.

which form the second part of verse 7 and the first part of verse 8 in the New King James Version. Beza's edition of the New Testament, known as the *Textus Receptus* (Received Text), includes them. Whether we include this passage amongst the raw materials for the doctrine of the Trinity depends, therefore, on the conclusion which we reach on the issue of the correct text. But that discussion is beyond the scope of these studies.

Old Testament

If we read the Old Testament without the light of New Testament fullness, we are bound to miss the clues to the trinitarian nature of God. But with that light shining on it, we find that the Old Testament contains numerous hints that the one God exists in three persons.

Why, then, was this truth largely concealed as long as the Old Testament age continued?

One reason must have been that it was God's intention first of all to establish the truth of the oneness of God in the face of the polytheistic religions of the time. Another reason is suggested by Louis Berkhof: "The Bible never deals with the doctrine of the Trinity as an abstract truth, but reveals the trinitarian life in its various relations as a living reality."[39]

So it is in relation to the work of redemption as that work reached its climax in the coming of Jesus Christ and the outpouring of the Holy Spirit that the doctrine burst forth into clarity. The doctrine of the Trinity was revealed in connection with the work of the Godhead for human salvation.

However, there are pointers to this doctrine even prior to the coming of Christ. Reymond lists eight categories of Old Testament evidence for the Trinity.[40] Seven are particularly compelling. I shall cite one example of each.

The use of plural pronouns for God

We find an example of this in the very first chapter of the Bible, where God says, "Let us make man in our image" (Gen 1:26). Gordon Wenham

---

39. Berkhof, *Systematic Theology*, 85.
40. Reymond, *New Systematic Theology*, 207–9.

writes: "It is now universally admitted that this was not what the plural meant to the original author."[41]

This may be true, but we must not overlook the intention of the divine Author. He could have inspired the original human author to give a hint of something beyond his own awareness.

God in one sense distinguished from God in another sense

Psalm 45:6 addresses a being who is called "God:" "your throne, O God, *is* forever and ever." But verse 7 then speaks of the one whom this being, God, knows also as "God:" "God, your God, has anointed you with the oil of gladness more than your companions." In the light of the New Testament, we understand these verses to be addressed to God the Son and to be speaking about God the Father.

The "angel of the LORD" both identified as God and yet distinguished from God

In Genesis 16:7 "the angel of the LORD" finds Hagar, and in verses 8–12 speaks to her. In the course of his speech he refers to the LORD, who has listened to Hagar in her affliction. But then in verse 13 Hagar's words show that she has recognized in the angel of the LORD none other than the LORD himself: "She called the name of the LORD who spoke to her, You-Are-the-God-Who-sees; for she said, 'Have I also here seen him who sees me?'" "The angel of the LORD" is the Son of God taking human appearance. The LORD to whom he refers is the Father.

God's Word or God's Spirit personalized

We do not have to wait for the New Testament revelation to realize that God's Word can be spoken of in personal terms. Psalm 107:20 says that God "sent his word and healed them." A word with healing powers, which is not merely spoken, but sent, is clearly a being with personal properties. God's Spirit too is personal. That is clear from Isaiah 63:10: "they rebelled and grieved his Holy Spirit." Only a personal being can experience grief.

---

41. Wenham, *Genesis*, 27–28.

The Messiah, as a divine speaker, referring to the LORD who sent him

Zechariah 2:10–11 is a remarkable passage in this respect:

> "Sing and rejoice, O daughter of Zion! For behold, I am coming and I will dwell in your midst," says the LORD. "Many nations shall be joined to the LORD in that day, and they shall become my people. And I will dwell in your midst. Then you will know that the LORD of hosts has sent me to you."

In verse 10 the LORD speaks to the "daughter of Zion," and promises to come and dwell in her midst. However, in verse 11 the same speaker makes reference to the LORD as a distinct being: "Many nations shall be joined to the LORD in that day." The speaker, the LORD, then repeats his promise to dwell in the midst of his people, and says that this will be conclusive evidence "that the LORD of hosts has sent me to you." Clearly, in the light of the completed revelation of the New Testament, God the Son is the speaker, and God the Father the sender.

The LORD, the angel, and the Holy Spirit depicted as distinct persons

In Isaiah 63:7 the prophet celebrates God's multitudinous lovingkindnesses towards Israel, mentioning his name, the LORD, three times. Throughout verses 7–10 the pronouns "he," "his," and "himself" occur 15 times, referring in each case to the LORD. Verse 8 says that he became Israel's Savior, but in verse 9 we hear that "the angel of his presence" also saved them. However, verse 10 speaks of their rebellion against him, but says that it was his Holy Spirit who was grieved by this rebellion.

The use of plural nouns to refer to God

Isaiah 54:5 says: "your maker *is* your husband, the LORD of hosts *is* his name." Both the words "maker" and "husband" are plural in Hebrew.[42] This may be a hint of the plurality which is present in the Godhead.

---

42. Cf. Motyer, *Isaiah*, 446, n. 1.

DOCTRINAL FORMULATION

The Early Creeds

The fullest statement of the doctrine of the Trinity from the early centuries is found in the so-called "Athanasian Creed."

Athanasius energetically defended the trinitarian doctrine against the Arians, who claimed that the Son of God was not fully divine, but the first created being. This creed was not written by Athanasius, but was named after him. It sums up the theology for which he fought. It was written in Latin sometime between the fifth and eighth centuries.

The relevant section reads as follows:

> We worship one God in Trinity, and Trinity in Unity; neither confounding the persons nor dividing the substance. For there is one person of the Father, another of the Son, and another of the Holy Spirit. But the Godhead of the Father, of the Son, and of the Holy Spirit is all one, the glory equal, the majesty coeternal. Such as the Father is, such is the Son, and such is the Holy Spirit; the Father uncreated, the Son uncreated, and the Holy Spirit uncreated; the Father incomprehensible, the Son incomprehensible, and the Holy Spirit incomprehensible; the Father eternal, the Son eternal, and the Holy Spirit eternal. And yet they are not three eternals but one eternal; as also there are not three uncreated nor three incomprehensible, but one uncreated and one incomprehensible. So likewise the Father is almighty, the Son almighty, and the Holy Spirit almighty; and yet they are not three almighties, but one almighty. So the Father is God, the Son is God, and the Holy Spirit is God; and yet they are not three Gods, but one God. So likewise the Father is Lord, the Son Lord, and the Holy Spirit Lord; and yet they are not three Lords but one Lord. For just as we are compelled by Christian truth to acknowledge every person by himself to be God and Lord; so are we forbidden by the catholic faith to say that there are three Gods or three Lords. The Father is made of none, neither created nor begotten. The Son is of the Father alone, not made nor created, but begotten. The Holy Spirit is of the Father and of the Son, neither made, nor created, nor begotten, but proceeding. So there is one Father, not three Fathers, one Son, not three Sons, one Holy Spirit, not three Holy Spirits. And in this Trinity none is before or after another, none is greater or less than another, but the whole three persons are coeternal, and coequal.

So that in all things, as aforesaid, the Trinity in Unity and the Unity in Trinity is to be worshipped.[43]

The teaching of the creed may be summarized in eight statements.

There is only one undivided divine substance

The Latin word *substantia* means the fundamental, underlying essence of something. It does not have the material connotations that the English word "substance" might imply. Here it refers to the fundamental Godness of God which can never be modified. There is only one such reality.

This divine substance is characterized by a number of attributes

Seven attributes in particular are mentioned in this creed: eternity, glory, majesty, infinity, omnipotence, sovereignty, and uncreatedness. No doubt these are intended only as representative examples.

Within this single divine substance there are three distinct persons, who are not to be confused with one another

The word "person" is used to emphasize the fact that the Father, the Son, and the Holy Spirit each has an individual personality. Each has a specific function within the total work of the Godhead. The Latin word *persona* comes from the verb *persono*, which means "to sound through," or "to resound." The divine reality sounds through all three persons. Each of them resounds with divine glory. But each person sings his own part in the harmony of the single divine music.

All three persons share all the divine attributes

The divine attributes are not shared out between the three persons. It is not that the Father has some of the attributes, the Son some others, and the Spirit a different set again. All three possess every attribute.

---

43. Athanasian Creed, 3–27.

Each person shares fully in divinity in his individual personhood

To take omnipotence as an example, God's omnipotence is not divided into three, so that the Father has one third, the Son another third, and the Spirit the remaining third of the total omnipotence of God. Rather, the totality of the divine omnipotence is present in the Father, and in the Son, and in the Spirit.

There are certain individual properties, which make the three persons truly distinct from one another

It is not just that there are three ways for God to be God. It is not that there are three choices with which God is faced, and from which he must choose how to reveal himself at any given moment. Rather, there are unique characteristics which mark the Father, but not the Son or the Spirit. There are unique characteristics which mark the Son. There are characteristics belonging exclusively to the Spirit.

The creed explains this in these terms. The Father was not made by anyone. He is neither created nor begotten. The Father has independent existence. He is not dependent on another being either to make him out of nothing or to give him birth from some pre-existing reality.

The Son is begotten. He was not made: he is not a creature. He is on the divine side of the absolute divide between God and creation. He is brought forth from the Father alone. He is the Father's offspring. Other creeds stress that this begetting of the Son is an eternal fact. Sometimes it is labelled "eternal generation," the word "generation" being equivalent to "begetting." There was never a moment when the Father existed alone without his Son. Nevertheless, the creed sees the Son's life as derived from the Father. This was an aspect of the early creeds which Calvin questioned, as we shall see later.

The Spirit was not made or created. He is genuinely God, and eternally so. But he was not begotten like the Son. He proceeds, again as an eternal reality.

There is an interesting difference in tense in the way in which the creed speaks of the Son and the Spirit. The Son was begotten. The Latin word *genitus* is in the past tense. The generation (begetting) of the Son was a unique event. It cannot be dated. It happened in eternity, not in time. But it is unrepeatable. On the other hand, the creed uses the present tense, *procedens*, when it speaks of the procession of the Spirit. The Holy

Spirit is every moment going forth from the Father and the Son. This procession is a permanent reality.

The vocabulary chosen for the creed here was borrowed from Scripture, which uses the word "begotten" of the Son on five occasions in John's writings, most famously in John 3:16. The Spirit is said to proceed from the Father in John 15:26. We shall consider this terminology in more details in the chapters on the Doctrines of Christ and of the Holy Spirit.

The three persons are equal

This is true in two ways.

First, they are equal in time. None of the persons comes before or after another. The begetting of the Son and the initial procession of the Spirit did not take place later than the origin of the divinity itself. God is eternally trinitarian. He was not a monad to start with, who at some point gave birth to his Son and put forth his Spirit. To be Father, Son, and Holy Spirit is the eternal nature of God.

Second, they are equal in status. The Son and the Spirit are not lesser deities than the Father. All three together are the one God. Without the Son and the Spirit the Father would not exist. To be Father, Son and Holy Spirit is what it is for the true God to exist at all.

This triune God is to be worshipped

The section of the Athanasian Creed quoted above begins and ends with a mention of the duty we have not just to think correctly about God, but to worship him.

The creed is not mere, bare, dry theology. It is an expression of faith and devotion. The very mystery of which it speaks should drive us to our knees in adoration. The arithmetical impossibility of working God out should prompt us to praise the Father, Son and Holy Spirit, the only true God.

The Reformation Confessions

The doctrine of the Trinity was not a matter of dispute during the Reformation. So the confessions did not make an elaborate declaration of this doctrine. A brief statement to the effect that there is one God in three persons was usually considered sufficient. Those confessions which did have more detail simply reproduced the language of the early centuries. Some of them included some selected quotations from the Athanasian Creed.

Modern Confessions of Faith

The Article on the Trinity in the Indian confession is brief. It is content to affirm the unity of God and his tri-personality. It insists on the equality of the three persons.

The Indonesian and Chinese confessions both have more to say, and they both echo the wording of the ancient creeds. The Indonesian confession clarifies the point that the generation of the Son is an eternal reality: "just as the Father is without beginning and without end, so also is the Son." Like the Athanasian Creed, the Chinese confession emphasizes the fact that worship is due to the triune God, and to no other.

Both of these confessions speak up against false definitions of the trinitarian nature of God. The Indonesian confession rejects two specific errors in connection with the Trinity: the idea that the Son and the Spirit are subordinate deities, and the idea that the Holy Spirit is God the Mother in relation to the Son. The section of the Chinese confession dealing with the Trinity finishes like this:

> We refute all mistaken explanations of the Trinity, such as one entity with three modes of expression (such as water, ice, and steam); or one entity with three identities (such as a person can be son, a husband, and a father, or as the sun, its light and heat).

Perhaps this is intended as a rejection of all attempts to find illustrations of the Trinity in the world of nature or in human experience. The confession recognizes that the mystery of the Trinity is so unique that any analogy is bound to be misleading. Perhaps the Chinese House Church leaders had in mind the words of Isaiah 40:18: "To whom then will you liken God? Or what likeness will you compare to him?"

HISTORICAL ELABORATION

In this section I want to do three things. First, we shall trace the route the early church traveled in coming to a worked out understanding of the truth of the Trinity. Next, we shall look at the trinitarian theology of Augustine and Calvin. Finally, we shall look at how Robert Letham connects the truth of the Trinity with the western classical music tradition.

The Route to a Full Trinitarian Understanding

In the early centuries various explanations of how God could be both one and three were put forward, which the Church then rejected. They came to be classed as "heresies."

This does not mean that the men who put them forward were necessarily heretical unbelievers. They may have been sincere Christians trying their best to delve as deeply as they could into the mystery of the Trinity.

The Church was thrashing this doctrine out for several centuries. Along the way they came to see that some attempts to explain the doctrine had been inadequate. To teach them later would be brazen heresy. But at the time they were well-meaning, though misguided, attempts to make progress towards a better understanding. The faulty attempts helped in that process. It was often against the background of what came to be recognized as unacceptable ways of describing the Trinity that genuine progress was made towards a correct understanding.

We can see the Holy Spirit at work in all the deliberations of the early Christians. He was leading them slowly but surely to the richest possible interpretation of the biblical data which must be gathered together into the doctrine of the Trinity.

Inadequate Explanations of the Trinity

We can identify five inadequate explanations which appeared prior to the Council of Nicaea in AD 325. All of them were motivated by the concern to safeguard monotheism, and to avoid any hint that Christians believed in three separate gods.

Economic Trinitarianism

This view dominated theological reflection during the second century. It taught that the Father is eternal God, and that he became a Trinity in order to conduct the divine economy, that is, to create, govern, and redeem the world. God's eternal nature is not triune. God's triune nature is a functional thing.

ADOPTIONISM

This approach emerged in the third century. It taught that Jesus was an ordinary man until his baptism, at which point he was adopted as the divine Son. The essential nature of God, however, remains unitarian.

MODALISM

This way of interpreting the Trinity, which also developed in the third century, taught that God is a unity, but that he has three different ways of being God for different purposes and at different times. Modalism held that the Father became the Son for a time, and later became the Spirit. This view is also known as "patripassianism," because it implied that it was the person of the Father who suffered and died on the cross. Its most famous representative was Sabellius, so it is also sometimes known as "Sabellianism."

SUBORDINATIONISM

Also dating from the third century, this inadequate explanation taught that the transcendent divine essence is a unity, and is found in God the Father. The Son and the Spirit are both eternal beings, but they derive their deity from the fullness of Godhead which is concentrated in the Father. That means that they are secondary gods, subordinate to the Father.

ARIANISM

In the early fourth century Arius, an Egyptian pastor, pushed subordinationism a step further away from an acceptable trinitarian understanding. The fundamental premise of Arianism was the unity of God. Arius taught that the Son is not a truly divine person. He is a creature of the Father. He is the first of God's creatures, and he was created prior to the creation of the world, but still he had a definite beginning and is not eternal. Arianism was condemned at the Council of Nicaea in the year 325.

The Orthodox Statement: homoousios

The Council of Nicaea used the Greek word *homoousios*, meaning "the same essence." The Nicene Creed affirmed that the Son is of identical nature to the Father. For the rest of the fourth century the appropriateness of the term *homoousios* was much debated. Some wanted a compromise term, *homoiousios*. This meant that the Son is of a similar essence to the Father, but not identical. The chief champion of Nicene orthodoxy was Athanasius. He insisted that the Son is begotten by the Father, not in a specific act, but as an eternal process. Moreover, this generation of the Son is not an act of the Father's will, but something intrinsic to the divine nature.

Up until now the main concern had been with the divine status of Jesus Christ. Once his full deity had been settled, the Church turned its attention to the Holy Spirit. The word *homoousios* was used of the Spirit too. Some people said this implied that the Father had two Sons, so the Cappadocian Fathers, Basil, Gregory of Nyssa, and Gregory of Nazianzen, thought through the different modes of origin of the Son and the Spirit.

In 381 the Council of Constantinople ratified the Nicene teaching. There is one God existing eternally in three persons. The Son and the Spirit are *homoousios* with the Father. The Son is begotten by the Father, and the Spirit proceeds from him.

The Trinitarian Theology of Augustine and Calvin

Robert Reymond argues that there is one great weakness in the trinitarian theology of the Nicene and Athanasian Creeds. There is an implicit tendency to subordinate the deity of the Son and the Spirit to that of the Father. The Father is seen as the fount and source of the Godhead, and deity passed from him to the Son by eternal generation and to the Spirit by eternal procession. The result of this way of putting it is that the Son and the Spirit derive their deity from the Father. They are not self-existent as divine persons. And yet, Reymond observes, part of the essence of true and full deity is self-existence.

Reymond refers also to the Irish Articles, a statement of faith prepared in 1615. It makes this comment on the doctrine of the Trinity:

> The essence of the Father did not beget the essence of the Son; but the person of the Father begets the person of the Son by communicating his whole essence to the person begotten from eternity.

Reymond argues that this suggests that the Son has no personal existence apart from the fact that the Father begets him. However, personal existence is essential to the nature of God. So this wording has the effect of making the deity of the Son secondary.

Reymond notes that, "in the sixteenth century, John Calvin contended against the subordinationism implicit in the Nicene language." The Nicene Creed said that Jesus Christ was "God from God." This implied that he drew his Godness from somewhere else, from outside himself. Calvin argued that the Son of God was *autotheos*—God from himself.[44]

The relevant passage in Calvin's *Institutes* is Book 1, chapter 13. Throughout the chapter Calvin declares his basic agreement with the traditional doctrine, and his general sympathy with the statements of the orthodox early church fathers. But the final couple of sentences relate to the distinction Reymond points out between Calvin and the earlier formulations:

> I have thought it better not to touch on various topics, which could have yielded little profit, while they must have needlessly burdened and fatigued the reader. For instance, what avails it to discuss . . . whether or not the Father always generates? This idea of continual generation becomes an absurd fiction from the moment it is seen that from eternity there were three persons in one God.

Calvin's concern always was to stay within the boundaries laid down by Scripture, to go as far as Scripture allows, and then stop. He sought to avoid mere speculation. He was, therefore, happy to speak of Christ as the Word, the Son, as begotten by God, and begotten by the Father. He was happy to speak of the Son as being from the Father, and the Spirit as being from the Father and the Son. But he was equally clear that, while, in terms of order, the Father is first, then the Son and then the Spirit, as regards the divine essence, there is no distinction. So, as Son, the second person of the Trinity is the Son of the Father, but as God, he is the Son from himself.

---

44. Reymond, *New Systematic Theology*, 317–41.

Calvin also points out the problems which arise from defining the Father as the essence of God, as if deity was transfused by him into the Son and the Spirit:

> On the supposition that the whole essence is in the Father only, the essence becomes divisible, or is denied to the Son, who, being thus robbed of his essence, will be only a titular God . . . . In this way, the divinity of the Son will be something abstracted from the essence of God, or the derivation of a part from the whole.

Calvin declares himself content with a sober definition according to the measure of faith set down in the Bible. This is what he says:

> When we profess to believe in one God, by the name "God" is understood the one simple essence, comprehending three persons . . . ; and accordingly, whenever the name of God is used indefinitely, the Son and the Spirit, not less than the Father is meant. But when the Son is joined with the Father, relation comes into view, and so we distinguish between the persons. But as the personal subsistences carry an order with them, the principle and origin being in the Father, whenever mention is made of the Father and the Son, or of the Father and Spirit together, the name of God is specially given to the Father. In this way the unity of essence is retained, and respect is had to the order, which, however, derogates in no way from the divinity of the Son and Spirit.

Calvin seems to be building here on the teaching of Augustine. He lived during the fifth century, and made one clarification of the doctrine of the Trinity. Whereas earlier theologians had tended to make the Father the starting point for their thinking, Augustine took the divine nature itself as his starting point. This divine essence is the Trinity, he taught.

If by now we find this entire matter completely baffling, we may be encouraged by this statement of Calvin's:

> But if the distinction of Father, Son, and Spirit, subsisting in the one Godhead (certainly a subject of great difficulty), gives more trouble and annoyance to some intellects than is meet, let us remember that the human mind enters a labyrinth whenever it indulges its curiosity, and thus submit to be guided by the divine oracles, how much so ever the mystery may be beyond our reach.

Robert Letham on the Trinity and Western Classical Music

In some beautiful sections of his works Robert Letham has pointed out how the diversity within creation is a reflection of the plurality within the one God, and that human creativity also reflects this diversity within unity. We are made in the image of the triune God, and so, not surprisingly, we find in human life emblems of the plurality within unity of the one who created us. One outstanding example which Letham uses to illustrate this point is western classical music,[45] which, he says, "demonstrates unity-in-diversity very clearly." He notes that "western classical music emerged in a culture formed by Christianity," that it is "a genre that owed its development to the Christian faith."

The key thing is the "tonal harmony" which characterizes western music, and which reflects the plurality within unity which the creator has built into his creation, and which is itself a reflection of his own plurality of persons within the unity of the one God. Letham says of classical music that

> its unity-in-diversity is heard in a variety of instruments combining to play one integrated piece. This is particularly obvious in chamber music, in which the various instruments can be distinctly heard within the overall score.

Letham's point is that classical music, in which different instruments play different parts to contribute to the one harmonious whole, could only have come about in a culture shaped by the Christian faith. Even those composers who were not themselves believers, were nevertheless influenced by the Christian tradition in the midst of which they grew up, and which gave the western world the ability to value unity-in-diversity and diversity-in-unity.

Letham draws a contrast with Muslim societies and the music which originates in Islamic contexts. He writes: "in Islam, unity trumps diversity. Allah is one, and the Muslim world is theoretically one *umma.*" As a result, western music, with its polyphony, different instruments playing different notes in one integrated score, is unacceptable in an Islamic context.

At the other extreme, as Letham also points out, is the postmodern trend. Today that emphasis seems to be in the process of demolishing our western tradition of unity-in-diversity. The clarion call now is "valuing

---

45. Letham, *Systematic Theology*, 284; *Trinity*, 530, 534–35, 538–39.

diversity," and, to quote Letham once more, "its tendency is for unity to be fragmented."

Both Islam and postmodernism are aberrations which reject the truth of one God in three persons. In opposite directions, the cultures which they promote cease truly to reflect the image of God.

Although Letham does not mention this specifically, what he says about orchestral music may surely be applied also to western choral music, in which different voices sing different parts in harmony. Perhaps we may extend this point to suggest that when congregations sing hymns in four-part harmony, the result is a noble reflection of the plurality within unity of the God whom we worship. As a result, such sung praise is the more enriching, and perhaps the more glorifying to the God whose praise we sing.

PRACTICAL APPLICATION

(1) We must believe everything which has been revealed about God, even where we cannot possibly understand it fully. We must struggle to understand as much as we can. But when we reach the limits of our finite ability, our reaction must not be rebellion and unbelief, but humility and worship.

(2) We must take care how we word our prayers. This is especially important for those of us who have been entrusted with the responsibility of leading God's people in prayer. Here are three examples of prayers which betray some confusion about the doctrine of the Trinity.

> Heavenly Father, we praise and worship you. You are the great and glorious God. We thank you for all your goodness to us. We praise you for your amazing mercy. We worship you as the God of love. We thank you for coming down from heaven and becoming a human being. We praise you for dying on the cross for our sins. In Jesus' name, Amen.

Perhaps the person who was praying here forgot how he had begun the prayer by the time he reached the sixth sentence. As a result, he carelessly spoke of the incarnation and crucifixion of the Father instead of the Father's Son. This echoes the ancient heresy of modalism.

> Dear Lord Jesus Christ, you are worthy of all our love and adoration. We praise you for your great glory. All honor and blessing belong to you. We thank you for sending your Son to live in

> this world and to die for our sins. We thank you for showing us
> your love in such an amazing way. In Jesus' name, Amen.

Here a prayer is addressed to God the Son. In principle, there is nothing wrong with that. However, Jesus did not send his Son. In fact he did not have any children. Some confusion about the respective roles of the Father and the Son has crept into this prayer.

> We give praise and worship to you, O God our Father. We thank
> you for sending your Son to be the Savior of the world. Fill us
> with your Spirit, that we may live for Christ in all things. We
> pray in your own worthy name. Amen.

Here is a prayer addressed to God the Father, but finishing, "in your name." This conflicts with the New Testament emphasis on praying in the name of Jesus. We have no authority to invent a formula which has no biblical warrant and to pray to the Father in his own name.

Of course, any of us can have a slip of the tongue from time to time. We certainly should not become hyper-critical of other people's prayers. But if we constantly make mistakes like these, it would suggest that we have not properly understood the truth of the Trinity. In that case we need to think it through seriously.

(3) We must rejoice that there is a trinitarian framework to our salvation. Father, Son and Holy Spirit are all equally committed to the joyful task of bringing many sons to glory. Jesus says, "No one comes to the Father except through me" (John 14:6). But this means that through him there really is a way back to God. And it means that the Father is one who desires that we should come, and who welcomes us with open arms when we do. For we may "testify that the Father has sent the Son *as* Savior of the world" (1 John 4:14). And since we received that salvation, "God has sent forth the Spirit of his Son into your hearts, crying out, 'Abba! Father!'" (Gal 4:6).

(4) We must preach the gospel of God. Earlier we saw how Charles Hodge suggested that the apostolic benediction in 2 Corinthians 13:14 was designed to keep the truth of the Trinity at the forefront of the Church's consciousness: "The grace of the Lord Jesus Christ, and the love of God, and the communion of the Holy Spirit *be* with you all."

The three qualities here associated with the three persons of the Trinity point us to the very heart of the gospel. Jesus Christ's grace is his willing saving work on behalf of sinners, who deserved nothing from him. God the Father's love is the ultimate motivation of his will to reconcile the world to himself in Christ. Although several ways of understanding the Holy Spirit's communion (or fellowship) have been suggested, the phrase is probably to be understood to mean that the Holy Spirit is the channel through which the desire of the triune God to be restored to relationship with sinners is realized. Matthew Poole says that it is the Holy Spirit "by whom the Father and Son communicate their love and grace to the saints."[46]

These three divine qualities—grace, love, and fellowship—are those by which the divine mercy becomes operative in our experience. As Murray Harris says, "it is through the grace shown by Christ in living and dying for men that God demonstrates his love and the Spirit creates fellowship."[47]

Our calling is to proclaim to a sinful world the grace of a triune God of love who recalls straying sinners into fellowship with himself. To be reconciled to him is to be "filled with all the fullness of God" (Eph 3:19) in his triune glory.

46. Poole, *Commentary*, 639.
47. M. J. Harris, "2 Corinthians," 406.

2

The Doctrine of Revelation

WE HAVE CONSIDERED THE doctrines of God's character of mercy and God's mysterious being as Trinity. But how can we know anything about God and his works? This is only possible because God has made them known to us.

God is so great and we are so small that it is impossible for us to find out anything about him unless he reveals it to us. And more than that, sin has blinded our minds, so that we have to pray, in the words of Psalm 119:18, "Open my eyes, that I may see wondrous things from your law."

We also have to remember that God has chosen not to reveal everything that he could reveal: "the secret *things belong* to the LORD our God, but those *things which are* revealed *belong* to us and to our children forever, that *we* may do all the words of this law" (Deut 29:29). This means that in all our attempts to formulate a tidy faith we must proceed with humility.

This text also reminds us that God's purpose in revealing certain things to us is not just to interest us or to amuse us, but so that we can do what he commands. Unless our study of Systematic Theology leads us into deeper obedience, we are just wasting our time.

The main source for God's revelation of himself and his truth is the Scriptures. However, when we do accept the inspiration, inerrancy, and authority of Scripture as the ultimate revelation, then we can say that there is a second form of revelation also—a revelation of God in creation. We can say so, only because Scripture itself speaks of this second source of revelation. We shall therefore divide our consideration of this doctrine into two parts, looking in turn at God's revelation in Scripture and in creation.

PART ONE: REVELATION IN SCRIPTURE

The doctrine of revelation in Scripture is the absolute foundation for every other doctrine. If we lose confidence in the Scriptures, that will have implications for what we say about everything else.

In Isaiah 40:5 the prophet assures us that "the mouth of the LORD has spoken." Earlier on the same prophet wrote: "To the law and to the testimony! If they do not speak according to this word, *it is* because *there is* no light in them" (Isa 8:20).

These words inform us that God's speech has been recorded for us in his Word: the doctrine of revelation becomes focused as the doctrine of Scripture.

In the story of Samuel, we learn that in his early years he "did not yet know the LORD, nor was the word of the LORD yet revealed to him" (1 Sam 3:7). By placing these two phrases side-by-side, God shows us that it is through his Word that we get to know him, and it is always through the Word of God that we get to know him better.

We are not to study the Bible just to become experts in theology. In our studies we are aiming to have a tidy faith so that we may grow in our knowledge of the Lord. "The LORD revealed himself to Samuel . . . by the word of the LORD" (1 Sam 3:21). As we proceed with these studies in Systematic Theology, let us pray that the result will be that the Lord himself is revealed to us afresh.

On the road to Emmaus, as Jesus spoke with Cleopas and his companion, "he expounded to them in all the Scriptures the things concerning himself" (Luke 24:27). In the end, all God's revelation leads to Jesus Christ. He is the true focus of all the Scriptures. The whole Bible is Christ-centered. We study it so that we may "grow in the grace and knowledge of our Lord and Savior Jesus Christ" (2 Pet 3:18).

BIBLICAL FOUNDATION

Old Testament

We shall look at just one passage in this connection. Psalm 19:7–11 is one of the main Old Testament contexts for establishing the doctrine of Scripture. We shall notice four things.

The Terms Used to Refer to God's Word

Six different terms are used. Taken together they refer to Scripture as a whole. Each term brings out a different aspect of God's Word.

Law (verse 7)

This translates the Hebrew word *tôrâ*. This does not only mean law in the sense of commandments. It means instruction. It is derived from the verb *yārâ*, which means "to show" or "to point out." This compares the Bible to a teacher. Just as a teacher points out to his students things that they would not and could not otherwise know, so Scripture shows us truth that we would otherwise be ignorant of, and so it instructs us. *Tôrâ* can also mean "direction," and *yārâ* can mean, specifically, "to show the way."[1] The Bible is like a signpost. God's Word shows us the way that we should go. It points us to Jesus, who said, "I am the way" (John 14:6).

Testimony (verse 7)

The Hebrew word which this translates is *ʿēdût*. It is derived from a word which refers to the testimony of a witness,[2] to the evidence which the witness presents. When a witness gives evidence in a court case, his testimony should be reliable. He is under a solemn charge to speak truthfully, so that his testimony cannot be refuted. The evidence he presents should be conclusive so that the case is clearly settled. The Bible certainly is reliable: nothing it says can be refuted, because everything it says is true. The Scriptures are not to be taken lightly. They proclaim a serious message about serious issues.

---

1. Tregelles (ed.), *Lexicon*, 208, 503; Enns, "Law," 893.
2. Schultz, "'ûd," 1576c–f.

The word *'ēdût* is also connected with the verb *'ēd*, which has the connotation of saying something again and again.[3] The thing about committing something to writing is that every time you read it you read the same words. And every person who comes to a written document reads the same thing. Again and again, repeatedly, always, the Bible is saying the same thing.

Subjectively, of course, there is such a wealth of truth in the Scriptures that we may go on and on discovering new things as we read the same words. However, what we discover is truth that has always been there. Only now our eyes have been opened to perceive it. The Bible is God's unchanging Word. It does not alter with changes of culture or fashion.

Statutes (verse 8)

This term speaks of the requirements of a properly appointed authority, the legislation passed by a properly constituted government.

When an election takes place, we may or may not like the outcome. But provided the result has not been rigged, provided there have been no threats or bribes, the outcome is constitutionally valid, and we have to accept it. We have to respect the decisions of the duly appointed authority. Everything in the Bible has been appointed by the God who is the properly constituted king over all. Our duty is to accept it.

Commandment (verse 8)

The Hebrew original here is *miṣwâ*. It is derived from *ṣāwâ*, which means "to give orders."[4] So this word draws attention to those aspects of the Bible which are more specifically directive. Scripture tells us what we ought to do, how we should behave. It reveals to us what sort of life God orders.

Fear (verse 9)

Normally we think of fear as an emotion inside us. Psalm 2:11 exhorts us to "serve the LORD with fear." We read in Proverbs 1:7, "The fear of the LORD is the beginning of knowledge." True knowledge starts with that subjective fear. But how do we obtain it? Here in Psalm 19:9 the Bible is

3. Cf. Schultz, "*'ûd*," 1576b.
4. T. F. Williams, "*ṣwh*," 776–77.

called "the fear of the Lord," because it is through God's Word that we learn to fear him, and so get to know him.

Judgments (verse 9)

This word means "decision" or "sentence." It would be used of the sentence passed by a court of law at the conclusion of a case, once the decision has been made that the accused is guilty.[5] The Bible pronounces God's decision about us. It announces his sentence against a world found guilty in sin. It rules that we are under condemnation, and so drives us in desperation to the Savior.

In the Psalm all six of these terms are followed by the phrase "of the Lord," translating God's covenant name, Jehovah. In Exodus 6:6–7 the Lord said to Moses:

> I *am* the Lord; I will bring you out from under the burdens of the Egyptians, I will rescue you from their bondage, and I will redeem you with an outstretched arm and with great judgments. I will take you as my people, and I will be your God. Then you shall know that I *am* the Lord your God who brings you out from under the burdens of the Egyptians.

These words explain what God's covenant name implies: it means that he is the God who liberates, rescues, and redeems his people, so that he and they can belong to each other in a commitment that cannot be broken. That is the God who speaks the Word of revelation. His Word is basically the revelation of his saving grace.

The first of these six words, *tôrâ*, is often used as a summary term for the Word of God as a whole. Although it is translated "law," we need to be clear that it means the whole of God's message of grace. The Bible recognizes no antithesis between law and gospel. The Dispensationalist tendency to characterize the Old Testament as a word of law and the New Testament as a word of gospel grace is quite false.

The Old Testament, just as much as the New, is the proclamation of the grace of God in the gospel. The New Testament continues and brings to its conclusion the gospel message which had been proclaimed in the Old Testament from the very beginning of Genesis onwards.

---

5. Culver, "*šāpaṭ*," 2443c.

The Qualities of God's Revelation

Each of these six terms is associated with an adjective which describes a quality of God's Word. Taken together they add up to the declaration that God's Word is of the highest possible quality.

PERFECT (VERSE 7)

This translates *tāmîm*. This is the same word that is used to describe a lamb as being "without blemish." If a lamb was to be good enough for a sacrifice it had to be sound, healthy, and complete. This emphasizes the truth that God's Word as given to us in the Bible is perfect. There is nothing at all wrong with the Bible. Nothing can be added, nothing needs to be removed.

Of course, when Psalm 19 was first written God's Word was not yet complete. This statement anticipates the day of full revelation with the coming of Christ. But it was also true, as regards the stage of progress in revelation which had then been reached, that there were no deficiencies in God's Word.

SURE (VERSE 7)

The original word is *'āman*. This word has a range of meanings. Its basic sense is "to be built," but it can also mean "to be supported," or "to be established," and sometimes "to be lasting," and "to be permanent." It would be used of a building that is built to last, a building that stands on a firm foundation, so that it is a safe place to be.[6] The Bible will stand firm for ever. Shifting human opinions may come and go, but God's revelation lasts, it is of permanent validity.

RIGHT (VERSE 8)

This translates *yāšār*, which means straight, whether upright (perfectly vertical), or level (perfectly horizontal).[7] In Ezekiel 1 we have an example of both uses of this word. In verse 7 the four living creatures' legs are said to be "straight"—up and down. In verse 23 their wings are said to be "straight"—from side to side. If a plumb line finds a wall to be completely

---

6. Tregelles (ed.), *Lexicon*, 36.
7. Wiseman, "*yāšār*," 930.0.

vertical, the wall could be described as *yāšār*. If a spirit level finds a ledge to be perfectly horizontal, the ledge could be described as *yāšār*. From whatever angle you examine the message of the Bible, you will find it to be just exactly right.

Yāšār can also mean "pleasing." Joab used this word when he said that David would have been pleased if Absalom had survived, even though he had become an enemy (2 Sam 19:6). The perfection of God's revelation is such that it is pleasing to those who receive it with faith and love.

Pure (verse 8)

Here the original word is *bar*. This term means "clean" or "choice." It comes from the word *bārar*, meaning "polished."[8] It is used in Isaiah 49:2: "He has made my mouth like a sharp sword; in the shadow of his hand he has hidden me, and made me a polished shaft; in his quiver he has hidden me."

It speaks of polishing weapons to make them bright and clean for a parade. In Psalm 19:8 this word points to the dazzling splendor of God's Word. The Bible puts any other message in the shade.

Clean (verse 9)

This translates *ṭāhôr*. It is the word that is used of the pure gold which had to be used in the construction of the tabernacle. For example, Exodus 25:17 says, "You shall make a mercy seat of pure gold." Pure gold is gold without any mixture of inferior contents. The Bible is God's truth, and there is not a scrap of error mixed up with it.

True (verse 9)

This translates *ᵉmet*, a term which speaks of something stable and firm, something reliable and trustworthy, something true and certain.[9] All these descriptions are applicable to God's Word. The Bible is unique, unrivalled, unbeatable, true. The LORD's revelation is beyond question.

---

8. Kalland, "*bārar*," 288.0.

9. Tregelles (ed.), *Lexicon*, 39.

In addition to these six adjectives there are two phrases in verse 9 which tell us more about the qualities of God's revelation.

First, it is "enduring forever." It will never ever be necessary to make any changes to the Bible. It will never become obsolete or out of date. No opponent will ever succeed in destroying it.

Second, it is "righteous altogether." The word "righteous" translates *ṣādaq*. It means "to be in the right." This word teaches us that there is nothing in the Bible that will ever be exposed as a sham, nothing that could ever be found out to be incorrect. The word "altogether" tells us that this is equally true whether you consider God's Word as a unified whole, or whether you delve into every particular part. Every detail of God's Word is right and true.

All six of these adjectives, and words similar to both these phrases are used in other parts of the Old Testament as descriptions of God himself. God's Word is as it is because God is as he is. The Bible reflects the character of the LORD who gave it. It derives all its qualities from him. By its very nature, it truly is a revelation of him, and we can rely on it.

The Impact of God's Word

Each clause in verses 7–8 ends with a statement about what God's Word does for those who receive it.

GOD'S WORD CONVERTS THE SOUL (VERSE 7)

The word "converts" translates *šûb*. It means "to turn back."[10] The picture is of the sinful soul glibly marching on in wilful unbelief, oblivious of the destruction that lurks just ahead. The person who is dead in sin is careering towards the edge of a precipice, and yet is totally unaware of the danger. The message of Scripture says, "Wake up! Be alert! Stop! Go into reverse!" The soul is rescued, revived, and it is the Word of God which is responsible for the sinner's new spiritual vitality.

---

10. Tregelles (ed.), *Lexicon*, 471–72.

GOD'S WORD MAKES WISE THE SIMPLE (VERSE 7)

The word translated "simple" is *pᵉtî*. It means "easily enticed" or "deceived."[11] It speaks of the gullible person, who can be led astray very easily. It speaks of the foolish person, who can be persuaded to do anything, however disastrous.

Here is a sad picture of human life in sin. We are prone to deception. We are hopelessly misled. We are naively open to listen to any voice. We are tragically misguided. We are led astray, enticed into wrong ways by the voices of unbelief. Then the Word of God speaks. It brings wisdom. It guides us, so that we can begin to live well. It sets us going in the right direction. It enables us to act with shrewd foresight.

GOD'S WORD REJOICES THE HEART (VERSE 8)

The Hebrew word translated "rejoices" is *śāmaḥ*. It means "to brighten," and so "to gladden," "to make joyful."[12] The life of sin is a miserable life. But when the Bible's message of grace and salvation and hope breaks into the sinner's heart, it brings light and gladness and true joy.

GOD'S WORD ENLIGHTENS THE EYES (VERSE 8)

Life in sin is like groping in the dark. When you grope in the dark you are in danger. You are exposed to threats which you can't see. The sinner is unaware of temptation or of impending judgment. To receive the message of Scripture is like having the light turned on. It is like having a torch shining on your pathway, or like the sunrise which ends the night.

The Power of God's Revelation

Verses 10–11 highlight three aspects of the response made by those who receive the Word, and thus underline its power.

---

11. Goldberg, "*pātâ*," 1853.0.
12. Tregelles (ed.), *Lexicon*, 461.

THEY LOVE IT (VERSE 10)

They find the message of Scripture more desirable than gold and sweeter than honey to their taste. To the true believer the Word of God is worth more than all the riches which this world can offer. In their love for the Bible, believers find it far more palatable than the richest delicacies that the most fashionable restaurant can serve up.

THEY ARE WARNED BY IT (VERSE 11)

The word translated "warned" is *zāhar*. The same word is used in two passages in Ezekiel (3:17–21, where the word appears in every verse, and 33:3–9). Here is Ezekiel 3:17: "Son of man, I have made you a watchman for the house of Israel; therefore hear a word from my mouth, and give them warning from me." The prophet Ezekiel was appointed "a watchman for the house of Israel." His task was to "give them warning" of the judgment of death hanging over the wicked, to turn them from their wicked ways, so that their life would be spared. The Bible warns us, so that we are constantly turned away from error and sin.

THEY ARE REWARDED IN KEEPING IT (VERSE 11)

We keep God's Word by believing it, by accepting it, by refusing to question it, by obeying it. This is not saying that salvation is a reward for our obedience. It is *in* keeping God's Word that the reward is enjoyed. The reward is not something received later as payment *for* keeping God's Word. The word translated "reward" is *ʿēqeb*. It is connected with the word *ʿāqēb*, which can mean "footsteps."[13] This suggests that the reward consists in following in the footsteps of our Lord. In his footsteps we find security and joy. This is a reward which is altogether a kindness of undeserved grace.

New Testament

We shall study two key New Testament passages on this theme.

---

13. Payne, "*ʿāqab*," 1676.0.

2 Timothy 3:15–17.

Three things stand out from this passage.

THERE ARE TWO WORDS FOR THE BIBLE

The plural word "Scriptures" (verse 15) translates the Greek word *gramma*, while the singular word "Scripture" (verse 16) translates *graphē*. The two terms are related, though slightly different in meaning. *Graphē* emphasizes the fact of writtenness, and so indicates the method by which God has chosen to get his Word to us. *Gramma* emphasizes the finished product, the document resulting from the act of writing and particularly its sacredness.[14] Together they emphasize that God has ensured that his revelation has been written down. We have his Word in writing.

THERE ARE TWO DESCRIPTIONS OF THE BIBLE

Holy (verse 15)

This translates *hieros*, a word used in only one other place in the New Testament, where it refers to the holy things of Old Testament worship, the sacrifices (1 Cor 9:13). Leviticus 22:3 makes it clear that the holy things were so sacred that to handle them while unclean was to profane the LORD's name, and resulted in banishment from his presence. The holy Scriptures are just as sacred. They are to be handled with extreme reverence. In Ezekiel 22:26 the LORD complains that the priests have profaned his holy things in that "they have not distinguished between the holy and the unholy." To treat the holy things as if they were merely ordinary was one way of profaning them. We need to remember that holy Scripture is no ordinary book. It must be held as unique and sacred. To read the Bible as if it is just like any other book is an act of profanity. We must read it with reverence, awe, and faith.

Given by inspiration of God (verse 16)

This phrase translates the single Greek word *theopneustos*. Its literal meaning is "breathed out by God." When we breathe out, we release air.

---

14. Mounce, *Pastoral Epistles*, 563–64.

When words are carried on the air we release, we speak: our breath is given a meaningful sound. This verse is telling us that to have the Scriptures is no different from God actually making sounds in the air for us to hear with our ears. If we want to know what God is saying, we must turn to the Bible. The Bible is his speech.

Theopneustos is related to the word *pneuma*, which means "Spirit." To say that the Scriptures are breathed out by God is to say that they are given by God's Spirit, that they are imbued with God's Spirit.

This applies to "all Scripture." The Bible as a whole is breathed out by God, and every separate bit of the Bible is breathed out by God. We cannot say that some parts of the Bible are more inspired than others. All of it is God's speech.

THERE ARE TWO THINGS WHICH THE BIBLE DOES

It is able to make you wise for salvation (verse 15)

The Bible has dynamic power. It has the ability to give us a clear understanding of the message of the gospel.

It is profitable (verse 16)

The Bible brings us countless benefits, huge advantages. It teaches us the truth. It convicts us of sin. It straightens out our distorted lives. It trains us in godly living. This function of God's Word has one goal in view: that the believer may be completely kitted out to live for God. The words rendered "complete" and "equipped" in verse 17 are related: "complete" translates *artios*, while "equipped" translates *exartizo*. Both are linked with the word *arti*, meaning "now." We are called to live for God appropriately for our own time and place. God has placed each of us where we are. We are to serve him using methods relevant to our own generation, in ways significant for our own context. To achieve that we need the Word of God.

One question arises from the study of these verses: since Paul's primary reference here is to the Hebrew Scriptures (the Old Testament), does this passage have anything to tell us about the New Testament?

Three other passages are helpful in answering this question.

In 2 Peter 3:16 Peter admits that in Paul's letters there are "some things hard to understand." He acknowledges that some people therefore abuse Paul's teaching "as *they do* also the rest of the Scriptures." Peter here puts the writings of his fellow apostle on a par with the accepted canon of the Hebrew Bible. That means that everything that 2 Timothy 3:15–17 has said about the Old Testament applies equally to Paul's letters.

However, if Peter is referring only to Paul's writings, what about the rest of the New Testament? Ephesians 3:5 links Paul with all the "holy apostles and prophets" as those to whom the Holy Spirit gave God's revelation. The phrase "apostles and prophets" should probably be understood to mean the apostles, who are prophets: the apostles are a prophetic group. Their description as "holy (*hagios*)," means "set apart." The apostles were specially called to be the official channel of the final chapter in God's revelation. They are the authentic interpreters of Christ and of the salvation which is given in him. Their writings are as much part of God's Word as the prophetic Scriptures of the Old Testament.

On the other hand, in 2 Peter 3:2 the apostles are distinguished from the prophets who went before. Here the word "prophets" refers to the men whose writings form the Old Testament Scriptures, in which the coming of Christ was predicted. However, Peter then sets the Lord's commandment through the apostles alongside the prophetic revelation in the Old Testament. The apostolic writings rank equally as Scripture. They are in fact the words of the Lord himself speaking through the men who are his mouthpiece.

These three passages show that everything that 2 Timothy 3:15–17 says about the Old Testament applies by extension to the New Testament too. The whole Bible is revelation breathed out by God.

2 Peter 1:19–21

From these verses we highlight four things.

THE TERMS USED FOR GOD'S WORD

The prophetic Word (verse 19)

This phrase translates *ho prophētikos logos*. The "pro-" bit of the word "prophetic" can mean either "before" or "above."[15] So this whole phrase can mean two things: (1) it can mean that the Bible declares things before they happen; (2) it can mean that the Bible is something spoken from above. Both are true. Some parts of the Bible are prophecies which foretell something in the future. Every part of the Bible is God speaking from above, making his revelation known.

Prophecy of Scripture (verse 20)

These words translate *prophēteia graphēs*. *Prophēteia* comes from the same root as *prophētikos*. It has the same significance: it refers to a word of truth, spoken from above. And the phrase as a whole spells out for us where we find the prophetic word—in the Scripture. The singular is significant. Although Peter uses the word in the plural in 2 Peter 3:16, here the singular emphasizes that there is a unity to the whole of God's revelation. Every part of the Bible is conveying the same message.

THE "CONFIRMED" PROPHETIC WORD

We are told in verse 19 that, once the prophetic word has been committed to writing in the Scriptures, it is "confirmed." This translates *bebaioteron*, which is the comparative form of the simple word *bebaios*, whose basic meaning is "stable," "sure," or "trustworthy," and is derived from the word *bainō*, meaning "to walk."[16] We could say that the Scriptures provide firmer ground, where we can tread with greater sure-footedness. However, this phraseology forces to ask what it is with which the Bible is being compared and found to be confirmed as having greater stability?

We find the answer in the previous verses. In verses 17 and 18 Peter describes that awesome moment when he was on the Mount of Transfiguration, when he and his companions heard the "voice which came from heaven," identifying Jesus as the beloved Son of God the Father.

---

15. Greenlee, *Exegetical Grammar*, 43.
16. Liddell & Scott, *Lexicon*, 125, 129; Thayer, *Lexicon*, 99.

Now, thirty years later, Peter looks back to that tremendous experience, and says that, for all the majestic glory of that occasion, it was not the greatest example of God speaking that he has ever known. We have the written Word of God in the Scriptures, and that is the more sure and stable prophetic word. The Bible is confirmed beyond voices from heaven. It provides a far firmer foundation for our faith. We are on much safer ground when we walk in the light of the written Word.

Even today, there is the temptation to look for voices from heaven. We sometimes wish that God would communicate to us directly. But we need to remember that even the apostle who heard an audible voice says that that experience was nothing in comparison with the Scriptures. If I claim that the Lord has told me something directly, there is no way of checking whether I am right. If I turn to the Scriptures, everything God has said is documented. The evidence of what he has revealed is there for all to see. It can be confirmed.

Some years ago a member of the British government had to resign. She had been accused of breaking the law. For a couple of weeks she kept denying it, both in Parliament and to the press. She clung on to her job. Then one day, a member of the opposition came across an email which proved that she was not telling the truth. She resigned the next day. She had no option. The documentary evidence was out in the open. As long as verbal accusations were being made and she was verbally denying them, no one could be sure who was right. The document clinched it.

In the Bible we have documentary proof of everything that God has said. It is far more certain and reliable than any guesses or claims I might make. It is the clinching evidence that we can rely on.

What we Know as a Matter of Primary Importance

We know "this first," says verse 20, that God's revelation in Scripture "is not of any private interpretation." The reference is to a possible private interpretation by the original human writer: it was not some idiosyncratic whim which prompted the prophets to speak. Their message did not find its source within themselves. Verse 21 explains: the Scriptures did not originate in a decision of the human will. The teachings of the Bible are not mere products of the human mind or imagination. Rather, "holy men of God spoke *as they were* moved by the Holy Spirit."

The word translated "moved" is the root from which we get our English word "ferry." On two of the occasions when I visited the Philippines I traveled from Manila to Iloilo by boat. The ferry moved me from my starting-point to my destination. As the prophets wrote their words, the Holy Spirit ferried them to the place where God wanted them to arrive. As a result, running through all the human features of the Bible, there is a divine quality. Every word is what God himself has spoken.

THE NEED THEREFORE TO HEED THE SCRIPTURES

This world is the dark place mentioned in verse 19. Ephesians 6:12 speaks of "the darkness of this age." Sin has cast a dark shadow across human existence. The Bible is a lamp, and it is an absolute necessity until "the day dawns" with the second coming of Christ.

That daybreak will be the time when "the morning star rises in your hearts." This refers to the climax and fullness of divine revelation which will impact the heart of every believer when we finally see the Lord. Until then we shall always need the revelation which we have now in the Scriptures.

The Scriptures are complete and infallible, but they are only for this life. Once we are in heaven there will be an even better revelation. The Bible will be superfluous then, just as a candle adds nothing to the brilliance of unclouded summer sunshine.

DOCTRINAL FORMULATION

The Early Creeds

The fourth-century Nicene Creed includes the words, "I believe in the Holy Spirit. . ., who spoke by the prophets."

This statement affirms that the voice of the Spirit of God is heard in the prophetic Scriptures. The reference to "the prophets" probably includes the writings of both the Old Testament prophets and the apostles whose prophetic calling has given us the New Testament.

In the original statement from Nicaea in AD 325 the doctrine of the Holy Spirit was confined to the words, "And [I believe] in the Holy Spirit." At Constantinople in AD 381, this was enlarged. The phrase, "who spoke by the prophets" was one of the additions.

In the early centuries of the Christian era, many local churches prepared their own creedal summaries, just as local churches often do today. The revision of the Nicene Creed at Constantinople was based on a local creed used in the church at Salamis, a city on the island of Cyprus, which included this clause in its creed: "We believe in the Holy Spirit, who spoke in the Law, and preached in the prophets, and descended at Jordan, and spoke in the apostles."[17]

The briefer addition to the Nicene Creed is probably intended as a summary of those words. The Holy Spirit spoke by the prophets in the sense of the Law and the Prophets of the Old Testament and the New Testament apostles. But the mention of the descent of the Spirit upon Jesus Christ at Jordan is a reminder that every word which he spoke was likewise the genuine voice of the Spirit of God. By setting the teaching of Jesus in the context of the references to the Spirit-inspired writing, speaking and preaching, both before and after his time, this sentence makes a wonderful point. To read the Scriptures is to hear the voice of Christ as authentically, as clearly, as if we had been there in Galilee when he was teaching here on earth.

In the following century the Chalcedonian Definition, having spelt out the truth of the two natures of our Lord Jesus Christ, adds this phrase, "even as the prophets from earliest times spoke of him."

Here is recognition that Christ is the heart, the focus, of all God's revelation. Everything contained in both the Old and the New Testaments points us to him.

The Reformation Confessions

The confessions typically include a list of the 66 books of the Old and New Testaments, and distinguish them from the Apocrypha. Several of the apocryphal books—Tobit, Judith, the first two books of the Maccabees, the Wisdom of Solomon, Ecclesiasticus, and Baruch, as well as some additional passages in the books of Esther and Daniel—had come into use on a par with the Scriptures in the medieval Catholic Church.

The Reformed churches reasserted the clear distinction between the inspired Scriptures and other religious writings, however valuable the latter might be as a source of historical information, or as objects of

---

17. Epiphanius, "Ancoratus," 37.

literary interest. The canonical books alone are the Holy Scriptures, the written Word of God.

The confessions then explore four themes as they develop the doctrine of Scripture.

The process by which the Scriptures were transmitted to the world

This is described in five stages.

(1) Scripture originated with God: Scripture does not find its source in human will; it comes from God.

(2) God revealed his Word to chosen men: the Scriptures were handed down by the Holy Spirit, as divine oracles were given to the prophets at various times and in various ways.

(3) God's Word was published to the world: through the preaching of the prophets and apostles God's revelation was passed on.

(4) God's Word was committed to writing: this is evidence of God's special care for us; it ensures that the truth is preserved.

(5) The Bible is the living voice of God: as he spoke to the prophets, so he still speaks to us through the Scriptures.

How the 66 books are identified as canonical

The confessions recognize the importance of asserting how we know that this particular set of books are the canonical Scriptures, and of spelling out the grounds on which we exclude the apocrypha. Three reasons are given for insisting on the distinctiveness of the books of the Bible.

THE CHURCH'S ACKNOWLEDGEMENT

The earliest Christians adopted the Jewish canon as its first Bible. Over a period of several decades the 27 books which make up our New Testament were added to the canon of Scripture. The church as a whole gave its common consent to the addition of these books. This does not mean that the church created the Bible, or decided which books to accept. It was more a case of the church recognizing which books did have divine authority.

An illustration might help us. A doctor is having difficulty deciding what treatment will be best for his patient. In the end he gives the patient a huge list of things to try out. "Then come back and tell me what has helped you," the doctor says. The patient returns at the appointed time. He hands the doctor a list, and says, "I've discovered that these 66 things help me." In the same way, the church made a discovery: these 66 books really do help us in our Christian life. They really do have the stamp of divine inspiration.

THE EVIDENCE WITHIN THE SCRIPTURES THEMSELVES

One such evidence is the fulfilment of prophecy. Another is the way in which the Bible's excellent quality reflects its divine origin. This is expressed beautifully in the Westminster Larger Catechism:

> The Scriptures manifest themselves to be the Word of God by their majesty and purity, by the consent of all the parts and the scope of the whole, which is to give all glory to God; by their light and power to convince and convert sinners, to comfort and build up believers unto salvation.

THE WITNESS OF THE SPIRIT

The Holy Spirit illumines the believer's heart, so enabling him to discern the supernatural quality of Scripture. This is a work of the Spirit which takes place along with the Word itself: as God's Word is preached or read, the Holy Spirit gives convincing witness of its truth and power.

It is sometimes claimed that this makes the discernment of the divine inspiration of Scripture a subjective or mystical experience, as if understanding comes in a revelatory flash. However, that was not what the Reformers meant. They understood that the Spirit uses the Scriptures themselves, opening a person's spiritual eyes to appreciate the objective marks of truth which are inescapably present in the Bible.

The obvious implication of recognizing the canon of Scripture

The term "canon" is derived from the Greek word *kanōn*, which means a rod. It referred to a straight rod used to measure or test something. The equivalent today would be a ruler. With a ruler we can draw a straight line, or check that a line is straight. We can measure a line.

By using this term we mean that the Bible is the standard by which everything must be measured. Christians find in the Bible the norm for what we must believe, how we ought to behave, how our worship should be regulated, what form our service for Christ should take.

The confessions often express this by describing the Bible as a rule. It is the rule of faith, the rule of truth, the rule of knowledge, the rule of obedience. Any merely human authority is to be rejected.

Five qualities belonging to Scripture

ITS SUFFICIENCY

By using this term the confessions were teaching that everything we need to know for Christian life, faith and salvation is found in the Bible. Nothing needs to be added or subtracted or altered in any way. The Reformers knew that there are things which God has not revealed, things which we shall never be able to discover in this life, or even in all eternity. However, God has left out of the Bible nothing which it is necessary for us to know, so we can approach the Bible with true gratitude.

ITS CLARITY

The clarity of Scripture is closely related to its sufficiency. There is an interesting statement in the Irish Articles which says that the Holy Scriptures "are able to instruct us sufficiently in all points of faith that we are bound to believe, and all good duties that we are bound to practice."

Those are wise words. They acknowledge that there are some things which do not come into the category of "bound to." The confessions note that some parts of Scripture are not crystal clear. They are open to differences in interpretation. However, everything which it is vital to believe or to practice is clear and plain. It follows from this that we should never insist on our own interpretation in issues of secondary importance. In such cases we must show tolerance and mutual respect, but in gospel essentials absolute unity is required.

Its infallibility

This is an obvious consequence of the fact that the Bible is inspired by the God of truth. Everything which Scripture says is beyond question. There are no errors of any sort in the Bible.

Its translatability

It is striking that some of the Reformers saw the possibility and the necessity of Bible translation as so important that they included it in their confessions of faith. The Irish Articles, for example, say this: "the Scriptures ought to be translated out of the original tongues into all languages for the common use of all men." In the light of such a confessional principle, I sometimes wonder—admittedly a bit mischievously!—whether those who insist on the use of the Authorized Version in today's society can truly claim to be "Reformed."

The confessions rightly saw that God's grace reached out to the world as a whole. They recognized that through translations of the Bible the gospel was to be published to all nations without exception. They saw translation as a necessary means of bringing people of every nation to the true knowledge of God. The Reformation was blessed with a great vision of Christianity as a missionary faith, because it had a vision of a God who is committed to extending salvation in Christ to the very ends of the earth.

It is true that the Reformers recognized the special importance of the Hebrew Old Testament and the Greek New Testament. Nevertheless, translations are still the sacred Scriptures. The Scriptures in the common languages of all the world's peoples are still the Word of God. This sets Christianity entirely apart from a religious system like Islam, which claims that the Qur'an can only properly exist in Arabic.

Its major thrust

The confessions often speak of the Bible's major scope, its general thrust. Whatever else it may contain, the main aim of the Bible is to proclaim the message of God's goodwill towards mankind in general. That goodwill is most especially declared in his benevolence towards sinners in Christ.

Modern Confessions of Faith

The Indonesian confession affirms, briefly, that the words of the Bible "are truly the Word of God." It insists on the sufficiency of Scripture in two respects: to reveal God and his will, and to teach us what we must believe in order to receive eternal life. It rejects all human wisdom that differs from God's Word.

The other two modern confessions go into greater detail on this topic. They both identify the 66 books of the Old and New Testaments as the inspired Word of God. Both recognize that it follows inevitably that the Scriptures are infallible, "the complete truth and without error," as the Chinese confession puts it. Consequently, as the Indian confession affirms, they are the only rule of faith and duty. The Chinese confession also emphasizes the Bible's main theme: it "clearly describes God's plan of redemption for man."

The Chinese confession adds that no changes to the Bible are permissible, defining it as the ultimate standard for faith, life, and service, and stating that it is never out of date. This leads into a section on the interpretation of the Bible. Any particular Scripture must be interpreted within two contexts: the historical context in which it was first given, and the overall context of scriptural teachings as a whole. The leading of the Holy Spirit is vital in the interpretation of the Bible. However, this does not mean that a purely individual and subjective interpretation is valid. The confession stresses two things: (1) the traditions of orthodox belief throughout church history must be consulted as we interpret Scripture today; (2) personal interpretation and subjective spiritualizing of Scripture is ruled out.

At certain points it is instructive to compare the Confession of Faith of the United Church of Northern India with the counterpart Confession of Faith of the South India United Church. The Southern Church had been founded in 1901. Its confession of faith seems to reflect the influence of western liberal theology. Its doctrine of Scripture is noticeably weaker than that of its northern neighbor.

The southern confession defines Scripture as the record of God's revelation, rather than according it revelatory status itself. Moreover, it does not see the content of the Bible itself as the Church's ultimate authority, but "the Holy Spirit speaking in the Scriptures." Such wording falls short of a fully biblical theology of the Bible, and risks opening the door to wayward subjective readings of the text. The northern church avoided this deficiency.

HISTORICAL ELABORATION

In this section we shall do three things. First, it will be useful to look briefly at the process by which the Church arrived at the final New Testament canon. Second, we shall read two classic statements on the doctrine of Scripture from different historical periods. Third, we shall consider some inadequate doctrines of Scripture, and seek to respond to them.

The Formation of the New Testament Canon

It is the process of formation of the New Testament canon which is of interest, because the canon of the Old Testament was inherited by the church from its Jewish roots.

> Christ passed on to his followers, as Holy Scripture, the Bible which he had received, containing the same books as the Hebrew Bible today. The first Christians shared with their Jewish contemporaries a full knowledge of the identity of the canonical books.[18]

However, by the end of the first century various new documents were circulating amongst the churches. As time went by their number increased. Not every church had access to every document. However, very early on the thirteen letters of Paul had already been gathered together into a collection, and by the middle of the second century the four gospels were also circulating together, indicating that "they were increasingly recognized as normative ecclesiastical documents."[19]

However, there were those who questioned whether the emerging consensus was correct. At the end of the second century Marcion drew up a list of New Testament books which included only Luke's gospel and ten of Paul's letters. He omitted the Pastoral Epistles. This provided an impetus for the church to think through the question of the canon. In response to Marcion, church leaders such as Irenaeus, reaffirmed the position of all four gospels and all thirteen of Paul's letters. In addition, Irenaeus included in his list of authorized books Acts, James, 1 Peter, 1 and 2 John, Jude and Revelation.

On the other hand, there were those who wanted to include additional books in the New Testament. Some churches accepted the remaining books which we now find in the New Testament—Hebrews, 2 Peter,

18. Beckwith, "Canon," 238.
19. du Toit, "Canon," 103.

and 3 John, while others were uncertain about their position. For a time, a number of other first- or early second-century writings were accepted as Scripture in some places.

In the middle of the third century Eusebius distinguished four categories of books claiming a place in the New Testament. First there were the acknowledged books—the four Gospels, the Acts of the Apostles, Paul's thirteen letters, Hebrews, 1 Peter and 1 John. These were universally accepted as true Scripture. Second, there were the debatable books—James, 2 Peter, 2 and 3 John, and Jude. Most Christians recognized these as canonical, but they were disputed by some. Third there were the compromised books—the Acts of Paul, the Shepherd of Hermas, the Revelation of Peter, the Letter of Barnabas, the Didache, and the Gospel according to the Hebrews. Although some earlier writers had included these in their lists of authoritative writings, by Eusebius's time, they were generally recognized not to be inspired Scripture. They were certainly of value for private reading, though they had to be read with discernment, since they were not infallible. Fourth, there were the heretical books—the Gospels of Peter, Thomas, and Matthias, the Acts of Andrew and the Acts of John. Some heretical sects included these in their Bible, but the orthodox Christian community universally dismissed them as fictional writings. The book of Revelation was in a category of its own. It was either fully accepted or completely rejected. Eusebius accepted it as valid Scripture, but he acknowledged that some Christians rejected it outright.[20]

By the later years of the fourth century the church saw that it was time to settle the issue of the canon. In AD 363 a Synod meeting at Laodicea decreed that books permitted to be read in the churches were "only the Canonical Books of the Old and New Testaments."[21] It did not, however, list these books. Such a decree does, however, prove that by then there was general agreement as to the limits of the canon. Four years later Athanasius wrote this in his annual letter to the churches in the area which he served as bishop:

> It is not tedious to speak of the books of the New Testament. These are, the four Gospels, according to Matthew, Mark, Luke, and John. Afterwards, the Acts of the Apostles and Epistles (called Catholic), seven, viz. of James, one; of Peter, two; of John,

20. Eusebius, "Church History," 3.25.
21. *Canons of the Synod held in the City of Laodicea*, Canon 59, 335.

three; after these, one of Jude. In addition, there are fourteen Epistles of Paul, written in this order. The first, to the Romans; then two to the Corinthians; after these, to the Galatians; next, to the Ephesians; then to the Philippians; then to the Colossians; after these, two to the Thessalonians, and that to the Hebrews; and again, two to Timothy; one to Titus; and lastly, that to Philemon. And besides, the Revelation of John.[22]

Athanasius's list corresponds exactly with the 27 books which make up the New Testament which we know. In AD 397 a Church Council meeting at Carthage published the same list. The canon was now definitively fixed.

However, we must never forget that it would be

a mistake to regard the official recognition of our present twenty-seven books by the church as the act which gave them their canonical status. The decisions of the church were in reality the acknowledgement of the intrinsic authority and power of these writings.[23]

Classic Statements of the Doctrine of Revelation in Scripture

Early Church Fathers: Origen

Origen was one of the first Christian writers to develop a doctrine of Scripture. He was born in Egypt towards the end of the second century. Early in the third century the Roman Emperor inflicted a harsh persecution on the Christians there. Most pastors were killed. Origen, who had been training in theology, found himself the senior Christian teacher in Alexandria, even though he was only in his early twenties. When he was 45 Origen moved to Caesarea as head of a theological training school. While here he wrote many volumes.

In all his writings Origen demonstrates a firm commitment to the Bible as the Word of God. One of his works has a section devoted entirely to the divine origin of Scripture.[24] He offers four proofs that the Scriptures are "inspired by the Spirit of God."

22. Athanasius, "Festal Letter," 5.
23. du Toit, "Canon," 104.
24. Origen, "De Principiis," 4.

The worldwide impact of the Bible

Origen notes that the Bible is unrivalled in this respect. Other writers might like to see their opinions changing the face of nations, but only the sacred Scriptures have actually achieved this.

The worldwide spread of the gospel

Origen describes the progress of the gospel across many nations. It has taken place in relatively few years, and has happened in spite of the persecution targeted against believers. Origen writes, "we have no difficulty in saying that the result is beyond any human power."

The fulfilment of the prophets' predictions

Origen shows most interest in the Old Testament predictions connected with the coming of Christ, especially those whose fulfilment required major changes in international politics. Here is proof of God's control of global affairs in order to bring about the fulfilment of what he had prophesied about Christ in his inspired Word.

The subjective experience of reading the Scriptures

If we read the Bible with care, attention, zeal, and reverence, we can trace its divinity. We feel our minds touched by the divine breath. We are then led to acknowledge that the words of Scripture are no mere human utterances, but the language of God.

Reformers and Puritans: Thomas Watson

After studying at Cambridge, Thomas Watson spent sixteen years as pastor of a congregation in the center of London. In 1662 Watson, along with many other puritans, was thrown out of the Church of England because its bishops were opposed to a thorough reformation of the church. For the next thirteen years Watson risked being fined or imprisoned by preaching from time to time at secret meetings whenever he could do so in safety. In 1675, the British government at last allowed Nonconformists to license premises for worship. Watson then became pastor of another London congregation.

One of Watson's published sermons is entitled "The Scriptures." Watson begins by giving seven arguments which prove the Bible to be the inspired Word of God: (1) it is ancient, and reaches further back in time than any other historical writing; (2) it has been miraculously preserved, despite the devil's attempts to destroy it; (3) its subject matter is beyond the power of human invention; (4) its predictions, sometimes looking many centuries ahead, have been fulfilled; (5) its human authors were willing to speak of their own failings in order to give all glory to God; (6) the Bible has transforming power in the lives of men and women; (7) the miracles which the Scriptures record demonstrate its divine origin.

Watson insists that Scripture is to be its own interpreter, and that its main subject is the way of salvation. He notes that God has appointed pastors in his church to expound the Scriptures for his people. This is not, however, to pin our faith upon mere men: God gives all his people the spirit of discernment so that they can tell whether what is preached is true to God's Word.

Watson then demonstrates that the truth of the inspiration of Scripture implies a rebuke on five types of people: (1) those who take away part of the Scripture; (2) those who neglect the Old Testament; (3) those who reject the Bible as a dead letter on the pretext that they have the Spirit; (4) those who simply do not bother to read the Bible; (5) those who put forward strange interpretations because they fail to compare Scripture with Scripture.

But the truth of the inspiration of Scripture also implies eight exhortations: (1) we must study the Bible reverently; (2) we must value the Bible more than gold; (3) we must believe everything which the Scriptures say; (4) we must love the Word; (5) we must conform our lives to the commands of Scripture; (6) we must contend for the Bible against those who oppose it; (7) we must give thanks to God for giving us the Bible; (8) if we have tasted the life-giving power of the Word, we must praise God for his saving grace.

Addressing Errors on the Subject of Revelation in Scripture

"The Fundamentals"

This was the title of a 12-volume series of journals which was published in America between 1910 and 1915. It was produced in response to a challenge to the traditional view of Scripture. The view that the Bible is the inspired and infallible Word of God was accepted virtually without question in the church until the mid-eighteenth century. Since then a new approach to the Bible had been gaining support.

This new view was anti-supernatural. It denied the possibility of miracles. It ruled out predictive prophecy. It reclassified many of the Bible's narratives as "myths." The Bible was regarded as a purely human work. It was marked by the fallibility which afflicts all human works. There was no ultimate authority in the message of the Bible. It was up to us to pass judgment on each part of the Bible to see whether it was true to the Christian spirit.

The people putting forward this new view were still prepared to speak of "inspiration," but they meant something very different from the normal meaning of the word. For these people "inspiration" meant that within this unreliable human book it was possible to come up against divine mystery. It was not that the exact words were inspired. The precise words were not important. It was that the writers were inspired men. They somehow possessed the divine Spirit to a remarkable degree, and when you read the Bible you could sometimes catch something of that mystical Spirit.

When a doctrine is challenged like that, it presents believers with a great opportunity to stand up for the truth. That is what the early twentieth-century Christians in America were doing through *The Fundamentals*. Altogether 90 articles were published in the series, and 29 of them had to do with the doctrine of Scripture.

James Gray, of Moody Bible Institute, wrote an article aimed at correcting the mistaken view of inspiration. He pointed out that "inspiration" refers to the writings, not to the writers. He explained:

> Moses, David, Paul, John, were not always and everywhere inspired, for then always and everywhere they would have been infallible and inerrant, which was not the case. They sometimes made mistakes in thought and erred in conduct. But however fallible and errant they may have been as men compassed with

infirmity like ourselves, such fallibility or errancy was never in any circumstances communicated to their sacred writings.[25]

In another article Leander Whitcomb Munhall, a Methodist evangelist, used the term "verbal inspiration" to teach that the very words of the Bible matter. It is not just that the thoughts of Scripture are of an elevated quality, but that the exact words are God-given: "if they were not, then the Bible is not inspired at all, since it is composed only and solely of words."[26]

Munhall quotes a number of other writers to support this point. One of them is Dean Burgon, who said,

> As for thoughts being inspired apart from the words which give them expression, you might as well talk of a tune without notes, or a sum without figures. No such theory of inspiration is even intelligible.[27]

Amongst the evidences for inspiration offered in *The Fundamentals* two were particularly favored by the contributors.

THE WITNESS OF CHRIST

An article by William Craven of Canada makes the following eight points: (1) the Lord never questioned the Jewish canon; (2) he never expressed doubt about anything that the Scriptures teach; (3) he accepted the narratives of Scripture as historically accurate; (4) he assumed that the Scriptures are from God; (5) he treated the Scriptures as God speaking; (6) he took it for granted that the Scriptures are authoritative and not merely human; (7) he taught the absolute infallibility of Scripture; (8) he declared that he himself is the fulfilment of the prophecies of Scripture.[28]

THE STRUCTURAL UNITY OF THE BIBLE

A. T. Pierson, who succeeded Spurgeon at the Metropolitan Tabernacle in London, points out that the harmonious teaching of the entire Bible is miraculous in itself:

25. Gray, "Inspiration," 138–39.
26. Munhall, "Inspiration," 159.
27. Quoted by Munhall, "Inspiration," 160.
28. Craven, "Testimony of Christ," 59–65.

> Here are some sixty or more separate documents, written by some forty different persons, scattered over wide intervals of space and time, strangers to each other. These documents are written in three different languages, in different lands, among different and sometimes hostile peoples, with marked diversities of literary style, and by men of all grades of culture and mental capacity, from Moses to Malachi. When we look into these productions, there is even in them great unlikeness, both in matter and manner of statement; yet they all constitute one volume.

Pierson stresses that all the diverse parts of Scripture are entirely at agreement. He concludes that there is no possible explanation except that God superintended the production of the Bible: "its unity is the unity of a divine plan, and its harmony the harmony of a Supreme Intelligence."[29]

The International Council on Biblical Inerrancy

When *The Fundamentals* series was being published the opponents of the historic doctrine of Scripture were liberal theologians. At the start of the twentieth century the Evangelical world was standing firm against the erosion of the biblical doctrine of revelation. However, by the end of the century some who would still claim to be Evangelicals were shifting their position. A view known as "Neo-Evangelicalism" became less clear on the inerrancy of Scripture.

Neo-Evangelicalism wants to accept the authority of the Bible, and yet it separates inspiration from inerrancy. The Bible was held to be infallible in matters concerning salvation, but its writers were claimed to be subject to the worldview of their time, so that in matters of science and history they may have made some errors. A leading example of this approach was Daniel Fuller, the founder of Fuller Theological Seminary in the USA. Robert Lightner explains Fuller's view of inspiration like this: it "makes sure that we have an authoritative record of all that God wanted to make known. But it was not God's intention or purpose to secure inerrancy in peripheral matters."

This raises the question, on what criteria do we decide what matters are "peripheral"? Lightner gives Fuller's answer: "'Peripheral matters' include scriptural data which have nothing to do with faith and life, such as minor historical details, grammatical constructions and the like."[30]

29. Pierson, "Organic Unity," 195–96.
30. Quoted by Conn, *World Theology*, 136.

However, we are on shaky ground here. How can we be certain that we have correctly identified those details which are "minor"? How can we be sure that a particular detail does not in fact have a bearing on faith and life? In 1976 Harold Lindsell wrote a book, *The Battle for the Bible*, in which he accused those holding a limited inerrancy view of opening the door to modernism.[31]

The danger in the theory of partial inerrancy is that our sinfulness is likely to make us weed out the bits of the Bible which we do not want to hear. It is the passages which rebuke us which we are likely to downgrade. It is those passages which correct wrong behavior, which re-direct warped thinking, which shape and alter disobedient lifestyles, which we decide to dismiss.

In response to this Evangelical shift, the International Council on Biblical Inerrancy was set up in 1978, with James Montgomery Boice as chairman. Boice has pointed out the fallacy of claiming that historical inaccuracies may still be consistent with infallibility in matters of salvation: "The Bible is a historical book, and Christianity is a historical religion. If the Bible errs in matters of history, Christianity itself is affected."[32]

Moreover, if we reject the doctrine of biblical inerrancy, this has a knock-on effect. It has implications for other doctrines and for aspects of Christian devotion. In John 10:35, Jesus says, "the Scripture cannot be broken." Donald Macleod makes this comment on these words:

> The Bible, in the judgment of Jesus . . . can't be wrong. It can't be false. It can't mislead. It can't deceive. It can't be violated . . . . Christ has said this book is infallible. He has attested it as the unbreakable Word of God, and it is because of his testimony . . . that [we] believe in the full, final, infallible authority of Scripture. I cannot see how one can be loyal to Christ and yet defy him on something as fundamental as his view of the status of the Bible . . . . Belief in the God-givenness of the Bible is simply an aspect of devotion to Christ.[33]

---

31. Lindsell, *Battle, passim*.
32. Boice, *Standing on the Rock*, 132.
33. Macleod, *Faith*, 14.

The Question of the Sufficiency of Scripture

At the beginning of the twenty first century a new challenge faces us. There is a tendency now to doubt the sufficiency of Scripture. Dr. Boice has observed how, in the work of the church, "the Bible is often laid aside and reliance is placed instead upon such extra-biblical props as sociological techniques, psychology and psychiatry, and what are called 'signs and wonders.'" He raises the following questions:

> Do we really believe God has given us what we need in this book? Or do we think we have to supplement the Bible with other man-made things? Do we need sociological techniques to do evangelism? Must we attract people to our churches by showmanship and entertainment? Do we need psychology and psychiatry for Christian growth? Do we need extra-biblical signs or miracles for guidance? Is the Bible's teaching adequate for achieving social progress and reform?

Boice insists that the Scriptures are sufficient for all times and in all areas of life. Because they are "the very words of God," they "are useful for dealing with any problem you will face in the church or out of the church, at this time or at any other period of history."[34] And we might add this. In the secular west, in the Islamic world, in the nations of Asia, in Latin America, anywhere and everywhere the Bible says it all.

In recent years there has been a new attack on the sufficiency of Scripture in the theory of "trajectory hermeneutics," developed by the Canadian theologian William Webb. He argues that the Bible traces a redemptive movement towards the ultimate ethic, and that we today need to apply the redemptive spirit of a text, not its bare words. Webb argues for what he calls "the X-Y-Z principle."

X represents the position held on an issue in the wider cultural world of Bible times. Y is the ethical assessment of the Bible on that issue for its own times. Z is the ultimate ethic towards which biblical statements are progressing. But the Bible did not reach the ultimate ethic. So we must go further, in line with the Bible's own redemptive spirit, along the trajectory of the redemptive movement of Scripture. Webb applies this in particular to gender roles and the ministry of women. He argues for complete gender equality without role differentiation, because

---

34. Boice, *Standing on the Rock*, 12, 133, 114–15.

that, he claims, is the direction towards which Scripture is tending, even though it has not yet arrived at that destination.[35]

Webb raises some important questions. We do have to interpret Scripture within our own cultural context in the light of its place within its own cultural context. However, if the Bible is not the revelation of the ultimate ethic, then how can we possibly know what the ultimate ethic is? If we deny the sufficiency of Scripture, we are left to flounder in a sea of speculation.

PRACTICAL APPLICATION

Charles Colson became a Christian around the time when he was imprisoned for his part in the Watergate scandal, which eventually brought Richard Nixon's presidency to an end. After his release from prison he became involved in a ministry working with prisoners. He admits that, at one time, the question of biblical inerrancy was of no concern to him. However, he became convinced of its importance when he saw the effects of different views of Scripture on the front lines of spiritual warfare in the prisons. This was his conclusion:

> The authority and truth of Scripture is not an obscure issue reserved for the private debate and entertainment of theologians; it is relevant, indeed critical, for every serious Christian—layman, pastor and theologian alike.
>
> My convictions have come, not from studies in Ivory Tower academia, but from life in what may be termed the front line trenches, where Christians grapple in hand-to-hand combat with the prince of darkness. In our prison fellowships, where the Bible is proclaimed as God's holy and inerrant revelation, believers grow and discipleship deepens. Where the Bible is not so proclaimed (or where Christianity is presumed to rest on subjective experience alone or content-less fellowship) faith withers and dies. Christianity without biblical fidelity is merely another passing fad in an age of passing fads.[36]

But for the application of the doctrine of divine revelation in an inerrant Scripture we can do better than to quote Charles Colson. Here are four texts from the Pastoral Epistles which refer to God's Word. They apply the truth about God's Word to the work of the ministry in particular.

35. Webb, *Slaves*, 30–66.
36. Quoted by Boice, *Standing on the Rock*, 112.

1 Timothy 5:17

Paul speaks here of elders "who labor in the word and doctrine." The word translated "labor" is *kopiaō*. It speaks of work that makes you tired, of exhausting effort. The same word is used in Luke 5:5 of the fishermen who "toiled all night." We should be toiling at the Scriptures. This word is also used in 2 Timothy 2:6 of "the hardworking farmer." We should be prepared for strenuous effort in the work of the gospel. It follows from the fact that the Bible is God's unchallengeable revelation. The Lord deserves the most energetic effort of which we are capable.

2 Timothy 2:15

Paul now compares Timothy, as the representative minister of God's Word of truth to "a worker (*ergatēs*)." This word is used of harvesters laboring in a cornfield (Matt 9:37–38), of grape-pickers in a vineyard (Matt 20:1–2), and of craftsmen at the smithies (Acts 19:24–25). A worker is prepared for hard graft in a hot environment.

Paul's exhortation to Timothy here begins "be diligent." This phrase translates the Greek word *spoudazō*. It could be translated "be in a hurry." It is an urgent matter to research the Scriptures so that we can proclaim the gospel message. It is a message for lost and dying sinners. They need to hear it now, and we should be eager to bring it to them. We must exert ourselves, putting every effort into the work.

The actual task of the gospel worker is described as "rightly dividing the word." This term (*orthotomeō*) means "to cut straight." It is found in the Greek translation of Proverbs 3:6: "In all your ways acknowledge him, and he will direct your paths." The idea of cutting a straight path brings to mind the picture of blazing a trail through the jungle and laying the tarmac for a new road. Our task as preachers is to carve out for our hearers a highway through the Bible. We are not to meander in obscurities, but to lay bare the essentials of God's gospel revelation in Jesus Christ.

2 Timothy 4:2

Paul urges Timothy to "preach the word." Because this word is divine revelation it must be preached. The verb here is *kērussō*, which is linked with the noun *kērux*. A *kērux* was a man with a commission to shout out an item of information for all to hear. He operated under the authority of another as spokesman. He had nothing to say except the message which his master had given him. He had to be totally dedicated to his task. The true preacher never expresses his personal opinion. He always declares what God has revealed in the Word of Scripture.

And, Paul continues, he must be "ready." He must stand poised. He must never be caught with nothing to say. He must be so familiar with the Word that whenever there is an opportunity to proclaim it, whenever a question is raised or a challenge is posed, he declares unhesitatingly what God says.

This readiness is necessary "in season and out of season." We must be ready when people are clamoring to hear. We must also be ready when being a preacher is a lonely and costly calling. The following verses (2 Tim 4:3–5) describe such a time, a time "when they will not endure sound doctrine," when they "will turn *their* ears away from the truth." At such times standing for God's Word may involve afflictions, but, nonetheless, we must "fulfil" the ministry of the Word. We must carry it through to completion in successive acts of proclamation.

Titus 1:9

An overseer must be one who holds fast "the faithful word." To describe God's Word as "faithful" is to say that it is trustworthy, reliable, dependable; it is free from error. The verb translated "holding fast" is *antechomai*. It speaks of loyalty. Jesus used it in Matthew 6:24, where he warned of the danger of trying to serve two masters: the danger for such a servant is that "he will be loyal to the one and despise the other."

The opposite of loyalty is to despise. This translates the verb *kataphroneō*, which means to have a low opinion of something. We are not to have a low opinion of the Scriptures. We are not to propagate our own ideas in its place. We must stand on the truth of God's Word with loyalty.

PART TWO: REVELATION IN CREATION

BIBLICAL FOUNDATION

Old Testament

We studied part of Psalm 19 in connection with revelation in Scripture. The opening verses of the same Psalm are relevant to this other aspect of God's revelation. We look, therefore at Psalm 19:1–4, where we focus on three things.

The sky is a revelation of God

The first verse tells us that "the heavens declare the glory of God; and the firmament shows his handiwork." The Hebrew word rendered "heavens" is *šāmayim*, and the word "firmament" (*rāqiyaʿ*) seems to define its meaning. It speaks of something which has been expanded and is spread out.[37] The last time these two words occurred together was in the account of creation. The phrase "the firmament of the heavens" occurs four times in Genesis 1 (verses 14, 15, 17 and 20), and it is clear from verse 8, which informs us that "God called the firmament heaven," that the two words refer to the same thing. We learn from verses 14, 15, and 17 that they refer to the place where the stars are and from verse 20 that it is the place where the birds fly. In other words, we are talking about the visible skies above us. And now the Psalmist tells us that the sky declares God's glory.

The wind is invisible, but we can see the branches moving on the trees and sometimes, when the wind is strong, we see branches blown down on to the road. God is invisible, but we can observe the effects of his reality.

God's glory is obvious from his "handiwork." This word translates the Hebrew term *maʿᵃśeh*. It can speak of a work which is a massive undertaking, a remarkable achievement, a real work of art.[38] It is used many times of the intricate work which went into the construction of the tabernacle and its equipment. It is used of the needlework in the curtains and the high priest's garments, of the metalwork for the altars, the candlestick, and the priest's chains, of engravings in stone, of the blending of the anointing oil, and of the expertise which went into the various artistic designs.

---

37. Tregelles (ed.), *Lexicon*, 454; Tsumura, "*rāqiyaʿ*," *passim*.
38. Cf. Tregelles (ed.), *Lexicon*, 282; cf. Durham, *Exodus*, 367.

All this was skilled work. And God's skill is seen in the sky. And in his artistic designs there is a declaration, a proclamation. God's splendor is published to the world.

This is true all the time

Verse 2 speaks of day and night, recognizing the two main ways in which we see the sky. (1) There is the daytime sky. Sometimes we bask in brilliant sunshine. At other times the sky is heavy with cloud. (2) There is the night-time sky. Some nights there is a magnificent display of stars. On other occasions we gaze up into an eerie mistiness.

But the transition between the two halves of the 24-hour period also exhibits divine majesty. (1) There is the transition from night to day. Think of the spectacle of the gradually growing light and beauty of the sunrise. (2) There is the transition from day to night. What amazing colors decorate the sky at sunset.

And the sky, with all its diverse faces, "utters speech," and reveals the knowledge of God. The word translated "utters" is *nāba'*. It means to spring up, to gush forth.[39] The same word is translated "flowing" in Proverbs 18:4. The sky just cannot help itself. By day and by night, the sun, the clouds, the light, the colors, the stars are just an overflow of revelation of God's abundant splendor.

The repetition of the words "day" and "night" emphasize the constant nature of this display of divine glory. From one day to the next, night after night, this revelation is unvaryingly there. Whatever the weather conditions, the sky in all its various moods is always a revelation of God.

This is true everywhere

There are two possible ways of translating verse 3. One possibility goes something like this: "There is no speech, nor is there language; their voice is not heard." This would mean that this eloquent revelation by the sky is not in words. It is not even audible to the human ear.

The other possibility is that of the New King James Version: "*There is* no speech nor language *where* their voice is not heard." The meaning, in this case, is that there is no human communication where the voice

---

39. Tregelles (ed.), *Lexicon*, 301; Beyer, "*nb'*," 15.

of the sky is unheard. In other words, there is no such place, because wherever you go, human beings are talking to one another.

My personal preference is for this latter translation. One of my reasons is that the word translated "voice (*qôl*)" sometimes means the sound of thunder, as, for example, in Psalm 77:18: "the voice (*qôl*) of your thunder *was* in the whirlwind." Perhaps Psalm 19:3 is saying that the revelation of God in the sky is thunderous: you just cannot miss it.

The alternative translation would then have to mean that the voice of the sky does not thunder. However, this would clearly be inappropriate on that understanding of the verse: the point surely would be that it does not make the faintest squeak. However, although the voice of the sky is silent, it is nonetheless thunderous. It is inescapable. It speaks in every place.

Another way in which *qôl* is sometimes used is to refer to the sound of music. It is used of the sound of instruments, and of singing. One example is 1 Chronicles 15:28, which speaks of Israel, as they brought the ark to the tabernacle, shouting "with the sound (*qôl*) of the horn, with trumpets and with cymbals, making music with stringed instruments and harps." The revelation in the sky is melodious and harmonious, and its song is heard everywhere.

Verse 4 continues this theme. The whole planet, to its remotest end, is exposed to the revelation of God in the skies. No tribe, however, isolated, is beyond its reach. That is why the apostle can quote this verse in Romans 10:18 as an assertion that sinful humanity is inexcusable. No one can say, "I never heard," because the skies are singing of God's glory, daily, nightly, incessantly, everywhere.

New Testament

The main New Testament passage on this theme is Romans 1:19–20. In these verses Paul speaks of the revelation of God in creation. He makes the following points.

God is the author of this revelation

Whereas Psalm 19 depicts the sky as speaking, here God speaks through his creation. God "has shown" the revelation to the world. The voice of the sky in the Psalm is, in fact, the mediated voice of God himself. James

Dunn writes: "God's knowability is not merely a characteristic or 'spin-off' of creation, but was willed and effected by God."[40]

The tense of the Greek verb is aorist. It speaks of a one-off revelation. Paul seems to mean that the act of creation was God's manifestation of himself. But Paul then goes on to say that what has been true since the creation of the world continues to be true: the attributes of God remain clear in the creation.

Not everything about God is knowable

These verses begin with the words, "what may be known of God." The apostle is recognizing that there are depths in the reality of God which human beings cannot penetrate. And there are aspects of the divine character to understand which far more is necessary than the available revelation in creation.

The apostle then clarifies what can be known about God from creation. There are two things.

The first is his eternal power. God is always able to do whatever he purposes to do. There is power inherent in his nature without any interruption.

Then, secondly, there is his Godhead. This word translates the noun *theiotēs*. This is the only place where it is used in the New Testament, but a related adjective, *theios*, appears three times. The way in which it is used helps us to get at what the apostle means here. In Acts 17:29, while preaching at Athens, Paul says, "we ought not to think that the divine nature (*theios*) is like gold or silver or stone, something shaped by art and man's devising." Here the apostle is emphasizing the unlikeness of God: he is not like anything else. He is distinct, separate, unique. Peter twice uses *theios* in 2 Peter 1:3–4. Verse 3 refers to "his divine power," and verse 4 to "the divine nature." By his power God "has given to us all things that *pertain* to life and godliness." His resources are infinite. And the divine nature is then portrayed as something of which we become partakers, "having escaped the corruption *that is* in the world through lust." This contrast with worldly corruption emphasizes the truth that God's uniqueness and distinctiveness is seen primarily in the fact that he is totally free from every hint of evil; he is a God of absolute purity and integrity.

---

40. Dunn, *Romans*, 57.

Here in Romans 1 Paul says that these two attributes are "manifest." God has brought out into the open the fact that he is an incomparably holy God, characterized by a unique power. In creation, these attributes of God are in full view. They are revealed to everyone.

This revelation in creation is seen in two places

IT IS SEEN IN HUMAN LIFE ITSELF

Verse 19 tells us that what it is possible for people to know about God "is manifest in them." The word "in" renders the preposition *en*. This implies that there is something intrinsic to the human personality which says, "there is a God." Paul will have in mind our moral sense, the conscience. Because we have been created in God's image, we have a feeling of accountability. This moral consciousness has been spoiled by sin, but not smashed completely.

IT IS SEEN IN THE WORLD

Verse 20 says that God's attributes are perceived "by the things that are made." Created things give shape and form in the human mind to the divine invisibility. Invisibility is a characteristic feature of God. Paul speaks of Christ as "the image of the invisible God" (Col 1:15). He ascribes praise to God as "the King eternal, immortal, invisible" (1 Tim 1:17). Moses, we read, "endured as seeing him who is invisible" (Heb 11:27). But created things give a sort of visibility to God—or at least to certain of his attributes. This vision of God is not physical but mental. Human eyes see the things that have been made, and the mind perceives the truth that God made them.

Unbelief is inexcusable

This passage ends with the statement that we have nothing to say in our own defense for our unbelief. The problem is not ignorance of the truth, but the fact that men "suppress the truth" (verse 18). In sin, people deliberately tread down the truth about God revealed in creation, until it is so hindered that they are no longer able to embrace it. G. I. Williamson puts it well. He says that the evidence of God's existence "is impossible to find when one is dead in trespasses and sins. But the evidence is impossible to escape anywhere when one is regenerated by God's Spirit."[41]

DOCTRINAL FORMULATION

Revelation in creation was not a doctrine that figured in the early creeds. Neither is it mentioned in the modern confessions which we are considering. Some of the Reformation confessions, however, did speak of God's revelation of himself in his works.

The Belgic Confession describes the universe as "an elegant book." It is comparing the creation to a play. Every created thing, great or small, is a character in the drama. And the impact of the whole is that we are led to the contemplation of God. The very fact of the existence of the created universe, with all its beauty, its order, the clear evidence of design, its immensity and magnificence, is a testimony to the reality of the Creator God.

But the confessions find this revelation, not only in the existence of the universe, but also in the preservation and government of creation. We can discern the signs of God's ongoing involvement with the things he has made. Every day, in his sovereignty, he directs the stars and planets, he oversees the movements of the animals and the seas. And in his providential control we see a revelation of his power, his wisdom, his goodness.

However, revelation in creation assumes prior faith. The sheer existence of anything at all may point inevitably to the existence of God. But to see in the preservation and government of the universe a revelation of God presupposes that we accept that God does preserve and govern all things. Unbelievers are unlikely to conclude from their observation of things that God is providentially ordering the course of creation. For the goodness, wisdom, and power of God to be seen in creation assumes that we already believe that God is a God of goodness, wisdom, and power.

That is probably why the Baptist Confession of 1689 alters the order of the Westminster Confession, on which it is based. The Westminster Confession begins with the revelation of God in creation. It notes the inadequacy of this revelation to give a saving knowledge of God. And so it moves on to the statement of supernatural revelation, culminating in the Scriptures.

---

41. Williamson, *Westminster*, 23.

The 1689 Confession retains all that. Its wording is precisely the same as Westminster, but it prefaces it with the sentence, "The Holy Scripture is the only infallible rule of all saving knowledge, faith, and obedience."

To begin with creation is to recognize that God is staring everyone in the face in his works, but only to leave them without excuse. People are blinded by sin. We are unable to see this revelation. The 1689 Confession begins with Scripture. It knows that it is only when God's saving grace revealed in the gospel has removed our blindness that the revelation in creation can tell us anything at all. Only then can this revelation be truly perceived.

HISTORICAL ELABORATION

This recognition that creation is a closed book until our sin-blinded eyes are opened by grace has led to some controversy over the validity of speaking of a revelation other than God's Word in Scripture and in Christ. There is a phrase in the Westminster Confession which refers to the manifestation of God by "the light of nature." But some people have taken exception to this expression.

Robert Shaw suggests that the confession meant that people can conclude that there is a God both from sense observation and through rational thought. Indeed, he says, they can reach no other conclusion. Through their senses people are acquainted with the works of God, and by reason they infer the excellence of the God who made them. Shaw claims that the universality of religion is evidence of this natural light within the human constitution which reveals the fact of God. Even professed atheists have qualms of conscience from time-to-time.[42]

However, to some people these ideas seem to imply that there is such a thing as "natural religion," which makes divine revelation unnecessary.

The concept of the light of nature underlies the various "proofs" for the existence of God which have been put forward. The Medieval Catholic theologian, Thomas Aquinas, stated five ways by which, he claimed, the existence of God could be proved.[43]

(1) There is the argument from motion. Observation of the world tells us that things are moving. Whatever moves must have been set in motion by something else, and that thing by yet another, and so on. But it

42. Shaw, *Confession*, 2–4.
43. Aquinas, *Summa*, 27–29.

is impossible to go back to infinity. If there is no first mover, then nothing moves. So this first mover is God.

(2) There is the argument from efficient cause. Nothing can cause itself, because it is impossible for something to precede itself. Every effect has a cause. So there had to be a first cause. And this is God.

(3) There is the argument from possibility and necessity. In nature, things may either be or not be. Anything that we see had a beginning, but eventually it decays. For now, it is, but it might not have been, and one day it will no longer be. But if absolutely everything was merely possible, then there must have been a time when there was nothing. What exists could only have a beginning as a result of other things already existing. So there has to be some being whose existence is not merely possible, but necessary. And this being is God.

(4) There is the argument from the gradation in things. Amongst existing things, some are better, others are less good, some are more noble, others less so. But this presupposes a standard, a maximum in goodness, nobility, or anything else. And this is God.

(5) There is the argument from the government of the world. Even inanimate things exist for a purpose. They were, therefore designed for that purpose. Only an intelligent being could have designed things. And this is God.

From here Aquinas argued that a certain knowledge of God is attainable by the exercise of the intellect. The human intellect needs the illumination of grace to lift it to a higher knowledge of God. Grace strengthens the natural light of reason. Nevertheless, that natural light is present, independently of God's illuminating grace.

The controversy over revelation in creation in Reformed circles arises from the suspicion that such a doctrine implies that the fall of human nature into sin is not total. To teach that grace merely assists human nature, as Aquinas did, conflicts with the truth that we need to be born again even to begin to see the kingdom of God. Moreover, it seemed to some Reformed thinkers that a doctrine of revelation in creation leads to the idea that fallen human beings can get to know God by their own powers, independently of the Scriptures and Jesus Christ.

This may be a fair criticism of Aquinas, but was it what the Westminster Confession meant?

Professor Berkouwer of Amsterdam has written a book entitled *General Revelation*. This is an alternative term for revelation in creation.

Berkouwer insists that we must carefully distinguish between natural theology and general revelation.[44] He denies the validity of the former concept, but affirms the reality of general revelation, but only because Scripture so clearly speaks of a revelation of God in creation and providence.

This doctrine is not talking about abilities in human nature, but about where God has set the revelation of himself. One focus of that revelation is creation. And the revelation is there, whether or not there is any power left in fallen humanity which is actually able to see it. The fact that, apart from God's saving grace, fallen human beings cannot see it does not take away the fact that the revelation is there. So we are without excuse.

Berkouwer also refers to Calvin's teaching on this subject. We find his teaching in Book 1, chapters 3–5 of the *Institutes*.

Calvin accepts that there is a sense of deity innate in man. The universality of the conviction that there is a God is evidence of this. The strength of this conviction is seen in idolatry. It is very hard for the human being to lower himself and set other created things above himself. Yet idolatry does just that. People worship wood and stone. This proves just how inescapable this innate sense of God is.

However, the truth about God is suppressed. Genuine godliness is absent. And yet man is inexcusable, because his ignorance is accompanied by pride and stubbornness. But God still desires the perfection of blessedness for his creatures. So he has manifested his perfections in the whole structure of the universe. Whenever we open our eyes we are compelled to behold him. And that proves man's shameful ingratitude. We don't burst forth in praise, but swell with pride and suppress the evidences of God. We ascribe wonderful events not to providence but to chance.

So Calvin says, "In vain for us, therefore, does creation exhibit so many bright lamps lighted up to show forth the glory of its Author." The invisible Godhead is represented by the display in creation, but we have no eyes to see it until we are enlightened through faith. So Calvin concludes:

> when Paul says that what may be known of God is manifested by the creation of the world, he does not mean such a manifestation as may be comprehended by the wit of man; on the contrary, he shows that it has no further effect than to render us inexcusable.[45]

44. Berkouwer, *General Revelation*, 61.
45. Calvin, *Institutes*, 1.3.1—1.5.14.

This debate about human ability when confronted by revelation in creation is not just a matter of vague historical interest. It has contemporary significance.

In his book *Mission and Meaninglessness* Peter Cotterell puts forward the thesis that "there is a divine self-revelation in creation which is not of itself salvific, but which may lead to the abandonment of human religious effort and to a flight to the mercy and grace of God."[46] Cotterell argues that people who have never heard the gospel, who have never heard of Christ, may be saved by Christ's passion as they seek God by faith, because they have perceived his eternal power and deity in his creation.

Cotterell bases this on Acts 17:27. Verses 24–27 read like this:

> God, who made the world and everything in it, since he is Lord of heaven and earth, does not dwell in temples made with hands. Nor is he worshipped with men's hands, as though he needed anything, since he gives to all life, breath, and all things. And he has made from one blood every nation of men to dwell on all the face of the earth, and has determined their preappointed times and the boundaries of their dwellings, so that they should seek the Lord, in the hope that they might grope for him and find him, though he is not far from each of us.

Cotterell reads verse 27 as a clear statement of God's saving purpose: general revelation may lead people to the grace of God.

Hywel Jones has written in response to this position.[47] He reads this text to mean not that many people will seek and find God through his revelation in creation, but rather that despite the revelation in creation people simply grope as in the dark, because their eyes are blinded by sin. Jones acknowledges that revelation in creation might lead people to a sense of the divine benevolence. However, we need more than the revelation in creation in order to know of God's grace. We need Christ.

PRACTICAL APPLICATION

(1) We may use aspects of the revelation in creation as a theme in our evangelistic preaching. Not that it is enough to preach on creation alone, but this doctrine may provide a point of contact with the unbeliever. It

---

46. Cotterell, *Mission*, 75.
47. Jones, *One Way*, 49.

may enable us to establish a relationship, so that we can go on to proclaim Christ.

The apostle Paul did this. We have mentioned his references to creation and providence in Acts 17:24–27. It is noticeable that, having spoken of creation, he went on, almost immediately, to preach Jesus. Here are verses 30 and 31:

> Truly these times of ignorance God overlooked, but now commands all men everywhere to repent, because he has appointed a day on which he will judge the world in righteousness by the man whom he has ordained. He has given assurance of this to all by raising him from the dead.

Earlier, in Acts 14:15–17 Paul had already used the revelation in creation as a preparation for the gospel. He urged his hearers to turn from the useless things of their pagan devotion "to the living God, who made the heaven, the earth, the sea, and all things that are in them," stressing the fact that "he did not leave himself without witness, in that he did good, gave us rain from heaven and fruitful seasons, filling our hearts with food and gladness."

It is true that there is no reference in this context to Paul preaching Christ on this foundation of the revelation in creation. However, the next verse (verse 18) suggests that this was because it was impossible for him to complete his message on that occasion: "with these sayings they could scarcely restrain the multitudes from sacrificing to them."

We may use the revelation in creation, then, as an argument to whet people's appetites to hear the gospel. All around us are the evidences of God's goodness. To fail to see them is, as Paul says in Romans 1:20, to be "without excuse." To point to this blindness is part of the way in which we must warn people of the wrath which they face, and is therefore a preparatory stepping-stone to the proclamation of the gospel.

(2) And as for ourselves, we may see the revelation in creation with eyes opened by the grace of God. This should lead us to worship the God of creation. Whenever we observe beauty and harmony in creation, it should remind us of the Creator and lead us into fervent adoration of him. Creation's intricate and awesome splendor should heighten our awareness of the Creator's eternal power and unique distinctiveness, leading us to contemplate him with reverence and awe. As we move around in the context of this created world, there should be a constant

song of praise in our hearts addressed to the God who made and governs and preserves all things.

(3) At the same time, we must never forget the implication of Paul's reference in Romans 1:19 to "what may be known of God:" there are things about God that we do not know and never will know. So the contemplation of created magnificence should also humble us before the Creator who is there revealed.

3

The Doctrine of Creation

THE FACT THAT THERE is a revelation of God in the creation leads us on to consider the doctrine of creation itself. The doctrine of creation divides into two parts. First, we consider the origin of this universe in which God's glory is displayed. Then we shall look at the present state of the universe.

PART ONE: CREATION IN ITS ORIGIN

BIBLICAL FOUNDATION

Old Testament

The passage detailing the creation of the world, Genesis 1—2 is the starting point of God's entire revelation. The first sentence of the Bible sets the context for everything that follows.

What does follow in the rest of Genesis is an account of the events leading up to the call of Abraham, and then the story of the establishment of the covenant. The covenant is then unfolded through the remainder of the Old Testament. It reaches its focal point in Christ, spreads worldwide through the New Testament era, and will reach its climax with the Lord's return.

The Bible is basically the story of God's mercy at work to the ends of the earth through the seed of Abraham. Creation is the stage on which the drama of divine mercy is acted out.

We shall look at Genesis 1:1—2:3 section-by-section. We omit verses 26–30 of chapter 1, which deal with the creation of man, as the doctrine of man will be considered as a separate subject.

Genesis 1:1

This verse reads, "In the beginning God created the heavens and the earth." And "these seven words [in the Hebrew text] are the foundation of all that is to follow in the Bible."[1]

The Four Components of this Text

In the beginning

"Beginning" translates the Hebrew word *rē'šît*, which usually "marks a starting point of a specific duration."[2] This is clear in Deuteronomy 11:12, which specifies a period running "from the beginning (*rē'šît*) of the year to the very end of the year." It is a characteristic of God to be "declaring the end from the beginning" (Isa 46:10), and Ecclesiastes 7:8 says that "the end of a thing is better than its beginning." Although Gordon Wenham points out that "more rarely" *rē'šît* "is used absolutely, with the period of time left unspecified," and thinks that is the case here with the beginning of time itself,[3] Sailhamer is probably right to see in the use of the word here a signal that the history now beginning will reach its climax in the consummation at the end of time. This reference to the beginning prepares us to anticipate the glorious end in store.

This emphasizes the truth that creation is the stage on which the Lord displays his mercy, and that mercy will finally and fully be seen in all the blaze of its glory at the end of all things. Creation is not an end in itself. It is just a beginning. The end is somewhere else. The end is something else. The end (the goal, the target, the aim, the purpose) for which this beginning is taking place is Jesus Christ. Throughout the history of

1. Sailhamer, "Genesis," 19–20.
2. Sailhamer, "Genesis," 20.
3. Wenham, *Genesis*, 14.

creation we are "waiting for the mercy of our Lord Jesus Christ that leads to eternal life" (Jude 21).

This text reveals a vital truth. Mere existence is not everything. There is a purpose higher than just being. The purpose of creation is to be a revelation of God, an exhibition of divine mercy. And the purpose of human life within the context of this creation is to see that revelation, to experience that mercy. In a sense we are anticipating in saying this, in that it was the fall which necessitated the revelation of God's mercy. However, from the very beginning of creation the Lord knew already the direction that things would take.

God

"The first subject of the Bible and Genesis is God."[4] The word here translated "God" is *ᵉlōhîm*. This divine title especially stresses God's sovereignty and his Saviorhood.[5] Wenham emphasizes the first of these divine qualities when he suggests that the use of *ᵉlōhîm* here "implies that God is the sovereign Creator of the whole universe."[6] But it is true that the sovereign Creator is also the merciful Savior. This title occurs many times in association with some of the terms which express the mercy of God. Here are just three examples.

First, in Genesis 24:27, Abraham's servant says, "Blessed *be* the Lord God (*ᵉlōhîm*) of my master Abraham, who has not forsaken his mercy (*hesed*) and his truth (*ᵉmet*) toward my master."

Then David's prayer in Psalm 51 opens with these words: "have mercy (*hānan*) upon me, O God (*ᵉlōhîm*), according to your lovingkindness (*hesed*); according to the multitude of your tender mercies (*rāḥam*), blot out my transgressions."

Finally, Daniel 9:9 says, "to the Lord our God (*ᵉlōhîm*) *belong* mercy (*rāḥam*) and forgiveness (*sᵉlîḥâ*)."

So the use of *ᵉlōhîm* signals that the God who created is the God who, in the developing context of that creation, will abound in mercy to his people. This very title underlines the fact that creation is just the beginning which establishes the context for the glorious end. And the end is the manifestation of God's saving mercy.

4. Procksch, *Genesis*, 438 (Quoted by Wenham, *Genesis*, 14).

5. J. B. Scott, "*ʾlh*," 93c.

6. Wenham, *Genesis*, 15.

Sailhamer points out that in Genesis 2:4 *ᵉlōhîm* is explicitly identified with the Lᴏʀᴅ, the God of Abraham, the God of Israel. He notes that the God of Genesis 1:1 "is far from a faceless deity."[7] He is none other than the God who is the Redeemer of his people. And the purpose of this opening sentence is to inform us that the God whom we already know in his mercy is himself the Creator of the universe.

Created

The verb *bārā'* appears 54 times in the Hebrew Scriptures. It usually has God as its subject, and its most common form is a qal perfect, emphasizing that when God created this was a completed action. There are just six exceptions, in five verses, where man rather than God is the subject of this verb (Josh 17:15 and 18, 1 Sam 2:29, and Ezek 21:19 and 23:47), and in these contexts "to create" is not a suitable rendering. It is true that it is rendered "make" in Ezekiel 21:19, but even when human beings use their creativity to make something, this is entirely different from God's creativity. A human being can only shape existing materials. When God creates, something entirely new and unprecedented comes into being.

That is why Genesis 1 does not speak of any raw materials out of which God created. They were part of his creation just as much as the finished product. Creation was out of nothing.

The heavens and the earth

This phrase refers to absolutely everything that exists without any exceptions at all. The entire universe is the handiwork of God.

Sᴏᴍᴇ Gᴇɴᴇʀᴀʟ Oʙsᴇʀᴠᴀᴛɪᴏɴs ᴏɴ ᴛʜɪs Vᴇʀsᴇ

Its status within the context of the chapter that follows

Some people have seen verse 1 as a title or summary, with verse 2 onwards expounding what verse 1 means. Others have seen it as the initial statement, describing the first act of creation, with verse 2 onwards describing subsequent creative actions.

---

7. Sailhamer, "Genesis," 20.

Wenham has presented cogent arguments against the view that verse 1 is a title. If the account of creation itself begins in verse 2, then there is no mention of the bringing into being of matter itself. This would seem to imply that matter was eternal, though in a chaotic state, and that creation was simply God putting it in order. Verse 1 must therefore be read as the statement of the first creative event. Only then, for the first time ever, did anything at all, other than God, begin to exist.

Its polemic against pagan polytheism

If thus understood, as the initial statement of the creation of the raw materials, the Bible's very first sentence is already a polemic against the polytheistic paganism of the ancient religious environment in which the faith of Israel was proclaimed. That is apparent in two ways.

First, the reference to creation in a general sense, to the totality of the universe, in the phrase "the heavens and the earth" opposes Canaanite theology. This claimed that creation was the ordering of pre-existing matter. The Bible insists that matter itself is the creation of God.

Second, there is the reference to the one *ᵉlōhîm*. Although this noun is plural in form, the verb is singular. Sailhamer makes this comment:

> by identifying God as the Creator, a crucial distinction is introduced between the God of the fathers and the gods of the nations, gods that to the biblical authors were mere idols. God alone created the heavens and the earth.[8]

Sailhamer cites Jeremiah 10:11 as conveying the same message: "the gods that have not made the heavens and the earth shall perish from the earth and from under these heavens." We might also mention Psalm 96:5: "all the gods of the peoples *are* idols, but the Lord made the heavens."

Its call to worship

This very first sentence of God's revelation in Scripture is already calling us to worship. It highlights the uniqueness of God, the splendor of his work, the dependency of all creatures. It is truly, as Wenham says, "a triumphant invocation" of God.[9]

---

8. Sailhamer, "Genesis," 20.
9. Wenham, *Genesis*, 10.

Genesis 1:2

In this verse we have a description of the universe immediately after God's first creative act. The raw materials, which are destined to become ordered and beautiful, have been brought into being. As yet everything is in darkness. The surface of the earth is entirely covered by water. God's Spirit is hovering. He is poised for action. He is waiting for the moment to begin.

The main issue raised by this verse is the meaning of the phrase "without form and void." "Without form" translates the Hebrew word *tōhû*, while "void" translates *bōhû*.

Wenham suggests that the two terms together mean "total chaos." He writes:

> frightening disorganization is the antithesis to the order that characterized the work of creation when it was complete . . . . The dreadfulness of the situation before the divine word brought order out of chaos is underlined.[10]

It seems to me very improbable that that is the significance of this phrase. Such an interpretation would seem to impugn the character and work of God. Could God really do anything "dreadful"? Surely there was no one there to be "frightened," except God himself—and that is hardly likely. We need a more positive reading of these words.

Sailhamer seems to be on the right lines when he says that this expression "refers to the condition of the land in its 'not-yet' state." Creation is not yet what it shall be. Sailhamer notes that the rest of the chapter will tell the story of the preparation of the land as a place for man to live. But as yet it is not inhabitable. Sailhamer points, pertinently, to Isaiah 45:18, where the word *tōhû* is also used:

> For thus says the LORD, who created the heavens, who is God, who formed the earth and made it, who has established it, who did not create it in vain (*tōhû*), who formed it to be inhabited: "I *am* the LORD, and *there is* no other."

Here *tōhû* contrasts with "inhabited."

However, even Sailhamer suggests that *tōhû* and *bōhû* "describe the condition of the land before God made it good."[11] This, again, seems, very questionably, to imply that God's initial act of creation was bad.

10. Wenham, *Genesis*, 15–16.
11. Sailhamer, "Genesis," 24.

Actually, however, it is not necessary to give *tōhû* and *bōhû* a pejorative sense. At this stage the earth is unformed and unfilled. The rest of the chapter will record its forming and filling. But God has not done that yet. But that does not mean that the earth is not yet good. It is absolutely as it should be for that stage in God's creative work.

It is sometimes alleged that Isaiah 45:18 contradicts Genesis 1:2. Genesis says that God created the earth *tōhû*. Isaiah says that he did not. However, Isaiah's point is that God did not create the world in order for it to be empty. That was not his ultimate intention, even though, of necessity, it began like that. Emptiness was the starting point of a route leading to fullness. God's final goal was that the earth should be inhabited, and that it should be a suitable home for man.

Isaiah 45:18 is linked to verse 17 by the word "for." Verse 17 says this: "Israel shall be saved by the LORD with an everlasting salvation; you shall not be ashamed or disgraced forever and ever." In describing the earth as a suitable home for man, the main thing is that it is a fitting location within which human beings could get to know the saving mercy of the Lord.

Genesis 1:3–25

We now hear the story of the forming and filling of the earth during six days. The six days occur in two corresponding sets of three. Having noted this pattern, we shall then observe some recurring features in this chapter.

THE THREE PAIRS OF DAYS

The first pair: Days One and Four

On Day One (verses 3–5) light is created. Light includes color. Light is a spectrum seen in the colors of the rainbow. Light and color are the source of aesthetic beauty. For God to create light first is for him to indicate the priority which he gives to beauty in his creation.

Corresponding to Day One is Day Four (verses 14–19), when the sun, moon and stars are created. Their purpose is to focus the light and to give structure to time.

It is sometimes objected that it is unrealistic for light to be created before the light-sources. Sailhamer argues that this was not in fact what happened. He suggests that the sun, moon and stars were created at the very beginning, and are included in the words "the heavens and the earth" in verse 1. Verse 3 then describes the first appearance of the sun through the darkness. Sailhamer then suggests a different translation for verse 14: "Let the lights in the expanse of the heavens separate the day from the night." This would imply that the lights were already there. On Day Four their function is being allocated for the first time.[12]

This seems to me an ingenious way of solving a difficulty which is itself only imaginary. It is not necessary to read verse 1 as meaning that every single component of the completed universe was in place from the start. To protest that God could not create light before creating light-sources betrays a poor view of the power of God.

In fact there is an important reason why God did not create the light-sources from the first moment of creation. He is emphasizing that he is himself the true light-source. Even the sun, so central to the solar system to which we belong, receives its light from God as the sovereign giver. This will become clear at the end; as Revelation 21:23 says, "the city had no need of the sun or the moon to shine in it, for the glory of God illuminated it. The Lamb *is* its light." Similarly, Revelation 22:5 reads, "there shall be no night there: they need no lamp nor light of the sun, for the Lord God gives them light."

Such a view would tie in with some observations which Wenham makes on Day Four:

> The creation of the sun, moon and stars is described at much greater length than anything save the creation of man . . . . The fullness of the description suggests that the creation of the heavenly bodies held a special significance.

The reason is that the sun, moon and stars held an important place in the thinking of Israel's neighbors. They were some of their most important gods. They were often credited with controlling human destiny—as is still the case today. Wenham notes four ways in which the Genesis account underlines its rejection of this understanding of the heavenly bodies.

(1) They were created by God. They are not gods, but creatures. They are not eternal, but transient.

12. Sailhamer, "Genesis," 34.

(2) The sun and moon are not referred to by their normal Hebrew names. They are called simply "the greater light" and "the lesser light." Their importance is thus reduced. They cannot be equated with any astral deities which the nations might foolishly honor.

(3) Their function is defined simply as lighting the earth. This is a lowly task compared with the elevated claims that Mesopotamian religion made for these entities.

(4) The stars are mentioned almost as an afterthought at the end of verse 16. It is as if the author says, "oh, I almost forgot: God made the stars too." He is laughing at the idea that they are the controllers of human destiny, worthy of veneration.[13]

The second pair: Days Two and Five

On Day Two (verses 6–8) the sky is created. Corresponding to this, on Day Five (verses 20–23), God creates the birds to fly in the sky, preceded by marine life.

The third pair: Days Three and Six

Day Three (verses 9–13) sees the appearance of the land, which is then covered with vegetation. The corresponding day is Day Six (verses 24–25). Now the land animals are created. Wenham notes that the correspondence between these two days is highlighted in the text by the repetition of the Hebrew verb *yāṣā'* ("to bring forth") in verses 12 and 24.

THE SIX RECURRING FEATURES

Creation took place by mere command

Seven times we read "God said" (verses 3, 6, 9, 11, 14, 20, 24). Each time God's command is followed by a phrase confirming that what was said actually happened. In verse 3 the phrase is "and there was." In verse 7 it is "and God made." In verse 21 we read "so God created." But the most frequent phrase is "and it was so" (verses 9, 11, 15, 24).

This draws attention to God's amazing power. He is not dependent on anything else at all. God is in total control, and creation is totally

13. Cf. Wenham, *Genesis*, 21.

under his control. We see the power of God's Word. The Word of God is creative and effective. Psalm 33:6 emphasizes this: "by the word of the Lord the heavens were made, and all the host of them by the breath of his mouth."

The entire universe was good

As it left the maker's hand, every single part of creation was good. Six times we hear that God saw that what he had just made was good. This phrase occurs every day except Day Two, and twice on Day Three (verses 4, 10, 12, 18, 21, 25).

In what sense were the elements of creation "good"? Sailhamer suggests that the word is used in the sense of "beneficial for man." He sees this as the reason why the word is absent from the account of Day Two:

> On that day there was nothing created or made that was, in fact, "good" or beneficial for man. The heavens were made and the waters divided, but the land, where man was to dwell, still remained hidden under the deep.[14]

I question this interpretation. Even though man was to dwell on land, the waters would be beneficial for man. Adam Clarke reports some scientific experiments on evaporation. They demonstrated that the quantity of water in creation is precisely what is needed to produce enough water vapor to cool the atmosphere and water the land.[15]

Wenham's explanation for the absence of the words "it was good" on Day Two seems more probable: "the separation of the waters was not completed until the following day." Also, I think Wenham's explanation of "it was good" is nearer to the point. He describes it as an "appreciation formula," and compares it to an artist admiring his own handiwork.[16] Creation was good in God's estimation. It was satisfying and glorifying to him. Its very existence brought God satisfaction. This passage highlights several features of God's creation which promote his glory. Verses 11–12 and 22–24 tell of the earth's productive capacity, and of its inbuilt potential for further development. Verses 20–21 stress the abundance which is found in God's creation. Verses 16–18 point to the orderliness, regularity, and predictability of creation.

14. Sailhamer, "Genesis," 27.
15. Clarke, *Commentary*, Vol. 1, 20.
16. Wenham, *Genesis*, 18.

God named the things he had created

On each of the first three days "God called" the thing he had created by its appropriate name (verses 5, 8, 10). Wenham explains: "in the Old Testament to name something is to assert authority over it."[17]

Creation took place by division

The Hebrew word *bādal* comes five times in this passage (verses 4, 6, 7, 14, 18). It is translated "to separate." In creating, God founded distinctions. The integrity of different aspects of creation was established at first by the LORD. The Creator ascribed to the various parts of his creation their proper functions. The use of created things is not something which can be decided by human whim.

Each category of living creatures was made "according to its kind"

This phrase comes three times in verses 11 and 12 with reference to the vegetation, twice in verse 21 with reference to the fish and the birds, and five times in verses 24 and 25 with reference to the land animals. This is an aspect of the differentiation which is built into creation.

Modern biology, zoology and botany have discovered the distinctions between order, family, genus, and species. But it was God who created these basic life forms. Wenham's comment is worth noting:

> There is a givenness about time and space which God has ordered by his own decree. The different species of plant and animal life again bear testimony to God's creative plan. The implication, though not stated, is clear: what God has distinguished and created distinct, man ought not to confuse. Order, not chaos, is the hallmark of God's activity . . . . Things are the way they are because God made it so, and men and women should accept his decree.[18]

17. Wenham, *Genesis*, 19.
18. Wenham, *Genesis*, 21.

God's creation is blessed by the Creator

Although a reference to blessing comes only once in this passage (verse 22), it will reappear in verse 28 and again in 2:3. It is a notable feature of the account. The Hebrew word translated "to bless" is *bārak*. Its form here is piel. This usually represents intent. God determined to bless the sea creatures and the birds. He blessed them thoroughly. Sometimes the piel can express repetition or permanence. God blessed his creatures again and again. Their blessedness was a constant state.

Wenham notes that "where modern man talks of success, Old Testament man talked of blessing."[19] But what is it to be blessed? Oswalt offers this answer: "To bless in the Old Testament means 'to endue with power for success, prosperity, fruitfulness, long life, etc.'"[20]

It is to live a life which fulfils the purpose of creation, and so to find contentment within the creation.

Genesis 1:31

The final verse of Genesis 1 begins "then God saw everything that he had made, and indeed *it was* very good." The superlative goodness of everything is being proclaimed. This sentence calls us to gaze with God on his pristine creation and to contemplate with enthusiasm the integrated goodness of the completed whole. It is now "very good." It is marked by exceeding goodness. It cannot be improved on. No one else could do the slightest bit better than the master Creator has done. When the separate pieces of creation were made, God pronounced them "good." Now, as he surveys the finished work he pronounces it "very good." Wenham says, "The harmony and perfection of the completed heavens and earth express more adequately the character of their Creator than any of the separate components can."[21]

Genesis 2:1–3

Two comments on these opening verses of chapter 2 are in order.

19. Wenham, *Genesis*, 24.
20. Oswalt, "*bārak*," 285.0.
21. Wenham, *Genesis*, 34.

THE SUMMARY OF THE WORK DONE

Creation is now "finished." The Hebrew word is *kālâ*, and in the original text it comes at the beginning of the verse, giving it emphatic status. It contains two ideas: the task is thoroughly accomplished, and God has ceased his work of creation.

GOD'S REST

This is depicted in verses 2–3. Here God sets a pattern and example for his human creatures. There is a certain rhythm of life built into creation which we ignore to our cost. From the very beginning one day in seven was set apart from the remainder of the week as an occasion for rest and refreshment. It is part of the very nature of creation that a rest day is needed. Later verses emphasize this point. Exodus 23:12 stresses that the refreshing rest is for everyone: "six days you shall do your work, and on the seventh day you shall rest, that your ox and your donkey may rest, and the son of your female servant and the stranger may be refreshed."

The word *nāpaš* (translated "refreshed"), with which the English translation of this verse concludes, means "to catch your breath" or "to renew your soul." But Leviticus 25:2 reminds us that the Sabbath rest is "to the LORD." The day spent aside from daily labor is an occasion for the contemplation of God's works, and for responding in worship.

New Testament

There are two additional aspects of the doctrine of creation taught in the New Testament.

Jesus Christ was the Father's Agent in Creation (Colossians 1:15–18)

This truth is mentioned briefly in Hebrews 1:2, and proclaimed at greater length in this Colossians passage, from which we can analyze Christ's role in creation by noting five elements.

THE CLAUSE, "THE FIRSTBORN OF ALL CREATION"

The title "firstborn" in verse 15 can indicate either priority in time or supremacy in rank. Curtis Vaughan sees both meanings here, but with the emphasis falling on the latter.[22] So the Son of God's love was there before all things (as verse 17 also says), and he is forever over all things.

Just because he is the Son of the Father's love, he must be superior to all created reality. He is distinct from creation. He is unique. He was therefore instrumental in the origin of the creation.

THE THREE PREPOSITIONAL PHRASES

Verse 16 tells us that all things were created "by him" (*en autō*—literally "in him"), "through him" (*di' autou*), and "for him" (*eis auton*—literally "towards him").

(1) "In him." This phrase portrays Christ as the sphere in which creation took place. He is like the container which holds the creation. The boundaries of creation are set by Christ. The universe is held in his hands, in his power. As verse 17 adds, "in him all things consist," which is to say that they stand together as a single, united whole in Christ. He is the context within which the Father created. The whole of creation is Christ-like. It reflects his nature. His pulse throbs through everything that God has made.

(2) "Through him." Christ is the Mediator in creation as well as in salvation. God created through Christ. The Son was the Father's agent. He was the Father's voice. Genesis 1 tells us that God created by speaking his Word. We know that Christ is the living Word of God. For God to say "Let there be" was to commission his Son to work in active power.

(3) "Towards him." Christ is the goal towards which the creation is traveling. God's original purpose was that creation should find its ultimate and final explanation in Christ alone. The only reason why anything exists is for the glory of Jesus Christ.

Perhaps this throws additional light on the word "good" in Genesis 1. We have seen that one interpretation of the word is good for the glory of God. But another way of understanding it is good and beneficial for man. If creation had Christ as its destiny, then ultimately "good" means suitable for him. The two understandings of "good" in Genesis 1 come

---

22. Vaughan, "Colossians," 182.

together in him. He is God who is glorified in creation. He is the true man, for whose benefit creation was made. God made all things as a present for his Son.

THE TWO VERB TENSES

In the phrase "in him all things were created" the tense of the verb is aorist (*ektisthē*). This draws attention to the initial event of creation. When God first made everything he boxed it up in his Son. Creation was not made free-ranging, open-ended, and unpredictable. It shares something of the constancy of Christ. On the other hand, the verb tense in the phrase "all things were created through him and towards him" is perfect (*ektistai*). This draws attention to the continuing reality of the created universe. To this very day, Christ's creative power sustains everything. Every single day, the movement of creation is towards him. Existence for his glory is a perennial feature of creation.

THE PHRASE "ALL THINGS"

Verse 16 elaborates on this phrase. It includes heavenly and earthly things, visible and invisible things, and four specific invisible things are mentioned: thrones, dominions, rulers and authorities. These are probably four categories within the angelic hierarchy. In Colossians 2:18 we read: "let no one cheat you of your reward, taking delight in *false* humility and worship of angels."

Evidently there were some at Colossae who were inclined towards angel worship. The apostle undercuts the idea that this could be valid: angels are just creatures. Others at Colossae seem to have been alarmed by demonic powers. That is presumably why Paul reassures them by telling them that Christ has "disarmed principalities and powers," by "triumphing over them" in his death on the cross (Col 2:15). Even evil spirits are not self-regulating, independent demigods. The demons too are mere creatures. Christ is above them all.

THE WORDS "WHO IS THE BEGINNING"

This title for Jesus Christ, used in verse 18, echoes the first verse of the Bible. The Greek word for "beginning" (*archē*) is the same word used in the Greek translation of Genesis 1:1. Just like *rō'š*, from the same Hebrew root as *rē'šît*, *archē* can mean "head." Creation exists with Christ as its head. It derives its very being from him. Already in the first sentence of Genesis there is an anticipation of the christological fulfilment. There is a profundity here which defeats our finite minds. How can we put this into words?

God's Pleasure is the Ultimate Purpose of Creation (Revelation 4:11)

In the New King James Version the final part of this verse reads as follows: "you created all things, and by your will they exist and were created."

However, there is a question about the most appropriate translation of the phrase "by your will." The Greek wording is *dia to thelēma sou*.

I would suggest that the New King James translation is poor at this point. The Authorized Version rendered these words like this: "thou hast created all things, and for thy pleasure they are and were created."

I think that the translation "for your pleasure" is to be preferred.

We have here *dia* followed by an accusative. The regular meaning of *dia* in this construction is "because of, on account of, for the sake of."[23] "By your will" would be a different construction, *dia* followed by a genitive: *dia tou thelēmatos*. That would see God's *thelēma* as the first cause of creation. However, the construction in this text suggests that God's *thelēma* is the final objective of creation.

So how should *thelēma* be translated? It is true that "will" is the usual rendering. But the Authorized Version translators were right to recognize that *thelēma* can have a secondary meaning—"pleasure." In fact, in the Greek translation of the Old Testament God's good pleasure is the normal meaning of *thelēma*.[24]

So Revelation 4:11 is saying that the reason why God created anything was to satisfy his own desire, to bring himself pleasure. That purpose was fulfilled, and so God pronounced his completed creation "very good" (Gen 1:31).

23. Wallace, *Greek Grammar*, 369.
24. Müller, "Will," 1019.

DOCTRINAL FORMULATION

The Early Creeds

We have seen already that the Apostles' and Nicene Creeds define God as Creator and speak of the universality of his creation. In its section on Jesus Christ the Nicene Creed also includes the phrase "by whom all things were made."

Although not precisely a creed, there is a creedal summary in Tertullian's work, *The Prescription Against Heretics*. Tertullian says that God is

> the Creator of the world, who, by his own Word coming down in the beginning, brought all things into being out of nothing; and this Word is called his Son, and appeared under the name of God in diverse manners to the patriarchs, was heard at all times in the prophets, and at last entered into the Virgin Mary by the Spirit and power of the Father, was made flesh in her womb, and, being born of her, went forth as Jesus Christ.[25]

Tertullian's theology here is thoroughly Christ-centered. By reference to the Word, he holds together the doctrines of creation, the Trinity, revelation and Christ. We can summarize his summary of the Rule of Faith in seven statements: (1) God created the world, defined as all things; (2) God created all things by his Word; (3) the Word was sent forth before all things; (4) God created all things out of nothing; (5) the Word by which God created all things is the second person of the Trinity; (6) the Word by which God created is also the Word by which he gives his revelation; (7) this Word, by which God created and reveals, is also the Word who became incarnate as Jesus Christ.

For Tertullian, creation, revelation and salvation are all part of a single enterprise, united in the person of Jesus Christ. Creation took place so that God could reveal his saving mercy.

The Reformation Confessions

The teaching of the confessions on creation can be summed up in nine statements.

---

25. Tertullian, *Prescription*, 13.

The Doctrine of Creation

God created everything

Some confessions elaborate on this basic statement by defining "everything." It means heaven and earth and all their contents, both visible and invisible, including the world of spirits.

The Belgic Confession points out that creation means more than mere existence. God gave every created thing "its being, shape and form." The exact proportions of things were the work of the Creator. He alone is the source of all beauty.

Creation was the beginning

The confessions are clear that nothing had any existence before God's work of creation. Time itself began with God's creative work. All things proceed from that one beginning.

In his exposition of the Westminster Confession Robert Shaw makes an interesting comment on the teaching that the world had a beginning:

> This will now be considered one of the most obvious truths that can be stated, but it is one which required to be confirmed by divine revelation. That the world existed from eternity was generally maintained by the ancient heathen philosophers. Some of them held that not only the matter of which the world is framed existed from eternity, but that it subsisted in that beautiful form in which we behold it. Others admitted that the heavens and earth had a beginning in respect of their present form, but maintained the eternity of the matter of which they are composed. That the world had a beginning is the uniform doctrine of the Scriptures.[26]

God created everything out of nothing

Several of the confessions simply, but clearly, affirm this truth. The Westminster Confession understands "out of nothing" to be implied by the word "create." In its statement that it pleased God "to create, or make out of nothing, the world" the clause "or make out of nothing" reads as a definition of the verb "to create."

---

26. Shaw, *Confession*, 60.

115

Creation was the work of the triune God

The confessions generally insist that God the Father, Son and Holy Spirit worked together in unity, equality, and oneness of purpose to bring about the creation of all things. Robert Shaw comments like this on the Westminster Confession:

> The work of creation is common to all the three persons of the Trinity . . . . We must not, therefore, suppose that in creation the Father is the principal agent, and the Son and the Holy Ghost inferior agents, or mere instruments. In all external works of Deity, each of the persons of the Godhead equally concur.[27]

Nevertheless, the confessions recognize that it is the clear teaching of Scripture that the instrumentality of the Trinity in creation is channelled through the Word. And this Word is not God's mere command. It is to be identified with the second person of the Trinity.

God created everything in six days

The English language confessions include this emphasis on the literal meaning of the six days of Genesis 1. The English puritan, Thomas Vincent, said:

> God created all things in the space of six days. He could have created all things together in a moment; but he took six days' time to work in, and rested on the seventh day, that we might the better apprehend the order of the creation, and that we might imitate him in working but six days of the week, and in resting on the seventh.[28]

Vincent is observing that for God to take six days over creation could seem unexpectedly long. He links God's decision to take six days with our apprehension of the order of creation. By this he does not mean the order in which things happened, but the orderliness of things. By portraying the orderly fashion in which God's creative work took place, according to a definite pattern, the Scriptures lift our sights and enhance our appreciation of the orderliness of the world in which we live. We are therefore stimulated to adore the Creator.

27. Shaw, *Confession*, 61.
28. Vincent, *Shorter Catechism*, 45–46.

God created everything very good

Robert Shaw interprets the confessions like this:

> Everything was very good; for it was agreeable to the model which the great Architect had formed in his mind from everlasting; it answered exactly the end of its creation, and was adapted to the purpose for which it was designed.[29]

"Very good," then, is a functional description. Creation fulfils its intended purpose. This raises a further question: what was the purpose of creation? The confessions give two main reasons for which God created. These form our next two strands in their teaching.

God created everything for the benefit of man

This applies even to the things of the invisible world. God created the angels to be his messengers in serving the elect.

God created everything for himself

God's own pleasure is the ultimate motive behind creation. No lesser reason is really required. God gave every created thing its own peculiar function to serve him within creation as a whole. In the creation the glory of God's power, wisdom, and goodness are made manifest. Vincent comments:

> God created all things for his own glory, that he might make manifest—1. the glory of his power, in effecting so great a work, making everything out of nothing by a word . . . ; 2. the glory of his wisdom, in the order and variety of his creatures . . . ; 3. the glory of his goodness, especially towards man, for whom he provided first a habitation, and every useful creature, before he gave him his being.[30]

Williamson points out the contrast with much modern dogma in these assertions of purpose: according to modern philosophy, "there is no ultimate reason for it all."[31]

29. Shaw, *Confession*, 62.
30. Vincent, *Shorter Catechism*, 47.
31. Williamson, *Westminster*, 41.

False teaching about creation is rejected

The Reformation confessions name two false views of creation which they reject, the teaching of Marcion and the teaching of Manicheanism.

MARCION

Marcion was born in Asia Minor and moved to Rome around AD 140. He believed that there was a complete antithesis between the Old and New Testaments. He held that they were inspired by different Gods. The God of the Old Testament was a God of justice, but not goodness, whereas the God of the New Testament was the God of love, the God of Jesus.

Marcion believed in the eternity of matter. He taught that the imperfections in the material world proved that it was not the creation of the good God. The good God was responsible only for the invisible world above us. The material world was the work of the other God.

However, the power of this other God was limited. So the formation of the material world involved him in a struggle. Under the impulse of Satan the material from which the world was formed resisted this God's attempt to give it shape. So the work of creation was only of limited success. This included the creation of man. However, the God of love took pity on man, even though he was not his own creature, and sent Christ to rescue him from the imperfections of the created order.[32]

The Reformation rejected such notions. There is only one God. He created everything, visible as well as invisible. And it was all very good as it came from the Creator's hand.

MANICHAEANISM

This philosophy developed in Persia. Its founder, Manes, was born about AD 215. He was 65 years old when he started propagating his teaching. It was based on Zoroastrianism.

Manes saw that life in this world was full of terrible contradictions. This led him to a dualistic view of the universe. He taught that there were two separate cosmic kingdoms, the kingdom of light or goodness, and the kingdom of darkness or evil.

---

32. Fisher, *History*, 58–59.

The kingdom of light, Manes said, is ruled by the primal God, and he is good. The kingdom of darkness is ruled by Satan and his demons. There is eternal opposition between the two kingdoms.

At some point Satan launched an invasion on the kingdom of light. God retaliated by creating the Archetypal Man. However, Satan won the battle, and stole some particles of light. He mixed them with some elements of darkness. God obtained this mixture, and from it he formed the visible world. His intention in doing so was to liberate the particles of light.

Satan then created Adam, the first human being in the visible creation. From the very first Adam was imbued with sin, but Satan put the particles of light into him to keep them more secure from God's attempts to retrieve them.

God sent prophets to the human race. They taught mankind about the imprisoned light. The aim was to set the light free to ascend to God and finish forever with any involvement in the material world. If they are not set free in the case of any particular human being, there are further cycles of life after death, so there is always a chance of redemption. Finally, when (or perhaps it is better to say "if") all the light is reunited with God, he will destroy the material universe, and there will again be a complete separation between the two spiritual kingdoms.[33]

To us this may seem a rather far-fetched philosophy. However, it continued, under various names, until the fourteenth century, and its influence lived on even after it came to an end as a movement. That is why, even in the sixteenth and seventeenth centuries, the Reformed confessions felt the need to repudiate it.

Modern Confessions of Faith

The modern confessions all treat this doctrine rather briefly. The Chinese confession is satisfied merely to say, "We believe that God created all things." The Indonesian confession acknowledges that God is the Creator of all things, both visible and invisible. A weakness in its wording, however, is that it sees the Father alone as the Creator.

The Confession of Faith of the United Church of Northern India makes two points in its brief affirmation of creation: (1) that all visible

33. O'Grady, *Heresy*, 65–66.

things were created by God; (2) that God created all things by the word of his power.

Presumably, the stipulation that visible things are God's creation is not intended as a denial that God created the things which cannot be seen, whether because they are intrinsically invisible, or because they are beyond the reach of human probing. The Indian Christians would certainly have acknowledged God's creation of the invisible realm.

However, the people who formulated this confession were not concerned to speak of things with which human beings can have no acquaintance. Their only interest was to proclaim the faith as it relates to human life. And it is in this visible world that human life takes place. From a human point of view, what matters is that our world is God's creation.

HISTORICAL ELABORATION

One issue which arises from the doctrine of creation concerns the six days of Genesis 1. Must they be understood literally as six days of 24 hours each?

There are some Christians who have been influenced by the theory of evolution, and who try to harmonize the biblical account of creation with the claims of evolutionary philosophy.

Evolutionists claim that the universe originated in a "Big Bang" as many as 20 billion years ago. Our solar system is said to have begun about 5 billion years ago. The origin of life in single-cell organisms is dated to 3 or 4 billion years ago, and the emergence of multi-cell organisms a couple of billion years later. The ancestors of man are reckoned to have appeared on earth a couple of million years ago, and human life as we know it, with its accompanying culture and civilization is thought to be between 5 and 10 thousand years old.

The issue is this: can these alleged billions of years somehow be fitted into the pattern of creation portrayed in Genesis 1? Can Genesis 1 be understood in such a way as to accommodate this vast time span? There are six ways in which Christians have sometimes tried to make the evolutionary timetable and biblical revelation fit each other.

(1) Theistic Evolution. This view accepts the entire evolutionary package, with the add-on that God started the whole process. With that common starting point, there are two variations of this theory: [a] Deistic Evolution teaches that God set things going, and then withdrew and

let it happen. [b] Providential Evolution teaches that the entire development from the amoeba to the ape to Adam was overseen and overruled by God.

(2) The Gap Theory. This claims that there is a break in time between the first verse and a half of Genesis 1 and the rest of the chapter. The first two sentences of Genesis say, "In the beginning God created the heavens and the earth. The earth was without form and void; and darkness *was* over the face of the deep." The gap theory argues that the billions of years of alleged geological formation come between those introductory words and the next sentence, which begins the account of the first day of the creation week: "And the Spirit of God was hovering over the face of the waters."

(3) The Restitution Theory. Like the gap theory, this view postulates a gap between the initial creation of the universe and God's creative work described in Genesis 1. In that gap the fall of Satan took place. His fall resulted in creation being thrown into chaos. This theory reads Genesis 1 not as the story of the original creation, but as an account of the restoration of the damaged cosmos.

(4) The Day-Age Theory. This asserts that "day" in Genesis 1 does not mean a 24-hour day, but a period of time which is unspecified, indefinite and lengthy.

(5) The Framework Hypothesis. According to this view, Genesis 1 is not an account of creation itself. It is the story of God's revelation of the fact of creation to his people. The six days form a framework within which God revealed creation. They are not the period during which the things mentioned were actually created.

(6) The "Ideal" Interpretation. This theory argues that, since God is outside time, reference to "days" when speaking of his work has no point of contact with earthly days, however understood, whether as periods of 24 hours, or as aeons of time. The word "day" is used to convey the idea of an aspect of divine creative activity. Six days highlights six aspects of God's creative work.

John Morris used to be Professor of Geology at the University of Oklahoma. He now works for the Institute of Creation Research, and has written a book entitled *The Young Earth*.[34] He argues that all these approaches are

34. J. Morris, *Young Earth, passim.*

flawed, and that the six days of Genesis 1 must be understood literally. He gives nine reasons.

Facts require interpretation

Morris points out that the evolutionary timescale is not a scientific fact, but a philosophy on the basis of which facts are interpreted. He observes that there is no dispute about the facts. The fossil record is there. Experiments have discovered how long certain observable phenomena would take to develop from scratch. However, every interpretation contains assumptions, and these determine the conclusion reached as the facts are examined.

Morris names the two chief assumptions of the evolutionary hypothesis. (1) The first is "uniformitarianism." This is the assumption that everything has always happened at exactly the same rate as we observe it happening now. (2) The second assumption is that everything started from scratch.

However, there is another interpretation which leads from the same evidence to a totally different conclusion—the hypothesis that God created everything in six days. This interpretation has two assumptions which are opposed to those of evolution. (1) The first is "catastrophism." This assumes that much of the fossil record and many observable phenomena on and below the earth's surface are the result not of slow, steady development, but of sudden change brought about by the worldwide flood. (2) The second assumption is that things did not start from scratch. Rather, the Creator made a functionally mature universe. That is part of what was involved in the pronouncement that everything was very good. Everything was in place which would enable things to function immediately for God's glory and for human benefit.

One example of how the universe was functionally mature from the beginning is seen in the light of the stars. Scientists have calculated that it would take billions of years for starlight to reach the earth. However, when God created the stars he also created the track of light visible to people on earth.

It is impossible to harmonize the Biblical and evolutionary accounts of origins

Morris draws attention to the different order in the appearance of things according to the two accounts. We may illustrate this in the form of a table:

Evolutionary Philosophy	The Bible
1. Matter existed in the beginning.	1. In the beginning was God, who created matter.
2. The sun and the stars appeared first and then the earth.	2. The earth was created several days before the sun and the stars.
3. The land appeared before the oceans.	3. The oceans were created before the land.
4. The sun was the first light source for our solar system.	4. Light was created before the sun.
5. The atmosphere was situated above one layer of water.	5. The atmosphere was situated between two layers of water.
6. The first forms of life were marine organisms.	6. The first life forms created were plants.
7. Fish evolved before fruit trees.	7. Fruit trees were created before fish.
8. Insects evolved before fish.	8. Fish were created before insects.
9. The sun predated the plants.	9. Plants were created before the sun.
10. Land animals appeared before sea mammals.	10. All types of sea creature predated the land animals.
11. Reptiles came before birds.	11. Birds were created before any land animals.
12. Evolution proceeded by way of death.	12. Human sin caused the entry of death into the world.

To try to harmonize these two accounts is futile. One attempt has been made by an astronomer called Hugh Ross. He suggested that the days of Genesis 1 overlapped each other. However, this only indicates the lengths to which it is necessary to go to try to marry the two hypotheses.

The old-earth hypothesis threatens the gospel itself

On the evolutionary model, death becomes a merely natural phenomenon. However, the basic assumption of the gospel is that death is the wages of sin. It follows that, before the entrance of sin the world as a whole was perfect, and death was unknown. To adopt the evolutionary approach is to undermine the entire structure of the Bible's story line.

Dating methods have been shown up as unreliable

If uniformitarianism is wrong, no effective dating method can be devised. But even on uniformitarian assumptions, the methods used are unsuccessful.

As an example Morris mentions the attempt to discover the age of a meteorite known as Allende. Scientists claim that it is 4.6 billion years old. A whole spectrum of dating tests was used, and the results ranged from 0.7 billion years to 16.49 billion years—a margin of error of over 2000%!

Morris explains that the conclusion that the correct figure was 4.6 was reached on the basis of a series of guesses, none of which could be proved, or even tested. Certain test results were excluded on the grounds that they seemed improbable. Yet probability itself was decided by assumptions which themselves were only guesses. The whole evolutionary approach is based on circular arguments.

Morris also mentions that archaeologists can date things that they discover on the basis of their historical knowledge. Carbon dating rarely agrees with what historians know. So they do not take it seriously.

Some evolutionary conclusions are incompatible with each other

Evolutionary geologists claim that the fossil record and radioisotope dating suggest that the earth is 5 billion years old. The seas are said to have emerged about 3 billion years ago. However, examination of the salt content in all the world's oceans demonstrates that the absolute maximum possible age of the seas is 62 million years—a discrepancy of nearly 5000%.

Many of the implications of the old-earth theory are illogical

If man really emerged from hominids who themselves first evolved a million years ago, and if population growth rates have always been approximately uniform, then the human population should by now have reached 10 to the power of 8600. In fact there are only about 8 billion people on earth today: that's less than 6 to the power of 13. And, Morris asks, why is there no trace of the bones of all the people who have died in the past?

There is plenty of geological evidence for a young earth

Here are just a few of the examples which Morris gives. There are ripple marks on lower layers of rock—proving that layers were formed on top of each other in rapid succession. There is fossil evidence of living things burrowing upwards to escape from a layer of rock laid in a catastrophe. Trees have been discovered fossilized in a standing position, passing through numerous rock layers—proving that successive layers are of a similar age.

Uniformitarian assumptions cannot incorporate the teaching about the curse on creation in Genesis 3

For this reason, such an assumption is incompatible with the Bible. On uniformitarian assumptions, only two options are available: (1) to argue that the description of creation as "very good" lies in the future, that evolution is still pressing onwards and progressing towards a perfect world, such as has never yet been seen; (2) to say that from the very beginning creation was subject to pain, suffering and death, and that these things are "very good," because they are intrinsic to the process of evolution. However, neither view is consistent with Scripture.

The argument that "day" can mean a long period of time in Genesis 1 is not borne out by biblical usage

Morris recognizes that the Hebrew word *yôm* ("day") can mean an indefinite period of time. However, he says, this is not a legitimate interpretation for Genesis 1. He gives the following reasons.

(1) Whenever *yôm* is modified by a number it always means a 24-hour day. Morris says that there are 359 examples elsewhere in the Old Testament.

(2) Whenever the phrase "evening and morning" occurs, it is always referring to a 24-hour day. Morris says that there are 38 examples elsewhere in the Old Testament.

(3) Morris refers to the reference to the six days in the fourth commandment in Exodus 20:11: "*in* six days the LORD made the heavens and the earth, the sea, and all that *is* in them, and rested the seventh day. Therefore the LORD blessed the Sabbath day and hallowed it." As a basis for the Sabbath commandment this reference to the six days of creation is most naturally read as meaning six days of 24 hours.

It seems to me that Morris has made the case for not attempting to combine Scripture with modern evolutionary accounts of origins.

However, it is sometimes argued that a non-literal understanding of "day" can be defended on different grounds and from a higher motive. It is said that the increased vastness of time that results leads to an enhanced perception of the glory of the Creator. It is claimed that this reading makes no concession to modern philosophy. The evidence offered is that some of the earliest Christian theologians, centuries before the time of Darwin, interpreted "day" in a symbolic fashion.

One defender of this viewpoint is Professor Donald Macleod. He writes:

> How can I possibly entertain the notion that these days are creation eras and not 24-hour periods? First of all, because that interpretation has a very honorable pedigree. It is completely false to imagine that it was only adopted by the church as a counsel of despair in the light of the challenge from Darwinism. It was the prevalent view of the fathers even before Augustine, and certainly from Augustine onwards.[35]

However, I think that Macleod is mistaken here. I have looked up every reference to the six days of creation in all 38 volumes of the American edition of the Edinburgh series of the writings of the Ante-Nicene Fathers and the Nicene and Post-Nicene Fathers. I could not find a single one who advocated the view that "day" means a long period of time. Indeed, some (including Basil, Ambrose and Augustine) were adamant, in contrast to the pagan philosophies of their contemporaries, that "day" means 24 hours, and that the earth is only a few thousand years old.

It is true that the fathers did sometimes take the six days in a non-literal way, but Louis Berkhof interprets them correctly:

35. Macleod, *Faith*, 58.

The opinion that these days were not ordinary days of 24 hours was not entirely foreign to early Christian theology . . . . But some of the Church Fathers, who intimated that these days were not to be regarded as ordinary days, expressed the opinion that the whole work of creation was finished in a moment of time, and that the days merely constituted a symbolical framework, which facilitated the description of the work of creation in an orderly fashion, so as to make it more intelligible to finite minds.

On the next page, Berkhof continues:

The prevailing view has always been that the days of Genesis 1 are to be understood as literal days. Some of the early Church Fathers did not regard them as real indications of the time in which the work of creation was completed, but rather as literary forms in which the writer of Genesis cast the narrative of creation, in order to picture the work of creation—which was really completed in a moment of time—in an orderly fashion for the human intellect. It was only after the comparatively new sciences of geology and palaeontology came forward with their theories of the enormous age of the earth, that theologians began to show an inclination to identify the days of creation with the long geological ages.[36]

It is true that Macleod tries to avoid capitulating to evolutionary philosophy. He admits that the Bible precludes

the notion that man is the result of an evolution, itself guided by natural selection and taking place through minute, chance variations over many millions of years. The Bible portrays man as new; and as the specific product of divine activity.

Macleod then proceeds to explain his personal view of the creation week:

within it there were long periods during which the procedures defined in Genesis operated in terms of the Lord's Word, "Let the waters bring forth," "Let the earth bring forth." These processes went on over many millions of years. The waters kept bringing forth and the earth kept bringing forth. But there are specific points in the process where God intervened, initiating a new departure.[37]

---

36. Berkhof, *Systematic Theology*, 152, 153 (Reymond, *New Systematic Theology*, 392, n. 9, makes the same point).

37. Macleod, *Faith*, 68.

However, I very much doubt that this can be carried through consistently. Two New Testament texts are vital for coming to a conclusion on this matter. Romans 5:12 tells us that "through one man sin entered the world, and death through sin, and thus death spread to all men, because all sinned." 1 Corinthians 15:21 presents a briefer summary: "by man *came* death."

Is it possible to maintain a millions-of-years process during which not one living creature died? Old earth theories inevitably teach that some species became extinct long before human beings were created. In that case, death is no longer the result of sin, but a merely natural problem. It will not do to say that these Scriptures are speaking only of human death, because the Romans text makes it clear that death came into the world as a whole through sin. This biblical link between sin and death makes me unable to hold to any other than the literal interpretation of Genesis 1.

PRACTICAL APPLICATION

Gordon Wenham seeks to analyze the picture of God and the world offered by Genesis 1. Some of the points which he makes have clear applicatory implications. Here are three of them.

First, the fact of creation tells us that God has no equals or rivals. This means that he alone is to be worshipped. We must avoid idolizing the things of this world.

Second, as Creator, God is also Law-giver. The Creator's authority is evident in his naming of the component parts of creation, in his appointment of the heavenly lights for a declared purpose, in the command given to the animals to be fruitful and multiply, and in his setting of bounds and defining of roles for his creatures. Wenham writes: "With this goes the corollary that all creatures will fulfil their divinely appointed role only if they adhere to God's directive." Clearly this applies equally to human beings. Our duty is to live in obedience to the God who made everything.

And third, the world reflects its Creator. The implication of this is that general revelation in nature leaves human beings without excuse if we refuse to acknowledge and submit to God.[38]

In addition, we may make the following points of application.

---

38. Wenham, *Genesis*, 37–38.

(1) We must remember that God created everything for the purpose of bringing honor and glory to himself. It follows that this is the ultimate purpose of our human existence too. The apostle reminds us of this in 1 Corinthians 10:31: "whether you eat or drink, or whatever you do, do all to the glory of God." Since, as Revelation 4:11 tells us, God created everything for his pleasure, our duty is to seek to live in such a way that we too bring pleasure to God's heart.

(2) To live to the glory of God is therefore a commitment which we must make from the earliest possible moment. Ecclesiastes 12:1 says, "Remember now your Creator in the days of your youth, before the difficult days come, and the years draw near when you say, 'I have no pleasure in them.'" The contrast here between "youth" and "the evil days" recognizes that old age is often a time of difficulty, tragedy and sadness. The pleasures of life may well be in the past by the time a person is old. However, even youth, with all its joys, falls short of what it should be if the Creator is forgotten. Moreover, to neglect the remembrance of the Creator during the days of youth may be to leave it too late: to remember the Creator early "is shown to be especially important in view of the gradual loss of vitality as age takes its toll of the body and brain."[39]

To remember God as Creator is to live in a constant attitude of gratitude. It is to cultivate a life of obedience. It is to take a serious-minded approach to life. It is to be a sincere worshipper. It is to seek God's forgiveness and to trust in his mercy offered to us in his Son.

(3) Psalm 89:12 says, "The north and the south, you have created them; Tabor and Hermon rejoice in your name." Tabor and Hermon represent the south and the north respectively. The parallel phrases "you have created them" and "rejoice in your name" demonstrate an equivalence in the Psalmist's mind between creation and joy. If the inanimate creation rejoices (metaphorically), so ought we to rejoice (literally) in God's creation. God "gives us richly all things to enjoy" (1 Tim 6:17). His creation is marked by abundant productiveness. We glorify him when we take pleasure, with gratitude, in his creation. He means us to enjoy the things which he has made.

We noted the connection between the light which God made on the first day of the creation week and color and beauty. It is right and proper that we truly appreciate and admire the beauty of creation, and allow the aesthetic splendor of God's creation to lead us on to the worship of the

---

39. J. S. Wright, "Ecclesiastes," 1192.

Creator himself, and to appreciate his own beauty. In the context of God's beautiful world we may live in complete contentment. Just as the Creator takes pleasure in the works of his hands, so one of the ways in which we glorify him is by taking pleasure in his works.

(4) We must stand against all astrological ideas, and avoid falling into the trap of taking a superstitious view of any created things, accepting that God made everything to serve his own purposes, and that the fate of every created thing, and the destiny of every human being is in his hands alone. He is in total control of everything that takes place within the confines of his creation, and is, therefore, to be adored and trusted. We do not need to fear anything in the created order, but may have peace as we live in God's world.

(5) We need to accept the structure which God built into creation by bringing everything into being in six days, and then resting on the seventh day. God has here established the model for our lives, and we ignore this pattern at our peril. We were created for six days' labor and one day's rest each week. There is no place either for overwork or for idleness. Moreover, the day of rest is also designated a day of worship, and we must never neglect attendance at the gathering together of God's people on the Lord's Day (Heb 10:25).

(6) We must reject all false teaching about the origin of the universe. Marcion's view of the eternity of matter has revived in modern times in the ridiculous notion of the big bang as the origin of the universe. Not only is such an idea utterly absurd, it is also a deliberate attempt to expel the Creator from the account of origins. The whole evolutionary hypothesis must be determinedly rejected by all who sincerely believe in a Creator God. The Bible is his word of truth, and therefore its account of origins is indisputably and unquestionably true. To deny the biblical account is really an expression of fundamental unbelief, however much certain people may try to combine the opposing and incompatible worldviews of creation and evolution.

(7) Since creation was accomplished through the second person of the Trinity, we miss the whole point of life in this created world unless we live by faith in him. Creation exists for the glory of the Lord Jesus Christ, and his glory is the point of our existence too. We must therefore repent of our unbelief, trust in him as our Savior and Lord, and live for him each day.

PART TWO: CREATION IN ITS PRESENT CONDITION

It is necessary to consider this aspect of the doctrine of creation as a separate subject because of the devastating results of the fall of the human race into sin. The repercussions of this failure extended far beyond human life alone, and had tragic implications for God's creation in its entirety.

BIBLICAL FOUNDATION

Old Testament

It is obvious that the present state of the earth is quite different from the Creator's original description as "very good." Genesis 3:17–19 explains the difference as the result of the curse on the ground (verse 17) which followed the entry of sin into the world.

What the curse means in practice is indicated by the reference to "thorns and thistles" in verse 18. "Thorns" translates the Hebrew word *qôṣ*. Elsewhere in the Old Testament this word has various connotations. It may speak of something that is only fit for rejection, as in 2 Samuel 23:6: "*the sons* of rebellion *shall* all *be* as thorns thrust away." Thorns are also depicted as responsible for turning joy to misery, as Isaiah 32:12–13 indicates: "people shall mourn upon their breasts for the pleasant fields, for the fruitful vine. On the land of my people will come up thorns *and* briers, yes, on all the happy homes *in* the joyous city."

Again, thorns make land unfit for cultivation. That is why Jeremiah 4:3 says, "do not sow among thorns." Furthermore, thorns may represent bitter disappointment, as in Jeremiah 12:13: "they have sown wheat but reaped thorns." Finally, thorns are a source of pain. Ezekiel 28:24 speaks of "a pricking brier or a painful thorn."

The Hebrew word for thistles is *dardar*. It comes only once more in the Bible, again along with *qôṣ*. Hosea 10:8 reads as follows: "the high places of Aven, the sin of Israel, shall be destroyed. Thorn and thistle shall grow on their altars." In this context the growth of thorns and thistles represents a situation where glory has departed (verse 5) and been replaced by shame (verse 6)—insignificance like "a twig on the face of the waters" (verse 7). The result is destruction.

Because of the curse, then, creation is now in a spoiled, flimsy, dangerous condition. This is a world which people find to be a constant source of frustrating disappointment. Creation is far removed from the glory of its origin.

The frustrating nature of the world as it is now is brought out in Genesis 3 by two words describing human experience on earth, the word "toil" in verse 17, and the word "sweat" in verse 19. "Toil" renders the Hebrew term *ʿiṣṣābôn*. This word has been used already in verse 16 of a woman's acute pain in childbirth. It is used only once more, in Genesis 5:29, where again it is connected with the curse as Lamech explains the name of his son, Noah: "this *one* will comfort us concerning our work and the toil of our hands, because of the ground which the LORD has cursed."

ʿIṣṣābôn is derived from the verb *ʿāṣab*, which may refer to physical pain, mental discomfort, emotional sorrow, or spiritual anguish.[40] To live as a frustrated human being in a cursed world is to have an ache in your body and grief in your heart, because the world in which we live is so badly damaged. As Ecclesiastes 10:9 recognizes, it is so often the case now that "he who quarries stones may be hurt by them." To have to labor in the painful conditions of the present creation is inevitably to sweat. And, as verse 17 makes clear, this is going to be true every single day. This reminds us that we should not expect too much in the present world. Our sights should be set on the new creation.

New Testament

Romans 8:18–22 is the predominant New Testament passage on the theme of creation in its present state. The passage is bracketed by two occurrences of the Greek word *nun*, translated "present" in verse 18 and "now" at the end of verse 22. We can divide what is said here about the present state of creation into two main themes.

Creation's Disappointment

The key word is "futility" (verse 20). This translates the Greek term *mataiotēs*, a word which speaks of emptiness or worthlessness, of something which lacks proper purpose.[41] It pictures creation as aimless, as missing its intended aim, just going round in circles, having been thrown off course and lost direction.

40. R. B. Allen, "*ʿāṣab*," 1666.0.

41. Thayer, *Lexicon*, 393.

Professor Dunn suggests two ways in which creation has become futile. (1) It fails to function as it was designed to do. (2) It has been accorded a role for which it was never designed.[42] On the first point, thorns and thistles had no place in God's blueprint. The need for ornamental plants and cultivated food to compete with weeds and pests for space, nutrients, and air was not God's first intention. As regards Dunn's second point, man now views creation solely in relation to himself, and so abuses it for selfish ends. He gives it a status which effectively turns it into an idol. He treats it as though it is an autonomous entity which can be studied and worked without reference to God.

Verse 20 reads, "the creation was subjected to futility, not willingly, but because of him who subjected *it* in hope." This gives rise to three questions.

(1) What is the force of the word "subjected"? This Greek word, *hupotassō*, means "put under." It speaks of something which has been brought under the total control of another.[43] Creation has come under the total control of futility. Futility now dominates the created order. Absolutely nothing goes as it should. Absolutely everything has gone off course.

(2) Who did the subjecting? There are two possibilities, and Bible scholars differ. Some suggest that man is responsible, that sin is the direct cause of this subjection.[44] Others read this verse in the light of Genesis 3:17, and understand Paul to mean that God subjected creation by imposing the curse.[45] This seems more likely. The words "in hope" imply that the subjection was intentionally only temporary. While human sin was certainly the indirect cause, it was the action of God which effected the subjection.

(3) Whose unwillingness is meant? Again there are two possibilities. It may mean that God had to subject creation to futility, but did it reluctantly. Or it may be that creation is being personified. As Dunn puts it, "creation was not party to Adam's failure but was drawn into it

---

42. Dunn, *Romans*, 470.

43. Cf. Moulton, *Lexicon*, 419.

44. So Chrysostom, "Romans," 784; Henry, *New Testament*, Vol. 7, 267; cf. Godet, *Romans*, 91.

45. So C. Hodge, *Romans*, 274; Cranfield, *Romans*, 414, along with nearly all modern commentators.

nonetheless."[46] Here it is probably not necessary to choose absolutely between these two options. There may be truth in both.

Creation's disappointment is depicted by a further four words.

(1) "Sufferings" (verse 18). The human experience of suffering within this world is a major symptom of the damage done to the creation by sin. These sufferings include illnesses and accidents, the grief of bereavement, natural disasters, such as earthquakes, volcanoes, storms and famines, and the inability of the nations to establish peace or eliminate poverty.

(2) "Bondage" (verse 21). Creation is enslaved. It is in a state of helplessness, possessed by a power greater than its own. Creation inevitably goes off course and can do nothing about it. It never achieves everything it was made for. Its potential is always restricted. Disappointment has creation in its grip.

(3) "Corruption" (verse 21). The Greek word is *phthora*. Paul uses it again in Colossians 2:22: having reminded us that in Christ we have died to the principles of the present world, and rebuked the tendency to continue living as if this world is everything by subjecting ourselves to unnecessary worldly regulations, he says that to be preoccupied with material things is to focus on "things which perish [*phthora*] with the using." Nothing in this world lasts: every aspect of creation has been ravaged by decay, and so perishes with use. Rot and rust, wear and tear—all these are evidences of the curse which has derailed creation.

(4) "Groans" (verse 22). The Greek word is *sustenazō*. Literally this means "groans together." The entire creation is at one in its groaning. Every created object lends its sigh to creation's enormous groan. This word depicts the grieving heart of the world. It is, of course, picture language. It is intended vividly to emphasize how great is the damage done to creation and how far the created order has been dragged down from the possibilities latent within it at the beginning.

Creation's Anticipation

The second feature of creation as it is now is that it is on the way towards its reconstruction. The apostle is still writing as if creation is a person. There is an element of hope. Creation has a sure and certain anticipation of something better to come. Beyond this interim period of pain there lies

---

46. Dunn, *Romans*, 470.

a glorious prospect for the entire world. It will at last "be delivered from the bondage of corruption," and restored to what it was in the beginning. The original plan will be restored. Things will no longer corrupt. There will be a new creation, liberated to develop its proper potential, in a state described as "the glorious liberty of the children of God." Creation's present anticipation of that future glory is brought out in two phrases.

(1) The creation "eagerly waits" with "earnest expectation" (verse 19). Two picturesque Greek words are used here. "Earnest expectation" translates the noun *apokaradokia*. This portrays someone leaning, straining forward, because of his intense desire for an event he is keenly awaiting.[47] Creation is standing on tiptoe[48] to see if the time is yet, trying at least to get a glimpse of what is so greatly anticipated. "Eagerly waits" renders the verb *apekdechetai*, which paints the picture of reaching forward with outstretched hand, attempting to grasp something really worth having. Taken together the two words convey creation's desperation for the repair of all things. We might compare it to the excitement of a child waiting for some very enjoyable experience, like Christmas, or the school holidays.

(2) The birth pangs (verse 22). Creation is now depicted as an expectant mother on the point of giving birth. All the sufferings and disappointments of life in the wreckage of creation as we know it in the present are like labor pains. They are the promise of the birth of the new heavens and the new earth.

DOCTRINAL FORMULATION

There is nothing in the early creeds, the Reformation confessions, or the modern confessions of faith relevant to this theme.

HISTORICAL ELABORATION

In recent times the biblical teaching on creation in its present condition has prompted concern on the part of Christians with environmental issues. This concern was started by Francis Schaeffer. In 1970 he wrote *Pollution and the Death of Man*. This was an attempt to offer a Christian

---

47. Thayer, *Lexicon*, 62–63; Moulton, *Lexicon*, 42.
48. N. T. Wright, *Romans*, 152.

view of ecology, which Schaeffer defines as "the study of the balance of living things in nature."[49]

Schaeffer's concern is with the way that human activity is leading to such things as water and air pollution, and destructive noise levels, especially in the world's large cities. As a result, the balance of nature is being destroyed.

Basing his argument on Romans 8 Schaeffer advocates "substantial healing."[50] Substantial healing falls short of perfect healing, but it is still evident and real. Schaeffer recognizes that the world will never be totally healed until Christ returns. But Christians are not just to sit back and wait for that day. By God's help, in the power of his Spirit, and on the basis of the work of Christ, we should be seeking to achieve at least this substantial healing of the planet. In anticipation of the perfection which Christ will establish at the end, we should be seeking to move things in that direction.

How is this achieved? Schaeffer's answer is by honoring each component part of the natural world on its own terms. We should not be destroyers of nature, but should treat God's creation with great respect. It may be legitimate to chop down a tree to build a house. However, it is never legitimate to chop down a tree just for the sake of it. As a part of God's creation, even a tree has value.

Schaeffer gives the example of a housing development to demonstrate the practical application of his thinking:

> Bulldozers have gone in to flatten everything and clear the trees before the houses are begun. The result is ugliness. It would have cost another thousand pounds to bulldoze round the trees, so they are simply bulldozed down without question. And then we wonder, looking at the result, how people can live there. It is less than human in its barrenness, and even economically it is poorer as the top soil washes away. So when man breaks God's truth, in reality he suffers.[51]

More recently John Davies, of New South Wales, Australia, has published a two-part series on a biblical theology of the environment in the magazine of Third Millennium Ministries. He sees environmental concern as

49. Schaeffer, *Pollution*, 8.
50. Schaeffer, *Pollution*, 47.
51. Schaeffer, *Pollution*, 56.

part of our duty of loving our neighbor, with particular reference to those neighbors in the generations yet to be born.

Davies notes that the industrial revolution has given us the capacity for large-scale environmental degradation. However, it is only in the past few decades that many of the consequences of industrialization have become apparent. A discussion of ecological issues has resulted, and Davies mentions Schaeffer's book as the most notable Christian contribution.

Davies structures God's revelation in Scripture around the three themes of creation, rebellion, and resurrection.

(1) Creation. The Bible portrays the earth and its teeming life as designed to exist under the care of human beings, and to find its value in relation to humanity before God. However, this is not merely a matter of economics: "there are the less quantifiable benefits of the richness, the beauty, and the diversity which God's creation brings into our lives, leading us to a greater appreciation of the wisdom and grandeur of God."[52]

(2) Rebellion. This human duty of care for creation still stands, but, because of human rebellion against the Creator,

> the world as we presently experience it is an aberration. Illness and death are abnormal experiences. Pollution, famine, and cyclones are the consequences (direct and indirect) of our rebellion.[53]

Davies sees God's curse as a deliberate pronouncement that all is not well with creation, that the order of things has been violated. We have to take seriously the curse and the world's fallen condition. Biblical realism refuses to imagine that we can usher in an environmental utopia. However, we are still to strive to overcome the effects of sin and the curse, at least in partial ways.

Davies recognizes that the frustrations built in to a cursed earth are made worse by human greed. Part of caring for a fallen creation is to rethink our attitudes towards economic growth and the expectation of constantly rising living standards.

(3) Resurrection. For the Christian, it is the resurrection of Christ which gives significance to the entire creation. The resurrection of his physical body is the promise of the renewal of the whole physical environment. Davies argues that the Christian community should be setting

---

52. Davies, "Environment," Part 1: Introduction and Creation.
53. Davies, "Environment," Part 2: Rebellion and Resurrection.

the lead in restraining the tendency to environmental degradation. Such degradation is a perversion of God's purposes.

Davies calls us to support any initiatives which foster care for God's creation. He challenges us to make personal adjustments in our lifestyle away from the consumer-driven greed of our generation.

PRACTICAL APPLICATION

John Silvius has expressed the practical side of the doctrine of creation in its present condition in terms of stewardship.[54] He lists the following areas of contemporary environmental concern: acid rain, water shortages, water supplies contaminated by toxic chemicals or disease organisms, expanding deserts, drought and famine, the diminishing quality of soil and air, and diminishing quantities of fuel supplies.

Silvius argues that concern for the environment and the earth's natural resources is part of our stewardship in the light of the Christian hope. Silvius says that the Christian steward of the earth must love the Creator and love the creation. Then he must understand his role as the Creator's steward within the creation. A steward is a manager of a home. As the manager of the earth as the human home, the Christian may not live in greedy and careless over-consumption of food, energy, and other resources. To do so would adversely affect our human neighbors, and the rest of God's creatures.

Silvius points out that the current reality is that 25% of the world's population consumes 80% of the world's energy and goods. Christians must challenge that situation, and clamor for equitability. In the end, environmental concern becomes an aspect of the demand for international social justice.

However, it seems to me that it is not just for the sake of our fellow creatures that we must care for the environment. We must thoroughly question a merely utilitarian approach to life. There is a remarkable passage, where the LORD is speaking, in Job 38:25–27:

> Who has divided a channel for the overflowing *water*, or a path
> for the thunderbolt, to cause it to rain on a land *where there is* no
> one, a wilderness in which *there is* no man; to satisfy the deso-
> late waste, and cause to spring forth the growth of tender grass?

---

54. Silvius, "Christian Stewardship," *passim.*

Grass grows even in uninhabited regions of the world. It is God's urge for beauty which is being satisfied. We must nurture beauty in the environment chiefly for God's sake. In a world so marred by ugliness because of sin, it is our duty to reject everything that makes ugliness worse and beauty less.

At the same time, we must, I think, take a humble approach to environmental issues. These days we hear a lot of talk about "saving the planet," and a major area of concern is so-called "global warming." We need to be careful not to buy into the discourse which credits the human race with total responsibility to foster change in this area. We must never forget that God remains in absolute control. Neither should we be taken in by the doom and gloom of those who, it seems, exaggerate the problem of global warming on the basis of what appears to be suspect science and a lack of historical awareness. Ancient Egypt experienced two periods of climate change nearly 1,000 years apart.[55] It seems that fluctuations in the sun's temperature are normal, and that periods when earth's temperature rises or falls markedly are part of the usual pattern of life in this fallen creation. Perhaps this is the reason for the climate change which we have experienced. If so, it is not something which should greatly alarm us, and it is quite outside our control. Our response is to trust in the merciful Creator.

In addition to these observations, we must also make the following points of practical application. We have to learn to live with the frustrations of life in a fallen creation. We must not entertain exaggerated expectations of what is possible in the here and now. The futility that now pervades all things is inescapable. To expect too much is to condemn ourselves to disappointment and even greater frustration. At the same time, though, we must live in hope. A new world is coming at God's appointed time, and we look forward with excited anticipation to that day when God will make all things new. In the meantime, we must strenuously avoid making idols out of any created things. This not only defies the creator, but also condemns us to constant misery, as nothing in this world lives up any more to its original promise.

55. Rohl, *Test of Time*, 14, 21.

4

The Doctrine of the Divine Decree

WE KNOW THAT CREATION has fallen from its original condition because of human sin. Has this made the world unpredictable, so that even God is no longer in control of what happens? Do things happen by chance, perhaps even taking God by surprise? The doctrine of God's decree is the answer to such questions. This doctrine teaches us that God has ordered everything that will happen. God's decree is rooted in his unique, unrivalled, unchallengeable authority.

BIBLICAL FOUNDATION

Old Testament

The New King James Version uses the noun "decree" in connection, unequivocally, with God on just six occasions (Pss 2:7; 148:6; Jer 5:22; Dan 4:24; Mic 7:11; Zeph 2:2), on five of them the Hebrew word underlying this translation being ḥōq. The one exception is the Daniel text where the original word is $g^e z\bar{e}r\hat{a}$.

Most of the occurrences of ḥōq in the Old Testament speak of a statute or commandment which God has prescribed for his people to obey. Its use to refer to God's sovereign, overruling decree, to "the order God has imposed upon his creation,"[1] is therefore somewhat exceptional.

1. Enns, "ḥōq," 250.

The verbal root from which the noun *gᵉzērâ* is derived has as its primary sense the meaning "to cut," and as a secondary meaning "to decide." The noun, however, "occurs only in the secondary meaning, decree."[2]

In addition to these six texts, there are passages where, although the specific word "decree" is not employed in the English translation, nonetheless the truth of the divine decree is being expressed. We shall consider the Old Testament teaching on this theme by reference to six passages, each of which brings out a different aspect of this truth.

Genesis 50:15–20

Following the death of their father, Jacob, Joseph's brothers are anxious that Joseph may now spot an opportunity to take revenge for their treatment of him. They pretend that Jacob has sent a message requesting Joseph's forgiveness for them. Joseph then reassures them in these words in verse 20: "you meant evil against me; *but* God meant it for good, in order to bring it about as *it is* this day, to save many people alive."

These words echo something which Joseph had said to his brothers on his own volition when he first disclosed to them his identity, and their initial reaction was one of dismay. His words in Genesis 45:5 were: "do not therefore be grieved or angry with yourselves because you sold me here; for God sent me before you to preserve life."

The Hebrew word rendered "meant" in 50:20 is *ḥāšab*. It means to devise a plan, to frame a purpose,[3] and denotes a plan which is prepared in advance before the work begins. Just as a garden designer or a fashion designer will form a mental picture and make sketches of the finished work before starting, so God sketched in his mind from eternity the course his creation would take, once he brought it into being. Joseph is expressing his confident conviction that, long before his brothers acted as they did, the Lord had drawn up a plan to get him to Egypt, and into a position of prominence there. This purpose was "for good." The Hebrew word used here, *ṭôb*, is the same as that used of the pristine creation. The good in view is the preservation of human life. John Sailhamer writes:

> Behind all the events and human plans recounted in the story
> of Joseph lies the unchanging plan of God. It is the same plan
> introduced from the beginning of the book where God looks

2. Carpenter & Nicole, "*gzr*," 847.
3. Wood, "*ḥāšab*," 767.0; Hartley, "*hsb*," 306–7.

out at what he has just created for man and sees that "it is good." Through his dealings with the patriarchs and Joseph, God had continued to bring about his good plan.[4]

Joseph's assessment of his own experience may be universalized. Whatever happens, behind it there is a divine plan, always intended to promote what is ultimately good. In his mind the Lord pictured what should happen to achieve the good. So whatever happens is the Lord's idea coming to reality. It is true that this may present us with mysteries which we cannot unravel. Calvin's comment on this verse faces up to that fact: Joseph

> skilfully distinguishes between the wicked counsels of men, and the admirable justice of God, by so ascribing the government of all things to God, as to preserve the divine administration free from contracting any stain from the vices of men. The selling of Joseph was a crime detestable for its cruelty and perfidy; yet he was not sold except by the decree of heaven. For neither did God merely remain at rest, and by conniving for a time, let loose the reins of human malice, in order that afterwards he might make use of this occasion; but, at his own will, he appointed the order of acting which he intended to be fixed and certain.

Calvin then continues, by elaborating on the fact that, although nothing happens apart from God's will, this does not make him responsible for the sinful actions of men, even though he appoints their actions and includes them in his plan. Calvin then issues this necessary warning:

> If human minds cannot reach these depths, let them rather suppliantly adore the mysteries they do not comprehend, than, as vessels of clay, proudly exalt themselves against their Maker.[5]

Psalm 115:1–7

The main thrust of this passage is the absolute contrast between the true God and idols. Idols are senseless human concoctions, unable to communicate. Their worshippers may pour scorn on the idea of an invisible God, but the Psalmist's response is to say that "our God is in heaven; he does whatever he pleases."

4. Sailhamer, "Genesis," 283.
5. Calvin, *Genesis*, 487–88.

The word "pleases" points us back behind what God does to his motivation. The Hebrew word is *ḥāpēṣ*. It means that God does whatever brings him pleasure and delight.[6] The grand purpose of everything is God's joy. The great purpose was drawn up with the divine happiness in view. God determined that all that happens will serve to make his creation completely attractive to him.

This word speaks of an emotional involvement in the planning. The same word is used in a human context of a young man falling in love with a woman. The divine decree is not some cold, calculating plan. It is something that the Lord is passionately committed to. God warms to his purpose. He finds it heart-warming. His plan was devised in the height of emotion.

In our planning we are often constrained. Circumstances beyond our control mean that we cannot always achieve our own pleasure. There are no such limitations on God: he is "in heaven," above the reach of hindrances and setbacks. He is free to bring about those things which delight his heart.

Psalm 148

This Psalm begins with an exhortation to the creation "in the heights"—to all that exists above the earthly level, both spiritual and physical, visible and invisible—to praise the Lord. Verses 5 and 6 state the reason why such praise is appropriate: "Let them praise the name of the Lord, for he commanded and they were created. He also established them forever and ever; he made a decree (*ḥōq*) which shall not pass away."

Our sights are being lifted to the sun, moon, and stars, and beyond them to the angelic hosts, as the Psalmist calls upon them to praise the Lord as the one whose decree directs their existence.

In verses 7–12 the Psalmist proceeds to survey the creatures in the sea, on the land, and in the sky, as well as their earthly environment, and then focuses on human beings of every class, category, and age, and calls on them too to praise the Lord's exalted name. The implication is that here on earth, just as much as in the heavens, everything is directed by the Lord's eternal, sovereign decree.

The Psalmist points out that the Lord's decree "shall not pass away." The verb used here, *'ābar*, has as its primary connotation the idea of

---

6. Wood, "*ḥāpēṣ*," 712a; cf. Talley, "*ḥpṣ*," 231–32.

movement.[7] In this context, the movement would be its disappearance: the divine decree cannot possibly vanish; there's no way in which it could possibly be deleted. Everything at every level of creation is continually driven according to God's decree.

Isaiah

Isaiah brings out this truth of God's decree in two key passages.

ISAIAH 14:24–27

Verse 26 speaks of a "purpose that is purposed." The two words are as closely related in Hebrew as they are in English: "purpose" translates the noun *'ēṣâ*, and "purposed" is its cognate verbal root, *yā'aṣ*. The verb means to deliberate, to determine, to devise.[8] The prophet is saying that the Lord has determined everything that will happen, and he has done so with deliberate, careful planning. The purpose in view is specific and particular, namely the downfall of Assyria.

However, the first and last verses of this passage suggest that this specific purpose is just one expression of a far larger, universal purpose. The word translated "purposed" in both verses 24 and 27 is again *yā'aṣ*. In verse 24 it occurs in parallel with *dāmâ*, translated "thought." The basic meaning of this verb, in the form in which it occurs here, is "to compare."[9] We may picture the Lord weighing up in his mind various options and then settling on which he will actually bring to pass. The main assertion being made here is that it is the Lord's purpose which gets fulfilled, and no human power can prevent it.

John Watts suggests translating *'ēṣâ* as "strategy," and makes an extended comment on its significance. Here are some extracts:

> The idea of God's control of events is common in . . . the Old
> Testament . . . . Yet apparently, Isaiah is the classic and perhaps
> the first book (and prophet) to speak of [the Lord's] plan on so
> universal a scale . . . . God stands in the center of his view of his-
> tory as the one who is acting. He has a goal in what he does. He
> is following a plan . . . . [Isaiah] sees his time in the light of the

---

7. Van Groningen, "*'āṣab*," 1556.0.

8. Gilchrist, "*yā'aṣ*," 887.0.

9. Hamilton, "*dāmâ*," 437.0; Konkel, "*dmh*," 967; cf. Tregelles (ed.), *Lexicon*, 119.

living God . . . . [God's] plan cannot be turned aside . . . . [Isaiah's prophecy] confronts the events of history with the reality of the living God whose acts and whose plan are becoming visible in the events of the day . . . . History is the work of [the LORD] of hosts, who is enthroned on Zion. It unfolds according to a plan which he has determined.[10]

In similar vein, Alec Motyer notes how Isaiah uses the crushing of the Assyrian threat "as an example of the way the divine hand governs all nations and executes an irresistible world purpose."[11]

ISAIAH 46:9–11

Four terms in this passage refer to the divine decree. "Counsel" (verse 10) translates *'ēṣâ* again. "Pleasure" (verse 10) translates *ḥēpeṣ*, which is cognate with *ḥāpēṣ* in Psalm 115:3. In the words "I have spoken" in verse 11 we have an indication of the ease with which God gets his will done. At creation he merely spoke, and it was done. In the same way, in the course of history, what he simply says is what happens. The words "I have purposed" (also in verse 11) render the verb *yāṣar*. It might be used of a potter moulding the clay.[12] In creating, God brought things into existence out of nothing. By his decree he shapes what is now there.

Each of these terms is linked with a phrase which affirms that God's decree is in fact fulfilled. God's plan stands (verse 10). It is brought to pass; it is done (verse 11).

There are two additional things to note here.

(1) God declares the end from the beginning. He is able to make known the ultimate destiny of creation, because in the beginning he planned both the destination and the route. He can make known everything that will happen, because he has determined from eternity what shall be. Motyer says that the one unique God "dictates the purpose within history," and adds: "he is sovereign, his purpose / plan / counsel is unalterable and is the product not of whim, but of his pleasurable will."[13]

(2) Only such a God is worthy of the title "God." The import of verse 9 is that the LORD is God, the only God, the incomparable God. Verse 10

10. J. D. W. Watts, *Isaiah*, 216.
11. Motyer, *Isaiah*, 146.
12. Tregelles (ed.), *Lexicon*, 205.
13. Motyer, *Isaiah*, 370.

then begins with a participle. This has the effect of making the verse say that this is what it means to claim that he is the unique and incomparable God: he decrees what shall be, and that is what happens.

Psalm 2:1–9

For our final passage we back-track to the first instance of the translation of the word *ḥōq* as decree. We have kept this passage till last, because it really brings us to the very heart of the divine decree, and therefore serves as a fitting climax to our study of the Old Testament teaching on this subject. Verses 7–8 read as follows:

> I will declare the decree: the LORD has said to me, "You *are* my Son, today I have begotten you. Ask of me, and I will give *you* the nations *for* your inheritance, and the ends of the earth *for* your possession."

It is impossible to dispute Campbell Morgan's comment that "to whatsoever king the words first applied, the singer was looking to the ideal King, and his song has found fulfilment in Christ."[14] These verses remind us that the main aim of God's sovereign decree is to secure the exaltation of Christ in the salvation of the world. The Psalm insists that this will take place regardless of the machinations of human rulers and their opposition to the LORD's Anointed. In principle, God has already set his king on his holy hill of Zion, and all he does is to laugh to scorn the presumptuous plotting of sinful man. To his Son he may pronounce with unabashed confidence that he will most definitely achieve the victory over every opponent, and possess the entire world at the appointed time. Henry Law brings out eloquently the gospel thrill implicit in the divine decree:

> Oh, wondrous thought! Before the birth of time eternal counsels willed the weal of man. A covenant of grace was firmly made. We live in hope of eternal life, which God, that cannot lie, promised before the world began. Jesus, in his love for souls, in tender zeal to fill our hearts with joy, and to cause the streams of peace to flow, announces the decree. By his Spirit he unfolds it. In his Word he writes the record. Here he displays important articles. It was decreed that honor should await him as God's co-eternal Son.[15]

---

14. Campbell Morgan, *Psalms*, 8.
15. Law, *Psalms*, 9.

New Testament

We shall divide the relevant New Testament texts into two categories.

General Statements of God's Decree

In Acts 15:14–18 James cites the prophets who foretold the ingathering of the Gentiles. Their prediction is evidence that God did not make a spontaneous, last-minute decision to call the Gentiles. God does not make any decisions "on the hoof." He does not merely react and respond to situations as they arise. "Known to God from eternity are all his works" (verse 18). He could therefore make his purposes known long ago.

The apostle Paul, in Ephesians 1:11, says that God "works all things according to the counsel of his will." "Counsel" renders the Greek word *boulē*. It speaks of a deliberate act of will, a determined decision. "Will" translates *thelēma*, which denotes God's pleasure in coming to his decision. "The counsel of his will" is therefore a decision made with delight. "Works" renders *energeō*. It means that God activates all things powerfully and effectively. He is the energizing dynamism behind all that happens. "God's unconditional freedom is affirmed, for whatever he has purposed is sure to be fulfilled."[16]

Hebrews 6:17 speaks of the "immutability of his counsel:" God's purpose is unchangeable in its character. Once God had made his decision in eternity past about the course of events in his creation, nothing could possibly change any single element in that plan.

Specific Statements of the Decree Relating to the Crucifixion of Christ

The purpose of God in the crucifixion of Christ is an illustration of the larger truth that everything is governed by God's decree. It is also the ultimate intention of everything else which God has planned.

Jesus himself said in Luke 22:22, "the Son of Man goes as it has been determined." The word translated "determined" is *horizō*. It means to mark out a boundary.[17] The Lord's pathway to death had been fenced in for him far in advance. God had fixed the boundary of Jesus' earthly life from eternity.

16. Lincoln, *Ephesians*, 36.
17. Liddell & Scott, *Lexicon*, 497.

Peter takes up this truth in Acts 2:23, seeing Jesus' death as a matter of "divine necessity."[18] He speaks of Jesus "being delivered by the determined purpose and foreknowledge of God." The words "determined" and "purpose" translate terms with which we are already familiar—*horizō* and *boulē* respectively. "Foreknowledge" renders *prognōsis*. It means more than that God knew what was going to happen. It has the sense of pre-arrangement.[19] God knew what was going to happen, because, long before, he had appointed that the death of Jesus must happen.

Similarly, when the early Christians met to pray in Acts 4:24–29 they acknowledged, in verse 28, that the events surrounding the crucifixion had been determined to take place by God's hand and purpose. "Purpose" again translates *boulē*, while "determined before" renders *proorizō*: it means that the matter was decided in advance. God's hand is a common metaphor for God's active power, his intimate control. It was God's decree which put Jesus on the cross. That assures us that the decree is rooted in God's saving mercy.

DOCTRINAL FORMULATION

The Reformation Confessions

The Early creeds did not spell this doctrine out. However, some of the Reformation confessions paid attention to it. We may summarize their teaching on this subject in nine statements.

God foreordained whatever comes to pass in time

God's decree relates to the created order of time and space. It relates to the whole duration of time and to the universality of space. Some of the confessions speak of God's decree in the singular, others use the plural. The decree may be considered as a unity. God made a single decision which relates to all the events of time. However, it is possible to analyze the decree into component decisions relating to each event. This reminds us that God's decree concerns both the totality of existence viewed as a consistent and coherent whole, and every intricate detail.

18. Longenecker, "Acts," 279.
19. Thayer, *Lexicon*, 538.

It is not that God just set the general trend, within which things crop up just as it happens. Neither did God make numerous little decisions and just hope that they would all fit together. Rather, he made a detailed decision about every tiny incident, in such a way as to ensure that all the incidents combine to make up his single determined purpose. Williamson explains:

> Since the Bible declares that the whole system of things is controlled by God, it declares with equal insistency that every single thing, however small and insignificant, is ordered by God ahead of time in his perfect plan.[20]

God's decree effectually works and disposes all things

There is no room for unanticipated problems. God is never in the position of having to modify his decree. He brings about precisely what he has planned, with no mistakes.

God's decree was made in eternity

The decree is God's definition of his eternal purpose. Every detail was worked out in detail before anything began to be. Donald Macleod says: "Before God spoke the universe into being God thought it. It was in his reason before it was spoken."[21] In his comments on the Westminster Confession Robert Shaw makes this statement:

> Everything which has happened and everything which is to happen, was known to God from everlasting. To suppose any of the divine decrees to be made in time, is to suppose the knowledge of the Deity to be limited.[22]

God's foreordination of all things was a totally free decision

The confessions speak of the decree as an act of the counsel of God's will, and of his will alone. God's will was not under constraint from some

---

20. Williamson, *Westminster*, 30.
21. Macleod, *Faith*, 40.
22. Shaw, *Confession*, 45.

power external to him. The decree was not merely the rubber-stamping of what God could see was going to happen anyway. That "would make God dependent upon something outside himself,"[23] in which case God would no longer be the highest authority, and so would not be truly God. He acted in sovereign freedom when he decreed whatever would happen. And in his freedom God is absolutely unrestricted.

However, the confessions stress that God's free will is both wise and holy. His purpose was not drawn up just on the basis of whim and fancy. As Thomas Vincent said, "God decreed all things according to the counsel of his will; according to his will, and therefore most freely—according to the counsel of his will, and therefore most wisely."[24] And there is nothing morally dubious in the decree, because it reflects the holiness of God.

God's decree is unalterable

God does not change, and so his decree is immutable. God never changes his mind. He is never forced to rethink. He is in total control.

The ultimate goal of God's decree is the glory of his name

Robert Reymond has said this:

> Just as the chief end of man is to glorify God and enjoy him forever, so also the chief end of God is to glorify and enjoy *himself* forever . . . . God loves himself with a holy love . . . . He himself is at the center of his affections . . . . The impulse that drives him, and the thing he pursues in everything he does, is his own glory . . . . That same concern—to glorify himself—is central to God's eternal plan.[25]

This is a truth which John Piper has worked at very thoroughly. His book *The Pleasures of God* is a series of meditations on the fact that "God delights fully in being God."[26]

23. Williamson, *Westminster*, 30.

24. Vincent, *Shorter Catechism*, 42.

25. Reymond, *New Systematic Theology*, 343–44.

26. Piper, *Pleasures*, 9.

We are not always able to unravel the mysteries of God's plan

God's decree stands, and what happens in time is always in accordance with his decree as he decreed it. This remains true, even though sometimes we may seem to hear something different. We need to remember that not everything has been revealed to us.

Three explanations must be added to the doctrine of the decree

GOD IS NOT THE AUTHOR OF SIN

Even though God embraced sin in his eternal plan, he is not responsible or accountable for sin. God is holy, and his holiness is not impugned by decreeing to allow sin to happen in his creation. As to why God allowed it, that is a question which we cannot answer. We need here, once again, to remember the words of Deuteronomy 29:29: "The secret *things belong* to the LORD our God, but those *things which are* revealed *belong* to us and to our children forever."

THE FREEDOM OF INTELLIGENT CREATURES IS NOT VIOLATED

God's foreordination does not mean that we are mere robots. It is not the case that we are simply programmed to act and react in specific ways. We cannot therefore excuse ourselves for our sins. It would be churlish to refuse to congratulate achievement in others. We never have any reason to complain that God is treating us as sub-human.

On the contrary, as Macleod points out, it is certain modern emphases that threaten to deprive us of freedom. Darwinism led to an approach in the human sciences which claimed "that human beings could not help the way they behaved. Their behavior was the result of various glands and other biological factors."

Therefore, one of the great problems of modern society has been the elimination of freedom. Macleod quotes Paul Johnson to the effect that the ideas of Marx and Freud combined to undermine personal responsibility, and the sense of moral duty. Macleod comments:

> Sociology, criminology, penology and psychology are largely based on the assumption that environment, education and genetic inheritance not only influence, but determine, human

behavior, and that individuals are therefore only minimally answerable for their own conduct.

However, the doctrine of God's decree asserts that

> I am free because God foreordained my freedom. I am not the plaything of pressure and circumstance, or even of internal and endocrinological factors. I am free. I make my own decisions. I am the cause, the ultimate, answerable cause, the responsible cause, of my own decisions.[27]

THE FACT OF SECONDARY CAUSES IS NOT DENIED

The first and ultimate cause of everything is God. His plan is the overarching reality. From it every individual event flows. From it the overall direction of the whole of creation stems. However, there are also secondary causes. These are causes within the system of things that we belong to, rather than the ultimate cause which stands outside and beyond our world.

A few years ago I fell off my bicycle and broke my hip. When friends asked me what caused my accident I did not reply, "God knocked me off my bike." Rather, I would say, "I took a bend too fast and skidded on some loose gravel."

It is true that the ultimate cause lies with God. But in explaining things from an earthly perspective, we refer to secondary causes.

God's decree is in Christ

One of the confessions backs up its teaching on the decree by reference to Colossians 2:3. This text refers to Christ, "in whom are hidden all the treasures of wisdom and knowledge." These treasures include God's decree: as early as the planning stage God, in eternity past, stored up his wisdom in Christ. This means that absolutely everything that exists is Christ-shaped. And that assures us that at the heart of everything that exists there stands the divine mercy which has been displayed in Jesus Christ.

---

27. Macleod, *Faith*, 43–44.

Modern Confessions of Faith

The Indonesian confession does not mention the doctrine of the decree. However, the other two confessions, although not addressing this doctrine specifically, do make indirect references to God's decree.

Confession of Faith of the United Church of Northern India

In the context of its statement on God's creation and government of the world, this confession affirms that "God works all things according to the counsel of his will." Consequently, all things "serve the fulfilment of his wise and good and holy purposes."

These words teach that God's will is the shaping factor which stands behind all contingent events. They also assert that history is the fulfilment of what God in his counsel has purposed. Moreover, God's purposes are characterized as wise, good, and holy. These terms make the point that, however things may sometimes appear to human perception, the reality is that God's wisdom ensures that what he has purposed is good. Even though evils may occur, God is always working towards the ultimate good. This is because his decree reflects his own character: he is holy, so his purposes are holy. They may never be challenged as lacking in moral integrity.

Confession of Faith of House Churches in China

This confession has just one relevant phrase in its section on the doctrine of God as Trinity, where it declares that "the Father plans salvation." This is, admittedly, only incidentally related to the present subject. It does, however, signal the Chinese church leaders' recognition that the Father drew up his plans from eternity. It also bears witness to their conviction that the salvation of his people stands at the very heart of the Father's eternal purpose.

HISTORICAL ELABORATION

Recent years have seen the rise of a movement known as "Open Theism." It began when five Canadian and American theologians collaborated to write a book entitled *The Openness of God*.[28] One of the participants, Clark Pinnock, followed it up a few years later with another book, *Most Moved Mover*.[29] Most of the contributors have also written briefer accounts of their position.[30] This movement rejects the Reformed doctrine of the decree.

Open Theists would insist that the Scriptures which we used earlier to teach the doctrine of the divine decree are only one set of texts. They do not dispute them. They accept that there are some things which God has planned from all eternity. However, there are other texts, they claim, which show that not everything is pre-planned.

According to Open Theism, the Bible is a real story, not the prescribed outworking of a pre-historical decree. There are aspects of the developing history of the world which God has left indefinite. The God of the Bible is one who relates to people in a personal way. He responds to situations. He is sometimes surprised by an unexpected turn of events. He can be grieved. He feels pain and pleasure. He may change his mind. He takes account of things when they happen and not before.

For Open Theism the sovereignty of God is general, not all-encompassing. While his goal is secure, he has no blueprint for the whole of time. He does not micromanage history. His strategies are flexible. True, he has planned some things, and nothing can frustrate his plans, but he has chosen not to predetermine everything that happens.

In his love, God gave human beings true freedom. He therefore leaves some of his works contingent on the actions and prayers of people. Human decisions are genuine and their consequences are often unpredictable. God's will is not always done. History is a real interaction between God and man, in which God has invited us into partnership with himself. God reacts to our choices and adjusts his own plans when necessary. The believer's confidence in such a world is that God is infinitely resourceful. He has the wisdom to handle any situation that might arise when it arises.

Open Theism has redefined the omniscience of God. He is omniscient in the sense that he knows all that there is to be known. His knowledge of the past and the present is exhaustive, but the future is not yet there to be known. The open aspects of the future, including the

28. Hasker, et al., *Openness, passim*.

29. Pinnock, *Most Moved, passim*.

30. I am basing this summary of Open Theism mainly on two articles: Pinnock, "Open Theism," and Sanders and Hall, "Does God know?"

actions of free creatures, are not yet reality, and so God cannot know them with certainty.

The Open Theists see important pastoral implications in all this. For one thing, God's will is not always done. The advocates of God's openness do not believe that the tragedies in human experience are willed by him, because this seems inconsistent with the biblical portrait of God as love. But a relational God is one who really is influenced by prayer. Prayer is not just a charade. Open Theism implies that passionate human living makes a true difference in the world.

To the charge that this leaves God "just fumbling along with the rest of us," John Sanders replies that Openness Theology does not mean that just anything might happen. God is at work to achieve his purposes, but he invites us to collaborate with him in the open part of the future.

One of the strengths of Open Theism is that it takes the Bible seriously. It refuses to explain any texts away in the interests of a preconceived theory. We need to look at the set of texts which, according to Open Theists, show that not everything is included in the infallible divine decree. We shall take them in biblical order, and seek to respond in each case to the challenge from Openness Theology.

Response to texts used by Open Theists

Genesis 22:12

This text contains the words of the angel of the LORD to Abraham after he has passed the test and proved himself willing to sacrifice Isaac. They include the words, "now I know that you fear God." The Open Theists argue that these words prove that God did not know for sure before this moment.

However, what the use of the "now" indicates is that God's knowledge has now been anchored in time. The Hebrew word for "now" (ʿattâ) is derived from ʿānâ, meaning "to respond."[31] God's knowledge is now a historical response to what has happened on Mount Moriah. However, this does not mean that he did not know before what would happen. It is simply that his previous knowledge was beyond this world of time.

---

31. Coppes, "ʿānâ," 1650.0.

Exodus 4:8–9

God is here speaking to Moses at the time of his commission at the burning bush, having given him two signs designed to convince the children of Israel that it truly is their God who has spoken to him. The key words here are "if" and "may." Verse 8 reads: "it will be, if they do not believe you, nor heed the message of the first sign, that they may believe the message of the latter sign." The word "if" appears again in verse 9. To the Open Theists it sounds as if God is unsure what will be the outcome of the signs he has given to Moses. However, Walter Kaiser notes that God is really quoting Moses' own sentiments back at him. In verse 1 Moses had said: "suppose they will not believe me or listen to my voice." What we have here is not an admission of divine ignorance, but a concession to Moses.

Deuteronomy 13:3

Moses tells the people of Israel that, when a prophet who tries to entice them after other gods successfully performs a miracle, this is a test which God has set "to know whether you love the LORD your God with all your heart and with all your soul." The Open Theists say that the words "to know whether" indicate that the LORD would not know the true state of heart of his people until the test had taken place.

However, there are other ways of reading this text. Calvin cites Augustine, who suggested that the LORD meant that the test would enable the people to know their own hearts. However, Calvin prefers to distinguish God's knowledge as it arises from his hidden wisdom, which needed no verification, and his knowledge arising from experience, which the test would provide.[32]

Isaiah

Sanders deals together with three passages from this prophetic book. In two of them the LORD's ability to predict the future is affirmed. In Isaiah 46:9–10 the LORD says, "*I am* God, and *there is* none like me, declaring the end from the beginning, and from ancient times *things* not *yet* done." This provides the evidence, as the LORD insists, that "I *am* God,

32. Calvin, *Books of Moses*, Vol. 1, 444–45.

and *there is* no other." A very similar statement is made in Isaiah 48:3: "I have declared the former things from the beginning;" this is followed by the testimony that the things predicted "came to pass." This passage continues in verses 4–5 by stating the reason why the LORD spoke predictively: it had to do with the obstinacy of the people: "before it came to pass I proclaimed *it* to you, lest you should say, 'My idol has done them.'"

Sanders alleges that the issue here is not foreknowledge but power. But this is unconvincing. It is true that God predicts because he has the power to do what he has said, but the predictive ability is more to the fore.

Furthermore, in the other passage which Sanders cites (Isa 41:22–23) the expected ability of "gods" to predict the future is stressed: "let them bring forth and show us what will happen; let them . . . declare to us things to come. Show the things that are to come hereafter, that we may know that you *are* gods." Geoffrey Grogan comments like this on these verses:

> The concept of deity is, in some ways, simple, combining superhuman power and the claim to human worship. It has many implications, however, and ability to predict is one of these. This is the basis of the argument here. If the gods of Babylonia and other nations have objective reality as deities, they should be able to predict the future and also to so interpret history that past and future are seen to be linked in one divinely controlled plan.[33]

Jeremiah 26:3; Ezekiel 12:3

We may deal with these two texts together, since they both contain the same Hebrew word, *'ûlay*, a particle which is "used to express doubt."[34] In the Jeremiah text it is rendered "perhaps:" "Perhaps everyone will listen and turn from his evil way, that I may relent concerning the calamity which I purpose to bring on them because of the evil of their doings." In the verse from Ezekiel it is translated "it may be:" "it may be that they will consider, though they *are* a rebellious house."

Both prophets are being commanded to preach publicly, Jeremiah orally, and Ezekiel in an acted parable. Perhaps God's Word will get a positive response. Open Theism claims that this indicates God's uncertainty.

---

33. Grogan, "Isaiah," 250.
34. Tregelles (ed.), *Lexicon*, 12.

However, it is better to see it as an indication of the genuineness of God's appeal, even though he knew what the outcome would be.

Jeremiah 32:24–25

The LORD told Jeremiah to buy a field in the vicinity of Jerusalem. However, the city and its surrounding countryside subsequently passed into the possession of the Chaldeans when they overran Judah as the instrument of God's judgment. In response, Jeremiah says: "you have said to me, O Lord GOD, 'Buy the field for money, and take witnesses'!—yet the city has been given into the hand of the Chaldeans." Hence, according to Pinnock, the LORD's direction proved to be unwise. Had the LORD known what the future held, he would not have given such an instruction.

Now it is certainly true that "the contradiction or absurdity of God's command to buy the field while the Babylonians are conquering the city"[35] is the first thing that strikes the reader. However, merely to highlight the apparent absurdity, as Pinnock does, is to ignore the context of the whole chapter.

The subsequent verses predict the restoration of God's people and their return to the land. The purchase of the field is a sign from the LORD and, on Jeremiah's part, an act of faith in his foreknowledge and sure planning. Charles Feinberg explains:

> The fall of the city and the divine command for Jeremiah's purchase of land seemed irreconcilable. The incongruity was plain. Why buy the field when it would soon be lost to the Babylonians? Yet in spite of the dire circumstances, God had commanded Jeremiah to buy the field and to do it publicly. It was a situation calling for faith in, and obedience to, the word the LORD had given him to proclaim.[36]

So far from being evidence of the LORD's limited omniscience, this text is actually testimony to his definite knowledge of the future—even at a time when the likelihood of such a future ever becoming reality was, to all appearances, remote.

---

35. Keown, Scalise & Smothers, *Jeremiah*, 157.
36. Feinberg, "Jeremiah," 584.

Jonah 3:10

This text tells us that, when the people of Nineveh "turned from their evil way" in response to Jonah's preaching, on seeing it, "God relented from the disaster that he had said he would bring upon them." Open Theists claim that the reference to God's relenting means that he changed his mind when Nineveh repented. However, Jonah's words in Jonah 4:2 show us that he recognized that this was the LORD's regular character: "you *are* a gracious and merciful God, slow to anger and abundant in lovingkindness, one who relents from doing harm."

So we do not have here a change of mind, so much as the enactment of the LORD's definite preference. The Hebrew word translated "relented" in 3:10 is *nāham*. Its basic sense has to do with pity or compassion. That characteristic of God led him to withhold the action which he had threatened.

All the LORD's warnings are conditional. Repentance always triggers his compassion. It had never been his intention to strike Nineveh in the face of their repentance. In fact, conditional warnings are part of God's strategy for evoking the desired and determined response. His normal method of procedure is indicated by Jeremiah 18:8: "if that nation against whom I have spoken turns from its evil, I will relent of the disaster that I thought to bring upon it."

There is a definition within Jonah 3:10 of the word "relented:" "he did not do it." The alteration was outward. It has nothing to do with the LORD's inmost knowledge of how things would turn out.

Jacques Ellul takes this a step further. He notes that *nāham* (which is sometimes rendered "repented") implies inner suffering, and comments: "when it is said that God repents, it means that he suffers, not that he changes what his justice has deemed necessary." Ellul discerns here a prophetic reference to Jesus Christ: in him God himself suffered the evil due in his justice to a sinful people, and so was free to put into effect his love to them without doing despite to his justice.[37]

---

37. Ellul, *Jonah*, 99–100.

Further texts which proclaim God's knowledge of the future

In addition to these Scriptures there are others which proclaim unequivocally God's absolute and detailed knowledge of the future. The following may be mentioned.

1 Samuel 8:9

At the time when Israel was clamoring for a king, the Lord spoke to Samuel like this: "You shall solemnly forewarn them, and show them the behavior of the king who will reign over them." The Lord was under no illusions as to how King Saul would turn out.

Psalm 139:2

This is the first of two verses from this Psalm which are relevant. It reads: "You know my sitting down and my rising up; you understand my thought afar off." The words "afar off" translate the Hebrew term *rāḥôq*. Sometimes it refers to a far away time. On several occasions it is translated "long ago" (2 Kgs 19:25; Isa 22:11; 37:26). Long ago in the past the Lord knew what the present would be, even in so secret a matter as David's innermost thoughts. On two occasions *rāḥôq* refers to the Lord's prediction concerning the distant future (2 Sam 7:19; 1 Chr 17:17).

Psalm 136:16

In this verse David proclaims: "Your eyes saw my substance, being yet unformed. And in your book they all were written, the days fashioned for me, when *as yet there were* none of them." Here again David is confident that the Lord had planned his life long before he was born. And the Lord's planning was not vague and general. The details of every day were written down.

Jeremiah 1:5

In similar vein, the Lord speaks to Jeremiah like this: "Before I formed you in the womb I knew you; before you were born I sanctified you; I ordained you a prophet to the nations." Even before Jeremiah was conceived, the LORD knew the way which he had appointed for his life.

Additional questions against Open Theism

Several other questions might be raised against the openness of God theology. Here are a few of them.

(1) If God is not in total control of everything, is there really any point in prayer?

(2) Is there in fact a problem with the idea that God can know in advance what free choices free agents would make? After, all even human beings can sometimes see things coming, as Proverbs 22:3 assures us: "A prudent *man* foresees evil and hides himself."

(3) Is Open Theism really an answer to the tragedies in human life? Could God not have intervened to prevent sin in the beginning?

(4) Does it really turn prayer into a charade to say that God has ordained whatever comes to pass? Has he not also ordained that he will act in response to the prayers of his people?

Open Theism is certainly correct to say that God is loving and responsive. He is not unaffected by human decisions. However, the idea that he is ignorant of what those decisions will be until they become present is hard to sustain from Scripture. It is true that the doctrine of the divine decree can be a problem to our finite minds. However, we must submit our thinking to Scripture, and accept what God has said, even where we cannot understand.

PRACTICAL APPLICATION

(1) This doctrine is a source of immense confidence. Nothing can happen which God has not planned. Absolutely everything has been conclusively arranged ever since eternity past. God is indeed in total control; everything that happens is God at work. We have no cause for anxiety, because we know that all the events of time are under the control of our omnipotent God of love.

(2) This truth underlines for us the fact that we are talking here about a God who is truly worthy of all our worship, the proper object of reverential fear. We may not be able to work out his strategies, but we

rejoice with comfort to know that everything that takes place is strategically planned by the God of infinite wisdom.

(3) The main reason why we can have such confident assurance, even in the face of life's uncertainties and sufferings is that the God who has decreed all things, and whose plan is being steadily worked out in the course of time, is none other than the God of mercy, who has determined to do us good. The very fact that the God of mercy is in ultimate control of all events gives us the absolute conviction that all must in the end be well, whatever the pains and difficulties and tragedies of the journey through life. This provides us with genuine consolation in life's difficult times. Even events which to us are inexplicable are not mere chaos.

(4) We may be blessed with full assurance of our eternal salvation: at the very heart of God's eternal decree is the exaltation of our Lord Jesus Christ via the events of his cross and passion. The determination that he would suffer for the sins of his people was part of the plan drawn up before the world began. In this fact, we have a cast-iron guarantee that our salvation cannot fail. The mercy of God is displayed supremely in Christ: at the center of the divine decree is our eternal salvation, and this is a reason for overflowing joy.

(5) The truth of the divine decree assures us that it is not only the overarching purpose of God in Christ and in history and on the global stage which is predetermined, but also the minute details of our personal everyday lives. Here, again, is a source of great confidence: the one who has mapped out our days is the Father who loves us and who has our best at heart. This means that, in all the struggles which life seems just to throw up, we can remain calm and at peace, because in reality we know, things are not merely thrown up, but have been wisely and lovingly planned from all eternity with a view to our ultimate and eternal well-being. In Romans 8:35–39 the apostle assures us of the implications of God's total sovereign control: it means that we are inseparable from his love.

(6) This truth is also a reason for deep humility, and that for two reasons. The first is that we have to admit that sometimes the reasons for God's decisions are beyond our capacity to understand. Many of the events of time baffle us. We may find ourselves tempted to question this biblical emphasis on the divine decree. But we have to submit to God's infinite wisdom even where we can make no sense of what is going on. We must be ready to admit our ignorance, and to submit with unquestioning trust, even when things are beyond our feeble and limited understanding.

Secondly, this doctrine reminds us that our freedom is subsumed under God's sovereignty. We are not autonomous. We are responsible to God, and we are also accountable for our own behavior.

5

The Doctrine of Providence

THE DOCTRINE OF PROVIDENCE explains how God's overall control works out in practice, year by year and from day to day. God's decree is his eternal ordination of all things prior to the beginning of time. Providence is the outworking of the decree in all the events of time.

When Paul was on trial before Felix, the spokesman for the Jewish leaders was Tertullus. He began his oration with these words, recorded in Acts 24:2–3:

> Seeing that through you we enjoy great peace, and prosperity is being brought to this nation by your foresight, we accept *it* always and in all places, most noble Felix, with all thankfulness.

Tertullus commends Felix for his foresight. This translates the Greek word *pronoia*. Actually, Tertullus is being rather flattering. The Jewish historian, Josephus, tells us that Felix was "disposed to act unjustly," and that he contrived the murder of the Jewish high priest.[1]

However, *pronoia* came to be used of God's providence. When Jerome translated the Bible into Latin, he used the word *providentia* to render *pronoia*. Both words speak of foresight, or advance understanding.

We may say that, in his foreknowledge, God has taken forethought with a view to the wise ordering of the world. God has advance knowledge

---

1. Josephus, "Antiquities," Book 20, 8.5.

of everything because of his decree: he himself planned it all. So he always acts advisedly. He does nothing rashly.

The word *providentia* occurs several times in the Jewish apocrypha. In the ways in which the word is used there we can see a distinction which theologians have made between God's general providence and his special providence.

God's general providence is his wise ordering of all the ordinary details of everyday events. One example is found in Wisdom 14:3. A seafarer is about to set sail. Credit is given to the skill of the workman who built the ship. But then this statement is added: "But it is your providence, O Father, that steers its course, because you have given it a path in the sea, and a safe way through the waves."

By God's special providence is meant the care and protection he displays towards his own people. 4 Maccabees 17:22 makes a reference to this: "divine providence preserved Israel that previously had been afflicted."

BIBLICAL FOUNDATION

Old Testament

We may analyze the Old Testament teaching on providence into three strands.

Preservation

Under this heading, we look at three texts.

GENESIS 8:22

Here we read, "while the earth remains, seedtime and harvest, cold and heat, winter and summer, and day and night shall not cease." This is the Bible's initial summary of the truth of divine providence. As long as earth's history continues, God promises that there will be no cessation of sowing and reaping seasons, of the alternations of the weather, of times of busyness and times for resting, of waking times and sleeping times. God will order things so that human life may continue. The food-production necessary to sustain human life will not be terminated.

"Cease" translates the Hebrew word *šābat*. It is the same word found in Genesis 2:2–3, which twice tells us that God "rested (*šābat*) on the seventh day from all his work that he had done." It is found also in the Sabbath commandment in Exodus 23:12, which says that "on the seventh day you shall rest (*šābat*)." God may rest; man must rest. But the seasonal rhythms of nature will never take a day off. Wenham writes: "God's assurance that these rhythms will be maintained is a mark of his continuing providential blessing on the world."[2]

Leupold reminds us that "the regular variation of times and seasons here promised is not to be regarded as merely natural, fixed by nature's ordinance, but as an outgrowth of God's specific promise."[3] In fact, nothing is "merely natural." Nature itself works according to God's providential arrangement.

Genesis 45:5–7

Whereas providence usually carries on in a gentle, behind-the-scenes fashion, there are occasionally remarkable, unexpected events which turn out with hindsight to be a plank in God's strategy of preservation. A case in point is found here in the experience of Joseph. Having just disclosed his identity to his brothers, he points to God's providential preservation of his people. He urges his brothers not to cave in to remorse because they sold him into Egypt, "for," he says, "God sent me before you to preserve life." He then adds a second reason why God sent him ahead: "to preserve a posterity for you in the earth, and to save your lives by a great deliverance."

Nehemiah 9:6

As the Levites lead the people in prayer, having acknowledged that the LORD alone has created the heavens and the earth and all that they contain, they affirm, "and you preserve them all." The only explanation for the world's continued existence is that God preserves it.

2. Wenham, *Genesis*, 191.
3. Leupold, *Genesis*, 187.

Provision

Psalm 65:9 speaks of God's providential provision on a global scale: "You visit the earth and water it, you greatly enrich it; the river of God is full of water; you provide their grain, for so you have prepared it."

But provision also takes place at a more particular level. From Job 38:41 we learn that God "provides food for the raven." And provision for the needs of his own people is something for which the Lord takes especial concern: as the opening words of Psalm 23 assure us, "The LORD *is* my shepherd; I shall not want."

Government

When the LORD finally appears to Job after his frustrating discussion with his friends, he does not answer Job's questions. Instead, in Job 38:16—39:30, he declares his awesome greatness in contrast with Job's inevitable ignorance in a world of baffling complexity. He assures Job that even a world of bemusing paradox is under his providential control.

The outline of this passage given by Elmer Smick is helpful.[4] He entitles this section "God as Ruler." Verses 16–38 of chapter 38 proclaim God as Ruler of inanimate nature. We see his rule over the depths and expanses (verses 16–18), over light and darkness (verses 19–21), over the weather (verses 22–30), over the stars (verses 31–33), and over the floods (verses 34–38). The rest of the passage proclaims God's rule over animate nature, including the areas of nourishment (38:39–41), procreation (39:1–4), wild freedom (39:5–8), intractable strength (39:9–12), incongruous speed (39:13–18), fearsome strength (39:19–25), and the flight of the predator (39:26–30).

The whole thrust of this passage is to declare "God's management of the universe."[5] At every level he is in control. He sustains all things. His signature is written across the whole creation.

We may analyze the Old Testament teaching about God's providential government into three strands; we shall use three texts from the Psalms to bring this out. Each states that God is King. This is an assertion of his providential government.

---

4. Smick, "Job," 1034.
5. Smick, "Job," 1035.

He is King over his inanimate creation, including the weather, as Psalm 93:1–4 shows, with its reference to the floods and the waves of the sea, than which "the Lord on high," whose "throne is established from of old" "*is* mightier."

He is also King also over the nations of the world. The sons of Korah speak of this in Psalm 47:7–8: "God *is* the King of all the earth; sing praises with understanding. God reigns over the nations; God sits on his holy throne."

Chiefly, though, God is King over his own people. Asaph writes in Psalm 74:12, "God *is* my King is from of old, working salvation in the midst of the earth." God is working all things to ensure the salvation of his people throughout the world.

The final Old Testament passage to which we refer, Psalm 104:3–30, brings together these three aspects of God's providence. "The theme of Psalm 104 is God's greatness in ruling and sustaining his creation."[6] Leslie Allen calls the Psalm "a sketch rather than an analysis."[7] But it paints a picture of the Lord who created the world as also the world's sole sustainer. "The Lord sovereignly rules over all creation and establishes order by his wise administration."[8]

Here are some of the areas in which God's providential sustaining is seen.

(1) His control of the waters (verses 3–8 and 25–26). Allen describes the typical ancient Israelite as a landlubber. The sea was traditionally an object of dread. Here, though, "water, the potent enemy of terrestrial life, has been harnessed to become its means of sustenance."[9]

(2) His provision for living creatures (verses 11–12, 14–18, and 27–28). All creatures are fed richly. All have somewhere to live. And this applies to the animals, birds, and sea-creatures as much as to human life. Some wild animals are terrifying to man, and none more so than Leviathan. But here Leviathan is depicted simply as the Lord's pet[10] (verse 26).

6. VanGemeren, "Psalms," 657.
7. L. C. Allen, *Psalms*, 49.
8. VanGemeren, "Psalms," 663.
9. L. C. Allen, *Psalms*, 46.
10. VanGemeren, "Psalms," 663.

(3) His regulation of time (verses 19–23). "The LORD is in control over the seasons and the alternation of day and night."[11] Allen writes:

> Animals prowling at night form a counterpart to man at work by day, all sharing in a divinely programmed cycle of activity. Human work belongs to a God-ordained pattern . . . . The Psalmist marvels at the order he can discern in the natural world.[12]

(4) His distribution of life and death (verses 29–30). Here is Allen's comment:

> All creatures, great and small, depend providentially on the LORD for food and for life itself . . . . God is their father-figure, and so they function as dependents in an extended family. They are at the mercy of God's outstretched hand or averted face. The power of life and death belongs to God.[13]

Our great reassurance in knowing that we are at God's mercy is that it truly is mercy which fills his heart.

This Psalm, then, reminds us that the LORD is not remote. He is daily involved in the existence of his creation. His involvement is direct and personal. It is not the involvement of someone who has wound up a toy and then keeps a watchful eye to make sure that it does not stop. Creation has not been left by God to continue by its own intrinsic power. Rather, it is more like a toy which needs pushing. The LORD carries the universe day by day.

Allen sums up the message of Psalm 104 like this:

> The world and its phenomena are regarded as windows through which divine activity of love and power may be glimpsed . . . . [The psalmist] subordinates nature and society to his basic belief in a transcendent, moral God of order . . . . The world's stability is divine stability writ large.[14]

Willem VanGemeren draws attention to the picture language of verses 3–4:

> The LORD's involvement in the world of creation comes to expression in the imagery of the chariot, the clouds, the wind, and the flames of fire. He sovereignly controls the elements, as if

---

11. VanGemeren, "Psalms," 663.
12. L. C. Allen, *Psalms*, 47.
13. L. C. Allen., *Psalms*, 47.
14. L. C. Allen, *Psalms*, 49.

> he "rides" on a chariot, using the wind, clouds, and lightning ("flames of fire") for his purposes . . . . The Creator-King is, as it were, driving his chariot, symbolic of his governance of his creation. All his created works reveal the splendor and wisdom of the Creator, because he remains constantly involved with his handiwork.[15]

So the universe is not a self-regulating system. It is not a self-contained entity. Its preservation, regularity, and fruitfulness are the direct result of the Creator's personal management from moment to moment. And the result is satisfaction for the earth (verse 13). The word translated "satisfaction" is *śāba'*. The same word is used in verse 16, where it speaks of abundance, and in verse 28, where it means fullness. For all the creatures on the face of the earth, the LORD's providence is generously enriching.

New Testament

We shall refer to six passages as we explore the New Testament teaching on this theme.

Matthew 5:44–45

Jesus points out that the weather is the same for evil and unjust people as it is for the just and good, because our Father in heaven "makes his sun rise on the evil and on the good, and sends rain on the just and on the unjust." The sun brightens the day for all people. The rain waters the crops indiscriminately.

Here is our Lord's answer to a modern heresy known as "the prosperity gospel." This error claims that becoming a Christian, and so "being good," is the route to enhanced prosperity. Jesus denies this. It is not so, because God's good gifts are showered equally on believers and non-Christians alike.

Jesus' words in verse 44 make it clear that this indiscriminate provision is an expression of divine love. We are commanded to love our enemies, because that is what God does. By distributing his kindness even-handedly he loves even those who do not love him. In this general, practical way, God loves his enemies no less than he loves his own people.

---

15. VanGemeren, "Psalms," 659.

What is clear from our Lord's words is, emphatically, that it is God who does this. He does not just sit back and let it rain, or stand back and let the sun shine. He makes the sun rise. Every day his universal love is displayed as every human being enjoys the light and warmth of the sun. Similarly, he sends the rain. Jesus is here tracing things back to their first cause, namely that God is indiscriminate in his kindness.

Matthew 6:26–33

Jesus now takes this a step further, teaching that God feeds the birds and decorates the flowers. In which case, he continues, posing a rhetorical question, "*will he* not much more *clothe* you, O you of little faith?" Of course he will not fail to look after the most valuable part of his creation—his people. "Therefore," Jesus concludes, we have no need to "worry, saying, 'What shall we eat?' or 'What shall we drink?' or 'What shall we wear?'" Our heavenly Father knows what we need, and as we "seek first the kingdom of God and his righteousness," we shall also receive everything else that we need.

Matthew 10:29–31

Jesus also teaches that the providence of God extends to the minutest details of the most trivial circumstances of the tiniest creatures. His point in these verses is that not even a small bird can fall to the ground unless God makes it happen. Calvin offers this comment:

> Christ gives a very different account of the providence of God from what is given by many who talk like the philosophers, and tell us that God governs the world, but yet imagine providence to be a confused sort of arrangement, as if God did not keep his eye on each of the creatures. Now, Christ declares that each of the creatures in particular is under his hand and protection, so that nothing is left to chance.[16]

However, as Matthew Henry says, what Jesus is chiefly asserting here is "that the providence of God is in a special manner conversant about the saints, in their suffering." They are "of more value than many sparrows," and therefore, he can say to each one of us, "the very hairs of your head are all numbered." That denotes "the account which God takes and keeps

16. Calvin, *Evangelists*, Vol. 1, 464.

of all the concerns of his people, even those that are most minute and least regarded."[17]

Don Carson issues this encouragement: "God's sovereignty over the tiniest detail should give us confidence that he also superintends the larger matters."[18]

Acts 17:24–26

Preaching to a pagan Gentile audience in Athens, the apostle Paul made five statements relevant to the doctrine of God's providence.

GOD IS INDEPENDENT OF HIS CREATION

He is not reliant on his creatures for the things he needs. Since everything is his creation, everything is also his possession. This text proclaims "the self-sufficiency and complete independence of God."[19]

God certainly is not in need of our help. The word translated "worshipped" in verse 25 is *therapeuō*. It is normally translated "healing." The reference is not to worship pure and simple, to worship as an expression of gratitude. The idea is worship misunderstood as a favor which man does for God, worship which supposedly is actually making a contribution to the divine glory.

This truth is the foundation for the doctrine of providence. The God of providence is sovereign.

GOD IS THE SUPREME GIVER

The Greek word *pas* (all) comes twice in verse 25. God gives all things to all people. No one has anything which he has not received from God. This applies to things as fundamental as life itself and the breath needed to sustain life.

The word rendered "breath" here is *pnoē*. It is the gentlest available term for a movement of air. Every single inhalation, however slight, is a gracious gift from God.

---

17. Henry, *New Testament*, Vol. 1, 225–26.
18. D. A. Carson, "Matthew," 255.
19. Schönweiss, *"deomai,"* 861.

GOD IS THE AUTHOR OF ETHNICITY

The human race is subdivided into different people groups. Ethnic diversity is an expression of God's driving passion for variety.

The word *pas* comes twice more in verse 26. God made all nations in all places. Wherever you go on the face of the earth, whatever ethnic group you find there has been constituted by the Creator.

This variety and diversity is not a valid ground for what is sometimes called "racism." In fact, the very idea that humanity is multi-racial is "racist"! This verse teaches that there is only one human race. God made us all from one blood. We share a common ancestry, stemming from the one pair in the Garden of Eden.

Richard Longenecker notes that the Athenians, to whom Paul is talking here, boasted that they were different from all other peoples.[20] They claimed that they originated directly from the soil of Greece. Paul demolishes such proud notions.

Because of our common descent from Adam and Eve genetic diversity developed gradually along with the migrations of people away from the Middle East. The diversity which we see today is the result of divine providence at work over many centuries.

GOD HAS DETERMINED NATIONAL DURATION

Migrations took place. Nations were formed. Governments were set in place. The time came when they collapsed. Perhaps the nation was overrun in war. Perhaps a people feeling oppressed rose up in revolution. Perhaps moral disintegration caused systemic weakness. But the length of time that a nation or empire or culture survives is determined and pre-appointed by the sovereign Lord. The word translated "periods" in verse 26 is *kairous*. It refers not to mere chronology, but to the power and influence of a nation for its time.

We need to take note of the words "determined" and "allotted." Two verbs are being used. The first is *horizō*. It means to set the limit, in this case, the temporal limit. The tense is aorist: it denotes a determination of timescale fixed in the past, in this case, in eternity. The other verb is *protassō*. It, too, means to determine something in advance. In this

---

20. Longenecker, "Acts," 476.

case the tense is perfect: it denotes that was determined still stands, and therefore inevitably becomes reality at the appointed time.

God has determined national location

The boundaries are fixed geographically as well as temporally. Migrations, ancient and contemporary, are all governed by the providence of God.

Colossians 1:17

Another of the New Testament emphases is the central role which Christ has in providence. In this verse Paul writes, "He is before all things, and in him all things consist." Providence, as we have seen, includes preservation. Here is a vital additional element to the truth of God's providential preservation: it is in Christ that all things "consist." This verb indicates that the creation is being kept intact. The unity of the universe is being upheld. There is a firmness about things which ensures that they do not fall apart. Everything has its place and remains there immovably. And the point of cohesion by which all things are preserved is found in Christ. "Apart from his continuous sustaining activity, all would disintegrate."[21]

The verb is in the perfect tense. It implies that all things were and still are held together. There has never been a moment when Christ could relax his sustaining hold. That would have led to total cosmic collapse. I wonder whether that is the reason for the midday darkness and the earthquakes when he died on the cross. Was creation thrown into turmoil because its center of unification was under threat?

Hebrews 1:3

The writer to the Hebrews also brings out this same point. God's Son is said to be "upholding all things by the word of his power." It is Christ who upholds the entire universe. The word translated "upholds" is *pherō*. It means "to carry." The Lord Jesus Christ is carrying creation so that it does not fall to destruction. He is moving it forwards towards its ultimate destiny.

---

21. O'Brien, *Colossians*, 62.

These last two texts emphasize the importance of something which T. H. L. Parker says about providence. He insists that

> we must resist the temptation to think about providence generally and independently of Christ. It would be possible to draw on certain Psalms and the Sermon on the Mount, for example, to make up a doctrine of God's relation to his creation which has nothing to do with Jesus Christ. But since it is in Christ that this relationship is established, an attempt to understand it apart from him would be a misinterpretation from the start. In Jesus Christ God has set up the relationship between himself and his creation.[22]

DOCTRINAL FORMULATION

The Reformation Confessions

The early creeds are silent on this subject. The teaching of the Reformation confessions may be summarized in eight points.

The meaning of providence

The confessions define God's ongoing relationship to his creation using a number of different terms. God is said to govern, to rule, or to direct, his creation. He preserves it and upholds it. He orders it and guides it. Creation is quickened and sustained by the Lord. The picture conveyed by the confessions is one in which God is totally involved in the life of the world. God holds creation in his hand, carrying it, shaping it, caring for it.

The scope of providence

God's providence extends to all things. The entire universe is subject to God. This applies to the actions of all God's creatures, from the greatest to the least. Providence may be seen as operating on two levels. God sets the overall cosmic direction. He also manages the smallest details. Robert Shaw quotes the words of one Dr. Dick on this point:

22. T. H. L. Parker, "Providence," 426–27.

> Some maintain only a general providence, which consists in up-
> holding certain general laws, and exclaim against the idea of a
> particular providence, which takes a concern in individuals and
> their affairs . . . . If God has certain designs to accomplish with
> respect to, or by means of, his intelligent creatures, I should like
> to know how his intention can be fulfilled without particular
> attention to their circumstances, their movements, and all the
> events of their life . . . . How can a whole be taken care of without
> taking care of its parts, or a species be preserved if the individu-
> als are neglected?[23]

Spelling this out in more detail, the confessions affirm that everything
that happens is disposed and ordained by God. Indeed, nothing can happen apart from his appointment. Every apparent accident occurs only at
God's command. Shaw sums up the scope of providence: it extends to
the inanimate creation, the whole animal creation, angels, both good and
evil ones, and the affairs of nations, families, and individuals.[24]

The character of God's providence

We may distinguish between the moral character and the practical character of God's providence. The confessions describe God's providence in
moral terms as just, right, good and holy. Practically, it is wise, but inscrutable. This last term amounts to an admission that we are not always able
to make sense of what happens. We therefore submit to a higher wisdom.

The basis of God's providence

There are two aspects to the underlying basis of providence: God's infallible foreknowledge, and the free counsel of his holy will. God knows
everything that will happen, and God decides everything that will happen. But which comes first? Does God decide on the basis of what he
knows, or does he know because he has already decided? This is a question which we cannot answer. Knowledge and decision are simultaneous
in the eternal God. We have to admit that in the doctrine of providence
there are mysteries which perplex us. We cannot expect to unravel every

---

23. Shaw, *Confession*, 66–67.
24. Shaw, *Confession*, 67.

mystery to our own emotional satisfaction. This doctrine lifts us up to trust and worship God.

The methods of providence

Many of the confessions note that God uses means to accomplish his purposes. Secondary causes come into play, and they operate according to their own nature. Of course, the means are ordained just as much as the end. This even applies to the evil choices and actions of sinners and devils, which God has wonderful ways of turning to good.

Shaw distinguishes between ordinary and miraculous providences. In ordinary providence God works "by means and according to general laws established by his own wisdom." A miraculous providence is when God chooses to work by his own immediate agency without the use of means.[25]

Providence and sin

The truths emphasized so far inevitably raise the question of the relationship of God's providence to sin considered as a hostile power, and to the individual sins of fallen angels and human beings. Here too we find ourselves in the realm of mystery. The confessions acknowledge that, if we truly believe in providence, we have to say that the entry of sin into the world was permitted by God in such a way that it was bound to happen, and that subsequent sins and all the effects of sin are carefully handled by God to promote ends which are morally praiseworthy.

In discussing the teaching of the Westminster Confession on this aspect of the doctrine of providence, Shaw notes two biblical examples of God's providential ordering of sin—the sale of Joseph by his brothers, and the crucifixion of Jesus. In both cases, greater good came about through the means of sinful choices and actions. In advance, God secured those sinful choices and actions with a view to that greater good.

However, the confessions are quick to assert that this does not make God the author of sin. God is not responsible for sin. Sinfulness comes from the creature, not from the Creator. Such teaching obviously causes us some uncertainty. To us it seems a contradiction to say that God

---

25. Shaw, *Confession*, 69.

decreed sin and yet that he is not the author of sin. Here is what Robert Shaw says about this:

> To solve the difficulty connected with this point, theologians distinguish between an action and its quality. The action, abstractly considered, is from God, for no action can be performed without the concurrence of providence; but the sinfulness of the action proceeds from the creature. As to the manner in which the providence of God is concerned about the sinful actions of creatures, it is usually stated that God permits them, that he limits them, and that he overrules them for the accomplishment of his own holy ends.

This still leaves unanswered the question, why did God choose to accomplish holy ends by that route in the first place? Shaw continues:

> The full elucidation of this abstruse subject, so as to remove every difficulty, surpasses the human faculties. We are certain that God is concerned in all the actions of his creatures; we are equally certain that God cannot be the author of sin; and here we ought to rest.[26]

This doctrine is bound to leave us with some loose ends which we cannot tie up. The confessions commend a humility which will bow before the secrets which are hidden from us. They warn us not to persist in questioning what is beyond our understanding.

The purposes of providence

What is God aiming at in providentially preserving and governing his creation and all its parts? The confessions mention three things. (1) The creation is providentially ruled so that every part of it may serve man, so that man may be better able to serve God. (2) Providence is designed for taking care of the people of God in particular: all things are disposed for the good of the church. As it says in 2 Chronicles 16:9: "the eyes of the LORD run to and fro throughout the whole earth, to show himself strong on behalf of *those* whose heart *is* loyal to him." (3) The highest appointed end of providence is God's own glory.

---

26. Shaw, *Confession*, 70.

The benefits of providence

The assurance that God's providence is ruling over all is of great benefit to the believer. It gives us peace to know that God is watching over us with fatherly care. It gives us a sense of safety to know that no enemy, human or demonic, can harm us without his permission. To know that nothing can happen to us by chance is a source of rich comfort. The doctrine of providence leads us to trust that God will provide us with all that we need, both materially and spiritually, and that he will turn every experience through which we pass to our good. We can therefore be patient in times of adversity, thankful in times of success, and confident as we face the unknown future.

It is in times of darkness and mystery that this doctrine really comes into its own. To know that all providences, even difficult ones, are for a purpose is an incalculable comfort to us. To know that nothing can do us ultimate harm is to see even our trials as blessings. Temporal evils there may be, but, because of providence, they will always turn out to be for our spiritual good.

Modern Confessions of Faith

Each of the modern confessions has something significant to say on this subject.

Confession of Faith of the United Church of Northern India

The Indian confession recognizes two strands to God's providence. It says that God both preserves and also governs all things within the visible world which he has created.

Here are words of comfort for human beings: even in this visible, physical world to which we belong, we are never in a situation where God's preserving and governing providence has been removed. Here, in this life as we experience it, every day we live within the sphere of divine government. All the time a loving God is preserving us and sustaining human existence.

This confession also makes the point that God "is in no way the author of sin." Without trying to unravel the mysteries of providence, it insists on the holiness of God, and refuses to deny his goodness by blaming him for the miseries which sin has caused.

Confession of Faith of the Huria Batak Protestant

God the Father in particular is described as "the Provider and the Lord of all things visible and invisible." This statement affirms God's sovereign providence, not only in our world, but throughout his entire creation. His providential provision and control extend to things invisible as well.

Some things are invisible simply because they are out of the range of human exploration. The remotest galaxies and the deepest depths of the sea bed would come into this category. Other things are intrinsically invisible by nature. This would include the realm of angels and spirits. But both types of invisible reality are held in the providential care and power of God.

However, this confession explicitly distinguishes the doctrine of divine providence from fatalism. It also includes a statement rejecting the practices of listening to fortune-tellers and reading one's fate in the lines of one's hands. A caring, loving God shapes our destiny by his providence, not some impersonal fate.

Confession of Faith of House Churches in China

Two words are used by the Chinese confession in speaking of God's providence: God controls all things; God sustains all things. These two terms echo the emphases in the Reformation confessions on God's government and preservation of creation. This confession stresses the fact that providence rules human history. God is described as "the Lord of human history," and it is within human history that God manifests his sovereignty.

This is not to restrict the sphere of providence to human history alone, as if God's sovereignty is not at work in the non-human part of creation, or in the personal histories of individual human beings. However, it is in human affairs that God's providence is of most interest to us, and it is on the historical stage that God's sovereignty is at work most powerfully. He is indeed King of the nations.

Chinese history has been at times illustrious, and at times excruciatingly painful. In both aspects of their history, the Chinese House

Church leaders want to trace the government of God. Even if, for them, God's providence has at times been most mysterious and inexplicable, yet they know that every Chinese government has been put in place by the sovereign Lord, and remains in place until he sees fit to remove it. That fact accounts for the sentiments expressed at the end of the section of the confession which teaches about the Church: "We are opposed to the church taking part in any activities that seek to destroy the unity of the people or the unification of the Chinese state."

Since it is the providence of God which has unified the Chinese State in the course of its history, it is not the calling of the Church to interfere with the workings of providence. The Church bows to the sovereign will of the Lord of history.

HISTORICAL ELABORATION

We shall now look at the writings of two men who celebrated the divine providence—the second-century French theologian, Irenaeus of Lyons, and the seventeenth-century English puritan, John Flavel.

Irenaeus

Irenaeus's life's work was to oppose Gnosticism, a heresy which invaded the church in the second century. His major work, *Against All Heresies*, includes an exciting and uplifting doctrine of providence.

Irenaeus taught that every aspect of everything that exists is a fruit of God's providence. There is a purpose to everything. Nothing happens "in vain." All that happens in the world is rooted in the purpose of God, and takes place with a view to the usefulness which God intended for it. Nothing happens "accidentally." Nothing simply appears. There are no chance events in God's world.

On the contrary, everything happens "with exceeding suitability." Irenaeus wrote in Latin, and the word which he uses here is *aptatio*. It is derived from a verb meaning "to adjust to fit." It could be used of tightening a belt to secure a piece of armor. It conveys the picture that every event in the story of the world is a minor adjustment which God makes to keep creation neatly tailored in its progress towards the fulfilment of his purpose. Every occurrence is a necessary modification to maintain the world's fitness as the realm within which God is working out his grand intention. This does not, of course, mean that God adjusts his plan as he goes along: it is picture language which serves to emphasize the totally detailed nature of that plan from the very beginning.

Irenaeus uses a musical image when he says that everything happens "in elevated harmony." Even when, to our limited perspective, things seem discordant, they are still playing together under the leadership of the divine conductor. The universe echoes the sublime exaltation of God.[27]

"God exercises a providence over all things," writes Irenaeus. Nothing is left outside the sphere of divine providence. Irenaeus explains this universal providence by saying that the Father "arranges the affairs of our world." Here is a comforting truth: even in the midst of life's struggles, we may rely on our Maker and Father, confident that, right here in this world, we are held in his mighty hand.

The word rendered "arranges" is *dispono*. It implies that God, with great care and deliberation, positions things, and times events, with precision. He secures regularity in creation, as opposed to haphazardness. He guards his handiwork meticulously. The word was sometimes used of a person's daily work. To be the managing director of the universe is how God is daily employed.

Irenaeus describes God as the ruler. Like a herdsman, God sets the direction with a clear aim in view. Like a horse rider, he steers things so that the correct direction is maintained and the intended destination is achieved. God's providential activity involves guiding the creation forwards to its appointed destiny, just as a helmsman or navigator guides a ship.

There is a practical application which Irenaeus makes. Providence should bring people to the knowledge of God. This is not something which will just happen incidentally. The experience of providence is something that people ought to seize on to lead them to the knowledge of the Lord himself. We have a duty actively to reap the benefits of the understanding of God's providence.

What Irenaeus means is that the very facts of order, purpose, harmony, security and provision in this world are making a statement that there is but one God who rules and governs absolutely everything. And these facts are staring all rational people in the face, if they will but take unprejudiced notice. Irenaeus admits that the ravages of sin mean that

---

27. Irenaeus, "Against All Heresies," 2.26.3.

people are moved only slightly. Nevertheless, there is something moving about a purposefully directed world. There is something inspiring and soul-stirring in the fact of providence. And this ought to alert God's creatures at least to the realities of his existence, his unity, his omnipotent greatness, and his universal overruling.[28]

Irenaeus goes on to point out that the supreme act of providence was the coming of Christ. This event, at a particular point in history, is supreme evidence of the divine ordering of all the events of history. But the wonder of this ultimate providence is that, although the coming of Christ took place at one time, its significance and impact are timeless, in the sense that its saving efficacy reaches to every time.

However, it is only believers who benefit from the saving power of Christ, and the providence of God in his coming was directed towards them particularly. Irenaeus recognizes that the original cause of the salvation of God's people was God's wise ordering of things. The outworking of that divine wisdom saw to it that the coming of Christ as Savior took place at the appointed moment as the central event of all history.[29]

Irenaeus writes like this: "It is the Father of our Lord by whose providence all things consist, and all are administered by his command."[30] The two parallel phrases here indicate two important aspects of the doctrine of providence for Irenaeus.

The two nouns "providence" and "command" tell us that God exercises his providence by issuing the all-powerful word of command. It is God's almighty Word which keeps all things in being. But Irenaeus has a particular type of command in view. The original word is *iussus*, which is derived from the verb *iubeo*. This means "to bid someone to be safe and sound." God's providence, for Irenaeus, is directed towards human safety in a sound world.

The two parallel verbs are "consist" and "administer." What is it for God to administer the world? It means that he secures its reliability and its harmonious continuation. The Latin verb *consto* suggests that the creation stands firm, settled and constant. We do not live in a world which is totally unpredictable, entirely random, or unreliably fluid. The providence of God ensures the stability which makes it possible for human life to go on.

---

28. Irenaeus, "Against All Heresies," 3.25.1.

29. Irenaeus, "Against All Heresies," 4.22.2.

30. Irenaeus, "Against All Heresies," 4.36.6.

John Flavel

In 1678 Flavel wrote *The Mystery of Providence*.[31] It is based on Psalm 57:2: "I will cry out to God Most High, to God who performs *all things* for me."

Flavel sets out to demonstrate how the believer can cope in times of distress. He finds the greatest support and comfort at such times to be the certainty that "there is a wise Spirit sitting in all the wheels of motion," so that even the evil designs of the enemies of God's people will be turned to their blessing and happiness. Flavel recommends that in the hard times of life we should reflect on our past experiences of God's providence at different stages of our lives.

He lists eight evidences that providence is overruling all things for the good of God's people: (1) we have experienced mercies beyond the ability of merely natural causes; (2) sometimes natural causes have come together in strange coincidences; (3) all attempts to destroy the people of God have proved ineffective; (4) sinners have often been turned out of the way of evil in remarkable fashion; (5) sometimes evils done to God's people have been repaid even here on earth; (6) the Scriptures describe exactly the experiences which God's people enjoy; (7) sometimes things turn out so well just in the nick of time; (8) and there are specific answers to prayer.

Flavel mentions six specific areas of life where the believer may meditate on providence: (1) our birth and upbringing; (2) our conversion; (3) our daily working life; (4) our family situation; (5) the way we have been preserved from evil; (6) the work of sanctification in our lives.

Meditation on providence, Flavel argues, is a Christian duty, and he gives advice on ways of doing it. First, though, he stresses one important factor. We must ensure that we see God as the author of all providences. This applies to sad afflictions as well as to comfortable providences.

Flavel then gives six pieces of advice for times of distress.

First, he says, we must ponder the sovereignty of God. We must remember that we exist by his will, and that everything that we have and everything that happens to us proceeds from his will.

Second, we must remember the grace and goodness of God. He reminds us that things are never as bad as they could be, and certainly nowhere near as bad as we deserve them to be. We must remember that our afflictions are only for the duration of this short life time, and things

---

31. Flavel, *Mystery, passim.*

will be better hereafter. If we are afflicted, we should see it as a mercy that we are not destroyed.

Third, we must perceive the wisdom of God. If we are afflicted it is because God knows that we need his rod of discipline. It is better to lose some of our cherished things now than to perish for ever.

Fourth, we must meditate on the faithfulness of God. He knows that it is better for us to suffer a little now than to suffer eternal punishment. His love does not pander to our fancies. It gives us what we need to do us good.

Fifth, we must recall the all-sufficiency of God. Whatever our afflictions might have taken from us, if we still have God, we have enough. Even though one pipe may be blocked God is still the fountain, and he remains as full as ever. We always find more in God alone than in any of the comforts we have lost.

Finally, we must see the unchanging nature of God. Our condition in life can change for the worse very suddenly. Two or three days may have brought unexpected sadness into our experience. But God remains what he was and where he was. The passage of time never changes him.

If we can learn to meditate on providence like this, Flavel assures us, we shall retain tranquillity of mind amidst all life's changes and uncertainties. We shall remain stable as the revolutions of things in this vain world circle around us.

But our meditations on providence here are at best partial. However, in eternity we shall have the opportunity for a full and entire survey of all the providences of God:

> O how ravishing and delectable a sight will it be to behold at one view the whole design of providence, and the proper place and use of every single act, which we could not understand in this world . . . . All the dark, intricate, puzzling providences at which we were sometimes so offended, and sometimes amazed, which we could neither reconcile with the promise, nor with each other, nay, which we so unjustly censured and bitterly bewailed, as if they had fallen out quite against our happiness, we shall then see to be to us, as the difficult passage through the wilderness was to Israel, the right way to a city of habitation.[32]

32. Flavel, *Mystery*, 22.

PRACTICAL APPLICATION

(1) Each of the three strands of providence has practical implications for our lives.

God preserves the world, and so we have nothing to fear. Even the world's weather-patterns are under his control. Since he sustains all things, we are safe at all times. There is an orderly stability to this world, in which we may therefore live with confidence and peace of mind.

God provides for our needs, and so gratitude is our appropriate response. All our needs are met: God supplies our food; "he gives his beloved sleep" (Ps 127:2). It may be that we have desires which remain unfulfilled. However, our confidence is that God is better able than we are to distinguish between our mere desires and our true needs, and that he will in consequence always do right. In his kindness he shapes his providence towards our satisfaction, and so we must respond in sincere and fervent praise.

God governs all things, and so we are assured of our safety in his world. His providence reaches to every level—the tiniest details as well as the largest developments. This means that we are never in ultimate danger anywhere, because our loving Father is watching over us wherever we may be. It follows that, even when things are difficult, we need not panic, because we have the confidence that no adversity can come our way without his permission, and that he ordains all things, even the hard things, for our good. We can cope in times of distress, because of our assurance that our God is working in all things for our good. If we are unable to discern how our afflictions are doing us good, we nonetheless trust him that in his wisdom he always does what is best, and we bow in humility before his power.

(2) We must therefore get hold of this assurance that God is in control, whatever may happen. We need never despair. We may not understand what his purpose is, but we do understand that his providence is never without purpose, and that his purposes are always for our ultimate good. Our confidence that God is in control may be boosted by considering obvious instances of his providence. We have been kept safe to live till today, when so many unknown dangers could have carried us out of the world already. God has nourished us daily. God's benevolence is indiscriminate: he is so favorable and generous to all people. Moreover, God's providence is furthering his own work. The Church still exists, the gospel is still being preached, even in difficult times. And it is towards

his own children that God's providence is especially tender. We may find comfort in the knowledge that the hairs of our head are numbered. We are being kept forever by the power of God. Our hearts do not need to be troubled. Even when there is a mystery to God's working, we trust him with humility.

(3) We may live at peace, because the God of providence is our loving heavenly Father. We are not only in safe hands; we are also in caring hands. The assurance of God's total involvement in all the minutest details of our lives is a source of great comfort. The fact that nothing ever happens merely by chance reminds us that we are being guided and kept for eternal blessedness.

(4) We may rejoice at the obvious instances of God's providence in our lives up until now. Moreover, we may rejoice at God's favorable generosity even to our sinful human race. Deep gratitude is the appropriate response when we ponder the numerous evidences of God's love for the world.

(5) We must carefully distinguish between the doctrine of providence and secular, atheistic fatalism. The God of providence is personal and loving. Providence is totally distinct from impersonal forces, and therefore, as the Indonesian Christians recognize, there is no place for stooping to astrology or fortune-telling.

(6) God's providence fosters a wonderful array of diversity and variety across his creation. That in itself calls for our admiration and our adoration of God.

(7) We must preach providence. We must preach it evangelistically. This doctrine is a powerful argument with sinners in calling them to repentance. God has been so kind to them every day. We must urge them to turn to him in gratitude and faith. God's providence is one of the ways in which his reality stares all people in the face, if only they had the eyes to perceive it. We must preach this doctrine to believers. They need to hear that God is in control. The realization that this is so will help them to rise above the mysteries of a bewildering life and to trust God without grumbling.

(8) We must praise God that his providential rule centers in Christ. The God of providence is the Father of our Lord Jesus Christ. "All of God's dealings with his creation are mediated through the Christ."[33] And

33. Reymond, *New Systematic Theology*, 400.

in his eternal purpose God determined that his Son would have a bride conformed to his image, and that he would have a special people residing in the glorified "new heaven and new earth" state, all to the praise of the glory of his grace. And *that* purpose he executed in and by his works of creation and providence.[34]

34. Reymond, *New Systematic Theology*, 414.

6

The Doctrine of Man

WHAT IS IT TO be human, and how do we account for both the amazing selflessness which we often see in people, and yet the horrifying degree of evil of which people are capable? The Scottish puritan, Thomas Boston (1676–1732), wrote a book entitled *Human Nature in its Fourfold State*. He explained the fourfold distinction as follows. First, we see man as God made him—in a state of innocence. Second, through sin, human nature has entered a state of corruption. Third, "in the state of grace" human nature is renewed in Christ. Finally, man's future state will be one of either perfect happiness or complete misery—"and that for ever."[1]

We will treat the third and fourth of these as aspects of the doctrine of salvation. For now our concern is Boston's first two categories. So we shall look at the doctrine of man in two parts. First, we consider man as creature, before moving on, in the second part of the chapter, to the theme of man as sinner.

Before proceeding any further, it is necessary to make one preliminary remark. Like Wayne Grudem, I am sensitive to the contemporary preference, when speaking of the human race in general terms, for using inclusive terms such as "humanity" or "humankind," rather than the word "man," which, it is claimed, degrades women as if they are less than fully human. However, I am in agreement with Grudem when he points out that the use of the word "man" to refer to the human race as a whole

---

1. Boston, *Human Nature*, 37.

is mandated by Scripture.[2] We see that in Genesis 1:27, where we read that God created man male and female, the word "man" translating the Hebrew word *ʾādām*, which, in chapter 2, becomes the personal name of the first human male whom God created.

PART ONE: MAN AS CREATURE

BIBLICAL FOUNDATION

We find the main biblical material on man as creature in the first two chapters of Genesis. From Genesis 3 onwards the rest of the Bible presupposes that the fall has taken place: man is a sinner, and there are only a few brief glimpses of what he was like before the fall. So it is mainly to the first two chapters of the Bible that we must turn for the scriptural doctrine of man as creature.

Genesis 1:26–28

In this passage God resolves to create man in his own image. There are two main emphases in these verses.

Man is one with the rest of creation

Man takes his place in the total context of God's creation. He belongs emphatically to this present created order. This is brought out in two ways.

(1) Man was created on the same day as the land animals. In one sense man is one of the animals. The human body is structured physiologically according to the same basic pattern as the bodies of mammals in general.

(2) Man was blessed in the same way as other created life. We read in verse 28 of God's blessing of man. It begins with these words: "Be fruitful and multiply; fill the earth." In verse 22 God has already spoken in very similar terms to the sea creatures and the birds: "Be fruitful and multiply, and fill the waters in the seas, and let birds multiply on the earth." Perhaps the blessing is pronounced on the sea creatures and birds representatively. This suggests that the entire creation exists under the divine blessing. And man shares in that blessing along with the rest of his fellow creatures.

2. Grudem, *Systematic Theology*, 439–40.

Man is distinct from the rest of creation

However, the greater emphasis is on the uniqueness of man amongst God's creatures. This fact is brought out in three main ways.

THE WORDING OF THE ACCOUNT OF THE CREATION OF MAN

The account of the human creation is worded differently from the earlier parts of the chapter. Two main differences may be observed.

(1) God expresses his intention to create man in more personal terms. He says, "let us make man" (verse 26). In creating other things God simply said, "let there be" (verses 3, 6, 14; cf. verse 9), "let the earth bring forth" (verses 11, 24), "let the waters abound" and "let birds fly" (verse 20). Further, this is the first time that the verb "make" (*'āśâ*) has been used of God's decision to create. All its previous occurrences have come in fulfilment statements (verses 7, 16, 25).

(2) The words "so God created" (verse 27) are also more personal than earlier fulfilment statements. They emphasize God's direct involvement in man's creation, in contrast to phrases such as "and there was" (verse 3), "and it was so" (verses 9, 11, 15, 24), or "the earth brought forth" (verse 12). The only previous use of the phrase "so God created" is in verse 21. The emphasis there is that the sea creatures which God created are "great" (*gādôl*): this word refers both to huge size and to vast numbers. It stresses the miracle of divine power that created out of nothing creatures as immense as these sea creatures—and so many of them! Man, too, is great, a magnificent element in God's world, the pinnacle of creation.

THE THEME OF THE IMAGE OR LIKENESS

This is the main way in which man's uniqueness is brought out in Genesis 1, and is the major emphasis in the biblical doctrine of man as creature.

In verse 26 God says, "Let us make man in our image, according to our likeness." Each of these pairs of phrases consists of a noun—*ṣelem* (image), and *dᵉmût* (likeness)—preceded by a preposition—*bᵉ* (in), and *kᵉ* (according to). So the full Hebrew clauses are *bᵉ ṣelem* (in the image), and *kᵉ dᵉmût* (according to the likeness).

In Genesis 5:3 the prepositions are occur in the same order, but with the nouns reversed: "in his own likeness (*bᵉ dᵉmût*), after his image (*kᵉ ṣelem*)." Moreover, either noun may occur alone: Genesis 5:1 says, that God created man "in the likeness of God," whereas Genesis 9:6 uses the alternative term: "in the image of God he made man." This implies that the terms are interchangeable. Genesis 1:26 probably uses both, rather than just one, for the sake of variety, vividness, and emphasis.

So what does it mean to say that man was made in God's image or likeness? Where is the resemblance between God and man? This passage suggests three possible answers to that question. It is not necessary to choose between them. They may all point to aspects of the image.

Man is God's representative on earth

It could be that the image is an alternative way of speaking of the dominion given to man over the rest of the creatures on earth (verses 26, 28). A human ruler will often set up an image of himself to symbolize his authority over his subjects. In many cultures human rulers are seen as representative of God, the carriers of the mandate of heaven. Similarly, in man, God has set up his image in the world to represent his authority over the whole of creation.

Man is a physical reflection of God

That sounds a strange thing to say. The divine nature is invisible, and God has no physical appearance. How can the human body be made in the likeness of God? However, an image is, by definition, something visible and physical. The human race is a physical embodiment of the divine likeness. Wayne Grudem helpfully notes the analogy between human abilities and qualities ascribed to God as one who sees, hears, and speaks; in these, and other, human functions there is a reflection of facts about God.[3]

This explains the prohibition in the second commandment against making images of God. To make an image of God is superfluous: God has already set up his image in the world from the dawn of time. And no image of human concoction could ever be as accurate a portrayal of God as the image which he designed.

Moreover, in Jesus Christ, God took physical form when he became man, and perhaps the image theme affirms that if God ever were to

---

3. Grudem, *Systematic Theology*, 448.

appear in physical form, it would have to be as a man. Man was originally created in the image of what God the Son would become. In creating man, God anticipates the incarnation of his Son.

Surely this lies behind the description of Christ as "the image of the invisible God" (Col 1:15). The word rendered "image" is *eikōn*, the same Greek word which the Septuagint uses in Genesis 1. Although many commentators explain this in terms of Christ's deity, it seems more probable, given the echo of Genesis, that Christ's humanity is in view: he is the authentic human being, "the proper man," as Luther put it.[4] Robert Wall writes correctly:

> Paul uses *image* to echo the biblical story of creation, when God created male and female in God's own image. Paul's ultimate point is that the Christ event brings to historical expression the ultimate purpose of God's creation of all human life.[5]

Man has the capacity for genuine relationship

It is important to notice the parallel clauses in verse 27. The first two clauses say exactly the same thing, but in the opposite order: God created man in his own image. The third clause changes the wording. Man's creation is still mentioned, but the reference to the image is replaced by the words, "male and female." This seems to define the image, in part at least, as being the gender distinctions which make human beings relational creatures.

Of course, animals also exist as male and female, but the text does not mention that specifically. It has no great significance in their case. Neither is the mandate to be fruitful and multiply the vital thing, even though this is linked with the distinction of gender, since exactly the same instruction was given to other creatures in verse 22.

It is only human beings who can relate to each other in a larger way than the merely physical, and this is an essential element in what it is to be human. The relationship between male and female is the basic relationship from which flows the possibility of all other relationships.

In this capacity for relationship, man reflects the nature of the creator. As Trinity, God exists eternally as a community of persons in

---

4. In the hymn, *A safe stronghold*, verse 2, line 3.
5. Wall, *Colossians and Philemon*, 67.

relationship. And as a relational creature, man is invited to enter into relationship with God himself.

In the times in which we live it is important to note also that Scripture knows only these two genders—male and female. The current emphasis on non-binary or transgender options is a travesty of reality, and a direct assault upon the Creator.

THE USE OF THE WORDS "VERY GOOD"

Man's uniqueness is emphasized thirdly by the use of the words "very good" in verse 31. Only now, only when man is created can creation's goodness be expressed in superlative terms.

Genesis 2:4–8, 15–25

Genesis 2 is a more detailed account of the events of the sixth day of creation. There are eight themes relevant to the doctrine of man as creature.

Man was created with a purpose.

The purpose of human life is defined in verse 5 as "to till the ground." This verb reappears in verse 15, translated this time as "tend," along with the additional purpose, to "keep it." Man was not created for idleness. "Work is intrinsic to human life."[6] Man's task is to work the land with a view to its productivity.

The verb translated "till" and "tend" (*'ābad*) is related to the noun *'ebed*, meaning "servant." By working the land, man's purpose in creation is to look after the earth as the servant of God. The verb translated "keep" (*šāmar*) means "to keep watch." It has connotations of loving care. There is no place for the abuse or the exploitation of creation in man's God-given purpose. Man must look after the world.

This purpose defines the dominion mentioned in chapter 1. Dominion is not domineering domination. It involves caring, tender nurturing.

---

6. Wenham, *Genesis*, 67.

Man is an integral part of the created order

Verse 7 tells us that man was made "*of* the dust of the ground." He is part of this world. In the Hebrew this is even clearer. The word translated "man" is *ādām*, while "ground" translates *ʾadāmâ*. John Sailhamer makes the following observation:

> The emphasis in chapter 2 on man's "creatureliness" is not without its importance. The notion than man's origin might somehow be connected with that of the divine is deliberately excluded.[7]

Man is distinctive within the created order

Despite man's integral part in creation, he is different from every other creature. He is unique. This truth is brought out in three ways.

MAN WAS *FORMED* BY THE CREATOR

This is stated twice, in verses 7 and 8. 'Formed' translates the Hebrew word *yāṣar*. Wenham notes that this speaks of "an artistic, inventive activity that requires skill and planning."[8] In Jeremiah 18:2 the same word is used for a potter. Man's formation was like the intricate moulding of clay. This divine artistry sets man apart.

MAN'S LIFE WAS GIVEN DIRECTLY BY GOD

Verse 7 tells us that the LORD God "breathed into his nostrils the breath of life." As a result, "man became a living being (*nepeš ḥayyâ*)."

It is not the status of "living being" which sets man apart. Verse 19 uses exactly the same term, here translated "living creature," of the animals and birds. It is how man became a living being which differentiates him from all other living creatures. In his case, this was not the result of the divine word; it was because he received a puff of divine wind. God gave man the kiss of life. Perhaps, in connection with man uniquely, the word "life" is already to be understood in the light of the

---

7. Sailhamer, "Genesis," 41.
8. Wenham, *Genesis*, 59.

richer connotations found in Jesus' statement in John 10:10: "I have come that they may have life, and that they may have *it* more abundantly."

MAN COULD FIND NO SUITABLE COMPANION AMONGST THE ANIMALS

In verse 19 the LORD brings all the animals in succession to man, because man is in need of a suitable companion. However, he could find no suitable helper amongst the animals (verse 20). In telling us this, "the author has assured the reader that man was *not like* the other creatures."[9]

Man was made for a life of joyful, aesthetic appreciation

There are four pointers to this in verses 8 and 15.

THE LORD PUT MAN IN A *GARDEN*

A garden is a place of beauty. The aesthetic sense is basic to human nature.

THE NAME OF THE GARDEN WAS *EDEN*

A related word is translated "pleasures" in Psalm 36:8. As Sailhamer rightly comments, "we may assume that the name was intended to evoke a picture of idyllic delight and rest."[10] God's intention was that human life should be a happy life. The pursuit of joy is basic to human nature.

THE GARDEN WAS *EASTWARD*

Wenham makes the following comment:

> In the east the sun rises, and light is a favorite biblical metaphor for divine revelation. So it seems likely that this description of "the garden in Eden in the east" is symbolic of a place where God dwells.[11]

9. Sailhamer, "Genesis," 47.
10. Sailhamer, "Genesis," 41.
11. Wenham, *Genesis*, 61.

This emphasizes the point that human life is intended for relationship with God. It is out of that highest of all relationships that true delight, real joy, genuine pleasure flow. As Psalm 16:11 says, "in your presence *is* fullness of joy; at your right hand *are* pleasures for evermore."

THE MAN WAS *PUT* IN THE GARDEN

This verb used in verse 15 to translate *yānaḥ* does not mean that God just plonked him down there. It implies that man was settled there comfortably. Sailhamer makes this comment: "Man was 'put' into the garden where he could 'rest' and be 'safe,' and man was 'put' into the garden 'in God's presence' where he could have fellowship with God."[12]

So the place of beauty and delight was also a place of peace and rest. Man was contented. Human life is intended to be a life of deep satisfaction. Man is not out of place, but at home within God's creation.

Man lives under God's authority

In verses 16–17 the LORD gives his human creature a command: "Of every tree of the garden you may freely eat; but of the tree of the knowledge of good and evil you shall not eat, for in the day that you eat of it you shall surely die."

Man is not an independent, self-governing agent. He is a responsible being. He is accountable to his maker. He is called to obedience. However, the law under which man is made to live is a "law of liberty" (Jas 1:25). The LORD allows man to eat of "every tree" except one. This implies that there were many trees, and illustrates God's lavish generosity. How constricted man would feel if the proportions were reversed, if, out of all the trees, he could only eat from one. But it was not that way round. Only one was forbidden, so man was given immense freedom. Nevertheless, should he abuse that freedom, the creator's authority is underlined by the death-threat.

---

12. Sailhamer, "Genesis," 45.

Human life consists in relationship, not in aloneness

The creator's comment, "*it is* not good that man should be alone" (verse 18), forms a surprising contrast with his repeated assessment in chapter 1 that creation was good! This "alerts the reader to the importance of companionship for man,"[13] and to the wonderful fact that human life reflects the trinitarian plurality within the single divine nature.

So God continues, "I will make him a helper comparable to him." The word "comparable" renders the phrase *k^e neg^{e}ddô*, which is unique to this passage. Its literal sense is "like opposite." It speaks not of mere identity, but of complementarity, found in "mutual support,"[14] and in the partnership which works together fulfilling different, but equally vital, roles. Matthew Henry long ago depicted the equality of the sexes by reference to the rib which God took from man in verse 21: the woman was

> not made out of his head to top him, nor out of his feet to be trampled upon by him, but out of his side to be equal with him, under his arm to be protected, and near his heart to be beloved.[15]

When God makes the woman, the man expresses his elation in a poetic outburst, where he describes the woman as "bone of my bones and flesh of my flesh" (verse 23). "This formula sets man and woman on an equal footing as regards their humanity."[16] However, the principle of male headship is also implied by the man's naming of the woman: to allocate a name implies seniority.

Monogamous heterosexual marriage is the only valid sexual lifestyle

Verse 24 defines the central expression of human relationality, as it highlights three elements in marriage. (1) Leaving: when a man marries, his primary obligations shift from his parents to his wife. (2) Being joined: a man and his wife are permanently stuck together as if by glue. (3) One flesh: sexual union is included here, but a marriage brings a unity which goes way beyond the physical.

---

13. Wenham, *Genesis*, 68.
14. Wenham, *Genesis*, 68.
15. Henry, *Whole Bible*, 7.
16. Wenham, *Genesis*, 70.

These days many governments have made so-called "gay marriage" legally possible. However, in the light of the creator's words right at the beginning, such a redefinition is a mere fiction. There is no such thing as a "marriage" between two men or two women, because the creator has already fixed the meaning of marriage. To pretend that homosexual marriage is a possibility is to defy the creator himself.

We need not be ashamed of being human

Verse 25 is the Bible's final word on man as creature. Human beings have nothing to be embarrassed about as regards their constitution by the creator. The word "naked" (*'ārôm*) speaks of being exposed. In their pristine condition, man and woman could be totally exposed to each other and to God. They had nothing to hide. There was openness and transparency.

DOCTRINAL FORMULATION

The Early Creeds

The creeds have very little to say about the doctrine of man as creature. There is only one relevant phrase. It comes in the Chalcedonian Definition, in the section referring to the two natures of Christ. It tells us that Christ was "truly man, consisting also of a reasonable soul and body."

This statement sees true humanity as having two aspects. First, the human being has a soul. This is mentioned first, as being the more important. It is the higher element in man. The soul is described as "reasonable." Man is pre-eminently a thinking being. That is what distinguishes him from the animals. In early Christian times the image of God in man was often defined as rationality.

Second, the human being also consists of a body. The physical aspect of man is not ignored by this creed, which is rejecting the Greek philosophical idea that the "real you" is the soul, and that the body is unimportant. The body is not something to be overcome. We are not intended to live in detachment from the material world.

The Reformation Confessions

Five themes may summarize the teaching of the confessions on man as creature.

God created man in his own image

The First Helvetic Confession describes man as "the most perfect image of God on earth," but several of the confessions consider the perennial question, what is the image of God in man? The two main answers are moral uprightness and rational wisdom. Everything about man as originally created was agreeable to the will of God, and he had a true knowledge of God and of spiritual realities. The 1644 Baptist Confession also includes the perfection of all man's natural capacities as an aspect of the image of God.

Two New Testament texts form the background to the confessions' definitions of the image: Ephesians 4:24 instructs us: "Put on the new man which was created according to God in true righteousness and holiness," while Colossians 3:10 informs us that we "have put on the new *man* who is renewed in knowledge according to the image of him who created him."

While the chief concern of these texts is the radical change involved in becoming a Christian, Paul's depiction of this change as re-creation and renewal in the image of God, implicitly offers a definition of what that image originally involved, namely righteousness and holiness, rooted in the knowledge of God which leads to knowledge of the proper way to live.

The confessions also raise the question, why is man created in the image of God? The Heidelberg Catechism replies: "that he might rightly know God his creator, heartily love him, and live with him in eternal blessedness, to praise and glorify him." This points us to the ultimate answer to this question: God created man in his own image so that God could glorify himself through the creature whom he had made.

Man as creature consists of body and soul

In some of the confessions there is, I think, at least the hint of a mistake when they talk about the human soul and body. Some of the confessions speak of man's original creation with an immortal soul and a mortal body.

I would want to make two comments on this wording.

(1) If death is the result of sin, then surely man, in his pristine created state, was not yet facing bodily death. The body was not mortal as first created.

(2) If the implication is that the soul is immortal naturally, whereas the body is only immortal as long as it is miraculously preserved alive, this conflicts with the statement in 1 Timothy 6:16, which says that God "alone has immortality." Even the human soul does not possess immortality as an intrinsic quality. That is true only of God. As first created, man was immortal in soul and body, but that immortality was conferred by the Creator. It was dependent upon the Creator's will. It was not somehow intrinsic to man independently of God's gift.

Man is the highest of God's creatures

Man is described as the principal of God's visible creatures, just as the angels are his principal invisible creatures. This need not imply that the invisible creatures are superior. The confessions are recognizing that God created an invisible, spiritual world, in addition to our material universe. However, "man was God's crowning work of creation."[17] We are greater than the angels because we are made in God's image, and the angels exist to serve us (Heb 1:14). The Westminster Confession affirms the ultimate superiority of humanity by pointing out that man was created "after God had made all other creatures."

Man was created as a being subject to God's law

The confessions acknowledge that the first man and woman received a command from God not to eat of the tree of the knowledge of good and evil. However, this is not their most important emphasis. They see the outward command as symbolic of the fact that God's law was written on the heart of man as creature. This inner inscription of divine law was

---

17. Williamson, *Westminster*, 43.

accompanied by the power to fulfil it, though not in such a way as to place man beyond the possibility of failure.

The confessions speak of this pristine law as a covenant, in which man was promised eternal life on condition of perfect obedience. The Belgic Confession calls it the "commandment of life." This emphasizes the point that obedience was the route to life, and that true life consists in obedience. As long as man and woman obeyed God's law, they enjoyed happiness in communion with God. However, in the case of disobedience, the law included the threat of death.

The human race was created initially as one couple

Genesis 1:27 makes it clear that God created man male and female. However, more specifically, the first father of the whole human race was Adam, who, while still in paradise, had as his wife Eve, "the mother of all living" (Gen 3:20). It was Adam and Eve as a couple whom the LORD blessed. Williamson sums up the unanimous opinion of the Reformation confessions in the statement that "the whole human race descended from one human pair."[18]

Modern Confessions of Faith

Of the three modern confessions with which we are concerned, only one has a significant statement about man as creature. The Indonesian confession mentions that Adam and Eve were created "good and able to act in conformity with God's will," but adds nothing by way of elaboration. The Chinese confession says that God "created man according to his own image," but makes no detailed explanation of this statement. However, the Confession of Faith of the United Church of Northern India has a more elaborate article on this theme.

This confession reiterates the main points from the traditional exposition of the doctrine of man as creature. Man exists as male and female, and human beings are created by God in his own image. The image is defined by reference to the two key New Testament texts (Col 3:10 and Eph 4:24) as knowledge, righteousness, and holiness. For this confession, the image is understood in entirely moral terms. The fact that

18. Williamson, *Westminster*, 43.

our first parents were free to choose between good and evil is mentioned, as is human dominion over all other creatures.

In his short exposition of this confession, William Stewart notes that talk about human dominion "expresses man's place in the universe." His created constitution and his God-given role "enabled him first to yoke a pair of bullocks to his plough and so win the crops by which not only he but also the bullocks are fed." Likewise, this God-given dominion

> enables him to use the treasures of coal and iron and oil which are hidden in the earth. God alone is the creator of all, but when he made man, he made someone who also could make new things, turning the raw materials of the earth and the dumb strength of animals to the making of finer things.[19]

The main distinctive element in this statement of faith comes with the sentence, "All men have the same origin, and are brethren." Here we see one of the chief implications of the Christian doctrine of man as creature: all human beings, of every ethnic group, every nationality, every social background, every level of educational advancement, all are brothers, by virtue of our common descent from Adam and Eve. Every time I see another human being, whoever he or she may be, I am looking at a more or less distant relative (see Acts 17:26).

HISTORICAL ELABORATION

In this section we shall look briefly at what the earliest Christian writers after the New Testament said about man as the image of God, and then at one representative modern theologian, G. C. Berkouwer.

Early Christian Perspectives

Writing towards the end of the first century, Clement of Rome defined man's understanding as "the express likeness of [God's] own image."[20] This identification of the image with rational understanding became commonplace in the early centuries, and human reason was located in the soul.

---

19. W. Stewart, *Faith We Confess*, 13–14.
20. Clement of Rome, "Corinthians," 33.

Many writers additionally saw a moral dimension to the image. Tertullian, for example, sees the likeness of God as consisting in holiness.[21] Early writers often combined these two elements in the image, as they saw the mind as the aspect of the human constitution which directs the moral life. So Clement of Alexandria notes that the divine likeness consists both "of doing good and of exercising rule," and locates government in the mind, as the ruling element in human life.[22]

There was a tendency amongst the earliest writers to make a distinction between the image, regarded as a perennial reality, and the likeness, seen as the future consummation of human character, which is in process of realization in the work of sanctification. Origen, for example, said that "man received the dignity of God's image at his first creation," but believed that "the perfection of his likeness has been reserved for the consummation."[23] However, this use of the Bible's dual terminology is justly recognized as invalid.[24]

Writing towards the end of the fourth century, Gregory of Nyssa gave more detailed consideration to the image of God, in his work *On the Making of Man*. Gregory recognizes that an image must have important points of difference from that which it reflects, but also states that "the image is properly an image so long as it fails in none of those attributes which we perceive in the archetype."[25] He therefore expects to find in human nature marks of all the divine attributes. So human dominion is an image of the divine sovereignty. The human senses are images of the divine powers of sight and hearing and so on. The divine incomprehensibility is mirrored by the complexity of the human mind. As God is the epitome of beauty, so there is a beauty about the human mind, which diffuses beauty throughout the human personality. Man's freedom of choice is an image of God's self-determination.[26]

After Gregory, the next writer to give extensive attention to the meaning of the image of God was Augustine in the early decades of the fifth century. Augustine shares the general view that the image has to do with human rationality.[27] However, in his work *On the Trinity* he insists

21. Tertullian, "Chastity," 1.

22. Clement of Alexandria, "Stromata," 2.19.

23. Origen, "De Principiis," 3.6.1.

24. Berkouwer, *Man*, 43, 68.

25. Gregory of Nyssa, "Making of Man," 16.12; 11.3.

26. Gregory of Nyssa, "Making of Man," 5–6; 11.2–4; 12.9–11; 16.11.

27. E.g., Augustine, "Confessions," 13.32.47.

that, since God is triune and man is made in his image, there must be an image of the Trinity in the human constitution.

Augustine discerns "a kind of trinity" in the human mind, which is manifested in the memory, the understanding, and the will. He then highlights images of the trinity in man's bodily nature, taking the sense of sight as his example, in which we find the thing which is seen, the form of what is seen as impressed on the eye, and the purpose of the will in equating the two. He admits that this is an inadequate image of the Trinity, because these three things are not equal and of one substance. He therefore returns to the inner man, and redefines this trinitarian image in terms of the image in the memory, the form of the image "when the mind's eye of the thinker is turned to it," and the purpose of the will in equating them. Finally, Augustine seeks an image of God in true wisdom, which is granted by God as a gift as man partakes of God himself.[28] This consists in remembering, understanding, and loving God.[29] For Augustine, this seems to be the true nature of the image: it is not merely a detached reproduction of God's trinitarian nature, but the reflection of the triune God himself as we focus our devotion upon him.

The Image of God as Discussed by G. C. Berkouwer

Professor Berkouwer devotes one chapter of his book *Man: the image of God* to the meaning of the image.[30] Having discussed and questioned various opinions, he then outlines his own reading of the subject.[31]

His emphasis is that, pre-eminently, it is Christ who is the image of God, and that, in him, human beings are renewed, enabling them to pursue the holiness in which the image of God becomes visible.

However, Berkouwer's distinctive and helpful contribution to this discussion is that he goes beyond the tendency to explain the image in merely individualistic terms, recognizing that the new life in Christ comes to expression primarily in the new community. In this new community, man discovers his true nature, his nature as God originally intended it to be. This is not a community in which differences are removed, but one in which difference is no longer a threat. It is a community rooted in

28. Augustine, "Trinity," 15.3.5.
29. Augustine, "Trinity," 14.12.15.
30. Berkouwer, *Man*, 67–118.
31. Berkouwer, *Man*, 98–118.

relationship with God, in which human beings give expression to their imitation of God as they relate to one another in love and mercy. It is a community in which mutual kindness, mutual love, mutual forgiveness, reflect the kindness, love and forgiveness of Christ.

Berkouwer thus finds the true meaning of the image of God in Jesus' summons in Matthew 5:48, "be perfect, just as your Father in heaven is perfect," and in Luke 6:36, "be merciful, just as your Father also is merciful." It is in this analogy of human life with the life of God that the image shines forth: the image of God in man does not come to expression in "awe-inspiring and spectacular deeds;" rather, it is seen in the sanctification of God's people, in their daily life in community as they conform to Christ in his life of obedient service.

In this connection, Berkouwer underlines the fact that our understanding of the image of God in the renewed community must be held in "unbreakable relation"[32] to Jesus Christ as himself the image of God. It is in the glory of Jesus Christ, and especially his glory in the gospel, that the splendor of God's glory becomes visible. And it is the privilege of man in the restored community in Christ to reflect the perfections of our Lord, as we undergo continuous renewal in his image.

Berkouwer acknowledges that the fulfilment of this likeness to God can only be eschatological. Nonetheless, as 1 John 3:2 insists, "now we are children of God," and as his children, we bear his image. The image is the call to the true destiny of the human race—in being conformed to Christ.

PRACTICAL APPLICATION

(1) We must cultivate relationship with God. An image is a reflection. When we look into a mirror we see our own face looking back at us. God sees in us a reflection of his own being, and we look back at him, in a more profound way than the reflection of our face in the mirror looks back at us. We truly gaze into the eyes, into the heart, of the God whom we resemble.

As the image of God, we were made for relationship with him. The biblical word for relationship is "fellowship" (*koinōnia*). It has to do with intimate sharing. We were created, as none of the other creatures were, for intimacy with our maker. The fact that we are able to have fellowship with the triune God ought to overwhelm us with astonishment. There is

32. Berkouwer, *Man*, 107.

always a danger that we stop short at a merely theoretical understanding of fellowship with God, and fail to plumb its depths as a reality in our experience. We should daily be going deeper into fuller and fuller intimacy with our heavenly Father.

(2) We must also cultivate relationships with other people. We have seen that relationality is part of what is meant by the divine image in man. Since the nature of God himself is focused in his mercy, our response, as his image, must be to put mercy into practice in all our dealings with other people. In human relationships, sin often leads to misunderstanding and hurt. How we react will often be the test of how well we have appreciated the way that God has made us as beings designed to reflect his mercy. To fail to live mercifully is to live contrary to our true nature as human beings.

(3) We must show respect for every other human being as a person created in the divine image. When you see God's image in every person who stands before you, all mistreatment of our fellow human beings, whether physical, verbal, or social, is ruled out. Moreover, the fact that our entire human constitution is created in God's image confers great dignity on the human body. It reminds us that the body is not some addendum to real humanity which can lightly be discarded; human bodies, our own, and those of other people, must be treated with respect.

(4) In Genesis 9:6 God imposed the death penalty for murder. Murder is such a serious crime, not only because it robs a fellow human being of life, but even more because it is a direct attack on the image of God, and therefore a head-on assault on God himself. The theory of evolution, with its claim that man has emerged from lower life forms, undermines human worth. It leads to forms of murder such as abortion and euthanasia. The idea of evolution is completely ruled out by God's revelation of man's origin.

(5) We must accept our calling to care for creation. God first placed man in his world to tend and keep it. That remains man's task in the world, and it affirms the genuine dignity in all forms of work. It also mandates science, research, experimentation, exploration, and discovery.

Do we become anxious as the boundaries of human knowledge and achievement are pushed further and further back? Do we fear that man is starting to "play God"? We need not usually worry. Generally, technological progress is simply man fulfilling his calling as the image of God with caring dominion in the world. Of course, knowing that we care for the world as God's delegates should put a restraint on the callous, uncaring approach to creation to which godless philosophies lead. But it should also excite us to discover as much as we possibly can about the workings of God's universe.

(6) We must remember that we exist under the authority of our creator. God gave a law to the first man and woman. He also wrote his moral law on their constitution. We still bear that moral law in our hearts. Moreover, that same law has been spelt out in the word of God. As creatures, we are accountable to our maker, and must endeavor constantly to abide by the law which he has given. This applies to individuals, communities, and nations. The alternative to obedience is to face judgment and death. As faithful citizens, God's people must constantly call the people around us back to the principles of God's word. However, God's law now serves to expose our failure and our inherent sinfulness. It therefore drives us to Christ for salvation and power from the Holy Spirit to live a new life in him.

(7) All idols must be abolished. Since we are the image-bearers of God, we must totally reject any form of idol worship. Physical idols made of wood or stone have no place, and any superstitious use of icons or pictures must be rejected. Equally, we may not concoct mental images of God devised by our fallen human imagination, nor idolize money or material things.

(8) We are to live continually to the glory of God. When the Pharisees asked Jesus whether or not they should pay taxes to the Roman authorities, he replied by asking for a coin. He showed them the image of Caesar on the coin, and said, "Render to Caesar the things that are Caesar's, and to God the things that are God's" (Mark 12:17). Just as the coin is Caesar's property because it carries his image, so man belongs to God, because we bear his image. To render to God what belongs to him is to live every moment for his glory.

PART TWO: MAN AS SINNER

BIBLICAL FOUNDATION

We face a difficulty at this point. The whole Bible after Genesis 2 tells the story of God's dealings with man as sinner. We therefore have to be very selective in deciding which passages to focus on as key texts.

Old Testament

Genesis 3

This chapter is fundamental for this subject: it explains how sin first entered the world. It describes the serpent's temptation of Eve and the fall of Adam. We shall expound its teaching under three main headings.

THE NATURE OF SIN

In essence sin is disobedience to God's command. 1 John 3:4 says, "sin is lawlessness," thus defining sin by reference to God's law. The attempt is sometimes made to trace a gradual fall into sin in Eve's interaction with the serpent in the early verses of the chapter, which reaches its climax in the act of disobedience in verse 6.[33] However, this is unwise. To be tempted is not yet to sin. Not until the fruit of the forbidden tree was actually eaten did the fall take place. At any point prior to that Adam and Eve could have pulled back and resisted the temptation.

In Romans 1:25 the apostle Paul says that man has "exchanged the truth of God for the lie, and worshipped and served the creature rather than the creator." This summarizes what happened at the fall. In taking the forbidden fruit, Adam and Eve turned their eyes away from the creator, giving to what God had made the place in their priorities which he alone should occupy.

Although it was not until the moment of disobedience that sin occurred, we certainly see in the tempter's strategy a deliberate plot to achieve that reorientation away from God. The temptation came from a serpent, identified in verse 1 as one of God's creatures: Eve is being manipulated into looking downwards, away from the creator to the creation. In the serpent's use of the word "indeed" (*'ap kî*) in verse 1, "there is possibly a touch of scepticism or at least surprise."[34] No doubt this is intended to sow the seed of doubt and so disincline Eve to keep her eyes on the LORD. In verse 5 the serpent offers Eve the possibility of being like God, a condition which would make continuing to serve and worship him superfluous.

By verse 6 the woman is being lured into craving what is good, pleasant, and desirable, and to chase after wisdom. However, she is being

33. E.g., Kline, "Genesis," 84.
34. Wenham, *Genesis*, 73.

enticed to seek it independently of God, in created things alone, as if the creation were a self-contained source of human fulfilment.

We have to consider the connection of Satan with the snake, and the role of Satan in the fall of man. Later Scriptures identify the snake with Satan. For example, Revelation 12:9 speaks of "that serpent of old, called the Devil and Satan." Satan dressed himself up in the serpent in order to achieve his aim.

In verse 4 the serpent contradicts God's warning of death in the event of disobedience. We are reminded of Jesus' words about the devil:

> he was a murderer from the beginning, and does not stand in
> the truth, because there is no truth in him. When he speaks a lie,
> he speaks from his own *resources*, for he is a liar and the father
> of it (John 8:44).

The devil lies in order to murder. He appears to have human benefit at heart, but this is just a "cunning" way of seducing human beings to their death.

This chapter also arouses our curiosity about the nature and timing of Satan's own fall. The Bible has very little to say on this subject. Passages like Isaiah 14:12–15 and Ezekiel 28:12–17 may possibly have a secondary reference to the fall of Satan, though Ellison disputes even this,[35] but in the first instance they are very clearly talking about Babylon and Tyre.

THE CONSEQUENCES OF SIN

In Genesis 3 we see how sin brings tension, friction, and hostility, and so disrupts the original harmony. Adam and Eve immediately tasted the bitterness of disappointment. The serpent had told them that their eyes would be opened and they would be like God (verse 5); however, when their eyes are opened, all that they see is that they are naked (verse 7). What a let-down!

Harmony now breaks down in man's relationship with God. Adam and Eve hide from God, naming fear as their motivation for this (verses 8, 10). Burdened now with a sense of guilt, they no longer welcome fellowship with their creator.

Moreover, the function of creation is distorted as a result of human sin: in verse 8 "the trees that God created for man to look at (2:9) are now

---

35. Ellison, *Ezekiel*, 108–9.

his hiding place to prevent God seeing him."[36] This is an illustration of the abuse of creation, the lack of harmony between man and his environment, which is the fruit of sin.

Very soon, human relationships are plunged into tension. In verse 12 the man blames the woman for the fall into sin. He tries to dodge personal responsibility. This becomes a perennial feature of human behavior: "people are inclined to justify their conduct by pointing to the circumstances and fate that God has allotted to them in life."[37]

God then responds to human disobedience by subjecting creation to the curse. Childbirth and food production will become painful experiences. The growth of weeds means that work, rather than being pleasurable service, becomes a frustrating chore (verses 16–19).

Finally, in verse 19, the LORD announces that man shall eventually die. The warning issued back in Genesis 2:17 had been no idle threat. It is true that physical death did not come instantaneously, but nevertheless, mortality is from now on an inescapable part of the human constitution. Survival is destined to become a struggle, and eventually death will defeat every person. Moreover, spiritual death did occur at that moment: there is now an impenetrable barrier between all human beings and their Creator.

THE PERMANENCE OF SIN

Genesis 3 should not be read as a pattern of every sinner's experience, despite the fact that some writers see it as symbolic of the temptations which we can face today.[38] It recounts the unrepeatable historical event by which sin first entered the world, with all its dire consequences for the human race. "Once sin happened, human history was forever changed."[39] Since Adam and Eve, no other human being has started with the same advantages that they had.

In verse 21 God provides clothes for the now sinful couple. Clothes are a reminder that sin is a permanent feature of human being. To be undressed is now a source of shame. This is where so-called naturists or nudists go wrong: to dispense with clothing is to claim to be sinless, and is therefore to live in contradiction of reality.

36. Wenham, *Genesis*, 76.
37. Cassuto, *Genesis*, 157.
38. E.g., Youngblood, *Genesis*, 53.
39. Leith, *Doctrine*, 105.

Every subsequent generation has begun life already in sin. The consequences of sin depicted in this chapter do not begin for each of us at the moment of our first personal sin. They are part and parcel of our situation in the world into which we are born. The expulsion from the garden represented an irreversible change in the human situation.

The biblical doctrine of man as sinner speaks of original sin and original guilt. We have inherited a human nature now corrupted and no longer in its pristine condition. Hence we are all guilty sinners from the moment our life begins at conception. Adam was the head and representative of the human race, and we were present in the garden "in his loins" (cf. Heb 7:10). He failed, and we all failed in him. Pollute a spring, and the whole river will be polluted. The human race now springs from a polluted source. Sin is a permanent reality in human life.

Genesis 6

In addition to that foundational account of the entrance of sin into the world, several other texts are worth mentioning which have a bearing on man's present sinful condition. We start with Genesis 6.

In verses 11–13 we have references to corruption and violence. We see such things constantly in the world in which we live. Governments are so often blighted by endemic failure. Terrorism threatens global stability. On a more personal level, various forms of cheating and cruelty take place. Verse 5 traces these things back to their root. The LORD is said to have seen the greatness of man's wickedness, "and *that* every intent of the thoughts of his heart *was* only evil continually." This is God's permanent assessment of human life since the fall, and all the violence and corruption throughout the world is the inevitable outcome of the inner life of man as sinner. Great wickedness stems from the evil heart.

The heart is the center of the human personality. It is the source of all our thinking and decision-making, our ideas, our planning. That is why this verse speaks of the intent of the thoughts of the heart, a phrase which speaks of human forethought by which behavior patterns are shaped and moulded.

But what a devastating critique of the human heart we are given here! Every intent and thought—with no exceptions whatsoever—is only evil: nothing but evil characterizes the human heart. And this is so continually: it is true all the time; there is no let-up, even for a moment, in the evil government of the human heart. Sin is an all-embracing reality which leaves no aspect of human life free from depravity. We might compare the words of Jeremiah 17:9, which also stress the deceit and rottenness at the center of human personality: "The heart *is* deceitful above all *things*, and desperately wicked; who can know it?"

Genesis 8:21

The common consent of the whole Bible concurs in this unfavorable assessment of man as sinner. The words of Genesis 6:5 are found in the preamble to the account of the judgment of the flood. After the flood we find that nothing has changed as far as the heart of sinful man is concerned. Now the LORD again makes a very similar statement: "the imagination of man's heart *is* evil from his youth."

We might feel inclined to protest at the severity and universality of this stricture. Surely even fallen man is capable of some good. That is true, though, as Brock and Sutanto have ably pointed out, this has to be traced not to some vestiges of good in man, but to the common grace of God.[40] From his point of view every action and every thought of man as sinner is tainted by evil. So the very best of which man is capable falls far short of any divine approval. Isaiah 64:6 puts it like this: "We are all like an unclean *thing*, and all our righteousnesses *are* like filthy rags." Even the worthiest human actions, now that we are sinners, are ultimately stinking, revolting and filthy, because of that deep-seated and incurable uncleanness which lies at the root of our being.

Psalm 51

When David, confronted by the LORD's challenge through Nathan the prophet, came to realize the guilt of his sin of adultery with Bathsheba followed by his murder-by-proxy of her husband Uriah, recorded in 2 Samuel 11, he wrote this Psalm.

The different terms which David employs in relation to his sin are significant. He speaks of his "transgressions" (*peša'*) [verses 1 and 3], his "iniquity" (*'āwôn*) [verse 2], and his "sin" (*ḥaṭṭā't*) [verses 2 and 3], and also uses the verb "sinned" (*ḥāṭā'*) [verse 4]. He attributes to his action the description "evil" (*ra'*) [verse 4]. In so doing he paints a picture of himself

---

40. Brock and Sutanto, *Common Grace, passim.*

as a rebellious, perverse, guilty wretch. At the end of verse 4 he acknowledges that God is just when he speaks, and blameless when he judges: he faces up to the fact that he is legitimately under God's judgment.

In verse 5 he adds, "I was brought forth in iniquity, and in sin my mother conceived me." David recognizes that his specific sin, like all sins, was an expression of the depravity of nature into which everyone is born. We do not become sinners by sinning: we sin because we are sinners by nature.

The words of verse 5 are crucial for a full understanding of the biblical doctrine of man as sinner. They are the key to the doctrine of original sin. The sad truth is that we originate as sinners. Sin is present in each of us from the moment of our personal origin, the moment of our conception within our mother's womb. This is God's devastating critique of humanity: each of us is "a sinner simply as a result of one's natural human descent."[41] No sin, however heinous, is merely a freak event. Every sin can be traced to its root in the human nature in which our personal existence shares.

New Testament

In the New Testament, there is such a wealth of material relevant to the theme of man as sinner that we shall have to be very selective. We shall focus on two key passages.

Romans 5:12–21

This is a complex passage, but we can tie its threads together in four statements.

THE ENTRY OF SIN INTO THE WORLD CAME ABOUT AS THE RESULT OF ONE ACTION BY ONE MAN

Verse 12 says that sin entered the world through one man, who is identified as Adam in verse 14, which also speaks of his transgression. Verses 15, 17, and 18 all refer to the one offense committed by one man, and verse 19 to "one man's disobedience."

41. Eichrodt, *Theology*, 268, n. 3.

These are all allusions to the initial sinful deed done in the Garden of Eden by Adam. That one event is the root of all the corruption and deviancy, and of every single sinful act, word, thought, desire, attitude, which has afflicted the world of men ever since. The four different words used combine to give a fuller picture of what sin entails.

(1) "Sin" (*hamartia*) means to miss the mark, and so suggests that sin entails failing to attain to a standard of achievement.

(2) "Transgression" (*parabasis*) is connected with the idea of deviation, so comparing sin to turning off the proper path and taking a wrong direction.

(3) "Offense" (*paraptōma*) conveys the thought of tripping up: sin involves stumbling along, and failing to make proper progress along the path that is right.[42]

(4) "Disobedience" (*parakoē*) exposes the source from which disobedience results, namely inattentive hearing.[43]

FROM THAT ONE EVENT SIN HAS INFECTED EVERY HUMAN BEING THROUGHOUT HISTORY

Verse 12 ends with the words "all sinned." The tense of the verb is aorist. It points to the primal sin of Adam, but regards it as the sin of every human being; we all fell in that initial fall. Adam's disobedience was not merely the pattern to which we all foolishly conform. Rather, Adam's fall was the moment when human nature itself was thrown off course. The entire human race fell on that day. Harrison explains this by reference to "the solidarity of mankind." He notes that the whole human race was in Adam; therefore, "what he did, his descendants, who were still in him, did also."[44]

Verse 19 makes the same point. By Adam's sin "the many were made sinners." "The many" here contrasts with "the one," and means all. All people were "made" sinners in the sense that "sinner" is the category into which they were placed.

---

42. Bauder, "Sin," 585.
43. Mundle, "Hear, Obey," 172.
44. Harrison, "Romans," 62.

THE RESULT OF THE ENTRY OF SIN THROUGH ADAM WAS THAT THE JUDGMENT OF DEATH CAME UPON EVERY HUMAN BEING

Verse 16 tells us that judgment followed hard on the heels of sin. But judgment (the Greek word is *krima*) may be favorable or unfavorable according to the circumstances. It stresses the need for a judicial decision one way or the other. So an immediate clarification of the situation is given: the sentence was condemnation (*katakrima*)—God's judgment was against the human race. In God's *krima*, the human race was found guilty. Verse 18 repeats this point.

What that sentence of condemnation leads to is also spelt out. Verse 12 says that sin brought death. Verse 21 says that sin reigned in death. Verses 14 and 17 tell us that death reigned. Death is sin's inseparable companion, and it conquered everywhere. Death spread to all people (verse 12); sin brought death to everyone (verse 21). It is not only sin which is universal. The effects of sin are universal too.

SIN AND DEATH ARE REALITIES EVEN WHERE GOD'S LAW IS UNKNOWN

Romans 5:13 says that "sin is not imputed when there is no law." In the absence of law you cannot calculate sin. Back in chapter 3 Paul has already stressed that the knowledge of sin comes through the law (verse 20). We can only define sin because God's law tells us what it is. However, even before God gave the law, sin was present in the world. The evidence is that during the period between the fall and the law-giving at Sinai, everyone still died, even though they had not sinned by breaking a specific commandment as Adam did (verse 14). God's judgment and sin's evil effects do not depend on clarity of definition.

These observations have clear implications for those today who are ignorant of God's law. They cannot excuse their sinfulness. And the proof that they cannot is that they still die.

In verse 20 Paul notes that "the law came in to increase the trespass"—to make it abundantly clear what sin is. The purpose was to ensure that people recognize that they have no excuse, to make it impossible for anyone to accuse God of injustice.

Ephesians 2:1–3

Here we find a succession or words and phrases which bring out the total devastation of the human personality by sin. We may make ten points.

MAN AS SINNER IS DEAD IN TRESPASSES AND SINS

Imagine a situation where noise and hubbub abounds. Workmen are in the street and their pneumatic drills are at maximum power. The children are laughing and shouting as they play their games. Pop music is blaring out of the radio full blast. And in the corner Granddad is snoozing soundly in his armchair. He is totally oblivious of all that is going on around him. We might say that he is "dead to the world."

When the apostle speaks of us as "dead in sin," that is the kind of picture that we must see. All around us creation shouts at us that God made it. The gospel is preached, crying out the offer of untold blessings in Christ. Our own conscience bellows at us that we need to repent of our godlessness. And yet we are dead to it all. We are sound asleep in unbelief.

A dead man is totally devoid of all ability. And there is nothing whatever that sinful man can do which counts for anything with God.

MAN AS SINNER LIVES AS A MATTER OF COURSE IN HIS SIN

In verse 2 Paul says that the sinner "walks" in sinful ways. Walking is a perfectly ordinary activity, and sin is our totally normal behavior. There is nothing out of the ordinary about the worst excesses in human vileness.

MAN AS SINNER FOLLOWS THE AGE OF THIS WORLD

The word "course" translates *aiōn*, which literally means age. The present age is being contrasted with the age to come. The present age is characterized by sin and death, and man is part and parcel of this current set-up. We are not mere victims of contemporary sinfulness. We are participants. We wholly belong.

The word "world" (*kosmos*) means human life structured without reference to God, indeed in opposition to God. The world is the godless organization of life. It describes the way in which man actively pursues godlessness in the entire framework of his life.

Man as sinner follows Satan

"The prince of the power of the air" is Satan. Demonic powers are here pictured as hovering in the atmosphere above the earth. The point of the metaphor is the ever-present proximity of evil power, and therefore the constancy of its influence.

Man is egged on in his sinfulness by Satan. We are not merely oppressed victims of Satan's malice, any more than we are the victims of the age of the world. The fact that we walk according to the prince of the power of the air implies voluntary choice. Man has deliberately aligned himself with the authority of the devil. We willingly side with evil in the cosmic battle against God. Satan is the democratically elected leader of fallen man.

Men as sinners are sons of disobedience

This means that disobedience is the primary feature of human life. As in the Garden of Eden, disobedience to God's commandments is the essence of sin. Having first got a foothold in human nature, disobedience has now totally taken over. As a result, constant, heartfelt, loving obedience to God is now a sheer impossibility.

The sinfulness of man is a universal condition

The word "all" in verse 3 rules out the idea that there might be any exceptions to this general truth.

Man as sinner is dictated to by fleshly lusts

The apostle speaks in verse 3 of our conduct taking place "in" the lusts of the flesh. In other words, fleshly lusts form the entire environment in which we move. The word "flesh" is a summary term for human nature in all its aspects. But human nature is out of control, because it is controlled by lust.

"Lust" (*epithumia*) is not necessarily a negative term, although in the majority of its New Testament uses it is employed in a negative way. The corrupted urges of fallen, sinful human nature direct what the sinner decides to do.

MAN AS SINNER DOES JUST WHAT HE PLEASES

Verse 3 continues with the observation that man as sinner carries out the desires of his flesh and his mind. Physical drives and ideas stemming from within man are what dictate our way of life. And all such drives and ideas arise out of the sinful nature. Consequently, man's course of life is intrinsically sinful. There are no inner depths of human nature left untainted by sin. Even the thoughts which control our actions are corrupt. So sin permeates the entire person.

MAN AS SINNER IS LIABLE TO GOD'S ANGER

Verse 3 describes human beings as "children of wrath." Wrath is what we deserve because of our rebellion against God. The entire life of man is now lived under the threatening cloud of God's righteous anger and the just judgment to come.

EVERY INDIVIDUAL HUMAN BEING IS SINFUL FROM BIRTH

This point is brought out by two phrases in verse 3. First, our position under God's wrath is said to be true "by nature." We did not come under that wrath gradually as time went by. We did not acquire the status "children of wrath" during the process of living and sinning. Our condition of liability before God comes about through our birth as human beings who are already sinners. Second, the words "just as the others" emphasize that no one at all can exempt himself from these indictments. "The others" refers to the whole of the rest of the human race. Every one of us is sinful. There are no exceptions.

The point is that sins express a sinful nature. They do not create it. The doctrine of original sin is indeed a correct exposition of biblical truth. We were all sinful from the moment of our origin. We all, without exception, originated as sinners. Human nature is now innately sinful. We have all inherited sinfulness from Adam as a result of the fall. Therefore, in its natural condition, humanity itself cannot escape God's wrath.

Andrew Lincoln makes a point which we must not overlook as we conclude our study of these key biblical texts about man as sinner:

> "By nature" should not of course be taken to mean that sin-
> fulness is of the essence of human nature . . . . Sin is always
> abnormal, a disorder, but in a fallen world the natural condi-
> tion of human beings involves experience of that abnormality
> and disorder.[45]

This is an important observation. This is why we have had to divide the doctrine of man into two parts. Man as sinner is not what the essence of created humanity ought to be. That is why we speak of fallen man: man has fallen from what he was made to be. Man as sinner is less than fully human according to the created essence of human nature.

DOCTRINAL FORMULATION

The Early Creeds

There is nothing specific to the doctrine of man as sinner in the early Christian creeds. However, there are some hints of the doctrine in the context of teaching on other subjects. That the human race is solidly sin-ful is an obvious implication of certain other truths proclaimed in the creeds. We can mention five things.

To be human is to need salvation

Both the Nicene Creed and the Chalcedonian Definition define the com-ing of Christ as "for us men and for our salvation." This phrase empha-sizes the fact that to be human is to be in need of salvation. Being human entails lostness and helplessness.

Man is a sinner in need of forgiveness

The Apostles' Creed affirms, "I believe . . . in the forgiveness of sins." The fact that such a statement is a plank in an ancient summary of the Christian faith indicates that the reality of human sinfulness is a basic truth. Man is a creature with sins that need to be forgiven.

The centrality of this truth is emphasized by a brief creed of the Ethiopian Coptic Church, dating from around AD 160. It sees the five loaves in the miracle of the feeding of the five thousand as symbols

---

45. Lincoln, *Ephesians*, 99.

of the five main truths in the Christian faith. While this is excessively imaginative, it is, nonetheless, instructive to note which five truths are listed. They are belief "in the Father, the ruler of the universe, and in Jesus Christ our Redeemer, and in the Holy Spirit, and in the holy Church, and in the forgiveness of sins."[46]

The forgiveness of sins is as foundational a doctrine as the three divine persons. Human sinfulness is the underlying assumption of the entire Christian system of truth.

The Nicene Creed acknowledges "one baptism for the remission of sins." This link with baptism is echoed in a statement in the Letter of Barnabas: "We go down into the water full of sins and uncleanness."[47] The word rendered "full of" (*gemō*) is used in classical Greek of loading a ship with cargo.[48] Man as sinner is absolutely laden with sin. Sin is the cargo we carry with us wherever we go. There is not even the tiniest area of the human personality where evil is not lurking. This same word is found in the New Testament when Jesus condemns the Pharisees because they are "full of greed and wickedness" (Luke 11:39; cf. Matt 23:25).

Kelly refers to the teaching given to baptismal candidates prior to their baptism during the second half of the second century. The emphasis was on "the release from the burden of sin, brought about by baptism."[49] The early Christians clearly saw that sin is a burden, a load, an intolerable weight that crushes and destroys fallen man.

Man stands under the divine judgment

The Apostles' Creed and the Athanasian Creed both say that Christ "shall come again to judge the living and the dead." The Athanasian Creed adds the observation that "all men . . . shall give account for their own works."

As in the Bible, the concept of judgment can refer simply to the objective assessment which could turn out either positively or negatively. However, the word comes to the fore in connection with sin, and the fact that man stands under God's just sentence of condemnation for his disobedience and rebellion.

---

46. J. N. D. Kelly, *Creeds*, 82.

47. Barnabas, 11.11.

48. Baldwin, "*gemō*," 743.

49. J. N. D. Kelly, *Creeds*, 162.

Human life ends in death

This fact is implied by the references to the resurrection of the body in the Apostles' Creed and the resurrection of the dead in the Nicene Creed, as well as by the slightly longer statement of the Athanasian Creed: "all men shall rise again with their bodies." The expectation of the resurrection assumes the fact of death. And, according to Scripture, death presupposes sin.

Sinfulness is a universal human phenomenon

The fact that sin afflicts all people universally and without exception is implied by a statement in the Chalcedonian Definition which says that Christ was, "as regards his manhood, like us in all respects, apart from sin." These words point to the fact that the rest of those included in the term "us" are sinners. Christ is unique in this respect. For the rest of mankind, sin is a universal reality.

The Reformation Confessions

There is a huge amount of relevant material in the confessions—far too much to be able to mention it all. We shall give a synthesis of the teaching of the various confessions, making 11 main points.

The sinfulness of the human race stems from Adam's rebellion

Under this heading, five themes may be listed.

THE ORIGINAL SIN WAS ADAM'S DISOBEDIENCE

The confessions summarize the biblical teaching: the woman was deceived by the serpent, and the man obeyed the woman's voice. But Satan was using the serpent as his instrument, and in obeying his wife, Adam disobeyed God. The original sin was the transgression of the creator's commandment.

As a result of his disobedience, Adam fell from his first condition of excellence

Adam fell into sin. The use of "fall" terminology indicates that man as sinner is in an inferior position to man as created. Sin involves loss. In the fall our first parents "lost all their excellent gifts," as the Belgic Confession puts it. The Second Helvetic Confession says that they "abandoned goodness and righteousness." To speak of the abandonment of these things indicates that this was no mere misfortune, but rather the deliberate rejection of pristine excellence.

Through Adam's sin, sin and death spread to all his descendants

The opening words of the Canons of Dort assume this New Testament truth: "As all men have sinned in Adam."

The guilt of the original sin is imputed to all people

The Westminster Confession includes the statement that our first parents, "being the root of all mankind, the guilt of this sin was imputed . . . to all their posterity."

Human nature was corrupted, and this corruption is passed on from generation to generation

In this sense "original sin" pervades the whole human race. That is to say, every human being is originally sinful, sinful from the time of his or her personal origin.

Several of the confessions stress the point that original sin is not the mere imitation by each generation of their parents. Rather, it is something hereditary. Infants are infected from the womb. The Canons of Dort make the point that this "propagation of a vicious nature" is an act of divine judgment.

Human nature is now fundamentally corrupted

The corruption of nature is described as "innate." Corruption is not something which just happens to become attached to the nature of a person in the process of exposure to a corrupt environment. It is present from conception.

Moreover, every human being is now wholly defiled in all the faculties and parts of soul and body. This rules out any exclusions, either of location or of degree.

In this connection, the word "depraved" is often used. It highlights the perversity at the very heart of man, the perversity in which man is totally immersed. A string of words is used to convey the utter corruption of human nature, including vain, perverse, wicked, and rebellious. Our natural inclination is always towards sin, and the image of God in human life has been utterly defaced.

Four other phrases are used in the confessions to convey the sense that human nature has been totally wrecked. We are dead in sin, servants of sin, slaves of Satan, and the subjects of death and calamity.

A corrupt nature gives rise to corrupt practice

Actual sins arise from original sin. Original sin is the root out of which grow the sad fruits of actual transgressions. Man is now averse to all good, and given over to all iniquity. Even what good remains in human life is constantly tainted by vice.

This corruption of nature is all-embracing

Every aspect of the human constitution is depraved by sin. Four aspects of this depravity may be noted in particular.

Man is afflicted by moral inability

Man now has no power to apply himself to good works. Of ourselves we are unable to do good, or even to think anything good. This sounds uncompromisingly absolute, but we must clarify what it means. This has been done in two ways. First, the Canons of Dort say that man is "incapable of any saving good." It is obviously true that men and women are capable of heroic feats of goodness. We observe many good deeds in human life and society constantly. It would be quite wrong to deny it. The point is that we are totally unable to be good enough to save ourselves from sin and misery. However, the second approach, developed particularly by the fathers of neo-Calvinism, Abraham Kuyper and Herman Bavinck, is perhaps more satisfactory. It is the recognition that all the goodness that continues in human life is a fruit of God's common grace, restraining the depravity which, otherwise, would be capable of nothing good whatsoever.[50]

MAN'S WILL IS NOT FREE TO CHOOSE GOOD OR EVIL

It is true that there is a "natural liberty" of the will, in the sense that no one is forced or determined to do anything in particular. However, the human will is no longer free to will what is good. Since the will is directed by a corrupted human nature, all that it can freely will is evil.

MAN'S MIND IS BLINDED

As a sinner, man's understanding is darkened. Consequently, he lives persistently in ignorance.

MAN'S SPIRITUAL PERCEPTION IS DESTROYED

Man as sinner has lost the light of God. He has no power in himself to know God properly. The Irish Articles say: "the condition of man after the fall of Adam is such that he cannot turn and prepare himself by his own natural strength and good works, to faith and calling upon God."

Sin has turned man into the enemy of God

The first sin is characterized as a revolt. In the Garden of Eden, Adam and Eve conspired against the sovereign majesty of God. Ever since that first sin, man has lost communion with God. All people are now alienated from God, in enmity against God, and prone to hate God. We have separated ourselves from God.

50. Cf. Brock & Sutanto, *Common Grace, passim.*

Sin has brought calamitous consequences upon the human race

All people are now children of wrath. We face experiences of wrath, both temporal and eternal.

Temporal experiences of wrath

The confessions mention two things in this category. (1) The effects of the curse which God imposed on the world in Genesis 3 are still evident. These include all the evils that afflict us, not only physically, but also as regards our reputation, or in the context of property, relationships, or work. À Brakel lists the following examples of such evils: "bodily want, sickness, discomfort, pestilence, war, times of scarcity."[51] All people everywhere live under this curse. (2) Eventually life ends in physical death, and this is a sign of God's wrath.

The eternal experience of wrath

The whole human race is under God's just condemnation. The Westminster Larger Catechism explains eternal death like this:

> the punishments of sin in the world to come are everlasting separation from the comfortable presence of God, and most grievous torments in soul and body, without intermission, in hell fire forever.

The confessions recognize that all sins are not of equal weight, even though they all arise from the same source. The corruption and unbelief which now lies at the heart of human nature is the fountain from which all sins spring. Nevertheless, some sins are more serious than others. However, the very least sin makes the offender liable to eternal condemnation.

God is not the author of sin

We noted this emphasis when considering the doctrines of God's decree and providence. A similar point arises in connection with the historical event of the fall. God permitted the fall, having purposed to order it to his

---

51. À Brakel, 412.

own glory. However, the confessions vehemently oppose the logic that claims that God was therefore the author of the first sin.

Adam and Eve sinned through their own fault. We all sinned in them, and bear our own guilt. And to this day we may never blame God for any sin. It is true that God sometimes hardens a sinner, and, as an act of judgment, gives him over to his sin. Nevertheless, it remains the case always that the sinner initiates his own sin.

The Second Helvetic Confession describes attempts to penetrate to the reasons why God permitted the fall as "curious questions." It is beyond the wit of man to find the answers to such questions. They are therefore best left humbly to the wisdom of God.

Sin is exposed by God's law

One of God's major purposes in giving his law was to define what sin is, and so to make a person conscious of his own sin and to bring him to self-awareness as a sinner. This is often referred to as the "first use" of the law. It is well put by the Canons of Dort: "the law of the decalogue, delivered by God to His peculiar people, the Jews, by the hands of Moses, . . . reveals the greatness of sin, and more and more convinces man thereof."

Sin has corrupted, but not totally annihilated, the image of God in man

Human talent is still very evident in works of skill, in intellectual endeavor, and in the arts and sciences. This is because God, in his mercy, has not allowed his image in man to be eradicated entirely. Good order in society may be traced back to the continuing glimmerings of natural light, which still remain in man even since the fall.

The teaching of Pelagius is rejected

At the time of the Reformation Pelagianism was a live issue. The Reformers saw that the teaching of medieval Catholicism had veered off in a Pelagian direction. Several of the confessional documents explicitly mention and reject Pelagian ideas, which always resurface frequently.

One of Pelagius's teachings was that original sin is spread by imitation. He did not accept the hereditary transmission of a guilty and sinful human nature. The confessions reject his teaching at this point.

Pelagius also asserted that an evil man has sufficient free will to do good when commanded. He failed to see that the human will is subject to the corruption which has afflicted human nature in its entirety. This error is also rejected in the Reformation confessions of faith.

Salvation from this state of misery is gloriously possible

The confessions are unanimous in celebrating the fact that God has graciously provided salvation for sinful man. This marvelous provision of salvation from sin is made in Jesus Christ, the Redeemer. However, at this point we move beyond the doctrine of man as sinner and anticipate the doctrine of salvation which will concern us later.

Modern Confessions of Faith

The Confession of Faith of House Churches in China refers in passing to sin and death, but has no statement devoted to this theme. The other two confessions speak on man as sinner at greater length.

Confession of Faith of the United Church of Northern India

We find here a succinct but comprehensive summary of the doctrine of man as sinner. It is worth noting especially the following four points.

(1) The confession says that our first parents, Adam and Eve, "sinned against God." This phrase recognizes that sin is always primarily Godward. Whoever else may suffer as a result of sin, God is always the prime victim.

(2) This confession recognizes the solidarity of the whole human race in Adam, our representative head. We were "in him" in the Garden. We sinned in him and fell simultaneously with him. So now all human beings start off on the wrong foot. We begin life in this world, not only corrupt, but also already guilty. The statement tells us that this is true of "all mankind by ordinary generation from Adam." This phrase stresses how all-encompassing this state of affairs is. There is no need of some

remarkable event to line us up with sinful Adam. Just to be descended from him in the ordinary way puts us in the class of sinners.

(3) We learn that actual transgressions are an addition to a guilty and corrupt nature which we possess from conception. Actual transgressions add nothing to our sinfulness, but they do make us guilty of our own sins as well as Adam's. However, the confession wisely recognizes that there are some human beings who are not capable of adding actual transgressions to their sinful nature. Children who die in infancy are in mind.

(4) The fact that all people without exception deserve God's anger and condemnation is stressed. Here there is no qualifying clause about capability. Even the child who dies in infancy deserves God's punishment by virtue of his participation in Adam's primal, representative sin. God's wrath is faced first in some of the frustrating and painful experiences of the present life, and ultimately in endless punishment beyond the limits of the present life.

Confession of Faith of the Huria Batak Protestant

We find two sections of this confession devoted to the doctrine of man as sinner. In the first it speaks mainly of the historical origin of sin in the fall of Adam. It then moves on to address the issue of the ongoing effects of Adam's sin in human life down to the present time.

In the first of these two sections the confession declares that Adam and Eve transgressed God's commandment. It states that sin is transgression. It thus reminds us that the very heart of sin is disobedience to the word of God, and so is an act of defiance against legitimate authority.

The exact wording speaks of "the commandment which God had given." This is probably a deliberate choice of words. It emphasizes that God's single law in the Garden was a gift, because it was designed as an opportunity to perpetuate human life in its created splendor. It also reminds us that the commandment was just one of the numerous gifts which the creator showered on his first human creatures. God is a giving God, and that is what makes sin so much the more despicable. Sin is monstrous ingratitude against a generous benefactor.

The confession alludes to the role of the devil in the fall of man. It does not refer to the serpent. As far as this statement is concerned, the only important thing is that the devil instigated the temptation. The serpent was a mere instrument, and as such does not need to be mentioned.

The devil is said to have seduced man, and the source of sin is attributed to him. It was the devil's desire to lead all people into sinfulness, and he achieved this by his sinister success in luring the representative head of the human race into disobedience.

Twice there is a reference to turning away from God. Adam turned away, and the devil desires that all people should turn away from God. Since the heart of sin is disobedience to the law-giver, sin inevitably involves turning away from him. And this involves turning our backs on the one who gives so generously. It involves placing ourselves in a position of ingratitude, where we can no longer appreciate God's lavish kindness, where we cut ourselves off from a beneficial experience of God's amazing love.

As we move on to the second section we are given more detail about original sin. The result of Adam's fall was that sin has been passed on to all his descendants. We inherit sin from the time of our conception, and sin is a power which enslaves us all. We cannot avoid disobeying God's law. As a result we face judgment and eternal death.

The final paragraph of this section specifies two false doctrines which are intentionally rejected by this statement. (1) It refutes the notion that children are not sinners from birth, that the heart of a new-born baby is like a blank sheet, which may go either way. (2) It opposes the idea that sin is caused by hardship or distress, and the associated idea that no one is truly guilty, that sin is a social reality, and people are mere victims.

HISTORICAL ELABORATION

I want to consider three key people from church history who were weak on the doctrine of man as sinner—Charles Finney, Pelagius, and Jacobus Arminius. Although we shall not take them in chronological order, I trust that the order in which we consider them will form a logical continuity.

Charles Grandison Finney (1792–1875)

Finney is an important character, because his teaching and practice set much of the direction for nineteenth- and twentieth-century western Evangelicalism. However, he was unsound in his exposition of many doctrines, including the doctrine of man. With regard to the Westminster

Confession of Faith, it is said that Finney "scorned its pessimistic attitude towards human nature and progress."[52]

Finney asserted that if God commands something, then it must be possible for human nature to achieve it. He argued that, since God commands absolute perfection, therefore absolute perfection must be possible for men and women. In saying this, he was influenced by the philosopher Immanuel Kant, who insisted that obligation implies ability. However, this teaching fails to recognize the distinction between human nature as created, which was indeed able to obey God, and man as sinner, who has lost that capability.

In response to Finney, Charles Hodge said this:

> It is merely a dictum of philosophers, not of common people, that "I ought, therefore I can." Every unsophisticated heart and especially every heart burdened with a sense of sin says rather, "I ought to be able, but I am not."[53]

Finney claimed that the doctrine of original sin is both blasphemous and nonsensical. He claimed that God's holiness is impugned by the idea that he is angry with people for possessing a nature which they did not consent to receive.[54] He therefore denied that human beings possess a sinful nature, and taught that Adam led his descendants into sin only by bad example. Guilt and corruption are not inherent, but are the result of bad choices made by each person.

Finney refers to Psalm 58:3, which reads, "The wicked are estranged from the womb; they go astray as soon as they are born, speaking lies." Finney comments:

> But does this mean that they are really and literally estranged from the day and hour of their birth, and that they really go astray the very day that they are born, speaking lies? This everyone knows to be contrary to fact.

Michael Horton comments tersely that Finney's question in the first sentence of the quotation really amounts to, "Is this verse really telling us the

---

52. McLoughlin, *Introduction*, vii.
53. C. Hodge, "Finney's Lectures," 254.
54. Finney, *Systematic Theology*, 297.

truth?"[55] Finney interprets the text to mean that "the wicked go astray from the commencement of their moral agency."[56]

Because of his unquestioning confidence in human nature, Finney sees conversion as the free act of the sinner himself. Conversion is a psychological experience, which involves the right application of the laws of the mind. The work of the Holy Spirit is limited to moral influence.

Finney insisted that the sinner has a duty to change his own heart. In a sense that is true, but Finney wrongly assumes that duty implies ability. He failed to see that a powerful work of grace is necessary to give any sinner the ability to carry out this duty.

Finney's influence comes down to the present day in the emphasis on decisions. "Decisionist" evangelism acts on the assumption that the human will has the ability to decide for itself to follow Christ. It proceeds as if the human will is the one part of human nature unaffected by the fall.

Pelagius

Finney-style decisionist evangelism is merely reviving the ancient heresy associated with the name of Pelagius.

Pelagius was born around AD 350. From about 380 he was teaching in Rome, where he wrote a series of works in which he questioned a number of Christian doctrines. His teaching was popularized by one of his followers, Celestius, in a book entitled *Against the Doctrine of the Propagation of Sin*. Celestius developed six teachings here.

(1) Even if Adam had not sinned, he would still have died. Celestius saw death as a purely natural phenomenon, not as God's punishment for sin.

(2) Adam's sin harmed only himself, not the whole human race. For Celestius, there was no such thing as inherited original sin.

(3) New-born children are in the same state as Adam before the fall. Celestius denied that every person is a guilty sinner in God's sight from birth. Sin is passed on only through bad example.

(4) It is not through Adam's sin that the whole human race dies. Celestius denied that Adam had a representative role on behalf of all his descendants.

---

55. Horton, "Finney's Attacks," 387.
56. Finney, *Systematic Theology*, 296–97.

(5) The Mosaic Law is as good a guide to heaven as the gospel. Celestius believed that human beings still have the strength of will to desire what is good and to do what is right. All that is necessary is that they hear the requirements of the law.

(6) Even before the advent of Christ there were men without sin. Celestius could make this assertion because, for him, sin is only external. He did not see sinful behaviour as the fruit of a sinful heart, which is present even if there is no obviously heinous sinful behaviour.

Celestius propagated these teachings in North Africa early in the fifth century. Here Augustine and Jerome led the fight against what they saw as serious errors. In AD 418 a church council meeting at Carthage declared Pelagianism a heresy. The council upheld the following three main truths.

(1) Death is not a natural evil. Rather it is the penalty imposed on man because of Adam's sin.

(2) Every person has inherited original sin from Adam. The Council referred at this point to Romans 5:12, which teaches that "the sin of Adam has passed upon us all." Therefore even new-born children already bear the taint of sin.

(3) Grace is not given just to help us to do what we can do anyway by our own free will. Pelagianism taught that grace only makes it easier for us to fulfil God's commands, but that we could do so, albeit with greater difficulty, without grace. By contrast, the Council insisted that grace is absolutely indispensable.

Whenever we read about theological controversies the vital question to ask is, which position most accurately represents the teaching of Scripture? In this case, as always, that is the issue. Which view of fallen man most truly expounds the Bible's teaching?

It should be clear from the key passages with which this chapter began that the Council of Carthage is in line with God's word, and that Pelagianism is far adrift from biblical theology. It is certainly true that Pelagianism in all its forms, including twentieth and twenty-first-century decisionism, flatters man. However, it robs God of his sole glory in the salvation of sinners.

Jacobus Arminius and the Synod of Dort

In the late sixteenth and early seventeenth centuries there was something of a re-run of this debate within the Reformed Church of the Netherlands. Jacobus Arminius was a pastor in the Dutch Reformed Church, but he reacted against an extreme Calvinist group led by Francis Gomarus, whose teaching seemed to Arminius to turn God into a tyrant.

One of Arminius's followers, Simon Episcopius, prepared a document entitled *The Remonstrance*. It set out five points in which the Arminians disagreed with Gomarus. They were as follows.

(1) It is God's eternal purpose to save those who believe and persevere. The grace of the Holy Spirit is the essential prerequisite for faith and perseverance.

(2) Jesus Christ died to obtain redemption for all. Faith is necessary for the enjoyment of this redemption.

(3) The human race in sin is totally depraved. The sinner has no free will, and is completely unable to think, will, or do, any good, or to exercise saving faith, without regeneration.

(4) The human being is in absolute need of grace to begin, continue, and accomplish, any good. This applies even to the regenerate. However, grace is not irresistible.

(5) On the question whether a believer can, through negligence, become devoid of grace, further study of the Scriptures is necessary.

On that final point, we might note in passing that it is an admirable quality to reserve judgment on any matter pending further study, where we are as yet unsure about Scripture's teaching. There is no virtue in asserting a view without sufficient certainty that it is consistent with the biblical position.

To respond to this controversy the Synod of Dort was convened in 1619. Its reply to the five points of Arminianism had four sections. On the third of Arminius's points there was no dispute, so the Canons of the Synod dealt only with Arminius's other four points. The Synod perceived that the problem with Arminius's teaching was its inconsistency. It agreed entirely with Arminius's teaching that man is totally depraved, lacks free will, that every aspect of human nature has been ruined by the fall, to such an extent that only divine regeneration can initiate the process of renewal, and that grace must have absolute priority in salvation. In which case, surely it is inconsistent to suggest that man has sufficient natural powers to resist grace, and that God merely confers the power freely to exercise the faith which participates in the benefits of redemption—or to choose to refuse to do so.

It is, incidentally, ironic, how those who today call themselves "Arminians" often take free will as their starting point. I wonder whether they realize that they are thereby flatly contradicting Arminius!

While recognizing that some of Gomarus's emphases were too extreme, the Synod of Dort also challenged the Arminian inconsistency. It insisted that God's grace accomplishes his saving purpose irresistibly, not by tyrannical force, but by gentle wooing. However, at this point we are wandering beyond the doctrine of man as sinner. Further consideration of the Canons published by the Synod of Dort must await our study of the doctrine of salvation.

PRACTICAL APPLICATION

(1) We must maintain constant humility before God. The doctrine of man as sinner definitely humbles us before a holy God. It reminds us that we are sinners by nature, by practice, by choice. It solemnly challenges us that we have nothing to boast about in the presence of God's majestic purity. We are rebels and law-breakers. We are wilful, self-indulgent transgressors. We are utterly lost in sin, hopelessly unable to mend our ways. These realities ought to humble us to the dust.

(2) We must maintain permanent awe and wonder at God's salvation. We are hopelessly unable to save ourselves. That is true. But God has saved us. God has provided a way out of sin. God has devised a means of rescue for fallen, lost mankind. It is too easy to become merely blasé about the gospel. When we recall the devastation of our nature by sin, and the immense cost to our Savior of redeeming us, we should be truly lost in wonder, love and praise.

(3) We must practice regular repentance. Repentance is not merely part of becoming a Christian. It is a daily duty incumbent upon us as believers. Unless we foolishly dare to claim that we no longer have sins to repent of, then we need to repent all the time. We remember how 1 John 1:8 challenges us in these words: "if we say that we have no sin, we deceive ourselves, and the truth is not in us." However, verse 9 continues with this comforting promise: "if we confess our sins, he is faithful and just to forgive us *our* sins and to cleanse us from all unrighteousness." At

the beginning of the next chapter John assures us that "if anyone sins, we have an advocate with the Father, Jesus Christ the righteous."

(4) We must have compassion for all our fellow-sinners. God's grace reaches out to all the world. There is no people group and no person beyond the scope of the divine mercy in Jesus Christ. We may never look down on other people in a snooty or supercilious way. We are no different from anyone else in terms of our sinful human nature. Only God can change us. Only God can change them. If we have been changed, then they can be changed. Our proper attitude to a sinful world is one of compassion. In this respect we must imitate our Lord himself, who, "when he came out, saw a great multitude and was moved with compassion for them, because they were like sheep not having a shepherd" (Mark 6:34). Jesus' parable of the two debtors, recorded in Matthew 18:23–33, intentionally rebukes any feelings of superiority which we may wrongly entertain.

(5) We must preach the gospel in total dependence on the Holy Spirit. We must never delude ourselves into imagining that it is within our power to persuade anyone to become a disciple of Jesus. Man as sinner is totally wrecked. No one can even begin to think about repenting and believing unless the Holy Spirit first works in his heart, and overrides his natural stubborn tendency to unbelief and defiance. Whenever we proclaim the gospel, we must remind ourselves earnestly that we are mere instruments; the sole agent in the conversion of a sinner is God the Holy Spirit. We preach prayerfully, urgently requesting that it might be his gracious pleasure to use even our ministry, so totally undeserving though we are.

7

The Doctrine of the Person of Christ

WHO IS JESUS CHRIST? What is special about him? Why do we claim that he is unique? How do we account for the unusual qualities which were evident in his life? But why was there also something so gloriously ordinary about him? Such questions bring us to the issue of Christology.

The answers to these questions center around the truth that Jesus Christ is both human and divine—fully human and fully divine, not merely half and half. He is neither fully divine to the detriment of his humanity, nor fully human to the detriment of his divinity. He is not so fully human that he is only a junior god, nor so fully divine that he is an incredible superman.

This is the mystery which we now seek to understand—at least to the extent that it is possible for finite minds to grasp it.

BIBLICAL FOUNDATION

Old Testament

Jesus came in fulfilment of prophecy. The person who came had been foretold through the centuries. That is what lies behind John the Baptist's question, "are you the coming one, or do we look for another?" (Luke 7:19).

This question takes up words from the Old Testament. For example, Zechariah 9:9 says, "Behold, your king is coming to you." But what sort of person will this coming king be?

The answer is that the Old Testament expectation was for a Savior who would be both human and divine. We shall glance at a small selection of the many relevant Old Testament prophetic texts.

Genesis 3:15

This has to be the starting-point for our survey of Old Testament christological prophecy. The LORD God says to the serpent after the entry of sin into the world, "I will put enmity between you and the woman, and between your seed and her seed; he shall bruise your head, and you shall bruise his heel."

Here we find the first declaration of the gospel of salvation for sinful man. Here, in merely embryonic form, is the initial proclamation of the coming of Jesus Christ as Savior. The coming deliverer will be the seed of the woman: he will be a genuine descendant of Eve, a true human being. There is perhaps an echo of Genesis 3:15 in Galatians 4:4, which says that God's Son was "born of a woman." He was altogether human. He will come to crush Satan's power by his own suffering.

Genesis 22:18

Here it is proclaimed that in Abraham's seed "all the nations of the earth shall be blessed." This is just one representative example of a host of texts in Genesis chapters 12—24 which speak of the seed of Abraham. The Hebrew word translated "seed" is *zera'*. It is an interesting word, because it is singular in form, but it may be used either individually or collectively: it may mean either one person, or it may refer corporately to all Abraham's descendants considered as a group.

In Galatians 3:16 Paul is inspired by the Spirit to recognize that the same Holy Spirit had a definite intention in inspiring Moses, as he wrote Genesis, to use this particular word. The singular form is crucial, because ultimately Abraham's seed is one person, and it is in that one person, Jesus Christ, that all God's promises are finally fulfilled: "now to Abraham and his seed were the promises made. He does not say, 'And to seeds,'" as of many, but as of one, "And to your seed," who is Christ." And as Abraham's descendant, Jesus Christ was just as human as his ancestor was.

2 Samuel 7:12–16; 1 Chronicles 17:11–14

Jesus Christ is also the Son of David, in fulfilment of the LORD's covenant, declared to King David in these two parallel passages, that a son of his would sit on the throne forever. The very first verse of the New Testament highlights the fulfilment of this covenant prophecy, as it identifies Jesus Christ as "the Son of David," the first of sixteen occurrences of this phrase in the Gospels.

It is instructive to compare 2 Samuel 7:14–15 with 1 Chronicles 17:13. In the former text God speaks as follows:

> I will be his Father, and he shall be my son. If he commits iniquity, I will chasten him with the rod of men and with the blows of the sons of men. But my mercy shall not depart from him, as I took *it* from Saul, whom I removed from before you.

By contrast, his words are reported in the parallel verse in 1 Chronicles like this: "I will be his Father, and he shall be my son; and I will not take my mercy away from him, as I took *it* from *him* who was before you."

The Chronicler omits the words, "If he commits iniquity, I will chasten him with the rod of men and with the blows of the sons of men." He is inspired to recognize that only a human being of whom it would never be necessary to say that, only a human being who never committed iniquity, could be qualified to be king forever. This can only be possible if the promised Davidic king is also divine.

Psalm 110:1

The opening words of this Psalm are: "the LORD said to my Lord." The LORD is God's personal name, Jehovah. He addresses another, called "Lord" (*ᵃdōnī*).

Jesus took up this prophecy in Matthew 22:42–45 (cf. Luke 20:41–44). He asked the Pharisees how, if the Christ is the Son of David, David could call him "Lord." He then quoted this Psalm, and asked the reverse of his initial question: "If then David calls him 'Lord,' how is he his son?" Walter Liefeld comments:

> Jesus' question is not intended to suggest that there could not be a descendant of David who was also "Lord," but that the seemingly irreconcilable has meaning only if he is more than just a human descendant.[1]

Jesus' point was that the Christ is both David's son and David's Lord. He is a divine-human Savior.

Isaiah 7:14

Here the prophet predicts the birth of a son to a virgin. He will be a human being, and will be named Immanuel, meaning "God with us." Matthew 1:23 insists that this prophecy was fulfilled in the birth of Jesus Christ. However, implicit in this name is an affirmation that the one who comes to be with us is God himself. Jesus Christ is also a divine person.

Daniel 7:13–14

Robert Reymond points to four pieces of evidence in these verses that the one described as "like the son of man" is also divine: (1) he has free access to the Ancient of Days; (2) he comes on the clouds: this is a metaphor which is reserved for God [cf. Nah 1:3]; (3) a universal and everlasting kingdom is bestowed on him; (4) the peoples and nations offer him worship—a valid alternative translation of the word "serve" in verse 14.[2]

In referring to himself so often as "the Son of Man," Jesus was implicitly claiming to be the fulfilment of Daniel's vision, and so asserting his own dual nature as both human and divine.

New Testament

That Jesus was a normal human being was quite obvious to his contemporaries. This is clear from the scornful words spoken by the people of his home town in Matthew 13:54–56:

> Where did this *man* get this wisdom and *these* mighty works? Is this not the carpenter's son? Is not his mother called Mary? And

---

1. Liefeld, "Luke," 1018.
2. Reymond, *New Systematic Theology*, 213.

> his brothers James, Joses, Simon, and Judas? And his sisters, are
> they not all with us? Where then did this *man* get all these things?

During the first 30 years of Jesus' life his friends and neighbors at Nazareth had not noticed anything which might have given them a clue that
he was anything more than an ordinary boy.

Indeed, the humanity of Jesus was so obvious that many of his
contemporaries, assuming that his clear claims to divinity were untrue,
classified him as a blasphemer. John 19:7 informs us that the clinching
argument at Jesus' trial, as far as the Jews were concerned, was that "he
made himself the Son of God." Because, if the claim was untrue, this man
certainly deserved to die.

But the testimony of the New Testament is that the claim is not
untrue. Jesus' hearers were misguided. However, the fact that it was possible for them to misunderstand does underline how clearly human, how
gloriously ordinary, the life of Jesus was to the observation of his fellows.

We shall focus on a representative selection from the numerous
relevant New Testament passages.

Luke 1:26–35

As the angel Gabriel appears to Mary, he greets her with the news that
she is to bear a son, and call his name Jesus (verse 31). Significant divine
terminology is used of the promised son in verses 32–33:

> He will be great, and will be called the Son of the Highest; and
> the Lord God will give him the throne of his father David. And
> he will reign over the house of Jacob forever, and of his kingdom
> there will be no end.

When Mary enquires, "How can this be, since I do not know a man?"
(verse 34), the angel gives this reply in verse 35: "*The* Holy Spirit will
come upon you, and the power of the Highest will overshadow you;
therefore, also, that holy one who is to be born will be called the Son of
God."

Here is a clear assertion of Jesus' full and true deity. He is to share
God's greatness; he is to be king forever, but only God is intrinsically
eternal; he is to be God's Son, conceived by the Holy Spirit.

The virgin birth did not cause Jesus' divinity. Kenneth Kantzer
makes the point that even a holy human mother could not produce

divine offspring.[3] Isaiah 7:14, part of which is cited in Matthew 1:23, says, "The Lord himself will give you a sign: Behold, the virgin shall conceive and bear a son." The virgin birth is the sign which enables us to identify which of the many babies born by women is God's Son.

Matthew 16:15–16

When Jesus asked his disciples who people were saying that he was, they reported the popular view that he was one of the prophets. These verses explain how Jesus continued, and how Peter responded: "He said to them, 'But who do you say that I am?' Simon Peter answered and said, 'You are the Christ, the Son of the living God.'"

An ancient writer comments like this on Peter's words: "If Christ is the Son of God, by all means he is also God. If he is not God, he is not the Son of God."[4] Whether Peter yet understood the fullness of content in the term "Son of God" is uncertain. However, Matthew certainly intends his readers to understand the larger significance of the title.

John 1

At several points this chapter emphasizes both aspects of Jesus' person. The opening phrase echoes the first words of the Bible, and verses 1–3 trace the existence of Jesus Christ, "the Word," right back to the beginning, and beyond. Jesus' pre-existence as God is a recurring theme in this Gospel.

In the first two verses the eternal Word is both distinguished from "God," and yet identified with God. This presupposes the truth of the Trinity: the Word has a distinct personal identity, and yet shares the nature of God.

The phrase "the Word was God" has been the source of some controversy. In Greek there is no definite article (the word "the") before the word for "God," even though it was present in the previous phrase, "the word was with God."

Some, such as the Jehovah's Witnesses, have claimed that this shows that Jesus Christ was less than fully and absolutely God. They translate "the Word was a god."

3. Kantzer, "Christmas," 15.
4. Epiphanius, "Gospels," 45.

On the other hand, Daniel Wallace insists that we must not translate the text in such a way as to impugn the deity of Christ. He points out that in that previous phrase "God" means the Father, but that the present phrase, "the Word was God," obviously cannot mean "the Word (the Son) was the Father." The absence of the article is intended, therefore, to maintain proper trinitarian distinctions: "it stresses that, although the person of Christ is not the person of the Father, their *essence* is identical."[5]

Verses 3 and 10 insist that the Word was the Father's agent in creation. This proves that Christ was there earlier than creation itself. Creation was the beginning of everything that is not God. Christ stands emphatically on the divine side of the creator-creature distinction.

Verse 14 declares that, in Jesus, "the Word became flesh." This term embraces everything which is involved in being human. Jesus became a true human being in every aspect of what humanity is.

However, the verse continues: "we beheld his glory, the glory as of the only begotten of the Father." The phrase "only begotten" translates the single Greek word *monogenēs*. This is the first of four occurrences of the word in John's Gospel (the others are 1:18: 3:16 and 18), and it is also used in 1 John 4:9. There is some debate about its precise meaning. Should it be translated, as in the New King James Version, "only begotten," or is the simple word "only," as in many modern versions of the Scriptures,[6] more accurate?

The answer depends on how we understand *-genēs*, the second part of the word. The noun *genos*, with which it is linked, can, in some contexts, mean "kind;" if that is in the background here, then *monogenēs* would mean "unique:" it would assert that Jesus Christ is the only one of his kind, that there is no other divine Son.

However, there are several problems with this view.

First, the absence of an additional noun in John 1:14 suggests that something more is involved than the mere description of Christ's uniqueness. The modern translations which want to translate *monogenēs* merely as "only" have to add the noun "Son," even though it is not present in the original Greek. If the word means "only begotten," on the other hand, it can stand alone without another noun. Jesus is *the* begotten of the Father, not a mere creature. He is the only person who is related to the Father by being begotten, rather than by being created.

5. Wallace, *Greek Grammar*, 268–69.

6. These include, e.g., the following English translations: ESV, Holman Christian Standard Bible, The Message, NEB, NIV, RSV, TEV (Good News Bible).

A second problem arises also in the translation of John 1:18, where there is a difference between Greek manuscripts. In some *monogenēs* is followed by the word "Son," in others by the word "God." Where a translation is following the textual tradition which reads "God," to translate *monogenēs* as "only" risks compromising on the truth of the Trinity, because it has the effect of distinguishing within the verse between "the only God" and "the Father." John's point is that the Son is the only person of the Godhead who is begotten, not that he is the only God, and he is certainly not denying the deity of the Father. It is surely significant that, while the early church fathers were divided on whether John 1:18 should read "only begotten God" or "only begotten Son."[7] they were nonetheless united in translating *monogenēs* "only begotten."

Thirdly, the -*genēs* ending and the noun *genos* do not mean merely "kind." Both Classical and New Testament Greek dictionaries, while including "kind" as a subsidiary meaning, define *genos* primarily in terms of race, descent, offspring, family, and birth.[8] Furthermore, even the Classical dictionary defines *monogenēs* as only begotten.[9]

A fourth consideration is that the word *monogenēs* is used elsewhere in the New Testament of ordinary human beings. Three of these occurrences are in Luke's Gospel (Luke 7:12; 8:42; 9:38). In each case the word refers to the only son or daughter born to the parent: the translation "only" is legitimate, because the implication is obvious that the parent had begotten the child. The word also appears in Hebrews 11:17, where Isaac is described as Abraham's "only begotten." Here, as in John 1:14, there is no accompanying noun. This means that the translation "only begotten" is required: the word "only" could not stand alone there.

In the fifth place, in every passage in John's writings where *monogenēs* is used, the related verb *gennaomai*, meaning "to be born," is also present in the immediate context (John 1:13; 3:3–8; 1 John 4:7). A contrast is therefore being drawn between the temporal experience of spiritual birth on the part of believers and the eternally begotten nature of the Son in his relation to the Father. Bob Letham writes: "it is impossible to eradicate the idea of begetting from this description."[10]

7. Elowsky, *John*, 54, n. 46.

8. Liddell and Scott, *Lexicon*, 140; cf. Thayer, *Lexicon*, 113–14; Moulton, *Lexicon*, 79.

9. Liddell and Scott, *Lexicon*, 451.

10. Letham, *Trinity*, 193–97; *Systematic Theology*, 114–17.

Sixthly, in a series of extracts from ancient commentators, every reference but one to the eternal Sonship of Christ in John's writings uses "begotten" terminology rather than "uniqueness" terminology. The one exception is a comment from Augustine on 1:18, though even he translates the Greek term into Latin as "only begotten" in verse 14.[11] It is surely significant, given the modern debate about the most appropriate translation of *monogenēs*, that our spiritual predecessors who commented on these texts understood the biblical language to mean more than merely "only;" they believed that "only begotten" was the full meaning of the word selected by John. And since most of them were native Greek speakers who lived within a few centuries of the time when the New Testament was being written, they, clearly, are far better qualified to assess the meaning of the word than people who live two thousand years later in a different cultural setting, and for whom Greek is a foreign language.[12]

These considerations all point to "only begotten" as the proper translation of *monogenēs*.

Verses 15 and 30 further emphasize the pre-existence of Jesus Christ by reference to John the Baptist's statement, "After me comes a man who is preferred before me, for he was before me." We know from Luke 1:36 that John was conceived six months before Jesus, so John cannot mean that Jesus predated him in time. He must have in mind an eternal priority. And Christ's eternal priority proves his deity.

However, John's words also affirm Jesus' humanity in a striking way. The word translated "man" is *aner*. This is not a generic word for human beings, but denotes specifically a male, a man as distinct from a woman. The fact that Jesus can be described in such a way emphasizes his true humanity: man was made in God's image male and female. Elsewhere this word is used of Jesus Christ in only two other places (Acts 2:22; 17:31). Just because it is so rare, it is notable. It underlines the real masculinity, and therefore the real humanity, of Christ.

Jesus was not gender-neutral. Theologians have sometimes spoken of Christ's "impersonal humanity." The intent in using this term is good. It aims to safeguard the unity of Christ's person, and to recognize that there was no human person of Jesus with a separate existence before the Son of God assumed human nature,[13] and that the human nature never acted independently. Nonetheless, the English translation is rather

---

11. Elowsky, *John*, 42–43, 46–47, 54–55, 125–26, 128; Bray (ed.), *James–Jude*, 213.

12. Cf. Letham, *Trinity*, 197–98.

13. à Brakel, *Reasonable Service*, 504.

unfortunate.[14] Can we even conceive of a human nature which is not personal?[15] The notion seems to make Jesus' humanity different from ours, an oddity—whereas he is an authentic human personality.

Twice in this chapter (verses 34 and 49) Jesus is called "the Son of God." Leon Morris notes that the use of the definite article emphasizes that Jesus Christ is indeed the only Son of God, not one amongst others, and the title "Son of God" puts a definite stress on Christ's deity.[16]

Philippians 2:6–8

This is probably the key passage for Paul's inspired contribution to New Testament Christology. Warfield suggests that the language in which the apostle here expresses Jesus' intrinsic deity is "as strong as any that could be devised."[17] Two phrases in verse 6 demand our particular attention.

(1) "Being in the form of God." The verb is a present participle, which expresses a permanent reality. Jesus Christ has never been anything other than in the form of God. The noun "form" (*morphē*) refers to his intrinsic, essential nature. This was not something merely incidental or external. Jesus Christ is absolutely God.

(2) He "did not consider it robbery to be equal with God." The sense seems to be that Jesus did not reckon that he needed to grab this equality with God, since it was something he already possessed, because he was divine in his very nature.

The apostle is equally insistent on Jesus' genuine humanity. The bridge between the deity and the humanity of Christ is found in the statement that he "made himself of no reputation." Warfield reads the emphasis here as falling on the word "himself," which Paul has placed ahead of the verb.[18] In becoming human, Jesus did not look to his own interests (cf. verse 4). He had every right to assert equality with God, yet he willingly renounced his entitlement to the continuing enjoyment of heavenly divine glory, and came to earth as a man.

We read in verses 7 and 8 that he came "in the likeness of men" and was "found in appearance as a man." On their own these two phrases

---

14. Cf. Berkhof, *Systematic Theology*, 322.

15. Cf. J. Murray, *Systematic Theology*, 137–38.

16. L. Morris, *John*, 167.

17. Warfield, *Christ*, 39.

18. Warfield, *Christ*, 42.

might suggest that there was only a similarity between Jesus Christ and a human being, that humanity was no more than a mask, an external appearance. However, two further phrases from those verses prove that this divine being really became human.

(1) "Taking the form of a bondservant." Here we have another instance of the word *morphē*. Servanthood became the essence of Christ's being. This implies his true humanity. To be human is to be the servant of God. However, human life as we know it has failed in this purpose. In Jesus, true service of God is restored. He is the authentic man.

(2) "He humbled himself and became obedient to *the point of death.*" God cannot die. That the Son of God did die emphasizes that he became truly human.

DOCTRINAL FORMULATION

The Early Creeds

On this occasion it is worth looking at each of the four ancient creeds in turn. This will enable us to discern the development and progress in the early church's perception of the truth about Christ's unique person.

The Apostles' Creed

This creed refers to Jesus Christ as the Father's "only begotten Son, our Lord," and then tells his story, without further reflection on his being, by referring to the following eleven key moments in his history:

1. his conception by the Holy Spirit;

2. his birth of the virgin Mary;

3. his sufferings under Pontius Pilate;

4. his crucifixion;

5. his death;

6. his burial;

7. his descent into hell;

8. his resurrection on the third day;

9. his ascension into heaven;

10. his present position seated at the Father's right hand;

11. his future coming as judge of the living and the dead.

In the context of Christology (Christ's divine-human person), we need to comment on the following four elements from this creed.

(1) The use of the phrase "only begotten" picks up the New Testament term *monogenēs*. This creed does not elaborate on what it means. However, it clearly implies that there is more to be said about Jesus Christ than merely the eleven items in his history which follow. There is a super-historical dimension to his person.

(2) This point is carried further in the phrase, "conceived by the Holy Spirit." This emphasizes the truth that Jesus was never, at any moment of his historical existence, anything other than God. "What but God could have been born from God?"[19]

(3) The reason for listing these eleven key elements is to stress the reality of Jesus' human experience. Though he was God from eternity, though conceived of the Holy Spirit, yet he really did live a human life.

(4) The words "under Pontius Pilate" in connection with Christ's suffering are deliberately intended to date these events. Kelly notes that the inclusion of Pilate in the creed stresses the fact that the saving story of Jesus is rooted in history. To date the events brings out the truth that these things did not happen just anywhere at just any time, and so the Gospel message "is not simply a system of ideas."[20]

The Nicene Creed

In the Nicene Creed we see the beginning of a movement from telling the story of Jesus to reflection on his being in the light of the purpose of his story. Like the Apostles' Creed, the Nicene Creed lists key moments in the historical existence of the Lord Jesus Christ, so emphasizing his human experience. However, this is preceded by a far more elaborate statement of the divinity of our Lord Jesus Christ.

The background is the Arian controversy. Arius was a leader in an Egyptian church. In the year AD 318 he began putting forward some teaching which was soon recognized as unsatisfactory.

---

19. Alcuin, an 8th century writer, cited by J. N. D. Kelly, *Creeds*, 378.
20. J. N. D. Kelly, *Creeds*, 150.

Arius taught that God was absolutely one and absolutely transcendent. God could be neither changed nor divided, so the divine essence could not be shared. Therefore, everything other than this unique and simple God was created by him out of nothing. And this included the Son or the Word.

For Arius, the divine transcendence meant that God needed an agent to carry out his desire to create a universe. So his first act of creation was to make the Word, the Son. The Word was, therefore, a creature. He was the first of all God's creatures, a perfect creature. He was of a different order from all other creatures, but he was a creature nonetheless. Like all God's other creatures, the Word was created out of nothing. He did not participate in the essence of God.

It follows that the Son had a beginning. True, his origin was before time, but he was not eternal. Before he was created he had no existence. For Arius, the Word was God's Son by adoption, not by nature. The Father alone is true God.

The Nicene Creed was drawn up to refute Arianism. It begins by piling up phrases designed to stress the Son's true deity. We may note five things about this creed.

(1) The word "begotten" appears three times. The middle one is the word *monogenēs*: Jesus Christ is "the only begotten Son of God." The other two translate a form of *gennaomai*: he was "begotten of the Father before all worlds," and he was "begotten, not made." Taken together, these phrases emphasize the Son's eternal divinity. He is not to be compared with any other being. His begetting predates absolutely everything else, and is distinguished from creation. Emphatically, he is not a creature.

(2) There are three clauses which clearly link the Son's nature as begotten with true divinity. He is "God of God, Light of Light, true God of true God." The creed is affirming the truth that the being of the Son was derived from the being of God in a sense that no creature can be. Every creature is of God, but no creature is *God* of God. "Light of light" echoes 1 John 1:5: "God is light and in him is no darkness at all." Since the Son of God participates in that pure light, he must be unequivocally God. Therefore, he can be called "true God." The fullness of deity is present in the Lord.

(3) The Son is said to be "of one substance with the Father." He shares the identical nature with God the Father. His eternal generation was out of the Father's very being. He participates absolutely in the divine essence.

(4) The uniquely divine function of creator is ascribed to the Son: "by whom all things were made." "All things" rules out any exceptions. The Son was not responsible merely for some elements in creation: the whole creation is his work. This again sets him plainly on the God side of the distinction between creator God and his creation.

(5) The incarnation is described as his coming down from heaven. The person of the Son did not begin when he was conceived in Mary's womb, even though his human experience began then. In the human embryo, growing within his mother, the Son of God was present. Indeed, the creed states that he "was made man," so giving the priority to his deity. The very word "incarnate" implies that the divine substance is the primary reality—not in the sense that his humanity was secondary, or less than genuine, but in the sense that the divine life of the Son of God predated his human life. The truth is that the divine Son was incarnated, not that the human person was deified. Nevertheless, the creed is stressing the real incarnation of the Word. The eternal Son of God really did become fully flesh, in all the various aspects of what it is to be human in body and soul.

The Athanasian Creed

Whereas the Nicene Creed presents the deity of Christ first before turning to his incarnation as man, the Athanasian Creed discusses his Godhead and manhood in tandem under the heading of incarnation. This section of the creed begins by explaining that confession of Jesus Christ as God and man is what follows from believing in the incarnation. The two natures of Christ are then stated in four parallel clauses.

(1) He is "God of the substance of the Father . . . ; and man of the substance of his mother." The word "substance" is intended to declare the real, full deity of the Son of God, and also to emphasize the fact that Jesus was as genuinely human as his mother was.

(2) As God, he was "begotten before the worlds," while, as man he was "born in the world." Eternal generation is set alongside a temporal birth. The divine nature had no beginning, and in sharing the eternal nature of God, the Son is seen to be really, truly, fully, genuinely divine. But looked at from the human side, he had a beginning. As such, he shares the temporal, transient nature of humanity, and so is seen to be really, truly, fully, genuinely human. In his divine nature, the Son was

there before the worlds, before any part of this universe was formed. In his human nature, he appeared in the normal way, at a particular point in time, in this particular world.

(3) He is "perfect God and perfect man." This emphasizes what has already been said. The creed then adds one further point: "subsisting of a reasonable soul and human flesh." This rules out the idea that Christ's human soul was replaced by the divine nature, as Apollinarianism claimed. If that had been the case, he would not have been perfectly human.

(4) He is "equal to the Father as touching his Godhead, and inferior to the Father as touching his manhood." The second part of this statement simply recognizes that God is greater than man, and that, for the sake of incarnation, Christ accepted that subordinate place. The first part is making the important point that, even during his incarnation, the Son was never anything less than truly divine. He was not a lower ranking god as compared with the Father. He had absolute equality with the Father in nature.

The Athanasian Creed then moves on to emphasize that the two natures were united in one person. There is only one Christ. It is not that there were two separate individuals within a single form. Two ways in which this unity of person might be expressed are ruled out.

(1) There was no "conversion." It was not the case that, in coming into contact with human flesh, the divine nature was changed into something less than it was before. Nor was the human nature changed into something higher than it was before as a result of its contact with divine power.

(2) There was no "confusion." The two natures, once united in the one person of Jesus Christ, did not become a third thing, neither truly God nor truly man. Christ did not possess a unique nature, either of deified humanity or of humanized deity.

Two phrases are then used to explain how the two natures in one Christ can be a reality.

(1) Manhood was taken into God. The divine nature comes first. The Son of God assumed humanity, but in such a way that neither the humanity nor his divinity were altered.

(2) There was a "unity of person." The unity of Christ was not in his nature. At that level there was duality. But in person he was one. Jesus was not schizophrenic. He did not have a double personality. He always thought, spoke, acted as one divine-human person.

The Chalcedonian Definition

It was this formula of two natures in one person which was expounded definitively by a council of pastors who met at Chalcedon in AD 451. Chalcedon was near Constantinople, by then the capital of the Roman Empire. The council sought to define once for all the church's understanding of the person of Christ, an aim in which they were largely successful. This Definition became the standard of orthodox Christology for the whole church for the rest of time. It asserts three main points.

JESUS CHRIST EXISTED IN TWO NATURES

The Definition expounded the truth about each nature in turn.

The divine nature

This was "complete:" the whole of God-ness was present in Christ. It was also "true:" Jesus was not merely godlike; he was really divine. He was "of one substance with the Father:" there was no difference at all between the divine nature as found in the Son and as found in the Father. Christ is "the only begotten Son of God, begotten of the Father before the ages."

As in the Nicene Creed, so the two occurrences of "begotten" in this phrase render respectively the different but related words *monogenēs* and *gennaomai.* The wording makes the second statement an elucidation of the preceding clause. As the only begotten Son, Jesus Christ was distinct from the creatures in that he was not made, as they were, but is eternal, and so is genuinely God. And the Father has no other sons by eternal generation.

The true deity of Christ is emphasized in another way too. Mary is described as "the God-bearer" (*theotokos*). Some have objected to this word. It is true that it has been abused. It has sometimes been rendered "mother of God," and associated with various erroneous teachings, of which four stand out: (1) the idea of Mary's perpetual virginity—the false claim that she never had an ordinary marriage relationship with Joseph; (2) the notion of the immaculate conception—the wrong idea that Mary had no original sin; (3) the error of Mary's assumption into heaven, claiming that she was translated into heaven in body and soul to become "Queen of heaven;" (4) the fatal idea that Mary is co-redeemer along with Jesus, or that she is the mediator between the sinful soul and her son.

However, the original intention in calling Mary "the God-bearer" was sound. Because Jesus was truly God and Mary was his mother, she was the bearer of God the Son in his becoming human. The point of the description is to assert the truth that the son she bore was unequivocally God. So there is no need to object to this term.

The human nature

As with Jesus' divinity, the Definition again uses the words "complete" and "true" of his humanity. This is then further defined. Jesus, as man, consisted "of a reasonable soul and body." He was not only physically human, with a constitution that was otherwise divine. He had intellectual, emotional, and volitional capacities which were also human.

He is said to be "of one substance with us." The Athanasian Creed speaks of Christ as "of the substance of his mother." Chalcedon rightly recognizes that he participates in the identical nature shared by all people, including, but not only, his mother. This wording guards against any heresy that might claim that Mary had a different type of humanity from the rest of the world.

So Jesus Christ was like us in all respects, the only exception being that he had no sin. He had the same physical frame, the same moral nature, the same feelings. He was susceptible to pain, to fear, to all the weaknesses of the flesh. His manhood was begotten of Mary in her virgin state. Otherwise, he had a perfectly normal human birth.

JESUS CHRIST EXISTED AS ONE PERSON

The Definition describes Jesus Christ as "one person and subsistence." Although he had two natures, nonetheless he had a unified experience of life and the world.

Three times we read that he was "one and the same Son," and twice we hear that he was at one and the same time both God and man. These phrases make two points. (1) There was never a moment when Jesus Christ was not one person in two natures. (2) It is never possible to analyze whether at any particular time he was operating as God or as man, because he always acted as one united person.

The Definition adds that Christ was not "parted or separated into two persons." Psychologically he was always an integrated personality.

IN THIS ONE PERSON EACH NATURE IS PRESENT IN ITS OWN INTEGRITY

The Definition makes this point by using four terms. Two of them we have already met in the Athanasian Creed: there was no "confusion" or "change" (equivalent to the Athanasian word, "conversion") of natures. This statement adds that the two natures co-existed in Christ "without division" and "without separation."

"Without division" disallows the idea that Christ was fifty-fifty God and man. It was not that he possessed some aspects of divine nature and some elements of human nature. He was truly and totally both divine and human: he had all of each nature.

"Without separation" entails the denial that the two natures were so completely divorced from one another as to create a dual personality.

The Definition sums up by speaking of "the distinction of natures being in no way annulled by the union, but rather the characteristics of each nature being preserved."

The Reformation Confessions

The confessions accepted the christological conclusions of the early church. Their echoes of Chalcedon may be briefly summarized under six headings. However, the Reformation made two distinctive contributions to our understanding of Christ,[21] and these we shall discuss in a little more detail.

Echoes of Early Christian Christology

JESUS CHRIST IS TRUE GOD

He was the Son of God from all eternity. He was eternally begotten, not made. He was of the same substance as the Father, and therefore is equal with the Father.

---

21. Beeke & Jones, *Puritan Theology*, 347–58.

JESUS CHRIST IS TRUE MAN

He possessed a soul as well as a body. He shared the common infirmities of human life, and was capable of suffering both bodily and in his soul. He was the same substance with us. The only way in which he differed was that he was sinless: unlike us, he fulfilled the law perfectly. The confessions often say that God the Son took on human nature: although the two natures were each perfect and complete, precedence is given to the divine nature.

JESUS CHRIST WAS CONCEIVED OF THE HOLY SPIRIT AND BORN OF THE VIRGIN MARY

No work of a man was involved in his conception and birth.

IN JESUS CHRIST HIS TWO NATURES ARE DISTINCT, YET INSEPARABLY JOINED

This picks up the ancient reference to the one person of Christ, in whom each nature retains its proper characteristics. The divine nature is uncreated and infinite. The human nature is finite.

IN THE UNION OF NATURES IN JESUS CHRIST THERE IS NO MIXTURE OF NATURES

The confessions insist that there was no absorption of one nature into the other.

BECAUSE OF THE UNION OF NATURES IN JESUS CHRIST, WHAT IS APPROPRIATE TO ONE NATURE IS SOMETIMES ASCRIBED TO THE OTHER

One pertinent example is cited. Acts 20:28 ascribes to the divine nature something proper to the human nature. Paul urges the Ephesians elders "to shepherd the church of God which he purchased with his own blood." Strictly speaking, the blood shed on the cross was the blood of the man Christ Jesus, but since he was a divine-human person, it can be called God's blood.

This fact is traditionally called the *communicatio idiomatum*, a Latin phrase meaning the interchangeability of attributes. This is well explained by John Murray:

> Whatever can be predicated of either nature can be predicated of the person. This is not . . . a communication or transfer of the attributes of one nature to the other. . . . What is true of either nature is true of the person, and the person may be designated in terms of one nature when what is predicated is true only in virtue of the other.[22]

So eternity is a property of Christ's divine nature, but it may legitimately said that Christ the person is eternal, even when reference is being made to him as a man. Conversely, to hunger and thirst is a property of Christ's human nature, but it may legitimately said that Christ the person hungered and thirsted, even when he is presented to our view as God. However, this must not lead us to infer either that Christ's humanity was eternal, or that his divinity hungered and thirsted. The distinction between nature and person is crucial here.

The Reformers' Distinctive Contributions

In Jesus Christ God became man
to fulfil three offices

The first distinctive contribution to Christology made by the Reformation was the emphasis on the threefold office of Jesus Christ as prophet, priest and king. The four catechisms which elaborate on this point, the Genevan, the Heidelberg, and both the Westminster Catechisms, treat it as the definition of the title Christ.

The Old Testament title "Messiah" is derived from the Hebrew root *māšaḥ*, which means "anointed." The Messiah is "the LORD's anointed." In the Septuagint *māšaḥ* is translated by *chrizō*, the root of the title "Christ."

In Isaiah 61:1 the LORD's servant says, "The Spirit of the Lord GOD *is* upon me, because the LORD has anointed me." In Luke 4:18–19 Jesus quotes Isaiah, and then, in verse 21, declares: "Today this Scripture is fulfilled in your hearing." He is claiming in himself the fulfilment of Isaiah's prophecy. Jesus is the Messiah, the anointed one.

---

22. J. Murray, *Systematic Theology*, 140–41.

In Old Testament times the three great offices of prophet, priest and king were instituted by anointing with oil. Here is one example of each.

In 1 Kings 19:16 the Lord instructs Elijah: "Elisha the son of Shaphat of Abel-meholah you shall anoint *as* prophet in your place."

In Exodus 40:13, Moses receives the following directions: "put the holy garments on Aaron, and anoint him and consecrate him, that he may minister to me as priest."

David makes provision for Solomon to be acknowledged as his successor at Gihon. These are his words, recorded in 1 Kings 1:34: "Let Zadok the priest and Nathan the prophet anoint him king over Israel."

In all three instances, the anointing with oil is symbolic of anointing by the Holy Spirit. The ritual represented the setting apart of the particular person to serve God with divine enabling. Jesus is called "Christ" because he is anointed by the Holy Spirit to be the complete and final fulfilment of these three offices.

(1) He is the prophet, who came into the world to bring the full and true knowledge of the Father and his will, and so to make his people true disciples of God. As prophet, his ministry answers to our ignorance.

(2) He is the priest, whose sacrifice appeases God's wrath, and who appears in God's presence on our behalf to obtain for us necessary grace. Through him we are reconciled to God, and have access to God. As priest, his ministry answers to our alienation from God and the imperfection of our best service.

(3) He is the king, who subdues our rebellion, rules our lives, and defeats our enemies. As king, his ministry answers to our utter aversion to God and our inability of ourselves to return to him.

The two states of Christ

The Reformation's second distinctive contribution to Christology was the exposition of Christ's two states, the state of humiliation and the state of exaltation.

It was a sixteenth-century Lutheran pastor, Martin Chemnitz, who first thought this issue through. The Lutheran Formula of Concord of 1576 alludes to it, and it is taken up by the two Westminster Catechisms. George Hendry explains that the doctrine "was not meant to displace the doctrine of the two natures, but to supplement it" by giving fuller recognition to the historical aspect of Christ's work.[23]

The state of humiliation entailed the events of his earthly life. Despite being the eternal Son of God, he was conceived and born; the circumstances of his birth were exceptionally lowly. He subjected himself to the law, which he obeyed perfectly. He experienced the miseries and conflicts of life on earth. He died, and his death involved the curse of the cross, in which he tasted the wrath of God. He was buried and continued for a time under the power of death.

In this connection, reference is made to Philippians 2:7–8: Jesus

> made himself of no reputation, taking the form of a bondservant, *and* coming in the likeness of men. And being found in appearance as a man, he humbled himself and became obedient to *the point of* death, even the death of the cross.

The Formula of Concord speaks of Christ's abstention during his state of humiliation from the majesty which was properly his. That is why it is possible to say that he "truly increased in wisdom and favor with God and men."

The state of humiliation continued until the resurrection. This was the stepping stone to the state of exaltation, which proceeded to his ascension and his position in glory at the Father's right hand. It will continue until its climax in his coming again in glory.

Christ's exaltation meant that he laid aside the form of a servant, and, even in his human nature, displayed the qualities of divine majesty. The truth of Christ's exaltation is rooted in Philippians 2:9–11:

> Therefore God also has highly exalted him and given him the name which is above every name, that at the name of Jesus every knee should bow, of those in heaven, and of those on earth, and of those under the earth, and *that* every tongue should confess that Jesus Christ *is* Lord, to the glory of God the Father.

Modern Confessions of Faith

All three of the modern confessions which we are using contain significant statements on the doctrine of the person of Christ. All are thoroughly in tune with the traditional christological affirmations of the church.

---

23. Hendry, "Christology," 59.

The Indian and Indonesian confessions both use the Chalcedonian "two natures, one person" terminology. The Indonesian reads, "Two natures are found in him, God and man inseparable in one person."

In line with the Christian tradition, all three confessions give primacy to Christ's divine nature. The Indian confession says that God sent his Son into the world, that the eternal Son became true man, while the Chinese document says that God's Son "comes to the earth by way of incarnation."

All three confessions are clear that Jesus Christ possessed both natures in their integrity and fullness: "Christ is true God but at the same time true man," is the Indonesian wording. The Son of God is described as "eternal" by the Indian Statement and as "only begotten" by both the Indian and Chinese texts. Both the Indian and Indonesian confessions recount his conception by the power of the Holy Spirit and his birth of the virgin Mary. The Chinese confession says, "In his perfect humanity he was tempted, though without sin." Temptability is recognized as a key characteristic of human nature. The Indian and Indonesian confessions each contain some distinctive statements which we must now observe.

Confession of Faith of the United Church of Northern India

There are two further points affirmed by this confession

IT IS IN THE LORD JESUS CHRIST ALONE THAT GOD HAS BECOME INCARNATE

The word "alone" in this confession is significant in the Indian context, where, as K. M. Sen notes, certain branches of Hinduism held "the theory of *avatāras*, that is of human incarnations of God."[24] Sen makes the point that, "Hindus accept many incarnations of God."[25] By contrast, the North Indian church asserts the uniqueness of Jesus Christ as the only true incarnation of God.

This point needs to be stressed overagainst all other religious claims that would similarly undermine the uniqueness of Christ. For example, Mahayana Buddhism deifies Buddha, and claims that he was "the

24. Sen, *Hinduism*, 76.
25. Sen, *Hinduism*, 73, n. 1.

incarnate Principle of Enlightenment in all men and in all forms of life," and that Jesus "was incarnate of the same Eternal Principle."[26]

The fact that Jesus Christ is the one and only God-man rules out all such attempts to find a point of identity between the work of any other religious leader, and what God did in becoming human in Jesus Christ his only Son. It renders illegitimate a syncretistic religious framework, combining Christian teaching with what are, supposedly, the best insights of other religions. It invalidates the use of confusing terms for "God," such as the prevalent use in Mongolian of *Burhan* to refer to the God and Father of our Lord Jesus Christ, even though Mongolian dictionaries consistently define the term as "Buddha," in line with evidence dating back at least to the ninth century AD.[27]

Christianity inevitably makes exclusive claims. This will always seem offensive to the unenlightened hearts of the unconverted. Gerhard Kittel described this as "the scandal of particularity."[28] Nonetheless, however scandalous it may seem, we must stand by the truth that Christ alone is God, Christ alone is the truth, Christ alone can save.

JESUS CHRIST CONTINUES TO BE TRUE MAN FOR EVER

This confession also acknowledges that when he ascended to heaven at the end of his earthly mission, Christ as God returned to his former place, but took with him the humanity which he had assumed. Our great comfort now, the truth that undergirds our hope, is that we are represented before the throne in heaven by a man, who understands us perfectly and pleads our cause effectively. Paul reminds Timothy that "*there is* one God and one mediator between God and men, *the* man Christ Jesus" (1 Tim 2:5). That mediatorial function is one which Jesus Christ continues to exercise now as a man. William Stewart makes this comment on this phrase from the Indian confession:

> When he became man it was not just for a time. If it had been so our hope would have gone, for then he would have returned to the Father leaving our manhood empty behind him. He did not do so. Having taken our manhood he has not given it up; he is "the firstborn of many brothers" (Rom 8:29), still our elder

26. Humphreys, *Buddhism*, 26.
27. Maue, "Three Languages," 63, 66–67, 71.
28. Cited by Whale, *Victor*, 81.

brother in the heavenly places . . . . He is no stranger to us, so we may come "boldly" where he has gone in our name.[29]

Confession of Faith of the Huria Batak Protestant

Here two errors related to the doctrine of Christ are explicitly refuted.

The first is the Roman Catholic elevation of Mary to a position of intercessor in rivalry to Christ.

The other is the idea that the Lord Jesus "is comparable with the prophets of the world." In the Indonesian context, this is no doubt primarily intended to distinguish Jesus Christ from the prophet of Islam, though the plural "prophets" affirms his uniqueness in comparison with any other prophets, whether true or false, including the genuine Old Testament prophets of Israel.

The truth motivating the rejection of both these errors is the absolute uniqueness of Jesus Christ.

HISTORICAL ELABORATION

In this section we shall attempt three things: (1) We shall look at some christological heresies from the early centuries. (2) We shall consider the teaching of certain contemporary cults. (3) We shall discuss the question, did the pre-existent Son of God possess a human nature?

Christological Heresies in the Early Church

On the way to the classic definition of the person of Christ spelt out at Chalcedon a number of inadequate Christologies were proposed and ruled out.

The early church had two paramount concerns, corresponding to the two main emphases eventually enshrined at Chalcedon. (1) There was the need to uphold the two natures of Jesus Christ as both God and man. (2) There was the need to insist that he was a single person.

Christological heresies then, as now, tended to err by exaggerating one of these two truths at the expense of the other. Some people were so motivated to uphold the truth of the two natures that they ended up

29. W. Stewart, *Faith We Confess*, 21.

dividing Christ's person into two. Others were so persuaded of the unity of Christ's person that they failed to do justice to the truth of the two natures.

A Heresy which Divided Christ's Person: Nestorianism

Nestorianism was the one main heresy in the early centuries which erred in the first direction. It was named after Nestorius, pastor at Constantinople from AD 428. This is unfortunate, because it was not his own teaching.[30] It was an excessively logical deduction from his way of wording things.[31]

The Nestorian controversy began with a sermon preached by Nestorius's assistant, Anastasius, in which he raised an objection to the description of Mary as *theotokos*, the God-bearer, the term which would later be included in the Chalcedonian formula.

It was at this time that the tendency to pay excessive devotion to Mary was on the increase. The title *theotokos* was being given greater prominence and significance. Originally the emphasis had been on the first part of the title, *theo-*. This put the stress on the full and genuine divinity of the one born of Mary. As Marian devotion began to develop, the emphasis was shifted to the second part of the title, *-tokos*. As a result, attention became focused on Mary's glory as Jesus' mother.

Anastasius said, "Let no one call Mary *theotokos*; for Mary was only a human being, and it is impossible that God should be born of a human being."[32] Nestorius was present as Anastasius preached, and he came out in support of his colleague. He agreed that Mary was only the mother of Jesus' human nature, and saw (correctly) that the divine and human natures in Christ were quite distinct. However, he spoke of Christ's unity as the "conjunction" of natures.

Nestorius's followers extrapolated this to mean that the union of natures in Jesus Christ was an alliance of two separate beings. The two natures co-existed in parallel, and Jesus was, in effect, two distinct persons. This deduction from Nestorius's teaching was condemned as "ungodly" and "impious"[33] at the Council of Ephesus in AD 431.

---

30. Cf. Prestige, *Fathers*, 120.
31. O'Grady, *Heresy*, 102.
32. Quoted by Socrates Scholasticus, "Ecclesiastical History," 1.32.
33. Council of Ephesus, "Decree," 441.

As a footnote to this controversy, we might note that Nestorians moved eastwards following their theological defeat. A separate Nestorian Church came into being, with Syria and Persia as its heartlands. The Nestorian Church was blessed with great evangelistic zeal, and its missionaries planted churches "all over Asia, from Arabia to China," and those indigenous Nestorian churches which survive today in Iran and Iraq "show no signs of possessing a heretical creed."[34]

Heresies which Denied Christ's Two Natures

Other major early christological heresies erred in the other direction. Four in particular stand out. In historical order of appearance they are:

1. Docetism, dating from the first century;
2. Adoptionism, dating from the second and third centuries;
3. Apollinarianism, dating from the fourth century;
4. Eutychianism, dating from the fifth century.

Adoptionism upholds Christ's human nature at the expense of the divine, Docetism and Apollinarianism uphold his divine nature at the expense of the human, while Eutychianism denies the fullness of both. We shall therefore deal with Adoptionism first, and then move on to the other errors.

A MERELY HUMAN CHRIST: ADOPTIONISM

Adoptionism taught that at Jesus' baptism the Christ descended upon him and indwelt him in a unique way from then on. Both before and after his baptism, Jesus was only a man in terms of constitution; the divine element was one of indwelling presence, not of nature. Jesus' experience, according to Adoptionism, was no different in kind from the experience of the believer indwelt by the Spirit. The difference was only that Jesus was indwelt to a far higher degree. This heresy safeguarded the unity of Christ's person by denying his divine nature.

34. O'Grady, *Heresy*, 104.

A MERELY DIVINE CHRIST

The two heresies which compromised on the human nature of Christ were motivated by the determination to emphasize the truth that he was divine. Even though it was not chronologically first, we shall look first at Apollinarianism, because it echoes the language of Adoptionism.

Apollinarianism

Adoptionism spoke of Godhead coming down to inhabit one who was truly, but only, human. Apollinarianism also speaks of God coming down, in this case to inhabit one who was only partially human. This heresy taught that the human body of Jesus was inhabited by the divine Son in the place where the human soul would normally be. Physically Jesus was human, but psychologically he was divine.

It was about the middle of the fourth century that Apollinarius began to put forward such ideas. He took up the words of John 1:14, "the Word became flesh," but he understood "flesh" to refer only to the physical frame of a human being: God the Son was united inseparably with a human body, but that was all.

Apollinarius described God incarnate as "a compound unity in human form."[35] However, the human form was not a nature in itself. To exist at all the human form needs to be animated. In an ordinary human being, the spirit animates the body. In Christ, it was the divine nature which animated his body.

Apollinarius therefore preserved the unity of Christ's person, but at the cost of losing the full two natures truth. At best the Apollinarian Christ had one and a half natures: he was fully divine, but his humanity was only partial.

Docetism

This was the earliest of those heresies which undermine the two natures of Christ by jettisoning his human nature. Its noble motivation was to uphold the true deity of Christ. However, it did this by claiming that his humanity was only apparent. All his human experiences were unreal. He

---

35. Apollinarius, *Letter to Dionysius*, 1.9, cited by Lietzmann, *Apollinarius*, 260.

just seemed to be born, to grow, to suffer, to die. The title of this heresy is derived from the Greek word *dokeō*, which means "to seem."

Docetism was rooted in the belief that the divine nature was unchangeable. God cannot go through experiences of growth or pain. Since Christ was genuinely God, all talk of change or suffering in connection with him is merely picture-language. These things did not really happen. Moreover, God does not have a body. For Docetism it followed that, since Christ is God, the body in which he seemed to live was just a phantom. Furthermore, even the human psychological and inner emotional life of Christ was just an appearance.

Already at the beginning of the second century, a mere seventy years after Jesus' death, resurrection, and ascension, Ignatius of Antioch had to argue strongly against this teaching. In his letter to the church at Smyrna he said that those who did not confess that the Lord was truly possessed of a body were in fact blaspheming him.[36] For Ignatius, blasphemy included the assault on our Lord's humanity as well as his deity.

Writing to the church at Tralles, Ignatius insisted that Jesus Christ

> was truly born, and ate and drank. He was truly persecuted under Pontius Pilate. He was truly crucified and died, in the sight of beings in heaven, and on earth, and under the earth. He was also truly raised from the dead, his Father quickening him.[37]

Here Ignatius uses the word "truly" four times, and connects it with seven different experiences in the human life of Jesus Christ. This is a polemic against those who claimed that all these things only apparently happened, because, they claimed, Christ was only apparently human.

A CHRIST NEITHER TRULY DIVINE NOR TRULY HUMAN: EUTYCHIANISM

Eutyches taught that Christ had only one nature after the incarnation, because his humanity was totally absorbed by his deity. The divine nature remained, but the human nature was swallowed up by it, in such a way that it no longer retained any distinct reality. However, in absorbing the humanity, the divinity was also altered.

---

36. Ignatius, *To the Smyrnaeans*, 5.2.
37. Ignatius, *To the Trallians*, 9.1–2.

In the end, the Eutychian Christ is neither divine nor human in the normal sense of either term. He becomes an oddity. He has a single nature which was an amalgamation of humanity and divinity.

This teaching was rejected by a church council meeting at Constantinople in AD 448, just three years before the publication of the Chalcedonian Definition.

Contemporary Cults

The main challenges in the area of Christology which we face today come from the cults. We shall look at three examples. The first two teach that Christ is not truly divine. The third differs from the others in that its Christ is truly God incarnate, but he is not absolutely identified with Jesus. In each case we shall base our summary on material found in the cult's own website.

Jehovah's Witnesses (also known as The Watchtower)

The teaching of the Jehovah's Witnesses is that Jesus is the greatest man who ever lived. However, he is not God, never claimed to be God, and credits Jehovah as his superior. He is one with God in purpose, but not in being. He is the promised Messiah, Jehovah's appointed king.

However, neither is Jesus a human being like other human beings. The Jehovah's Witnesses claim that he was created in advance of everything else, and that, prior to the rest of creation, he had a pre-human existence as a mighty spirit-person in heaven, enjoying intimate fellowship with Jehovah. This teaching resembles that of the Arians.

At the appointed time, God transferred the life of this spirit-creature to the womb of the virgin Mary, and Jesus became the son of God. While using this term, the Witnesses do not mean that Jesus was God. He was a human son of God, as was Adam. But where Adam failed, Jesus remained without sin.

During his childhood and adolescence Jesus had no recollection of his pre-human existence. That memory was evoked when the heavens were opened to him at his baptism, which the Witnesses, in line with ancient Adoptionism, see as a crucial moment in his human career. As holy spirit descended upon him, Jesus was born again, so entering into a new relationship with God, becoming God's spiritual son. From then on Jesus carefully imitated his Father, and became the perfect reflection of God on earth. His life becomes the example which all people ought to follow.

When he died, Jesus laid down his perfect human life in sacrifice, having completed what was necessary to enable others to be set free from death and sin. In that event his human life, including his body, was sacrificed forever. He was not raised from the dead bodily; his resurrection was a spiritual restoration to his pre-human glory, pending his return in kingdom power and glory.

It is clear that this teaching falls way short of what the Bible affirms about the eternal Son of God. Such a "Christ" can have no saving power, and to follow him is to be forever lost.

Mormonism (also known as the Latter Day Saints)

After the Jehovah's Witnesses the Mormons are probably the next most significant of all the cults. They claim to believe "in Jesus Christ as the Savior and Redeemer of the world," and refer to him as "the Only Begotten Son of God the Father." The Mormons accept the virgin birth of Christ. They describe him as "both mortal and divine," but this "divinity" is not equal to that of his Father: "they are one in purpose, but they are two separate beings." This is not to be understood in a trinitarian sense of the distinction of persons within the one Godhead. The key words are "purpose" and "separate." Mormons see the unity between the Father and the Son only as one of shared purpose; at the level of being, they are quite separate. Jesus is referred to as the Son of God, but he is not truly God in a full sense: he does not share the Father's nature.

This is connected with the Mormon doctrine of man: being created in God's image, we are all "divine in our nature and purpose." Christ too was "created in his image," and therefore is no different from other people. Moreover, Mormonism teaches that all human beings possess a pre-mortal life, such that Christ is not unique in that respect.

In Mormon teaching Jesus is different, only in that he was the one whom God chose to serve his saving purpose. But he is not truly God. This, again, falls short of the New Testament teaching, where Jesus Christ insists not only that he does the works of his Father (John 10:37), thus sharing a common purpose, but also that he and his Father are one (John 10:30).

Eastern Lightning (also known as The Church of Almighty God)

Eastern Lightning first appeared in China in 1991. It divides God's Salvation "Management Plan" into three stages, named in turn the ages of law, grace, and the kingdom. At each stage God is known by a different name—first Jehovah, then Jesus, then Almighty God. This seems to resemble the ancient Modalist heresy, locating the entirety of God in a different person at different times and for different purposes.

During the second stage, Jesus is the Christ, and is God incarnate. However, Jesus and the Christ are not totally equated. According to this teaching, during the third stage the Christ reappears, but in a different person, a woman from Henan province in eastern China. She is "the last Christ." In her, God is incarnate again under the title Almighty God: as Christ, "she does not only have a normal humanity, but has a full divinity." Her words are God's word for the present age of the kingdom, because what she says "is completely from the divine substance she possesses;" consequently, "she can express the truth at any time and in any place."

The appearing of the Christ in China in a hidden way is the precursor to God's conquest of every nation. No longer is Christ the Son of the Jews, but the Lightning of the East, which flashes to the west.

Although ostensibly orthodox in its statements about Jesus, this cult falls foul of the New Testament emphasis that Jesus is the Christ—not just one of the Christs. The Church of Almighty God is one of those movements which Jesus warned us against when he said, "many will come in my name, saying, "I am the Christ," and will deceive many" (Matt 24:5).

Did the Son of God have a Human Nature Before the Incarnation?

On first hearing it, this question may sound a bit arcane, the answer being so obvious: in the incarnation the Son of God became man, and this implies that he assumed a nature which he had not previously possessed. However, the notion that Christ's pre-existence included humanity has surfaced occasionally over the centuries, and even today it is a genuine issue for some believers. The idea was put forward by Isaac Watts in the eighteenth century,[38] Phillips Brooks in the nineteenth,[39] and Charles

---

38. I. Watts, *Glory of Christ*, 146–255.
39. Brooks, "Eternal Humanity," *passim*.

Pridgeon in the twentieth,[40] and has resurfaced significantly in China in the twenty-first century.[41]

Isaac Watts thought that Christ's human soul had to be pre-existent so that he could consent to the work of atonement. The covenant of redemption required two distinct parties, God and man; it could not merely be an agreement internal to the Godhead. Moreover, in the incarnation Christ is said to have taken flesh—or a body, but the Bible does not say that he took a human soul.

Phillips Brooks described our Lord as the eternal Christ, and reads this title as including both the divine and human elements. He saw the eternal humanity of God the Son as the "the perfect archetype and pattern" of our humanity, the image of what we would be. From here Brooks deduces the thought that our humanity is an exalted thing, because its pattern was "part and parcel of the everlasting Godhead." So we are not insignificant creatures, but dignified and worthy beings.

Pridgeon's claim was that if Christ did not assume humanity until his incarnation but continues thereafter as the God-Man forever, then there was an addition to the Godhead, which implies that Godhead was previously deficient. Pridgeon distinguishes the uncreated deity of Christ from his created humanity, which, nonetheless, he defines as eternally created before time.

There are several points of resemblance to this teaching in the writings of some contemporary Chinese Christian theologians. Here is Zeng Shao Kai's summary of their position:

> Their proposal is that Christ's human nature is uncreated and eternally within his divine person, and this human nature is the "image of God" in which human beings are created. On this view, Christ would be the archetypal human. According to their proposal, the incarnation would be Christ's act of taking on merely human flesh, but not human nature, which already subsists within Christ's person from all eternity without the body.[42]

The reference to an uncreated human nature goes further than Pridgeon's teaching that Christ's human nature was created, albeit eternally, but the claim that Christ's pre-existent human nature is the image of God in which human beings are created is similar to the teaching of Brooks.

---

40. Pridgeon, *Is Hell Eternal?*, Ch. 17.

41. Baugus, *Christological Confusion*, Part 5.

42. Zeng Shao Kai, *Ghost of Apollinaris*, para 1.

The idea that, in the incarnation, Christ took on merely human flesh resembles one of Watts's emphases.

Watts and Pridgeon both offered scriptural support for the idea of Christ's eternal humanity, and they use many of the same texts.

Amongst the texts cited by both writers are John 3:13 and John 6:62, both of which refer to the descent of the Son of Man from heaven and his return in the ascension. Assuming that the title "Son of Man" emphasizes Jesus' humanity, Pridgeon infers its pre-existence, while Watts deems the depiction of the incarnation as a change of place as more appropriately applied to a human nature than to divinity. In the same connection both writers cite Ephesians 4:9–10, which Pridgeon takes to mean that Christ's identity was the same as he descended from heaven and when he returned to heaven, implying the pre-existence of both natures.

Again, both Watts and Pridgeon mention Philippians 2:6–7, where Christ is said to have divested himself of some of his pre-incarnate glory. Watts sees this as impossible for the divine nature, and Pridgeon says that the divine nature could not be tempted to grasp equality with God: being already divine, there was nothing to be grasped. However, the Son might have faced the temptation to try to make his humanity equal with God.

However, these arguments fail to do justice either to biblical teaching or to the theological grappling of the early church. Addressing the above points in the order mentioned, the following observations may be made.

(1) Watts, in his claim that a pre-existent humanity was necessary for the covenant of redemption and for Christ to assent to the work of atonement, overlooks the representative role that the Son of God willingly embraced in anticipation of his incarnation. Though not yet a human being, he accepted responsibility on behalf of those with whom he would, in time, identify.

(2) The word "flesh" as used in the New Testament does not mean only physical flesh. It is a comprehensive term for everything involved in being truly human. God the Son assumed an entire human nature. Zeng Shao Kai aptly compares the teaching that the Son of God assumed only a body to Apollinarianism.[43]

(3) The inference which Brooks makes from the title "Christ" is dubious. The word refers to the promised and anointed king, and the phrase "eternal Christ" is nowhere found in Scripture.

---

43. Zeng Shao Kai, *Ghost of Apollinaris*, para. 21.

(4) The claim that Christ's eternal humanness is the reality on which human nature in general is modelled falls foul of the biblical teaching in two ways: in the first place, an image is not the same thing as the original reality; and second, we were made in the image of God, not of pre-existent humanity.

(5) Although all these writers try to avoid this trap, there is a danger in proposing eternal humanity in Christ that the divine-human divide breaks down. Some of Brooks's statements on human worthiness come perilously close to this error. It is particularly problematical where the word "uncreated" is used of Christ's humanity. However, even Pridgeon, who recognizes the created nature of Christ's humanity, even if eternally created, runs this risk: since eternity is a divine quality, the notion of eternal humanity threatens to deify human nature, and so to undermine the difference between the Creator and the creature. This may then lead to the view of salvation which involves the rediscovery of the innate divine spark in human nature. This suggests that Leo the Great, already in the fifth century, had a point in characterizing this teaching as blasphemous and impious.[44]

(6) Pridgeon's claim that a denial of eternal humanity in the Son of God means that an addition to Godhead took place in the incarnation overlooks the absolute distinction of natures on which orthodox Christology has insisted. The incarnation neither added anything to, nor subtracted anything from, the Godhead of the second person of the Trinity. True, God the Son assumed an additional nature, but it was added alongside perfect deity in the one person of the God-man. Therefore, the assumption of humanity in the incarnation in no way implies any previous deficiency in Christ's deity. Zeng Shao Kai explains this point well: "the relation between Christ's human nature and divine person is not to be understood as 'part of the whole,' but rather a relation of communion: Christ assumed human nature in such a way that it is inseparably united to his divine nature in his divine person with abiding distinction."[45]

(7) In handling the texts quoted Watts and Pridgeon overlook a point noted earlier in connection with the Reformation Confessions of Faith: the union of natures in Jesus Christ makes it possible to ascribe to him what is characteristic of one nature, even when he is being referred to as he bears the other. However, to ascribe to Christ as man what

---

44. Leo, "Tome", 6.
45. Zeng Shao Kai, *Ghost of Apollinaris*, para. 2.

properly pertains to the divine nature does not mean that his humanity shares in the eternity of his divinity: "the attributes of one nature have not become those of the other nor can be predicated of it abstractly. Divinity did not suffer. Humanity is not eternal."[46] As Donald Macleod explains, "whatever he did was done by the Son of God . . . . A nature did not do it. *He* did it."[47]

In addition to these points, Charles Hodge makes two further observations. First, he points out that this theory is rooted in an inadequate view of humanness:

> The Bible in teaching that the Son of God became man, thereby teaches that he assumed a true body and a rational soul. For neither a soul without a body, nor a body without a soul, is a man in the scriptural sense of the term. It was the Logos which became man; and not a god-man who assumed a material body.[48]

Second, he fears that this elevation of Christ's human nature places him beyond the reach of human sympathy. He is no longer human in every way that we are, sin excepted. His humanity is not the same as ours.[49] This suggests that the doctrine of Christ's pre-existent humanity threatens to undermine the effectiveness of his work on our behalf, and so is also fatal for the truth of atonement.

The fact is that in the incarnation "the Word [the divine Son] became flesh [a human being]" (John 1:14)—and it is impossible to *become* what one already *is*. The Son of God assumed a nature which he had not previously possessed.

PRACTICAL APPLICATION

In a sense our next two doctrines—the atonement and salvation—are the practical application of the doctrine of Christ. As some of the early creeds explained, it was "for us men and for our salvation" that God's only Son came down from heaven. So we shall not deal here with the saving application of the doctrine of Christ; that will come up in the subsequent chapters. At this stage we shall note some applications associated with different aspects of Christology.

46. L. Riissen, quoted by Heppe, *Dogmatics*, 442.
47. Macleod, *Faith*, 127.
48. C. Hodge, *Systematic Theology*, Vol. 2, 427.
49. C. Hodge, *Systematic Theology*, Vol. 2, 427–28.

(1) Jesus Christ is the fulfilment of Old Testament prophecy. The fact that the Messiah came as promised is the evidence *par excellence* that God keeps his word. As the apostle declares, "all the promises of God in him *are* Yes" (2 Cor 1:20). The coming of Christ is, therefore, the guarantee that we can trust everything which the Bible says. We may confidently trust in the Lord.

(2) Jesus Christ is truly divine. Since the Lord Jesus Christ is genuinely divine, worship is the entirely proper response to him as the divine Son.

Moreover, the fact of Christ's deity tells us that God has come to us in person to save us. He did not delegate this responsibility to some other being. Jesus Christ is "God with us" (Matt 1:23). This demonstrates how seriously God takes the work of human salvation. It ought to provoke a response of wonder and gratitude.

(3) Jesus Christ is truly human. There was an amazing human ordinariness about Jesus. He knew human weakness, he experienced temptation. This is a source of immense comfort. It assures us that in all our human struggles, we have a Savior who has been there, who understands from the inside what we are going through. He is not a mere onlooker on our plight. He is a participant. He can, therefore, sympathize with us, as Hebrews 4:15 assures us. And as we look to him for the sympathy that we need, we can "come boldly to the throne of grace, that we may obtain mercy and find grace to help in time of need" (Heb 4:16). We can pray with confidence, certain that God will not reject us, because the representative human being is at his side. Mercy and grace according to our need are ours for the asking.

But Jesus Christ is a sinless man. In that respect he is unlike us. Yet this feature of his life has important implications for us. Jesus has placed before us a demonstration of what it looks like to live according to the image of God. He has held up a portrait of real humanity, a pattern for us to emulate.

Those who reduce the work of Christ to that of setting an example fall far short of the truth. Nevertheless, it is true that part of his work was setting us an example. The apostle Peter writes, "Christ also suffered for us, leaving us an example, that you should follow his steps" (1 Pet 2:21). The way in which Jesus suffered without protest is exemplary. Equally, the way in which he lived before his final suffering is exemplary. He himself said, "I have given you an example, that you should do as I have done to you" (John 13:15).

(4) Jesus Christ fulfils the three great offices. He is our prophet. So we must listen to God's word as it comes to us in him. Moses said, "The LORD your God will raise up for you a prophet like me from your midst, from your brethren. Him you shall hear" (Deut 18:15). We must learn from him, understand what true discipleship entails, and obey his commands.

He is our priest. So we must recognize the futility of all our works and service independently of him. We must receive from him the grace which we daily need.

He is our king. So we must gladly submit to his rule over our lives. Psalm 2:6 tells us that God has appointed Christ as king. Verses 10–12 then warn us of the need to be wise, to "serve the LORD with fear," to "kiss the Son,"—"an ancient mode of doing homage or allegiance to a king,"[50] and to take refuge in him.

(5) Jesus Christ is absolutely unique. As the God-man, Jesus Christ is peerless and unrivalled. No other prophet, priest or king can claim divine honor. That is why he is the only way to the Father. That is why Peter could say, "nor is there salvation in any other, for there is no other name under heaven given among men by which we must be saved" (Acts 4:12). So our task is to preach him to all people. Every nation and people group, every individual person, has the need and the right to hear of Jesus Christ, for he is the only hope for the whole world.

The uniqueness of Jesus Christ has to be fearlessly proclaimed over-against all other religions and ideologies. It is one of the chief distinguishing marks of true faith in God: no other religion can claim that in its founder God became human.

---

50. Alexander, *Psalms*, 26.

8

The Doctrine of the Atonement

THIS CHAPTER LEADS US to the very hub and kernel of biblical truth. It brings before us the most central doctrine of the Christian faith. It gets us right to the heart of the wonderful grace of God, focused as it is in the glorious reality of Christ's atoning work on the cross. But what was it that he achieved by his death? The astonishing reality is that Christ's atonement made an impact upon God, and that God himself initiated it for that purpose.

In Psalm 85:10 we read these words: "Mercy and truth have met together; righteousness and peace have kissed." In the death of his Son, God ensures that his true righteousness on the one hand, and, on the other, the mercy that leads to peace, are united in such a way that neither is compromised. Mercy is not withheld: sinners are forgiven; but neither is the righteous punishment for sin overlooked: it falls upon Christ. As a result, the divine holiness is honored, the divine anger turned away from the sinner, and the divine mercy extended to a rebellious world. As we ponder this theme, may our hearts overflow with praise to the Lord.

BIBLICAL FOUNDATION

Old Testament

We must always remember that the Old Testament sacrificial system was a pointer to Christ in types and shadows. Every Old Testament sacrifice was a signpost to Calvary. In itself the Old Testament sacrificial system had no saving power. This is stated explicitly in Hebrews 10:1–4. Nonetheless, the principles brought out in the sacrificial system were all fulfilled in Christ and his atoning work. Read correctly, they are powerful illustrations of his work, which did take sins away, and so perfected his people in God's sight for ever. In Christ alone we find the final reality of atonement, but it is prefigured in the Old Testament shadows. The rich Old Testament background will prepare the way for a doctrinally satisfactory and warmly satisfying understanding of what Jesus did for us all.

The Hebrew word usually translated "atonement" in the English Bible is *kāpar*. In the Septuagint it is generally translated *exilaskomai*, and the New Testament uses the related term *hilaskomai* and a number of cognates.

There is an instance of *kāpar* in Genesis 6:14, where it is translated "cover." It is sometimes suggested, therefore, that the basic idea in atonement is the covering of sin. However, this seems unlikely: some scholars think that there are two quite separate Hebrew roots both spelt *kāpar*. They conclude that the root meaning "atonement" has no connection with covering: rather its basic idea is to appease by the offering of a substitute.[1]

The first occurrence in Scripture of the *kāpar* root with which we are concerned is found in Genesis 32:20. Jacob's words as he prepared to meet his brother Esau for the first time since, twenty years earlier, he had deceitfully secured the blessing intended for his brother, were: "I will appease (*kāpar*) him with the present that goes before me, and afterward I will see his face; perhaps he will accept me."

Back then, those twenty years ago, Esau had plotted murder, and Jacob had had to flee for his life. Now, hearing that Esau is on the way to meet him with a huge army, Jacob is "greatly afraid and distressed" (verse 7). So he prepares a huge present, designed to negate Esau's anger, and to secure acceptance.

---

1. Cf. R. L. Harris, "*kāpar*," 1023a.

Here *kāpar* refers to an atonement between men, making it a useful text for understanding the general principles which also underlie God's atonement. The word rendered "present" (*minḥâ*) is a regular Old Testament term for an offering.

These observations lead us to expect to find the following features in the Old Testament teaching on atonement: (1) it will involve an offering; (2) it will pacify God's legitimate anger; (3) it will result in undeserved acceptance.

It is true that, with regard to that third feature, Jacob feels compelled to add a "perhaps." How glorious it is that there is no uncertainty about the impact upon God of Christ's atoning offering!

We shall look at three key Old Testament passages relevant to the theme of atonement.

Exodus 11—12

The Passover, narrated in these chapters, is a signpost to Calvary, illustrating some of the principles of atonement. In 1 Corinthians 5:7 Paul describes Christ as "our Passover."

The Passover was God's provision to deliver his chosen people, not only from Egypt, but also from his own judgment on their sin. The need of a Passover sacrifice arose from God's declaration in Exodus 11:4–5 that, on that fateful night, "all the firstborn in the land of Egypt shall die." No firstborn would be excluded, from the family of Pharaoh, down to the family of the lowest of the female servants.

Back in Exodus 4:22, the LORD had said, "Israel *is* my son, my firstborn." Morally, there was no distinction between Egyptians and Israelites. Both were equally sinful. Consequently, the death-threat against the firstborn impinged on Israel as much as on Egypt. And since Israel was the LORD's firstborn, the judgment that every firstborn would die would mean that the entire Hebrew nation would be wiped out.

However, in Exodus 8:23 the LORD says to Pharaoh, "I will make a difference between my people and your people." This is the second of four such statements in the course of the judgments on Egypt (cf. Exod 8:22; 9:4; 11:7). In the other three cases the ordinary Hebrew term for a difference (*pālâ*) is used. However, Exodus 8:23 employs a rare form of the verb *pādâ*—the word *pᵉdût*, which is found only in three other places in the Old Testament. Its meaning is best brought out from Psalm

130:7–8, which says that with the LORD of mercy there is "abundant re-demption (*pᵉdût*)," on the basis of which "he shall redeem (*pādâ*) Israel from all his iniquities."

The basic meaning of "redemption" is a price paid to secure release, in this case from sin and its corollary, death. Exodus 8:23 is indicating that what makes the difference between Israel and Egypt is not a mere whim on God's part, but a costly ransom. This is because Israel needs to be delivered not only from slavery in Egypt, but also from his iniquities (Ps 130:8). Israel can only survive the final plague, if a price is paid to avert the death-threat which God's anger inevitably imposes on sinful people.

That price was the death of the lamb. The people were required to take one lamb per household (Exod 12:3), kill it (verse 6), and then "take *some* of the blood and put *it* on the two doorposts and the lintel of the houses" (verse 7). The LORD then assures them in verses 12–13 that, when he passes through the land of Egypt to strike all the firstborn, he will pass over the people of Israel, because "the blood shall be a sign for you on the houses where you *are*." As a result the plague would not bring destruction to the houses marked by the blood.

According to Leviticus 17:14 blood is the life of the flesh. But blood is life as long as it remains within the flesh. Visible blood is a sign that something is wrong. Shed blood is death. Leviticus 17:11 says that blood on the altar makes atonement for the soul: it is the sign that the life of the sacrificial victim has been given up to death in the place of the sinner condemned to death, whose own life is therefore preserved.

At the Passover the blood was a sign that a death had already taken place in the Israelite homes. Exodus 12:30 tells us that "*there was not a house where there was* not one dead." That was equally true of both the Hebrew and the Egyptian houses. The difference was that in the Hebrew homes the dead one was the lamb, whose life substituted for the life of the LORD's firstborn. Now, as the LORD passed through Egypt, he was free to pass over the houses with the sign of substitution-ary death around their doors.

Leviticus 1:1—6:7

This is the main Old Testament teaching passage on atonement. It con-tains the regulations for the five types of offering which the LORD required of Israel—the burnt offering (chapter 1), the grain offering (chapter 2), the peace offering (chapter 3), the sin offering (4:1—5:13), and the trespass offering (5:14—6:7). Here the principles of atonement are laid down as the foundation of Israel's covenant life.

The main offering was the burnt offering. Two of these had to be offered by the entire community every day, one in the morning and the other at twilight, as Exodus 29:38–39 explains. Verse 42 comments that this was to be the regular practice "throughout your generations."

The first reference to atonement in our passage comes in 1:4, in connection with the burnt offering. The offerer had to "put his hand on the head of the burnt offering." This action was a symbolic way of saying, "this animal represents me and takes my place in the present situation."

In the next verse the animal is killed. This is what the offerer, as a sinner, deserves, because "the wages of sin is death" (Rom 6:23). However, as the burnt offering, the representative animal dies instead of the sinner. Atonement involves the substitution of one for another.

Leviticus 1:4 assures the offerer that the substitutionary offering "will be accepted on his behalf:" the LORD accepts the death of the sacrificial animal in lieu of the punishment of the person. The person lives, freed from the death sentence, because the sacrifice has died instead.

Three times in Leviticus 1 the burnt offering is described as "a sweet aroma" (verses 9, 13, 17). This phrase is repeated in chapter 2 (verses 2, 9 and 12) in connection with the grain offering, in chapter 3 (verses 5 and 16) in connection with the peace offering, and in chapter 4 (verse 31) in connection with the sin offering. Each of the offerings has its own distinctive significance, but this is a common characteristic of offerings in general.

The Hebrew word translated "sweet" is *nîḥôaḥ*. This word gets to the heart of the biblical concept of atonement. Amongst its definitions one meaning offered is "tranquillizing."[2]

In the film *We Bought a Zoo* there is a vivid scene where a bear confronts the zookeeper, Benjamin Mee, who's carrying a gun. To begin with Benjamin tries talking nicely to the bear, but the bear continues to threaten. Benjamin then gets ready to use his gun, only to have it knocked out of his hand by the bear, whose face is now right up against Benjamin's and who seems to be on the point of devouring him, when, all of a sudden, the bear flops to the ground and lies motionless at Benjamin's feet.

---

2. Brown, Driver, & Briggs, *Lexicon*, 629.

Thanks to one of Benjamin's colleagues, out of sight on the screen, the bear has been hit with a powerful tranquillizer, and so Benjamin is safe.

Perhaps there is a helpful illustration of atonement here. Like Benjamin in the film, we may try to placate God's wrath by our own supposed niceness, only to find that it counts for nothing in the light of his holiness and purity. We may obstinately oppose the idea that God should judge sin, pointing our gun at his anger, so to speak. But it's only when, from beyond the immediate scene of our lives, the LORD's anger is hit by the powerful "tranquillizer" that is the sacrificial death of the Lord Jesus that we are safe from its just and righteous threat.

We might perhaps question the appropriateness of this way of speaking, on the grounds that a tranquillizer wears off after a while. We probably make the assumption that the tranquillizer in the film later wears off, and the bear is up and running again, but we don't learn that from that particular scene. And that is the point of an illustration: we may never press it beyond its limits. The bear has been tranquillized and is lying on the ground, totally inactive. That is where we finish.

In the same way, whatever may be the aftermath of the human practice of tranquillization, the biblical illustration stops at the point where God's anger against every kind of sin—sins of niceness as well as sins of aggression against God—lies motionless at our feet, so to speak, totally inactive! We certainly do not need to be frightened of the vivid words with which the Holy Spirit has inspired his chosen writers to bring God's truth to life. The "tranquillizer" by which God's anger is hit is not the kind that wears off after a while. The root word from which *nîḥôaḥ* is derived is *nûaḥ*, which has "overtones of finality."[3] Its root meaning has to do with rest.[4] The effect of atonement, we may say, is that God's anger against sin is laid to rest once and for all. Jesus' death has "tranquillized" the LORD's anger against the sins of his people, not just temporarily, but eternally.

However, rather than majoring on the etymology of the biblical terms, it is perhaps better to look at how the Bible outworks the concept of the sweet aroma, the "tranquillizing aroma." The first biblical instance of the word *nîḥôaḥ* is in Genesis 8:21, and that verse is crucial for understanding its significance. Noah has offered burnt offerings,

---

3. Coppes, "*nûaḥ*," 1323.0
4. Tregelles (ed.), *Lexicon*, 307–8.

and the LORD smelled a soothing (*nîḥôaḥ*) aroma. Then the LORD said in his heart, "I will never again curse the ground for man's sake, although the imagination of man's heart *is* evil from his youth; nor will I again destroy every living thing as I have done."

It is interesting that Noah offered a burnt offering over nine hundred years before the law of the burnt offering was spelt out to Moses. The need of an offering was imprinted on the human conscience ever since sin had first disrupted man's relationship with his creator. When Noah made his offering, the LORD smelled its soothing, its "tranquillizing," aroma.

What that means, and what resulted, is revealed by what the LORD goes on to say. He acknowledges the universal, perennial, and deep-seated reality of human evil, and yet pledges that he will withhold the curse and the punishment which this sinfulness deserves. It is the LORD's just anger against human sin which, we might say, has been forever laid to rest by the burnt offering. The LORD said emphatically to Noah, "never again," and it is those two words which get us to the heart of what atonement is all about. God's anger is permanently extinguished for all time. Never again will it surface with reference to those who are concerned in the sacrifice. In the case of Noah's offering, that was the entire world.

In the case of the Levitical sacrifices, those concerned are his own people. The purpose of the Levitical sacrifices was to prefigure the ultimate sacrifice of our Savior at Calvary, to point us forwards to their fulfilment in him. In this case the divine anger towards them is permanently laid to rest for all eternity. As a result, sinners though we are by nature, we are forever freed from the danger of punishment. We are forgiven (cf. Lev 4:31). Never again will we have to face the judgment which our sin deserves.

But this is to anticipate. We need first to consider one more of the Old Testament signposts to Calvary.

Leviticus 16

This chapter describes the procedures for the Day of Atonement. Although that title does not appear in chapter 16, it is used in Leviticus 23:27–28, which cites the same date as in Leviticus 16:29.

On this day five sacrificial animals had to be presented—a bull, two rams, and two goats. The bull was a sin offering for the priest, the goats a sin offering for the people. The two rams were burnt offerings, one for the priest and the other for the people (Lev 16:3, 5).

The background to the Day of Atonement was death because of sin. Verse 1 refers back to Leviticus 10:1–2, when Aaron's sons "offered profane fire before the LORD, which he had not commanded them," and so "died before the LORD." Leviticus 16:2 highlights the permanent deadliness of God's holy presence in a sinful environment.

The purpose of the Day of Atonement was to avert this death-threat. Four of the five animals died instead. They represented the sinful people and fulfilled a substitutionary role, dying in their place. The death required by God's just anger was fulfilled in the sacrifices, and so his anger towards the people was "turned away," to use another biblical term.[5]

The animal which was not sacrificed to death was the scapegoat (verses 8–10). Because of some alleged uncertainty about the meaning of the Hebrew word ᵃzā'zēl, many modern translations have left it untranslated, and refer to this second goat as the goat "for Azazel." This is rather unfortunate: it gives the impression that Azazel is a name, and has given rise to the absurd notion that this goat is presented to a demon.[6]

The older translators showed greater wisdom. They recognized ᵃzā'zēl as a combination of the two Hebrew words ᵉz ("goat") and ᵃzal ("to go away"), and so rendered it by such phrases as "the goat that goes away."[7] This coheres with the explanation given in the text: this goat was "released" (verse 26) "into the wilderness" (verse 10).

The traditional title "scapegoat" conveys this understanding, but combines it with the recognition that, as the goat went away, it took with it the people's guilt, another clear aspect of the ritual as described. In verse 21 we hear how Aaron laid both hands on the head of this goat, and confessed over it all the sins of the people. This is described in verse 10 as making atonement over it. It symbolizes the goat's representative and substitutionary role. The goat stood for the people, as the embodiment of their guilt. It was then led out into the desert, and never seen again. Its complete disappearance symbolizes the total removal from God's sight of the people's guilt.

The two goats as a pair clearly made up one sin offering, as verse 5 indicates. Verse 15 describes the sacrifice on the altar of the first goat. This goat died in the place of the people, over whom hung the threat of

5. Isa 12:1; Dan 9:16; Hos 14:4.

6. E.g., Moore, "Azazel," 421.

7. Cf. Tregelles (ed.), *Lexicon*, 354.

death because of sin. The second goat—the live goat, the scapegoat—served as a vivid display of the removal of sin and guilt resulting from the transfer of punishment to the first goat. The first goat signified the "means and essence" of atonement, the other "its effects."[8]

Verses 14–15 also prescribe the sprinkling on the mercy seat of the blood of the two sin offerings. The phrase "mercy seat" translates *kappōret*, which is connected with the word for atonement (*kāpar*). R. Laird Harris therefore makes a valid point when he suggests that "atonement place" would be a better translation than "mercy seat," since the emphasis in the vocabulary is on the atonement itself, rather than on the mercy which provided atonement.[9]

Exodus 25:22 explains the significance of the mercy seat, the atonement place. The LORD says: "there I will meet with you, and I will speak with you from above the mercy seat, from between the two cherubim which *are* on the ark of the testimony." This is where the LORD meets his people to speak with them. But this is possible only when his anger has been satisfied—otherwise his word would have nothing but killing power. Atonement is essential before God can meet and speak with his people. However, the wonderful result of atonement is that his word is life-giving, because his anger truly has been laid to rest, never again to surface against his people.

The Day of Atonement procedures also indicate a secondary significance of atonement. Verse 30 says, "on that day *the priest* shall make atonement for you, to cleanse you, *that* you may be clean from all your sins before the LORD." A sinful people is unclean (verses 16, 19), but atonement also achieves cleansing, alongside the cancellation of God's legitimate anger.

It just remains to exclaim: this is amazing! All praise to the God of astonishing steadfast love and mercy!

New Testament

We shall summarize the New Testament teaching on atonement by reference to five key passages.

---

8. So Seiss, *Types*, 296.
9. R. L. Harris, "Leviticus," 589.

Ephesians 5:2

We start with this text because there is a clear link with the Old Testament teaching which we have just been considering. It must therefore rank as one of the most important New Testament comments on this theme. Paul speaks of how Christ has "given himself for us, an offering and a sacrifice to God for a sweet-smelling aroma." The phrase rendered "sweet-smelling aroma," is *osmē euōdias*—the exact phrase used in the Septuagint for "sweet aroma." Paul here is taking up the chief feature of the Old Testament sacrificial system, and highlighting its ultimate fulfilment in Christ. His death on the cross is the true reality, to which the Old Testament sacrifices pointed: it has, we might say, forever "tranquillized" God's anger against sinful people, so that God can now say that he will never again punish our sins.

Matthew 20:28; Mark 10:45

In these two parallel verses, which are worded identically, Jesus' gives his own account of his work: "the Son of Man did not come to be served, but to serve, and to give his life a ransom for many." In the verses leading up to this statement he has had to rebuke the disciples for the ambition that led to rivalry. This needs to be replaced by a servant attitude, of which he is the supreme example. In his case, the heart of that service was the giving of his life as a ransom. This translates the Greek word *lutron.*

Don Carson claims that *lutron* was most commonly used of the price paid to liberate a slave.[10] However, it seems to me that, in biblical usage, while the notion of the emancipation of slaves is certainly present,[11] the more important emphasis is on the ransom as the price paid to release from the threat of death: there are far more texts which make that link.[12]

God's promise in Hosea 13:14 gets us to the heart of the matter: "I will ransom them from the power of the grave; I will redeem them from death." Moreover, the death from which the ransom redeems is specifically the judicial death of condemnation: "The LORD redeems

10. D. A. Carson, "Matthew," 433.

11. Exod 21:8; Lev 19:20; 25:48–49, 51–52, 54; Num 35:32; Deut 24:18; Lam 5:8; Mic 6:4.

12. Exod 13:13; 15, 21:30; 30:12; 34:20; Lev 27:29; Num 3:12, 46, 48–49, 51; 18:15–17; 35:31; 2 Sam 4:9; 1 Kgs 1:29; Pss 7:2; 34:22; 49:7–8, 15; 103:4; 119:154; 144:10; Prov 13:8; Hos 13:14.

the soul of his servants, and none of those who trust in him shall be condemned" (Ps 34:22).

Here, then, Jesus is defining his own life, surrendered in death, as the price paid to effect our release from the death which is our condemnation because of our sin and guilt. His death is the payment which satisfies a holy and angered God. We stand under the sentence of death, but God executed our sentence on Jesus Christ. He died under the divine judgment. As a result, we no longer face the sentence passed against us as guilty sinners.

Warfield notes that Jesus' words "could not fail to determine for his followers their whole conception of the nature of his redemptive work."[13] We therefore find that the concept of the ransom permeates the New Testament teaching on Christ's death.

The preposition "for" (*anti*) means "instead of." It "denotes substitution, equivalence, exchange."[14] As Wessel puts it, "what should have happened to them happened to him instead."[15] In 1 Timothy 2:6, Paul says that Christ Jesus, "gave himself a ransom (*antilutron*) for all." Here is a deliberate echo of Jesus' words, except that Paul uses a compound term which includes the preposition *anti* as a prefix. This makes explicit the truth that the ransom took the form of the substitution of one life for another. The death of Jesus was the payment for sin.

John 1:29

Early on, as his ministry was about to begin, Jesus approached John the Baptist, who announced: "Behold! The Lamb of God who takes away the sin of the world!" A lamb was acceptable for various of the Old Testament sacrifices. John depicts Jesus as the ultimate fulfilment of what the sacrifices represented. He is the true Lamb of God, towards which they were mere pointers. Jesus' role was to achieve definitively what the Old Testament sacrifices could only symbolize: to be the sweet aroma which eternally lays the divine anger to rest. As the Lamb of God, Jesus takes away the world's sin. He removes sin from its position as the magnet that attracts God's wrath, and so protects us from condemnation. He brings us into the position where God can say to us, "never again will you face my judgment."

---

13. Warfield, *Christ*, 464.
14. D. A. Carson, "Matthew," 433.
15. Wessel, "Mark," 721.

Romans 3:24–25

Paul proclaims that we are justified freely through faith by God's grace "through the redemption that is in Christ Jesus, whom God set forth *as a* propitiation by his blood."

"Redemption" translates the compound term, *apolutrōsis*, which Warfield calls "the specialty of New Testament usage." He points out that the prefix, *apo-*, draws attention to the deliverance from death which is the result of atonement, while the second part of the word, *-lutrōsis*, implies that it is through the payment of a ransom price that the deliverance is achieved.[16] This ransom price is "in Christ Jesus." He himself was the payment. His life laid down in death met the cost of our salvation.

"Propitiation" translates *hilastērion*. This is the regular Septuagint translation of *kappōret*, the mercy seat. Jesus Christ is the true fulfilment of everything which the mercy seat symbolized. The mercy seat was the place where God and his people met in true fellowship, because it was the place where atonement was achieved, where God's anger was permanently laid to rest. Our Lord is now that place. In him we meet with a God whose anger will never again burn towards us.

This passage stresses that atonement is made in Jesus' blood. His shed blood is the sign that his life has been surrendered in lieu of ours, in order to pay the penalty which we owed to God for our sin. He died as a substitutionary sacrifice. Dunn explains Paul's meaning in terms of "sacrificial interchange," which means that "the sinner lives, the sinless dies . . . . As the sinner's sin was transferred to the spotless sacrifice, so the spotless life of the sacrifice was transferred (or reckoned) to the sinner." Moreover, God put him forward. This phrase "underscores the divine initiative," and emphasizes that "it was God himself who acted" in the death of Christ.[17]

1 John 2:2; 4:10

We look, finally, at these two verses from John's first letter. The first reads: "he himself is the propitiation for our sins, and not for ours only but also for the whole world," while the second explains that "in this is love,

---

16. Warfield, *Christ*, 465–66.
17. Dunn, *Romans*, 170–72.

not that we loved God, but that he loved us and sent his Son *to be* the propitiation for our sins."

Both verses contain the word *hilasmos*, translated "propitiation." Whereas *hilastērion*, used in Romans 5, points to the mercy seat, the place of atonement, this related word draws attention to the means of atonement, the atoning sacrifice itself.

We may note the following four points with reference to this pair of verses.

(1) Both include the phrase "for our sins." It is sins which make an atonement necessary.

(2) The Greek text of 1 John 2:2 includes the word *autos*. This puts emphasis on the fact that he himself is the propitiation for our sins. Jesus did not merely offer a sacrifice; he was the atoning sacrifice for sin.

(3) 1 John 4:10 tells us that the Father sent him for this purpose. There is no divide between the Father and the Son. The Son did not offer himself on his own initiative in the hope of seizing favor for us from a reluctant Father. It was the Father who initiated the entire process of atonement.

(4) The basis of the Father's atoning purpose was love. The sending of the Son to die on the cross was the highest expression of love; it was the very epitome of love. The cross of Jesus is the love of God.

DOCTRINAL FORMULATION

The Early Creeds

The doctrine of atonement is not addressed as such in the early creeds. However, five pointers towards it are worth noting.

The creeds jump from the birth to the death of Jesus

The Apostles' Creed says that Jesus Christ was "born of the virgin Mary, suffered under Pontius Pilate." Likewise, the Nicene Creed records that Jesus Christ "was incarnate by the Holy Spirit of the virgin Mary, and was made man; and was crucified also for us under Pontius Pilate." The Athanasian Creed jumps from a statement of the truth of the incarnation to the fact of Jesus' suffering: "God and man is one Christ, who suffered for our salvation."

Gareth Brandt criticizes the creeds on this score. He argues that they are inadequate, because they totally bypass Jesus' life. His teaching and miracles are totally overlooked.[18] However, I would suggest that Brandt's criticism is misplaced. What the early creeds are doing is to point us straight to the very heart of what Christ is all about.

Those early Christian theologians had a sound biblical insight. They recognized that what sinful man most needs is not a religious teacher, not an example whom we can aspire to follow, not someone to sort out the problems of mortal life. What sinful man most needs is a Savior who suffered for our sins and made atonement, and so the creeds come directly to this main point.

The creeds pile up terms to portray the fact of Christ's death

The Apostles' Creed is the fullest. It uses four different words—suffered (used also in the Nicene and Athanasian Creeds), crucified (repeated in the Nicene Creed), died, and buried (used again by the Nicene Creed).

Kelly suggests "that the details of the Lord's experiences were elaborated so as to underline the reality of his death."[19] For the early church was well aware that if anything in the experiences of the Lord needed underlining, it was his death. That was the vital thing, the most important of all his accomplishments.

The creeds are clear that the real purpose of the incarnation was a saving purpose

The Nicene Creed explains that Jesus Christ came down from heaven "for us men and for our salvation," words which are repeated in the Chalcedonian Definition. The Athanasian Creed abbreviates them by saying that Christ "suffered for our salvation." The Nicene Creed says also, "he was crucified for us." These are obvious echoes of New Testament terminology, especially the phrase "for us." The purpose of Christ's coming was to save us from sin.

18. Brandt, "Radical Christology," *passim.*
19. J. N. D. Kelly, *Creeds,* 383.

The creeds teach Jesus' descent into hell

In both the Apostles' Creed and the Athanasian Creed, references to Jesus' suffering are followed by the statement, "he descended into hell." The meaning of this clause has been the subject of discussion and controversy both in the early centuries and in more recent times. One viewpoint, represented by William Cunningham, is that, since this statement is found merely in the creeds and not in the Bible, "we are under no obligation to explain or to believe it."[20] However, Cunningham then spends two pages discussing it at some length!

Kelly notes that the early church assumed that the descent took place during the three days that Christ's body was in the tomb. Its purpose was defined differently by different early writers: some saw it as the declaration of his victory to the faithful departed, others as the release of their souls to glory. Some writers combined both. By the end of the second century the tendency was to interpret the descent into hell as Christ's opportunity to tread down the demonic powers in order to bring man safely home to the heights of heaven.[21]

Calvin also understood the purpose of the descent to hell to be the liberation of fallen man, though he stressed that the victory by which Christ trod down the powers of hell took place on the cross. He descended to hell as he suffered its agonies in our place. This raises a question. Why does the creed mention Jesus' descent to hell after his burial if it happened before—on the cross? This is Calvin's answer:

> after explaining what Christ endured in the sight of man, the Creed appropriately adds the invisible and incomprehensible judgment which he endured before God, to teach us that not only was the body of Christ given up as the price of redemption, but that there was a greater and more excellent price—that he bore in his soul the tortures of condemned and ruined man.[22]

If Calvin is correct to understand this clause in this way, then the creed hints at the truth of substitutionary atonement, though without spelling it out in detail.

---

20. Cunningham, *Historical Theology*, Vol. 1, 90–91.

21. J. N. D. Kelly, *Creeds*, 380–81.

22. Calvin, *Institutes*, 2.16.10.

The creeds mention Christ's resurrection, ascension,
and present position at the Father's right hand

The Apostles', Nicene, and Athanasian Creeds all mention all three of these events. While not strictly part of the doctrine of atonement, they are historical proof that Christ's death did successfully atone for sin. As Kelly says,

> The first- and second-century Christian who expressed his faith in [these events] understood them as implying that Christ had beaten down the hostile powers opposed to him, and consequently to his church.[23]

The Reformation Confessions

The confessions often quote the creeds on this subject. We shall look first at the main themes in the confessional doctrine of the atonement, and then at some additional emphases.

The Main Themes

We may identify three main themes in the teaching of the confessions on the atonement.

THE ATONEMENT AS A SACRIFICE

The description of Jesus' death as a sacrifice is found in most of the confessions. It is the only atoning sacrifice, and it was offered both for our actual transgressions and also for our original guilt. The sacrificial nature of Jesus' death is associated with his perfect obedience. He was the Lamb of God without blemish, and his innocence was declared by Pilate his human judge. Several of the confessions allude to the letter to the Hebrews, and describe Christ as our high priest. As such, he presented himself to the Father on our behalf.

---

23. J. N. D. Kelly, *Creeds*, 151.

THE ATONEMENT AS A SUBSTITUTION

The confessions state that our iniquities were laid on Christ, that he willingly bore the curse and punishment for our sin, and felt and suffered the Father's wrath, which sinners deserved. "He was wounded and plagued for our transgressions," as the Scottish Confession puts it. As a result God's wrath was appeased. The language of judicial exchange is present in some of the confessions: God's judgment was directed at his Son, so that his mercy and goodness come to us.

THE ATONEMENT AS A SATISFACTION

This gets us to the heart of the Reformation teaching on atonement. Almost all the confessions speak of the "satisfaction" which Christ made for the sins of his people. The Heidelberg Catechism explains: "God wills that his justice be satisfied, therefore we must make full satisfaction to the same, either by ourselves or by another."

The Canons of Dort point out that God's justice requires our sins to be punished, "not only with temporal but with eternal punishments, both in body and soul; which we cannot escape, unless satisfaction be made to the justice of God."

The Westminster Confession connects satisfaction with a purchase price:

> The Lord Jesus, by his perfect obedience, and sacrifice of himself . . . , has fully satisfied the justice of his Father, and purchased not only reconciliation, but an everlasting inheritance in the kingdom of heaven, for all those whom the Father has given to him.

It is worth pausing to look at the idea of satisfaction in more detail. Reymond[24] traces the origin of this understanding of atonement to Anselm and his work, written in 1098, whose title translates as *Why Did God Become Human?*[25]

In the early medieval period the idea was around that Christ's death was a ransom paid to the devil to get him to set people free from his clutches. John Leith still defends this notion.[26] However, Anselm rightly

---

24. Reymond, *New Systematic Theology*, 1121–23.
25. Anselm, *Cur Deus Homo?, passim.*
26. Leith, *Doctrine*, 154–55.

rejected it: God owed the devil nothing. What needed addressing was not the devil's usurped rights of ownership, but God's offended honor. Christ's death was a vicarious satisfaction offered to God the Father in his capacity as the legal representative of the whole Trinity.

Anselm argued that God's infinite holiness made even the tiniest sin infinitely culpable and the sinner liable to infinite wrath.

Anselm's understanding of satisfaction is based on a principle of justice applicable in the medieval world: human beings come in family units, and an offence committed by one family member could be compensated for by another member instead of the offender himself. In the incarnation, God the Son became a member of the human family so that he could discharge the debt accrued by the human race.

Because of God's infinite holiness, man's infinite blameworthiness, and God's infinite wrath, satisfaction requires an infinite payment. But such a payment is only possible by a sinless being whom God accredits with infinite worth. And that has to be God himself. The incarnation was therefore necessary so that the cross of Jesus could repay God for the injury done to his honor by sin.

The Additional Emphases

Four points are worth making.

THE SUFFERING OF JESUS CHRIST WAS BOTH PHYSICAL AND SPIRITUAL

Several of the confessions stress that Christ suffered in both body and soul, making the point that bodily suffering alone would not have been enough to make atonement. The cruel death of the cross involved him facing the wrath of his Father, and so experiencing the terrible punishment merited by our sins.

THE BASIS OF THE ATONEMENT WAS THE DIVINE MERCY

The confessions acknowledge the justice of God in demanding atonement for sin. They also praise the mercy of God for providing it. The Belgic Confession says that God gave his Son to die "out of mere and perfect love." It was infinite mercy which lay behind God's giving of his Son.

THE CONFESSIONS COMMENT ON THE DESCENT INTO HELL

The Westminster Larger Catechism uses this phrase, but seems simply to understand it as another way of speaking of Jesus' burial:

> Christ's humiliation after his death consisted in his being buried, and continuing in the state of the dead, and under the power of death until the third day; which has been otherwise expressed in these words, he descended into hell.

The Heidelberg Catechism is closer to Calvin's understanding. It asks, "Why is it added, 'He descended into hell?'" The answer goes:

> That in my greatest temptations I may be assured that Christ my Lord, by his inexpressible anguish, pains and terrors, which he suffered in his soul on the cross and before, has redeemed me from the anguish and torment of hell.

This aptly sees the reference to Christ's descent into hell as a thorough summary of the entire doctrine of the atonement. Substitution and exchange are being declared here.

THE RESURRECTION WAS A REALITY

The resurrection was God's declaration that he was indeed satisfied with the death of Christ. The cross really achieved what it set out to do: by giving his life Jesus made satisfaction for human sin to divine justice.

But such comments only make sense if Christ truly did rise from the dead. If Jesus was merely raised spiritually, then the entire doctrine of the atonement falls to the ground. A real, bodily resurrection is a necessity if the atonement is a fact.

The confessions therefore condemn those who deny a true bodily resurrection. As the apostle says, "if Christ is not risen, your faith *is* futile; you are still in your sins!" However, we may truly praise God, because a few verses later he continues, "But now Christ is risen from the dead" (1 Cor 15:17, 20).

Modern Confessions of Faith

The three confessions which we are using add little in the case of this theme. The traditional elements in the doctrine of atonement are touched upon fairly briefly. All three statements mention the facts of Jesus' death on the cross and his burial, as well as the resurrection, ascension, and Jesus' present position seated at the Father's side.

The language of sacrifice is used: both the Indian and Indonesian confessions describe the Lord's death as a "perfect sacrifice." The shedding of Jesus' blood is mentioned.

Jesus' death, we are told, was offered for our deliverance from sin, death, and the devil's rule, and for our reconciliation with God. The Indonesian confession acknowledges the "remission of sin which Jesus Christ procured through his death." It insists that we cannot be redeemed by our own good works, or by any power of our own, "but only from the grace of God and through the redemption of Jesus Christ." It sees the descent into hell as an experience which Jesus suffered after his burial. The Indian confession rightly notes that Jesus' perfect obedience to God's law was the basis for his sacrificial self-offering. Similarly, the Chinese confession states that he was without sin, and emphasizes the voluntary nature of his sacrifice.

Although the Chinese confession does not mention it, the concept of propitiatory sacrifice is found in Chinese history. Chan Kei Thong notes that, for 4,000 years, Chinese Emperors represented their people in an annual sacrifice to the supreme God. He traces the awareness of the need for sacrifice to settlers in China dispersed after Babel. He points out that this awareness predated the Levitical instructions, and was known to the earliest generations of mankind, including Noah.

The sacrificial animals offered by the Chinese Emperor had to be without blemish. On the way to the place where they were slain, they passed through a gate called "The Gate of Hell." This, Thong suggests, indicates an ancient Chinese understanding that the death penalty rightly due to the worshippers was being borne instead by the sacrifice. Thong writes: "the Chinese shared with the Hebrews an understanding that God demanded propitiation for sin and required that it be a perfect and excellent sacrifice."

Thong describes this ancient Chinese tradition as a signpost to the substitutionary, atoning death of Jesus Christ.[27] As such, the memory of this historic annual sacrifice may well be a point of contact for directing the Chinese people to the ultimate unblemished sacrifice which God has provided for the sins of the world, the sacrifice of his own dear Son.

---

27. Thong, *Faith of our Fathers*, 113–51.

HISTORICAL ELABORATION

I want to focus on three issues in this section. First, we shall look at the debate about penal substitution. Second, we shall consider the question whether atonement is primarily a matter of propitiation, or whether the concept of "expiation" is more appropriate. Third, we shall discuss the issue of the extent of the atonement.

The Penal Substitution Debate

The truth of penal substitutionary atonement is often challenged. During the first decade of the twenty-first century, Steve Chalke and Alan Mann wrote a book in which one section rejects this doctrine.[28]

They claim that the view that Jesus was punished in our place because of God's anger towards sinners contradicts the statement "God is love." Taking John 3:16 as their starting point, they ask how it is possible to believe that a God of love would suddenly vent his anger on his own Son and punish him for sins he didn't even commit. They claim that this turns the cross into "a form of cosmic child abuse."

This silly comparison shows that Chalke and Mann have lost sight of the trinitarian nature of God, and overlooks the fact that Jesus on the cross was not a child, but a mature adult with a will of his own, who chose to co-operate with the Father's will. Chalke and Mann fail to see the togetherness of Father and Son in the plan for the ransom of sinners. Moreover, they have forgotten that this plan was drawn up in eternity: it was no sudden impulse. Garry Williams points out that the punishment of the Son by the Father is clearly taught in Scripture, for example, in Isaiah 53:6.[29]

Chalke and Mann replace the truth of penal substitution with a theory of absorption:

> On the cross [Jesus] absorbed all the pain, all the suffering, caused by the breakdown in our relationship with God and in doing so demonstrated the lengths to which a God who is love will go to restore it.

The last part of that statement is not totally wrong, but it begs the question: how does the cross demonstrate the lengths to which divine love

---

28. Chalke & Mann, *Lost Message*, 181–85.
29. G. J. Williams, "Penal Substitution," 178.

will go if absorption of pain is not the same as the bearing of guilt and punishment?

Chalke later wrote an article in which he made some additional points.[30] He concedes that the doctrine of penal substitution teaches that it was love which led God to punish his Son in place of sinners, but, he insists, the basic underlying picture is a God of wrath. This, Chalke claims, contradicts what Jesus says about the Father in the parable of the prodigal son: he does not punish, but runs and welcomes. The message of the cross is that God, in great love, intervenes to put right the broken relationship with a world out of harmony with his purpose.

Chalke is clearly weak on the doctrine of sin. Moreover, to emphasize the truth of God's love to the exclusion of holiness and wrath is clearly to present an unbalanced and unbiblical picture of God.

Chalke also claims that penal substitution makes all but the last weekend of a thirty-three-year incarnation unnecessary. He asks why, if God needed a sacrifice in order to forgive, didn't Jesus just come and die? However, Jesus' life is not irrelevant. For him to be able to lay down in death a sinless life, that life had first to be lived.

Chalke asserts that atonement is multifaceted. Substitution may be one element, though he denies that this substitution is penal. It is true that there are other facets to the biblical doctrine of the atonement in addition to penal substitution. James Packer notes that, in addition to the God-ward doctrine of satisfaction through the substitutionary punishment of sin, there have been two other ways in which Christ's death has been explained: (1) the cross reveals God's love, and changes our lack of God-ward motivation; (2) the cross is Christ's victory over demonic powers, and liberates us from their power.

Packer acknowledges the truth in these other explanations. However, neither of them is coherent without the third. The reason why we need to be both changed and set free is precisely that we have sinned against our maker, stand under his judgment, and therefore need a propitiatory sacrifice by a substitute who bears our guilt and punishment, and so turns God's rejection of us into acceptance.[31]

Chalke claims that no single theory of atonement can sum up the breadth and depth of the cross. He may be right about the breadth, but as for the depth—penal substitution is the indispensable explanation.

30. Chalke, "Crosspurposes," *passim.*
31. Packer, *Cross, passim.*

Propitiation or Expiation?

We noted how the Day of Atonement regulations included reference to cleansing as a secondary aspect of atonement. It is sometimes claimed that this is not secondary, but the primary purpose, and that the most appropriate word to sum up atonement is not "propitiation," which implies that atonement is directed towards God to nullify his anger, but "expiation," implying that atonement is directed towards sinners to cleanse our hearts from sin.[32]

John Hartley, for example, argues that, in the Old Testament passages to do with sacrifice, atonement most frequently results in forgiveness of sin. He claims that these passages do not mention God's wrath, that for God to display wrath is rare, and that the focus of the sacrifices is not kindled anger, but potential anger. Without expiation there is a risk of facing God's anger, but the sacrifices expiate sin and God's anger is not kindled.[33]

However, this distinction between kindled and potential anger is a dubious basis for Hartley's claim. It overlooks the fact that God's anger is always smouldering in the background, because the world is sinful. There is an ever-present danger that God's wrath will erupt unless it is appeased and pacified. The only reason why sinners are not destroyed is precisely that God's anger remains unkindled because of the atoning sacrifice. Hartley also overlooks the substitutionary nature of sacrifice. Another dies instead: punishment does fall, but it misses the sinner, because it alights on his substitute. God's wrath is diverted, but it is still expressed.

The appeasement of God's wrath "must be central" to the concept of atonement.[34] The primary direction of atonement is God-ward. Its primary purpose is to avert judgment. Its primary meaning is propitiation. Expiation from the sin which calls down that judgment is a secondary purpose.[35]

32. So Dodd, *Bible and the Greeks*, ch. 5; Hartley, *Leviticus*, 62.
33. Hartley, *Leviticus*, 65.
34. Budd, *Numbers*, 196.
35. Cf. L. Morris, "*hilastērion*," *passim*.

The Extent of the Atonement

Two Views of the Issue

Here is the second of the five points raised by the Arminians in *The Remonstrance* during the controversy in the Netherlands:

> Jesus Christ, the Savior of the world, died for all men and for every man, so that he has obtained for them all, by his death on the cross, redemption, and the forgiveness of sins; yet that no one actually enjoys this forgiveness of sins, except the believer.

Then John 3:16 and 1 John 2:2 are quoted.

In response, the Canons of Dort acknowledged that Christ's death was "abundantly sufficient to expiate the sins of the whole world," and that the gospel promise and appeal "ought to be announced and proclaimed indiscriminately and without distinction to all peoples and to every person." The Canons then explain that God's sovereign will was, through the preaching of the gospel, to bring Christ's salvation to his elect, and to justify them through faith. His purpose was that Christ, by his blood, "should efficaciously redeem out of every people, tribe, nation, and language, all and only those who were elected to salvation from eternity."

Here we have two different views of the extent (and therefore also of the purpose) of the atonement.

The Arminian view teaches that Christ died for everyone to make salvation possible. Salvation becomes actual through faith. God's purpose in Christ's death was to put a potential salvation on offer.

The Reformed view teaches that Christ died for the elect actually to save them. Through faith this actual salvation is applied. God's purpose was to save his people from their sins.

The issue is this: has Christ's atonement rendered complete satisfaction to God's justice and nullified his anger against every single individual human being, or specifically against those whom the Holy Spirit leads to trust in the work of Christ?

The biblical language about atonement is very definite. The sacrifice of substitution is the sweet aroma, as a result of which something changes in God: he is no longer angry. It follows that, if Christ died for everyone, then God is angry with no one, and so everyone must be saved. If an Arminian then protests that he is not a universalist, there is only one alternative. He must say that God is not angry with anyone but still punishes some anyway. The Arminian God then becomes an unjust ty-rant, or a sadistic joker.

Scriptural Support for the Reformed View

However, we need to be able to back up the Reformed view from Scrip-ture. Robert Reymond offers a range of biblical evidences for the doctrine that the atonement was particular and definite, rather than universal and indefinite in its design.[36] Two of his points are particularly helpful.

(1) The language of Scripture is particularistic. We read that Christ died for his people (Isa 53:8; Matt 1:21), for his sheep (John 10:11, 15), for his church (Acts 20:28; Eph 5:25). In John 10:26 Jesus says, "You do not believe because you are not part of my flock." He makes it clear that we do not become his sheep by believing. Rather, it is his sheep who become believers.

(2) The way in which the Bible speaks of atonement makes it neces-sarily particular rather than universal. Reymond notes the four preposi-tions used in the New Testament.

[a] *peri*. Christ died *for* others. An example is 1 Peter 3:18: Christ "suffered once for sins, the just for (*peri*) the unjust."

[b] *huper*. Christ died *on behalf of* others. For example, Romans 5:6 says, "Christ died for (*huper*) the ungodly."

[c] *dia*. Christ died *for the sake of* others. 1 Corinthians 8:11 is our example. It speaks of the brother "for (*dia*) whom Christ died."

[d] *anti*. Christ died *instead of* others. The example is Mark 10:45: Jesus says that he came "to give his life a ransom for (*anti*) many."

Although some of these prepositions can sometimes have a more general sense, their overall combined implication is that Jesus actually paid the penalty for those for whom he died, and therefore every one of them is actually discharged from guilt.

Since God is just, the fact is that he will never inflict punishment twice for the same sin. Consequently, a universal atonement must logi-cally lead to universal salvation. If we deny that universal salvation is biblical, we have to affirm particular atonement.

Reymond quotes a splendid passage from Spurgeon, who insists that Christ's death secured the salvation of the elect. Therefore, "they not

---

36. Reymond, *New Systematic Theology*, 673–82.

only may be saved, but are saved, must be saved, and cannot by any possibility run the hazard of being anything but saved."

Reymond also points out that the idea of universal atonement really means that Christ did not actually substitute for anyone and that his death actually guarantees the salvation of no one. All that it does is to make everyone somehow saveable. That would mean that, in the end, salvation depends not on God's work in Christ, but on man's response. It leads to a doctrine of salvation by human merit.

The Arminian evangelist can never know whether anyone will ever respond to the gospel. Arminianism implies that heaven could have remained for ever empty. What a gloomy idea that is! It is enough to drive the preacher to despair, to make him give up.

The Reformed evangelist, on the other hand, knows that there is a people whom Christ has died to save, and that these people will definitely come to Christ in response to the preaching of the gospel. That gives him a great encouragement to go on preaching. His labor in the Lord will not be in vain. God will save his people. Heaven shall be populated with ransomed sinners.

Scripture's Universal Texts

Having said all that, there are Scriptures which appear to say that Christ's atonement is universal in scope. Jesus died for all; he died for the world. It is necessary to give attention to these expressions. Waldron rightly points out that they often mean "all nations." He writes: "universal terms are often directed against Jewish exclusivism."[37] The gospel door is now wide open to the Gentile world also. However, this national definition cannot account for all the apparently universal texts of Scripture.

TEXTS CITED IN *THE REMONSTRANCE*

The Remonstrance cited two texts, and we shall start by looking at them.

---

37. Waldron, *Modern Exposition*, 164.

John 3:16

This is probably the best known gospel verse in the whole Bible. It connects God's giving of his only begotten Son with his love for the world. Two things may be said about the word "world" in this verse.

(1) It has ethical connotations. It is defined by certain other statements in John's writings. His fullest account of the world in this ethical sense is found in 1 John 2:15–16:

> Do not love the world or the things in the world. If anyone loves the world, the love of the Father is not in him. For all that *is* in the world—the lust of the flesh, the lust of the eyes, and the pride of life—is not of the Father but is of the world.

In the light of those words, to hear, "God so loved the world," is to be invited to celebrate the amazing wonder of divine love.

(2) There is a sense in which it is true that "world" here does have a universal sense. Often "world" refers to God's entire creation project, especially as it comes to its highest expression in human life. And there is a universal love of God which lies behind the giving of his Son. However, that is not yet to say whether the atonement which the Son made is intended to save the whole world. The implication of the words "whoever believes" is that there is a limitation to the effects of God's love. Particular atonement is the manifestation of a universal love.

1 John 2:2

The New King James Version renders this text correctly when it says that Christ is the propitiation, not only for our sins, "but also for the whole world." Other versions often insert the words *the sins of* into the phrase "for the whole world." This is because the phrase "the whole world" is in the genitive case (*holou tou kosmou*), and therefore could refer to something pertaining to the world—namely, its sins. However, the preposition "for" (*peri*) is one which, in any case, takes the genitive, so the insertion is not essential.

"The whole world" should, I think, be understood as the entire creation. God's anger blazed against creation itself, where man, the creature who stood at the apex of that creation, had led the entire universe into a condition of fallenness. Christ's death on the cross appeased that anger against creation as a whole, so that the world is preserved for the preaching of the gospel.

The Old Testament speaks on several occasions of atonement being made for the environment in which the sinful people moved. For example, Aaron had to make atonement "for the tabernacle of meeting which remains among them in the midst of their uncleanness" (Lev 16:16).

Maybe Jesus' atoning sacrifice achieved something similar for this entire universe groaning under the weight of human uncleanness. If this is a correct reading, there is no evidence here for a universal atonement in the sense of an effective propitiation for every human individual.[38]

OTHER RELEVANT TEXTS

In addition to those two texts there are others where the "all nations" interpretation is not obviously appropriate. We shall note three representative examples.

Romans 8:32

This text illustrates how, sometimes, the word "all" is qualified by the text itself. We are reminded here that God "did not spare his own Son but delivered him up for us all."

So, yes indeed, Jesus was delivered up "for us all," but the word "us" helps to define the word "all."

Suppose I'm attending a meeting in London on a day when gale force winds are blowing and the rain is torrential. I might say to my fellow participants, "Isn't the weather is wild for us all today!" What do I mean by "us all"? I might mean "everyone who is in London right now." But probably, I am speaking with a more limited intention, meaning "all of us who are at this meeting." I will certainly not mean "everyone who inhabits planet earth." The shared context—London, and that particular meeting—already places a restriction on the scope of the word "all."

So it is in this text. Those included in "us all" are defined by the context. In the surrounding passage Paul speaks of those who are predestined, called, justified and glorified (verse 30), of God's elect (verse 33), who are inseparable from his love in Christ (verses 35–39). So "us all"

---

38. Cf. Bayes, "Propitiation," *passim.*

means all of us of whom these surrounding descriptions are true—we are the ones for whom God gave up his Son.

2 Corinthians 5:14–15, and 19

It is true that there are some texts where, taking their statements at face value, it is hard to see how they can have any other than a genuinely universal sense. This passage is an obvious instance, with its statements that "one died for all," and that God in Christ was "reconciling the world to himself." However, this does not mean that such expressions should be read in a way which contradicts the definiteness of God's atonement for his elect people.

Gresham Machen argues that the context concerns Christ's relation to the church. He concludes that "all" in verses 14 and 15 means every one of his people, and that there is no implication that Christ died for all people, whether or not they become Christians.[39] Reymond notes that "world" in verse 19 is not preceded by the definite article in Greek, and sees this as limiting the application of the statement. It is not the whole world which is in view, but *a* world of people who form a subset of that whole.[40]

However, it is hard to disagree with Albert Barnes, who argues that "all" in verses 14 and 15 refers to every human being without exception, and says that this "is the plain and obvious meaning of the expression— the sense which strikes all men, unless they have some theory to support to the contrary." Similarly, on verse 19 Barnes writes: "The world here evidently means the human race generally," and finds evidence in this text "that God designed that the plan of salvation should be adapted to all men."[41]

On the basis of his reading of these texts Barnes argues that God provided a universal atonement, but decreed in election to apply its benefits only to his elect. This resembles the teaching known as Amyraldianism, named after the seventeenth-century French Protestant theologian, Moise Amyraut.

Amyraut offered a modified version of Calvinism which reversed the logical order of two of God's decrees. Traditionally, Reformed

---

39. Machen, *God Transcendent*, 146–47.
40. Reymond, *New Systematic Theology*, 698.
41. Barnes, *New Testament*, Vol. 6, 116, 130.

theology placed God's election of his people first, followed by the decree to provide a definite atonement to save them from their sins. According to Amyraut, God first decreed to provide a universal atonement conditional upon faith. However, knowing that no sinner could exercise faith by his own free will, God then elected a people to whom he would grant the gift of faith and the benefits of the atonement.

The weakness in this approach is that it threatens to undermine the truth of penal substitution. If Christ died instead of everyone, then how can anyone die for his own sins? If someone else does something instead of me, then I do not also have to do it myself. Logically, Amyraldianism should lead to universalism. The decree of election prevents Amyraldianism from going in that direction, but, as Warfield has pointed out, this simply highlights the inconsistency and instability of the position.[42]

How, then, should texts like these be read, without capitulating to Amyraldianism?

Machen is right that we need to note the context in which these apparently universal statements occur. However, I am not sure that his summary of the context as Christ's relation to the church is correct. Rather, Paul is defending his evangelistic ministry.[43]

In chapter 3 he rejoices to be a minister of the new covenant. In chapter 4 and the first part of chapter 5, he points to the things that sustain him in this ministry, despite the setbacks and sufferings. Then from verse 11 he begins to speak of the persuasive nature of his ministry of reconciliation, motivated by the fear of the Lord and the love of Christ.

It is in this context that Paul refers to Christ's death for all in order to reconcile the world to God. The issue is not the doctrine of the church, but the practicalities of gospel outreach. Paul is convinced that he must preach the gospel to every creature. The fact is that Christ "died sufficiently for all, but efficiently for the elect only."[44] Where the context concerns gospel motivation, it is the universal sufficiency of the atonement which is in view: this is what impels the apostle to preach persuasively to everyone, appealing to them all to be reconciled to God.

---

42. Warfield, *Plan, passim.*
43. Cf. Belleville, *2 Corinthians,* 60.
44. Quoted, e.g., by Turretin, *Institutes,* 459.

1 Timothy 2:1–7

Here is another example of a text which sounds universal in its scope. However, the fact that Christ Jesus "gave himself a ransom for all" (verse 6) does not mean that all human individuals without exception will be ransomed from eternal death. The context defines the apostle's intention. The phrase "all men" has already appeared twice in this passage. In verse 1 Paul urges prayer for all men, including those in authority. The reason for this is that God desires all men to be saved (verse 4), and it is this which is undergirded by the truth that Christ gave himself a ransom for all. In verse 7 Paul sees this as the reason for his appointment as a preacher to the Gentiles. Here again, the context is the scope of gospel ministry. Since Christ is the only mediator, since his ransom is universally sufficient, there is a mandate to pray for, and to preach to, absolutely everyone.

"Limited Atonement"?

This is the title sometimes given to the understanding of the doctrine of the atonement which we have been defending. The point is that the ransom price was not paid for all people, but for a limited number—the definite number of God's elect. However, "limited atonement" is a rather unfortunate label. It risks conveying the impression that the Reformed faith believes that God's elect is a very limited number in proportion to the human race as a whole. This, though, has not been the conclusion drawn by those who hold to a Reformed theological position.

George Marsden summarizes Jonathan Edwards's theology like this:

> God's trinitarian essence is love. God's purpose in creating a universe in which sin is permitted must be to communicate that love to creatures. The highest or most beautiful love is sacrificial love for the undeserving. Those—ultimately the vast majority of humans—who are given eyes to see that ineffable beauty will be enthralled by it.[45]

Edwards believed that the vast majority of the human race was included in God's saving purpose in Christ.

This view was common amongst earlier Reformed theologians. In Romans 5:18–19 we read these words:

---

45. Marsden, *Jonathan Edwards*, 505.

As through one man's offence *judgment came* to all men, resulting in condemnation, even so through one man's righteous act
the free gift came to all men, resulting in justification of life. For
as by one man's disobedience many were made sinners, so also
by one man's obedience many will be made righteous.

Here is Charles Hodge's comment on these verses:

We have no right to put any limit on these general terms, except
what the Bible itself places on them . . . . All the descendants of
Adam, except Christ, are under condemnation; all the descendants of Adam, except those of whom it is expressly revealed
that they cannot inherit the kingdom of God, are saved.

Hodge continues by noting that the apostle

does not hesitate to say that where sin abounded, grace has
much more abounded; that the benefits of redemption far
exceed the effects of the fall; that the number of the saved far
exceeds the number of the lost.[46]

The same view—that God's elect includes most people—is put forward
by Lorraine Boettner. Commenting on God's purpose in Colossians 1:18
("that in all things he [Christ] might have the preeminence"), he writes:

When the doctrine of election is mentioned, many people immediately assume that this means that the great majority of
mankind will be lost. But why should anyone draw that conclusion? God is free in election to choose as many as he pleases,
and we believe that he who is infinitely merciful and benevolent
and holy will elect the great majority to life. There is no good
reason why he should be limited to only a few. We are told that
Christ is to have the pre-eminence in all things, and we do not
believe that the devil will be permitted to emerge victorious
even in numbers.[47]

C. H. Spurgeon shared this view. He writes this:

I believe there will be more in heaven than in hell. If you ask
me why I think so, I answer, because Christ, in everything, is to
"have the pre-eminence," and I cannot conceive how he could
have the pre-eminence if there are to be more in the dominions
of Satan than in paradise. Moreover, it is said there is to be a

---

46. C. Hodge, *Systematic Theology*, Vol. 1, 26.
47. Boettner, *Predestination*, 130.

multitude that no man can number in heaven; I have never read that there is to be a multitude that no man can number in hell.[48]

B. B. Warfield speaks of "the relatively insignificant body of the lost" as contrasted with the number of the elect, the tree which shades the whole world,[49] embracing "the vast majority of the human race."[50]

W. G. T. Shedd has also written on the vast numbers who will be saved by Christ's atonement. Speaking of the "larger hope," Shedd sets out to answer those who view Calvinism as a pessimistic doctrine, consigning the vast majority of the human race to eternal misery. To the contrary, he argues, Calvinism "teaches that an immense majority of the human family will be saved by the redemption of the dying and risen Son of God."[51] Later he elaborates on this in this paragraph:

> It is utterly improbable that such a stupendous miracle as the incarnation, humiliation, passion, and crucifixion of one of the persons of the Godhead, should yield a small and insignificant result; that this amazing mystery of mysteries, "which angels desire to look into," and which involves such an immense personal sacrifice on the part of the Supreme Being, should have a lame and impotent conclusion. On *a priori* grounds, therefore, we have reason to conclude that the Gospel of the Cross will be successful, and the Christian religion a triumph on the earth and among the race of creatures for whom it was intended. But this can hardly be the case, if only a small fraction of the human family are saved. The presumption, consequently, is that the great majority of mankind, not the small minority of it, will be the subjects of redeeming grace.[52]

Albert Barnes also concurs with this point of view. This is what he says:

> More *will* probably be actually saved by the work of Christ, than will be finally ruined by the fall of Adam. The number of those who shall be saved from all the human race, it is to be believed, will yet be many more than those who shall be lost. The gospel is to spread throughout the world. It is to be evangelized. The millennial glory is to rise upon the earth; and the Savior is to reign with undivided empire. Taking the race as a whole, there

48. Spurgeon, *New Testament*, Vol. 4, 785.
49. Warfield, *Biblical Doctrines*, 65.
50. Warfield, *Tertullian and Augustine*, 263–64.
51. Shedd, *Calvinism*, 116.
52. Shedd, *Calvinism*, 125–26.

is no reason to think that the number of those who shall be lost, compared with the immense multitudes that shall be saved by the work of Christ, will be more than are the prisoners in a community now, compared with the number of peaceful and virtuous citizens.[53]

These writers and preachers typically use three arguments to defend the idea that the vast majority of people will finally be saved.

(1) They point to the vast numbers of people who have been and are being saved throughout history and today from every part of the world.

(2) They held that all who die in infancy are numbered amongst the elect. The biblical evidence for this is not conclusive: it is possible, indeed probable, though not clearly revealed. If true, it will presumably include all miscarried babies and aborted foetuses.

(3) They believed that the gospel will finally triumph globally, and that every nation will visibly become part of the kingdom of Christ in accordance with the Father's promise to his Son to make all nations his inheritance (Ps 2:8).

Shedd also adds a fourth, rather more contentious, argument. He refuses to rule out the possibility that the Holy Spirit might work in regenerating power independently of the preaching of the gospel in the hearts of those who have never had the opportunity to hear the word proclaimed.[54]

To these arguments, I would also add the observation that we have no idea how often God may work in someone's heart on his or her death bed, even in the final few minutes of earthly life, or perhaps in the moment of trauma immediately preceding a tragic and untimely death. Perhaps in such circumstances the Holy Spirit might suddenly open someone's eyes to see the salvation that is in the Lord Jesus Christ, and enable the faith that receives him. How many people may have been saved just in the nick of time, so to speak? I would not rule out the possibility that there may be a staggering number in glory of whom this is true. It would certainly be a magnificent testimony to the amazing mercy of God.

The fact is, there is an elect to be saved. Christ has made atonement for the sins of his people, and they must believe on him. They are "a great multitude which no one could number, of all nations, tribes, peoples, and tongues" (Rev 7:9). But God knows their number, and, in his Son,

53. Barnes, *New Testament*, Vol. 4, 136–37.
54. Shedd, *Calvinism*, 128–29.

he has secured their eternal salvation. Because of the truth of "limited atonement" we may preach the gospel with unlimited expectancy, with immense anticipation, with intense excitement, with thoroughgoing confidence, with joyful hope. The Lord will save every single one of his people for whom Christ has died!

PRACTICAL APPLICATION

(1) The first application of this doctrine is evangelistic. It could be that you are reading this book, but you have never yet trusted in the atoning work of Christ. He is the sacrifice, substitute, and satisfaction for our sins. Faith in him is the only hope of escaping God's anger and judgment. Without him we are hopelessly lost, liable to the punishment which our sins deserve. But Christ died to suffer that punishment. Without him, we face eternal punishment, but he has paid the debt by his life-blood poured out on the cross. God's anger is turned away forever from all those who pin their hopes on his Son. As Paul and Silas said to the Philippian jailer, "believe on the Lord Jesus Christ, and you will be saved" (Acts 16:31). Never again will you face God's judgment.

(2) We must keep studying the biblical teaching on atonement. The truth of the atonement is absolutely foundational. If we make a mistake at this point, the entire Christian faith collapses. So we must continue to study the biblical teaching on this theme. There is mystery and profundity involved in it. There is enough wealth of truth here to keep us learning all our life long.

(3) We may stand secure in what Jesus Christ achieved in the atonement.

One week the children's Sunday School was about to begin. One of the Sunday School teachers, Anne, walked up to her pastor and said that she was not going to teach Sunday School any more. With that she walked out. The pastor went to see her a day or two later. She told him that she felt too unworthy to serve the Lord in that way.

It is dreadfully possible for the forgiven Christian to fall back into a sense of guilt which totally disables us for Christian service. That is because we are not focused properly on the finished work of Christ on the cross. Jesus has completely discharged our debt, removed our guilt from God's sight, totally and eternally cancelled God's anger against us.

We truly are forgiven; God never again recalls our sin to mind. We honor him as we live in the secure joy of this truth.

Thankfully, the sequel to Anne's story was a happy one. With some gentle pastoral instruction and exhortation, she came to see that her worthiness was not the issue. Jesus had paid the price in full for every sin that she had ever committed and ever would commit. In him, she was totally accepted by a holy God, who now delighted in her because of Christ. The next Sunday she was back at her post as a Sunday School teacher.

(4) We are to enjoy fellowship with God. The Old Testament mercy seat was the place of meeting with God (Exod 25:22). Because of Calvary, we may meet with God in rich fellowship. Christ suffered "that he might bring us to God" (1 Pet 3:18). We must be very careful not to allow the idea of being brought to God to become merely theoretical. The atonement is the basis for a rich spiritual experience of God, which will overwhelm our souls with wonder.

(5) We must never boast about ourselves. After explaining the glorious truths associated with the redemption and propitiation achieved in Christ, Paul insists that they exclude boasting (Rom 3:24–27). We cannot save ourselves, so we have nothing to boast about. We do not make even the tiniest contribution. Therefore, "he who glories, let him glory in the Lord" (1 Cor 1:31).

(6) We respond in heartfelt worship. As Moses concluded the Passover instructions, "the people bowed their heads and worshipped" (Exod 12:27). Included amongst the instructions were directions as to how the event was to be commemorated annually from then on. There had to be a combination of holy assembly and feasting (Exod 12:14–16). Hushed awe and exuberant joy combine to make up our appropriate response to what God has done in Christ on the cross. We are subdued with staggering wonder that mercy should go to such lengths. We revel in the overwhelmingly happy results which have come to us.

(7) We must remember that we now belong to Jesus Christ. As long as we live in the body here on earth, we belong to the one who bought us at the price of his own life-blood. Paul reminds us in 1 Corinthians 6:19–20 that we are not our own, having been "bought at a price." So we are to live every moment for his glory. He died "that those who live should no longer live for themselves, but for him who died for them and rose again" (2 Cor 5:15). Romans 8:3–4 reminds us that Christ was condemned in our place, "that the righteous requirement of the law might be fulfilled in us who do not walk according to the flesh but according to

the Spirit." Obedience and blamelessness are constantly held before us as the only valid way to respond to the high cost which Jesus paid to save us.[55] And this is not mere moralism: it involves the imitation of Christ.

(8) We serve the one who has so mercifully provided atonement for our sins. As Hebrews 9:14 tells us, the blood of Christ will "cleanse your conscience from dead works to serve the living God." One way in which those of us who are called to preach serve him is in evangelism. Christ was made sin for our sake, and so "the ministry of reconciliation" has been entrusted to us: we become "ambassadors for Christ:" we issue the appeal to receive the grace of God in this day of salvation (2 Cor 5:18—6:2).

As we go forth with the gospel of redeeming grace in a crucified Savior, let's maintain the vision of a world in which grace abounds more than sin, and so pursue the conversion of countless millions from every nation. There is an elect out there to be saved. So we preach with bold confidence. The gospel is God's alarm, for calling to Christ all for whom he died. So we preach him to all. We appeal to people's consciousness of sin and need, and then point them to the Savior who died on the cross to satisfy God's just anger against sinners, so that never again will they have to face his wrath for their sins.

And let's pray that we may be the kind of preachers who really grasp and convey the wonder of what God has done in Christ, that we—and our hearers—may be moved to the very depths of our being by the mercy that has provided atonement for sin. God forbid that we should preach the atonement in an abstract, academic way. May God enable us to preach it with passion, and also with genuine love for the Savior and for the people he came to save.

---

55. E.g., Col 1:22; Titus 2:14; 1 Pet 1:2, 18–22; 1 John 2:1–6; Rev 14:4–5.

9

The Doctrine of Salvation (1)
The Three Tenses of Salvation

THE DOCTRINE OF SALVATION is potentially a very large theme. The word "salvation" could sum up God's entire plan and activity since the fall of man into sin. This would include the history of Israel and cosmic renewal at the end of time. Our concern is more limited. We shall focus on the personal experience of salvation following from the atonement achieved at Calvary.

We sometimes speak of three tenses of salvation. Am I saved? I might answer, quite rightly, "Yes, I have been saved." But it would be equally correct to reply, "I am in the process of being saved," or "Not yet, but I will be saved one day." We are saved already from sin's penalty; we are being saved from sin's power; we shall finally be saved from sin's presence.

The New Testament speaks of salvation in these three different ways. Sometimes it sees salvation as a completed event: Paul assures his readers, "by grace you have been saved" (Eph 2:8). At other times being saved describes ongoing Christian experience: so Paul refers to "us who are being saved" (1 Cor 1:18). Again, salvation may be portrayed as a future prospect: "now our salvation *is* nearer than when we *first* believed" (Rom 13:11).[1]

1. Cf. Pink, *Eternal Security*, 7; D. W. H. Thomas, *All the Way Home*, 139;

A word of caution is in order, though. Bob Letham, while distributing the various elements of salvation between the three tenses, adds the comment that "each has past, present, and future dimensions." He elaborates on this by noting that the elements of salvation fulfilled at the start of the Christian life continue "to have significance and reality thereafter," and that "the final and eschatological aspects of salvation have a present reality to them."[2]

What is noteworthy is that those writers who emphasize these three tenses of salvation tend to limit their comments to three elements of salvation—justification (past), sanctification (present), and glorification (future). Typical is Derek Thomas. Having outlined the three tenses in general terms, he then says: "at every stage—justification, sanctification, glorification—we come with empty hands, seeking mercy from our heavenly Father."[3]

For that reason, in this chapter we shall consider those three subjects—the essential aspects of salvation—before moving on to look at other facets of salvation in the following chapters.

PART ONE: THE PAST TENSE (JUSTIFICATION)

We were justified fully the very moment we put our trust in Christ, and we remain in a justified condition for evermore. Justification is a past event with permanent consequences.

This theme is focused in two biblical word groups—*ṣādaq* terminology in Hebrew, whose root meaning is "conformity to an ethical or moral standard,"[4] and *dikaios* vocabulary in Greek, which has to do with the fulfilment of obligations.[5] It is important to keep in mind that the twofold English terminology of "justice" and "righteousness" are both translating these same sets of words from the original biblical languages.

Lloyd-Jones, *Romans*, 131–32.

2. Letham, *Systematic Theology*, 613, 615.
3. D. W. H. Thomas, *All the Way Home*, 140; cf. Lloyd-Jones, *Romans*, 131–32.
4. Stigers, "*ṣādeq*," 1879.0.
5. Seebass, "Righteousness," 353.

BIBLICAL FOUNDATION

Old Testament

Psalm 5:12 says, "you, O LORD, will bless the righteous (*ṣaddîq*)." Proverbs 12:28 adds, "in the way of righteousness (*ṣᵉdāqâ*) *is* life." These verses show how crucial righteousness is. It is the condition for enjoying God's blessing, which sets us on the road to true life.

However, in the book of Job a vital question is raised by three different speakers. In 9:2 Job asks, "how can a man be righteous (*ṣādaq*) before God?" Then in 15:14 Eliphaz agrees with this sentiment: "What *is* man, that he could be pure, and *he who is* born of a woman, that he could be righteous (*ṣādaq*)?" Finally, in 25:4, Bildad repeats the same point: "How then can man be righteous (*ṣādaq*) before God?" The implication of these rhetorical questions is that it is totally impossible for a human being to be righteous by God's perfect assessment.

In each case the word rendered man is *ᵉnoš*, derived from *ʾānaš*, meaning incurably sick.[6] Human life is incurably sick in a moral sense: righteousness is a sheer impossibility. Isaiah 64:6 insists, "all our righteousnesses *are* like filthy rags." The very best that human beings can offer is stinking, filthy, and offensive to a holy God.

How, then, may any human being enjoy the blessing which leads to life? The Bible's wonderful answer is that unrighteous man can be reckoned righteous in God's sight by God's own amazing grace. We shall look at three Old Testament texts which stress this theme.

Genesis 15:6

Here we are told that Abram "believed in the LORD, and he accounted it to him for righteousness (*ṣᵉdāqâ*)."

The LORD had promised Abram innumerable offspring. All appearances seemed to make this an idle dream: Abram continues childless, and a servant looks likely to inherit his estate (verses 2–3). All that he has to go on is God's bare word of promise, which God repeats in verse 5: "Look now toward heaven, and count the stars if you are able to number them." And he said to him, "So shall your descendants be." Then comes verse 6, telling us that Abram believed the LORD. "Believed" translates the

---

6. McComiskey, "*ʾānaš*," 135.0

Hebrew term *'aman*. It means that Abram stood firm in the certainty that God would do what he had said, despite appearances.

In Romans 4:17–22 Paul expounds this text. First he explains how Abram believed: he describes three features of Abram's faith. (1) He was confident that God raises the dead and creates out of nothing: he was assured that God can do what is naturally impossible. (2) He held on to the conviction that God is reliable even when circumstances seemed desperate. (3) He accepted with full conviction that God is able to do what he says.

Paul then concludes, "and therefore 'it was accounted to him for righteousness,'" citing the last part of the Genesis text.

Faith is confidence in the truth and reliability of God's promise. The promise to Abram (of offspring to an elderly couple) could only be fulfilled supernaturally. For Abram to believe it was to place himself in a position of total dependence upon God in humble recognition of his own helplessness—and that is always the essence of true faith.

So the LORD "accounted it to him for righteousness." The word "it" does not refer only to Abram's faith, but to the entire phrase "believed in the LORD." It was not Abram's mere believing that counted. It was the fact that it was God whom he trusted. He relied on the one whom Jeremiah called, "The LORD our righteousness" (Jer 23:6; 33:16).

However, this was not the first time that Abram had demonstrated faith. Back in Genesis 11:31, he had left Ur of the Chaldeans, in obedience to the word of the LORD, and set out "to go to the land of Canaan." The destination is named with the benefit of hindsight: all that the LORD actually told Abram was to go "to a land that I will show you" (Gen 12:1). Hebrews 11:8 finds this a defining moment of faith in the story of Abraham: "By faith Abraham obeyed when he was called to go out to the place which he would receive as an inheritance. And he went out, not knowing where he was going."

Why, then, it was not until Genesis 15:6 that it (believing the LORD) was said to be accounted to Abram for righteousness? A. W. Pink suggests that it was because of the direct connection at this point with the promise of the offspring, the promise which, according to Galatians 3:16, finds its ultimate fulfilment in Christ. The faith which is counted for righteousness is specifically faith in him. Pink sums up: "there is no justification apart from Christ."[7] We can legitimately say that it was Christ himself who was counted to Abram for righteousness.

Habakkuk 2:4

This verse portrays a contrast between the just, or the righteous (*ṣaddîq*), who "shall live by his faith," and the one who is proud—the conceited person who has an inflated view of himself, who brashly acts in self-confidence—that is the unrighteous person. So righteousness is implicitly defined as the humility which relies on the LORD and not on self. That is why the life of the righteous is connected to "his faith." Although the word rendered "faith" (*ᵉmûnâ*) can also mean "faithfulness," Calvin seems right to exclude that meaning from this context, insisting that the issue here is not human integrity.[8] People have faith when they "venture their all" upon God's promise.[9]

The book begins with Habakkuk perplexed on behalf of the righteous within the nation of Judah. Violence, iniquity, and lawlessness are rampant. The righteous are surrounded by the wicked (1:4), and yet the LORD seems to do nothing about it, even though the righteous cry for help. However, the LORD assures the prophet that he is taking action: he is raising up the Babylonian Empire. The Babylonians will march out and seize the surrounding nations. In the process they will be the agent of God's punishment of his own people. This merely adds to Habakkuk's perplexity: how can a pure and holy God countenance using such an evil, idolatrous empire? How can he sit idly by as the wicked swallow up the righteous?

The LORD then speaks the words of our verse. When the catastrophe strikes, when the kingdom of Judah is overrun, the righteous will survive by faith: it is not their own ingenuity that will get them through. In themselves they are utterly helpless. Only trustful reliance on the LORD will save them. Faith is the confidence that God is doing what is right, however strange his providence may seem.

The apostle Paul quoted this text on two occasions (Rom 1:17; Gal 3:11). He takes up Habakkuk's stress on human helplessness, and the need for a faith that depends upon God alone for salvation. He recognizes that

7. Pink, *Genesis*, 168.

8. Calvin, *Minor Prophets*, 75.

9. Henry, *Whole Bible*, 1164.

it is through faith alone that the believer is counted as righteous. The verse is cited also in Hebrews 10:38. Here faith is connected with endurance. The righteous is contrasted with the person who draws back and is destroyed. Righteousness is linked with a trust in God that perseveres and survives in the face of every challenge.

Isaiah 53:11

This whole chapter is prophetic of Christ, the LORD's archetypal Servant. The particular words in which we are interested are these: "by his knowledge my righteous (*ṣaddîq*) servant, shall justify (*ṣādaq*) many. For he shall bear their iniquities." Here we see that the righteousness of the many stems from God's righteous servant, who bears their iniquities and communicates his righteousness to others.

The righteousness of God's people is all down to the work of Christ, the LORD's true servant. Our justification is rooted entirely in him. The link with the fact that he bore our iniquities is vital: justification is based on atonement and substitution. Paul echoes this verse when he writes, "by one man's obedience many will be made righteous" (Rom 5:19).

New Testament

We shall trace some of the more important uses of *dikaios* vocabulary, focusing on three New Testament passages.

Luke 8:9–14

It is surely significant that the first New Testament reference to the justification of sinners is found in Jesus' own words in verse 14 of this passage. Jesus here tells the parable of the Pharisee and the tax-collector, both of whom "went up to the temple to pray" (verse 10). In the final verse Jesus explains that it was the tax-collector who "went down to his house justified *rather* than the other," and also adds the reason why this was so: it had nothing to do with his own moral superiority; from a merely human perspective, he was no doubt vastly morally inferior. The key, says Jesus, is that "everyone who exalts himself will be humbled, and he who humbles himself will be exalted."

The Pharisee's problem was that he was exalting himself. Verses 11–12 give us the content of his prayer: "God, I thank you that I am not like other men—extortioners, unjust, adulterers, or even as this tax collector. I fast twice a week; I give tithes of all that I possess."

The tax-collector, by contrast, humbled himself. He "would not so much as raise *his* eyes to heaven, but beat his breast, saying, 'God, be merciful to me a sinner!'" (verse 13).

To exalt oneself is absurdly unthinkable in the presence of the God who truly is the exalted one. To humble oneself is to look away from oneself entirely, recognizing, as the tax-collector did, that our only hope lies elsewhere—in the mercy of God. So Jesus is not teaching justification by humility! Rather, humility is the acknowledgement that nothing in us has any justifying worth at all.

Verse 9 notes that the parable was addressed to "some who trusted in themselves that they were righteous." Self-trust is exemplified by the Pharisee, but it is the diametrical opposite to the humility which looks entirely away from self to the mercy of God. Those whom Jesus was addressing must have been quite disconcerted to hear that their self-trust does not after all result in righteousness. But what amazing good news that even a wretch like the tax-collector may be justified because of God's mercy!

Romans 1—8

The book of Romans is the major New Testament source for the theme of justification. It is such a big theme in this letter that our study will have to be selective rather than exhaustive.

In 1:17 the apostle quotes one of the Old Testament texts which we have considered, Habakkuk 2:4. He tells us that in the gospel, "the righteousness of God is revealed from faith to faith; as it is written, 'The just shall live by faith.'" Martin Luther explained the meaning of the phrase "the righteousness of God" in this place like this:

> "The righteousness of God" must not be understood as that righteousness by which he is righteous in himself, but as that righteousness by which we are made righteous (justified) by him.[10]

---

10. Luther, *Romans*, 18.

To reach this conclusion was a liberating experience for Luther, and Herman Ridderbos describes this understanding of the phrase as "established."[11] It does, indeed, go back to the early church fathers.[12]

Paul says that God's righteousness is revealed in the gospel. Back in verses 3–4 he has defined the content of the gospel as Jesus Christ himself. The righteousness of God by which we are reckoned righteous is precisely the righteousness revealed in his life. It is on the basis of faith that we receive this righteousness, and the result is that the person who has been made righteous can experience and enjoy true life.

When we reach Romans 3, verse 20 begins with the word "therefore" (*dioti*), which signals that we have here the conclusion of an argument. The argument begins at verse 10, where Paul quotes Psalm 14:3: "there is none righteous, no not one." The following verses drive this point home. In the previous chapter the apostle had linked righteousness with God's law. The law defines righteousness. However, the fact of universal unrighteousness means that no one can be justified by obeying the law—there is no one, other than Christ, who has kept the law perfectly.

Against that sad background, verses 21–28 make the glorious declaration of justification by faith. In verses 21–22 Paul returns to the theme indicated in Romans 1:17: there is a righteousness which God confers. The righteous life of Christ is reckoned as ours. This is a righteousness which meets the standards of his law, and yet it is a righteousness "apart from the law." That is, it is not obtained through our own obedience to the law—which the previous passage has demonstrated is impossible.

So if this acceptable righteousness cannot be obtained by our obedience to God's law, how do we get it? Verse 22 supplies the answer: the Greek text reads, *dia pisteōs Iēsou Christou*. Recently it has become common to read this as a subjective genitive, and so to translate it "through the faith of Jesus Christ," implying that what justifies us is Jesus Christ's own faith.[13] However, traditionally the phrase was understood as an objective genitive, "through faith in Jesus Christ," meaning that "Jesus Christ" is the object of the believer's faith.

Trevin Wax notes that none of the native Greek speakers amongst the early church fathers read the phrase as a subjective genitive. Neither, indeed, did they explicitly reject such a reading: they do not even seem

11. Ridderbos, *Paul*, 163.
12. See Bray (ed.), *Romans*, 29–31.
13. Cf. Bird & Sprinkle (eds.), *Faith of Jesus Christ, passim*.

to be aware of it as an option.[14] This suggests that the objective reading is more likely to be correct.

This does not, of course, mean that it is our act of believing which ultimately justifies us: the apostle insists in verse 24 that we "are justified freely by his grace." Since it is a gift, there is nothing that we have to do, nothing that we can do, to earn that righteous status. Our faith is not meritorious. To believe is simply to entrust ourselves to Christ, to receive the righteousness which he has earned on our behalf.

However, in giving righteousness freely to unrighteous people, is God not compromising his own righteousness? That is the issue which lies behind verses 25–26. Here Paul reminds us that God set Christ forth "*as* a propitiation by his blood." That is to say, God's anger was tranquillized forever, his justice was fully satisfied, by the sweet aroma of Christ's sacrifice of his righteous life on the cross. He then explains that, because of the atonement which Jesus Christ achieved, God is both just and the justifier. He is just, because he did not pass over former sins in the sense of never taking any action against them. Rather, the day eventually came—at Calvary—when all sins, past, present and future, were conclusively punished. And therefore God is the justifier: he may legitimately, justly, accept as righteous all who are joined to Jesus Christ, because their sins have been punished in him. Verse 28 sums up: justification (being counted righteous in God's judgment) is received by faith.

Paul continues expounding this truth of justification by faith in Romans 5. Verses 16–21 form part of the passage which presents the parallelism between Adam and Christ. Verses 16 and 17 emphasize the point that justification is a free gift, and then verse 18 refers to Jesus Christ's "righteous act (*dikaiōma*)" which leads to our justification.

Here Paul stresses how our justification is linked with Christ's righteousness: it is his obedience which God accounts to the believer in justification (verse 19). Cranfield writes,

> By Christ's *dikaiōma* Paul means not just his atoning death, but the obedience of his life as a whole, his loving God with all his heart and soul and mind and strength, and his neighbor with complete sincerity, which is the righteous conduct which God's law requires.[15]

---

14. Wax, 'Faith,' *passim*; cf. Dunn, *Paul*, 379–85.
15. Cranfield, *Romans*, 289.

Verse 21 makes a comparison. On the one hand, "sin reigned in death." But the comparison cannot be straightforward, "grace reigns in life." There has to be a middle term: grace reigns "through righteousness to eternal life." God's grace cannot simply write sin off. A satisfactory righteousness has to be provided, and that righteousness is "through Jesus Christ our Lord." It is his righteous life of obedience which is accounted ours by grace.

In Romans 8:33, the apostle ponders the possibility, "Who shall bring a charge against God's elect?" Immediately he answers his own rhetorical question: "*It is* God who justifies." This does not mean that God who justifies brings charges. It means that, just because it is God who justifies us in Christ, no charges against us are admissible. The God who has justified us no longer presses charges against us. Even if Satan, other people, or our own consciences condemn us, God simply disallows all charges to stand.

To be justified is to be unchargeable! It is to be placed beyond the reach of any accusatory charges. We can never be called in question. We shall never be prosecuted for our sin. God has already found us not guilty in Christ. We are acquitted. Even at the final judgment, when charges against us are called for, the response will be total silence. Hallelujah!

Galatians 2:16

This has been described as "one of the most important verses in the Bible."[16] It effectively makes the same point three times. Its main thrust is to pose the question as to how we are justified, how we are to obtain God's verdict of approval. By means of its threefold repetitions it answers that question first negatively and then positively, and there is a perfect balance between the negative and positive parts of the verse.

The negative answer is "not by the works of the law." Galatians 3:11 later makes the same point. According to Galatians 3:21–24, it never was God's intention that the law should have life-giving power. Its purpose was to steer the Jews to Christ, to keep them on track for his coming so that they could be justified by faith.

And so the positive answer given in Galatians 2:16 is this: we are justified by faith in Jesus Christ. Paul is stressing the vital place of believing faith directed towards Christ.

16. Boice, "Galatians," 448

God can declare us acceptable in his sight only because of what Jesus did. And we obtain that righteousness by believing, that is, by entrusting ourselves to him, by relying exclusively on what he has done. In the next verse Paul speaks of our being justified in Christ (*en Christō*). God's grace places us into Christ, and so he, the holy one, sees us as righteous.

DOCTRINAL ELABORATION

The Early Creeds

The whole doctrine of salvation is summed up in the Apostles' Creed in the single phrase, "I believe in . . . the forgiveness of sins." The Nicene Creed also refers to "the remission of sins." Commenting on this clause of the Apostles' Creed, Augustine emphasizes the lavish generosity of God's forgiveness:

> Let none say, "I have done this or that sin: perchance that is not forgiven me." What have you done? How great a sin have you done? Name any heinous thing you have committed, heavy, horrible, which you shudder even to think of: you have done what you will: have you killed Christ? There is no deed any worse than that, because also there is nothing better than Christ. What a dreadful thing is it to kill Christ! Yet the Jews killed him, and many afterwards believed on him . . . : they are forgiven the sin which they committed.[17]

Kelly sums up the early church understanding of forgiveness in two ways: (1) the cancellation of past trespasses; (2) release from the burden of sin.[18]

The Reformation Confessions

Nine themes may sum up the teaching on justification in the confessions.

Justification entails forgiveness of sin

The French Confession speaks of justification as a consequence of the forgiveness of sins: "all our justification rests upon the remission of our

---

17. Augustine, "Creed," 15.
18. J. N. D. Kelly, *Creeds*, 162.

sins." Other confessions reverse the order, portraying justification as the root of forgiveness. Perhaps forgiveness is so much part and parcel of justification that it is impossible to say which comes first and which follows. So perhaps the Belgic Confession is right when it says that "our salvation consists in the remission of our sins for Jesus Christ's sake, and that therein our righteousness before God is implied."

Forgiveness is defined to mean that God no longer remembers our sins or our corrupt nature. Because we are forgiven, we are justified from past, present, and future sins.

Justification goes way beyond forgiveness

However, in that justification means that God accounts and accepts the forgiven sinner as righteous, justification goes way beyond mere forgiveness, even though the two things are very closely connected. Forgiveness is the negative side: our terrible sinfulness is no longer held against us. Justification is superlatively positive: God does not merely see us as not-sinful any more; he regards us as positively righteous, as those who have not merely avoided the errors condemned by the law, but also as those who have perfectly fulfilled all the positive goodness implicit in the law.

Justification comes to us freely, by sheer grace

The confessions insist that justification is of God's mercy. All the glory for our justification is therefore God's. The reason is that it is based on Christ's sacrifice. The Westminster Larger Catechism asks, "How is justification an act of God's free grace?" The answer reads:

> Although Christ, by his obedience and death, made a proper, real, and full satisfaction to God's justice on behalf of them that are justified; yet inasmuch as God accepts the satisfaction from a surety, which he might have demanded of them, and did provide this surety, his own only Son, imputing his righteousness to them, and requiring nothing of them for their justification but faith—which also is his gift, their justification is to them of free grace.

Justification glorifies God's justice as well as his mercy

The reason why this statement is true is that Jesus' sacrificial death provided satisfaction to God: the demands of his justice were fully met. We are justified because our ransom has been paid in full. By his life and death Jesus completely discharged our debt. However, it was the divine mercy which gave the Son of God up to the death of the cross.

Justification means the imputation of Christ's righteousness

All the holy works which Jesus Christ did, he did for us and in our place. Since he fulfilled the law for us, God accepts his righteousness as ours, as we trust upon him. The Irish Articles point out that in and by Christ "every true Christian man may be called a fulfiller of the law; forasmuch as that which our infirmity was not able to effect, Christ's justice has performed."

Therefore, as the Heidelberg Catechism affirms, our standing with God now is "as if I had never committed nor had any sins, and had myself accomplished all the obedience which Christ has fulfilled for me."

Christ's righteousness is embraced by faith alone

We need to notice four things on this point.

JUSTIFICATION IS APART FROM WORKS.

In fact justification is apart from any other means at all. There is nothing in man which is even a partial cause of justification. There is no merit or virtue in us whatsoever. This is because the righteousness which is approved before God's tribunal must be absolutely perfect. It must conform in every detail, however minor, to God's law. Yet even our very best works are defiled by sin. We are worthy only of God's hatred. So if we look for something in ourselves as a reason for our being justified, we inevitably end up restless and troubled.

WHAT IS MEANT BY "FAITH"

This is defined as the personal appropriation of the promises in which God declares his love and offers life through Jesus Christ. By faith we make a particular application to our own hearts of all that Christ has done.

THE FAITH THAT JUSTIFIES MUST BE "TRUE FAITH"

To say that true faith is the only faith that will justify implies that there is such a thing as false faith. So the Irish Articles, for example, explain:

> When we say that we are justified by faith only, we do not mean that the said justifying faith is alone in man, without true repentance, hope, love, and the fear of God (for such a faith would be dead and cannot justify).

True faith, that is to say, is the kind of faith which James 2:22 tells us Abraham exemplified, a faith that "was working together with his works," and so "made perfect" by them. When James continues, two verses later, "a man is justified by works, and not by faith only," he was not opposing the position which the confession would later state in the words, "we are justified by faith only." His point is that true justifying faith does not remain on its own. It is invariably accompanied by the works which provide the evidence that it is genuine. A mere profession, unsupported by the fruits by which we know it to be real faith, is simply equivalent to the kind of faith which, according to James 2:19, a demon has: it cannot save, it does not justify.

However, the Articles quickly go on to point out that we may not therefore conclude that there is justifying merit in our repentance, hope, and love. Indeed, there is no justifying merit in any of our works subsequent to faith: they are merely the fruits which grow on the tree of genuine faith. But our faith, our trust, is only in God's mercy and Christ's merits.

IT IS NOT FAITH ITSELF THAT JUSTIFIES

As we have stressed in our study of the New Testament teaching on this theme, so the confessions emphasize that there is no worthiness in the act of believing. It is definitely not our believing which is accounted as righteousness. Rather, our faith is the instrument by which we embrace

Christ as our righteousness. Faith is the cord which keeps us in communion with Christ and his benefits. What faith does is to send us directly to Christ for our justification.

The decree of justification and actual justification

The Westminster Confession insists on an important distinction. The justification of the elect was decreed in eternity, but this is not the same as their actual justification: the decree and the actualization of justification must be distinguished. Our justification is not actual until the Holy Spirit has applied Christ to us.

The confession is here rejecting the idea of "eternal justification" which arose in the context of the seventeenth-century antinomian controversies, and has been put forward by various Reformed thinkers since. It claimed that justification in a believer's experience was merely the declaration of his justification which had been an eternal reality.

Berkouwer admits that this teaching desires to honor God's free grace and the exclusive significance of Christ's righteousness, and to avoid turning faith into a meritorious work. Nevertheless, he insists, the justification of a sinner is one of God's historical works, and certain texts become meaningless if the elect are already justified prior to their own act of believing.[19] Most notable among these is Ephesians 2:1–3:

> You . . . were dead in trespasses and sins, in which you once walked according to the course of this world, according to the prince of the power of the air, the spirit who now works in the sons of disobedience, among whom we all once conducted ourselves in the lusts of our flesh, fulfilling the desires of the flesh and of the mind, and were by nature children of wrath, just as the others.

The results of justification

We find mention in the confessions of the following benefits flowing from justification: confidence in approaching God with a conscious freedom from fear; perfect freedom from the wrath of God in this life; peace; no condemnation before God's tribunal; and eternal life.

---

19. Berkouwer, *Faith and Justification*, 146–49, 159.

Justification is the same in both Old and New Testaments

The identity of justification throughout time is stressed in the Westminster standards. The need to make this point arises from the fact that there have always been those who have taught the sort of dispensationalism which maintains that the Old Testament and the New Testament reveal two different ways of salvation, two distinct methods of justification. The claim is that the Old Testament saints were justified by keeping the law, whereas New Testament believers are justified by God's grace in Christ.

Robert Shaw elaborates on this point helpfully:

> Though "the righteousness of God" is now more clearly manifested by the gospel, yet it was witnessed by the law and the prophets. And those under the Old Testament who laid hold upon that righteousness by faith were as really and fully justified as believers under the New Testament. Paul, accordingly, adduces the justification of Abraham as an example of the method in which believers in all ages must be justified. Though the everlasting righteousness was not actually brought in until Christ "became obedient unto death," yet the efficacy of his death extended to believers under the former, as well as the present, dispensation.[20]

Modern Confessions of Faith

The main feature in all three of the modern confessions with which we are concerned is the emphasis which they place on faith as the condition of salvation.

The Indian confession refers to the benefits which come to those who believe in Christ and are saved by him. Similarly, the Indonesian confession teaches that we obtain the redemption of Jesus Christ through faith, and that in this redemption we receive the remission of sin which the Savior procured for us by his death. Again, the Chinese confession says, "Anyone who repents, confessing his or her sins, and believes in Jesus as the Son of God . . . shall be saved." By this faith we are justified and we become the sons of God.

These confessions are not giving faith the status of a meritorious work. The Chinese document insists that we are saved by grace through faith. Faith is the appropriating channel, but the grace of God is the

20. Shaw, *Confession*, 136.

initiating source, the foundational basis. The Indonesian statement notes that faith "is the work of the Holy Spirit:" believing is not an act which stems from human power.

The Indian confession acknowledges that justification, along with adoption, is chief among the benefits received by those who believe in Christ, but the Indonesian confession is the only one of the three which offers a definition of justification. It does so in these words: "God regards such faith as righteousness before him."

At first sight these words might seem to locate righteousness in our act of believing, rather than in the righteousness of Christ imputed to us through faith. However, this may not be the intention. The key word may be "such:" it is such faith as has already been defined within this article of the confession which God regards as our righteousness. This type of faith is the work of the Holy Spirit; it must be distinguished from good works and from any other human power operating independently of the grace of God. The confession does not intend faith as a vague abstract thing, but that faith which is directed towards the God who has acted for our salvation in Jesus Christ, and which relies on him alone.

There is one other point worth noting. The Indian confession says this of Jesus Christ: "For sinful man he perfectly obeyed the law of God." Although this is not explicitly related to justification, it may well be that the confession is assuming such a connection.

HISTORICAL ELABORATION

Since the 1970s the so-called "new perspective" on the apostle Paul has developed. It emphasizes the Jewish background to Paul's writings, and recognizes that authentic Judaism was a grace-based faith, and not a religion of works. However, it tends to overlook the fact that the Pharisaic Judaism, which was Paul's background, had wandered from the truth, as Jesus' criticisms of the Pharisees in the Gospels show.

Amongst other things, this teaching offers a "new perspective" on what Paul meant by justification. One of the leaders in this development, Tom Wright, has written a book on this subject.[21] It was prompted by a book by John Piper, in which he questioned whether Wright had properly understood Paul.[22]

---

21. N. T. Wright, *Justification, passim.*
22. Piper, *Justification, passim.*

Wright recognizes that Paul's doctrine of justification uses the imagery of a divine law court. Justification is the judge's verdict in someone's favor, which acquits him of all charges levelled against him, and clears him of guilt. If the defendant is actually guilty, justification also entails forgiveness. However, Wright disputes the notion of imputed righteousness. He argues that justification has nothing to do with moral character, and says, correctly, that the law was never intended to be a ladder for the accumulation of merit. To claim, therefore, that Christ obeyed it to secure a moral righteousness which could be reckoned to his people misses the whole point of the law. Wright claims that Paul never speaks of the imputed righteousness of Christ, and suggests that the idea is absurd: a judge cannot transfer his own righteousness to a defendant.

Wright sets justification in the context of God's covenant with Abraham: through Abraham's family, Israel, God covenanted to undo and repair the damage to the world caused in Adam. Wright notes that, in the later chapters of Deuteronomy, where righteousness is mentioned frequently, the context is covenantal. As Israel's Messiah, Jesus is the true Israelite in whom the covenant is fulfilled by his obedience to the death of the cross. Those who are justified in the present era are those who believe in Jesus as Lord, and the basis of their justification is his faithfulness to God's covenant purpose. The status granted in justification is membership of God's covenant family; in Jesus, this now extends beyond Israel to incorporate Gentiles also.

Wright also sees a future dimension to justification. The final judgment will be on the basis of works. Those who, by the power of the Holy Spirit, have begun to do the works which meet with God's approval will be justified on that day.

We must now assess Wright's theology. I would raise the following points.

(1) Wright is correct to define justification as God's legal declaration that a sinner is acquitted, but wrong to deny that it has any moral aspect. We have to ask on what grounds God can make such a declaration? Surely it is only by imputing an acceptable moral character irrespective of the sinner's own character that God may do this. To deny this jeopardizes the holiness of God. Wright overlooks the truth that justification is rooted in Christ's moral achievement. The truth of imputed righteousness is in fact present in Scripture. This seems the best way of understanding 2 Corinthians 5:21 and Philippians 3:9, notwithstanding Wright's alternative readings. Moreover, although Wright focuses on Paul's theology, we must

formulate doctrine in the light of Scripture as a whole, and the truth of imputed righteousness is taught in other places in the Bible, for example, in the imagery of "the robe of righteousness" (Isa 61:10). Moreover, that there is a moral dimension to the definition of righteousness is clear from plenty of texts in the Pentateuch, including the later chapters of Deuteronomy with their covenantal emphasis. Paul insists that the law was given to expose sin (Rom 3:20). This implies that it does define moral righteousness—otherwise it could not perform that exposing function.

(2) Wright fails to distinguish clearly between what justification is and what it implies. He says that justification involves membership of God's covenant family. This may indeed be a consequence, but it is not what justification is. What it is, is precisely what the Reformers saw—the imputation of Christ's righteousness. Wright's account begs the questions why and how the believer in Jesus is declared to have the status of covenant family member. Surely that is only possible as the family likeness, exemplified by Christ, is reckoned to the believer's account.

(3) Wright seems to underplay God's trinitarian nature. It is not that the judge transfers his own righteousness to sinners. The judge is God the Father, but what he reckons to the believer is the righteousness of Christ his Son.

(4) There are dangers in Wright's emphasis on eschatological justification. We acknowledge that such a concept is present in the New Testament—in Romans 2:13 most notably. However, I fear that Wright's exposition undermines the truth of justification in Christ alone through faith alone. This would demolish our confidence in Christ as our only hope at the last judgment. The law is the standard, though not the ground, of eschatological righteousness.[23] The law is certainly the criterion by which judgment will be made: "the doers of the law will be justified," Paul writes, but no one will be declared righteous on that day because they have obeyed the law. All who are justified on that final day will be justified because of something which God will do. True, he will do it for those who, by the grace of the Spirit, have begun to be doers of the law, though not because they have begun to be doers, but exclusively because of what Christ did for them. I am not persuaded that Wright is sufficiently clear about such distinctions.

23. Cf. Cosgrove, "Justification," 657, 659–63.

I find myself, therefore, concerned that Wright, along with many other adherents to the "new perspective," has sidelined or discarded some vital elements of the traditional Reformed understanding of justification.

PRACTICAL APPLICATION

(1) We must face up to our own unrighteousness. It is always tempting to assume that things are not quite as bad as the Bible suggests, that our condition is not as totally hopeless as Scripture portrays. However, we must make sure that we are constantly aware that our natural condition is one of helpless unrighteousness before God. There is nothing that we can do to make ourselves acceptable to him. All our boasting is excluded (Rom 3:27). Unless we rightly see ourselves as God sees us, we will not understand our need to be justified in Christ, and therefore will not "seek to be justified in Christ" (Gal 2:17). That would be an eternally fatal mistake.

In our gospel preaching, too, we must seek to make crystal clear to our fellow sinners their hopeless state outside of Christ, that they too may both appreciate and appropriate what God has done for them in him.

(2) We must have a true justifying faith. Since we are justified as we believe on Jesus Christ, we need to be clear what it means to believe. Genuine faith is not mere assent to the truth, nor is it a mystical feeling. Truly to believe is consciously to entrust oneself, one's eternity, into the safe hands of Jesus Christ. However, we must never trust in our faith. Our faith is only any use as it causes us to trust in Jesus Christ. Having spoken of Christ as our righteousness, the apostle then adds the challenge, "he who glories, let him glory in the Lord" (1 Cor 1:30–31).

(3) We must rejoice in the truth of imputed righteousness. God graciously reckons the righteousness of Jesus to our account. In Christ the ungodly are rendered acceptable to him. That is something for which we should be profoundly grateful, and in which should ecstatically rejoice. It is our only hope. We should be deeply thankful to Jesus Christ that he lived the life of sinless perfection where we failed to do so, and that his life of faithful obedience is the basis of our justification. We must pray that we may be helped truly to love the Lord Jesus from the depths of our hearts.

As we proclaim the gospel, we must ever remember that this is the main thing which we offer to our fellow sinners. We offer them Christ for righteousness, and so hold real hope before them.

(4) We must enjoy the benefits of justification. "Having been justified by faith, we have peace with God through our Lord Jesus Christ" (Rom 5:1). To know that we are at peace with the God from whom we were once estranged is a source of great comfort. Peace with God leads to a calm sense of inner peace: we have nothing to fear when the Lord is our God.

This peace follows from the fact that justification is always complete, permanent, irreversible. The resurrection of Christ is the proof that what he did really has justified his people (Rom 4:25). We really are saved by his blood from the wrath of God (Rom 5:9). The blessing of total forgiveness is ours. "*There is* therefore now no condemnation to those who are in Christ Jesus" (Rom 8:1). We must believe it, and never condemn ourselves. No charges will ever be pressed against us again.

(5) We must beware of slipping back into works religion. The apostle asks, "having begun in the Spirit, are you now being made perfect by the flesh?" (Gal 3:3). It is so easy, having believed on Jesus Christ, having understood that we are justified by faith, then to imagine that we have to maintain our justified status by our own effort and works. We need to develop the mindset that rests totally on what Christ has done for our standing with God. The peril of failing to think in these terms is a depressing loss of assurance.

(6) Our lives must show the fruit that follows from justification. Although we are justified solely on the basis of what Jesus did through believing on him, our new status nevertheless gives us the desire and impetus to be "filled with the fruits of righteousness" (Phil 1:11). Good works cannot justify us, but they do flow from justification as its inevitable consequence. To claim that we are justified when we are persisting either blatantly or casually in sin is to make a spurious claim. Our works do not justify us, but our justification does issue in a changed life.

(7) We must accept all our fellow justified believers. That is one of the main messages of the book of Galatians. Paul sees the doctrine of justification by faith as the answer to Peter's reluctance to share fellowship with Gentile Christians (Gal 2:11–16). The implication of the fact that I am justified by faith in Jesus Christ is that I must freely and lovingly accept everyone else who is also justified by faith in Jesus Christ. Even though we may have different cultural emphases, different personal preferences, on issues that are not vital to the gospel, I must commit myself to undiscriminating fellowship with all the Lord's people.

(8) We must avoid driving a wedge between the Old and New Testaments. We must make sure that we do not fall into a dispensationalist trap which separates the work of God before and after Christ. True, there is a major element of newness with his coming, but it is newness within an overall continuity. We must never lose the sense of the unity of God's plan of salvation throughout all time. We must cherish the fact that we belong with the saints of Israel before Christ came.

PART TWO: THE PRESENT TENSE (SANCTIFICATION)

The words "sanctification" and "holiness" are effectively synonymous. Both translate words from the same biblical roots, *qādaš* in Hebrew and *hagios* in Greek. These terms can be used in two ways. We speak both of "definitive" and of "progressive" sanctification. We shall concentrate on the second of these, the ongoing, present experience of growth in holiness. However, a brief word about the first is in order.

"Definitive sanctification" refers to the fact that at the moment of our justification we were set apart as God's and for God. It is mentioned in Hebrews 10:10: "we have been sanctified through the offering of the body of Jesus Christ once *for all*." John Murray defines definitive sanctification in terms of the decisive break with sin and the world which is bound up with the fact that we died with Christ.[24] Donald Macleod finds three strands to definitive sanctification: (1) we now belong to God and exist for God's use; (2) our identity is radically altered: the old man is dead and we are new creatures in Christ: (3) we are united with Christ, branches of the vine, members of his body.[25]

So holiness is our starting-point: it was "in holiness" that we were called (1 Thess 4:7). But on that basis our sanctification is God's will (1 Thess 4:3)—that we should progress and grow in holiness in the course of our Christian lives: "by one offering he has perfected forever those who are being sanctified" (Heb 10:14).

It is important that we maintain a clear distinction between sanctification and justification, and avoid any confusion. Justification has to do with our position, sanctification with our practice. Justification confers a righteous standing; sanctification develops a righteous character. In justification righteousness is accredited to us; in sanctification righteousness

---

24. J. Murray, *Systematic Theology*, 277–84.
25. Macleod, *Faith*, 176–79.

is outworked within us. Justification is God's gift before we have done a single good work; sanctification consists in the good works which follow from justification.

We must also be careful never to base justification on sanctification. Our good works are not the basis on which we are justified. Rather, they are the fruits of the fact that we are already justified.

On the other hand, while we must never confuse justification and sanctification, neither must we separate them. A claim to be justified which is not backed up by progressive sanctification is a spurious sham. We must never think of justification as being saved, and sanctification as something else which follows salvation. You cannot receive Christ as Savior one day, but postpone receiving him as Lord until a later time. Sanctification is part of salvation, not something additional, and certainly not an optional extra. If we are not being sanctified, then we are not saved, we have not been justified. If Jesus is not Lord of our life, neither is he our personal Savior; we are still in our sins.

BIBLICAL FOUNDATION

Old Testament

We shall look at the Old Testament teaching on this topic in two sections.

"The Holiness Code"

This is the title which has been given to Leviticus 17—26: "it emphasizes God's moral standards for his people."[26] The Hebrew words *qādaš* (to sanctify) and *qōdeš* (holiness) occur over 50 times in those chapters. Many of the references are to holy things, days, places, and to God's holy name. Our concern is those texts which voice God's demand that Israel should be a holy people. The key verse is Leviticus 19:2: "Speak to all the congregation of Israel, and say to them: 'You shall be holy, for I the LORD your God *am* holy.'"

Similar words occur in Leviticus 20:26: "You shall be holy to me, for I the LORD *am* holy and have separated you from the peoples, that you should be mine." This note of demand has already been sounded twice in Leviticus 11:44–45.

26. R. L. Harris, "Leviticus," 502.

The main emphases of the holiness code are sexual purity, family relationships, and regard for the property, life, welfare, and reputation of the neighbor.[27] These are the ingredients of holiness in God's definition.

It is against the background of this understanding of holiness that the prophets battled with the tendency to define holiness in terms of mere religious observance. The people came to rest satisfied with the outward ritual, and assumed that this made them holy. The prophetic challenge had to remind them that the LORD was looking for outward and inward moral commitment, and that these were the things which they needed to work at. We may cite three examples of this later appeal.

First, we turn to 1 Samuel 15:22. The LORD has commanded Saul to subject everything belonging to the Amalekites to total destruction. However, Saul disobeyed. He spared the best of the sheep and cattle, on the pretext that they were to be sacrificed to the LORD. Samuel's reply first asks whether the LORD has "*as great* delight in burnt offerings and sacrifices, as in obeying the voice of the LORD?" The answer then follows: "to obey is better than sacrifice, *and* to heed than the fat of rams."

Next, Isaiah 1 is a message of judgment because of the wickedness of the people. If the people protest that they are assiduous in keeping the requirements of offerings and sacrifices, the LORD's response is that he is thoroughly fed up with their sacrifices, which no longer give him any delight. The people are merely trampling his courts and bringing futile and abominable offerings. Their religious life has become burdensome to the LORD, and he will no longer take any notice (verses 11–15). The reason is signalled right at the end of verse 15: "your hands are full of blood." The remedy is a total renewal of moral commitment which must pervade the whole of society, as demanded in verses 16–17:

> Wash yourselves, make yourselves clean; put away the evil of your doings from before my eyes. Cease to do evil, learn to do good; seek justice, rebuke the oppressor; defend the fatherless, plead for the widow.

Then again, in Amos 5:21–24 we find another similar indictment of Israel's ceremonial life, as the LORD declares his hatred of Israel's feasts and assemblies. He indicates his rejection of their offerings and their sung praise. In verse 24 God highlights what he is really looking for: "let justice run down like waters, and righteousness like a mighty stream."

27. R. L. Harris, "Leviticus," 525.

Israel is a redeemed people. They have been liberated from bondage and rescued from sin and judgment. But that has all happened with a purpose in view. They are to be the nation in the middle of the world where God's holiness is reflected, so that the whole world may see what human life in the image of God is really supposed to be like.

> The character of God is behind all his commandments. Among the sensual and foolish deities of antiquity, no god could ground all moral duty in his divine character; only the God of Israel could.[28]

True faith and moral living are, therefore, intimately bound up together.

There is an interesting feature which we must note in Leviticus 20:7–8: Verse 7 begins with the challenge, "consecrate yourselves," and verse 8 ends with the statement, "I *am* the LORD who sanctifies you." The words "consecrate" and "sanctifies" both translate the same Hebrew verb, *qādaš.* God says, "sanctify yourselves—because I sanctify you." This brings together the twin poles of human responsibility and divine power in sanctification. The Lord's transforming grace gives the redeemed person a new power to "be holy," as it says in the middle of verse 7, and a new will to develop a holy lifestyle; the beginning of verse 8 spells out what that involves: "you shall keep my statutes, and perform them."

The Place of God's Law

Numbers 15:40 is an important verse, because it answers the question, how do we know what holiness is? It tells us that holiness is spelt out in God's commandments. To be holy is to obey God's law.

This is an important point, for two reasons. In the first place, we can never dare to claim to be holy if we are not actively obeying God's commandments.

On the other hand, a Christian culture can easily impose on people requirements and taboos which are not found in Scripture. This may apply to an entire national culture where Christianity has made an impact. Or it may apply within the culture of a particular church fellowship. However, conformity to man-made demands and avoidance of man-made restrictions have no part in holiness. It is only things which God commands and forbids which have any place in the definition of holiness. We have no right to impose on one another duties which are not

28. R. L. Harris, "Leviticus," 602.

biblical. Neither is anyone under obligation to conform to such cultural norms as are not found in Scripture.

New Testament

The Levitical challenge to a holiness which reflects the LORD's character is quoted in 1 Peter 1:16: "it is written, 'Be holy, for I am holy.'" Jesus also alludes to it in Matthew 5:48: "you shall be perfect, just as your Father in heaven is perfect."

Commenting on Peter's text, Edwin Blum defines holiness as "loving conformity to God's commands and to his Son."[29] Those words indicate a new element as we turn to the New Testament: the holiness of God has now been lived out in practice for us to observe in the incarnate life of the Son of God.

John Murray insists that the New Testament emphasis on definitive sanctification does not mean "that no place remains for a process of mortification and sanctification by which sin is more and more put to death and conformity to holiness progressively attained."[30] We shall look at four passages which refer to progressive sanctification.

Romans 6

This chapter demonstrates how the possibility of progressive sanctification is rooted in the reality of definitive sanctification. To be sanctified progressively is to become what, definitively, we already are.

In verse 1 a question is posed. It arises naturally in the light of the truth of justification by grace: "shall we continue in sin that grace may abound?" Substantially the same question is repeated at verse 15: "shall we sin because we are not under law but under grace?"

The chapter falls into two balanced parts. Each states two spiritual truths, followed by an exhortation. Both the truths in each section are aspects of definitive sanctification. The exhortation is to a consequent progressive sanctification.

---

29. Blum, "1 & 2 Peter," 224.
30. J. Murray, *Systematic Theology*, 294.

The first truth: we died to sin

This is stated succinctly in verse 2, and then expressed in five different ways in the following verses: (1) we were baptized into Christ's death [verse 3]; (2) we were buried with him [verse 4]; (3) we were united with him in death [verse 5]; (4) "our old man was crucified with *him*, that the body of sin might be done away with" [verse 6]; (5) we died with Christ [verse 8].

The second truth: we walk in newness of life

This truth is stated explicitly in verse 4, and is also expressed in terms of union with Christ in his resurrection (verse 5), and living with him (verse 8). Our confident assurance, according to verse 9, is that the resurrection places Christ (and us in him) on the other side of death, beyond its reach, for ever.

Christ is viewed here in his representative capacity. He died and rose again in our name. The passage does not mean that it is impossible for a believer to commit a sin, but that a decisive break with the old life has taken place, so that we can no longer live in sin or be slaves of sin.

The exhortation

This now follows in verse 11: "reckon yourselves to be dead indeed to sin, but alive to God in Jesus Christ our Lord." In other words, we are to count on this being true and calculate, on the basis of the facts, what this will entail in practice. Paul is not telling us to pretend or imagine that we are dead to sin and alive to God. He is reminding us that, definitively speaking, in Christ, that is the way it is. Therefore we must work out what that means and live accordingly. And verse 12 spells out what it does mean: we must close down sin; we must choose to disobey its desires. The verb "reckon" in verse 11 is a present tense: if we are to live out this reality, we must constantly, repeatedly remind ourselves of it.

The first truth: we are set free from sin

Verse 18 gives the summary statement of this truth. The verses around elaborate on it. Sin used to have dominion, to dominate and exercise governmental power in our lives, but it no longer does (verse 14). We used to be sin's slaves or puppets, but when we heeded the gospel all that changed (verse 17).

The second truth: we have become slaves of righteousness

This also is stated in verse 18. As verse 16 has made clear, some kind of slavery is unavoidable. It is impossible to live without an ultimate commitment to something. Therefore the converse to freedom from sin is a binding obligation to obedience. And the word "obedience" defines God's law as the pattern for the believer's life.

Verses 20–23 spell out the opposite outcomes of these two alternative slaveries: slavery to sin leads to shame and death, whereas slavery to God leads to sanctification and life.

The exhortation

The exhortation in this part of the chapter is summed up in the words, "present your members" (verses 13, 19). In the rest of the passage this exhortation is expressed both negatively and positively. Negatively, we are no longer to present our members "*as* instruments of unrighteousness to sin" (verse 13), "as slaves of uncleanness, and of lawlessness *leading* to *more* lawlessness" (verse 19). Positively, we are to present our members "*as* instruments of righteousness to God" (verse 13), "as slaves *of* righteousness for holiness" (verse 19).

The use of the word "members" is interesting. It serves to break down holy living into its component parts. I must think how I will use my eyes, my mouth, my ears, my hands, my time, my work, my leisure, my family life, and so on, in obedience to God. The word "members" means every element of everything that I am. This makes sanctification more concrete, and therefore more manageable, more achievable, but also more challenging, than thinking vaguely about everything at once.

1 Thessalonians 3:12—4:8

The opening verses of this passage indicate the progressive nature of sanctification: the goal is total blamelessness, but this will not be fully achieved until the coming of the Lord. The route to the goal is increasing and abounding love.

The main point of this passage is that the chief expressions of Christian holiness in a world of uncleanness are abstinence from sexual immorality and faithfulness in marriage. F. F. Bruce comments helpfully on this point:

> Chastity is not the whole of sanctification, but it is an important element in it, and one which had to be specially stressed in the Greco-Roman world of that day . . . . Christianity from the outset has sanctified sexual union within marriage . . . ; outside marriage it was forbidden. This was a strange notion in the pagan society to which the gospel was first brought; there various forms of extramarital sexual union were tolerated and some were even encouraged . . . . When the gospel was introduced into pagan society, therefore, it was necessary to emphasize the complete breach with accepted mores in this area which was demanded by the new way of life in Christ.[31]

In the climate of the present day, we need to clarify that sexual immorality includes lesbian and homosexual relationships, and that faithfulness in marriage means specifically and exclusively heterosexual marriage.

1 Thessalonians 5:23

As the apostle approaches the end of this letter, he prays for the Thessalonians that God would "sanctify you completely." These words have given rise to the teaching that it is possible for us to attain to entire sanctification in this life. However, the rest of the verse, in which Paul enlarges on this summary request, defines what the prayer means, and shows that such an interpretation is not valid: the prayer continues by asking that their "whole spirit, soul, and body" may "be preserved blameless at the coming of our Lord Jesus Christ." This demonstrates that to be sanctified "completely" does not mean absolutely and totally in every aspect of life,

31. Bruce, 1 & 2 Thessalonians, 82.

so that we become entirely sinless. It means that sanctification should be progressing steadily in parallel in every dimension of our personality.[32]

Since this is the prayer of an inspired apostle we can be sure that it will most definitely be answered—and not only for the Thessalonian Christians, but for all believers.

Additionally, Warfield notes that in this letter the apostle has given instructions about the meaning of sanctification for various areas of life. However, he does not want his readers to think that those examples are the only areas where sanctification is necessary. So now he emphasizes the point that every aspect of life without exception must be sanctified.[33]

Hebrews 12:3–14

This passage reminds us that we sometimes need chastening in order to promote our growth in holiness. However, it also assures us that life's chastening experiences are sent by a heavenly Father who loves us, and who allows us to undergo disciplinary difficulties with the express purpose of sanctifying us: he chastens us "for *our* profit, that *we* may be partakers of his holiness" (verse 10).

Verse 14 says this: "Pursue peace with all *people*, and holiness, without which no one will see the Lord." From these words we notice three things.

(1) Holiness is essential to salvation. Final salvation—that glorification in which we see the Lord face to face—is the outcome of the present development of salvation, which is sanctification. That in turn is the fruit of the justification which is our initial salvation. The three tenses of salvation are interdependent and inseparable. There is normally no direct jump from justification to heaven without sanctification forming the pathway (we do, of course, recognize that, as with the thief on the cross, there may occasionally be abnormal cases).

(2) Holiness is something which we must strive for. The Greek word is *diōkō*. It has the sense of being in hot pursuit, of running fast after something to make sure that it does not get away. It is an active, eager, energetic term. We do not just sit around waiting for God somehow to "zap" us with holiness. We have to reach out for it.

---

32. Cf. L. Morris, *Thessalonians*, 181; S. Gordon, *Five Marks*, 312.
33. Warfield, *Entire Sanctification, passim.*

(3) Holiness is linked with peaceable relations with other people. There is no such thing as being holy in relation to God independently of how we relate to our fellow human beings.

DOCTRINAL FORMULATION

The Reformation Confessions

The early creeds are silent on this theme, but the teaching of the confessions on sanctification may be summarized in seven points.

Sanctification is essential for salvation

Salvation is impossible without holiness. Strictly speaking, sanctification is part of salvation. The confessions see it as a blasphemous delusion to imagine that Christ is present in a person in whom there is no evidence of sanctification. As the Scottish Confession says,

> We fear not to affirm that murderers, oppressors, cruel persecutors, adulterers, whoremongers, filthy persons, idolaters, drunkards, thieves, and all workers of iniquity have neither true faith, nor any portion of the spirit of sanctification, which proceeds from the Lord Jesus, so long as they obstinately continue in their wickedness.

The Irish Articles include this statement: "all that are justified are likewise sanctified, their faith being always accompanied with true repentance and good works."

It is necessary to stress this, because the doctrine of justification by faith alone could be misconstrued to mean that good works are no more necessary after conversion than before. However, this was emphatically not the teaching of the Reformation. The reformers saw sanctification as inseparably joined to justification.

The confessions are clear that justification is not a hindrance to holy living. It does not make us careless about holiness of life. On the contrary, true justifying faith is never unfruitful: it always gives birth to good works, and excites us to put them into practice. The confessions illustrated this from horticulture. Just as a plant thrives in well fertilized good soil, so Christ is the soil in which the life of holiness thrives.

Holy living is inevitable in a believer

Part of what God does in saving us is to renew us by the Holy Spirit. He gives us a new heart and restores us to his image. So the old man dies. The believer is marked by sorrow for sin, hatred of sin, a turning from sin, and deliverance from bondage to sin. The new man, characterized by joy in God, begins to live the new life. He delights in living according to God's will, and, to quote the Scottish Confession again, "he begins to hate that which he loved before and begins to love that which he hated before."

The inevitability of sanctification is linked with the sources from which it comes. It does not arise from our own free will, or any other power or ability of our own. Rather, God determines us to what is good. We are sanctified by the virtue of Christ's cross and resurrection, the indwelling of the Holy Spirit, and the grace received through faith. The instrument of sanctification is the word.

However, the believer is not passive in sanctification. There is no place for negligence. Duties must be performed diligently in order to stir up the graces of the Spirit within. So backsliding is not impossible. Where negligence sets in, backsliding occurs. But even this is used by God's grace: when the believer is restored, he lives with greater care.

Sanctification is real and possible

Robert Shaw notes that these terms are intended to oppose the antinomian teaching that the only sanctification that a believer receives is the holiness of Christ by imputation, which leaves sinful human nature in a believer basically unchanged:

> Sanctification includes the mortification of sin in the members. It includes also the fruit of the Spirit—as love, joy, peace, long-suffering, gentleness, goodness, faith, meekness, temperance. These are personal things; they are wrought in the hearts of believers and produced in their tempers and lives.[34]

Sanctification proceeds by battle

Although sinful lusts are weakened in a believer, they do not die out overnight. So the Christian life is one in which the flesh and the Spirit are

34. Shaw, *Confession*, 142.

battling it out. However, the outcome of the battle is not in doubt. By the Spirit's strengthening, the believer is enabled to overcome sin and grow in grace, to die to sin more and more.

Holiness is defined by God's moral law

Sanctification can be defined as walking in the works which God prepared beforehand for us to do (Eph 2:10). That will have a particular application which will be different in the case of each person. However, God's general will for all his people is spelt out in his moral law, which is summarized in the ten commandments. The Westminster Confession stresses the point that it is only by reference to God's commandments that works can be classified as good, "and not such as, without the warrant thereof, are devised by men out of blind zeal, or upon any pretence of good intention."

Even then, for works to be counted good, they must proceed from true faith. Sanctification always follows justification. It never comes before, or instead of, justification, and may never be equated with it. There are two reasons for this. (1) It is God who begins the work of salvation in each believer, and it is God who continues it: so the whole work of our salvation brings praise to God's grace, undeserved as it is by us. (2) In this life no believer attains perfection: all we manage are the small beginnings of holiness; so there is no foundation for salvation in our sanctification.

Because the law was seen as the definition of holiness, the Reformation catechisms gave detailed consideration of the ten commandments. They considered what each commandment forbids, what it requires, what reasons there are for it, and what further implications it entails.

The Heidelberg Catechism asks why God so strictly enjoins the ten commandments upon us, since in this life no one can keep them? It gives two reasons: (1) so that we learn more about our sinful nature to keep us depending on Christ's righteousness; (2) so that we continue to pray for the grace of the Holy Spirit to change us.

God rewards good works

The confessions are clear that obedience to the law has no saving merit. Nevertheless, they affirm that God is genuinely pleased with believers' good works and rewards them. The reward is itself the crowning gift of grace. Just as God freely and graciously accepts the person of the believer, so he accepts the believer's works, as he looks upon the believer in Christ.

There are motives to sanctification

The greatest motive is our thankfulness for redemption, as the heading of the third part of the Heidelberg Catechism says. But the answer to the first question in that section adds three further motives—the glory of God, personal joy, and effective witness:

> Since, then, we are redeemed from our misery by grace through Christ, without any merit of ours, why must we do good works?
>
> Because Christ, having redeemed us by his blood, also renews us by his Holy Spirit after his own image, that with our whole life we show ourselves thankful to God for his blessing, and that he be glorified through us; then also, that we ourselves may be assured of our faith by the fruits thereof; and by our godly walk may win others also to Christ.

Modern Confessions of Faith

It will be helpful to look at each confession in turn on this subject.

Confession of Faith of the United Church of Northern India

This confession touches on the doctrine of sanctification in two of its articles. It says that, in those who have embraced Jesus Christ, the Holy Spirit works "all the fruits of righteousness." William Stewart's comment on this phrase is worth noting:

> We are "engrafted into Christ," so that it is now his own life which is lived in us, and as our will is renewed a different fruit begins to appear. True, it may be, as the greatest saints have known, that while we are in this world the pull of the "old Adam" is still there. But this is no longer the whole truth nor the most important truth, for now there is in us a new source of life, even the life of Christ which the Holy Spirit makes effective in our wills, and it is that new life which appears in the "fruit of the Spirit" which is "love, joy, peace, longsuffering, kindness,

goodness, faithfulness, meekness, temperance." Let us pray that such a lovely fruit may be brought forth in our lives today.[35]

The next article speaks of "sanctification through the indwelling of the Spirit," and explains that those who "believe in the Lord Jesus Christ as their Savior" are commanded "to live a humble and holy life after his example, and in obedience to God's revealed will." We see here two sources for guidance in holiness—the written word of God and the incarnate life of Christ, which is a perfect reproduction of the law of God. However, we can only follow either guide with the power of the Spirit to purify us.

Confession of Faith of the Huria Batak Protestant

One complete article is entitled *With Regard to Faith and Good Works*. It begins with the words, "good works must be fruits of faith," and then proceeds to deny the possibility of receiving righteousness or salvation by doing good works. It is by Christ alone that we are forgiven and reconciled to God. The opening words could be read as insisting that true faith will always bear fruit in good works, and that would certainly be true. However, the main emphasis is on the uselessness of any good works which are not the fruits of faith: any attempt at self-salvation by good works is doomed to failure.

The article continues with the words, "we have to follow the ten commandments." It is indeed the ten commandments which define true holiness. However, again the main emphasis is that good works alone without faith are not a proper basis for life. So it must be the Holy Spirit who moves us to do good works. Unless he is their source, the statement points out, even good works become sins.

The previous article makes one specific statement about sanctification. It affirms that "everything God created is good." This implies that no food is prohibited: as we receive it with thanksgiving, it is sanctified. But the main issue addressed is the fact that no one "becomes holy by abstaining from certain foods." Only faith receives holiness from God. The kind of asceticism which demands abstention from certain foods, whether on the basis of cultural heritage or of religious tradition is a perversion of the gospel. The confession backs up this point by reference to Paul's opposition to Jewish food laws.

---

35. W. Stewart, *Faith We Confess*, 26.

It is likely that a particular Indonesian issue lies behind this article. There are perhaps two possible reasons for its inclusion.

(1) It may be targeted at the Muslim context. It has been noted that the Batak people are divided into several sub-groups. Christianity has prospered especially amongst the Toba, whereas others, such as the Mandailing, remain largely Muslim. Consequently, the Mandailing do not wish to be associated with the Toba, "who regularly eat foods that are considered unclean to Muslims."[36] Perhaps the confession is underlining the need to make a complete break with the surrounding Muslim culture, and not to try to carry over Muslim dietary prohibitions into the Christian definition of holiness.

(2) On the other hand, there are some Pentecostal groups in Indonesia who have made it their practice to reject any traditional cultural practices which they see as having some lingering connection to heathen animism. This includes rejecting many traditional foods—"a situation that has resulted in deep relational rifts in families and in the larger communal network."[37] Maybe it is that kind of exclusiveness which the confession is opposing. It recognizes that, whatever associations any particular food may once have had, abstention from it has nothing to do with progress in holiness.

Whatever the precise local reason for this article, it makes a point of general relevance. Any culture or sub-culture may develop prohibitions, not stated in Scripture, against eating certain foods or drinking certain things. In such a situation, those who abstain often feel superior in holiness to those whom they judge to be weaker Christians who happily partake of the prohibited food or drink. We all need to be reminded that sanctification has nothing to do with what we eat and drink or what we choose not to eat and drink. As the apostle writes in Romans 14.17: "the kingdom of God is not a matter of eating and drinking but of righteousness and peace and joy in the Holy Spirit."

Confession of Faith of House Churches in China

Here there are two phrases relating to our present theme. The confession opposes the idea that the believer is free to sin because he is under grace. This is a clear rejection of antinomian ideas. The confession links this

---

36. Hodges, *Voice of Grief*, 74.
37. Hodges, *Voice of Grief*, 361, n. 104.

teaching with the version of "once saved, always saved" which leads to a cocksure certainty which breeds a casual carelessness about the Christian life. The confession rightly sees that such an attitude is not that of a true Christian. By contrast, the confession defines the work of the Holy Spirit as leading believers to obey Christ, "thereby bearing abundant fruit of life."

HISTORICAL ELABORATION

We shall consider two main issues in this section, first perfectionism, and then the place of God's law in the life of the Christian believer.

Perfectionism

An Outline of its Teaching

The most consistent form of perfectionism teaches that sanctification can be complete, that sin can be totally eradicated from the life of a believer, even while he is still on earth. There are also various modified forms of the teaching.

John Wesley taught a doctrine of "perfect love," of which the essence is obedience to the law of Christ. For Wesley, the perfect Christian was not free from weakness, and yet the sanctifying power of the Spirit enables him to employ his own powers in total accordance with the master's will. Wesley had great confidence in the Holy Spirit's power as greater than the power of sin.

Wesley defined the perfect Christian as one who loves God with all his heart, soul, mind, and strength. God is his joy and desire. He is always happy, because he is happy in God. Perfect love casts out fear, so the perfect Christian is always rejoicing whatever his circumstances. His heart is lifted up to God without interruption. He loves his neighbor as himself and he loves his enemy. He is pure in heart, because love has purified his heart from envy, malice, wrath, and every unkind temper, and from pride. The perfect Christian's one desire is to do God's will, so he keeps all the commandments.

Wesley did not believe that perfection was a condition from which it was impossible to fall. Neither did he describe it as "sinless perfection" although he did not object if others wanted to use that term.

Wesley taught that perfection was acquired instantaneously: it "is always wrought in the soul by a simple act of faith."[38] However, that moment was both the culmination of a gradual work, and was always followed by further gradual development.

Wesley's importance was that he sowed the seed for the holiness and "higher life" teaching which flourished in the nineteenth century. It began to be developed in the 1830s by Charles Finney and Asa Mahan.

Finney defined "entire sanctification" as "that state of devotedness to God and his service required by the moral law."[39] However, to make entire sanctification possible on this definition he had to redefine moral law. He argued that the law cannot require more than man has the natural ability to perform, because law always appeals to voluntary powers. Finney accepted that human moral power was reduced, though not destroyed, by the fall, but, he claimed, God has adapted his law, and with it the definition of perfection, to human weakness. As a result, by exercising what powers he has, the Christian can keep the law perfectly.

Finney also taught a decisive anointing of the Holy Spirit as the impetus to sanctification. His followers developed this idea, and it came to the fore in what has become known as the "Keswick teaching."

Since 1875 an annual convention has been held in the English Lake District town of that name. Its purpose is stated to be "for the deepening of the spiritual life." One of the early influences on the leaders of the Keswick movement was Hannah Pearsall Smith. Sensing her weakness, she began to feel and to teach that Christ delivers completely from the power of sin.

The key word in the traditional Keswick teaching was "counteraction:" believers, burdened by the power of sin in their lives, may find this power broken by a new counteractive power imparted in a definite experience.

Evan Hopkins, who wrote the standard work on Keswick teaching,[40] claimed that the power of sin is stronger than the renewed nature implanted at regeneration. However, in the blood of Christ there is a source of spiritual power for sanctification. The indwelling Christ fills the believer's soul with love. This is a decisive crisis experience. It then becomes an easy matter to obey God's law. The believer attains holiness by union with the indwelling Christ. So the Christian life is not one of

38. Wesley, *Christian Perfection*, 112.
39. Finney, *Sanctification*, 15.
40. Hopkins, *Law of Liberty, passim.*

effort, discipline, struggle, or striving. A favorite Keswick hymn spoke of "holiness by faith in Jesus, not by effort of thine own."[41]

A Critique

B. B. Warfield has written a critique of these approaches to sanctification. We shall focus on just one chapter, entitled "The Higher Life Movement."[42] Here Warfield assesses the teaching of William Boardman and Robert and Hannah Pearsall Smith. Their views are important: as a result of the Keswick Convention, their teaching has had widespread influence in Evangelical circles. Here are Warfield's main criticisms.

PERFECTIONISM TENDS TO DIVIDE SALVATION

Justification and sanctification are separated from each other, and each is obtained by a distinct act of faith. Warfield describes this as "a doctrine of salvation, not by faith, but by faiths."

PERFECTIONISM DIVIDES CHRIST

Jesus Christ as our righteousness and as our sanctification are distinguished from each other. The Higher Life movement divided these two aspects of his work. However, Warfield says, Jesus is one and complete. It is impossible to have him as our righteousness without also having him as our sanctification.

The position which Warfield is opposing here surfaced again more recently in a Dispensationalist context through the teaching of Zane Hodges. He taught that it is possible to receive Jesus as Savior at one time, and only later receive him, as Lord of one's life. He even implied that a person could still be saved, even if they never reached this second phase.

John MacArthur led the way in the fight against this view. His position was nicknamed "Lordship salvation," because he rightly insisted that the only people whom Jesus saves are those who receive him as Lord.[43]

---

41. From *Church of God, beloved and chosen*, by Frances Ridley Havergal (1836–1879).

42. Warfield, *Perfectionism*, 216–311.

43. MacArthur, *Gospel, passim*.

Perfectionism makes the human will the decisive factor in salvation

The Keswick teaching was that full surrender is the route to sanctification. It implies that God is helpless until we surrender to him.

Perfectionism has a reduced idea of what God accomplishes in saving a sinner

Perfectionism does not expect a gradual eradication of the sinful nature towards the day of complete blamelessness at the second coming. This is because it does not locate holiness in the believer's nature. Its only expectation is that faith will keep us doing holy actions. So we are not freed from sin itself, but only from sinning.

Perfectionism has an inadequate concept of sin

Only conscious sin is treated as sinful. So sanctification is defined as freedom from conscious sin, and perfection means freedom from all consciousness of sin resulting in peace and rest. This means that perfection is not measured by an objective standard, but by subjective feeling.

This leads to some odd conclusions. A mature believer, living a godly life, who is becoming increasingly aware of his own sinfulness, is regarded as less "perfect" than a new convert who has no sense of condemnation, even though, very obviously, he has not yet broken free from the anti-Christian morals of his pre-conversion state. There is, therefore, in perfectionism a tendency towards antinomianism. Warfield says: "in order to vindicate the perfection of the Christian, the perfection of his perfection is sacrificed."

Perfectionism is driven by impatience

It is no doubt an admirable desire that we should be perfect now. Yet perfectionism grows out of a frustration with God's slow method of purifying the heart through the conflicts and trials of human experience. Warfield defines this as

> an attempt to substitute a doctrine of perfectionism for the doctrine of perseverance, and to discover the completeness of

salvation in what we find in our possession, rather than in what we shall be, which an apostle tells us is not yet made manifest.

The Law in the Life of the Believer

The Reformation confessions taught (1) that the law is divisible into three parts—ceremonial, civil, and moral, and (2) that the moral law (summarized in the ten commandments) is permanently binding on all people everywhere, including believers, for whom it is the rule of life. Both parts of this teaching have come under attack, so we shall consider each in turn.

The Threefold Division of the Law

John Reisinger claims that the idea of the threefold division originated with Thomas Aquinas in the thirteenth century.[44] However, this is incorrect. The theory of divisions within God's law in Christian thought goes back at least to the second century in the writings of both Barnabas and Justin Martyr. It is true that early writers spoke of two, rather than three, parts: they saw the civil law as particular applications of the moral law.[45] Moreover, Jewish interpreters of the Hebrew Scriptures also recognize a threefold distinction within the law. Boaz Cohen sees the references in texts such as Deuteronomy 6:1 to "commandments, statutes and judgments" as corresponding to three parts of the law, which he entitles ceremonialism, jurisprudence and ethics; he, too, sees the ten commandments as moral principles.[46]

Actually, it is very difficult to reject the threefold distinction with consistency. Edgar Andrews claims to reject the idea that the law is divided into different parts, and yet admits that it has two aspects:

> In the first part (or aspect), we see what a holy God required of his people, and what penalties were applied to those in Israel who broke his commandments. In the second aspect we see the provision God made for the forgiveness and reconciliation of those who sinned. This second aspect prefigured the work of Christ.[47]

44. Reisinger, *Tablets*, 14.
45. Bayes, *Threefold Division*, 6.
46. Cohen, *Law*, 188–89.
47. Andrews, *Free*, 89.

Moreover, Andrews says, "Those who are Spirit-led will fulfil the righteous requirements of the law."[48] It is hard to see what difference there is between these righteous requirements and the moral law.

In fact, Scripture itself assumes distinctions within the law. We have already cited 1 Samuel 15:22, Isaiah 1:11–17, and Amos 5:22–24, where the prophets prioritize obedience to God's commandments above sacrifices, even though these were also commanded. In other words, moral law takes precedence over ceremonial law.

The same distinction is assumed in the New Testament. For example, 1 Corinthians 7:19 reads, "circumcision is nothing and uncircumcision is nothing, but keeping the commandments of God *is what matters.*" Jesus told the rich young ruler, "if you want to enter into life, keep the commandments." The man responded, "which ones?" He was probably not looking for a list of specific commandments, but wanted to know which part of the law was the most important. Jesus then emphasized the importance of the moral law as summarized in the ten commandments (Matt 19:17–19).

Therefore, although the terms "moral," "civil," and "ceremonial" are not found in the Bible, it is true to say that "these theological designations collect important biblical teachings into brief phrases."[49]

The Moral Law as the Believer's Rule of Life

Those who reject the threefold division claim that the whole Law of Moses is one entity, and that we have to be under either all of it or none of it. However, the Reformation taught that, while the civil and ceremonial law were abrogated, God's moral law is the believer's rule of life. However, there are some godly people who deny that Christians need the moral law. They do not advocate lawlessness; they just do not believe that the route to sanctification involves the law.

Within this general framework there are two distinct approaches. On the one hand there is New Covenant Theology. This distinguishes the law of Christ from Old Testament law, and argues that the Christian believer is to be directed only by the New Testament. On the other hand, there is Doctrinal Antinomianism. This believes that holiness is brought

---

48. Andrews, *Free*, 293.
49. Chantry, *God's Righteous Kingdom*, 113.

about in the believer by the immediate work of the Holy Spirit, without the instrumentality of law. We shall look briefly at each in turn.

New Covenant Theology

John Reisinger represents this school of thought. He understands the ten commandments to be the foundation document of the legal covenant given to Israel at Sinai. It was given for a particular historical epoch only. It was part of the old covenant, and when the old covenant was terminated by the coming of Christ, the ten commandments were rendered obsolete.[50] However, Reisinger is absolutely clear that there is a revealed will of God for the new covenant believer, namely the teaching of Jesus and the authoritative apostolic exposition of that teaching.[51]

The difference between this position and that of the Reformation confessions really concerns one issue: is the Lord's Day the Christian Sabbath? New Covenant Theology recognizes that nine of the ten commandments are restated in the New Testament, and are, therefore, part of the teaching of Christ by which the Christian life is directed. However, it sees the Sabbath commandment as abrogated in Christ, whereas most of the confessions saw the Lord's Day as the continuation of the Sabbath commandment in the new post-resurrection situation. This is, therefore, slightly tangential to the larger issue of sanctification.

Doctrinal Antinomianism

This represents a more serious departure from the Reformed position. We shall take Michael Eaton as our example. We must stress that doctrinal antinomians do not teach practical antinomianism. They do believe that holiness is necessary, that holiness of life must follow from the initial experience of salvation. The issue is, how is it achieved?

Eaton sees the law's power as consisting wholly in the fear of punishment. He denies that God uses such a power towards Christian believers. The power for godly living comes from glimpsing God's mercies in Christ. So the instrument of sanctification is the gospel, and the power for sanctification comes directly from the Holy Spirit. Eaton agrees that the believer today fulfils the moral part of the law. However, he does this,

50. Reisinger, *Tablets*, chs. 4 and 8.
51. Reisinger, *Tablets*, 95–96.

not because the law is itself his rule, which he strives to obey, but incidentally, because that is the way that the Spirit leads, and we walk by the Spirit.

This does not mean that the Holy Spirit uses no principles at all, but the principle is the law of love, and love never leads into sin. Eaton acknowledges that "some verses from the law are picked out and applied to the Christian," but, he says, "Paul was not expounding the Mosaic law! He was putting into his own words the kind of thing that he knows the Spirit will lead us into."[52]

This suggests that doctrinal antinomianism is not really possible. How did Paul know what the leading of the Spirit would be in practice? Surely from God's law! If he was not expounding the Mosaic law, why did he allude to some verses from the law? And if sin has no place in a holy life of love, how are we to know what things are sinful and so are to be avoided? We have to give God's law some place.

But even apart from the inconsistencies in doctrinal antinomianism, we must also recognize that the vital role of the Old Testament law as the Spirit's instrument in our sanctification is the consistent teaching of the New Testament. We shall look at a few selected texts.

First, we hear the words of the Lord Jesus in Matthew 5:17–19, where he gradually narrows things down. In verse 17 he speaks of the Law and the Prophets—the entire Old Testament revelation—and says that he did not come to destroy them. Then in verse 18 he refers only to the Law, the five books of Moses, which will not pass away, before focusing specifically on the moral law, which is spelt out in commandments, mentioned in verse 19. These, he says, are the measure of greatness in the kingdom of heaven. That these are the moral commandments, of which the ten commandments are the summary, is clear from the passage which follows.

According to the new covenant promise, which is twice quoted by the writer to the Hebrews (Heb 8:10; 10:16), it is emphatically God's law which is written on the heart of the believer. In chapter 8 the prophet's reference to Israel is quoted, but this is omitted in chapter 10: the writer recognizes that the new covenant promise extends to all the world.

Next, in Romans 2:14–15 the apostle Paul teaches that Gentile Christians, "who do not have the law by nature" (which is how I think

---

52. Eaton, *Godly Life*, 20, 92–93.

this phrase should be punctuated),[53] are recognized by the fact that they now keep the law. In verse 26 also Paul speaks of an uncircumcised man who "keeps the righteous requirements of the law."

Later, in Romans 8:4. Paul explains the purpose of God's condemnation of our sin in the flesh of Christ: it is "that the righteous requirement of the law might be fulfilled in us who do not walk according to the flesh but according to the Spirit." The Spirit's work is to fulfil the law's righteous requirement in us. Verse 7 notes that it is a mark of the fleshly mindset not to submit to God's law, and that mindset contrasts with the mindset of the Spirit.

Finally, James 2:8 says this: "if you really fulfil *the* royal law according to the Scripture, "You shall love your neighbor as yourself," you do well." James sees the love command as the summary of the entire law, and understands that it is a duty of believers to fulfil the law. In 2 John 6, John is clear that we do not merely fulfil the law incidentally as we love, but we express love as we deliberately "walk according to his commandments," for the commandments amplify the content of real love.

PRACTICAL APPLICATION

(1) We must make sure that becoming holy is our great aim, the main goal of our lives. It is far more important than making money, progressing up the career ladder, gaining qualifications, or anything else, however worthy and legitimate in themselves, those other things may be.

For those of us called to pastoral ministry, the pursuit of holiness is also more important than seeing souls saved or seeing church growth. Robert Murray M'Cheyne is famously reputed to have said, "my people's greatest need is my personal holiness." If we neglect our personal holiness, we shall undermine our own ministries. As Paul reminds Timothy, it is those who are holy who are "useful for the master" (2 Tim 2:21).

(2) We must remember that holiness is intensely practical. There is always a temptation to turn holiness into something mystical and otherworldly, whereas the scriptural call is "present your bodies a living sacrifice, holy, acceptable to God" (Rom 12:1).

It is true that holiness involves separation from evil and from the world. That was God's plan for his people from the beginning. He said to Israel in Leviticus 20:26: "you shall be holy to me, for I the LORD *am*

53. Bayes, *Weakness*, 104.

holy, and have separated you from the peoples, that you should be mine." When, many years later, the people of God had mixed itself with the peoples of other lands, this was condemned as a trespass (Ezra 9:2).

However, what is in view is a moral separation, a separation from the worldly ethos, not the sort of separation which withdraws from society into a supposedly holy ghetto. Scripture portrays holiness as mainly to do with the practicalities of daily life in this world. It is, of course, true that holiness is birthed in the place of prayer, but there is far more to holiness than private devotion.

The great holiness text, "you shall be holy, for I the LORD your God am holy" is followed by the instruction, "every one of you shall revere his mother and his father" (Lev 19:2–3; cf. 20:7–9). The family is a major formative sphere for developing holiness.

From the home, we move out into the wider society, as the place where we put holiness into practice. The practical nature of holiness is clearly taught in the New Testament. This is what Colossians 3:12–14 says:

> As *the* elect of God, holy and beloved, put on tender mercies, kindness, humility, meekness, longsuffering; bearing with one another, and forgiving one another, if anyone has a complaint against another; even as Christ forgave you, so you also *must do*. But above all these things put on love, which is the bond of perfection.

Holiness is largely about how we relate to other people in a fallen world, where sin constantly cries out for forgiveness. Our holiness can often be measured by how we react in difficult relational situations.

In Titus 1:7–8 Paul states some of the qualifications for eldership: an elder must not be "self-willed, not quick-tempered, not given to wine, not violent, not greedy for gain, but hospitable, a lover of what is good, sober-minded, just, holy, self-controlled."

Holiness is connected with a self-discipline which avoids scandalous sins, but which is also honest and kind in dealings with other people. And the elder is not supposed to be a super-Christian. These will be the marks of every Christian as we grow towards maturity.

(3) We must make a habit of meditating on God's moral law, which is a summary of the holiness which he requires. The ten commandments are at the heart of that summary. That is why holiness and obedience are often mentioned side-by-side, as, for example, in Deuteronomy 26:18–19. Here keeping the commandments is a defining feature of a

people holy to the LORD. The apostle Peter also defines holiness in terms of obedience, recognizing that this entails a clear break with our past life (1 Pet 1:14–16).

Those of us who are preachers and pastors must not shy away from the task of teaching the ten commandments to our people. We should expound them as Jesus did in the Sermon on the Mount, where he corrected Pharisaic misinterpretations of the commandments and clarified their original meaning, demonstrating their far-reaching demands for our inner impulses as well as our outward actions. As well as preaching the positive commands given by God, we must also avoid the kind of legalism which would impose on other people's consciences any requirements not found in Scripture. Of course, before we preach God's law to others, we must preach it to ourselves.

(4) We should work out what holiness means in detail. It is possible to speak of holiness in such vague and general terms that we are left in the dark as to what it really means in practice. This is where the emphasis in Romans 6:19 on presenting our members to God is so helpful: we must consider what it is to be holy in every separate dimension of life. It would be so easy to be striving after holiness in some areas, while totally neglecting it in others. We must remember that sanctification touches on every part of our being and every aspect of our living. We must not neglect any part of it.

(5) We must remember that we have to work at holiness. Sanctification does not just happen to us without our effort. The apostle says, "pursue . . . holiness" (Heb 12:14). Progress in holiness is gradual, and we must see it as our daily responsibility to sustain a holy walk.

Holiness will never come easily, because of the powerful remnants of our sinful nature. We cannot expect to get to heaven unless we can say with the apostle, "I have fought the good fight" (2 Tim 4:7). We long to be overcomers, but we cannot win unless there is a battle. Those of us who preach God's word must be careful not to misrepresent the truth by conveying the impression that the Christian life is an easy life.

(6) Particular care must be taken in the area of sexual purity. Sexual sin is not the worst of sins. It is not in a league of its own. It is no more sinful than the pride that congratulates self for the avoidance of sexual sin. Nevertheless, sexual sin is unusually destructive. As it says in 1 Corinthians 6:18, "he who commits sexual immorality sins against his own body." No doubt this is why the apostle almost equates sanctification and sexual purity in 1 Thessalonians 4:3–5.

That passage also makes the point that sexual purity is one of the most powerful characteristics of the people of God as distinct from the world. Sexual temptation is particularly strong, and the devil tends to latch on to it to try to drag Christians down. We must pay heed to the apostle's words in 1 Corinthians 9:27: "I discipline my body and bring it into subjection, lest, when I have preached to others, I myself should become disqualified."

To help in this, we must endeavor to avoid all contaminating influences: avoid reading unsavory material; avoid looking at disgusting images, whether in print or on film, on television or on the internet. The apostle's advice in Philippians 4:8 is salutary: "finally, brethren, whatever things are true, whatever things *are* noble, whatever things *are* just, whatever things *are* pure, whatever things *are* lovely, whatever things *are* of good report, if *there is* any virtue and if *there is* anything praiseworthy— meditate on these things."

(7) We must also meditate deeply on God's grace. There can be no more powerful motive to holy living than to ponder God's amazing grace to us in Christ. We should spend much time meditating on the depths of his love, the intensity of Christ's sufferings. When we see what agonies our sin imposed on our Savior, we shall surely want to avoid sin as much as we can. When we ponder the promises of mercy all summed up in Christ, we shall be able to act upon the words of 2 Corinthians 7:1: "having these promises, beloved, let us cleanse ourselves from all filthiness of the flesh and spirit, perfecting holiness in the fear of God."

PART THREE: THE FUTURE TENSE (GLORIFICATION)

So where does it all lead? We have been justified in Christ, and for the rest of our lives are in the process of being made new by God's sanctifying work within us. Now we must set our sights on our future destination when our salvation will finally be complete, when sin shall be no more. The key word which expresses the future hope is "glory." The future tense of salvation is therefore summed up in the word glorification.

Glorification is a New Testament theme. In the Old Testament we find hints and glimpses of the final glorification of God's people, but this truth was not fully disclosed until Christ came. Thereafter, the New Testament is full of the hope of glory, although we have to bear in mind that "it has not yet been revealed what we shall be" (1 John 3:2). We cannot give a fully detailed account of what glory will be like.

BIBLICAL FOUNDATION

Romans 8:18–30 is, in fact, the only passage where the actual word "glorified" is used to refer to the future glory of Christ's people, as distinct from the glorifying of God the Father or God the Son. We shall therefore focus just on this single passage.

Our prospect is defined in these verses as complete conformity to God's glorified Son in the setting of a renewed creation. Paul introduced the theme at the end of verse 17: we shall "also be glorified together" with him. Glory is something which we shall enjoy together with Christ, because it is final, complete Christlikeness. However, this prospect awaits us "if indeed we suffer with *him*."

In verses 18–25 Paul anticipates the time when we shall be glorified with Christ. Verse 18 is a summary of the whole section: "I consider that the sufferings of this present time are not worthy *to be compared* with the glory which shall be revealed in us." There is simply no comparison between our sufferings now and the surpassing glory then. Two illustrations of that fact are suggested.

The first is the picture of a balance sheet, suggested by the word "consider" (*logizomai*). The apostle imagines our present sufferings in the debit column, and the future glory on the credit side. As he considers one in relation to the other, he concludes that the glory so far exceeds the suffering that it is impossible to balance the account.

The second is the picture of a pair of scales. This is suggested by the word "worthy" (*axios*). In one pan is our present suffering. In the other is the future glory. The weight of glory is so immense as to make even the heaviest of present day trials seem as light as a feather (cf. 2 Cor 4:17).

Our present sufferings are, therefore, the foundation and inspiration of our hope. However, it is not only Christian believers who suffer now and anticipate glory. In verses 19–22 Paul shows that the future glory will include the restoration of the entire creation. This will take place on the day of "the revealing of the sons of God." It is when God's children are finally glorified that the entire creation will simultaneously be set free and made new. Thereafter we shall live in a glorified world in which nothing will ever get damaged or wear out.

In verses 23–25 the apostle speaks in more detail of what that ultimate glory will mean for us. It is interesting that he puts things in the order that he does. Human future salvation is the catalyst of cosmic redemption, yet Paul deals with the cosmic aspect of salvation first. It is first in importance. God is not satisfied just with saving souls. His real goal is to rescue his whole creation project, to present it to his Son as his eternal inheritance. Our salvation is part of that larger purpose.

These verses depict our future glory using the metaphor of a harvest. Already, we enjoy a foretaste of glory. The Holy Spirit is "the firstfruits." The firstfruits are the initial representation of the full harvest. They are a few of the fruits of the crop which have ripened ahead of the rest. They are the guarantee that the rest of the harvest will, in due course, be gathered in. So our present experience of the power of the Holy Spirit in our lives is the guarantee that the future glory is a reality. Because of the joy of the foretaste we groan for the full reality.

But what will that reality be like? The apostle highlights two things.

First, it will mean our adoption. Back in verses 15–16 Paul has told us that we are already adopted by the Father as his sons, and so "the Spirit himself bears witness with our spirit that we are children of God." As yet our adoption is not publicly confirmed, but on that glorious day the whole world will know. Our faith will be vindicated.

Second, the physical redemption of our bodies will take place. This presupposes resurrection, and reminds us that our resurrection bodies will be completely free from decay. Death will be destroyed, and all the marks of mortality will be a thing of the past. This includes the ageing process, illness, pain, vulnerability to accidents, and so on.

Verses 24–25 remind us that "we were saved in this hope." Christian hope is not uncertain. It is sure and definite, but what we hope for is unseen because it is as yet future. As long as we remain on earth, the greater part of our salvation is still to come, as the fact of suffering proves. So "we eagerly wait for *it* with perseverance."

In verses 26–30 Paul speaks first about an uncertainty—"we do not know" (verse 26), and then about a certainty—"we know" (verse 28). Our uncertainty is how best to pray for our own progress towards glory, but here the Spirit helps. The certainty is that "all things work together for good to those who love God."

In this context, the "good" is our progress towards glory—our complete conformity to the likeness of Christ (verse 29). To be glorified will mean that in every aspect of our whole personality we become replicas of Jesus. That, the apostle reminds us, is what we were predestined to be. And what is "good" for us now is to be moving little-by-little closer to that goal.

In verses 29–30 Paul traces the stages in a process leading to glorification. All the things which he mentions except the last one happened for every believer in the past, whether in eternity or time. We have already been foreknown, predestined, called, and justified. The final thing is still future, and yet the apostle again uses the past tense: "whom he justified, these he also glorified." Although the process has not yet culminated in glory, Paul is so confident in a God of absolute faithfulness that he knows that it is as good as done.

Further, the apostle does not mention sanctification, even though it comes between justification and glorification. He is so certain that those who are justified will be finally glorified that he omits that link in the chain. God will complete the work of glorifying us, of making us forever Christlike, in sanctification now, and in glorification at the end.

DOCTRINAL FORMULATION

There is surprisingly little treatment in the creeds, the confessions, or the modern statements of faith of the theme of glorification as an aspect of salvation. It is dealt with more in the context of individual eschatology. Perhaps this reflects the worthy fact that the chief concern of these historic statements is life in and for Christ in the here-and-now.

The early creeds have two articles which are relevant, affirming belief in the resurrection, and in everlasting life. However, by placing these articles at the end of the creeds, the early church sets them in an eschatological context. We shall therefore consider them under the heading of Eschatology.

Of the three modern confessions of faith which we have been surveying, only one—the Indian confession—has a mention of glory in its article on salvation. It includes "eternal glory" in a list of the four chief benefits which come to believers as their salvation. William Stewart describes the new life in the Holy Spirit as "the prelude to 'eternal glory' for which we were made."[54]

When we turn to the Reformation confessions, we find that there are two documents which do mention glorification.

54. W. Stewart, *Faith We Confess*, 30.

The Canons of Dort

Here glorification is defined as reigning with the Lamb in heaven. It is the final stage in the entire process of salvation. The entire process is designed to demonstrate God's mercy, and so provoke praise for his glorious grace. So when we are finally glorified, God's grace will be finally displayed in the fullness of its splendor: that those who were sinners should share the throne with the Lamb of God—what a mercy!

The Westminster Larger Catechism

This document refers to our communion in glory with Christ. This emphasizes the point that our glorification is a participation in his glory. This participation is seen in two ways. First, it is seen now, as the first-fruits, in our love, peace, joy, and hope. Second, it will be seen at the resurrection in our final perfecting.

HISTORICAL ELABORATION

There is not a great deal to write about under this heading for this theme. Perhaps because the issue of glorification has never been particularly controversial, it has not figured much in theological debate. We shall refer to just one brief article by John Murray, entitled "The Goal of Sanctification."[55]

Murray's central point is that glorification is the goal of sanctification. He thus holds together the present and future aspects of salvation. Indeed, he defines glorification as "the consummation of the sanctifying process." He says two main things.

First, since the chief end of everything is God's glory, that must be the chief end of our glorification. Murray sees this as the reason why believers must appear before the judgment seat of Christ. The prerequisite to our eternal happiness is the vindication of God's glory. That must include adjudication of the lives and the sins of believers. But our judgment will not fill us with dismay. It will enhance our appreciation of the wonders of redeeming grace. As long as our mindset is God-centered, we will find the final perfect adjudication of everything, including our own lives, the source of the highest joy. "The bliss of heaven is not constituted

---

55. J. Murray, *Systematic Theology*, 313–17.

by forgetting sin, but by glorying in the redemption that washed from sin and made us white in the blood of the Lamb." That is why we "rejoice in hope of the glory of God" (Rom 5:2), which Murray takes to mean that we rejoice as we look forward to God himself being glorified.

Second, Murray sees our glorification as the final stage of Christ's glorification. He draws attention to the final clause of Romans 8:29, God's people are destined "*to be* conformed to the image of his Son, that he might be the firstborn among many brethren." This is what it means for us to be glorified—that we conform to the image of the Son. Glory is nothing apart from that conformity. As Murray comments, "God himself could not contemplate or determine a higher destiny for his creatures."

However, while we are glorified in Christ, he too is glorified in us. And, as this text makes clear, our conformity to him—our glorification—is in order that he may be pre-eminent, that being one significance of the title "firstborn." That is the ultimate goal. Christ remains the pre-eminent one. "The glory of God is always supreme and ultimate. And the supreme glory of God is manifested in the glorifying of his Son." However, he is to be the firstborn "among many brethren." His pre-eminence has no meaning independently of his relation to them: he is glorified in community with his people. Here is a truth which "staggers our thought by reason of its stupendous reality:" the ultimate glory of Christ is inextricably tied to the glorification of his people.

PRACTICAL APPLICATION

(1) We must be God-centered in our vision. We must ensure that the glory of God in the glorification of Christ is the dominating vision in our hearts. It is in God's glorification in Christ that we shall reach our highest joy. Our joyful privilege is to seek his glory. We must strive to overcome the tendency to put ourselves at the center, just longing for our own glory, from lesser motives, such as the desire to be free from earthly pain, frustration, and restriction. Neither must we let lesser goals, such as the hope of reunion with loved ones, become the center of our hope. Christ is the loved one we are eager to see: we must ensure that we love him so much that we long to see him, and pray that God will daily deepen our love for him, so that he alone is the center of our affections now, and the focus of our eternal hope.

God the Father and God the Son are the light in which Christians will live their eternity. This is the consummation of God's goal in all of history—to display his glory for all to see and praise. The prayer of the Son confirms the purpose of the Father: "Father, I desire that they also whom you gave me may be with me where I am, that they may behold my glory which you have given me; for you loved me before the foundation of the world" (John 17:24).[56]

(2) We must constantly be amazed by grace, never ceasing to be astonished at the mercy which God has shown us in Christ. We must ponder constantly the fact that we are destined to share the glory of the only begotten, eternally beloved Son of the Father. We must meditate daily on the wonder that Christ's pre-eminence will be associated with our glorification. We should be humbled that God should confer upon sinners like us such an overwhelming privilege. We should be praising him constantly for the honor which he has bestowed on us in uniting us with Christ now and for ever. 1 John 3:1–3 expresses the wonder of it, and verse 3 reminds us that wonder and praise has its practical outworking in the purity with which our growth in Christlikeness starts. We must remember that the apostle describes conformity to the Son of God as our "good" (Rom 8:29). It really is good for us to become more and more like Jesus. Glorification is the goal of sanctification: we strive after glory by striving after holiness.

(3) Let us keep the vision of glory bright in our hearts. A future vision is vital. We must rejoice in the hope of glory. The anticipation of future glory must always be our most powerful inspiration. We must actively cultivate that anticipation. If our future vision grows dim, we face either of two dangers.

First, we may become overly despondent and depressed at the state of the world and at our own painful experiences. To keep reminding ourselves that these things, however grim, are brief in comparison with eternal glory will protect us from despair.

On the other hand, we may find the things of the present time too attractive. We shall become too much at ease in this life. Then the passing away of the transient things of time will be a shock to our system, and we shall not be ready and eager to leave them behind when the time comes to enter into glory.

56. Piper, *Desiring God*, 238.

Those of us called to minister God's word should hold the hope of glory before our people regularly. That alone will sustain them through the inglorious moments of the present life, and provide the check they need against being "conformed to this world" (Rom 12:2).

(4) We are to enjoy the foretaste of glory even now. The Holy Spirit is the firstfruits of eternal glory. Life in the Spirit is that blessed foretaste of better things to come. Our joy is to be penetrating ever deeper into the things of the Spirit. We must beware of allowing the truth of the Holy Spirit to become merely theoretical. We should be living in the Spirit's power, developing the Spirit's mind, with its associated life and peace (Rom 8:5–7), cultivating the Spirit's desires, and producing the Spirit's fruit in our hearts and lives (Gal 5:17, 22). As we walk in the Spirit, so our minds are filled with expectancy as the glory of the future shines its light into the present.

(5) The vision of future glory helps us to see our sufferings in perspective. In a godless world, every Christian should expect to "endure hardship as a good soldier of Jesus Christ" (2 Tim 2:3). We should, indeed, regard it as a privilege to be "counted worthy to suffer shame for his name" (Acts 5:41). And we must ever remember that our present suffering "is working for us a far more exceeding *and* eternal weight of glory" (2 Cor 4:17). That will help us to keep our sufferings in proportion and not exaggerate them to the point where they drag us down into misery, and so cease to be a blessing to us.

(6) Let us be longing for Christ's return. We must remember that the fullness of glory will not be experienced by any of us until it is experienced by all of us. While each believer at death will go to "be with Christ" in a condition which Paul describes as "far better" (Phil 1:23), it is only when our bodies are raised from the dead at Christ's second coming that our glorification will be finalized.

10

The Doctrine of Salvation (2)
Further Aspects of Salvation

In addition to the three fundamental elements of justification, sanctification, and glorification, there are many more aspects to salvation. In this chapter we shall consider five of the most important ones: regeneration, union with Christ, reconciliation, adoption, and perseverance.

PART ONE: REGENERATION

Regeneration is the starting-point of the entire experience of salvation. It is the essential prerequisite for justification. It makes it possible for the sinner to exercise justifying faith. That is not primarily a chronological, but a logical, statement. The exact sequence is a divine mystery.

BIBLICAL FOUNDATION

Old Testament

We shall look at three Old Testament passages relevant to this subject. In all three the Old Testament is looking forward. These passages are all predictions of what will come as a result of the work of the Messiah.

Deuteronomy 30:6

We hear in this verse of the LORD circumcising people's hearts, with the result that they will love the LORD with all their heart and soul, in order that they may live. These words occur in the context of the promise of return after exile. Moses is looking forward to the days of the Messiah and the new covenant. At that time there will be total commitment to the LORD. But for that to be possible, circumcision of the heart will be necessary, and that is something which only the LORD himself can do.

Calvin comments that Moses indicates that "a divine remedy was needed, namely, that God should renew and mould their hearts." He equates this with "the Spirit of regeneration."[1]

Circumcision, the sign of belonging to the old covenant community, was intended to point to this deeper reality of circumcision of the heart (regeneration). That is the source of new covenant membership. In Romans 2:29 Paul defines this as the work of the Spirit.

Jeremiah 30—32

In these chapters the LORD promises to restore the fortunes of Israel and Judah, and to renew the covenant commitment that he will be their God and they his people. He affirms his steadfast love and faithfulness, and assures them of a hope-filled future. At the heart of these chapters we find the new covenant promise (Jer 31:33–34). These verses affirm that the central element in the new covenant is that the law will be written upon people's personalities. As a result they will possess true knowledge of the LORD. Any covenant which does not include the regeneration of the human personality in order to defeat the power of sin, is inevitably doomed to failure. That is the problem which the new covenant overcomes.

The prophet returns to this theme in the next chapter (Jer 32), where, in verses 39–40, he quotes the LORD's promise to give his people "one heart and one way," the purpose being "that they may fear me forever." Verse 40 takes this same issue a step further. Having reaffirmed his intention to "make an everlasting covenant" with his people in which he "will not turn away from doing them good," the LORD explains in these words how this will be achieved: "I will put my fear in their hearts so that they will not depart from me."

1. Calvin, *Books of Moses*, Vol. 3, 284–85.

The covenant response is one of complete, wholehearted devotion to the LORD. God's people fear him, not because they observe him from afar, but because he has put his fear within them. The verb "fear" in verse 39 translates *yārē'*, while the noun in verse 40 is the cognate term *yir'à*. In Deuteronomy 10:12 *yārē'* occurs alongside obedience, service and love. To fear the LORD is to respond appropriately to him because of the great respect which we have for him. But only when God changes our hearts is such a response possible.

Ezekiel 11:19–20 and 36:24–27

After the opening message of assurance, the early chapters of the book of Ezekiel are mainly words of judgment and warning. However, at the end of chapter 11, there is a sudden gleam of light, as the re-gathering of Israel after the exile is prophesied. However, restoration to the land will not be enough. The LORD must also work within the people, and so, in verses 19–20, he says this, in words that echo those of Jeremiah:

> I will give them one heart, and I will put a new spirit within them, and take the stony heart out of their flesh, and give them a heart of flesh, that they may walk in my statutes and keep my judgments and do them.

God's real purpose in restoring Israel is a spiritual one. It will involve renovating the people from the depths of their personality. Like Jeremiah, Ezekiel uses the phrase, "one heart," and also refers to "a new spirit." This is a prophecy of the inner working of the Holy Spirit, by whose power sinners are made new. The result of the Spirit's inner working is that a heart that was hardened against the LORD is changed into a heart that beats with the desire to do God's will.

Ezekiel then returns to the theme of judgment. There are a few more bright moments of hope, but judgement is the major emphasis. However, the theme of the new heart and the new spirit recurs in chapter 36. Verses 24–25 speak of the re-gathering of Israel to the land, and of the far more important work of cleansing them from the uncleanness caused by idolatry.

Verses 26–27 then clearly state the truth that a new heart and a new spirit entails the presence of God's Spirit within. In these two verses the phrase "I will" is repeated three times. This serves to stress that all this is the work of the LORD: "I will give . . . , I will take . . . , I will put . . . ." "I will" is also understood, though not written in the English translation, in front of the verbs "put," and "give" (in its second occurrence) in verse 26 and "cause" in verse 27. Here is a sixfold commitment on the part of God, in which, in effect, he says, "I will achieve your regeneration." Regeneration is not a work which a person can do for himself. A divine initiative is needed. Regeneration is a total, all-encompassing renovation of the human personality, which is entirely the work of the Holy Spirit.

New Testament

We now come to the age of fulfilment, and see how these Old Testament predictions came about. The word "regeneration" comes only twice in the New Testament (Matt 19:28 and Titus 3:5), and only one of them is relevant to our theme. More noticeable is the language of spiritual birth. We shall focus on four contexts.

John 3:3–8

This is, arguably, the main passage in the New Testament on the theme of regeneration. Talking with Nicodemus Jesus starts by saying, "unless one is born again, he cannot see the kingdom of God" (verse 3). As the conversation continues, we may analyze Jesus' teaching into four themes.

(1) Regeneration (being born again) is indispensable: "you must be born again" (verse 7). The point of the reference to seeing the kingdom of God (verse 3) is that without regeneration we have no spiritual vision, no insight into spiritual matters. We are spiritually blind. The gospel makes no sense, and it is impossible to become a believer, unless we are born again. In verse 5 Jesus makes the point that without regeneration we are not part of God's kingdom. And that applies even to this Jewish ruler (verse 1), who is the leading teacher of his generation (verse 10).

(2) Being born again is a work of the Holy Spirit. This is what Jesus says in verse 5. To be born again is not something which an unconverted sinner can do. Jesus does not command Nicodemus to be born again. He informs him that it is necessary, and then points out that the Spirit has to do it. The point of verse 6 is that nothing which human ability can achieve can be enough to generate spiritual life. The phrase "born again" (*gennaō anōthen*) can equally validly be translated "born from above." This emphasizes the fact that only God can do this.

(3) Being born again is a marvel, and yet not a marvel! Jesus' teaching here is a marvel to Nicodemus (verse 4). His question, "how can a man be born when he is old?" does not necessarily mean that he is thinking in merely materialistic terms. Merrill Tenney suggests that he may be asking how it can be possible to have a radically new start once we are set in our ways?[2] It is true, it requires a miracle. And yet this fact is not to be marveled at (verse 7). The sinful life is as Nicodemus fears; regeneration must, therefore, be a supernatural work of the Spirit.

(4) Being born again by God's Spirit is not something that we can control. The movements of the Holy Spirit are as unpredictable as the wind (verse 8). In October, 1987, a British weather forecast assured everyone that the rumor that a hurricane was approaching southern England was untrue. Just a few hours later southern England was indeed hit by its worst storm for nearly 300 years! Eighteen people were killed. Fifteen million trees were brought down, blocking roads and railways, crushing cars, and damaging buildings. Electricity cables were wrecked, so that most of south-east England was blacked out. Usually, of course, a forecast predicts the weather more accurately than that, but there is no equivalent way of predicting the work of God's Spirit.

Jesus' main point is that to become a true Christian the first thing needed is a change of heart by the Holy Spirit's power. We are helpless until God works in us. However, Nicodemus is not left merely groping in his helplessness. In verses 12–15 the message of the cross is proclaimed, and Nicodemus is urged to believe in Jesus. It is as the gospel message is proclaimed that the Holy Spirit does his secret work of regeneration.

Titus 3:5

We turn next to the one text where the word "regeneration" (*palingenesia*) itself appears, used relevantly to this theme. It is used in parallel with the term "renewing," which indicates that regeneration entails making us new people through the infusion of spiritual life. This is the work of the Holy Spirit. Regeneration also involves "washing." It is the first stage in the process of cleansing from sin's defilement, as a new heart is created by the Spirit. Verse 7 indicates that regeneration by the Holy Spirit leads on to justification by grace. Until the Spirit has made us spiritually alive, justifying faith is impossible.

2. Tenney, "John," 47.

1 Peter 1

Being born again is mentioned twice in this chapter. First, verse 3 says that God "according to his abundant mercy has begotten us again." Then in verse 23, the apostle says that we have "been born again, not of corruptible seed but incorruptible, through the word of God which lives and abides forever."

We notice three things here.

(1) Regeneration is God's work. As verse 3 insists, he has caused it to happen. In both verses the passive voice of the verb is used. This also draws attention to the fact that this is God's work.

(2) The basis of regeneration is God's mercy. Verse 3 makes this point. The fact that it is "according to mercy" means that God was under no obligation to give us rebirth. It was a free choice on his part. We had no right to expect to be given spiritual life. The fact that we have received this gift is evidence of God's stupendous kindness.

(3) The means of regeneration is the word of God. Our emphasis on the sovereignty of the work of the Spirit in regeneration could make it sound rather mystical. It is certainly a mysterious work, but verse 23 makes it clear that the Spirit normally employs the word as an instrument of rebirth. Generally, regeneration takes place in a hidden way as a person hears the gospel preached. As a result, that person believes. That is why, when Jesus told Nicodemus about the new birth, he also told him about the cross and called him to believe. God's word is compared here to an incorruptible seed. It has to be incorruptible if it is to produce a spiritual life which is beyond the danger of perishing.

1 John

The Greek verb *gennaō* (born) comes ten times in 1 John. It is used once on its own (5:1), and nine times in two different phrases—"born of God" (3:9 [twice]; 4:7; 5:1, 4, 18 [twice]), and "born of him" (2:29; 5:1).

John uses this word as he points to the evidences of regeneration. These include the practice of righteousness (2:29), the avoidance of sin (3:9; 5:18), love for one another (4:7; 5:1), the belief that Jesus is the Christ (5:1), love for God (5:1), and overcoming the world in faith (5:4).

Regeneration is a work of God. We cannot examine people's hearts to see whether it has taken place. However, there are signs of its reality on the surface of our lives. If these are missing, there is reason to doubt whether regeneration has actually taken place. The importance of 1 John is that it reminds us of the need to examine ourselves to ensure that we are not deluded when we claim to be born again.

DOCTRINAL FORMULATION

The Reformation Confessions

We may summarize what the confessions say on this theme under five headings.

Why regeneration is necessary

Many of the confessions preface their statements on regeneration with a comment about the human plight which makes regeneration a necessity if anyone is to receive spiritual life. For example, the Scottish Confession says: "by nature we are so dead, so blind, and so perverse, that neither can we feel when we are pricked, see the light when it shines, nor assent to the will of God when it is revealed."

This explains why so many people remain unmoved by the thrilling truths of the gospel even when we are able to declare them brimming over with excitement and enthusiasm. Until the regenerating grace of the Spirit works within them, they cannot and will not turn to God, and have no motivation for reformation of the depraved human nature.

The agent of regeneration

The confessions saw regeneration as a supernatural work, powerfully performed by God alone through the agency of his Holy Spirit. It is not by any natural powers, and not by free will, that we are born again, because, of ourselves, we are unable to think even one good thought.

It is not even the case that the Holy Spirit regenerates us with our co-operation. In regeneration we are completely passive. That is why the confessions could characterize regeneration as an astonishing, mysterious, and ineffable work.

Because regeneration is God's work, it follows that it is a work of grace. If we have been born again, that does not give us any cause at all for self-glorification. The only legitimate response is thankfulness.

How regeneration is defined

Regeneration involves enlightenment of the mind to understand spiritual truth and renewal of the will. Echoing the Old Testament, the confessions speak of the gift of a new heart and spirit, and echoing the New Testament, they speak of being made alive and of newness of life.

The Holy Spirit illuminates the darkened mind, and so gives understanding of spiritual things. He also softens the hardened heart and transforms the will, so that the sinner, previously bent on disobedience, becomes inclined instead to obey the will of God.

The means of regeneration

The confessions are clear that the tool which the Holy Spirit uses in enacting the new birth in a sinner is the gospel. The Spirit's inner call to the sinner to believe occurs alongside the external call of the word. Furthermore, in his providence, God so arranges things that those whom he purposes to regenerate do in fact hear the gospel preached to them.

That, at least, is the normal method, though, with pastoral wisdom, the Westminster Confession concedes that we must allow for the abnormal: in some special cases regeneration may take place independently of the preaching of the gospel. It mentions infants who die in infancy, and others whose mental incapacity leaves them "incapable of being outwardly called by the ministry of the Word." Such, the confession insists, may be "regenerated, and saved by Christ, through the Spirit, who works when, and where, and how he pleases."

Regeneration and human nature

Although regeneration is a work in which God is the sole agent, this does not mean that he treats people as "senseless stocks and blocks," to quote the Canons of Dort. In other words, he does not violate the human will. Rather, the Canons continue, the grace of regeneration

> spiritually quickens, heals, corrects, and at the same time sweetly and powerfully bends it, that where carnal rebellion and resistance formerly prevailed, a ready and sincere spiritual obedience begins to reign; in which the true and spiritual restoration and freedom of our will consist.

This means that, even though the human being is passive at the moment of regeneration, the result is that he actively believes and repents.

Modern Confessions of Faith

The Chinese confession is the only one of our three modern confessions to use the phrase "born again." It comes in the section on the Holy Spirit: "The Holy Spirit illuminates a person causing him to know sin and repent, to know the truth, and to believe in Christ and so experience being born again unto salvation."

It is a moot point whether the order in which faith and regeneration are mentioned here reflects a less than robustly biblical understanding of the logical order in which the components of a salvation experience take place, or whether it is merely imprecise wording.

Although neither the Indian nor the Indonesian confessions contain an explicit reference to being born again, both make reference to things which we have seen belong to the content or to the results of regeneration. In the Indian statement on the Holy Spirit, the description of his work is tantamount to a definition of regeneration: he

> makes men partakers of salvation, convincing them of their sin and misery, enlightening their minds in the knowledge of Christ, renewing their wills, persuading and enabling them to embrace Jesus Christ.

Likewise, the Indonesian statement says that the Holy Spirit calls the congregation of God's people. Although calling may be distinguished from regeneration, the two are intimately related. This confession also rejects the idea that "the Holy Spirit can descend upon man through his own power without the gospel."

Here is a recognition that the Spirit's normal way of working is by the use of means, in particular the word of the gospel. The confession is probably not intending to deny that there may be abnormal situations where the regenerating work of the Holy Spirit takes place apart from the preached word. It is, however, insisting that, in no case is it human power which results in a sinner's conversion.

What is clear in all three confessions is that regeneration is firmly recognized to be a work of the Holy Spirit. None of the confessions has an article devoted exclusively to regeneration. All three embed their description of regeneration within their statement on the Holy Spirit. This reflects a clear understanding of the helplessness of sinful man to initiate his salvation. The deadness of man in sin makes the power of the Holy Spirit the indispensable necessity if we are to be born again.

HISTORICAL ELABORATION

Here we shall consider two issues. The first is the rise of a man-centered approach to regeneration in decisionist evangelism in recent decades. The second is the question whether regeneration takes place entirely in a moment of time.

The Man-centered Approach to Regeneration

A typical example of this is found in a brief pamphlet by an American pastor called George Cover. The title is *How to be Born Again*.[3] The first six sections define the new birth and the need for it. Then we come to section 7, which asks the question, "How can a person be born again?" There are two subsections. The first concerns "God's Part." God's part in our regeneration is summarized in three things: (1) Jesus Christ died in our place; (2) he forgives sins; (3) he gives spiritual life.

The second subsection is the part of the pamphlet in which we are mainly interested. It is entitled "Your Part," and outlines four steps, which, it claims "will result in the new birth." Here they are.

(1) Choose to be born again. This point is amplified with these exhortations: "Choose the way of Jesus instead of the way of Satan; choose to call on the Lord for salvation. Choose whom you will serve."

(2) Believe on the Lord Jesus Christ, the Son of God. To believe is then defined as "absolute trust."

(3) Receive Christ.

(4) Repent. There then follows an explanation of what this means: "Be sorry for your sins—confess them—leave them."

In themselves, these are admirable exhortations. However, they are set in the context of an evangelistic approach which misleads people into thinking that being born again is a matter of personal choice, and that it results from faith and repentance.

This is at odds with the biblical emphasis, which puts things in the opposite order: faith and repentance are the results of being born again,

---

3. Cover, *How to be Born Again*, *passim*.

and we are totally dependent on God for the gift of new life. There is nothing that we can do to secure it.

Sometimes this approach reduces regeneration to a trivial formula. People are urged to say the rather trite "sinner's prayer," confessing their sins and inviting Jesus into their life, and then are assured that they are now born again. All this is a far cry from the biblical emphasis on our utter dependence on the grace of God and the power of the Holy Spirit. The tendency to portray regeneration in such easy terms stems from the lack of a proper awareness of the depth of human sin and depravity, resulting in a large number of people "who thought they were saved because they prayed a certain prayer, but they lacked a biblical understanding of salvation and were in reality not saved."[4]

This approach finds its roots in the teaching of Charles Finney, to whom we have already referred. Samuel Baird once said that Finney intended "to make regeneration so easy that men may not be discouraged from attempting to do it."[5] We scent already Finney's mistaken notion that regeneration is something that we do.

In 1849 Finney preached a sermon on regeneration. He argued against the teaching that a person is passive in regeneration. Finney defined regeneration as a change of character, and that, he said, requires voluntary action on the part of the sinner. His argument was that since character depends on will, therefore a change of character requires a change of will, and that is a change which man voluntarily chooses.[6]

It is true that, for Finney, there is divine influence. However, this influence does not supersede human agency. Rather, it brings change about by man's own agency. Regeneration then consists in voluntary consecration to God. There is no profound recognition here of the implications of the imagery of rebirth. An unborn baby has no control over his own conception. He cannot be commanded to step out into the world. It simply happens to him at the appropriate moment.

We may contrast Finney's words with the teaching of Charles Haddon Spurgeon a generation later. This is what he said about regeneration:

> It is a great mystery. Certainly it is entirely *superhuman*. We cannot contribute to it. Man cannot make himself to be born again. His first birth is not of himself, and his second birth is

---

4. Platt, "The 'Sinner's Prayer'," *passim*.

5. Quoted by I. H. Murray, *Revival*, 365.

6. Finney, *Regeneration*, I(4), II(1).

not one jot more so. It is a work of the Holy Spirit, a work of God. It is a new creation; it is a quickening; it is a miracle from beginning to end.[7]

Regeneration as a Process

Peter Masters has argued strongly against an all-at-once view of regeneration, and in favor of the idea that regeneration is an elongated process.[8] In this he is in line with Puritan theology.[9]

The "all-at-once" view expects a convert to be completely born again in an instant, such that, immediately, he repents and believes. It does not anticipate a struggle to find the Lord, or the need for the preacher to offer the blessings of salvation as something future. Masters refers to John Murray as the main proponent of this view. He cites Murray as claiming that all the elements of conversion, including calling, regeneration, justification, and adoption, occur simultaneously.

By contrast, Masters argues that the biblical position is that regeneration takes place over a period of time. Citing Berkhof,[10] Masters distinguishes two parts of regeneration, which he calls generation and bearing.

> In other words, the first imparting of spiritual life does not include the full bestowal of spiritual consciousness, and all the graces. There is an *initial* regeneration, usually regarded as instantaneous, and this give rise to a birthing process, in which that life is subsequently manifested outwardly.

The first part of regeneration is a secret work of God in which the sinner is totally passive. It enables him to understand and respond to God's word. However, the entirety of regeneration is not accomplished in the moment of generation, and the process of bringing forth, which includes conviction of sin, repentance, and faith, takes place gradually through a process of persuasion. In this part of regeneration, the convert is not passive, but is drawn consciously to salvation. "Initial regeneration brings to life a capacity to respond and to "embrace" what the gospel call offers."

7. Spurgeon, "Simplicity," 7.

8. Masters, *Physicians*, 95–110.

9. Beeke & Jones, *Puritan Theology*, 464.

10. Berkhof, *Systematic Theology*, 465.

Masters sees this as the position of "authentic, mainstream Calvinism," represented in the Reformed confessions of faith. I suspect that this may well be why some of the confessions link regeneration with sanctification, rather than justification.

Masters argues that the all-at-once view is fatal for directness in evangelistic preaching. It results in the loss of an emphasis on persuasion. However, the elongated view

> means that the preacher is privileged with *genuine instrumentality* by the Spirit in bringing men and women to Jesus Christ. He knows that as he preaches, the Spirit may work in some heart a work of initial regeneration. Then, using the preacher's continuing exhortations, the Spirit will draw the sinner through the resulting process of conviction and faith.

Moreover, the elongated view is consistent with the scriptural emphasis on the conscious blessings of salvation following repentance and faith.

To some extent, this may be merely a debate over the use of words. Masters agrees that the initial implanting of new life is instantaneous and unconscious. There then follows a conscious conversion process. Some may prefer to restrict the term "regeneration" to God's initial work, and use an alternative term for the ensuing process. There need be little difference between the two views. The first implanting of the seed of life and its subsequent gestation are two parts of one process. Whether we restrict the term regeneration to the first part, or use it as to cover the entire process is less important than that we recognize the validity of the distinction between the two parts of the total experience.

However, Masters's main point is crucially important. If our theology disables us as genuine gospel preachers, if it renders us incapable of making direct, powerful gospel appeals, then something is indeed seriously wrong.

PRACTICAL APPLICATION

(1) We need to recognize the absolute need for regeneration. We must never forget in all our gospel work that it is not in the power of those to whom we preach to convert themselves. Before they can respond to the word, the Holy Spirit must plant within them the seed of new life.

Neither may we ever imagine that it is in our power to persuade sinners to turn to Christ. We must preach persuasively, but even when we have done our best, the work is the Lord's; we are mere instruments in his hands. All our gospel endeavors must therefore be saturated in prayer. Prayer signals our awareness of our total dependence on God.

But perhaps you yourself are not yet born again. Plead with God to send his Holy Spirit to open your eyes, enliven your will, and lead you to faith in Christ. You cannot regenerate yourself, but the gospel commands appeal to you to turn from sin and entrust yourself to Christ. Your responsibility right now is not to try to delve into the mysteries which are hidden in the wisdom of God, but to repent and believe.

(2) We are to preach the gospel. Although we cannot regenerate a sinner, we can administer the tool which the Holy Spirit normally uses to bring new life. We must energetically preach Christ and the cross, just as Jesus himself did when talking with Nicodemus. It is our privilege to call people to faith and repentance, and to do so with assured confidence that it is this message which the Holy Spirit will empower for the regeneration of those who will be saved.

(3) We must praise God for his mercy in granting us new life. The regeneration of a sinner is a gift of God's free mercy, as 1 Peter 1:3 reminds us. None of us has any claim on that mercy. If we have been born again we cannot congratulate ourselves. It is entirely due to God's stupendous kindness. It is absolute grace, undeserved favor. We should never let a day go by without praising him from the bottom of our heart for his gracious goodness. And so we rejoice constantly that the Holy Spirit has made it possible for us to repent and believe.

(4) We need constantly to examine our lives for the evidences of regeneration. In his first epistle the apostle John mentions six tests of a truly regenerate heart. We must all apply them to our own lives.

One test is doctrinal—the belief that Jesus is the Christ (5:1). Ask yourself, then, do I truly believe what the Bible teaches about the Son of God, without any hesitation?

One test concerns our attitude to God—that we love him (5:1). Ask yourself, then, do I really love God, and can I speak like that without a hint of embarrassment? This was Moses' longing for Israel in Deuteronomy 30:6, that heart-circumcision would lead to a love for the LORD which would captivate their entire personality. When I ponder the mercy which lies behind everything which he has done for me, both in my natural life, and in the saving work of Christ, how can I help but love him?

One test has to do with our relationship to our fellow believers—we must love one another (4:7; 5:1). Ask yourself, then, do I love all the other

Christians whom I know? It may be easy to speak of a theoretical love for Christians whom we have never met. It is more challenging sometimes to love those whom we see every day, but that is where the real test comes. Christians are not perfect, and loving some of them can be difficult. But if I am born again, I have a new power to love the unlovely, which reflects the love of Christ.

Three tests relate to our personal moral life—the practice of righteousness (2:29), the avoidance of sin (3:9; 5:18), and the overcoming of the world in faith (5:4). Ask yourself, then, am I resisting temptation and striving to do what is right in every situation?

These tests are not preaching perfectionism. They are not intended to deflate the humble believer who is still struggling with sin, and who knows that so often his love grows cold. None of us measures up totally, but do you have sincere desires to live as the regenerate should? That is the issue. For if you do, you can be sure that the Holy Spirit who first planted the seed of new life in your heart will also nurture it and bring it at last to maturity. If not, then, as Jesus said to Nicodemus, "you must be born again" (John 3:7).

PART TWO: UNION WITH CHRIST

John Murray describes union with Christ as "the central truth of the whole doctrine of salvation,"[11] and for some of the puritans, union with Christ was the "chief blessing a Christian receives from God."[12] For that reason we address this theme next, immediately after the initial topic of regeneration. Murray's words might sound rather strange, as it seems that union with Christ has become something of a neglected topic. As Kevin DeYoung says, "union with Christ may be the most important doctrine you've never heard of."[13]

BIBLICAL FOUNDATION

Two strands of New Testament teaching are the basis for this theme: the concept of abiding in Christ, introduced by the Savior himself and taken

---

11. J. Murray, *Redemption*, 170; cf. Letham, *Systematic Theology*, 597; Philip, *Union*, 1.

12. Beeke & Jones, *Puritan Theology*, 483.

13. DeYoung, *The Hole*, 94.

up by the apostle John, and Paul's frequent phrase "in Christ." We shall look at each of these in turn.

"Abiding in Christ" in John's Writings

John's Gospel

The main passage in the gospel on this theme is 15:1–10. It is linked with the fact that Christ is the true vine in which his disciples are the branches. The command to abide in him appears first in verse 4. The word translated "abide" (*menō*) has connotations of staying put, and that with settled continuity.[14] Jesus is making the point that, just as the branches derive all their life and nutriments from the root of the vine, and cannot be fruitful, or even survive, once chopped off, so it is only through our union with him that we receive the spiritual nourishment which imparts ultimate significance and enables our lives to count in his service.

Two specific fruits which grow on the branches which are ingrafted into Christ are mentioned—effective prayer (verse 7) and obedience (verse 10), which Jesus goes on in the subsequent verses to define as obedience to the specific commandment to love one another.

No doubt part of the meaning of abiding in Christ is the subjective fellowship, the experienced communion, which we can enjoy with our Savior: "abiding in Christ means to maintain unbroken fellowship with him."[15] However, behind that is the objective fact that we are totally dependent on him for everything involved in salvation and spiritual life.

There is a mutuality to this abiding: "abide in me, and I in you," is what Jesus says. On the subjective level there is a two-way relationship, but this is brought about, objectively, by the indwelling of Christ in the believer by his Spirit. Jesus amplifies the concept of mutual abiding in two ways.

First, in verse 7 he speaks of his words abiding in us. Matthew Henry is surely right to comment that we see here "how our union with Christ is maintained—by the word." He continues, "if the word be our constant guide and monitor, if it be in us as at home, then we abide in

---

14. Cf. Liddell & Scott, *Lexicon*, 435; Moulton, *Lexicon*, 263.
15. Ladd, *Theology*, 278.

Christ, and he in us."[16] This underlines the importance of a disciplined life of Bible reading.

Second, Jesus speaks of our abiding in his love (verse 9). This has to be understood as his love for us, as is clear from the parallel with the Father's love for his Son. Christ's love is "the atmosphere in which the disciple lives."[17]

The result of faithful abiding in Christ leading to much fruitfulness, Jesus says in verse 8, is the glory of God. A modern illustration, taking up Jesus' use of the word "branches," might say that any particular branch of a company gets all its stock from the head office, and cannot survive if it cuts itself off from the central supplier. Conversely, all the profits made by each branch contribute to the success of the company as a whole. Abiding in Christ is, therefore, "the pulse beat of the believer."[18]

1 and 2 John

In these letters John takes up this strand of Jesus' teaching, using the verb *menō* 25 times, on all but two occasions translated in the New King James Version by abiding vocabulary. One of the exceptions is 1 John 3:9, where the context suggests that "abides" would have been a helpful translation. We shall summarize John's teaching on this theme in these letters under five headings.

THE LOCI OF THE BELIEVER'S ABIDING

John speaks first of abiding in him (1 John 2:6). In the context the identity of "him" is ambiguous. However, in the light of five later appearances of such phraseology (1 John 2:27, 28; 3:6, 24; 4:13), it probably means Christ, rather than God.[19] That said, abiding in God is a term which John does use (1 John 4:15–16), and in 1 John 2:24 he speaks of abiding "in the Son and in the Father."

In addition to these references John speaks of abiding in three further loci. (1) We abide in the light (1 John 2:10). Since Jesus identified himself as the light of the world, this may be an alternative way of

16. Henry, *New Testament*, Vol. 5, 181.

17. Westcott, *John*, 219.

18. Unmack, "Abide," 16.

19. Against Candlish, *1 John*, Vol. 1, 91–92, 104, and Marshall, *Epistles of John*, 127.

speaking of abiding in him. (2) We abide in love (1 John 4:16). (3) We abide in the doctrine of Christ (2 John 9). In the light of verse 7 this probably means the doctrine which teaches that the human Jesus is the Christ, over against the docetic teaching which John has had to oppose.

THE MUTUALITY OF ABIDING

As in the teaching of Jesus, John too brings out the two-way nature of this abiding. From 1 John 3:24 we learn that "he" abides in us. Once again, there is ambiguity here. "He" refers back to the previous verse, but both God and his Son are mentioned there, and the statement that he gave us the commandment to love one another is equally ambiguous, though it is possible that the reference is to the Son, in which case he is probably the divine person in view in the next verse. However, in 1 John 4:12–16 we hear four times that God abides in us, and back in 2:27 John has said that "the anointing which you have received from him abides in you," and in 3:9 has spoken of God's seed abiding in the person who has been born again, both of which are probably references to the Holy Spirit.[20] Certainly, it is by the Spirit who has been given to us that we know this mutual abiding (1 John 3:24; 4:13). There is a trinitarian abiding in the believer.

As a consequence of the abiding of God in his people, eternal life and the love of God also abide (1 John 3:15, 17). The means by which this all takes place is the word of God, which has been heard from the beginning (2:14, 24), as a result of which the truth also abides in us (2 John 2).

THE EVIDENCES OF TRUE ABIDING

John lists six evidences which validate any claim to be abiding in God: (1) we walk as Jesus walked [1 John 2:6]; (2) we love one another as brothers [1 John 2:10; 3:14, 15, 17; 4:12], and so keep Christ's commandments [1 John 3:24]; (3) we overcome the wicked one as a result of the strength derived from the word of God abiding in us [1 John 2:14]; (4) we do the will of God [1 John 2:17]; (5) we confess that Jesus Christ is the Son of God [1 John 4:15]; (6) we avoid sin and transgression [1 John 3:6, 9; 2 John 9].

It is clear that, for John, abiding is not merely a theoretical notion. It has practical consequences which are indispensable.

20. So King, *Fellowship*, 56, 74; Hannah, *1, 2, and 3 John*, 121, 139.

A Happy Result of Abiding

John also states a further consequence which flows from abiding. We contemplate the coming of Jesus with shameless confidence (1 John 2:28).

The Eternal Nature of Abiding

John writes, "he who does the will of God abides forever" (1 John 2:17). Although there is an experiential and subjective side to abiding, as is clear from the command in 2:28 to abide in him, John Hannah rightly says that the apostle's emphasis is not on this merely temporal aspect.[21] The eternal and objective side of abiding is dominant in John's letters.

"In Christ" in the Letters of Paul

This phrase, and various equivalent phrases, occur in all of Paul's letters with the one exception of Titus. Rather than attempting an exhaustive survey of the apostle's use of such terminology, we shall take as an example Colossians, one of the two letters where this theme is most prominent. We shall trace the theme through the epistle in order.

The phrase first occurs in the second verse of the epistle, where its recipients are designated "saints and faithful brethren in Christ." Definitive sanctification is probably in view in the description "saints . . . in Christ." "When by faith we were united to Jesus, his holiness became ours,"[22] and the power to remain faithful derives from our being in him.

Verse 4 speaks of the Colossians' "faith in (*en*) Christ Jesus." While, faith is the gateway into union with Christ, that point is usually expressed using the preposition *eis,* as in 2:5. In the present context, however, Paul is portraying faith in Christ as "the sphere in which they move."[23]

Verse 14 states that it is Christ "in whom we have redemption." Herbert Carson says: "it is not merely that he is the agent, but it is through union with him that we are redeemed."[24]

In verse 18 Paul introduces to the Colossians his comparison of the church to the body of which Christ is the head. This emphasizes the

---

21. Hannah, *1, 2, and 3 John,* 167; see also 89.
22. Appéré, *Mystery of Christ,* 19.
23. H. M. Carson, *Colossians and Philemon,* 30.
24. H. M. Carson, *Colossians and Philemon,* 40.

inseparable union between Christ and his people. The theme recurs in verse 24 and in 2:19, where the apostle describes the church's God-given growth as the result of the spiritual nourishment which flows from the head to all the members, compared to joints and ligaments, as they hold fast to him.

We saw how, in John's writings, there is a mutuality in the concept of abiding, and Paul, too, can speak not only of our being in Christ, but also of Christ being in us. In 1:27, he refers to "Christ in you, the hope of glory," which is the elucidation of a mystery pertaining to the Gentiles. Given the fact that the Gentiles had for centuries been spiritual outcasts, the very fact that Christ can now indwell them is a staggering demonstration of the astonishing grace of God. And his indwelling presence guarantees for us Gentiles a future of eternal glory.

En route to the fulfilment of that glorious hope the interim goal is ongoing spiritual progress so that on that final day we may be presented "perfect in Christ Jesus" (verse 28). Our growth now and our perfection then will flow out of our union with Christ.

Verses 6 and 7 of chapter 2 speak of three realities which the apostle prays that the Colossians may experience in Christ—walking, being rooted, and being built up. Two further illustrations of union with Christ are implicit in the latter two terms: "he is at once the deep genial soil of your life and growth, and the corner-stone of your ascending structure."[25]

The phrase "in him" recurs in verse 10, where believers are described as being "complete in him." This follows the statement in verse 9 that "in him dwells all the fullness of the Godhead bodily." Those words bring out another aspect of union with Christ: its basis is found in the fact that the Son of God united with his fully divine nature a bodily existence as a human being. The incarnation is the essential prerequisite for union with Christ. The word "bodily" is not meant to exclude other dimensions of human personality, but simply to emphasize the astonishing miracle that God the Son, who shares the invisible, spiritual divine nature, should have taken the entirety of human nature into eternal union with that divine nature, and to convey the simple truth that it is only because of the visible aspect of his human nature that we can have any inkling of the miracle of the incarnation at all. But it is because of that amazing accomplishment that we find completeness in him. The word "complete" is

---

25. Moule, *Colossian Studies*, 129.

plēroō, which picks up the word *plērōma* ("fullness") from verse 9. This suggests that these words of Carson's are apposite:

> if in Christ the fullness of Godhead dwells, then this has profound consequences for his people. They are "in him" by a spiritual union, which means that they share his life. Hence they share his *plērōma*; and so are partakers of the very nature of God.

Carson continues by noting that the completeness in view includes the overcoming of the human incompleteness imposed by the fall.[26]

At 2:11 Paul speaks of our having been circumcised in Christ. This leads on to a cluster of expressions in the following two verses, where "with him" replaces the customary "in him," but is tantamount to the same idea of union with him: we were buried and raised with him in baptism, and we have been made alive together with him.

The circumcision in view is "the circumcision of Christ"—a circumcision which we receive through him. It is a "circumcision made without hands," a spiritual reality, "which is wholly the work of God,"[27] and which Paul defines as "putting off the body of the sins of the flesh." This is the fulfilment of the Old Testament portrayal of the true meaning of physical circumcision as the circumcision of the heart, which entails the abandonment of stiff-necked rebellion against the ways of the LORD (Deut 10:16), and whole-hearted love for the LORD (Deut 30:6).

This spiritual circumcision has come about as a result of our total identification with Christ which is expressed in baptism, in which we are both buried and raised with him. Baptism signifies our incorporation into the central event which lies at the very heart of the Christian faith. Christ's death and resurrection are pertinent to us, because we were there in principle when they took place, as he died and rose again as our representative. Baptism brings out into the open that hidden union with Christ which we already had at that time.

As a result, we were "made alive together with him," a single word (*suzōopoieō*) in Greek, the prefix (*su-*) bringing out that togetherness, our union, with Christ. The distinction between being raised with Christ and being made alive with him is probably between the initial event and the ongoing result.

---

26. H. M. Carson, *Colossians and Philemon*, 64–65.
27. Martin, *Colossians and Philemon*, 82.

It seems to me that it is reading too much into these verses to claim, as Hendriksen does, that "baptism has taken the place of circumcision." Rather, Paul deals in parallel with true circumcision as a spiritual reality and baptism as a significant symbol of that spiritual experience. Neither can Hendriksen's attempt to use this passage to validate infant baptism be defended.[28] It goes far beyond what the apostle actually says to draw such an implication from the fact that infants were circumcised in Old Testament times.

The practical implications of this union with Christ in his death and resurrection are then expounded in the passages beginning at 2:20 and 3:1 respectively. Having died with him, we must make a decisive break with "the basic principles of the world," and having been raised with him, we must "seek those things which are above." The rationale for this is that, having died with Christ, our life is now "hidden with Christ in God." It is this phrase, from 3:3 which gets us to the heart of the teaching of this passage on our union with Christ, who is then described as being himself "our life" (3:4).

The fact that our life—our true spiritual life in union with Christ—is hidden may include the thought that "the world does not see this new life which the believer has experienced."[29] However, there may also be a deeper significance. The word rendered "hidden" is *kruptō*, for which Moulton offers as a subsidiary definition "to lay up in store."[30] We might say that our life in Christ is under divine protection; it is "out of danger."[31] Our union with him is invulnerably eternal.

The next two relevant texts bring out again the converse of our being in Christ. According to 3:11 he is "in all" his people, irrespective of their ethnic, religious or social backgrounds. Union with Christ is the universal reality and experience of all believers, such that, while retaining their distinctiveness, they "find a unity in him."[32]

In 3:16 Paul explains how this indwelling of Christ is sustained: it is when the word of Christ dwells in us. The word then proves to be the vehicle of Christ's own indwelling presence and our experience of union

---

28. Hendriksen, *Colossians*, 116, and 116, n. 86.
29. H. M. Carson, *Colossians and Philemon*, 80.
30. Moulton, *Lexicon*, 242; cf. Thayer, *Lexicon*, 362–63.
31. Calvin, *Philippians, Colossians, and Thessalonians*, 207.
32. H. M. Carson, *Colossians and Philemon*, 85–86.

with him. As Appéré explains, "Christ's presence in us does not come about through a mystical experience but through biblical teaching."[33]

It remains to notice the three occasions towards the end of this letter where Paul uses the formula "in the Lord." All have to do with practical Christian living—the submission of a wife to her husband (3:18), and the exercise of Christian ministry (4:7, 17). The wording expresses two thoughts. First, the word "Lord" indicates that practical service, whether private or public, is an act of obedience to Christ as Lord. But second, the preposition "in" reminds us that it is our union with the Lord which provides the ultimate context in which our lives of service take place.

DOCTRINAL FORMULATION

The Early Creeds

The phrase in the Apostles' Creed, "the communion of saints," can be read as having a bearing on this theme. It has been pointed out that the word rendered "saints" is ambiguous. In both Greek and Latin it could be either masculine or neuter, which means that it is possible to translate the phrase, "the communion with holy things."

Of course, Christ is not a "thing," but, as Cranfield rightly points out, "the holy things" include "all that God has done, is doing, and will do for us in Jesus Christ."[34] Packer comments that "holy things" would include the word, the sacraments, worship and prayer, and that this points further to the truth "that in the church there is a real sharing in the life of God."[35] This is well brought out in the following statement by Pannenberg:

> The church must be understood primarily as the communion with Christ which is mediated through preaching and the ordinances of the church, which guarantee the individual communion with Jesus Christ . . . . The ministry of preaching is there to mediate communion with Christ.[36]

33. Appéré, *Mystery of Christ*, 108.
34. Cranfield, *Creed*, 64.
35. Packer, *Christian*, 65.
36. Pannenberg, *Apostles' Creed*, 150.

The Reformation Confessions

Some of the Reformation confessions take up this early creedal phrase, "the communion of saints," and read it as a reference to the saints' communion with Christ. The Heidelberg Catechism takes it to mean that all believers, "as members of Christ, have part in him and in all his treasures and gifts." The Westminster Confession, and those based on it, contain a chapter entitled "The Communion of Saints." It begins by referring to the saints as "united to Jesus Christ, their head," in which position they "have fellowship with him in his graces, sufferings, death, resurrection, and glory." This may refer both to the benefits which are received in union with Christ because of his own experiences, and also to the participation with him in such experiences.

In connection with the theme of abiding in Christ we had reason to comment on its objective and subjective aspects. This duality is equally true in the confessions, in some of which this word "communion" tends to point to the subjective, and the word "union" to the objective, side, albeit that it would be a distortion to limit the reference of either word to one particular aspect. We shall look initially at the use of this vocabulary, and then trace the use in the confessions of Paul's "in Christ" formula.

Union with Christ

The Westminster Larger Catechism gives this summary of the confessional teaching on this doctrine:

> The union which the elect have with Christ is the work of God's grace, whereby they are spiritually and mystically, yet really and inseparably, joined to Christ as their head and husband.

Union with Christ is described here by means of four words. (1) It is a spiritual reality—brought about by the work of the Holy Spirit. (2) It is a mystical thing, because it is "a profound mystery;"[37] Williamson comments:

> It is in truth something that we can know only because it is revealed by God. We could not know it by self-examination, nor by insight into our own experience. And this is because it far transcends all other union and communion that we know.[38]

37. Shaw, *Confession*, 272.
38. Williamson, *Westminster*, 197.

(3) It is real: its mysterious nature notwithstanding, it is not merely a flight of imagination. (4) It is unbreakable: we are inseparable from our Savior for all eternity; a point made in several confessions is that, even in death, both the soul and the body of a believer remain united to Christ pending the ultimate union in glory.

This paragraph of the catechism also picks up two of the biblical metaphors depicting our union with Christ: he is the head and his members are his body, and he is the husband, his people being his bride. Such illustrations are found frequently throughout the confessions. Other comparisons are with the vine and its branches, a house and its inhabitants, a foundation and the building erected upon it, and a shepherd and his flock.

The Genevan Catechism says that by virtue of this union we "become partakers of all his blessings." The confessions in general see all the benefits of salvation as flowing from union with Christ. Specifically mentioned are justification, adoption, sanctification, perseverance, and the glory of the life to come. This underlines the centrality of this theme of union with Christ in Reformed theology.

The confessions often comment on union with Christ in their sections on the sacraments, which, according to the Scottish Confession, seal in believers' hearts the assurance "of that most blessed conjunction, union, and society" which they have with Christ. Baptism is a sign to the believer of "of his being engrafted into Christ," as the 1689 Baptist Confession puts it, and the Lord's Supper is a witness and confirmation of this union.

The Baptist Confession of 1644 goes a step further in its treatment of this theme, speaking not only of union with Christ, but also of union with God, Father, Son, and Holy Spirit. Its compilers were clearly echoing John's trinitarian emphasis on abiding, seen in his first letter.

Communion with Christ

That it would be an exaggeration to limit the meaning of "communion" to the subjective aspect is clear from the statement in the Genevan Confession that God, in his goodness, "received us into the communion of his Son Jesus," a phrase which points rather to the objective element of this doctrine. Nonetheless, the Westminster Larger Catechism says that true believers "enjoy communion" with Christ, and enjoyment is clearly a subjective experience.

Communion with God is seen as part of the experience of man before the fall. Back then Adam and Eve "were happy in their communion with God," as the Westminster Confession says. There is a sense in which communion with Christ is the restoration of that pristine experience.

Once again, the Lord's Supper is understood to be for believers a sign, a bond, and a pledge of the true spiritual communion which we have with Christ.

The Westminster Larger Catechism has a section which traces communion with Christ in the believer's experience from its inception to its eternal fulfilment in three stages. The entire experience from beginning to end it entitles "communion in glory."

The first stage is communion in glory with Christ in this life, which is described as

> the firstfruits of glory with Christ, as they are members of him their head, and so in him are interested in that glory which he is fully possessed of; and, as an earnest thereof, enjoy the sense of God's love, peace of conscience, joy in the Holy Ghost, and hope of glory.

The second stage of communion in glory is that which believers "enjoy immediately after death." It consists in the instantaneous perfecting in holiness of their souls, as they are

> received into the highest heavens, where they behold the face of God in light and glory, waiting for the full redemption of their bodies, which even in death continue united to Christ, and rest in their graves as in their beds.

The third and final stage is communion with Christ as it is "at last perfected at the resurrection and day of judgment." This is portrayed eloquently in the statement that, on that day, the righteous shall be

> filled with inconceivable joys, made perfectly holy and happy both in body and soul . . . in the immediate vision and fruition of God the Father, of our Lord Jesus Christ, and of the Holy Spirit, to all eternity.

This is then defined as "the perfect and full communion," which believers "shall enjoy with Christ in glory."

These comments demonstrate how this concept straddles the objective and subjective definitions.

"In Christ"

The confessions use this Pauline terminology, or the equivalent wording, "in him," very frequently. The Genevan Confession makes a summary statement which says that Jesus Christ is given to us by the Father "in order that in him we should recover all of which in ourselves we are deficient." Later it speaks of our living in him: he is our life-source; true life can be experienced only in this wonderful union.

The confessions speak of our salvation being in Christ, and highlight a number of specific salvation benefits which are ours in him. Interestingly, the one most often mentioned is election in Christ. The Westminster Larger Catechism relates this to the covenant of grace in these words: "the covenant of grace was made with Christ as the second Adam, and in him with all the elect as his seed."

The other facets of salvation mentioned we shall simply list without detailed elaboration. It is in Christ that we are justified, in him that our sins are forgiven. In him we receive redemption, reconciliation, and adoption. We are new creatures in Christ, created in him for good works. In Christ we are given spiritual life, and all that is needed to nourish that life so that in him we experience spiritual growth. We have joy in Christ, and our service is in him, and finally it is in him that we shall be glorified. These observations underline again the centrality of this concept, notwithstanding the absence of specific chapters devoted to the theme.

Recognizing the mutuality in the New Testament teaching on this theme, we note another set of blessings which the confessions view in Christ. God's grace comes to us in Christ, and, by his mercy, it is in him that we are freely accepted. In Christ God has become our Father, and he now looks upon us only as we are in him. Our good works, imperfect though they be, are nevertheless accepted in Christ.

Finally, we cite this vital comment found in the Genevan Catechism: "whatever gifts are offered us in Christ; we receive by the agency of the Spirit."

Modern Confessions of Faith

Only one of the three modern confessions with which we have been concerned, the Chinese confession, has any reference to this theme, and then only incidentally. In its section on the church it includes a reference to the growth of all the members of the body "into Christ who is the head," and to the unity of the universal church in Christ. This focuses exclusively on the corporate aspect of union with Christ, based on the New Testament image of the head and the body.

HISTORICAL ELABORATION

John Fesko identifies Bernard of Clairvaux as one of the leading Medieval theologians to expound the doctrine of union with Christ, and Girolamo Zanchi as one of the Reformation scholars who gave seminal thought to this theme.[39] We shall therefore look in turn at one work from each of these two writers, before turning to an early twentieth-century writer, Wilhelm Bousset. Finally, we shall summarize the helpful teaching on this theme in the third volume of Joel Beeke and Paul Smalley's *Reformed Systematic Theology*.

Bernard of Clairvaux

Bernard was the abbot at a monastery in Clairvaux, eastern France, in the early twelfth century. Ellison notes that even "in the dark night of medieval superstition," God always "preserved a handful of the faithful."[40] Bernard, I'm sure, was one such. We shall look at his series of sermons to his monks on the Song of Solomon, a key exposition of union with Christ.[41]

Bernard reads the Song as a celebration of the love between Christ and his church, and introduces the word "union" in the very first sermon. He refers to "endless union with God," and speaks of the "nuptial union with the divine partner." Bernard sees marriage as the primary illustration of this union between Christ and his church: "no sweeter names can be found to embody that sweet interflow of affections . . . than Bridegroom and bride."

---

39. Fesko, "Union," 424, 426, 435–36, 440–41.
40. Ellison, *Ezekiel*, 118.
41. Bernard, "Sermons on the Song of Songs," *passim*.

Union with Christ is a corporate reality, though Bernard also acknowledges that the experience of this union is a personal one, which each believer must pursue in his own experience, and, in fact, this becomes the more dominant emphasis in these sermons. Bernard speaks of the union "between the Word and the soul," and says that the enlightened mind, "joined in truth to God, is one spirit with him." This union is a spiritual experience, involving "the ecstatic ascent of the purified mind to God, and the loving descent of God into the soul."

Bernard majors on the subjective side of union with Christ: his abiding presence is an "intimate experience" of unreserved joys. Bernard gives an eloquent account of this experiential union in these words:

> "he who is united to the Lord becomes one spirit with him," his whole being somehow changed into a movement of divine love. He no longer has the power to experience or relish anything but God and what God himself experiences and relishes, because he is filled with God. But God is love, and the deeper one's union with God, the more full one is of love.

This experience is obtained through contemplation. Bernard presents two sides to this. In the first place, there is "that contemplative gift by which a kind and beneficent Lord shows himself to the soul with as much clarity as bodily frailty can endure." On the other hand, there is the believer's responsibility to cultivate "ecstatic repose," by which obscure mysteries may be penetrated: in practice contemplation means retreating to the quiet place to focus one's thoughts on God alone.

Bernard finds the basis of our union with Christ in the fact that he united in his one person the divine and human natures. As Mediator, Jesus is God's kiss bestowed on the world, and, "joined to him in a holy kiss," we become "one spirit with him." Behind that union of the divine and human in Christ there lies the indivisible unity of Father, Son and Holy Spirit, into which the bride of Christ is embraced.

Nonetheless, there is a significant difference between the union of the Godhead and the mutual abiding between the Savior and the soul. The unity of the Godhead is a unity of nature, whereas the "blissful unity" between the believer and Christ involves conformity of will and affection in the bond of love. Bernard elaborates on this vividly: he says that the person "who cleaves perfectly to God" is

> he who, dwelling in God, is loved by God and, reciprocating that love, draws God into himself. Therefore, when God and

man cleave wholly to each other—it is when they are incorporated into each other by mutual love that they cleave wholly to each other—I would say beyond all doubt that God is in man and man in God.

However, the personal experience of union with Christ is not the same for every believer. Since purity of heart is its vital prerequisite, Bernard sees this as something which we attain as we mature in spiritual life. It is necessary to break with sin and the world, and to increase in the virtue of love, if union with Christ is to be a living reality. This, though, is no ground for pride or for the adulation of mature believers themselves: the praise belongs to God alone.

Bernard traces our union with Christ back to the eternal predestination "by which God loved his chosen ones and endowed them with spiritual blessings in his Son before the world was made." In that sense the elect have been abiding in God from everlasting. In the course of time, when they begin to love God reciprocally, he begins to abide in them, and they "become sharers in the inheritance of the Son." This union with Christ is then carried on through time until the ultimate union is realized on the final day of glory, when

> the Word and the soul shall love each other with a pure and perfect love, they shall know each other fully, they shall behold each other clearly, they shall be united to each other firmly, they shall live together inseparably, they shall be like each other absolutely.

In the meantime, the life of the believer will inevitably be burdened by affliction, hardship, pain, suffering, and miseries. Such things are designed by the Lord to bring humility to fruition in the lives of his beloved ones, and in that humility they are brought closer to God.

Bernard highlights the amazing nature of this mutual abiding of God and the soul. It is not a loving union between equals. The "supreme felicity" of the soul is rooted in "the amazing condescension" of God. God's love has been despised, and yet it recalls the soul that spurned it. And now the Bridegroom looks happily on the soul which has been made like him, and allows that soul to look upon him. In this union God "finds pleasure for himself in our advancement towards perfection." As a result, he unites us the more closely to himself.

Girolamo Zanchi

In 1542 the Catholic Church in Italy revived the practice of Inquisition to root out what it considered to be heresy.[42] Zanchi was one of a number of Italians sympathetic to the Reformation who fled to Switzerland to escape. He spent several months in Geneva, where he benefitted from the ministry of John Calvin.[43] In 1586 he published his *Confession of Christian Religion*.[44] Chapter 12 addresses the necessity of union with Christ.

Zanchi uses a vivid range of terms to express the concept of union with Christ. We are united to him, made one with him, joined and knitted together with him; we are grafted or ingrafted into Christ, incorporated into him, we cleave to him and participate in him; we are coupled to him and abide in him; with him we have conjunction and communion.

He also employs a range of descriptive words to convey the nature of our union with Christ. Although it is secret and mystical, that is to say, invisible to the human quest for evidence and therefore truly a mystery, it is nonetheless real, true, and near. It is spiritual, because it is brought about by the Spirit and by our faith, which is itself a product of the Spirit. It is essential and substantial, in the sense that union with Christ is more than just receiving some spiritual gifts, but is the genuine communication to us of the very flesh, blood and soul of the Savior.

Zanchi's starting point is the affirmation that Christ was righteous, and therefore eternal life is his due, but that he achieved this not for himself alone: righteousness, eternal life, redemption, and salvation, while remaining and abiding in him, are also communicated from him to all those who, by the regeneration of the Spirit, are made one with him. These are the elect, who, from the beginning, were chosen for, and predestined to, salvation in Christ. That comment, at least implicitly, dates the origin of the union from the very beginning when we were chosen in Christ.

The role of the Holy Spirit is stressed quite emphatically by Zanchi. We come to Christ by our spirit, because he first comes into us by his Spirit. We embrace him by faith, because he first, by his Spirit embracing us, stirred us up to faith. We, therefore, cannot be united to him unless he first unites himself to us by the Spirit.

Zanchi picks up several biblical metaphors to portray the union. He refers to Christ as the head and his people as the members of his

---

42. Linder, "Rome Responds," 416.
43. Farthing, "Zanchi," 1076; Fesko, "Zanchi," 42.
44. Zanchi, *Confession, passim.*

body, to the vine and its branches, the tree and its olive-bearing boughs, a foundation and the stones which form the building thereon, and to a husband and wife.

Zanchi distinguishes three stages in union with Christ.

The union of nature

This was achieved when the person of God the Son assumed human nature into the unity of his person, coupling to himself by the Spirit our flesh and blood. The purpose was that he should live a life of perfect fulfilment of God's law, of perfect obedience to his Father, even unto death, in which he offered up his flesh as a sacrifice for our sins, so purging them, and obtaining eternal salvation for us, in order to make us partakers of it along with him.

The union of grace

It is this aspect of the union on which Zanchi enlarges most extensively, indicating that he saw it as the real heart of the subject. It means that Christ unites all the elect into one mystical body with himself, and into participation in his divine nature. This involves both the communication of himself to us and the incorporation of us into himself by the Spirit, who unites all his people as one body in Christ, the head. The church is one new man in Christ, because the same Holy Spirit is in him and in us. Zanchi explains this in these words: "by the Spirit of Christ, we, although remaining on the earth, yet are truly and really coupled with the body, blood, and soul of Christ, reigning in heaven." This is all entirely by grace alone.

When he first mentions this second dimension of union with Christ, Zanchi describes it as "daily made in the persons of the elect, which yet go astray from the Lord." Strangely, he says nothing more about the need for union with Christ to be daily renewed, but he does refer to the instruments through which it is maintained on a regular basis, namely preaching and the sacraments, and he defines this communion with Christ as their "principal end." As we hear the word preached and participate in the sacraments, particularly the Lord's Supper, our grafting into Christ by the Spirit is constantly sustained, and so our abiding, in this case, perhaps, as a matter of subjective experience, is continually revitalized.

The union of glory

Regarding this aspect of union Zanchi says that it entails being "with the Lord in our persons when they shall be present with him: namely when God shall be all in us all." It will be fulfilled when we are all assumed "into everlasting glory with Christ."

Wilhelm Bousset

James Dunn notes that, at the start of the twentieth century, the focus of interest in Pauline studies swung from doctrine to experience. He identifies Bousset as one of the chief exponents of an approach to union with Christ construed almost exclusively as a matter of inner experience.[45] Our focus will be on one section of Bousset's work,[46] where he surveys Paul's use of "in Christ" terminology, and claims that Paul "sounds one entirely new note, and it becomes the dominant: the intense feeling of personal belonging and of spiritual relationship with the exalted Lord."

Bousset labels this approach "Christ piety" and "Christ mysticism." He compares this mystical approach to the Christian life to a fire, and speaks of the "glowing passion" with which Paul embraces the Lord as the one living and governing his life. Bousset argues that Paul's Christ mysticism has little to do with the historical Jesus: only his death and resurrection feature. Rather, it is "the pre-existent supra-terrestrial Christ" who is "the principle of the new Christian life."

Behind the personal mysticism of the apostle, Bousset discerns a mysticism of the community and the sacraments. The Christian community is the new man, the body whose head is Christ, and the living experience of Christ as present in the community, especially as it gathers for worship is a powerful, tangible reality. In that setting, the individual ceases to be, becoming merged into the whole. This is something which is "experienced in vital reality." In the worshipping assembly "the Lord fills the believers, who, like a mirror, take upon themselves the splendor of his light, his presence."

Bousset offers an explanation of the sacraments in this context. The Lord's Supper is "a mystical personal union of the community with its head." Through participation in the one bread, the community

---

45. Dunn, *Paul*, 391.
46. Bousset, *Kyrios Christos*, 153–60.

experiences fellowship with the exalted Lord. In this union with him, the worship service is characterized by rejoicing. Likewise, in baptism the "sacramental intimacy of the Christians with Christ" is accomplished.

Out of his intense involvement in the mysticism of the worshipping community, where Paul himself experienced the living presence of Christ, so the argument goes, his own personal "Christ piety" was ignited. As a result, he extends this mystical approach beyond the community to the individual believer also. This personalizes the idea of union with Christ. Baptism is now seen as an act of initiation in which the mystical believer "is merged with the deity, or is clothed with the deity," and so "a mysticism of a more personal note struggles free and flies upward with freer strokes of the wings."

What this means is that the total personal life of the believer becomes an "ardor of experience." The Christian lives and dies with Christ, and the Lord governs his entire personal life. He experiences the Lord as a present power, a "supra-terrestrial power which supports and fills with its presence his whole life." The believer's own life is then characterized by the joy that marks the assembled church, and the act of worship and the Christian life as a whole become interwoven. "Christians have become one with the Son, and hence themselves have become sons."

To conclude this summary of Bousset's doctrine of union with Christ, I quote, from a later section of his book, two sentences which sum it up well:

> Paul's preaching of the *en Christō einai* (being in Christ) means a new world. It means the ministering absorption of the individual will in one great surpassing, world-embracing will which is expressed in the totality of a comprehensive fellowship, the triumphant awareness of being incorporated into a power that moves from victory to victory.[47]

Although Bousset's account is rather esoteric and biblically dubious in nature, nonetheless, that there is an experiential aspect to union with Christ is a truth which we must uphold.

---

47. Bousset, 168–69.

Joel Beeke and Paul Smalley

Beeke and Smalley's work includes two chapters on union with Christ.[48] Where Bousset strays to the extreme of reducing union with Christ to a matter of personal, mystical experience, these writers maintain a biblical balance, distinguishing between union and communion with Christ:

> Union with Christ is the oneness, bond, and established relationship between him and his people. Communion with God is the active exercise and enjoyment of the graces of that union— living fellowship with God.

Beeke and Smalley include amongst a list of false views of union with Christ the "unbiblical mysticism," such as that represented by Bousset. Referring to a contemporary of his, Adolf Deissmann, they note how this approach, by treating Christ as a universal spirit, depersonalizes him and divorces him from the historical person of Jesus of Nazareth,

The title of these two chapters is "Union with Christ by the Spirit," words which recognize the role of the Holy Spirit in uniting us with Christ, and so applying salvation to our lives. The first chapter signals Old Testament typological material which forms the background to the New Testament doctrine of union with Christ. We shall proceed directly to the second chapter where the doctrine is more explicitly outlined.

Five elements in the truth of union with Christ are distinguished.

(1) We were united to Christ in election, chosen in him by grace before the foundation of the world. In the covenant of grace, the Son committed himself to do everything which his earthly life would involve in the name of those who had thus been united to him. This is "the foundation of all other aspects of union with Christ."

(2) There is the union in the incarnation, by which the Son of God joined himself to us. He took upon himself "a common nature with all human beings, but his incarnational union joins him particularly" to those given him by his Father to save. The incarnation is "the indispensable basis" for our union with Christ.

(3) We have union with Christ in his death, resurrection, and ascension. This is possible only because of the underlying union established in election and incarnation. Christ and his people are "regarded as one." It can therefore be said that we died and rose with him, and are seated with him in the heavenly places, because he did these things in our name, on

---

48. Beeke & Smalley, *Systematic Theology*, 227–66.

our behalf, because we were joined to him. Every present aspect of salvation flows through our union with Christ in these key events. Because of the union, everything which he achieved is our possession in him. This is an objective state, an abiding reality, and a historical fact.

(4) We enjoy union with Christ by the work of the Spirit who applies salvation to us personally. Although a reference to the Holy Spirit is included in the title of these chapters, the first three aspects of union with Christ really precede, from eternity, the Spirit's direct work of application. Now, however, we recognize that it is the Spirit who establishes this vital union with Christ in our life and experience on the basis of those preceding aspects of union. He does this by working faith within us, and so leading us into "the bond of love" by which we are united to our Savior.

(5) We shall be united with Christ in glory for ever. Then, "the exaltation that we already share by virtue of our covenantal union with him will become ours in actual possession."

Beeke and Smalley then underline once more the distinction between the two dimensions of union with Christ, the first of which is foundational for the second. First, there is the "federal and representative" union, which concerns Christ acting for us. Second, there is the "spiritual and vital" aspect, the "mystical union," as experienced and felt in our personal lives. The word "mystical" denotes the mysterious nature of the union: quoting A. A. Hodge, the authors say that it "transcends all the analogies of earthly relationships, in the intimacy of its communion, in the transforming power of its influence, and in the excellence of its consequences."

The doctrine of union with Christ is summed up by Beeke and Smalley in these uplifting words: "In short, God has made Christ to be everything to the believer. Christ does not merely dispense his benefits, but gives himself to us, and in him we have all."

PRACTICAL APPLICATION

(1) We are commanded to abide in Christ, so that is what we must do. There is an urgency about this command, so we must commit ourselves to serious obedience. Abiding in Christ involves conscious dependence upon him, reminding ourselves constantly that without him we can do nothing. It also means conscious, unbroken, joyful fellowship with our Savior, cultivated in the place of prayer, where we commune with him.

There is much to be said for the practice, in addition to our regular times set aside for prayer, of maintaining a constant conversation with the Lord as we go through the hours of every day. This will ensure that union with him is a feature of our daily life, that we relish God alone more and more as time goes by. Prayer is, indeed, according to Jesus himself, one of the fruits of abiding in him. To abide in Christ is to find in Christ the sphere, the environment, the atmosphere, for our entire existence. It is to be rooted in him as the source of our whole life. We must pray for the grace to live this out in practice.

(2) Another of the chief fruits which is a sign of our union with Christ is that we obey his commandments, focused especially in the commandment that we love one another. We need, therefore, to make the commitment to abide in love towards our fellow believers, in the congregation to which we belong, and beyond. Such a commitment will exercise a control over our tendency to be unloving when we are upset by the actions of other believers, or when we simply want our own way. True love will go out of its way to ensure that we deal with all our fellow believers in kindness, patience, honesty, seeking their good above our own preferences. Our lives must be lives of devoted service, not of self-seeking pride. Our motivation for loving our fellow believers is the fact that our Lord and Savior has loved us. We must abide in his love, and make sure that our reciprocal love for him has abiding reality. Then our love for one another will be a response to, a reflection of, his love for us, and an expression of our love for him. We must meditate regularly on his love—its cost, its basis in his grace and mercy, its selflessness—in order truly to love others as he has loved us.

(3) In addition to love for our brothers and sisters in Christ, there are other indispensable consequences of union with Christ. These may form a check list against which we may measure ourselves to ensure that we are not merely saying that we abide in Christ when the evidence is not there to back up the claim. These evidences include that we walk as he walked—that our lives are a clear imitation of his; that we overcome the evil one—resisting temptation in the power of the Spirit; that we do God's will—obeying not only the love command, but all his commandments; that we maintain a faithful confession of Jesus as the Son of God—rejecting all christological heresies; that we avoid sin—striving against the remnants of sin in our lives; that we reject stiff-necked rebellion—loving the Lord wholeheartedly; that we make a decisive break with this world—seeking, rather, the things above; that we develop purity

of heart and mind—avoiding all contamination by the unclean things of this world; that we grow in humility—recognizing that Christ is our all, and that we amount to nothing without him. We need to be constant in prayer that the Lord will enable us sincerely to display these consequences of abiding in our lives, preserving us in the way of obedience until the end.

(4) Since our union with Christ is maintained by his word abiding in us, we also need to ensure that we spend adequate time in Bible reading and Bible study. How much time is available for these pursuits will vary according to our different life-situations, but each of us, in our particular circumstances, must make God's word a priority in our schedule. In addition to our private times of prayer and Bible study, we must be faithful in attending the gatherings of the people of God when the word is preached and when the Lord's Supper is celebrated, for these are the instruments by which our communion with Christ is sustained and deepened. Every time that we participate in the Lord's Supper, we should do so expectantly—expecting truly to participate in him, resisting the temptation to regard it as merely symbolic. Those of us who have a responsibility to preach the word should remember every time we do so that ours is a solemn responsibility; on each occasion we should pray that the Lord will use his word not merely to instruct his people, but to nurture their union with Christ.

(5) By the grace of Christ, we shall be one with him for the eternal future. Knowing this ought to fill our hearts and lives with peace. It is a source of comfort in times of trial, a source of strength in times of difficulty, a source of hope in times of uncertainty, a source of resilience should we have to face persecution, to suffer with him being a reason for joy. Even when our time to die comes we remain inseparable from Christ: body and soul will both abide in him until that joyful day when they are reunited at his return. We therefore look forward to his return with shameless confidence.

(6) We have seen that the alternative to abiding in Christ is to be abiding in death. The unconverted person is dead in sin, and is destined, unless the position changes, to eternal death, an endless death in agony and torment, separated for ever from the love of God in Christ. If you are reading this book, but that is still the position that you are in, please let me exhort you to seek the Lord while he may be found. Put your trust in the Savior who died for sinners to secure eternal life for all who believe. If you do this, you will enter into union with him, and you will then be

inseparable from him for all eternity. In the meantime you will anticipate that full and perfect communion when you share his glory in the world to come.

(7) The fact that we are united to Christ is a reason for fervent praise. There are many aspects of this doctrine that drive us to praise. We are blessed with a sense of God's love, our conscience is at peace, we are filled with joy in the Holy Spirit and blessed with the hope of glory. We have the power to remain faithful because we are in him: for that we should be full of gratitude. We are complete in him: this enables us to rise above our weaknesses and shortcomings, to resist the pressure to cave in to despondency at the things that are beyond us, recognizing that in him we have everything that we need, and that from him we receive the grace and strength to fulfil everything that is his will for us.

PART THREE: RECONCILIATION

One of the greatest wonders in the work of salvation is that we who by nature were God's enemies should be changed into those whom he befriends. This is another facet of our Lord Jesus Christ's glorious achievement.

BIBLICAL FOUNDATION

Reconciliation is a theme found exclusively in the New Testament, and only in the writings of Paul. The fact that it is nowhere explicitly anticipated in the Old Testament Scriptures surely emphasizes the astonishing wonder which reconciliation with God truly is: it is indeed a phenomenal expression of his mercy.

We shall look at two of the four contexts in which Paul addresses this theme.

Romans 5:9–11

Here the apostle sets justification and reconciliation in parallel. Douglas Moo raises the obvious question, "does this suggest that they mean the same thing?" His reply is as follows:

Not at all. Rather they are two ways of describing what happens when God first accepts us. He declares us innocent and absolves us from punishment for our sins ("justify"), and he removes the hostility that existed between us and him because of that sin ("reconcile"). The former is a judicial idea, the latter a relational one.[49]

Cranfield observes that Paul uses the word "reconciliation" alongside a reference to justification to express the deeply personal nature of the relationship between God and his redeemed people, a quality which the word "justification" in itself does not convey.[50]

We note four points relevant to this theme of reconciliation.

We used to be God's enemies

The word so rendered is *echthros*, which is connected with the verb meaning "to hate." The word can have either an active or a passive meaning. In this context, therefore, it may speak either of our enmity against God or of our being on the receiving end of God's enmity. Commentators divide over this question, but perhaps Matthew Henry is wise to write, "This enmity is a mutual enmity, God loathing the sinner, and the sinner loathing God."[51]

We are now reconciled to God

This point is made three times, twice in verse 10, and once in verse 11, where the verb is replaced by the equivalent noun, "we have now received the reconciliation." All three verbs ("reconciled" in the two instances in verse 10, and "received" in verse 11) are aorist: this emphasizes the fact that our reconciliation is a single once-for-all event, completed conclusively in a moment of time. The word "now" in verse 11 draws out the truth that the ramifications of that event are ongoing, and are still applicable in the here and now.

The words which the apostle uses are *katallassō* (the verb "to reconcile") and *katallagē* (the related noun "reconciliation"). Their primary

---

49. Moo, *Romans*, 172–73.
50. Cranfield, *Romans*, 267.
51. Henry, *New Testament*, Vol. 7, 231.

sense has to do with an exchange, in this case the exchange of hostility for friendship.

Reconciliation was achieved through the death of Christ

This point is made in both verses 10 and 11, with slightly different terminology used in each case. Verse 11 attributes our reconciliation to the mediating work of the Lord Jesus Christ. Verse 10 calls him God's Son, and specifies that it was by his death that we were reconciled to God. Verse 10 is therefore making the main point, which verse 11 reiterates more briefly.

The chief thrust of verse 10 is to attribute the work of reconciliation entirely to God. The passive voice of the verb, "we were reconciled," portrays reconciliation as something which we received, not something which we achieved. It was God the Father who gave his Son to die in our place. Reconciliation was both at his initiative, and also his action.[52]

Moreover, it was the death of the Son which was crucial. That was the defining moment when reconciliation was conclusively achieved. This is because reconciliation required the hostility of God towards sin to be set aside in our case. For that to be possible his just anger had to be expressed elsewhere. It was that eternal wrath which the Son willingly endured in our name on the cross. As a result, the Father's antipathy towards us was overcome.

The result is overwhelming joy

This is the key message of verse 11. But it is joy "in God." He is its source, its reason, its target, its object. Charles Hodge comments:

> The benefits of redemption are not all future. It is not only deliverance from future wrath, but the joy and glory of the present favor and love of God, that we owe to Jesus Christ.[53]

Stuart Olyott sums it up like this:

> The Christian life is a life of joy! . . . He is a reconciling Father who has brought us near in Christ. This causes our hearts to leap with joy, exultation, rapture and ecstasy . . . . The reconciliation

52. Dunn, *Romans*, 260.
53. C. Hodge, *Romans*, 140.

is complete. Salvation is a present reality. Our hearts are bursting with joy, gratitude, and appreciation, and most of all with worship for *him*![54]

2 Corinthians 5:18–21

Paul is celebrating the privilege of gospel ministry. The ministry of reconciliation has been given to him and his colleagues (verse 18); the message of reconciliation has been committed to them (verse 19). As they issue the urgent appeal, "be reconciled to God," they do so on Christ's behalf and as the very mouthpiece of God himself (verse 20). Paul is clearly elated by the sense of privilege in being called to proclaim the message of reconciliation to this sinful world. It is a privilege which should both humble and thrill all of us who are called to be preachers of the gospel.

However, interspersed with this celebration of his calling, Paul gives some instruction on the nature of reconciliation. In verse 18 we read that God "has reconciled us to himself." Here again the fact that reconciliation is a divine initiative and accomplishment is stressed. Moreover, it was "through Jesus Christ," a point repeated in verse 19: "God was in Christ reconciling the world to himself."

Paul is not here teaching universalism. This is one of nineteen occurrences of the phrase "the world" in Paul's Corinthian correspondence. He has portrayed the world as a place of foolishness (1 Cor 3:19), a sphere which is passing away (1 Cor 7:31), a realm under condemnation (1 Cor 11:32). Read in the light of such a perspective on "the world," verse 19 serves to emphasize the tremendous condescension on God's part—that it should be this world to which he has reached out in Christ is a remarkable thing.

Verse 19 also elucidates the meaning of reconciliation: it is that God "is not imputing their trespasses to them." The cause of the alienation between God and man is our trespasses. The Greek word is *paraptōma*. The prefix *para-* can mean "from," or "beside," or "near." The rest of the word, *-ptōma*, is derived from the verb *piptō*, to fall. To trespass is to fall away from where we ought to be. It is to stop beside the destination, instead of reaching it fully, the destination here being total obedience to God's requirements. It does not matter how near we may be to an

---

54. Olyott, *Gospel*, 44.

authentic lifestyle. Unless we fulfil God's law absolutely and completely, we are trespassers. And that is the universal human condition.

That condition merits nothing but the counting against us of our trespasses. In this case the word is *logizomai*. It has the sense of reckoning up, calculating the extent, keeping an account. If God keeps an account of our sins, entering them day by day into his ledger under our name, then his hostility towards us inevitably mounts up, as he calculates the increasing extent of our rebellion against his ways.

We are reconciled to God when he ceases doing his calculations, when he ends his reckoning up the number of our sins, when he tears our page out of his ledger and stops keeping an account of our misdeeds.

But how may God legitimately do this without compromising his own justice? Verse 21 explains: "he made him who knew no sin *to be* sin for us, that we might become the righteousness of God in him."

This verse is "a declaration of the ground on which reconciliation has been effected and is available."[55] The key is what God did in Christ, his sinless Son: "he made him to be sin." This phrase can be understood in two main ways. Some people take it to mean that the Father offered the Son as a sin offering. In the Greek translation of the Old Testament the term for a sin offering is sometimes abbreviated to "sin" (*hamartia*). One example would be Leviticus 4:24. Barnes favors this reading.[56]

The other way that this verse can be understood is that God made his Son the very personification or embodiment of sin, and treated him as a sinner deserves to be treated—condemned, punished, made the target of the eternal and just wrath of a holy God. This reading is preferred by Philip Hughes, who writes, "God the Father made his innocent incarnate Son the object of his wrath and judgment, with the result that in Christ on the cross the sin of the world is judged and taken away."

Hughes adds the comment, "in this truth resides the whole logic of reconciliation."[57] Our sin has been conclusively dealt with: we have become righteous in Christ with a righteousness which is the exact match of God's righteousness. Nothing remains to foster any hostility on God's part towards us; we are reconciled.

---

55. Hughes, *Second Epistle to the Corinthians*, 211.

56. Barnes, *New Testament*, Vol. 6, 133.

57. Hughes, *Second Epistle to the Corinthians*, 213.

DOCTRINAL FORMULATION

The Reformation Confessions

We can identify six main themes relevant to this subject in the confessions.

The need for reconciliation

Reconciliation is necessary because we are guilty, unworthy sinners, who are unacceptable to God. We are alienated from God, afar off, and by nature children of wrath.

The basis for reconciliation

On the one hand the confessions state the negative point that our own works cannot be the basis for our reconciliation. This is because of the "imperfection of the best of our services," as the 1689 Baptist Confession words it. On the other hand, they detail a fourfold positive basis.

CHRIST'S TWO NATURES

Because the Son of God assumed human nature, and continues forever as both divine and human, he is able to reconcile humanity and God. The Genevan Catechism explains well:

> Was it of consequence then that he should assume our nature? Very much so; because it was necessary that the disobedience committed by man against God should be expiated also in human nature. Nor could he in any other way be our Mediator to make reconciliation between God and man.

CHRIST'S OBEDIENCE

This point is stressed especially by the Westminster Confession and those derived from it, the Savoy Declaration and the 1689 Baptist Confession. It was, in part "the perfect obedience" of the Lord Jesus by which reconciliation was procured.

Using a different word ("innocence") Zwingli's Articles also mention this as a basis for reconciliation: "The sum and substance of the

Gospel is that our Lord Jesus Christ, the true Son of God, has . . . with his innocence released us from death and reconciled God."

CHRIST'S DEATH

Having mentioned Christ's obedience, the British confessions also specify Christ's sacrifice as the purchase price for reconciliation. The Thirty-Nine Articles elaborate in these words: Christ "truly suffered, was crucified, dead, and buried, to reconcile his Father to us."

CHRIST'S PRIESTHOOD

A number of the confessions explicitly link the reconciling work of Christ with his priestly office. For example, the Genevan Catechism asks, "To what is the office of priest conducive?" The answer begins with these words: "First, by means of it he is the mediator who reconciles us to the Father." Without mentioning the priestly office, the Genevan Confession nevertheless connects reconciliation with part of the priestly function: "being in our own nature enemies of God and subjects of his wrath and judgment, we are reconciled with him and received again in grace through the intercession of Jesus Christ."

The confessions are declaring that the entire basis for reconciliation is all of Christ. As the Augsburg Confession succinctly summarizes: we "trust that for Christ's sake we have a God who has been reconciled."

The parties to reconciliation

While the fact that the Lord Jesus Christ reconciles God and man is obvious, two points found in the confessions are noteworthy.

(1) A universal reconciliation is explicitly ruled out. It was only for the elect that reconciliation was achieved: Jesus purchased reconciliation "for all those whom the Father has given unto him," to cite the Westminster Confession.

(2) The frequency with which the confessions speak of the reconciliation of God to us, rather than the other way round, is noteworthy. The Irish Articles may be representative: Christ "was crucified, and died to reconcile his Father unto us." This implies that God's just anger is an even more serious obstacle to friendship than our sinful rebellion.

The result of reconciliation

This is expressed by the 1644 Baptist Confession, which echoes the words of Romans 5:11:

> All believers . . . have this as their great privilege of that New Covenant, peace with God, and reconciliation, whereby they that were afar off, were brought nigh by that blood, and have (as the Scripture speaks) peace passing all understanding, yes, joy in God, through our Lord Jesus Christ.

The ministry of reconciliation

The Canons of Dort pick up Paul's words in 2 Corinthians 5:18, concerning the "ministry of reconciliation:"

> What, therefore, neither the light of nature nor the law could do, that God performs by the operation of the Holy Spirit through the word or ministry of reconciliation; which is the glad tidings concerning the Messiah, by means whereof it has pleased God to save such as believe.

The Lord's Supper and our reconciliation

The Genevan Catechism relates the participation of believers in the Lord's Supper to this theme, particularly in connection with the sharing of the bread. It asks the question, "What then have we in the symbol of bread?" The answer reads as follows: "As the body of Christ was once sacrificed for us to reconcile us to God, so now also is it given to us that we may certainly know that reconciliation belongs to us."

To eat the bread at the Lord's table, this document expects, will wonderfully strengthen our assurance of God's grace towards us in Christ.

Modern Confessions of Faith

The Chinese confession contains no reference to reconciliation. Each of the other two confessions mentions it briefly. Both highlight the basis of the reconciliation, referring to the two natures of Jesus Christ the Son of God, and to the perfect sacrifice by which he offered himself. To these two elements in the basis of reconciliation the Indian confession adds also the Lord's perfect obedience. In the same context, the Indonesian confession makes mention of the reason why reconciliation is necessary, arising from "all the sin of mankind."

In a later article the Indonesian confession, having ruled out good works as a route to "righteousness, life, comfort, or salvation," offers this summary statement: "Christ alone can grant remission of sins and can reconcile man with God."

HISTORICAL ELABORATION

As far as I am aware, no book devoted to the subject of reconciliation appeared during the patristic period. However, one early writer, Augustine, makes frequent reference to it: mentions of reconciliation are scattered throughout his works. First I shall draw these references together and systematize the main themes which he links with this doctrine.[58] Then we shall look at a series of articles on the doctrine of reconciliation written by Arthur Pink and published in his monthly magazine, *Studies in the Scriptures*.

Reconciliation in the Writings of Augustine

The problem which reconciliation addresses is the separation of the human race from God because of sin, wickedness, and ungodliness. There is now "a wide gulf between God and the human race." We are alienated from him, and have become his enemies. As a result, God's wrath threatens us. He has become our adversary.

It follows from these insights that reconciliation entails "the termination of the enmity produced by our sins." God's "wrath comes to an end." So Augustine asks the rhetorical question, "what is 'to be reconciled' to him but to have peace with him?" From enemies we are transformed into friends and children.

Augustine eloquently expresses the result of reconciliation: it "is carried to the very length of bringing us to the enjoyment of that perfect

---

58. The following works of Augustine will be alluded to: "Enchiridion," "Gospels," "John," "Merits and Forgiveness," "New Testament," "Rebuke and Grace," "Reply to Faustus," "Trinity."

blessedness, which is thenceforth incapable of further addition." Consequently, we "take delight" in our reconciliation.

Augustine regularly, and logically, connects reconciliation with Christ's role as the mediator. Being both human and divine, he is qualified to reconcile sinful humanity with a sinless God. This he achieved by his death, which was "the sacrifice of peace."

The reason why Christ's death is the basis of reconciliation is that, through it, "the separating wall, which is sin," is removed. Augustine emphasizes the fullness of reconciliation when he speaks of "the abolition of all sin." Consequently, "purified and atoned for, we are reconciled" to God.

Augustine is insistent that there is no other basis for reconciliation than the work of Christ. We are deceived by the devil if we seek reconciliation through angels or prayer or learning or visions, all expressions of our own arrogance. We can cling neither to our own merit, nor to "sacrilegious imitations, or curious arts that are impious, or magical incantations."

Having said that, Augustine recognizes that there are things which we must do by way of response to the reconciling work of Christ. Repentance of sin and faith in Christ are vital. "He who disowns Christ . . . finds no reconciliation to God."

The application to human souls of the reconciling work of Christ Augustine links closely to the church's sacramental ministry. It is as we are washed in baptism, and commit ourselves to the love of our Christian brothers and sisters within the fellowship of the body of Christ that reconciliation is received. Our reconciliation is sustained as we feed on the flesh and blood of Christ.

Notwithstanding those comments, Augustine clearly affirms that the grace of reconciliation "is conferred in the church by the Holy Spirit." Whatever duty we may have in responding to the work of Christ, the basic truth is that it is only "by his gracious help" that "the enmity of our ungodly condition" may be terminated.

One point which Augustine is careful to stress is that reconciliation to God through Christ finds its starting point in the gracious love and goodness of God himself. There is no divide within the Godhead: it is "the merciful reconciliation of God," by which he "has reconciled us to himself by Christ." Augustine elaborates on this point. Describing God's love as "incomprehensible and immutable," he continues:

For it was not from the time that we were reconciled to him by the blood of his Son that he began to love us; but he did so before the foundation of the world, that we also might be his sons along with his only-begotten, before as yet we had any existence of our own. Let not the fact, then, of our having been reconciled to God through the death of his Son be so listened to or so understood, as if the Son reconciled us to him in this respect, that he now began to love those whom he formerly hated, in the same way as enemy is reconciled to enemy, so that thereafter they become friends, and mutual love takes the place of their mutual hatred; but we were reconciled to him who already loved us, but with whom we were at enmity because of our sin.

A. W. Pink on the Doctrine of Reconciliation

Pink notes the neglect which the doctrine of reconciliation had suffered. He wrote to redress the balance. His articles follow an orderly sequence which I shall follow here.[59]

First Pink considers the need of reconciliation. Two parties—God and man—are at variance; man has revolted from God and trespassed his commandments. This stems from the rebellion of Adam, the representative head of the human race, as a result of which all his descendants enter the world as guilty sinners, alienated from the life of God, and exposed to his wrath. Moreover, we are complicit with Adam in his rebellion: we ourselves disobey God's law. Sin has made "a real, a broad, a fearful breach" between God and us, as a result of which "fallen man is separated from God, he is an object of abhorrence to God, he is under the wrath of God, he is in bondage to Satan, and so under the reigning power of sin that he hates God."

Pink then asserts that God alone is the author of reconciliation. It originated in God's unfathomable love, was determined according to the good pleasure of his will, and planned in a wisdom which ensured that neither divine justice nor divine mercy was compromised.

By that wisdom, a mediator was appointed who, though divine, took to himself human nature. Pink emphasizes the covenantal basis for reconciliation: the Father appointed the Son to be the head and Savior of his elect, and the Son consented to act as his people's representative, to satisfy the demands of the law on their behalf by living a life of perfect

59. Pink, "Reconciliation," *passim.*

obedience, and to endure in their place the curse and penalty of the broken law, by offering himself as a satisfaction for their sins, so appeasing the divine wrath. As a result, "the breach between God and his sinning people has been righteously healed."

Pink then goes on to insist on the two-sided nature of reconciliation. Not only do sinners need to be reconciled to God, but, equally, a holy and offended God requires reconciling to his people. Pink acknowledges that this may sound strange after his affirmation that God is the author of reconciliation, which is the outflow of his love. However, we must distinguish God as the Father of his elect whom he views in Christ with an everlasting love, from God as the Judge of his people as he views them in Adam with holy indignation. Pink insists that it was specifically for the elect, the church which is his body, that Christ secured reconciliation.

He notes the balance in Paul's treatment of reconciliation: in some of his letters the reconciliation of the individual believer is prominent, whereas other epistles focus on the reconciliation of the body, the church, of which the individual believer is a part. The emphasis on the church includes the reconciliation in Christ of Jews and Gentiles, "two diverse peoples who had for many centuries been widely separated, and bitterly hostile to each other."

Pink also highlights another aspect of the theme of reconciliation. Christ's work as mediator also "closed the breach which existed between the celestial hosts and the Church," and, indeed, secured the reconciliation of all things to God. Where the hosts of holy angels shared God's disgust at Adam's sin, the blood of the cross has reunited them with the human race in Christ. The disruption introduced into the universe by sin has now been repaired, perfect concord is restored.

Next Pink considers the human reception of reconciliation. "Mutual alienation requires mutual reconciliation." Christ has appeased God's wrath and removed his hostility to us, but reconciliation is not finalized until we are turned away from our opposition to him. To show how this takes place Pink lists three prerequisites cited by the puritan, Thomas Goodwin: we must be convinced that we are enemies to God, and that he is therefore an enemy to us; we must see the danger of our position when God is our enemy; we must understand that God is ready to be reconciled.

We must then come, as those who are condemned, to seek God's favor in Christ, renouncing every other friendship which is incompatible with friendship with God. Pink sums up this point in these words: "Our reconciliation to God (through the renewing of the Spirit) is the sure consequence of his reconciliation to us, and a faith which works by love, which goes out in acts of holy obedience, is the evidence of our new birth and of our having entered into covenant with God."

Pink next sets out the results of reconciliation: we are restored to life; we receive pardon from God; we have peace with God; we are brought into God's favor; we are given access to God; we receive the sanctifying gifts of the Spirit; God accepts our service; we are eternally secure; God is for us; we look forward to "the beatific vision."

Pink ends by considering the practical challenge of this doctrine. He offers this succinct, but searching, summary: "Those who are at peace with sin are at enmity with God; but those who are reconciled to God are antagonistic to sin." He then documents the marks of true friendship, which should be evident in the attitudes of those reconciled to God: we delight in his company; we enjoy the freedom of unburdening our hearts to him; we seek his guidance; we seek to avoid offending him; our hearts are drawn out in confidence towards him.

Pink poses a question: "If the wrath of God is removed from me and I am now taken into his unclouded and everlasting favor, how shall I . . . best show forth my gratitude?" He offers seven answers: (1) by fervent praise; (2) by care to please God; (3) by trusting him; (4) by cherishing his peace; (5) by using access to God; (6) by rejoicing in him; (7) by devotedness to God.

PRACTICAL APPLICATION

(1) We must maintain our sense of wonder at the truth of reconciliation with God. It is so easy to become over-familiar with gospel doctrine, to allow the truth to become merely theoretical, and so to start taking everything for granted. We then lose our sense of amazement at what God in Christ has achieved on our behalf: that we who were dire enemies of the God of surpassing holiness should now be regarded by him without a hint of hostility towards us is phenomenal. It should captivate our imagination. We need to ensure that we meditate daily on the glorious fact that God has been reconciled to us and we have been reconciled to him.

(2) We must cultivate relationship with the God who has become our friend. In human life friends seek out one another's company. They talk incessantly on their phones, they text each other constantly. If God

is our greatest friend, then we should be no less enthusiastic about developing an ever-deepening relationship with him. We should talk to him without ceasing, listen to his word, and seek through the Scriptures to hear his voice and to encounter him in his love. The believer's walk with the Lord must be deeply personal. We must beware of settling for shallowness in our walk with him. When we participate in the Lord's Supper, we must make sure that it is more than merely a symbolic act of remembrance—that the Lord himself will draw near and excite us with the truth that his work on the cross has reconciled us to God; we must pray that our heavenly Father will manifest his presence to our hearts afresh as the reconciled God.

(3) We may have every confidence in God. He is now our friend. He will not let us down. We may trust him in all things. Then we shall know ourselves to be at peace with him, and he will fill our hearts with that peace which surpasses all understanding. When we know that God is our greatest friend, an all-powerful friend, then we have no reason to be anxious whatever may transpire. Our times are in his hands. We can maintain our confidence in him in the darkest times as in the brightest. The one who is in total control of all that is going on, who is shaping all events in accordance with his infinitely wise eternal plan and purpose is our best friend. He will not let us down.

(4) We should be filled with joy that we are reconciled to God. Paul reminds us that we "rejoice in God through our Lord Jesus Christ, through whom we have now received the reconciliation." A joyful heart and a joyful countenance—these are the proper fruits of the knowledge that reconciliation with God is the reality.

(5) We must live out the evidences of reconciliation in our daily life, seeking to live in obedience to our heavenly friend. Our overriding desire will be to please the God to whom we are reconciled, to spend our lives in devotion to him. May God grant us the grace to fulfil these fruits of reconciliation in our lives.

(6) It is our joy and our privilege to be involved in the ministry of reconciliation. As it was for Paul, so for us it should be a thrill to share in gospel ministry, in proclaiming to sinners the reconciling work of Christ on the cross, and appealing to them to be reconciled to God. This is a truth which we may preach with excitement. But we must preach it with humility, always remembering that only the Holy Spirit can bring it to life in our preaching and in the understanding of those to whom we preach.

Our ministry must therefore be permeated by prayer, asking the Lord that it may truly be a ministry of reconciliation.

(7) We must practice reconciliation in our relationships with other people. It is an interesting observation that this is the context of the first New Testament reference to reconciliation, when Jesus says,

> if you bring your gift to the altar, and there remember that your brother has something against you, leave your gift there before the altar and go your way. First be reconciled to your brother, and then come and offer your gift (Matt 5:23–24).

Such reconciliation will be the natural and spiritual outflow of our reconciliation with God. Knowing that our offended Creator has acted to re-establish relationship with his offending creature should give us every incentive to make amends whenever we are aware of friction with other people. We can never protest that we have been offended by anyone else to the degree that we have offended God. Our response to his mercy towards us can surely be nothing other than to show mercy to those who have wronged us, and to seek mercy where we have caused upset to others. To go through the motions of worshipping God while we are at odds with a brother or sister in Christ will reduce our devotions to mere hypocrisy. We who have been reconciled with God have no excuse for failing to be reconciled with other people. Rather, we have the most powerful motivation imaginable.

(8) We must be reconciled to God. By nature we are all children of wrath. Until we repent of our sins and believe on the Lord Jesus Christ we remain in enmity to God. However, we may hear the apostle's appeal, "be reconciled to God" (2 Cor 5:20). The appeal is one of encouragement. There is desperation and urgency there, no doubt, but Paul uses a word which suggests God's constant invitation to find comfort in becoming reconciled. Nothing can bring greater or deeper comfort than knowing the most fulfilling friendship of a reconciled God, who will no longer regard us with hostility, but will surround us forever with his amazing love.

PART FOUR: ADOPTION

It is amazing to think that when he saved us, God the Father adopted us as his sons and daughters alongside his only-begotten Son, and that we now take our place as members of his family. So deep is this relationship that Jesus even said in prayer to his Father: you "have loved them as you have loved me" (John 17:23).

BIBLICAL FOUNDATION

While some Old Testament texts may hint at the LORD's adoption of Israel, the actual term is nowhere used in the Old Testament, although Paul does so use it in Romans 9:4, mentioning it first in his list of Israel's privileges. However, because this application of the term is unique, we shall focus on those New Testament contexts where adoption vocabulary is used with reference to believers in Christ.

Romans 8:15 and 23

The interesting thing here is that, within the space of a few verses, Paul uses the metaphor of adoption in two different ways. In verse 15 he refers to the adoption which "you have received," whereas in verse 23 we are still eagerly waiting for it: there are both past and future dimensions to adoption.

There has been considerable debate about the background to Paul's use of the adoption metaphor, some scholars tracing it back to the implicit Old Testament teaching about Israel's adoption, others finding decisive the Roman background of Paul's own time.[60] Maybe this is one of those debates where an either-or conclusion is not essential. Perhaps it was Paul's Roman background which fed into his reading of the Old Testament Scriptures, enabling him to apply the idea of adoption to Israel in Romans 9:4.

Everett Harrison points out how, in Roman law, adoption entitled the adopted son to inherit the adoptive father's possessions. The word translated adoption is *huiothesia*. Literally it means to be placed, or appointed, as a son. And this placement was made with a view to the inheritance.[61] Adam Clarke notes that it was a person of property who had no children of his own who would adopt a member of another family into his own family, and the adopted son, upon the death of the adoptive father, would inherit the estate.[62] Verse 17 describes us as heirs. A future

---

60. J. M. Scott, "Adoption," 16–17.
61. Harrison, "Romans," 93.
62. Clarke, *Commentary*, Vol. 7, 234.

inheritance is in prospect. Integral to our adoption, even in the present, is that future expectation.

Verse 15 indicates that the application of adoption is the work of the Holy Spirit, and contrasts it with the slavery that would cause us to fall back into fear. Adoption therefore implies a liberty which leads to fearless confidence. This is the fruit in the present of the fact of adoption in the past, as we enjoy a permanent awareness of God's Fatherhood.

It is the future inheritance to which verse 23 is pointing. Verse 19 tells us that "the creation eagerly waits for the revealing of the sons of God." The adoption of verse 23 is the same thing as that revelation. The idea is of a coming day when God will bring out into the open the register of his people. He will announce to the entire assembled creation who the sons are whom he has adopted. In that instant, every child of God will be transformed as we enter into our resurrection bodies. Our humanity will be totally renovated, and our bodies from then on will be free from pain, disease, and death.

Galatians 4:4–7

Verse 5 refers to our adoption, and, once again, it is linked with the status of heir. The shift from the first person ("we") in verses 4–5, to the second person ("you") in verses 6–7 is noteworthy. The apostle starts by referring to the Jewish believers, and then moves on to address the Gentiles.

The earlier verses of the chapter spoke of the Jews as heirs while still not yet of age, while living under the law as their tutor. At that time they had not yet entered into all the privileges of sonship. It was the redemption accomplished by Christ which brought them to maturity and so entitles them to live visibly as sons, with all the responsibility which adulthood entails. However, this sonship has always been adoptive, not natural.

Verses 6 and 7 apply this adoption to sonship to the Gentiles also, so that they too are heirs. The use of the first person ("our") in the middle of verse 6 is striking: by that word the apostle brings the "we" and the "you" together into one united body, adopted by the Father as his son and heir. When all things are finally made new, there will be no ethnic divisions cutting through the restored humanity.

Ephesians 1:3–6

Paul now defines adoption as that for which we were predestined. Andrew Lincoln comments, "Sonship is a benefit of the salvation of the end-time and it comes to those included in the Son through whom that salvation has been inaugurated."[63]

The note of inheritance is present once again in the context of these verses. Verse 11 speaks of the inheritance which we have obtained in Christ, and mentions predestination once more, linking it with the inheritance. As in his other letters, here too Paul associates adoption with the work of the Holy Spirit. According to verse 14 the Holy Spirit "is the guarantee of our inheritance until the redemption of the purchased possession."

Charles Hodge discerns a threefold purpose in God's adoption of his children: (1) we participate in his nature through becoming conformed to his image; (2) we enjoy his favor as the special objects of his love; (3) we are heirs, who will eventually participate in the glory and blessedness of God.[64]

DOCTRINAL FORMULATION

The Reformation Confessions

While most of the confessions mention adoption, few elaborate on it. There are two exceptions, the 1644 Baptist Confession, and the Westminster Confession along with those based on it—the Savoy Declaration and the 1689 Baptist Confession. Even in these documents we find less attention than to other topics. We shall look in turn at the 1644 Confession and the set of documents stemming from Westminster.

First though, it is worth noting in passing the two most common points made by the other confessions. (1) We find a frequent connection made between adoption and predestination: adoption is one of the benefits which flow from the electing love of God. (2) A link between adoption and baptism is also common: baptism is the seal or pledge of our adoption, by which God acknowledges us as part of his household.

---

63. Lincoln, *Ephesians*, 25.
64. C. Hodge, *Ephesians*, 35.

The 1644 Baptist Confession

Two themes are particularly highlighted in chapter 27 of this document.

ADOPTION IS BASED ON THE UNITY OF BELIEVERS WITH THE TRIUNE GOD

God, Father, Son, and Holy Spirit in all his fullness is "one with all believers." Conversely believers are "one with him," and "all believers by virtue of this union and oneness with God, are the adopted sons of God."

ADOPTION LEADS TO HEIRDOM

Believers are one with God, particularly in this case, God the Son, "in his inheritance and in all his glory." This point is elaborated in the following statement: as the adopted sons of God believers are "heirs of Christ, co-heirs and joint heirs with him of the inheritance of all the promises of this life, and that which is to come." This well captures the essence of the New Testament truth of adoption: it is relevant both for this life, but also looks forward to the ultimate inheritance in the life to come.

The Westminster Confession

The Westminster Confession, the Savoy Declaration, and the 1689 Baptist Confession, unusually amongst the Reformation Confessions, each contains a chapter devoted to this subject, entitled, "Of Adoption." We may analyze the teaching of this paragraph under six headings.

ADOPTION IS LINKED WITH JUSTIFICATION

Justification and adoption are co-extensive. Every sinner who is justified by faith is also and simultaneously adopted into the family of God. This is something which God vouchsafes: there is an absolute guarantee to this effect.

ADOPTION IS IN AND FOR JESUS CHRIST

The Lord Jesus Christ is God's "only Son" by nature, but his people are granted the joy of sharing in his sonship. But we are also adopted "for him." Those words underline the truth that the entire work of salvation is primarily for the glory of Christ. His atoning work has earned him the name which is above all names. The fact that sinners are saved contributes to his glory.

ADOPTION IS ENTIRELY BY GRACE

We are said to be "partakers of the grace of adoption," words which emphasize our own utter helplessness and God's unspeakable kindness in bringing us into his family. In their even briefer comments on adoption some of the other confessions signal this same essential point. The Genevan Catechism says that we are sons of God, not from nature, but because God has put us in that place. The French Confession comments that our entitlement to adoption is not in any good works of our own, not even those performed since we were justified by faith.

ADOPTION MAKES US GOD'S CHILDREN

We are said to be "taken into the number" of God's children. These words point to the vastness of God's family: he has a huge number of children. To be part of that great family is an enormous privilege.

GOD'S ADOPTED CHILDREN ENJOY THE LIBERTIES AND PRIVILEGES OF THEIR POSITION

The word "liberties" echoes Paul's teaching in Romans 8:15, contrasting the fearful bondage of unbelief with the freedom granted by the Spirit of adoption. The sense and the outworking of this privilege are definitely enjoyable: it is a matter of joyful experience to be an adopted son of the living God—far more than a mere theoretical theological doctrine. The Westminster Shorter Catechism says that we "have a right to all the privileges of the sons of God," stressing the gracious entitlement conferred by our being placed into the position of adopted children. The Confession goes on to list several of these liberties and privileges.

God's name is put on us

In adoption God makes us a special people for himself. He happily identifies us as his own, without a hint of reluctance. In today's society, when a child is adopted into a new family, there is a change of surname: the child's legal surname becomes that of the adopting family, and the birth surname no longer has any validity. So God's name is our new identity. Bearing God's name, we belong to him. We are no longer our own. Satan no longer has any legitimate claim upon us. The matter is settled eternally.

We receive the Spirit of adoption

This makes the point that, while adoption has a legal basis, it is far more than merely a legal transaction. The Spirit seals it to our hearts. Adoption leads on to a wonderful life within the joyful fellowship of the children of God.

We have access with boldness to the throne of grace

Hebrews 4:16 is in the background here. That verse reads: "let us therefore come boldly to the throne of grace, that we may obtain mercy and find grace to help in time of need." As long as we live in a broken world in bodies marred by the fall, with a sinful nature still lurking within us, we are in a "time of need." We face difficulty, weakness, uncertainty, doubt, anxiety. However, at any time we have access to our gracious Father. He sits on the throne, in total control. He never loses his grip either on global affairs or on our personal situation: he is well able to provide the help that we crave. In its only other New Testament occurrence the word translated "help" (*boētheia*) is used of "cables" to undergird a ship which was in danger of sinking (Acts 27:17). How often we feel in danger of sinking under the weight of life's trials. Well, we have an even stronger support than that ship had through the cables which were passed underneath it: we have the grace of God to see us through to safety. So we come to our heavenly Father, not with a shy hesitancy, but with bold confidence, and we receive a ready welcome.

We have an assurance of God's Fatherhood

As God's adopted family, we can cry in genuine prayer, "Abba, Father," thus readily taking our place alongside God's only-begotten Son (Mark 14:36). We are truly fathered by God. In practice, as the Confession continues, that means that we are "pitied, protected, provided for, and chastened by him as by a father." The Westminster Larger Catechism puts it like this: we are "under his fatherly care and dispensations." We know that everything that crosses our path comes only by his permission: it is an arrangement made by our Father out of his magnificent care for us, his children.

As God's adopted sons, we are destined to receive the inheritance

So far this article has focused on the blessings of adoption in the present age. However, the chapter ends with a future perspective. God's adopted children will never be cast off; we are sealed with the ultimate future in view, and we shall inherit the promises. We are the "heirs of everlasting salvation."

Modern Confessions of Faith

Both the Indonesian and Chinese confessions are marked by the complete absence of any reference to adoption. The Indian Confession mentions it twice in passing in its article on salvation. The first occasion occurs in a synopsis of Ephesians 1:4–5, and the article goes on to include "adoption into the number of the sons of God" in a list of the chief benefits accruing to "those who believe in Christ and obey him."

HISTORICAL ELABORATION

In recent years Tim Trumper has conducted significant research into this topic. We shall start this section by surveying his findings.[65] Trumper mentions Irenaeus and Calvin as the foremost contributors to the discussion of adoption in the course of Christian history. We shall therefore

---

65. Reference will be made to four articles: Trumper, "Fresh Exposition: I, II;" "Metaphorical Import;" "Slaves to Sons."

go on to look at their comments on the subject. Referring to Calvin, Trumper says that "we find the doctrine peppered throughout his writings." The same is equally true of Irenaeus. We shall focus here on just one work by each writer.

Tim Trumper

Trumper notes that the subject of adoption has suffered from extreme neglect in the history of theology: few confessions have a chapter devoted to the subject, and theological works tend to conflate adoption with other subjects, and so miss the distinctive teaching of the adoption metaphor.

Trumper draws attention to the future aspect of *huiothesia*, emphasized in Romans 8, but also hinted at in Galatians 4 and Ephesians 1 by references to heirdom and the inheritance in the contexts. He arranges the references to adoption according to their place in the order of salvation.

Ephesians 1:4–5: predestination to adoption

Rooted in the grace of God, adoption stems from God's election. Its instrumental cause is Christ's redeeming work on the cross. Its purpose is glory, as God's adopted family "anticipate with hopeful longing the grand family gathering planned for the end of the age."

Romans 9:4: the privilege of adoption

Israel's adoption occurred at Sinai following its redemption from Egypt, and marked its inauguration as a nation. Israel had the status of the LORD's firstborn son, and the LORD's commitment to his people was "undying."

Galatians 4:4–5: the reception of adoption

"The Father adopts his redeemed by uniting them to Christ," whose work marked the transition from the old covenant, in which Israel was like a child under age, to the new, in which Jews and Gentiles, united in fraternal communion, enjoy the full privileges of mature sons. Trust in Christ is inspired by the Spirit, who gives believers freedom and enables them to enjoy relationship with the Father.

Romans 8:15–16: the assurance of adoption

Believers receive assurance of this relationship through the Spirit of adoption, who witnesses with their spirits that they are indeed the children of God.

Romans 8:22–23: the consummation of adoption

At the end of the age God's adopted children will enter fully into the blessings of the inheritance. Adoption coincides with glory, entails the revealing of the sons of God, and will mean the perfect fulfilment of freedom for God's children. The New Testament hope is the enjoyment of the inheritance shared with Christ in a creation redeemed from its corruption and filled with God's presence. This consummation is what adoption inherently is, "so long as we understand that it publicly ratifies the adoption received in principle the moment there occurs union with Christ in his Sonship."

Irenaeus

In his work *Against Heresies*[66] Irenaeus's discussion of adoption has very much a trinitarian flavor. We shall comment first on this aspect of his thinking, before looking at how he connects adoption with the inheritance.

Adoption and the Trinity

Irenaeus writes of the adoptive work of the triune God in his united operation. He says that the Word of the Father grants the Spirit after the manner of adoption. More elaborately, he says that God is seen "adoptively" through the Son and shall be seen paternally in the kingdom of heaven. It is the Spirit who prepares human beings in the Son, the Son who leads them to the Father, and the Father who confers the incorruptible life

66. Irenaeus, "Against All Heresies," Books 3–4.

which comes from seeing God. Those who see God receive the true and eternal life, which is found in that fellowship with him, which is "to know God, and to enjoy his goodness."

However, as well as speaking of the interconnected work of the three persons of the Trinity together, Irenaeus also identifies distinct roles for each of the three persons.

ADOPTION AND THE FATHER

We are adopted by the Father, and it is by means of adoption that God calls his people: becoming the sons of God is intrinsic to the nature of being his people. To be adopted is to receive from the Father the fellowship with himself which is freedom, so that God's children cry, "Abba, Father." In a wonderful passage Irenaeus says that God is ungrudging when he grants us, by means of adoption, to know him as Father; thus to know him is to love him wholeheartedly, with the far greater love and veneration that a son has for his father than a slave for his master.

ADOPTION AND THE SON

The Father adopts us through his Son. We possess the adoption as we "believe in the one and true God, and in Jesus Christ the Son of God." Irenaeus's main concern at this point is to emphasize that it is because the eternal Son of God became human that we humans may be taken into him as sons of God by adoption. He explains this eloquently:

> By no other means could we have attained to incorruptibility and immortality, unless we had been united to incorruptibility and immortality. But how could we be joined to incorruptibility and immortality, unless, first, incorruptibility and immortality had become that which we also are, so that the corruptible might be swallowed up by incorruptibility, and the mortal by immortality, that we might receive the adoption of sons?

ADOPTION AND THE SPIRIT

The Holy Spirit announced through the apostles the arrival of "the fullness of the times of the adoption," which equates to saying that the kingdom of heaven has drawn near. Irenaeus says that God pours out his

Spirit by means of his adoption of sons, by which he seems to mean that, as his adoption of sons is realized as they trust in Christ, simultaneously the Spirit starts to indwell them.

Adoption and the inheritance

This aspect of the theme Irenaeus explains by understanding the recipient of adoption, the church, as the seed of Abraham, to whom is given both the adoption and the inheritance promised to Abraham, namely its place in the kingdom of heaven, which it will receive at the resurrection of the just. God adopts believers as his sons, and, at the proper time, bestows "an incorruptible inheritance, for the purpose of bringing man to perfection."

Calvin

In his *Institutes*[67] Calvin refers quite frequently to the adoption of Israel, beginning with Abraham. This was a "visible image of a greater benefit," namely the adoption of a people in Christ.

Six times Calvin refers to "gratuitous adoption," thus emphasizing the absolute grace that underlies God's adoption of his people. There is nothing in human nature to motivate God to adopt us as his sons: all the glory for adoption must be ascribed to God alone. We can subdivide Calvin's teaching on this subject into five themes.

The trinitarian framework for adoption

Like Irenaeus, Calvin brings out the trinitarian basis of adoption.

It is God the Father who takes us as his sons, admits us to his family, and relates to us with a strong fatherly affection. Adoption is closely related in Calvin's thought to the truth of election: it is those whom God has chosen whom he adopts as sons.

However, those whom God has adopted have been chosen in Christ Jesus. Adoption is dependent on his vital role as Mediator. Only by becoming human could the Son of God "make that which is his by nature to become ours by grace:" we are God's sons in "holy brotherhood" with him.

---

67. Calvin, *Institutes, passim.*

430

One of the New Testament titles for the Holy Spirit is "the Spirit of adoption." He is to God's children the earnest and seal of their adoption.

Adoption, faith, and good works

Calvin stresses that human works carry no merit and cannot avail for adoption. Nevertheless, the gift of good works is the evidence that we have received the Spirit of adoption. Good works stem from faith, which itself finds its source in the Holy Spirit. Believers have Christ as their model; their lives should reflect his image.

Calvin is prepared to speak of our dedication to a life of Christ-like righteousness as the condition of our adoption. This is a work of the Spirit within us, but Calvin is clear that we have a responsibility to devote ourselves to the task of living as God's adopted sons. He distinguishes between, on the one hand, "the first cause" of the saints' access to the kingdom of God, which is the Lord's adopting mercy, and, on the other hand, "the manner" by which our sonship is maintained, namely that we are born again by the Spirit and display the fruits of it.

Individual and corporate aspects of adoption

Calvin maintains a balance between the individual and the corporate aspects of adoption. God has elected certain individuals for salvation. However, all these individuals belong to the one seed, connected to one another in Christ, the Head. The true church consists only of those who "by the gift of adoption are the sons of God, and by sanctification of the Spirit true members of Christ." Baptism serves as the badge of adoption.

The results of adoption

Calvin refers to some of the fruits of adoption in the Christian life. It releases us from the bondage of a conscience oppressed by the fear of death. It enables us to cry out to God as "Abba, Father," encouraging us to pray with boldness as we make known our requests to God. It is the reason for the blessings which we daily receive from the hand of God. It admits us to the hope of immortality.

Adoption and the eternal inheritance

Calvin recognizes the New Testament connection between adoption and the inheritance. As partners with God's only Son, to whom the inheritance properly belongs, God's adopted sons have their inheritance in the heavenly kingdom.

Calvin notes how "Paul gives the name of adoption to that revelation of adoption which shall be made at the resurrection," defined in Romans 8:23 as "the redemption of our body." He underlines this point in these words: "let it be a fixed principle in our hearts, that the kingdom of heaven is not the hire of servants, but the inheritance of sons, an inheritance obtained by those only whom the Lord has adopted as sons, and obtained for no other cause than this adoption."

Calvin's final reference to adoption is followed by this statement:

> Christ is the only food of our soul, and, therefore, our heavenly Father invites us to him, that, refreshed by communion with him, we may ever and anon gather new vigor until we reach the heavenly immortality.

PRACTICAL APPLICATION

(1) Our study of this theme ought to lead us to celebration: we should be full of praise for the amazing reality of adoption. We who were slaves of sin, have been adopted by God alongside his only-begotten Son. We have become members of God's family, and he is our tender, loving heavenly Father. This is truly a cause for wonder and joyful gratitude. What astonishing grace God shows towards unworthy rebels!

We must be grateful to the Father who chose us for himself before time began and then sent the Spirit into our hearts to seal our adoption as sons.

We must be grateful to the Son who entered into this fallen world and shared our sorrows and bore our sins, in order to unite us with himself in his inherent glory. We must be grateful for his incarnation which enabled him to serve as the mediator in whom we are changed into the children of God.

We must be grateful to the Spirit who has worked in our hearts to give us faith, and to enable us to imitate the Savior, and so display the true evidence of our adoption. We must be grateful to him also as he bears witness with our spirits that we are the children of God, and as he guarantees to us the inheritance to which we look forward.

Everett Harrison sums up appropriately: "How unexpected and how breathtaking is the gracious provision of God!"[68]

(2) We must make daily use of the present benefits of adoption. The Spirit of adoption sets us free from the bondage of a conscience tormented by sin, and gives us the amazing liberty to come constantly before our Father with boldness and confidence. We may cry to him as "Abba, Father," and present our prayers with the absolute guarantee that we shall be heard and received and welcomed into his presence. Given this wonderful provision, how foolish we would be to neglect the life of prayer. Let us daily cultivate our relationship with our Father and go deeper in the knowledge of his love as the days go by. Let us love him wholeheartedly, as those who are no longer slaves, but sons.

(3) We must live up to our new identity in Christ. As those adopted in Christ into the family of God our identity has been transformed. No longer are we sinners in God's sight, but sons. Then it is our duty to live up to this reality, to ensure that we manifest in our daily living the family likeness. This is a far-reaching challenge; it is one to which we can only measure up by the power of the Spirit of adoption. Let us be constant in prayer that he will work within us as we commit ourselves to this task.

(4) We must rejoice in the fact that God's family transcends all ethnic divisions. It is not only that Jews and Gentiles are one in Christ: people of every nation, tribe and language are brought together in the Father's family. The family gathering on the last day of the present age will include representatives of every people group in the human race. The implication is that there is no place for any sense of ethnic supremacy now. All thoughts of superiority must be banished from our minds and hearts. We should joyfully embrace all who know and love our Lord Jesus as our brothers and sisters, adopted with us into the most wonderful family the world has ever known. Whoever, we are, we must be humble enough to learn from our brothers and sisters, wherever they may come from, and put away all ideas that we know better. We shall then be truly enriched by our relationships as the family of God, to belong to which is an inestimable privilege.

(5) We must be full of anticipation as we wait for our final adoption. A day is coming when our adoption will be ratified and completed. On

---

68. Harrison, "Romans," 93.

that day all the pains and diseases of the present time will be finished with forever. All the groanings of a time of frustration will fully and finally be over and done with. All our spiritual longings will be fulfilled. Death will be no more, and all God's children will share in the inheritance due by eternal right to God's dearly beloved Son and due to us by virtue of our union with him. To ponder these realities with craving and anticipation must be a source of the richest comfort in the trials of our earthly journey.

One of the trials of the present time is that we may well have to suffer for the sake of the name of Christ. How wonderful a thing it is to know that on that final day the Father will own us as his children before the eyes of a watching world. We shall be vindicated. In the meantime, let us wait patiently and press on with certainty towards the day when we shall finally receive the fullness of our eternal inheritance, when Christ shall at last receive the fullness of his glory.

PART FIVE: PERSEVERANCE

Can a Christian lose his salvation? Or is a believer eternally secure, once saved, always saved? The doctrine of the final perseverance of the saints assures us that God's electing grace never stalls. All whom he has chosen from eternity and called in time shall persevere to the end. This theme points us to the future hope when our salvation shall be finalized, but also brings out the present challenge to continue living the Christian life authentically, to press on to the very end.

BIBLICAL FOUNDATION

Old Testament

The promises of the LORD's faithfulness to Israel may be embraced by the Christian and applied to the believing life today. We shall look at three examples of these promises.

Deuteronomy 7:9–11

Verse 9 teaches that the LORD's faithfulness to his covenant is the basis of his people's assurance. He is unfailingly dependable—"for a thousand generations." The LORD "would be true in his covenant love toward his people into the distant future."[69] We today may, likewise, be certain that the God who first laid hold of us in Christ will never relinquish his hold. For the Christian believer, the distant future becomes the eternal future. God's reliability will never fail as long as eternity endures!

Verse 11 draws the inference that God's people must keep and observe all that he commands. Perseverance to the end does not mean that we float effortlessly to heaven, that God's faithfulness carries us home, while we sit back and relax! It means that there is a persevering in obedience that we actually have to do. But we can do it, because our faithful God supplies the grace and strength that we need.

Isaiah 49:15–16

These words form the LORD's reply to an exclamation made by Israel in anxious fear: "the LORD has forsaken me, and my Lord has forgotten me" (verse 14).

However, the LORD responds, it is most unlikely that a mother's love would fail, and it is even less likely that God's love should fail. Indeed it is impossible. God has taken his people into his very personality. They have been inscribed, or engraved, into him. A piece of him has been cut away, as it were, to make room for them. Here we see an Old Testament anticipation of the New Testament reality that we are chosen in Christ. This inscription is on the LORD's hands, implying that his people are held, carried, protected.

The verb rendered "inscribed" (*ḥāqaq*) could be used for enacting a law. The LORD has imposed on himself a law which forbids him to delete his people's names from his heart. They are as secure as his unalterable word.

Jeremiah 31:3–4

The LORD declares that his love for his people spans eternity. An everlasting love is one with no beginning and no end. Here is a love which is never interrupted even for a moment. An everlasting love is made concrete in continuous faithfulness.

---

69. Kalland, "Deuteronomy," 71.

Verse 4 is the consequent promise: even though, at times God's people feel forsaken, he remains their faithful God, and will return.

> Here Jeremiah underscores the LORD's inexhaustible patience— the basic concept of his constantly wooing his people and drawing them to himself. What comfort was theirs in the recognition of such perpetual love![70]

New Testament

The New Testament teaches in many places that God keeps his people to the end. We shall just glance at four examples.

John 10:27-29

From these verses we notice five things.

(1) Eternal life is Jesus' gift to his sheep. In John's writings the word "eternal" can denote life of a new quality. However, the idea of endless continuation is also present. If what Jesus gives is endless life, then the Christian cannot lose it. If he could it would not be endless!

(2) Jesus' sheep are his Father's gift to him, and having given, the Father will not take away again. The implication is that Jesus' sheep are preserved for ever.

(3) Jesus states that "they shall never perish." He uses very emphatic language, including two words both meaning "not" (*ou* and *mē*), and the phrase *eis ton aiōna* ("unto the age"), that is the eternal age. So Jesus is saying that his people "shall not perish, no, certainly not, not for all eternity."

(4) It is impossible for anyone to snatch Christ's people out of his hand. It is equally impossible to snatch them out of the Father's hand. Believers are securely held in this double grip, "All the resources of God are committed to their preservation."[71]

(5) This eternal preservation is the outcome of Christ's people following him. It is not something that merely happens irrespective of our personal effort. We are preserved for eternity as we persevere in following our Lord to the end.

---

70. Feinberg, "Jeremiah," 566.
71. Tenney, "John," 112.

Philippians 1:3-6

As so often at the beginning of his letters, the apostle thanks God for his work in the lives of believers. He rejoices in the outward evidences of that inward work of grace. Then he assures the Philippian Christians "that he who has begun a good work in you will complete *it* until the day of Jesus Christ."

The word rendered "until" is *achri*. It implies that God will complete the work not only at that final moment, but every moment leading up to that final moment. The Lord who has begun the work of grace in his people is maintaining it constantly. The end time completion will be the fulfilment of his daily keeping power along the way.

The completion of our salvation has to be God's work, because of our weakness: left to ourselves, we could not persevere to the end. And Paul assures us that God will not reverse his work where he has once begun it.

1 Peter 1:3-5

Here the apostle assures us that our heavenly inheritance is being reserved for us, and we are being kept for it. The word "kept" (*phroureō*) means surrounded by a defense. This implies that, without such divine protection, we would be helplessly vulnerable to the attacks of the devil through this hostile world. However, God's dynamic power is our defense, and we enjoy his protection through faith.

This reference to the believer's faith again emphasizes the important point that the truth of the perseverance of the saints does not mean that we just sit back and let God carry us to heaven while we enjoy the ride. Rather, it means that the saints are the people who do actually persevere to the end.

Matthew 24:13

We return now to listen again to Jesus himself. Here he says, "he who endures to the end shall be saved."

Jesus makes endurance to the end a sort of "condition" of salvation. This endurance is essential to prove the reality of our profession of faith.

Our final salvation depends on us keeping going through the time of our present salvation until we reach the end.

The word "endures" (*hupomenō*) implies that the route through life to final salvation will not be an easy one. There are many trials to be endured, some of which will be extremely severe. That has indeed been the theme of the preceding verses. Jesus has spoken in verses 9–10 of tribulation, martyrdom, hatred, and betrayal. In the parallel passage in Mark 13, which builds up to the same statement, "he who endures to the end shall be saved" (verse 13), he has also mentioned specifically, trials in court and the treachery of family members (verses 9–12).

However, the believer endures all such things, and comes through to the very end, because, in all the battles and hardships, he has been sustained by the preserving power of God. He therefore does persevere to the end. Again we see that the keeping power of God is no excuse for complacency. We have to do the enduring. We can do it, because God's preserving power works through our persevering effort.

> Jesus is not here setting forth a doctrine of salvation by works. He is rather emphasizing that genuine faith will issue in Christian living that will endure trial and persecution.[72]

DOCTRINAL FORMULATION

The Reformation Confessions

The teaching of the confessions on this subject falls into two main themes.

Believers certainly persevere to the end

True faith is never finally or totally extinguished. These two words "finally" and "totally" come up in several of the confessions. Their use recognizes that true faith may waver or become weak. However, a true believer's faith can never disappear altogether.

It is true that, in the worst times of doubt and despair, faith may seem completely to have died. However, that is never the final condition of the true believer. He is bound to return to a stronger faith. In times

---

72. Wessel, "Mark," 747.

of backsliding, the believer is deprived of all comfort. Nevertheless, the Lord keeps his grip on him, and draws him back in time to a joyful faith.

The most succinct summary of this theme is found in the 1644 Baptist Confession:

> Those that have this precious faith wrought in them by the Spirit can never finally nor totally fall away, and though many storms and floods do arise and beat against them, yet they shall never be able to take them off that foundation and rock which by faith they are fastened upon, but shall be kept by the power of God to salvation, where they shall enjoy their purchased possession, they being formerly engraven upon the palms of God's hands.

It is the power of God which enables believers to persevere

The confessions speak of the believer's powerful preservation in faith. They point out that the same power that brings conversion also carries the soul through all duties, temptations, conflicts and sufferings. The faith that God gives makes us continue in the way to the end. So God, who begins the work of salvation, also completes it.

Modern Confessions of Faith

There is no reference to this theme in the Indian confession. However, the other two confessions do mention it.

Confession of Faith of the Huria Kristen Batak Protestant

The Indonesian confession has two references to the preservation of God's people by the Holy Spirit, both set within the context of other discussions. The first occurs in the context of the doctrine of the Holy Spirit, part of whose work is to preserve the congregation of the church "in faith and in holiness through the gospel to the honor of God." The other context is the doctrine of the church, although here the preservation of the congregation is individualized: the church is defined as "the assembly of believers in Jesus Christ, who are called, gathered, sanctified, and preserved by God through the Holy Spirit."

It is worth highlighting three things here.

(1) The preservation of God's people by the Holy Spirit is understood in both corporate and individual terms. It is the church as a whole which is preserved, but the church constitutes the people who are believers, and each one is preserved personally.

(2) Preservation is not understood in isolation. It is in faith and holiness that the church is preserved. This implies a duty on the part of the believing community to maintain purity of doctrine and of life. When those qualities are absent we are not talking about the true church which the Holy Spirit is preserving. Faith and holiness are the things which bring honor to God.

(3) Preservation is a link in a chain of graces effected by the Holy Spirit. The church is "called, gathered, sanctified, and preserved." The entire work of salvation from start to finish is a supernatural work, which only God, by the agency of the Spirit, can achieve. Moreover, the entire work is one. It can be analyzed into its various components, but the full "salvation package" must stand or fall together. There is no preservation where there is not also calling, gathering and sanctification. However, where these various things are integrated together, there we observe the miracle of God's saving work.

Confession of Faith of House Churches in China

The Chinese confession devotes one sentence to this theme: "We believe that God will preserve his children in Christ to the end, and we also believe that believers should firmly believe in the truth to the end."

Those words are found in its statement on salvation. This confession upholds the biblical balance between the preserving power of God and the duty of believers to persevere to the end. This duty is described as believing in the truth. No doubt, behind this there lies the recognition that a genuine belief in the truth will issue in a transformed life of growing Christlikeness.

The emphasis on perseverance in believing the truth may reflect a context of persecution, with the temptation to deny the faith, to abandon the truth, in order to preserve one's earthly life and comforts. Enduring to the end, especially where allegiance to Christ is costly, means holding fast to the faith, and willingly to suffer for the sake of the name.

HISTORICAL ELABORATION

We shall cover two issues now. First we shall look at the debate about perseverance at the Synod of Dort. Then we shall consider the meaning of those Scriptures which appear to teach that a Christian may fall away.

The Synod of Dort

The Arminians raised the issue of the perseverance of the saints in the fifth article of their "Remonstrance" at the Synod of Dort.

Referring to John 10:28, they acknowledged that no one can pluck a true believer out of Christ's hands. Whatever trials and temptations the believer may face, the power of the Holy Spirit is given to enable him to win the victory. However, the article went on, believers are kept from falling if they are ready for the conflict and desire God's help in an active way. The article then concluded with these words:

> But whether they are capable, through negligence, of forsaking the first beginnings of their life in Christ, and of again returning to this present evil world, of turning away from the holy doctrine which was delivered them, of losing a good conscience, of becoming devoid of grace, that must be more particularly determined out of the Holy Scripture, before we ourselves can teach it with the full persuasion of our minds.

We must admire those seventeenth-century Arminians for their readiness to admit their uncertainty, and for their recognition that the answer to their uncertainty has to be found in Scripture.

The Synod's response may be summarized under seven points, as it sought to help the Arminians to reach biblical certainty on this matter.

(1) It is impossible for any Christian to persevere in his own strength. This is because of the remains of indwelling sin.

(2) God, in his mercy, confirms and powerfully preserves his people to the end in a state of grace.

(3) If a believer becomes negligent in prayer and watchfulness there is a very real danger that he will fall into serious sin. This will result in the loss of joy. Repentance is the only route to recovery.

(4) However, God never wholly withdraws his Holy Spirit. He never permits his children to fall so far as to lose their justification and adoption. He never allows them to come after all to eternal destruction.

(5) When a believer sins, God preserves the seed of regeneration in his heart. At last he renews the believer to repentance. This leads the believer to work out his own salvation with greater diligence.

(6) It is not human strength, but God's mercy, which keeps his children from totally falling from grace. The Canons then give reasons for confidence in God's mercy: a total fall is impossible,

> since [God's] counsel cannot be changed nor his promise fail; neither can the call according to his purpose be revoked, nor the merit, intercession, and preservation of Christ be rendered ineffectual, nor the sealing of the Holy Spirit be frustrated or obliterated.

(7) Assurance of salvation is possible. There are three ways in which assurance may be obtained: from faith in God's promises, from the testimony of the Holy Spirit, and from a serious and holy desire to do good works. Assurance is not guaranteed to the believer all the time, though, and is never a reason for pride. Rather, it is a cause for joy, and a motive to pray that we may do the works which express gratitude to God for our salvation.

The "Christians-can-fall-away" Passages of Scripture

Those who deny the certainty of final perseverance point to several passages of Scripture in support of their position. The most famous such passage is Hebrews 6:4–8. Some Arminians understand these verses to mean that a truly converted person can fall away and lose his salvation. This goes beyond the uncertainty which Arminius himself expressed. Some of his followers conclude that apostasy to eternal destruction is certainly possible for a true believer.

Take John Wesley for example. He understands verses 4–5 to refer to a genuine believer, one born of the Spirit, whose sins have been forgiven, who has known the witness and the fruit of the Spirit, and who has obtained the hope of immortality. Then, on verse 6, Wesley says:

> Here is not a supposition, but a plain relation of fact. The apostle here describes the case of those who have cast away both the power and the form of godliness; who have lost both their faith, hope, and love, and that wilfully. Of these wilful apostates he declares *it is impossible to renew them again to repentance* (though they were renewed once).[73]

---

73. Wesley, *New Testament*, 824.

However, this seems an unsatisfactory way of reading such texts, since it is at odds with the general tenor of Scripture. Salvation is God's work, rooted in his electing grace, bought at the high cost of the blood of his Son, sustained by the power of his Spirit. How, then, can a true Christian fall away to eternal perdition?

Another reading of this passage, favored by both G. H. Lang and R. T. Kendall,[74] claims that the issue is not the loss of salvation but the loss of reward at the judgment seat of Christ. Kendall notes that this also entails the loss of the present experience of "rest." Lang based this view on the Old Testament parallelism. Although many Israelites fell in the wilderness, not a single one was allowed to return to Egypt.

However, from the language of the passage it does seem that eternal salvation is in view. The illustration in verse 8, with references to cursing and burning, suggests so. How, then, is it to be understood?

Robert Reymond mentions two possible ways of understanding this passage compatible with Scripture as a whole.[75]

(1) It may assume a doctrine of "temporary faith:" the subject is not a true believer, but someone who makes an empty profession of faith. He appears to be a Christian. But when he falls away it becomes clear that he was a sham.

(2) Such warnings may be means to the end of perseverance. God's goal is the final perseverance of every one of his people. The means by which he secures this goal is by warning of what will happen if they do not persevere to the end: they will be lost. The result of the warning is that their perseverance to the end is secured.

On another relevant text, 1 Corinthians 8:11, Charles Hodge makes a comment similar to Reymond's second suggestion:

> The Bible telling those for whom Christ died that they shall perish if they violate their conscience, prevents them transgressing, or brings them to repentance. God's purposes embrace the means as well as the end. If the means fail, the end will fail. He secures the end by securing the means . . . . There is not only a possibility, but an absolute certainty of their perishing if they fall away. But this is precisely what God has promised to prevent.[76]

---

74. Lang, *Hebrews*, 93–101; Kendall, *Once Saved*, 140–42.

75. Reymond, *New Systematic Theology*, 788–89.

76. C. Hodge, *Corinthians*, 149.

This is the approach which I find most convincing. I once lived in a city not far from the sea. The road to the sea ended on a cliff top. Just before the end of the road there was a sign illustrating a car going over a cliff. It was a warning: that is what will happen if you drive any further! Supposing the local council had said, "no car has ever driven over the cliff, so we might as well remove the sign." We would think that they were very foolish. It was the presence of the sign which ensured that no car had ever driven over the cliff. If the sign were removed, probably there would be a dreadful accident the very next week.

In the same way, God's warning signs in Scripture stop us going over the cliff of apostasy to our eternal destruction. They are a means of grace to keep us pressing on in the present towards the goal of eternal salvation.

PRACTICAL APPLICATION

(1) We may have every confidence in God. He is faithful, and we praise him for that fact. We may be sure that he will keep us to the end. It is true that the Christian life is a hard, uphill struggle. But we can be encouraged: the almighty power of God is on our side to enable us to press on to the end. We must beware, when the struggle is strenuous, of caving into doubt. It is when the battles are fiercest, when the darkness is deepest, when the opposition is most intense, that we are vulnerable. But these are the very times when we need to draw encouragement from God's promise, "I will never leave you nor forsake you" (Heb 13:5).

(2) We must preach this encouragement to those to whom we minister. Those in our pastoral care need constant encouragement. Like us, they face the discouragements and challenges of life in a fallen world. They need to see that they are not on their own. They need regular reminders of the love of Christ, the presence of God, and the power of the Spirit. We must make sure that we are truly ministers of grace to our people, not increasing their burdens, but comforting them in their afflictions, just as the apostle Paul did (2 Cor 1:3–4).

(3) Persevere! This is really the main application of this doctrine. Perseverance is not something that just happens to us. We have to do the persevering. We persevere in faith, in good works, in all the duties of a Christian commitment. There is no place for laziness or complacency in the Christian life. The Christian calling is a 24-hours a day, 7-days

a week calling. The devil never takes time off, and we must be on our guard against his devices all the time. We are to keep on keeping on, and face the fact that, if we fail to persevere to the end, there will be no salvation for us. 1 Peter 1:9 says that "the salvation of your souls" is "the end of your faith." If faith falters before the end, salvation will not be the outcome. Hebrews 3:14 reminds us that "we have become partakers of Christ if we hold the beginning of our confidence steadfast to the end" (cf. Heb 3:6). So hold on! Press on!

(4) We must use the means which help us to persevere. Although we must do the persevering to the end, we cannot do it in our own strength. God's power is vital. So we must never forget our own weakness. But at the same time, we must remember that God has given us the means to draw on his power. They include prayer, watchfulness, his word. We must be very careful not to neglect these means of endurance to the end, but to make constant use of them. "Let us run with endurance the race that is set before us" (Heb 12:1), and keep this promise from Revelation 2:26 constantly in mind: "he who overcomes, and keeps my works until the end, to him I will give power over the nations."

11

The Doctrine of Salvation (3)
Its Eternal Basis: Election

OUR SALVATION IS ROOTED in the eternal, electing love of God in Christ. The truth of election is the starting point for the whole process of salvation. We are justified, sanctified, and glorified, regenerated, united with Christ, reconciled, adopted, and enabled to persevere, all because, before the foundation of the world, God chose us in his Son. We have had reason to refer to election and predestination in connection with the doctrine of salvation a number of times already; now it is time to home in on this theme specifically.

BIBLICAL FOUNDATION

Old Testament

There are two aspects to the truth of election in the Old Testament. The first is the election of Israel, and it is into the people of God first defined as Israel that new covenant Gentile believers are ingrafted; moreover, Israel's election sets the pattern for God's election of each member of his people. Second, there is the election of Christ—the chosen one *par excellence*. It is in him that we are God's elect. We shall look at one passage relating to each aspect.

The Election of Israel

Deuteronomy 7:6–8 develops the thought that the LORD chose Israel to be "a people for himself." We note the following truths about election from this passage.

THE BASIS OF ELECTION IS LOVE

Verse 7 says that the LORD "set his love" on his people. The Hebrew word (*ḥāšaq*) speaks of a strong attachment which delights God as the lover. It brings out the wonder of divine love.

THIS LOVE IS ENTIRELY SELF-MOTIVATED

Verses 7–8 stress the total lack of merit on Israel's part. There was nothing impressive about them to evoke God's love. The love in which election is rooted finds its cause in God alone. Kalland speaks of Israel's status as the elect people as a "gratuitous position," and writes, "it is the character of God, rather than any excellence in the people that accounts for the choice."[1]

ELECTING LOVE IS TIED UP WITH COVENANT FAITHFULNESS

Moses points out in verse 8 that the LORD had sworn on oath to the patriarchs that he would be God to them and to their descendants. So the continuing choice of Israel represents God's faithfulness to his word.

THE RESULTS OF ELECTION

Two results for Israel of their elect status are mentioned: (1) they were delivered from slavery in Egypt [verse 8]; (2) they were constituted a holy people to the LORD [verse 6].

This latter point is not holiness as merit, "but purely a matter of grace."[2] It means that they were set apart to belong exclusively to the LORD. As his treasured possession the LORD greatly valued his exclusive prize.

1. Kalland, "Deuteronomy," 71, 86.
2. Christensen, *Deuteronomy*, 156.

The Election of Christ

In Isaiah 42:1–4 the LORD, through his prophet, speaks of his servant, whom he describes as "my elect one *in whom* my soul delights!" Sometimes Isaiah uses the term "servant" of Israel, but there are eight occasions where the term is used, but he is clearly not speaking of Israel. The term "servant" is "the most prominent personal, technical term to represent the Old Testament teaching on the Messiah."[3] This text has a clear Messianic reference.

Jesus was chosen to be the LORD's servant. Motyer notes that "my servant" used "without any qualifying proper name" suggests "'my pre-eminent servant:'" Jesus Christ is the "one who embodies true servanthood."[4] Because he is God's chosen, and the object of divine pleasure, he receives divine support in being filled with God's Spirit to fulfil his God-given earthly ministry.

New Testament

Our main concern now is the fact that God has chosen his people for salvation, both as a people, and each member individually. However, first we shall briefly note some New Testament references to the election of Israel and the election of Christ.

The Election of Israel

This is the theme of Romans 9—11. In the opening verses of chapter 9 the apostle is grieving because his fellow Jews, by and large, did not recognize Jesus as their Messiah. This leads to the question, voiced in verse 6, whether God's promises have failed. In verses 6–13 the apostle discerns the answer in a distinction between ethnic Israel—the children of the flesh, and the true Israel—the children of the promise. This distinction was already apparent in Israel's history: Abraham had two sons, but only through Isaac was the offspring named; Rebecca had two sons, yet God chose Jacob not Esau, and Jacob was chosen, not on the basis of works which he had done (he was chosen before he was born!), but "that the purpose of God according to election might stand."

3. Kaiser, "*ābad*," 1553a.
4. Motyer, *Isaiah*, 319.

But if God chose Jacob and bypassed Esau, is he not then unfair? That is the question which verse 14 asks. In verses 15–16 Paul insists that this is quite the wrong way of looking at things. If God dealt with us in strict fairness and justice, there would be no hope for anyone. Rather, it is all about mercy, mercy undeserved and free, mercy which is at his disposal entirely. Verses 17–18 then teach that God has a purpose in the hardening of Israel, as he did in the case of Pharaoh, namely that the name of Christ should be declared throughout the world. Through the gospel God is enlarging the sphere of his mercy, and how can that be considered unfair?

But now another question arises in verse 19. Is God unreasonable? How can he punish sin when he himself hardens the sinner? Paul's immediate answer is in the form of a counter-question, "but indeed, O man, who are you to reply against God?" (verse 20). Who do we think we are to dare to make such accusations against God? But in verses 21–33, Paul develops his answer. The gist of this passage amounts to this: just look how patient God is. The Gentiles have been brought in, so God's mercy has been extended universally. A remnant of the Jews has been preserved, because God moderates judgment.

Chapter 10 begins with prayer, and the first 17 verses indicate the twofold thrust of the prayer, for the salvation of Israel, and for preachers of the gospel.

Then at verse 18 the apostle returns to the question of Israel. Their problem is not that the gospel has not been preached to them. And that leads to a further question in the first verse of chapter 11: "has God cast away his people?" Is their election finished? And Paul's answer in verses 1–6 is no, not at all, for there is still "a remnant according to the election of grace." There were some Jewish believers in Paul's day, as there have been since. So, while Israel as a whole missed out on salvation in Christ, the elect within Israel have come to him (verses 7–10).

Now another question is posed in verse 11: "have they stumbled that they should fall?" Although God chose a remnant within the Jewish nation to be saved in Christ in the present time, is it the end for Israel as a nation?

In verses 11–22 Paul answers by explaining God's twofold purpose at this stage of history. He is bringing salvation to the Gentiles and thereby provoking jealousy on the part of Israel.

Then, in verses 23–29, the apostle turns to Israel's future. If they repent, they can yet come into the fold of the gospel. And in any case their hardening is only temporary. The day will come when "all Israel will be saved" (verse 26). This possibly means that the whole of the final generation of Jewish people before the Lord returns will recognize Jesus as Messiah, a point which we shall discuss further in the final chapter, on the Last Things. The basis for this expectation is God's faithfulness to his covenant promise: "concerning the election *they are* beloved for the sake of the fathers" (verse 28). Ultimately God's election will embrace the whole nation, because God loves the Jews.

Although these chapters have to do with the election of Israel, the pattern established in God's dealings with his ancient people holds true for the doctrine of election more generally. God's choice predates our existence. Election does not take our works into account. It is entirely on the basis of God's free mercy.

The Election of Christ

In 1 Peter 2:4 and 6 "the election of Jesus Christ as God's instrument of salvation"[5] is emphasized: he is God's chosen and precious cornerstone, even though men rejected him. Peter is probably referring to the resurrection as the point at which God's election of Jesus Christ was made public. That was the moment of reversal when the stone rejected by men was shown to be God's chosen.

To speak of Jesus as God's elect is to focus on his incarnate life. However, as in the principle set out in Romans 9, his election predated his incarnation. It was not God's response to what Jesus actually did. It was God's eternal purpose to choose Jesus Christ to be the Savior of the world.

The Election of Sinners for Salvation

There are too many passages relevant to this theme to look at them all. We shall therefore select just three key texts.

EPHESIANS 1

Most especially, verses 3–6 and 11–12 are fundamental for this subject. Verse 4 teaches that God chose us, and tells us three things about this.

---

5. Michaels, *1 Peter*, 99.

(1) We were chosen in Christ. He is the eternal representative of all his people. In verse 6 there is a parallel phrase—in the Beloved. Christ is God's truly beloved one, and all the elect are caught up into that inner-trinitarian love. Jesus mentioned this in his prayer to his Father in John 17:23–24: the Father has loved his disciples even as he has loved the Son, and this is the love by which the Son was loved "before the foundation of the world."

(2) We were chosen before time began. This emphasizes that God's choice "was a free decision not dependent on temporal circumstances . . . , provoked not by historical contingency or human merit."[6]

(3) The goal for which we were chosen was that we should be holy and blameless in God's sight. This goal is fulfilled in the process of sanctification in the course of the Christian life.

In verses 5 and 11 a different verb is used: we were predestined. From verse 5 we learn three things about election.

(1) Predestination is rooted in divine love. The words "in love" at the end of verse 4 may be connected either with what precedes or with what follows. Although our translation connects them with what precedes, there is much to be said for connecting them with what follows in verse 5, "having predestined us." The doctrine of election may never be construed as cold and abstract. It pulsates with the passion of everlasting love.

(2) Another goal of election is highlighted: we were predestined to become adopted sons of God. This goal is realized initially at the moment of a sinner's conversion.

(3) The basis of our election was "the good pleasure of his will." This emphasizes God's sole sovereignty in salvation. The word translated "good pleasure" (*eudokia*) speaks of something which seemed good to God. It brought God delight and satisfaction to contemplate the salvation of his elect. God really enjoys saving sinners. That is why he chose some.

Verse 11 also speaks of God's purpose in which election is rooted. However, a different word (*prothesis*) is being translated here. This refers to a plan which someone works out in advance, and stresses again that the initiative in salvation lies entirely with God.

Both these verses stress that the ultimate goal of election is the glorification of God as the God of grace: it is precisely by the fact that he chooses sinners for salvation that God is revealed to be truly a gracious

---

6. Lincoln, *Ephesians*, 23.

God; the existence of a body of redeemed sinners puts the grace of God on display.

1 THESSALONIANS 1:4–6

The apostle declares that he knows that his Thessalonian readers are numbered amongst those whom God has chosen. It was not that, as an inspired apostle, he had been given special insight. Verse 5 begins with the word "for." Verses 5–6 are the explanation as to how Paul knows.

First, he knows that the Thessalonians are chosen because of how the gospel came to them. It came with the manifest power of the Spirit accompanying the preaching of the word. This made it obvious that God meant to save these people at that time, proving that he had chosen them in eternity. Whenever God has his elect to save, he will ensure that the Holy Spirit is working mightily through the preaching of the gospel.

Then again, Paul knows that the Thessalonians are chosen because of the way in which they responded to the gospel. They received the word with joy, even though it meant affliction. This was so remarkable that such joy could only have had its origin in the Holy Spirit.

This passage reminds us that it is impossible to read God's secret decree. However, there is no reason to doubt God's electing purpose wherever we see a response to the gospel which can only be explained as the work of the Holy Spirit.

2 TIMOTHY 2:8–10

There is one other important point relating to the truth of election which this passage emphasizes: the doctrine of election does not lead to inactivity.

It could be possible to adopt the following sort of attitude. If God has chosen who is to be saved, then it is pointless to preach the gospel, because the elect will get saved anyway.

However, that is not at all a genuinely Christian way of looking at things, because it is totally unbiblical. It overlooks the fact that God has not only chosen who will be saved, but also how they will be saved. The normal method by which the elect are saved is through the preaching of the gospel. It is when we engage in gospel work with strenuous effort that the elect are gathered to Christ.

We do not know who the elect are, but we do know that there is an elect. So the doctrine of election gives us an immense impulse to preach the gospel to every creature, and to put up with whatever it costs to make sure that every elect sinner gets saved. As Paul writes to Timothy he is in prison for the sake of the name and the gospel of Jesus Christ. However, he is willing to endure whatever it takes to make sure that the elect do obtain salvation through hearing and believing the gospel.

DOCTRINAL FORMULATION

The Reformation Confessions

We can outline the teaching of the confessions on this doctrine in ten sections.

What election means

The confessions define election as God's choice to deliver some from the curse and from condemnation. Conversely, election means that God has chosen them for life, for eternal salvation, for holiness, and for glory. Ultimately, it is this election which is the cause of their salvation.

When election took place

The confessions stress the fact that God's decree of election took place before the foundation of the world. It is an eternal decree.

The basis of election

This is stated both negatively and positively.

Negatively, the basis of election is not any foreseen faith, perseverance, or good works in those elected. They are no different from, no better than, the rest of mankind.

Positively, it is God's eternal and unchangeable counsel which is the only basis for election. The elect are chosen in God's purpose. The cause of election is found only in God's good pleasure. So the elect are chosen totally because of God's goodness, by grace and mercy alone.

They are chosen freely—without any consideration of human qualities or qualifications.

Election and love

To say that God's elect were chosen before the foundation of the world is another way of saying that they are loved with an everlasting love. The confessions are clear that election is not a cold, abstract theory. The doctrine of election throbs with love, it vibrates with passion.

The ultimate goal of election

The confessions recognize that the goal of all things is the glory of God. This must, therefore, also be the goal of election. Election promotes the glory of God as it displays the glory of his grace and the riches of his mercy.

Election in Christ

The confessions teach that "God has elected us, not directly, but in Christ," to cite the Second Helvetic Confession specifically. The election of sinners is indirect, in the sense that it is by virtue of our union with Christ that we are chosen. He is the true elect human being. He is chosen representatively, and his people are given to him by his Father, and are caught up into his election. The truth of election in Christ means that from eternity the Father nominated as Christ's body all those sinners whom his Son would in time redeem. Christ and his members, considered as a single entity, is the object of divine election. The Westminster Larger Catechism says that "the covenant of grace was made with Christ as the second Adam, and in him with all the elect as his seed." As the 1689 Baptist Confession explains, our election is therefore

> founded in that eternal covenant transaction that was between the Father and the Son about the redemption of the elect; and it is alone by the grace of this covenant that all the posterity of fallen Adam that ever were saved did obtain life and blessed immortality.

The Scottish Confession further elaborates on this truth. It tells how

> that same Eternal God and Father, who of mere grace elected us
> in Christ Jesus his Son, before the foundation of the world was
> laid, appointed him to be our Head, our Brother, our Pastor, and
> great Bishop of our souls.

It then goes on to speak of the necessity of Christ's incarnation in order that he might become the sole mediator who overcomes the enmity
between God's justice and our sins. Later this confession refers to "that
most blessed conjunction, union, and society, which the elect have with
their head, Christ Jesus."

This truth leads the Second Helvetic Confession to exhort us, "Let
Christ, therefore, be the looking glass, in whom we may contemplate
our predestination." Berkouwer notes that the truth of election in Christ
"takes away all our self-esteem." He comments, "the election of God is
an election of mercy precisely because it is election in Christ."[7] We find
meaning only by virtue of our association with Christ, the worthy one.

Election appoints the means of salvation

Recognizing that God in his electing grace appoints some people for
salvation, the confessions are equally clear that the means by which the
elect are brought to a saving knowledge of Christ are also appointed by
God from eternity.

He ensures that in due time the elect hear the gospel and are called
through the preached word by the Holy Spirit. By grace they obey the
gospel call, believe on Jesus Christ, and are kept by the power of God to
persevere to the end. The external word of the gospel and the internal call
of the Holy Spirit together form the appointed means by which the elect
are brought to salvation in Christ.

Even the time of our conversion is not in our own power. This explains an answer that William Carey once gave to an Indian man who
asked why the gospel had not come to India sooner. Carey replied that
God's judgment sometimes allows a nation to sink into ever deeper sin
until his appointed time to visit with salvation. When that time comes,
Carey said, "by the diffusion of gospel light, the wisdom, power, and
grace of God will be more conspicuous."[8]

---

7. Berkouwer, *Election*, 142, 149.
8. Cited by Wells, *Vision for Missions*, 13.

What of those unable to be called by the gospel?

As we have observed previously, some of those involved in drawing up the confessions were aware that there are people who cannot benefit from the appointed means to salvation. They had two categories of people in mind: infants who die in infancy, and those of limited mental capacity who cannot understand the gospel even if it is preached to them. Does this automatically mean that they cannot be numbered amongst the elect? The Westminster Confession recognizes that there will be elect sinners among such categories of human beings. They "are regenerated, and saved by Christ, through the Spirit, who works when, and where, and how he pleases."

The necessity for election

Divine election is an absolute necessity if anyone is to be saved at all, because all people are by nature dead in sin. Unless God chose some for salvation, no one could be saved, because no one is able to respond to God's call unaided.

The elect are a definite number

There is no possibility that the number whom God has chosen for salvation can be either increased or decreased. God made his choice in eternity and it stands for all eternity. The Westminster Confession comments, "From the free and unchangeable love of God the Father" there flows "the immutability of the decree of election."

As for how great a number the elect might be, the confessions do not speculate. However, we have already seen, in connection with the doctrine of so-called "limited atonement," how a number of the great Reformed theologians and preachers of the past believed that God has chosen the overwhelming majority of the human race for salvation, that he has refused to leave the devil with the larger share. Certainly the Scripture clearly says that there will be "a great multitude which no one could number, of all nations, tribes, peoples, and tongues, standing before the throne and before the Lamb" (Rev 7:9).

The fact that the number exceeds human counting ability demonstrates its vastness. The fact that it is only human counting ability that it exceeds demonstrates that God knows the definite number of his elect. This implies the amazing, heart-warming truth that he knows each one of us personally. The hugeness of the number does not cause God to look at his elect in purely impersonal terms.

Modern Confessions of Faith

The doctrine of election features in only one of the three modern statements which we are using. The Indian confession affirms the truth of election by reference to Ephesians 1:4–6. However, it is set within an affirmation of the free offer of the gospel to all people:

> While God chose a people in Christ before the foundation of the world, that they should be holy and without blemish before him in love, having foreordained them to adoption as sons through Jesus Christ unto himself, according to the good pleasure of his will, to the praise of the glory of his grace, which he freely bestowed on them in the Beloved, he makes a full and free offer of salvation to all men.

In coupling the doctrine of election together with God's free offer of salvation to all, this confession is totally in line with the biblical emphasis. The truth of election must never become an excuse for inactivity. It should never be construed as a reason for half-heartedness in gospel endeavors. We do not know who God's elect are. We do know that the preaching of the gospel is the Holy Spirit's normal tool for calling them to Christ.

There is a danger that we can tie ourselves in knots trying to avoid giving the impression that we think that Christ died to save all people. We can feel inhibited to issue the gospel appeal because we do not want to seem to suggest that sinners can come to Christ by their own power. The "whosoever will" of the New Testament can become muted in our effort to preserve our Reformed credentials! The Indian confession avoided falling into this trap.

HISTORICAL ELABORATION

Here we shall do three things. First, we shall pay another visit to the Synod of Dort, and look at its teaching on election. Second, we shall consider some common objections to this doctrine. Third, we shall address the issue of the free offer of the gospel in the light of the doctrine of election.

The Synod of Dort

The first article of the Arminian Remonstrance asserted that it was God's eternal, unchangeable purpose in Christ to save those who believe in Jesus and persevere to the end. The article added that this purpose was determined before creation, and that faith in Jesus is only possible through the grace of the Holy Spirit.

On this definition, election is not of persons, but of conditions. God did not purpose to save particular individuals, but to save any who would fulfil the conditions of exercising faith and persevering in it.

Admittedly, the Arminians recognized that the grace of the Spirit was necessary for anyone to be able to fulfil the conditions. Nevertheless, God's election before the foundation of the world was not concerned with particular people, only with general principles.

The Canons of Dort responded with this definition of election:

> Election is the unchangeable purpose of God, whereby, before the foundation of the world, he has out of mere grace, according to the sovereign good pleasure of his own will, chosen from the whole human race, which had fallen through their own fault from their primitive state of rectitude into sin and destruction, a certain number of persons to redemption in Christ.

In the surrounding context the Synod elaborated on this basic definition. It insisted that the gift of faith itself proceeds from God's eternal decree. God did not merely foresee various qualities of human actions, and select some of them as the condition of salvation. God was pleased to adopt out of the sinful human mass some particular persons as a people for himself. Their hearts are changed just because they are elected.

The Canons are clear that the elect were not chosen because they were better than the rest. Though they were no better, they were given to Christ to be saved by him. They were chosen both to grace and to glory, both to salvation and to the way of salvation. They were chosen to be called by the word and the Spirit, to be justified, sanctified, preserved, and glorified. Consequently, not one of the elect can be lost. Their number cannot be diminished, because the decree of election is as unchangeable as God himself. So the basis of election was not some foreseen faith, obedience, holiness, or anything else in man. Rather, the elect were chosen to all these things. Election is the fountain of every saving good. The sole cause of election was God's good pleasure which proceeds from everlasting love. So the ultimate goal of election is the demonstration of divine mercy.

The Canons raise the question of infant deaths. The answer given is that believers, because of the covenant of grace, may be confident that their children dying in infancy are numbered amongst the elect.

Objections to the Doctrine of Election

Wayne Grudem considers several typical objections.[9] Some of his answers I have modified a little, to make them, in my judgment, more adequate.

Election means that we have no choice
whether we accept Christ or not

This confuses choice with freedom. We are not free, because we are in bondage to sin. So the only choice which we can make is one which accords with our sinful nature: we reject Christ. However, when the Holy Spirit regenerates our will, it becomes our genuine choice to believe on Christ.

Election makes us puppets or robots, not real persons

This is not true, because we have a will. Even if our will is in bondage to sin, it is still our personal will which we exercise. When our will is liberated from bondage by the Holy Spirit, we exercise our will. However, a sub-human thing, such as a robot or a puppet, has no will of its own.

Election means that unbelievers never had a chance to believe

The implication is that God is unfair. However, the unbeliever wilfully refuses to believe. It is true that he refuses because his will is bound by his nature as a sinner. Nevertheless, it is still his own will which he exercises.

9. Grudem, *Systematic Theology*, 674–75, 680–84.

God is certainly not unfair. Fairness would consign us all to hell without exception. That even one person is enabled to believe on Jesus Christ means that God is operating in a completely different realm: we are in the realm of gracious mercy, not strict justice.

It is unfair if God is going to save some that he does not save all

This argument is based on an intuitive human sense of fairness, namely that there should be equality of treatment wherever that is possible. However, we are wrong to presume that our intuitive sense of what is appropriate in inter-human relationships can be projected on to God.

The Bible says that God desires to save everyone, so the doctrine of election results in an inconsistency in Scripture

We need to remember that God's revealed will must be distinguished from his hidden will, and that his desire must be distinguished from his decision. For reasons known only to himself, God may decide not fully to satisfy his own desire.

Election amounts to fatalism

This is not so. A mechanistic, impersonal picture of things is a far cry from the biblical vision of salvation as the work of a personal God who is motivated by love.

The Free Offer of the Gospel

There is a point of view which maintains that, since God has elected some to salvation, he makes no genuine gospel offer to any except his elect. The advocates of this position argue that it would be insincere of God to offer salvation to those whom he has not chosen for salvation, and that insincerity is impossible on God's part. Therefore it is improper for a preacher to offer Christ to his hearers indiscriminately.

By contrast, Maurice Roberts[10] defines the free offer as "the invitation given by God to all sinners to believe in Jesus Christ, with the promise

10. Roberts, "Free Offer," *passim.*

added that if they do so believe they will at once receive forgiveness of sins and eternal life." He draws out the following implications of the free offer:

> The offer is made for all who hear it, whether they be elect or not. The offer is not to be restricted or modified by the preacher in his presentation. The offer is an expression of love and grace on God's part towards sinful, unbelieving men. The offer is sincere on God's part, and it is genuinely and well meant. The offer is addressed to sinners as they are and requires of them repentance and faith.

Roberts finds the logic of this position in a distinction between God's genuine desire and his decreed will. Scripture teaches that God "desires all men to be saved" (1 Tim 2:4), that he is "not willing that any should perish but that all should come to repentance" (2 Pet 3:9). It also teaches that he guarantees the salvation of the elect. So Roberts concludes,

> both are stated as revealed facts in Scripture. The way to interpret Scripture is not to stress one truth to the detriment of the other but to hold both truths at the same time. So we affirm both God's eternal election and his well-meant offer to all sinners who hear the gospel. We are obliged to do this because this is how God himself reveals his will to us. Put simply, it is this: God has fixed the number of the elect from eternity past; yet God desires every sinner who hears his gospel to receive it and to be eternally blessed in Christ . . . . The preacher's duty is not to stumble over this mystery but to be zealous in persuasively offering and passionately presenting Christ to sinners—to *all* sinners.

Stuart Olyott points out that Jesus, in effect, refers to God's election in Matthew 11:25–27. He talks about God hiding and revealing truth according to his own will. However, in the very next verse he issues this general invitation: "Come to me, all *you* who labor and are heavy laden, and I will give you rest." Olyott points out that this "all" is universal, because everyone in the world is weighed down with a burden of sin, whether or not they recognize it, whether or not they feel it.

> There is *no one* he doesn't invite! He invites them *all*! And your invitation to come to Christ must be as open as that if you are going to minister like he did. It must be as free, as unembarrassed, as uninhibited, as unreserved and as *universal* as that. If it is not, you and your Master will have parted company.[11]

---

11. Olyott, *Ministering*, 57–58.

PRACTICAL APPLICATION

The Reformation confessions devoted much space to the issue of the practical relevance of the doctrine of election. We shall base this section around six areas of practical implication which they suggest.

Comfort and Assurance

We cannot read our elect status directly, but faith in Christ is the fruit of election: only the elect can obey the command to embrace Christ for salvation. If, therefore, our unfeigned trust is in Christ alone to save us, then we may deduce our election indirectly.

Since the believer's faith arises from God's electing love in eternity, it is securely established. To realize this leads to full assurance of faith. That, in turn, produces solid comfort especially in times of trial, and great joy at all times. In 2 Thessalonians 2:13–14, the apostle reminds the Christians to whom he writes of their election to salvation, sanctification, and glory. In verses 16–17 he then prays for their comfort rooted in grace:

> Now may our Lord Jesus Christ himself, and our God and Father, who has loved us and given *us* eternal consolation and good hope by grace, comfort your hearts and establish you in every good work and word.

It is just because we anticipate a comfortable eternity that we can be comforted in the midst of life's trials. This is not merely the result of a logical inference concerning the doctrine of election. The marvelous truth is that, to those whom he has elected, God gives himself, his presence, his daily help. As Moses said to the Israelites, because the LORD "loved your fathers, therefore he chose their descendants after them; and he brought you out of Egypt with his presence" (Deut 4:37).

Humility

When we grasp the doctrine of election all pride is demolished. We can glory only in the Lord. The fact that we are saved is not a mark of our superiority. It stems totally and only from the Lord's grace. Colossians 3:12 includes humility in a list of graces appropriate to "*the* elect of God." We had to humble ourselves to become Christians; daily humiliation follows. If we understand God's free electing grace, then we can never look down on others, we can never be gripped by a judgmental spirit, we can never feel self-satisfied that we are living a Christian life. It is all of grace. It is grace from first to last.

Love for, and Praise to, God

Admiring reverence is the only conceivable response when we are captivated by the undeserved kindness which we have received. The Canons of Dort put it like this:

> The sense and certainty of this election afford to the children of God additional matter . . . for adoring the depth of his mercies, for cleansing themselves, and rendering grateful returns of ardent love to him who first manifested so great love towards them.

Diligent Striving

The Second Helvetic Confession refers to the question addressed to Jesus in Luke 13:23, "are there few who are saved?" Jesus did not answer the question directly. His attitude was that curious prying into mysteries is fruitless and irrelevant. Rather, the Lord responded to this question with the words, "Strive to enter through the narrow gate." The issue is not "how many are saved?" but will I be saved?

Jesus assures us that there is an open door, because God has chosen to save people. Therefore everyone should seriously seek salvation in Christ. So the doctrine of election includes the commands to repent and to believe on Jesus Christ for salvation.

The doctrine of election also requires diligent striving on the part of those called to be preachers of the gospel. When the eternal destinies of our fellow sinners are at stake, we cannot have a casual attitude. Urgent prayer, and effortful proclamation of Christ are demanded of us.

We must have Good Hope for all People

The Second Helvetic Confession says, "we must hope well of all, and not rashly judge any man to be a reprobate." Lorraine Boettner expands on this practical implication of the truth of election. He writes:

> The doctrine of predestination . . . impresses upon us the fact
> that our salvation is purely of grace, and that we were no better
> than those who are left to suffer for their sins. It thus leads us to
> be more charitable and tolerant towards the unsaved.

Later on Boettner adds this further observation. He reminds us that a church which holds to the doctrine of election will be "truly broad and tolerant." The reason is that such a church recognizes as true Christians "any who trust Christ for their salvation, regardless of how inconsistent their other beliefs may be."[12]

Boettner's point is that, since God's election is unconditional, even theological accuracy may not be made a condition of divine acceptance. We are under obligation to accept all whom the Lord accepts. The apostle Paul says as much in chapters 14—15 of Romans. He refers to a dispute amongst Christians about acceptable foods. He insists, "let not him who eats despise him who does not eat, and let not him who does not eat judge him who eats; for God has received him" (Rom 14:3).

Probably those final words, "for God has received him" should be linked with both the preceding clauses. They are equally a reminder to "him who eats" and is tempted to despise the abstainer, and to "him who does not eat" and is prone to judge the eater. Wherever we stand on whatever issue, we may neither despise nor judge any of those whom God has welcomed because he chose them in Christ before the foundation of the world, however vehemently we may disagree with them on certain matters. That passage comes to its conclusion in these words: "receive one another, just as Christ also received us, to the glory of God" (Rom 15:7). To fail to accept our fellow believers is to insult Christ and to deprive God of his proper glory. If we truly understand the doctrine of election, we shall have wide open, welcoming hearts.

"Make your Call and Election sure"

These words are taken from 2 Peter 1:10. The doctrine of election will not lead to a careless or complacent Christian life. How do we make our election sure? How can it be unsure, if it is rooted in God's eternal purpose of love? Edwin Blum notes that the verb "make" is in the middle voice. This

---

12. Boettner, *Predestination*, 332, 353.

can imply "make for yourself."[13] The issue is not the certainty of election as such, but the personal certainty that I am indeed one of God's elect.

How, then, do we attain this assurance? Verses 5–7 form a list of qualities which ought to supplement the faith of every believer:

> giving all diligence, add to your faith virtue, to virtue knowledge, to knowledge self-control, to self-control perseverance, to perseverance godliness, to godliness brotherly kindness, and to brotherly kindness love.

We make our calling and election sure to ourselves by diligently striving to cultivate these qualities. Election is the appointment not just to final salvation, but to every component of salvation along the way. We are called to holiness and obedience, to a life bearing the fruits of Christlikeness that validate our profession of faith. Peter adds in verse 8: "if these things are yours and abound, *you* will be neither barren nor unfruitful in the knowledge of our Lord Jesus Christ."

Calvin agrees that we must make our election sure to ourselves, but also adds one other comment: holiness of life also gives certainty to other people, to our fellow believers, that we are truly the elect of God:

> Purity of life is not improperly called the evidence and proof of election, by which the faithful may not only testify to others that they are the children of God, but also confirm themselves in this confidence.[14]

---

13. Blum, "1 & 2 Peter," 270.
14. Calvin, *Catholic Epistles*, 377.

12

The Doctrine of the Holy Spirit

WE LIVE IN THE age of the Spirit. The truth about the Holy Spirit really ought to promote great expectations on our part. He is the source of all our power for Christian life and ministry.

Both the biblical words translated "spirit" (*rûaḥ* in the Hebrew Old Testament and *pneuma* in the Greek New Testament) can also mean wind or breath. So the Holy Spirit may be compared to God's breath, and "ultimately breath signifies activity and life."[1] To speak, then, of God's Spirit is to emphasize that God is the living God, who is incessantly active. However, what becomes increasingly clear as God's revelation in Scripture progresses is that talk about his Spirit is more than merely a reference to divine life and activity: the Spirit of God is personal—and the early church drew out the implications of this in its explanation of the truth of God's triune nature.

BIBLICAL FOUNDATION

Old Testament

It is often claimed that the presence and work of the Holy Spirit was far more restricted in Old Testament times than in the New Testament, that the earliest Old Testament texts portray the Spirit's work as "a temporary

1. Payne, "*rûaḥ*," 2131a.

endowment for a specific task."[2] One example which seems to support this claim is Samson: we read several times of the Spirit coming upon him (Judg 13:25; 14:6, 19; 15:14).

However, this is not true without qualification. Ronald Youngblood points out that "such a view overlooks the indispensable animating role of the Spirit in effecting spiritual renewal in the Old Testament," and also disregards David's prayer, "do not take your Holy Spirit from me" (Ps 51:11).[3] Those words imply that David was well aware of the Spirit's permanent presence (cf. 1 Sam 16:13), a reality which he dreaded losing.

The Old Testament contains many indications that believers then knew a far more profound experience of the Spirit than merely a temporary endowment for a specific task. God said that Caleb "has a different spirit in him" (Num 14:24). Joshua was "a man in whom *is* the Spirit" (Num 27:18). The work of the Spirit was evident in both Elijah and Elisha (2 Kgs 2:9, 15).

Brian Edwards, while recognizing that "there is a new era of the work of the Spirit with the coming of the Messiah," nevertheless rightly insists that "under the old covenant the Spirit was at work both in the individual and in the community."[4] John Owen reminds us that "everything that is *good*, even under the Old Testament" is assigned to the Holy Spirit "as the sole immediate author of it."[5]

We shall select four representative texts and passages to illustrate the Old Testament teaching on the Holy Spirit.

Genesis 1:2

God's Spirit is mentioned as early as the second verse of the whole Bible. He is hovering over the pristine creation, as yet unformed and unfilled. He is poised in readiness to begin implementing what the divine word will demand. We learn that God's work of creation was accomplished by his Spirit.

The word translated "hovering" (*rāḥap*) reappears in Deuteronomy 32:11, which compares the LORD's care for his people to a parent eagle training its young to fly. The eagle stirs up the nest so that the baby bird

2. Budd, *Numbers*, 268.
3. Youngblood, "1 and 2 Samuel," 686.
4. B. Edwards, *Pray for Revival*, 51, 67.
5. Owen, "Holy Spirit," 151.

falls out. At first the baby does not know how to spread its wings, and seems to be plummeting to its death. In ample time, the parent bird, having hovered above, now swoops underneath, catches its young, and carries it back to the safety of the nest.

The verbal connection between these two verses implies that it is the work of the Holy Spirit to preserve God's creation. He hovers ready to prevent its collapse. That was so at the moment of initial creation, and it remains the task of the Holy Spirit every day. Were the Holy Spirit ever to relax his preserving power, then God's creation would most certainly disintegrate. Creation has no intrinsic self-preserving capacity. The Holy Spirit is "the source of all order, life and light in the universe. He is the divine principle of all movement, of all life, and of all thought in the world."[6]

The role of the Spirit in relation to creation is emphasized in a number of Old Testament contexts. The beauty of the heavens is the work of God's Spirit (Job 26:13). The renewal of the earth and the mating of the animals every Spring are attributed to God's Spirit (Ps 104:30; Isa 34:16), and it is the Spirit of the LORD who directs the movements and the stopping places of all the animals (Isa 63:14). Every detail in creation is "implemented by his Spirit."[7]

In connection with the doctrine of creation, we noted how the New Testament speaks of God the Son as the agent of creation, and the one in whom all things hold together (Col 1:16–17). How does the emphasis in Genesis 1:2 relate to that truth? We have to remember that all God's external works, including creation, are works of the triune God, in which Father, Son, and Holy Spirit share unitedly. We cannot separate the two persons of the Son and the Spirit. The Holy Spirit is the Spirit of Christ, and it is by the Spirit's presence that Christ's power is exerted.

Exodus 35:30–35

We read here of a practical wisdom which God gave the artisans called to make the equipment for the tabernacle. Bezalel and his assistants are filled with wisdom, understanding, knowledge, and workmanship, to enable them to design and do the work. The Hebrew word rendered "filled"

---

6. Warfield, *Biblical Doctrines*, 107.
7. Motyer, *Isaiah*, 272.

denotes an abundant fullness.[8] But at the head of the list of attributes with which they are filled stands the statement, "he has filled him with the Spirit of God." The Spirit was the source of their skill and knowledge, the fountain from which all their ability flowed.

Perhaps this is just one particular example of the universal truth that all human abilities find their source in the Holy Spirit. In the parallel passage in Exodus 31:6 God says: "I have put wisdom in the hearts of all the gifted artisans." Perhaps those words carry us beyond the immediate context of the construction of the tabernacle. Isaiah 28:24–29 depicts all human skill, even in tasks connected with farming, as coming from the LORD of hosts. John Calvin, acknowledges that Bezalel's call was special, because of the unique task to which he was appointed. He then continues: "no one excels even in the most despised and humble handicraft, except in so far as God's Spirit works in him," and this is true, not just in spiritual gifts, "but in all the branches of knowledge which come into use in common life."[9]

Isaiah

A recurring theme in this book is that when the promised Messiah comes he will be anointed by the Holy Spirit. In the use of the word "rest" (*nûah*), Isaiah 11:2 implies that the Spirit of the LORD will take up permanent residence in Christ.

The initial reference to "the Spirit of the LORD" is amplified by three pairs of qualities which will result from the anointing of the Holy Spirit: Christ will know true wisdom and understanding, will possess real counsel and might, and will be blessed with genuine knowledge and fear of the LORD.

Alexander notes that "the qualities enumerated are not to be confounded as mere synonyms, nor on the other hand distinguished with metaphysical precision."[10] All six terms are related to the work of the Spirit as the instructor. Each brings out a different aspect of the Spirit's revelatory function, and together they express the fullness of divine understanding granted to Jesus Christ.

Albert Barnes asks and answers a pertinent question:

8. Van Pelt & Kaiser, "*ml'*," 939.

9. Calvin, *Books of Moses*, Vol. 3, 291.

10. Alexander, *Isaiah*, 220.

> If it be asked how one, who was divine in his own nature, could be thus endowed by the aid of the Spirit, the answer is, that he was also to be a man descended from the honored line of David, and that as a man he might be furnished for his work by the agency of the Holy Spirit. His human nature was kept pure; his mind was made eminently wise; his heart always retained the fear and love of God, and there is no absurdity in supposing that these extraordinary endowments were to be traced to God.[11]

According to Isaiah 42:1–4, the rule of God's righteous servant will be marked by gentleness, determined perseverance, and justice embracing all nations. The source of this achievement is found in God's words in verse 1, "I have put my Spirit upon him." The verb "put" is *nātan*, which can mean "to give," denoting that the Spirit is the Father's gift to his Son. Matthew 12:15–21 highlights the fulfilment of this passage in the ministry of Jesus.

In chapter 61:1–3 Christ himself speaks prophetically. He takes up the reference in the earlier chapters to the Spirit being upon him, and uses the word "anointed." The Hebrew term is *māšaḥ*, the root of our word "Messiah." Jesus expressly applies this passage to himself in Luke 4:16–21.

Joel 2:28–32a

A key feature of the Old Testament's future hope is the promise of the outpouring of the Spirit. These words of Joel are central to this issue. These are the verses to which Peter alluded as he preached in Acts 2, on the Day of Pentecost.

In verse 28 the LORD says that "it shall come to pass afterward that I will pour out my Spirit on all flesh." The word translated "afterward" is sometimes used in the Old Testament in an eschatological sense, but may be merely a general reference to future time. The question must therefore be raised as to which sense is to be understood here.

When Peter quoted this passage in Acts 2:17–21, "afterward" was rendered "in the last days." Reading the Old Testament in the light of the New, as we always must, determines that here the Hebrew word should be understood eschatologically. The prophet is looking forward to

---

11. Barnes, *Old Testament*, Isaiah, Vol. 1, 223.

something which God will accomplish during the final epoch of history, during the period inaugurated by the coming of Christ.

What that accomplishment will be is the pouring out of his Spirit on all flesh, which in the immediate context of verses 28–29 is elaborated to mean both genders, all age groups, and every social class, though, as Acts 2 makes clear, it also refers to the expansion of the reach of the gospel to the entire human race. The result will be the proclamation of the Word of God, here depicted in terms of prophecy, dreams and visions.

Verses 30 and 31 refer to wonders which will take place. Specifically, the sun will be turned to darkness, and the moon to blood. This is sometimes read as a description of eschatological upheavals, but this seems to be a misreading. Verse 30 dates these things before the coming of the great and awesome day of the LORD, that is, before the day of Christ's return in judgment. They are things that happen throughout the age between Pentecost and the second coming.

We must read these verses in the context of this whole passage: their fulfilment is the outpouring of the Spirit, resulting, as verse 32 adds, in the salvation of all who call on the name of the LORD. The significance of the imagery is that the Holy Spirit will cause the glory of the Lord Jesus Christ to outshine everything: in comparison with him, even the sun will seem dark, and so people will call on his name for salvation. The word "everyone" throws open the invitation to salvation to the whole world. That is to be the scope of the Holy Spirit's ministry in the gospel age, as foreseen by Old Testament prophecy.

New Testament

The New Testament is so full of references to the Holy Spirit that we shall have to be very selective. The Spirit is mentioned as early as the first chapter of the New Testament, where twice, in verses 18 and 20, we hear that Jesus Christ was conceived in Mary's womb by the Holy Spirit. The Spirit plays a prominent role in Jesus' ministry: he descends at his baptism; he leads Jesus both towards his temptations, and back to commence his ministry; he is involved in Jesus' exorcisms, in his death, and in his resurrection.

Our concern now will be the New Testament teaching on the role of the Holy Spirit in the life of the church and the believer. We shall look first at three key passages, and then at the theme of the baptism of the Spirit, which brings together a number of texts.

Three Key Passages

JOHN 14—16

In these chapters we hear Jesus' own most extensive teaching on this subject, given in the course of his farewell address in the upper room.

In John 14:16–17 Jesus uses two titles for the Holy Spirit.

First, he is the Helper. This title reappears three times later in these chapters (John 14:26; 15:26; 16:7). It renders the Greek term *paraklētos*. Etymologically this refers to one who is called alongside. The implication is that the Spirit is at the side of Jesus' followers to help them. A theme which runs through the New Testament is that the Holy Spirit helps the church and individual believers by empowering us for Christian mission and witness.

Second, he is "the Spirit of truth." This is the first of three occurrences of this title (cf. John 15:26; 16:13). A few verses earlier (John 14:6), the Lord Jesus called himself "the truth," and then in John 17:17 he identifies God's word as the truth. Jesus Christ is the embodiment of God's word, and the Holy Spirit is the invisible, spiritual representation of Christ.

We are told both negatively and positively of the Spirit's destination.

Negatively, he is not received by the world, and indeed, it is impossible for the world to receive him. This is linked with the world's inability to see or know the Spirit. This, of course, refers to the absence of eyes of faith to penetrate beyond the merely visible.

Conversely, the gift of the Spirit is portrayed positively as being to Jesus' disciples. He will be with them, remaining with them forever, and he will not merely be with them, but also in them. As a result, they will know him, with "a knowledge grounded in personal experience."[12]

In John 14:26 we have one of only two recorded occasions in John's Gospel (cf. John 20:22) where Jesus uses the full term "Holy Spirit." This name draws attention to the Spirit's participation in the divine holiness, and so underlines his true divinity.

The Spirit's work now begins to be defined. Its first element is a teaching ministry. The two ideas of teaching and bringing to remembrance

---

12. Thayer, *Lexicon*, 118.

what Jesus has said are more or less identical concepts. The Holy Spirit is not the source of fresh teaching, so much as the authoritative interpreter of the words of the Lord. He enables the disciples to grasp Jesus' teaching in depth.

That the Spirit's message is not a new and independent revelation, but an exposition of the teaching of Christ, must be true, since Christ is God's final word (Heb 1:1–2). The Spirit's interpretative ministry comes to fruition in the definitive apostolic interpretation of Jesus in the books of the New Testament.

In John 15:26 Jesus says of the Spirit, "he will testify of me." This shows that the Spirit also has an evangelistic role. His task is to enable the world to receive the testimony to Jesus through the preaching of the gospel by the disciples. It is such an encouragement as we evangelize to know that we are not on our own, that we are simply the mouthpiece of the Spirit.

In this verse the Lord introduces another term: the Spirit "proceeds" (*ekporeuomai*) from the Father. This word denotes a movement from one place to another. The form of the verb (*ekporeuetai*) includes the sense of independent action. Although the Father sends the Spirit, at the same time, the Spirit carries himself forth on his mission. This double truth again underlines the real personal divinity of the Holy Spirit.

Jesus' next reference to the Spirit comes in John 16:7–11. He links the coming of the Spirit with his own departure. His return to glory via the cross was the moment when the new covenant promise, predicted in the Old Testament, would be fulfilled. Jesus is reminding his disciples that "as long as he was with them in person, his work was localized;" however, the Spirit's coming "would equip them for a wider and more potent ministry."[13]

Jesus now brings out yet another aspect of the Spirit's work: he will have a convicting ministry. The verb translated "convict" in verse 8 (*elenchō*) occurs also in John 3:20, translated "exposed." Its use there helps to elucidate its significance: an evildoer will avoid the light "lest his deeds should be exposed," conclusively exposed, that is, as evil.

We may summarize verses 8–11 as follows: it is the work of the Spirit to convince the sinful world that the primary sin is failure to believe in Christ, that the absence of Christ from the world and his presence in heaven vindicates his righteousness, despite his condemnation by the

13. Tenney, "John," 157.

world, and that his condemnation by the world therefore turns out to be the world's condemnation by God.

John 16:13–15 sums up what Jesus has already said about the teaching and evangelistic aspects of the Holy Spirit's ministry, but adds one further element in his work. He has a prophetic ministry: "he will tell you things to come." Certainty about the future hope for Jesus and his kingdom is needed for the encouragement of the church in darker days. The Lord taught about the future, the end of the age, his return, and part of the Spirit's role of bringing Jesus' teaching to remembrance will be to enable the apostles to give clear expression to the eschatological truth about Jesus.

1 Corinthians 12—14

Here we find the apostle Paul's main teaching on the work of the Spirit in the life of the Christian church. The precise understanding of some of what is said here is open to debate. The main issue is whether it was God's intention that all the gifts of the Spirit mentioned in these chapters would be permanent realities (the charismatic view), or whether they were a temporary provision pending the completion of God's revelation in the New Testament Scripture (the cessationist view).

This leads to a difference in the exegesis of these chapters. On the charismatic view the passage is prescriptive, extolling the purpose of the gifts. On the cessationist view the passage is regulatory, restricting the unhelpful outcome of the gifts.

It is not my intention to enter that debate at any length. There is plenty of teaching here on the Holy Spirit on which everyone can agree. That will be our focus. It is worth noting these words, written by John Chrysostom around AD 300:

> This whole place is very obscure: but the obscurity is produced
> by our ignorance of the facts referred to and by their cessation,
> being such as then used to occur but now no longer take place.[14]

If ignorance of the nature of the gifts was a fact a mere 250 years after the canon of Scripture was completed, how much more is it the case in the twenty-first century! That observation should caution all of us against being too dogmatic about what these chapters are referring to.

14. Chrysostom, "Corinthians," 384.

Paul starts by identifying the topic of this section of the letter: the first verse of chapter 12 tells us that it is about "spiritual *gifts*." The initial point is the Spirit's loyalty to Christ: verse 3 insists that it is by the Spirit that we recognize the Lordship of Jesus. When the Lordship of Christ is obvious in the church, that is the most important sign that the Spirit is at work.

Verses 4–6 use three synonymous terms in parallel: gifts, ministries, and activities, but each is a "manifestation of the Spirit" (verse 7). The various expressions of spiritual life are ways in which the invisible divine Spirit is brought into view. "Gifts" underlines the truth that every manifestation is given undeservedly by sheer grace. "Ministries" stresses that every manifestation must be used with a servant-spirit. The word behind "activities" draws attention to the truth that such service is only possible when divine energy is supplied.

Nine manifestations of the Spirit are then listed, and verse 11 emphasizes the fact that the distribution is according to the Spirit's will.

However, the specific matter of the Spirit's manifestations is part of a larger issue. Verses 12 to 27 portray the church as a body into which the Spirit has placed us individually, with all our differences of cultural background and personality, and therefore with differing potential to contribute to the life of the church. Verse 28 mentions eight roles within the church, four of which are not found in the earlier list of manifestations, so a total of 13 activities is catalogued in the chapter.

Two phrases require particular attention. Verse 13 reads as follows: "by one Spirit we were all baptized into one body—whether Jews or Greeks, whether slaves or free—and have all been made to drink into one Spirit."

This is the only place where the New Testament uses the language of baptism in association with the Holy Spirit in individual terms. It probably refers to water baptism, as employed by the Holy Spirit as a means of grace, while to "drink into one Spirit" probably speaks of the inward work of grace, which is the essential counterpart of the external sacrament. The point is that only through the power of the Spirit can anyone become a Christian. Paul twice insists that this twofold reality applies to all of us. As Clement of Alexandria noted, it is not the case that some believers are enlightened, while others are less perfectly spiritual; everyone "is equal and spiritual before the Lord."[15]

15. Clement of Alexandria, "Paedagogos," 1.5.31.

The Spirit is not mentioned in chapter 13, where love is depicted as the indispensable ingredient in the exercise of spiritual gifts. Chapter 14 then returns to the way in which manifestations of the Spirit must function. They are to be desired (verse 1), but are only to be used for building up the church (verses 3, 5, 12). This drives home what the apostle has said in the brief digression about the use of tongues in verses 2–11: speaking meaningless mysteries has no value for the church as a whole. Verses 14–16 speak of the Spirit and the mind in parallel. These are sometimes read as contrasting ways of praying and singing, but it is equally possible that Paul's point is to equate the two: true Spirit-led prayer and song will always engage the mind. Certainly, the following verses stress emphatically the duty of all to ensure that everyone present at a meeting can understand. When that happens, the potential for the Spirit to bring conviction is immense (verses 24–25).

GALATIANS 5:16–25

In this passage the apostle depicts a contrast between two opposing sets of desires—those of the flesh and those of the Spirit. To "walk in the Spirit" is to fulfil his desires and to avoid giving ourselves fleshly gratification, as he works within us the genuine desire to do the things that please the Lord. Walking in the Spirit is later distinguished from living in the Spirit (verse 25). What, then, is the difference?

We need first to note that the word "walk" in verses 16 and 25 translates two different terms in the original Greek. In verse 16 the term is *peripateō*, the normal word for strolling along; this denotes the unhurried regularity of life's progress. To "walk in the Spirit" is persistently to live as directed by the Holy Spirit, making gradual but steady progress. The word used in verse 25 is *stoicheō*. This speaks of "leading a closely regulated life, living according to definite rules."[16] The implication is that God's law is the tool which the Spirit uses to direct the Christian life. It is true that verse 18 has said, "if you are led by the Spirit, you are not under the law." However, "the law" should probably be understood there, in line with the dominant usage in Galatians, in an epochal sense, as the entire Old Testament system before the fulfilment in Christ. Certainly, the age of the Spirit has superseded "the law" understood in that sense. Nevertheless, it is clear from Galatians 5:13–14 that the apostle still sees,

---

16. Esser, "stoicheia," 452.

within the life of the Spirit, a role for the law, understood as its moral demands independent of its former epochal function.

Verses 19–24 contrast "the works of the flesh," which "those *who are* Christ's have crucified," with "the fruit of the Spirit." We are given some examples of works of the flesh, and a list of nine qualities which characterize the fruit of the Spirit (verses 22–23).

We need to notice three things.

(1) The contrast between works and fruit reminds us that fleshly behavior stems from our very nature as sinners, and therefore is a set of works which we do. By contrast, the transformed life of the believer is one whose qualities do not grow out of the natural soil of our own hearts: it is produced by the indwelling Spirit.

(2) The contrast between the plural (works) and the singular (fruit) is probably significant. The Spirit-led life is an integrated unity, whereas the fleshly life is a disorderly chaos.

(3) At the end of verse 23 we read that there is no law against the fruit of the Spirit. This may well be an example of a rhetorical device known as "litotes." This means that a negative expression, often incorporating a double negative, is used as way of strongly asserting its positive counterpart. We have here a double negative ("against" and "no"), and the meaning is that "the fruit of the Spirit is in complete accordance with the law."[17] This would emphasize the point that the chief instrument which the Holy Spirit uses in shaping the life of the believer is God's revealed law. We are not helpless robots, merely manipulated by the Spirit: the Spirit works through our minds and hearts, and energizes us to obedience.

The Baptism of the Holy Spirit

John the Baptist told his hearers that the one who came after him would baptize them with the Holy Spirit (Matt 3:11; Mark 1:8; Luke 3:16; John 1:33). After his resurrection, the Lord Jesus refers back to John's words: "you shall be baptized with the Holy Spirit not many days from now" (Acts 1:5).

The baptism with the Spirit has sometimes been misunderstood. The Acts of the Apostles makes it clear that it is an alternative term for Pentecost.

17. Bayes, *Weakness*, 168.

In Acts 11 the apostle Peter is reporting on the events at the home of the Roman centurion, Cornelius, recorded in the previous chapter. Peter has been called to account by the church at Jerusalem for eating with Gentiles, but he recalls how, as he preached the gospel, "the Holy Spirit fell upon all those who heard the word" (Acts 10:44). He refers back to Jesus' quotation of John: he "remembered the word of the Lord, how he said, 'John indeed baptized with water, but you shall be baptized with the Holy Spirit'" (Acts 11:16). He continues by pointing out how "God gave the same gift to them as he gave to us" (verse 17), alluding there to Pentecost. The Gentiles' experience is a further fulfilment of John's reference to the baptism of the Holy Spirit, akin to what had taken place at Pentecost, which was its initial fulfilment.

We need to note the variety of terms which are used here. Acts 10:44 says that the Holy Spirit "fell" on the hearers. Peter picks up this word in Acts 11:15. Acts 10:45 uses the phrase "poured out," repeating a word used in the quotation from Joel in Acts 2:17–18. Peter employs it again as he explains the Pentecost events in Acts 2:33. It is used again in Titus 3:6. In Acts 10:47 we hear that the Gentiles "received" the Holy Spirit. Peter used the same word in Acts 2:38, at the end of his Pentecost sermon, as he promised those who repented that they would receive the Holy Spirit.

Two of these words ("fell" and "received") are used again with reference to the Holy Spirit later in Acts. Both appear in tandem in Acts 8:15–17, where another event akin to Pentecost has taken place, this time in Samaria. Paul also uses "receive" in Acts 19:2. Having met some disciples in Corinth, he asks them. "Did you receive the Holy Spirit when you believed?" On discovering that they are as yet only disciples of John the Baptist, he preaches Jesus, they believe and are baptized, and then, we are told, "the Holy Spirit came upon them" (verse 6). Here we have yet another term occurring in parallel with "receive," and it is the same verb which is used in Matthew 3:16 of the Holy Spirit "alighting" on Jesus at his baptism.

It seems, then, that the New Testament uses a variety of terms, all of which describe Pentecost and later similar events. We need not overpress any distinctions between them. Taken together, they are various ways of speaking of the same phenomenon—that of which Pentecost in Acts 2 is the prototype. On that occasion the Spirit was poured out on Jews in Jerusalem. In Acts 8 the Spirit falls upon Samaria. The events in Acts 10, which Peter describes in chapter 11, witness an outpouring of the Spirit upon Gentiles, and in Acts 19, there is a further coming of the Spirit on to more distant Gentiles.

It appears that there was a Pentecost-like event every time that the gospel broke new ground. The movement corresponds roughly with the outward expansion of gospel witness in the power of the Holy Spirit which Jesus indicated in Acts 1:8: "in Jerusalem, and in all Judea and Samaria, and to the end of the earth." Witness took place in Jerusalem/Judea (Acts 2), Samaria (Acts 8), and then made its first inroads towards the end of the earth (Acts 10—11 and 19). With each new stage of gospel progress a baptism with the Spirit took place.

"Baptism with the Spirit" is, therefore, primarily a geographical thing. It defines the coming of the gospel to a new locality or a new cultural sphere. It is equivalent to what, today, we call "revival." It takes place whenever the gospel penetrates a new area or a new people group, or perhaps when the gospel recaptures lost ground with renewed power. Albert Barnes develops this thought in his notes on the book of Acts.[18] In his introduction he says,

> This book shows that revivals of religion are to be expected in the church. If they existed in the best and purest days of Christianity, they are to be expected now. If by means of revivals the Holy Spirit chose at first to bless the preaching of the truth, the same thing is to be expected still. If in this way the gospel was at first spread among the nations, then we are to infer that this will be the mode in which it will finally spread and triumph in the world.

Then, amongst his comments on Acts 2, Barnes notes that Peter's explanation of what happened on the Day of Pentecost teaches us

> that revivals of religion are to be expected as a part of the history of the Christian church. He speaks of God's pouring out his Spirit, as what was to take place *in the last days*, that is in the indefinite and large tract of time which was to come under the administration of the Messiah. His remarks are by no means limited to the day of Pentecost. They are as applicable to future periods as to that time; and we are to expect it as a part of Christian history, that the Holy Spirit will be sent down to awaken and convert men.

18. Barnes, *New Testament,* Vol. 3, v, 35–36.

We might add that, in times of revival, the awakening and converting of people will take place in large numbers.

DOCTRINAL FORMULATION

The Early Creeds

The section on the Holy Spirit in the Apostles' Creed merely affirms that the Holy Spirit exists: "I believe in the Holy Spirit." Commenting on the creed around the year 400 Rufinus observed that "by the mention of the Holy Spirit, the mystery of the Trinity is completed." It does indeed seem that this reference to the Holy Spirit is there for little more than the sake of completeness, though Rufinus also notes that to confess belief *in* the Holy Spirit serves to identify the Holy Spirit with God, and gives him equal status with the Father and the Son, who, according to the creed, are also believed *in*.[19] The only other relevant point made in the Apostles' Creed is that it was through the Holy Spirit that Jesus Christ was conceived.

The Nicene and Athanasian Creeds are more elaborate, and we can summarize their teaching on the Holy Spirit under five statements.

The Son of God was incarnate of the Holy Spirit by the virgin Mary

There is a difference of emphasis between the Apostles' and the Nicene Creeds. The Apostles' Creed draws attention to the miracle of the virgin birth: that was achieved by the power of the Holy Spirit. The Nicene Creed draws attention to the fact that the person conceived in the virgin's womb was none other than God in human form—and it was that which really demanded the exertion of the Holy Spirit's power.

The Holy Spirit is a distinct person within the Godhead, and at the same time equally divine with the Father and the Son

All the divine attributes are as applicable to the Holy Spirit as to the Father and the Son, and yet it would be wrong to divide God into three: threeness relates to the persons, and yet there is oneness as God.

---

19. Rufinus, "Apostles' Creed," 35–36.

The Nicene Creed calls the Holy Spirit "Lord." This may be equivalent to the affirmation in the Athanasian Creed to the effect that the Father is Lord, the Son is Lord, and the Holy Spirit is Lord, and yet there are not three Lords. That is to say, the use of the word "Lord" is a way of stating the full deity of the Holy Spirit. The Nicene Creed also insists that the Holy Spirit is equally worthy of worship and glory with the Father and the Son.

The Holy Spirit is the lifegiver

This is an echo of biblical language. The creed uses a noun, but it is equivalent to the verb in John 6:63 ("it is the Spirit who gives life") and 2 Corinthians 3:6 ("the letter kills, but the Spirit gives life"). In the former Scripture the reference is to the life given in regeneration. In the latter context the new covenant experience is in view, and it can be summed up in that all-encompassing word, "life," whereas, when the law is received as mere "letter," it is deadly. New covenant life is the fruit of the Spirit's presence.

The Holy Spirit spoke by the prophets

The creeds are clear that whenever we read or listen to the Bible, we are hearing the voice of the Spirit.

The Holy Spirit proceeds from the Father and the Son

The Athanasian Creed sought to express the interrelatedness of the persons of the Trinity, while preserving the essential distinctions between them, by deliberately using varied but specific vocabulary. It says that the Father was neither created nor begotten, that the Son was not created, but was begotten, and that the Holy Spirit was neither created nor begotten, but proceeds. The word "proceeds" was borrowed from John 15:26, where Jesus refers to "the Spirit of truth who proceeds from the Father."

Those words look forward to the outpouring of the Spirit for his temporal mission after Christ has accomplished redemption, but Palmer Robertson thinks that this temporal procession must be rooted in an eternal procession of the Spirit from the Father and the Son.[20] It seems

20. Robertson, "Holy Spirit," 72.

that the composers of the creed also saw the procession of the Spirit at Pentecost as a reflection of eternal realities within the divine being.

Christ speaks of the Spirit's procession from the Father only. The earliest form of the creed also stopped with the statement that the Holy Spirit "proceeds from the Father." The words which form our heading for this point are taken from the version of the creed which became normative for the Latin-speaking churches of western Europe and North Africa from the eighth century, speaking of procession from the Father and the Son. This involved the insertion in the Latin edition of the creed of just one additional word—*filioque*—meaning "and the Son." This was one of the issues which led to a divergence from the Greek-speaking churches of Eastern Europe and the Middle East, culminating in a complete division in 1054. The eastern churches continued to speak of the Spirit's procession from the Father alone. They were happy to say that the Spirit proceeded from the Father through the Son, but since the oldest form of the creed read "who proceeds from the Father," they preferred not to tamper with the established wording.

It is necessary to try to understand the issues at stake in this disagreement. We must note first that both sides were driven by exactly the same motivation—to safeguard the unity of the triune God. They differed over how best to maintain this truth.

The main thing which those who added *filioque* to the creed were aiming at was to avoid any implication that the Father was somehow more divine than the Son. Kelly defines it as a cardinal premise of Augustine's

> that whatever could be predicated of one of the persons could be predicated of the others. So it was inevitable that he should regard the denial of the double procession as violating the unity and simplicity of the Godhead.[21]

Underlying this was the view that the Trinity starts from the one Godhead, Father, Son, and Holy Spirit all sharing equally in the one divine nature.

By contrast, eastern writers tended to see the Father as the starting-point of the Trinity, and as the source of the Son and the Spirit. From a western viewpoint, this seemed to put the co-equality of the three persons at risk, even though that was definitely not the intention of the eastern churches. Ted Campbell's explanation of the issue at stake is succinct and helpful:

21. J. N. D. Kelly, *Creeds*, 359.

Western theologians argued that adding the words "and the Son" was a more appropriate expression of the equality of the persons. Without these words, they argued, God the Father would appear to be the only source of the Godhead, and so could be seen as having priority over the Son and the Holy Spirit. Eastern theologians reasoned differently. The expression "from the Father" (without "and the Son") expressed better the equality of the persons, as they saw it, since it would be unbalanced to have the Son originating from the Father only, and the Spirit originating from the Father and the Son.[22]

Robert Reymond suggests that on this question both eastern and western theologians were going beyond Scripture and into the realms of speculation. He comments like this:

> There can be no question that the Holy Spirit is a divine person who is the Spirit of God and of Christ, and that he "proceeded" or "came forth" from the Father and the Son at Pentecost on his salvific mission. But *we must not attempt to define, beyond the fact of the clearly implied order, a modal "how" of the Spirit's spiration.* It is enough to know that the Scriptures affirm that this title distinguishes a third subjective conscious self in the depth of the divine being.[23]

The Reformation Confessions

It is often regarded as strange that the Reformation confessions do not devote a section to the person and work of the Holy Spirit. This is not because of any lack of interest in the subject: the confessions are packed with references to the Spirit. In almost every section he is mentioned somewhere. This demonstrates the profound conviction on the part of the Reformers that the gospel is a supernatural message, and that the work of the Spirit is basic to the entire Christian life, and to all spiritual experience. So all-pervading is the reality of the Spirit that it seemed superfluous to include in the confessions a special section devoted exclusively to the doctrine of the Holy Spirit.

We shall note nine themes connected with the Holy Spirit. The content will show how comprehensive is the confessions' treatment of this doctrine.

22. Campbell, *Confessions*, 85.
23. Reymond, *New Systematic Theology*, 336 [italics original].

The Nature of the Holy Spirit

On this point the confessions follow the early creeds. They insist that the Holy Spirit is true and eternal God. He is the third person in the order of the Trinity, and shares the same essence as the Father and the Son. Three particular words are used to emphasize the Holy Spirit's full and true deity: he is co-essential, co-eternal, and co-equal with the Father and the Son. The confessions speak of the majesty and glory of the Spirit, which is identical with that of the Father and the Son. It follows that the Spirit is to be worshipped with the Father and the Son. Although the confessions describe the Holy Spirit as eternal power and might, and as the virtue, power and efficacy of the Father, this must not be read as in any way denying his own individual personhood.

Not surprisingly, given their western provenance, the confessions cite the western version of the creeds, and state that the Spirit proceeds from the Father and the Son. Several confessions note that the procession is eternal.

With reference to the Westminster Confession Robert Reymond suggests that its framers were deliberately taking their stand with the ancient creeds, but also draws attention to the reserve shown in the wording of the confession, which is not as elaborate in its speculation as were the creeds. This, he suggests, may well indicate the intention to see procession only as a statement of order, and not of being.[24]

Palmer Robertson defends the addition of the word *filioque* in that it "binds the person and work of the triune God into an indivisible unity," and avoids undermining the equality of the Son with the Father. He notes the danger of viewing the work of the Spirit apart from the redemption achieved by Christ, so that communion with the Spirit becomes more significant than Christ's atonement, and the inner illumination of the Spirit is treated as though it can occur apart from the Word of God. He makes the following comment on much contemporary Evangelicalism:

> Exclusive concentration on the working of the Spirit in the soul has virtually excluded an awareness of the fact that the Spirit proceeds in his work only from the sacrificed Son of God.[25]

On this point Robertson quotes Edwin Palmer, who said that "a denial of the *filioque* leads to an unhealthy mysticism," because a failure to

24. Reymond, *New Systematic Theology*, 340.
25. Robertson, "Holy Spirit," 72–74.

recognize the procession of the Spirit from the Son "tends to isolate the work of the Holy Spirit in our lives from the work of Jesus."[26]

The Holy Spirit and the Scriptures

Not only did the Scriptures originate from the Holy Spirit, but in their permanent existence they are the voice of the Spirit. Ultimately, he wrote the Bible, moving men of God to write down exactly what God intended them to say. Therefore, whenever we read God's Word as given by the prophets and apostles, we are listening to the Holy Spirit. Moreover, the whole counsel of God is found in the Scriptures. Because they are Spirit-inspired, their sufficiency is guaranteed. It follows that no new revelations are possible. The closure of the canon was final.

It is by the powerful witness of the Spirit that believers are convinced that the Scriptures are indeed God's Word. There is an inward persuasion in our hearts which assures us that the books of the Bible have divine authority and are infallibly true. This is not something merely mystical. It is by the Word itself that the Spirit's persuasion comes. He enables us to understand and perceive in our hearts as the Word is read or preached that it is the voice of God which we are hearing.

The confessions also stress that the Holy Spirit alone is the true interpreter of Scripture. The Spirit can never contradict himself. If any interpretation of one part of Scripture involves a contradiction with another part, then it is clear that the human interpreter has misunderstood the Spirit's meaning. Any controversy over the meaning of Scripture can only be settled by careful examination of what the Spirit says throughout the Scriptures.

The Reformers were clear about the central message which the Spirit preaches in the Word. It may be summed up in these words from the Heidelberg Catechism: "The Holy Spirit teaches us in the gospel . . . that the whole of our salvation depends upon that one sacrifice of Christ which he offered for us on the cross."

The Holy Spirit in the Old Testament

The confessions are clear that the Holy Spirit has been an active agent in history from the very beginning. He was involved in the event of creation,

26. Palmer, *Holy Spirit*, 18.

and it is through his preserving work that the creation is maintained in existence and stability from day to day. He makes the glory and majesty of God everywhere present throughout creation.

Moreover, the Holy Spirit was active during the old covenant epoch in applying God's grace to the hearts of his people. The confessions are clear that the covenant of grace under the Old and New Testaments is one and the same: for God's elect since the dawn of time, forgiveness of sins and eternal salvation has been through faith in Christ. However, the covenant was differently administered before his coming, and the Old Testament administration was by promises, prophecies, sacrifices, circumcision, and so on—types which were designed to sustain the forward-looking faith in Christ of God's people at that time. Nonetheless, it was by the operation of the Holy Spirit that the old covenant was effective.

The Holy Spirit and Jesus Christ

The work of the Holy Spirit flourished in the life and ministry of Jesus Christ. The secret power of the Spirit came upon Mary so that the miraculous conception took place in her womb. It was the Holy Spirit who ensured that the one conceived was truly the Son of God. It was also by the power of the Spirit that the Son of God assumed human nature.

The work of the Holy Spirit is apparent at Jesus' baptism. He appeared in the form of a dove, symbolizing, as the Westminster Larger Catechism puts it, that Jesus "was anointed with the Holy Ghost above measure; and so set apart, and fully furnished with all authority and ability, to execute the offices of prophet, priest, and king."

It was through the power of the Holy Spirit that Jesus lived a life of perfect obedience, and through the eternal Spirit that he offered himself up as a sacrifice to God. Moreover, the outpouring of the Spirit was a benefit which followed from the ascension of Christ into heaven.

The Holy Spirit and the Beginning of the Christian life

The confessions are clear that no one can come to Christ apart from the work of the Spirit. Without his working we would all remain dead in trespasses and sins, enemies of God, and ignorant of Christ. We can have no spiritual life until we are quickened by the Spirit. The Spirit effectually calls God's elect to Christ and applies Christ to the sinner, so that the sinner becomes a partaker of all Christ's benefits.

All saving graces come from the Holy Spirit. The confessions explicitly mention the following.

(1) Illumination. The Spirit removes the darkness from our minds and gives us inward enlightenment so that we can understand the gospel.

(2) Regeneration. By the Spirit we are born again, as he works in the depths of our personality. The nature of regeneration is elaborated by the terms quickening and renewal, and in regeneration the Holy Spirit takes possession of our heart.

(3) Faith. The Spirit kindles upright faith in our hearts. Faith is not a mere deposit placed within us. The Holy Spirit works faith by changing our wills so that we become willing and able actually to believe. The Spirit's persuasion is mighty and effectual, yet it is still true to say that we do the believing. True faith is a trust from the heart—genuine, sincere and personal—relying on God to save us for Christ's sake.

(4) Justification. It is the Holy Spirit who applies justification to the life of the believer.

(5) Repentance. This involves turning from sin to God when the sinner has come to understand both the danger and the filth of sin so much that he laments and hates it, and resolves to walk in obedience because he has seen God's mercy in Christ. This too is a work of the Spirit in the heart of a sinner.

(6) Cleansing. The Heidelberg Catechism notes several times that sins are washed away and our pollution is cleansed by "the blood and Spirit" of Christ. It is a spiritual work to apply the blood of Christ to the soul, and the Holy Spirit carries it out by his power.

(7) Union with Christ. The Holy Spirit dwells both in Christ and in us. Consequently, by his effectual and vital influence, he engrafts us inseparably into Christ, and it is through his work that we partake of Christ and his benefits.

(8) Adoption. Since the Holy Spirit is the Spirit of adoption, it is through his work that we who once were children of wrath become children of God. Part of what adoption entails is that the Spirit of God's only begotten Son is given to us.

The Holy Spirit and the Continuation of the Christian life

The Holy Spirit is God's gift to his people. The new covenant believer receives a rich experience of the Spirit of God. However, the confessions are careful not to divide Christ and the Spirit: by his Spirit it is Christ who nourishes and strengthens our spiritual life. Under this heading we may note three things.

THE HOLY SPIRIT SANCTIFIES

It is the Holy Spirit who renews us in the image of God, and changes us little by little into the likeness of Christ. By his indwelling the Spirit operates as our sanctifier. Sanctification involves increasing purity of life. We die more and more to sin and lead a life defined by growth in holiness. This includes separation from the world, and is expressed in good works. The confessions use various phrases to express the means by which sanctification takes place. Our hearts are governed by the Spirit, by the Word, and by Christ through his Spirit.

One central theme running through the confessions is that God's moral law, summarized in the ten commandments is the believer's rule of life, and is the major tool of the Spirit in the work of sanctification.

This is important, because it means that the Spirit's method in sanctification is not one which dehumanizes us. The Spirit does not make us holy while we sit back and do nothing. He infuses grace for sanctification and enables us to exercise that grace. He bows our hearts to obedience so that we actually become heartily willing to live for God. The Westminster Confession puts it like this: "The Spirit of God subdues and enables the will of man to do freely and cheerfully that which the will of God revealed in the law requires to be done."

This does not mean that we have to wait for some special motion of the Spirit: our responsibility, because we have the influence of the indwelling Spirit, is to stir up the grace of obedience. Failure to do so grieves the Spirit.

THE CHRISTIAN EXPERIENCE OF THE HOLY SPIRIT

The believer's body is the temple of the Holy Spirit. The Spirit dwells in our hearts by faith. This means that the place of the Holy Spirit in the

Christian life is not merely theoretical. We may have, and ought to long for, true spiritual experience, genuine experiences of the Holy Spirit. The confessions particularly mention the following experiences.

(1) Fellowship with Christ. The confessions speak of fellowship with Christ in his graces, sufferings, death, resurrection, and glory. This is a glorious fellowship.

(2) Sealing. The confessions understand this as the Spirit's work of strengthening and increasing our faith in God's promises for our deepening comfort. It can be neither frustrated nor obliterated in the true believer. It also refers to the Holy Spirit as the first instalment of our eternal inheritance, the foretaste of glory. The practical result of this sealing is that our minds are drawn upwards so that we seek the things that are above.

(3) Assurance. Closely related to the experience of sealing is the believer's assurance of eternal life. This is the fruit of the Spirit's witness that we are indeed the children of God. One route to assurance suggested by the Westminster Larger Catechism would seem to be of only limited value: it suggests that believers may attain assurance "by the Spirit enabling them to discern in themselves those graces to which the promises of life are made." R. T. Kendall is, I think, right to argue that this route is actually fatal for assurance, because it bases assurance on sanctification and not on Christ.[27] Assurance is far firmer when the Holy Spirit turns our eyes upon Jesus alone.

(4) Prayer. To pray acceptably we need the help of the Holy Spirit, which comes in two ways. He enables us to understand what we should pray for, and he quickens our hearts so that we really want to pray.

(5) Battle. It is a result of the Spirit's presence in our hearts that the Christian life is a battle. Sinful infirmities also remain within us, so that the flesh and the Spirit fight against each other. Through the Spirit the believer must fight against the sinful nature. The Spirit enables us to resist filthy pleasures, to groan for deliverance, and to triumph over sin. Victory is progressive though: by the strength of the Spirit the regenerate nature increasingly overcomes, and the power of the flesh cannot extinguish the Spirit's work. The Holy Spirit never ceases to support the believer so that we stand in the hour of temptation.

(6) Comfort. The Holy Spirit is the comforter, and in the face of the battle, his comfort is what we need.

---

27. Kendall, *English Calvinism, passim.*

(7) Peace. Part of Christian experience of the Spirit is peace of conscience in the knowledge that sins are forgiven entirely through the grace of God without any merit on our part. To be released from the quest for worthiness is a liberating experience. It flows from being at peace with God through the love of the Lord Jesus Christ.

(8) Joy. This is one of the benefits accompanying and flowing from justification. The confessions see joy as virtually the defining characteristic of the Spirit's work in the believer's heart.

THE HOLY SPIRIT AND PERSEVERANCE

The confessions are clear that our final perseverance is dependent upon the Holy Spirit. We are too weak of ourselves to endure to the end. However, because the Spirit indwells, we are assured that we shall persevere to the end.

The Holy Spirit and the Consummation of the Christian life

The resurrection of the bodies of the just to honor at the last day is defined as a work of the Spirit.

The Holy Spirit and the Church

In defining the church the confessions refer to the Spirit: the true church is composed of the faithful, called out of the world by the Holy Spirit. He it is who gathers, defends, preserves, and increases the church. There are some elements of the work of the Spirit more particularly associated with the corporate life of the company of believers.

By the Spirit all believers are baptized into the one body. Just because there is one Spirit, there is but one church, and it is kept by the Spirit in the unity of the true faith.

The Spirit governs the church. He does so for Christ by means of the Word. Another way of putting this is that, by the Spirit and the Word, Christ as King governs his people.

Office and service in the church are the gift of the Spirit. By the Spirit Christ bestows heavenly gifts amongst the members of the church. The Spirit works through the various ministries of the church, making them effective. However, chief amongst the Spirit's gifts is Christ's own nearness to his people through his Spirit.

Christian worship, guided by the word, requires the empowering of the Spirit. This is particularly true in the use of the sacraments. Reformation theology understood the sacraments to be more than mere symbols: they were means of grace. However, their impact is dependent on the work of the Spirit as he works in our hearts as we receive them by faith. The Spirit confirms, strengthens, and increases our faith as we use the sacraments, causing us inwardly to receive what the sacraments outwardly represent. The outward washing of baptism represents inner cleansing—and that is achieved by the Spirit. The bread and wine represent Christ as our spiritual nourishment—and through the signs the Spirit leads us to the reality. The Heidelberg Catechism summarizes by saying that

> the Holy Spirit teaches us in the gospel, and assures us by the sacraments, that the whole of our salvation depends upon that one sacrifice of Christ which he offered for us on the cross.

The Holy Spirit and the Work of the Gospel

The Holy Spirit was active in the ministry of the apostles, and continues to energize all gospel preaching throughout the course of Christian history.

It is striking how frequently the phrases "Word and Spirit" or "Spirit and Word" occur in the confessions. The Reformers were absolutely clear that the Spirit works in conjunction with the Scriptures. They stressed this point repeatedly.

This is emphatically so when the gospel of Christ is preached. God's "Word and Spirit only do sufficiently and effectually reveal him unto men for their salvation." These words from the Westminster Larger Catechism are not pointing to two separate sources of saving revelation, either of which might operate alone, the Word or the Spirit. The linking word "and" ties Word and Spirit together, indicating that there is only one source of revelation—Word and Spirit in harmony. The Word is a dead letter until it is taken up powerfully by the Holy Spirit, and the Spirit says nothing except what he says in the Word. God's way of working for the salvation of sinners is explained by the Canons of Dort like this: he causes the gospel to be externally preached to them, and power-fully illuminates their minds by his Holy Spirit, that they may rightly understand and discern the things of the Spirit of God.

There is just one necessary qualification which the Westminster Confession makes to this vital emphasis on the unity of Word and Spirit. It says,

the grace of faith, whereby the elect are enabled to believe to the saving of their souls, is the work of the Spirit of Christ in their hearts, and is ordinarily wrought by the ministry of the Word.

The word "ordinarily" does concede that occasionally, though unusually, the Holy Spirit may work independently of the Word. There may rarely, though genuinely, be a direct and immediate work of the Spirit in the hearts of those "incapable of being outwardly called by the ministry of the Word," which includes those who die in infancy, and others whose mental incapacity renders normal understanding of the Word impossible.

Normally though, our evangelistic responsibility is twofold: to preach the gospel word, and to pray that the power of the Spirit may fall upon the preaching. Every gospel preacher must seek to preach in the power of the Spirit. Preaching cannot achieve anything unless it is in demonstration of the Spirit and of power. Prayer is vitally important as the pre-eminent signal of our awareness of our helpless dependence on the Holy Spirit.

However, the Westminster Larger Catechism contrasts preaching in the demonstration of the Spirit and power with words of merely human wisdom. This implies that there is an assumption that all sound biblical preaching is by definition in the demonstration of the Spirit. The confessions therefore display the genuine expectation that the Spirit will move in mighty power whenever the true gospel is preached.

Furthermore, the promise of the Spirit is the gospel promise *par excellence*. The gospel message is an invitation to men and women to have their lives transformed by the impact upon them of divine power.

Modern Confessions of Faith

The three modern non-western confessions which we have been using deliberately echo many of the emphases found in the early creeds. All three mention the Holy Spirit in their explanation of the truth of the Trinity. The Chinese confession rejects the idea that the Holy Spirit is only a kind of influence: he is emphatically a person of the Trinity. It defines the Spirit as "the Spirit of God, the Spirit of Christ, the Spirit of truth, and the Spirit of holiness," and therefore adds that he, along with the Father and the Son, receives worship. The Indonesian and Chinese confessions specifically mention the eternal nature of the Spirit in expressing his full divinity.

All three confessions stand with the early western tradition in affirming the double procession of the Spirit, though the Chinese confession avoids the term "proceeding," and says that "the Holy Spirit is sent by the Father and the Son." This represents the admirable desire to avoid wandering into speculation beyond the clear limits set by Scripture.

The Indian and Indonesian confessions both refer to the conception of Christ by the power of the Spirit.

Moreover, these confessions also stand firmly with the faith as understood by the Reformation. The Indonesian and Chinese confessions agree in defining the Scriptures as ultimately the work of the Holy Spirit, who inspired them. Quoting 2 Peter 1:21, the Indonesian confession notes that it was the Spirit who moved men to write. The Chinese confession also notes the implication of this truth:

> in seeking to understand Scripture, one must seek the leading of the Holy Spirit and follow the principle of interpreting Scripture by Scripture, and not taking anything out of context.

All three confessions allot most of their space in discussing the Holy Spirit to his role in human salvation. We shall refer to each in turn.

Confession of Faith of the United Church of Northern India

This confession focuses on the work of the Holy Spirit in the individual heart. It affirms that it is the Spirit who makes people partakers of salvation, and under that heading lists five specific things which he does: (1) he convinces people of their sin and misery; (2) he enlightens their minds in the knowledge of Christ; (3) he renews their wills; (4) he persuades and enables them to embrace Christ as Savior; (5) he works in believers all the fruits of righteousness.

This last point is elaborated by the statement that it is through the indwelling of the Spirit that believers are sanctified. In this gracious work, the Holy Spirit uses the means of grace, especially the word, the sacraments, and prayer. A further note observes that the working of the

Holy Spirit and reception by faith are essential if the sacraments are to be of any benefit. Clearly William Stewart is correct in his interpretation of this confession: "That men are saved is not at all their doing; it is always the work of him who has laid hold on them, and their acceptance of his choice of them is the work of the Holy Spirit."[28]

Confession of Faith of the Huria Kristen Batak Protestant

The Indonesian confession alludes to the fact that the faith and the good works of the individual believer are the Spirit's work. Indeed, good works not urged by the Spirit become sinful. However, the main emphasis in this confession is more corporate. It stresses the role of the Spirit in calling, gathering, teaching, and sanctifying the church, and preserving the church in the faith and in holiness through the gospel. The church is the temple of the Holy Spirit, and the Spirit is himself one of the gifts of Christ to the church. One of the reasons stated for keeping the Lord's Day is that this was the day on which the Spirit was outpoured, and this confession includes "the feast of the outpouring of the Holy Spirit" in a list of church festivals which are to be celebrated. It is indeed, the only festival mentioned which is not focused primarily on an event in Christ's experience. This is testimony to the absolute importance which the Indonesian Christians attached to the person and work of the Spirit.

The Indonesian confession explicitly rejects several erroneous notions. It refutes a version of the doctrine of the Trinity which taught that the Holy Spirit is the Mother, corresponding to Father and Son, presumably a teaching that was current in their context in the 1950s. Whatever the contemporary background, the idea of the Holy Spirit as the Mother in the Godhead has surfaced from time to time since the early days of the church. Augustine, writing in the fifth century, had to refute those who thought "the Holy Spirit to be the mother of the Son of God, and the wife of the Father."[29]

More recently, several theologians have suggested that the Holy Spirit should be referred to as "she." Clark Pinnock is one example. He claims that this "would call attention to facets of the Spirit's work which appear feminine—Spirit as life giver, birthing, comforting, God's loving breath." He claims that this "could enrich religious experience by allowing

---

28. W. Stewart, *Faith We Confess*, 25.
29. Augustine, "Trinity," 12.5.

us to access the Spirit's feminine side."[30] Part of his argument is that the Hebrew term for Spirit is feminine, as are many of the Old Testament images used with reference to the Spirit of God. The Indonesian confession rightly reminds us that this is out of step with Scripture as a whole. The Greek word for Spirit is neuter, and yet the New Testament does not refer to the Spirit as "it," but uses a personal pronoun—though not "she," but "he." While recognizing that we cannot project on to the persons of the Godhead human gender identity, it is nevertheless important to respect the way that the Holy Spirit speaks of himself.

This confession also rejects five "doctrines that falsely call upon the name of the Holy Spirit," a reminder that misrepresentation of the Holy Spirit falls foul of the third commandment. A brief comment on each is in order.

(1) There is the idea that the Holy Spirit can descend on man through his own power independently of the gospel. The confession is dissociating itself from any mystical experiences which might be construed as "spiritual," where Christ is not being preached and believed on. The Holy Spirit only works in people's hearts as the representative of Jesus Christ.

(2) The claim is rejected that it is only in times of ecstasy and speaking in tongues that the Spirit descends. The confession recognizes that the work of the Spirit is much larger than merely the impartation of extraordinary experiences. He is also quietly at work in the more regular experiences of church life.

(3) The Indonesian church disowns the teaching that the use of medicine is unnecessary, that in times of illness it is sufficient to pray to the Holy Spirit. Here the confession gratefully acknowledges medical discoveries and abilities as a providential gift of the Spirit, and so discountenances any supposition that the use of medicine reflects a lack of trust in God.

(4) The confession denounces false prophecies made in the name of the Spirit. It does not define how such prophecies would be recognized. Presumably there is some background which is not explicitly stated, where the Indonesian churches had been troubled by words, claiming to be Spirit given, but which were clearly incompatible with Scripture, or which had bad consequences in church life.

---

30. Pinnock, "Role of the Spirit," 48.

(5) The confession resoundingly challenges the false notion that a Christian can claim to be Spirit-filled, while leading a dissolute life. Since he is the Holy Spirit, holiness will be the inescapable mark of his presence.

Confession of Faith of House Churches in China

The Chinese confession speaks of the Holy Spirit as the person of the Godhead who implements salvation. Jesus rose from the dead and ascended into heaven in order to receive the promised Holy Spirit. The Holy Spirit now manifests the Son, and illuminates a person so that he may know his own sin and his need of repentance, and so that he may recognize the truth in order to believe in Christ and experience the new birth. The order in which faith and regeneration is mentioned is a little misleading.

To all those who have been born again and become believers Jesus Christ gives the Spirit. The inclusion of the word "all" is important and encouraging. As believers we receive the Spirit through faith, and, in so doing, we receive assurance of salvation, as the Spirit bears witness with our spirit that we are God's children. Without defining precisely what is meant, the confession says, "through faith and thirsting, Christians can experience the outpouring and the filling of the Spirit." The Holy Spirit leads believers into the truth, so that we may understand and obey the word of Christ, and bear abundant fruit in our lives. In the Christian life we pray in the Spirit.

This confession also pays attention to the role of the Spirit in the church. He "gives all kinds of power, and manifests the mighty acts of God through signs and miracles." This confession clearly expects miraculous signs to be a permanent feature of church life. The diversity of gifts of the Holy Spirit given by God to the church is intended to manifest the glory of Christ. The Chinese confession explicitly rejects the cessationist position on the gifts of the Spirit, though without adopting a specifically charismatic stance. It refuses equally to forbid speaking in tongues and to insist upon it as an evidence of salvation. The main thing is that in the Spirit the church is united as one in Christ.

HISTORICAL ELABORATION

According to Gerald Bray, "Basil of Caesarea was the first person to write a major theological treatise devoted exclusively to the Holy Spirit," and

John Owen was "the author of perhaps the greatest book on the Holy Spirit ever written."[31] We shall look at each of these two writers in turn.

Basil

Basil was born during the early decades of the fourth century, and was converted when in his mid-twenties. Eight years later he was ordained to the Christian ministry, and became the senior pastor at Caesarea in AD 370, when he was about 40 years old. He held this position for just under ten years, until his relatively early death.

Basil wrote his treatise *On the Holy Spirit*[32] around the year 375. In it he refers twice to a heretical group known as the *pneumatomachi*, a combination of the two Greek words *pneuma* (Spirit) and *machomai* (to fight). The adherents of this group were therefore dubbed "fighters against the Holy Spirit." It was in response to their teaching that Basil wrote this work. The central theme of the teaching of the *pneumatomachi* according to Basil was the subordination of the Spirit to the Father and the Son. They saw the Spirit as inferior in dignity, because he was separated from them by an interval of time. In other words, they denied the eternity of the Spirit.

In another work, Basil claims that the *pneumatomachi* taught that that the Holy Spirit was a created servant.[33] This may be an over-statement. The *pneumatomachi* certainly denied the Spirit's equality of nature with the Father and the Son. However, they did not usually define him as a created being, but saw him as occupying a middle position, neither truly God nor absolutely a creature.[34] Basil may be conflating the views of the *pneumatomachi* and the Anomoeans, derived from the Greek word *anomoios*, meaning "unlike." Basil refers to Aetius, a leader of the latter group, as "the champion of this heresy." The Anomoeans did, indeed, place the Holy Spirit firmly on the creature side of the creator-creature divide. In AD 381 the Council of Constantinople rejected both views.[35]

The great burden of Basil's work is to assert unequivocally the essential equality of the Spirit with the Father and the Son. Emphasizing

31. Bray, *God Has Spoken*, 610, 934.

32. Basil, "Holy Spirit," *passim*.

33. Basil, "Letter 140," 2.

34. cf. Jackson, "Preface," 117; J. N. D. Kelly, *Doctrines*, 260; Lampe, "Christian Theology," 112.

35. Toom, *Trinitarian Theology*, 20.

that the Holy Spirit is worthy to be exalted and glorified as God, he says that he "is in his nature divine, in his greatness infinite, in his operations powerful, in the blessings he confers, good" Basil there summarizes the four approaches which he uses to establish his point. We shall look briefly at each in turn.

The divine nature of the Spirit

Basil proves this point in two main ways. First, he notes the titles which Scripture gives to the Spirit. Titles such as Spirit of God, Spirit of our Father, Spirit of Christ, and Spirit of the Lord all demonstrate his inseparability from the other two persons of the Trinity. Titles like Spirit of truth, of wisdom, of knowledge, of holiness, and of grace, also establish this unbreakable connection.

Second, Basil looks at the language of Scripture. There are many scriptural references which use identical terminology for the Spirit as for the Father and the Son. Moreover, the conjunctions and prepositions which link references to the three persons point to their equivalence at the level of being. The most obvious example is the baptismal formula. Since baptism is in the name of the Father, the Son, and the Holy Spirit, the three are set on a level by regular liturgical usage.

The infinite greatness of the Spirit

Basil lists many of the divine attributes which the Spirit possesses: he is eternal, spiritual, unchanging, omnipotent, self-sufficient, omnipresent, supreme in intelligence.

The powerful operations of the Spirit

Basil revels in the magnitude of the Spirit's works. His operations are ineffable and innumerable. Basil sees the Spirit at work since the beginning of creation, and throughout the whole of creation. Not a single gift reaches creation without the Holy Spirit.

It was by his power that the powers of heaven were established. He established the good angels in holiness. Their inability to fall away from the good is by his operation. It is by the Spirit's empowering that the unfallen angels constantly praise their creator.

Basil traces the operations of the Spirit under the old covenant: "the blessings of the patriarchs, the succor given through the legislation, the types, the prophecies, the valorous feats in war, the signs wrought through just men"—all were accomplished through the grace of the Spirit.

Next the operations of the Spirit are evident in the incarnate life of our Lord. The Spirit's anointing descended upon him at his baptism, and everything which Jesus did, he did with the co-operation of the Spirit. In his victory over temptation, his miracles, his healings, the expulsion of demons, we see the Spirit at work with the Son.

The Spirit is at work in the church, establishing order and conferring gifts. The Father is the fountain of spiritual gifts; the gifts are sent by the Son, and the Spirit is the distributor.

His operations will again be evident at the time of the Lord's second coming. The resurrection of the dead, the judgment of the lost, the conferring of the crown of righteousness on believers—all these will be accomplished through the presence of the Spirit.

The good blessings conferred by the Spirit

At certain stages of his writing Basil focuses on the Spirit's work in the souls of believers. He confers spirituality by drawing people into fellowship with himself. This leads to spiritual understanding, spiritual joy, and the reality of abiding in God. The Holy Spirit brings us into the state of fullness of blessing in this world and in the world to come.

Basil is clear that it is impossible to have faith without the presence of the Spirit. It is he who makes us partakers of the grace of Christ. He alone enables us to worship, to call on the Father as his children by adoption. As the Spirit of knowledge, he enlightens us to fix our eyes on the beauty of Christ, the image of the invisible God, and through the image to be led up to the supreme beauty of the invisible Father.

The Holy Spirit is the unction, the quickening power, of all that is represented in baptism. He is the Lord of life, who raises us from spiritual death and renews us to our original life. He frees us from sin's slavery, and enables us to mortify sin. The fruit of holiness in our lives is the work of the Spirit. He enables our transmutation from a merely sensuous life to one marked by heavenly conversation.

The Spirit is the earnest of all the good gifts promised and held in store for us; by his presence we enjoy the first fruits of eternal glory.

Ultimately he will complete our restoration to paradise, our ascension to heaven, and the full enjoyment of blessing

John Owen

Owen wrote his comprehensive work on the Holy Spirit[36] to counter erroneous views, prevalent in his day, about the activity of the Spirit in the work of the gospel. Since similar errors resurface repeatedly, it is well to be aware of them, so that we may be prepared to resist them. We shall, therefore, glance at Owen's account of the errors which he is opposing, and his response. He refers to four overlapping categories of error.

(1) He mentions those who affirm that the Holy Spirit is a personal being, yet deny his deity, defining him as the highest of angelic creatures. Owen refers to the "Mohammedans" as a prime example. He admits that this issue is not his major concern, but comments briefly that the way in which Scripture speaks of the Spirit rules out this interpretation of his person: such things are ascribed to his action that it is impossible to defend the notion that he is not divine.

(2) This error is the reverse of the first. It involves affirming the divine nature of the Spirit, but denying that he is a distinct personal being. "Holy Spirit" is reduced to a reference to God's almighty power in action. Owen names Socinianism as the prime example of this in his day. It is part of his purpose to uphold orthodox trinitarian teaching against this heresy. Owen maintains that the Bible's frequent ascription to the Holy Spirit of personal properties clearly attests that he is a person. Amongst his evidence he cites the wording of the baptismal formula (Matt 28:19), and the ascription to the Spirit of a will as, for example, in John 3:8 and 1 Corinthians 12:11.

(3) There are the Quakers, the chief representatives in Owen's time of the tendency to devalue the Word of God through an over-confidence in personal spiritual experience. This led to a subjective doctrine of the Holy Spirit. Owen rebuts this teaching occasionally, fearing that the "extraordinary power" which acted upon the Quakers was actually devilish in its origin. However, this is not his chief target.

(4) The final error entails assenting to the doctrine of the Holy Spirit within an orthodox trinitarian framework, but resting content with a theoretical understanding that makes his work in gospel ministry and

---

36. Owen, "Holy Spirit," *passim.*

Christian life as good as irrelevant. Owen groups together a cluster of emphases under this heading. It includes some who poured scorn on those who emphasized the Spirit's role in conversion, unfairly implying that they were no different from the fanatics who were Owen's concern in the third category of errors. This "open and horrible opposition" to the Holy Spirit and his work in the world was Owen's main concern. Since it remains a constant threat, we shall focus on this issue.

Owen's conviction is that the effectiveness of gospel ministry depends on the work of the Spirit. There is no spiritual or saving good except as bestowed by God's Spirit. "Take away the Spirit from the gospel," he writes, "and you render it a dead letter." Yet in his day there were those who taught that the Word of God was a book to be preached and studied merely cerebrally. Owen saw that to separate the Spirit from the word is to destroy the gospel, because God's promise "is, that his word and Spirit shall go together." Our desire should therefore be for "real effusions of the Spirit upon the ministers of the gospel."

Amongst those who impugned this aspect of the truth Owen refers to two in particular.

(1) Johannes Crellius, who taught that, since the Holy Spirit is promised to those who repent and believe (Acts 2:38), the act of believing is therefore our own, and not itself a fruit of the gracious operation of the Spirit.

(2) Samuel Parker, who maintained that "all that the Scripture intends by the graces of the Spirit, are only virtuous qualities of the soul."[37] He rejected the genuineness of all claims to direct experiences of the Spirit on the grounds that "the conditions upon which the promise of the Spirit is entailed agree equally to Christians of all times and places." Consequently he assumed the presence of the Spirit, and denied any purpose in praying for his grace. Moreover, Parker claimed that the Spirit works as he "joins in with our understandings, and leads us forward by the rules of reason and sobriety." Consequently, "whatever assistances the Spirit of God may now afford us, they work in the same way, and after the same manner, as if all were performed by the strength of our own reason."[38] It is said that Parker equated the belief that the Holy Spirit is present in the congregation or the believer with a mystical idealism stemming from the philosophy of Plato.[39]

37. S. Parker, *Discourse*, 72.
38. S. Parker, *Defence*, 333–34.
39. Pocock, Schochet, & Schwoerer, *British Political Thought*, 177.

Owen sees such teachings as essentially Pelagian, since they deny "the effectual and ineffable operation of the Holy Spirit" in regeneration. Instead, such teachings attribute moral reformation to human power as if our intellectual and volitional faculties are undamaged by the fall. Owen outlines these errors in greater detail, and then gives a biblical response.

He acknowledges that there are Scriptures which promise the Spirit as a consequence of faith. However, he insists, we must properly distinguish what is promised to those who are already regenerate from the promise of the Spirit for regeneration—a work which is wholly his.

The error which Owen is addressing limits the work of the Spirit towards the unbeliever to "moral suasion." Owen uses the word "suasion" in contrast with a persuasion which is inevitably effective. The teachers with whom he is concerned saw the Spirit's work as that of advice, encouragement, urging, which may or may not be effectual, because ultimately it is the will of the person which decides for or against Christ.

On this understanding God's method of working towards the lost is to declare to all people the doctrine of the law and the gospel, in a rational appeal to the human will and affections. The truths taught are seen as so congenial to human nature that only a mind overpowered by sin could reject them. However, the doctrine of God's Word is backed up with promises and warnings designed to overcome the power of sin. This teaching sees the bare Word of God through the ministry of the church as sufficient to accomplish the salvation of sinners.

Owen does not disagree with this as a description of God's usual external method. However, the missing ingredient is the internal work of the Holy Spirit upon the unregenerate sinner. The teachers of this error might pay lip service to the work of the Spirit; however, they limit his role to an external appeal to the human mind and will. But, Owen insists, without his gracious infusion of a principle of spiritual life, there is no possibility that anyone will respond positively to the preaching of the gospel, however commanding the preacher's powers of oratory may be. Even the most spectacular use of the outward means is not all that is necessary for regeneration. To imagine that it is, betrays a false doctrine of fallen human nature: it is to fail to see the depravity of every part of the human constitution: intellect, will, and affections are all unable to apprehend, respond to, or delight in, spiritual truth. Owen compares this error to offering arguments to a blind man urging him to see.

Owen points out that when we pray for God's grace to convert, we mean far more than a mere influence which leaves the final choice in the hands of the sinner. Indeed, he says, if the final choice is left to the sinner, it is pointless to pray at all. Rather, our prayer is that God by the gracious power of his Spirit will actually work regeneration in human hearts. The role of the Spirit is not merely an external moral influence, but a direct, internal, powerful, effectual, infallible, irresistible, victorious work. It is the raising of those who are helplessly and hopelessly dead in sin to new life in Christ.

Therefore, Owen concludes, the mere teaching of the Bible can never be enough. In all our gospel work we must pray for the outpouring of the Spirit.

PRACTICAL APPLICATION

(1) We must acknowledge that the Holy Spirit is God's supreme gift. The covenant promises of God are summed up as the promise of the Spirit. All the manifold blessings of salvation are rolled into one in the gift of his presence. If we do not receive him, we receive nothing else. Receiving him, we receive all things. As any gift merits heartfelt gratitude and sincere expressions of thankfulness, so then, by God's grace, may we be readily forthcoming in our appreciative response for such a stupendous demonstration of generous kindness.

(2) We must remember that everything good in creation is from the Holy Spirit. This should move us to praise and worship whenever we observe beauty in the world. When we admire the works of human skill, we ought to be led upwards to adore the God whose Spirit activates human ability. We ought to give thanks to God every time we benefit from gifts such as medical provision. He it is who, by his Spirit, confers all that benefits us in life.

(3) We must receive the Sprit's teaching. Our Lord Jesus defined the Spirit's ministry primarily in terms of teaching the truth, and specifically, the truth of what he himself had taught. This includes the Spirit's inspiration of all Scripture as the authentic witness to Christ. Our duty, therefore, is to be good learners, humble students of the Bible, ever seeking the Spirit's guidance into a full and correct understanding of the word of Christ. As we do this, we should give the Holy Spirit the credit and the glory for all the wonderful things which we learn in the course of our Christian growth.

(4) We must acknowledge the need of the Spirit for conversion. It is only through the power of the Holy Spirit that anyone can be converted. He alone can convict of sin, plant the seed of regeneration, and impart new life. He alone can renew the fallen will and enlighten the fallen understanding. He alone can actualize all the blessings involved in turning from sin and trusting in Christ. To remember this will decrease our foolish sense of competence in evangelistic work and will increase our necessary sense of total reliance on God by his Spirit as we seek to reach out to the lost. If you are not yet a believer, do not imagine that it is in your power to turn to Christ whenever you choose. We are absolutely dependent on God's grace by his Spirit. But since he is a God of grace who does give the Spirit, we may plead with him for the grace that grants us the power to repent of sin and trust in the Savior.

(5) We must recognize our utter dependence on the Holy Spirit in the Christian life. We are nothing, we have nothing, we achieve nothing, apart from the work of the Holy Spirit within us. Knowing this rules out pride in anything we are or do, whether in personal spiritual development, or in the work of ministry. The Holy Spirit alone produces the fruits of regeneration in our lives. None but he can seal to our hearts assurance in the work of Christ. Only he can make us holy. Only he can strengthen us for the fight of faith. He alone can work within us the varied graces of salvation, such as deep peace, sweet comfort, overflowing joy. Only he empowers us for Christian service. It is the Spirit alone who moves us to pray and instructs us how to pray. It is the Spirit who grants us the grace to persevere to the end, and so preserves us for everlasting life. He alone is entitled to any of the credit. Our duty is to praise God with humility for the action of his Spirit.

(6) We must stir up the grace of obedience in our lives. To recognize our dependence on the power of the Spirit is not to cave in to fatalism. The idea that we "let go and let God" do everything is not biblical. Because God has given us his Spirit and renewed our fallen nature, we are called to walk in his ways. God guides us by his law in the paths of righteousness, and our task is to strive to obey. That is how we live as subjects to the Lordship of Christ. It is true that the Holy Spirit must enable us for such obedience. We can only strive in his power, but strive we must. Our need of the Spirit's power must not become an excuse for laziness or carelessness in the Christian life.

(7) We should seek the experience of Christ which the Spirit brings. The Christian life should never be a dull routine or a tedious chore. It

should always be a rich experience of fellowship with Jesus Christ by the power of the indwelling Holy Spirit. We should seek this constantly. If ever we fall short, we need to repent, and to realign our priorities. If the felt presence of Christ fades in our experience, we must seek again the fullness of the Spirit to give Christ's presence genuine, living vitality in our hearts, our minds and our affections.

(8) By the Spirit, we anticipate glory. He is the firstfruits of glory to come. We should live constantly with the prospect of eternal glory bright on the horizon of our consciousness. It is the presence of the Spirit in our hearts which enables us to live in this world with that world in us. We must not settle for a merely theoretical doctrine of the Spirit, but daily seek the reality.

(9) We must ensure that the Spirit is given his rightful place in church life. The Spirit places us within the body of Christ, the church, maintains the unity of the church, uses the means of grace to sanctify and edify the people of God, directs our worship by the word, enlivens it by his presence, and gives to the members of the body the gifts by which each one serves for the common good. Whatever our particular gift and calling may be, we should fulfil it with a servant heart, not for our own kudos.

(10) We must not sever the work of the Spirit from the work of Christ. We have been alerted to the danger of a concentration on the Holy Spirit disconnected from the work of Christ. Our salvation is rooted in the work of Jesus on the cross and in resurrection. The Spirit's function is to point to him. If we start to become preoccupied with the Holy Spirit and find our excitement in what we suppose to be his activities divorced from the work of Jesus Christ as the Lamb of God, we grieve the Spirit. The measure of genuine spiritual experience is the extent to which it is Christ-centered.

(11) We must plead for the power of the Spirit in gospel ministry. No gospel effort can ever be successful independently of the presence and power of the Holy Spirit. Without his direct operation the word is a mere dead letter, and our gifts, however great, are weak and useless. We need the Spirit's power in personal witness and in Christian mission. Evangelism without the Spirit is empty talk. Only he can vindicate the message of Christ. Only he can enable sinners to receive the truth about Christ and so turn to Christ and be saved. Only he can convict of sin and move an unbeliever to repentance and faith. We must preach the gospel of Christ. But we must also pray that the Spirit will energize the message, empower the preaching, grant the grace of regeneration to our hearers,

and glorify Jesus as the Savior of sinners. Gospel endeavor without prayer will always be fruitless. It is by fervent prayer that we signal our awareness of our total dependence on the power of God by his Spirit. We must pray that the Holy Spirit will be outpoured, that revival will occur, that he will cause the glory of Christ to outshine the sun. In all this we can be thoroughly encouraged to evangelize the nations brimming with hope, just because the Father has promised to pour out his Spirit: we are not left to our own feeble devices.

13

The Doctrine of the Church

THE SUBTITLE OF THIS book is *Systematic Theology from a Reformed Baptist Perspective*. In the doctrines which we have covered so far, there is little that is distinctive in the Reformed Baptist position. It is now, as we come to church-related issues that the Baptist position becomes significant.

The New Testament word for church is *ekklēsia*. It is formed from two words, *ek*, meaning "out of," and *klēsis*, which means a call or invitation. The word is used in a secular sense in Acts 19, which refers to "the lawful assembly" (verse 39) at Ephesus. The Greek city-states were governed by an assembly in which all citizens were entitled to participate. The assembly had to be run in line with procedures laid down in law.

The use of this word for God's assembly suggests that the church is a company of people called to come out of the godless world, and invited to come together. It must be organized in line with the procedures laid down in the Word of God.

At one point the Ephesus assembly descended into confusion (Acts 19:32). Everyone was talking at once and it was total uproar. The town clerk had to rebuke the unjustifiable uproar (verse 40). There is a warning there for us: even God's church can become disorderly, in which case challenge and reformation are needed.

BIBLICAL FOUNDATION

Old Testament

Two of the New Testament occurrences of *ekklēsia* point us back to the Old Testament foundations for the doctrine of the church. In Acts 7:38 Stephen refers to Moses as having been "in the congregation (*ekklēsia*) in the wilderness." Quoting Psalm 22:22, Hebrews 2:12 reads: "in the midst of the assembly (*ekklēsia*) I will sing praise to you." The Old Testament people of God is regarded as the prototype church.

In the Septuagint, most of the uses of the word *ekklēsia* refer to a specific gathering of the people. We shall focus on two of the main passages, both from the book of Deuteronomy.

Deuteronomy 4:10–13

The Septuagint version of verse 10 refers to the gathering of the people at Sinai (also known as Horeb) to receive the law; it speaks of "the day in which you stood before the LORD our God in Horeb, on the day of the assembly (*ekklēsia*)."

The words "on the day of the assembly" are not present in the Hebrew text, but are borrowed from Deuteronomy 18:16, which also refers to the same gathering. The Hebrew word for "assembly" is *qāhēl*. It depicts the people as gathered together in answer to God's call:[1] Moses thus continues by citing the LORD's words: "Gather the people to me."

Moses is reminding the people of what their parents' generation had experienced at Sinai, but he addresses his hearers as if they had been there. This is typical of this book. In Deuteronomy 5:2–3 Moses says: "the LORD our God made a covenant with us in Horeb. Not with our fathers did the LORD make this covenant, but with us, who are all of us here alive today." Moses means that the Sinai covenant was not made only with the exodus generation. It is not a matter of mere historical interest. Because God's people are spiritually united across the generations, and because the record in Scripture of God's dealings with his people gives contemporary significance to historical events, it is as if every generation had been present at Sinai. It is noteworthy that the Sinai gathering is designated "the assembly." It was the assembly *par excellence*, the definitive gathering of the people of God.

1. Coenen, "Church," 296.

The LORD now goes on in the rest of verse 10 to explain the purpose of this assembly. The initial purpose was that the assembled people might hear the word of God. The ultimate purpose was that they might fear the LORD.

Verses 12 and 13 then amplify these two things. In verse 12 the experience of hearing the LORD's word is described: "the LORD spoke to you out of the midst of the fire. You heard the sound of words, but saw no form; *you* only *heard* a voice." Verse 13 then elucidates the meaning of fearing the LORD: "he declared to you his covenant which he commanded you to perform, the Ten Commandments." To fear the LORD is to obey him.

In this passage we find a preview of what we are to expect in our gatherings as the church today. We assemble to hear the word of God. That is why the preaching of the word must always be central in Christian worship. But this hearing of the word is never an end in itself: its ultimate purpose is to give impetus to the life of faith and obedience, to train us to fear the LORD.

Deuteronomy 23:1–8

In these verses the Septuagint uses the word *ekklēsia* five times. They anticipate the day when Israel will be settled in the promised land. Certain categories of people—those with damaged bodies, illegitimate ancestry, or a foreign background—may not "enter the assembly of the LORD," first at the tabernacle and later in the temple. This is a pointer to the holiness and separation demanded of those who belong to God's church.

New Testament

Jesus refers to the church on only two occasions. We shall look first at his teaching on this subject, and then look at two passages from Paul's letters.

Jesus' References to the Church

MATTHEW 16:18

Having ascertained from the disciples the popular misconceptions of his identity, and then elicited from Peter the confession, "You are the Christ, the Son of the living God" (verses 13–16), Jesus then says: "you are Peter, and on this rock I will build my church (*ekklēsia*), and the gates of Hades shall not prevail against it." Six points may summarize the teaching of this passage.

The church is the continuation of the Old Testament assembly

The use of *ekklēsia*, borrowed from the Septuagint, to translate Jesus' words indicates that everything taught by the Old Testament about God's assembly is relevant also to the New Testament church: the church is indeed a people committed to holiness and separation, gathered to hear God's word with a view to fearing and obeying him.

The church is defined in relation to Jesus

He refers to it as "my church." It is his possession, his property, a community which revolves around him. Membership of the church is restricted to those who have genuine faith in Jesus Christ.

There is only one Christian church

Jesus' use of the singular noun is significant: the worldwide people of God across all the generations of the Christian era is a single entity. Notwithstanding the divisions, differences of emphasis, diversity of culture, disagreements over practice, debates about theology, nonetheless all true believers belong to the one universal church.

Jesus is the builder of the church

It is not our work. Paul and Apollos fulfilled their God-given roles in establishing the church, but only "God gave the increase" (1 Cor 3:6).

The church is built on a rock

Its foundation is solid and stable. Christ builds his church to last. Satan and godless people may try to destroy it, but the Lord will always have his people in this world.

The *Catechism of the Catholic Church* interprets this text to mean that "the Lord made Simon alone, whom he named Peter, the "rock" of his church." Alluding to verse 19, that quotation continues:

> He gave him the keys of his church and instituted him shepherd of the whole flock. The office of binding and loosing which was given to Peter was also assigned to the college of apostles united to its head. This pastoral office of Peter and the other apostles belongs to the church's very foundation and is continued by the bishops under the primacy of the Pope.

In rejection of this view, three other interpretations of the rock have been put forward: (1) Christ himself is "this rock;" (2) the rock is Peter's confession in verse 16; (3) the rock is Peter in his representative capacity as the leader of the apostles.

Don Carson, however, makes the following claim:

> if it were not for Protestant reactions against extremes of Roman Catholic interpretation, it is doubtful whether many would have taken "rock" to be anything or anyone other than Peter.[2]

However, it is not entirely true that the alternative interpretations represent a Protestant reaction against Roman Catholicism. As early as the fourth century, Chrysostom understood the rock to be the faith of Peter's confession.[3]

Perhaps the true reading incorporates something of all the various opinions. The rock is the apostles as a body, here represented by Peter, as those by whom the truth about Christ, the ultimate foundation, was confessed. And all who hold to that faith are part of Christ's church.

The gates of hell shall not prevail against the church

Gates prevail by staying shut. The church is on the march, battering hell's gates with the preaching of the gospel. Satan's kingdom is ransacked as sinners, destined for hell, already experiencing a living hell, are brought to saving faith in Christ, escaping Satan's clutches via the demolished gates.[4] What a word of reassurance as we preach the gospel!

---

2. D. A. Carson, "Matthew," 368.
3. Chrysostom, "Matthew," 702.
4. See Bayes, *Revival*, 37–40; cf. Passantino & Passantino, *Gates of Hell, passim.*

A Tidy Faith

Matthew 18:15–17

This passage deals with the issue of church discipline, which, sadly, is sometimes necessary. However, church discipline only begins after two previous steps have been taken. Jesus lays down a four-stage approach to dealing with sin in his church.

The private word

Verse 15 raises the question, if you are aware that another member is sinning, to whom do you speak about it? The answer is that member. The church is not a place for gossip. The hope is that you will gain the brother, that you will win him for what is right.

The two or three witnesses

In verse 16 the Lord says that, if the sinning member does not respond to the private word, you must approach him again with a small number of other members as witnesses. This ensures that in any discussion with the erring member, it is not just your word against his.

The matter brought to the church

Next, in the first part of verse 17, the Lord's instruction is that if the member still does not respond, the entire congregation must call him to repentance (verse 17a).

Excommunication

Finally, in the rest of verse 17b, Jesus addresses the situation if there is still no response. In that case church discipline comes into play. However, it is always exercised in the hope of recovery and return. He is to be treated as a Gentile and a tax-collector—precisely the people whom Jesus came to save.

Two Passages on the Church from Paul's letters

EPHESIANS 5:22–33

The apostle uses marriage as a picture of the relationship between Christ and the church. Our concern is the teaching about Christ's relationship to the church; we shall extract that, and bypass the instructions regarding marriage.

Paul's starting point is that, as its Savior, Christ is also the head of the church (verse 23). Verse 24 notes that, as his body, the church comes under Christ's authority: it "is subject to Christ." The word translated "subject" (*hupotassō*) means "to place oneself under." It speaks of something willingly undertaken. Christ's headship is not a tyranny grudgingly acknowledged, but something in which the church delights. This is because of the salvation which Christ has achieved for her.

Verse 25 enlarges on Christ's role as head and Savior: it is rooted in the fact that Christ "loved the church." The aorist tense of the verb indicates that a specific event is in mind, which the rest of verse 25 identifies as Christ's giving of himself on the cross for the church. This wording implies that the church was, in principle, in existence at the time of Christ's death. It assumes the truth of election: that body of people whose names were written in heaven before the foundation of the world constitute the church.

Verse 26 defines Christ's purposes for his church as her sanctification and cleansing, and explains that this takes place "with the washing of water by the word." This phrase has been read in two main ways. It has been understood to refer to two complementary things: baptism in water, as a sign of the Spirit's work, and the preaching of the word.[5] On the other hand, it may be a double description of one reality—the sanctifying power of the word of God when taken up and applied by the Holy Spirit.[6]

The latter seems to me the more probable reading. The word is like water: it is the primary means of the church's cleansing. Paul's phrase therefore echoes the words of Jesus in John 17:17: "Sanctify them by your truth. Your word is truth." Jesus used the word *logos* for "word," drawing attention to God's word considered in itself. Paul's term, however, is *rhēma*, which emphasizes the spoken word: the preaching of God's word

---

5. Lincoln, *Ephesians*, 375–76; Hendriksen, *Ephesians*, 252.
6. E.g., Simpson, *Ephesians*, 131–32.

in the hearing of the people is the chief means by which Christ cleanses and sanctifies his church. Preaching is therefore the highest function which the church performs.

Verse 27 looks forward to the day when the church's cleansing and sanctification will be completed, and Jesus will "present her to himself a glorious church, not having spot or wrinkle or any such thing, but that she should be holy and without blemish." On that final day the church will be morally perfect when it is presented to Christ in glory. Every stain of sin will have been purged away.

In verse 29 we read that Christ nourishes and cherishes the church. Verse 30 states the reason: "for we are members of his body." This phrase individualizes and personalizes all that has been said. The church is the sum total of all its members, and Christ's profound care for each one is as intense as his committed care for the body as a whole.

1 TIMOTHY 3

The word *ekklēsia* appears in verses 5 and 15 of this chapter. The first occurs within a section where Paul outlines the qualifications required of those who are to fulfil the two permanent church offices, while Paul's primary concern in the later part of the chapter is appropriate behavior in "the church of the living God." These will be the two aspects of the teaching on the church which we shall consider now.

The permanent church offices

Elders

In the opening verse our translation refers to "bishops," translating *episkopos*, literally meaning overseers. This term is used also in Titus 1:7, but in that chapter (verse 5) the same officer is called an "elder" (*presbuteros*). Since this is the more common term, it is the one which we shall employ.

The summary qualification for an elder is that he "must be blameless" (verse 2). There is nothing about his character on which anyone can seize to make an accusation. The apostle then goes on to show how that quality will be evident in three different spheres.

(1) It will be evident at home. He will be "the husband of one wife." Paul is probably not ruling out the possibility of a single man becoming

an elder, but in days when polygamy was rife, a married elder had to be monogamous. Today, a divorced man who has remarried is probably not eligible for eldership. Verses 4–5 emphasize that a potential elder should be "one who rules his own house well." His children must be submissive. The home will be known for the peace which flows from obedience. Inability to maintain discipline at home disqualifies a man from trying to maintain it in the church.

(2) It will be evident in the church. Personal graces will be displayed in his manner of life (verses 2–3). He will be a man of calm spirit who is able to exercise self-control and live an orderly life. He will be generous in hospitality, and will deal with people fairly and patiently. Conversely, he will not get drunk; he will not be contentious, nor insist on his own way, and he will not be in the Lord's service just for what he can get out of it. In these qualities, do we not see the character of Christ? The church's leaders should resemble him.

(3) It will be evident in the world. Verse 7 says that "he must have a good testimony among those who are outside." If a man senses that God is calling him to ministry, and his current employer's reaction is, "Great, I'll be so glad to see the back of him," the church should probably think twice before appointing him an elder!

If we were to press all this very rigorously, there would be no elders in any church anywhere! When we read such a list of personal graces, we all feel disqualified. None of us measures up. But what is in view here is not perfection but direction. An elder's general behavioral trends should be clear. That is why a recent convert cannot be appointed (verse 6). There must be sufficient time for the fruit of a man's profession of faith to be tested.

It is notable that Paul mentions only one qualification which concerns the elder's duty in the church—the ability to teach (verse 2). God sees how we live as far more significant than what we can do. However, the Bible does not leave it to us to devise the elder's duty: "able to teach" translates the word *didaktikos*, which is used elsewhere only in 2 Timothy 2:24. Its context there sheds light on its meaning. The Lord's servant must be "gentle to all, able to teach, patient."

Apt teaching will be accompanied by gentleness and patience. The skilful teacher will not become frustrated and get angry. He will slowly lead his hearers forwards towards maturity at the rate that they are able to grasp the truth. Calvin comments, Paul "commends wisdom in applying the word of God judiciously to the advantage of the people."[7]

Deacons

The word "deacon" (*diakonos*) means "servant," and those appointed to this office serve the church in various ways. To serve as a deacon is to exercise a practical, supportive, behind-the-scenes ministry. Nevertheless, the qualifications listed for deacons in verses 8–9 and 12 are very similar to those for elders. A deacon must have a serious approach to life and his words must be trustworthy. He must not over indulge his appetites or be motivated by greed. He must have a sound grasp of the truth, and this must be reflected in a pure lifestyle. He must be faithful in marriage and competent as a father.

Just because the main focus of diaconal service is not spiritual ministry, it does not follow that deacons may be unspiritual men. In fact, these qualities are really a description of any genuine, maturing Christian. Testing for work as a deacon is vital (verse 10). A man should be functioning diaconally before being appointed to the diaconate.

Verse 11 can be understood in either of two ways. It may refer to the wives of deacons, as in the New King James Version. However, the Greek word *gunē* can mean either wife or woman. So this verse may be read as indicating that women may legitimately be appointed as deacons. This seems likely, given that there is no equivalent comment in the verses about elders.

Appropriate behavior in the church

In verse 15 Paul explains that he is writing as he does so that "you may know how you ought to conduct yourself in the house of God, which is the church of the living God, the pillar and ground of the truth."

Timothy was ministering in Ephesus (1 Tim 1:3), the city which saw itself as "temple guardian of the great goddess Diana" (Acts 19:35). In contrast to that lifeless goddess, the church belongs to the living God, the true God, the God who is real, alive, active, the very life-giver. It is just because the church belongs to him that behavior within it is such an important issue.

7. Calvin, *Timothy, Titus, and Philemon*, 80.

The apostle goes on to describe the church in two ways.

(1) It is "the house of God." The word *oikos* refers to the entire family that inhabits a house. God is the Father of his adopted family, his household. We must all therefore behave in a way that reflects the family likeness, and which avoids bringing shame on the family.

(2) It is "the pillar and ground of the truth." The words "pillar" and "ground" are synonyms, used together for the sake of emphasis. They convey the idea of sturdy support. The church is a strong column which holds the truth up and makes it visible. The church preserves the truth in the world, preventing it from falling into oblivion.

DOCTRINAL FORMULATION

The Early Creeds

The creeds were trinitarian in structure, and the doctrine of the church is set within the section on the Holy Spirit; it is one of "the fruits of the Spirit in action."[8] The Nicene Creed reads, "We believe in one holy, catholic and apostolic church." The Apostles' Creed refers to "the communion of saints." We therefore divide this section into five parts.

The church as one

The second-century writer, Hermas, noted that the church includes all God's elect, even those who have already "fallen asleep."[9] The unity of the church is not just a feature of any particular generation, but throughout time there is only one church, composed of all who believe.

The church as holy

This is the oldest descriptive term for the church, found already in statements pre-dating the creeds. The term "holy church" refers not to moral holiness, but to the church's special relationship to God. Another second-century theologian, Justin Martyr, links the church's holiness with God's sovereign election of his people.[10] Kelly connects it with election, with

8. J. N. D. Kelly, *Creeds*, 155.
9. Hermas, "Shepherd," 2.4; 3.5.
10. Justin Martyr, "Trypho," 119.

the glorious destiny awaiting the church, and with the fact that she is indwelt by God's Spirit.[11] Ferdinand Kattenbusch points out

> that the concepts of the holy and the heavenly are most closely related in the thought of the time, and that the holy church as here mentioned is probably thought of as a branch or colony upon earth of the City of God which is in heaven.[12]

The church as catholic

The Greek word *katholikos* means universal. Kelly notes that the term eventually came to mean the one "great church" as distinct from the heretical rivals which began to spring up. However, when Ignatius first introduced it of the church, early in the second century, his emphasis was that a local Christian congregation only had "reality, life, and power in proportion as it formed part of the universal church with its spiritual head," Jesus Christ. As Cyril of Jerusalem explained, the church was catholic or universal in the sense that it was "spread throughout the whole world."[13] Stewart notes that catholicity first expressed the church's consciousness of its mission, which extends the benefits of salvation to all peoples, excluding none.[14]

The church as apostolic

This word emphasizes the link with the foundational apostles. No church is genuine unless the doctrine which it teaches is that which the apostles taught. This term, therefore, places the word of God firmly at the center of church life. Unless all that we do is rooted in Scripture, we have ceased to be authentically the church.

---

11. J. N. D. Kelly, *Creeds*, 158.
12. Cited in A. Stewart, *Creeds*, 55.
13. J. N. D. Kelly, *Creeds*, 385.
14. A. Stewart, *Creeds*, 56.

The church as the communion of the saints

In the New Testament "saints" are all those set apart in Christ by faith. In the church all true believers share in mutual fellowship. Kelly cites the late fourth-century writer, Nicetas, who said:

> From the beginning of the world, patriarchs, prophets, martyrs, and all other righteous men who have lived, or are now alive, or shall live in time to come, comprise the church, since they have been sanctified by one faith and manner of life, and sealed by one Spirit and so made one body, of which Christ is declared to be the head.[15]

Nicetas thus defined the church as all the redeemed throughout time. To be part of God's people today is to belong to God's one people drawn from every generation. The ultimate communion of the saints is focused at any given time in the fellowship of the church on earth.

The Reformation Confessions

The confessions reiterate the teaching on the church found in the early creeds. The church is one, not by external uniformity, but in the truth. The church is holy, because the people who comprise it are called out of the world and its universal allegiance to sin. The church is catholic, found in all the world and across the whole of time. The church is apostolic, founded on the apostles' teaching. The church is the communion of saints, as all believers have fellowship with one another in love, and benefit from one another's gifts and graces. The additional teaching of the confessions may be divided into two main parts.

The Church Universal

DEFINITION

For the confessions "church" is really synonymous with "elect." The church is that multitude of people chosen by God throughout time, who are led by the Spirit to embrace Christ by true faith. This traces the church back into the eras before the coming of Christ.

---

15. Cited by J. N. D. Kelly, *Creeds*, 391.

Sometimes we call Pentecost "the birthday of the church." This is appropriate if we are talking specifically of the New Testament church. However, the confessions recognize that the church since Pentecost stands in continuity with all believing people from Adam onwards, and that they are just as much part of the universal church as we are.

The word "church" emphasizes the corporate nature of God's people. The confessions, like Scripture, use singular nouns in defining the church: it is Christ's body, bride, flock, kingdom, and temple. The church is not just an agglomeration of individuals, but a "community of faith in which individuals [find] their proper place."[16]

CHRIST IS THE HEAD OF THE CHURCH

This truth led the reformers to reject the papacy. The idea that the pope is the universal head of the church on earth as Christ's deputy was seen as an affront to the Lord. It implied Christ's absence, whereas the Lord is present with his people, personally performing the duty of universal pastor of his church. The reformers believed that the pope, in usurping the role of Christ's deputy on earth, makes himself the man of sin, the antichrist. Today we are less certain that we can positively identify the pope with antichrist, even if we judge the Roman Catholic system to be anti-Christian. Peter Masters suggests that the final antichrist might be a particular pope, the Roman Catholic Church, or an atheistic ideology.[17]

THE CHURCH INVISIBLE AND VISIBLE

Some of confessions distinguish the invisible church (all the elect) from the visible church, which includes all who are associated with the church on earth. This distinction is motivated by the recognition that, in the present, sinful world, there are people in the church who are not genuine believers. Moreover, the Westminster Confession defines the visible church as all who profess faith "together with their children."

By contrast, the 1689 Baptist Confession insists that what becomes visible on earth is precisely the invisible church, and that only genuine believers are truly part of it. Some of those present in a church are members of the visible church, and some are not, such as seekers or

16. Bray, *God Has Spoken*, 90.

17. Masters, *Baptist Confession*, 74.

hypocrites. So this confession makes no reference to believers' children. While they participate externally in the visible church, they are not part of the church until they personally profess repentance and faith.

Robert Shaw argues for the inclusion of believers' children within the definition of the visible church on three grounds.

(1) In civil society, children enjoy the same privileges as their parents: it is reasonable to suppose that the kingdom of God will be not less favorable to children than the kingdoms of this world.

(2) The Old Testament covenant extended to parents and their children (e.g., Gen 17:7), and there is no word in the New Testament of the exclusion of children.

(3) Jesus says, "Let the little children come to me, and do not forbid them; for of such is the kingdom of God" (Luke 18:16).[18]

The Baptist would respond as follows to these points.

(1) The New Testament equivalent of children in Israel is babes in Christ—those newly born again, not those young in years.

(2) The New Testament makes clear that it is those who are Christ's who are Abraham's seed (Gal 3:29). Paedobaptists have to admit that not all the children of believers become Christians. To claim that they are included in the covenant therefore undermines the faithfulness of God.

(3) We do let the children come to Christ: children can be converted, and therefore we ensure that they hear the gospel. However, until they profess faith, they are not members of the visible church.

THE CHURCH MILITANT AND TRIUMPHANT

The church militant consists of those believers at present on earth, waging war against the world, the flesh, and the devil. The church triumphant comprises believers already in heaven, discharged from the battle, and enjoying their share in Christ's victory.

OUTSIDE THE CHURCH THERE IS NO SALVATION

This statement is true by definition when it refers to the invisible church, since the church is the assembly of the saved. The Scottish Confession explicitly rejects the view that those who live moral lives are saved whatever religion they profess. It insists that those given to the Son by the Father

18. Shaw, *Confession*, 264–65.

will come to him in faith. Underlying this is the conviction that God in his sovereign providence ensures that all his elect do hear the gospel.

This statement is also made with reference to the visible church. In this case it is qualified. Thus the Second Helvetic Confession states that outside the visible church "there is no certain salvation," while the Westminster Confession says "there is no ordinary possibility of salvation." The words "certain" and "ordinary" reflect the pastoral wisdom which allows for exceptional cases: some genuine believers may, through force of necessity or weakness be absent from the church, or a Christian's faith may falter without being totally extinguished.

GOD PRESERVES HIS CHURCH

The true church faces intense opposition in this world. Sometimes it may seem to be reduced to virtually nothing. However, God always preserves a witness. Robert Shaw points out that this is no guarantee of

> the permanent continuance of the church in any particular country where it has once been planted; but we have the most solid ground for assurance that, in one place or another, Christ shall have a seed to serve him and to perpetuate his name as long as sun and moon endure.[19]

The Local Church

THE NEED FOR LOCAL CHURCHES

The confessions recognize that the subdivision of the one holy, catholic, and apostolic church into many congregations is a matter of necessity: it is impossible for all the members of the universal church on earth at any one time all to meet together. Local companies of believers must be established in every place so that meetings for worship can happen.

THE MARKS OF A TRUE CHURCH

Reformed theology identified three essential marks of a true church.

19. Shaw, *Confession*, 267.

(1) The gospel is faithfully preached, heard and kept. This wording stresses the responsibility of all the members of the congregation. It is not the preacher alone whose work defines the church. The French Confession expresses the point like this: "where the word of God is not received . . . there is no church."

(2) The sacraments are properly administered. This was understood to mean that the sacraments must be regulated by God's word, and used along with the exposition of the word. This entailed rejection of the Catholic view, which claimed that the sacraments have an intrinsic power of their own. This corrupted them into idolatry.

(3) Church discipline is uprightly administered. A true church nurtures holiness. A lax approach to discipline disqualifies a church from being recognized as true. I like the way in which Heinrich Heppe puts this: he speaks of "the serious and zealous practice of disciplined Christian life."[20] "Church discipline" suggests an occasional requirement at times of crisis; the disciplined Christian life is how it should be at all times: a true church is one where discipleship is expressed in daily life.

MEMBERSHIP OF A LOCAL CHURCH IS A DUTY

The confessions stress that joining a true church is an obligation, and that failure to join entails disobedience to the word. The Baptist confessions clarify that this is applicable to believers, and add that it is so when there is opportunity, acknowledging that exceptional circumstances may occasionally make church membership impossible.

For the 1689 Confession, church membership involves placing oneself under the church's government, and therefore also, if necessary, under its reproof. Membership is voluntary: the church comes together by willing agreement. The 1644 Confession emphasizes that the faults of other members and the corruptions which arise in church life are no grounds for leaving a church. The Reformers valued the church so highly that they regarded schism as a serious sin. However, they did distinguish schism from separation, which they considered necessary if a professing church made a major departure from truth or holiness.

---

20. Heppe, *Dogmatics*, 669.

THE RESPONSIBILITIES OF CHURCH MEMBERS

The confessions mention nine duties which pertain to church members: (1) to attend public worship; (2) to maintain unity; (3) to promote peace; (4) to affirm the church's doctrine; (5) to submit to the church's discipline; (6) to serve one another; (7) to relieve the needy; (8) to edify one another; (9) to love one another.

INTER-CHURCH RELATIONS

All the reformers recognized the equality of all churches. They rejected the claim made by the church at Rome to be the senior church in the entire world, with its bishop as the chief pastor. However, there is a difference of emphasis between the confessions that advocate Presbyterian church government and those from a Baptist perspective.

The Presbyterian view

This holds that church councils are part of the church's God-given structure, serving to edify and protect the churches. Acts 15 is seen as the prototype church council. The circulation of its decree is evidence for the authoritative status of decisions of wider groups of congregations, which are binding on the churches. However, it is true that councils can err, so their decisions must not be elevated to the level of a rule of faith, a position held only by God's word.

The Baptist view

The notion of a governing body over a group of congregations is generally rejected by Baptists. Rather, each particular church is complete in itself, and church government is focused on the congregation. No seat of government exists beyond the local church. Messengers from a group of churches might sometimes meet to discuss matters of mutual relevance, and such meetings will report back to the churches. However, the wider body may not impose its decisions on the churches.

That said, the Baptist confessions do oppose the extreme independency which can end in total isolation. The 1644 Confession insists that particular congregations should receive one another's counsel and help.

The 1689 Confession puts the obligation on every church to pray for all the churches, and for neighboring churches to have fellowship amongst themselves in order to promote peace, to increase love, and to enlarge opportunities for mutual edification. Underlying these emphases is the awareness that all churches are members of the one body under Christ as the one Head.

CHURCH OFFICERS

Some of the confessions speak of three offices—pastors, elders, and deacons, while others equate pastors and elders, and therefore see only two offices. Both positions agree that Scripture dictates church order, but disagree as to its exact meaning. No one may take it upon himself to become a church officer. Officers must be appointed by the church, as it recognizes those men who have a commission from God.

Church officers dare not mix Scripture with their own imaginations. All their authority is derived from God's word. The Second Helvetic Confession notes that the word translated "servants" in 1 Corinthians 4:1 (*hupēretas*) literally means "under-rowers." It emphasizes a subordinate position under a superior. A rower in a boat does not look where he is going; his eyes are fixed on the cox, whose responsibility it is to set the direction. So church officers must not be looking around for ideas. They must look to Christ alone. It is Christ speaking through the word who sets the agenda for his church.

In addition to the requirements for church officers spelt out in the Pastoral Epistles, the Second Helvetic Confession lists five practical considerations.

(1) They must have sufficient consecrated learning. While they must know what to teach, "sufficient" learning is enough: high academic qualifications are not needed. Their knowledge must be consecrated to God, not paraded for their own reputation.

(2) They must have pious eloquence. They need to be able to communicate clearly and helpfully, and that ability must be consecrated to the Master's use.

(3) They need simple wisdom. They do not need to be sophisticated and erudite, but they do need to understand the word of God, and to see how it applies in different situations.

(4) They must be men of moderation. This general term would rule out extremists, men who are over-indulgent, men of fiery temper, and so on.

(5) They must have an honorable reputation. Churches must avoid appointing rogues!

The confessions mention six purposes for which officers are appointed: (1) to organize and administer the assemblies which the church holds for edification; (2) to exercise leadership; (3) to ensure that true doctrine is maintained; (4) to correct error; (5) to deal with disciplinary matters; (6) to ensure that the poor and needy are helped.

THE PASTOR'S WORK

The Second Helvetic Confession analyzes all a pastor's duties under two headings.

(1) Gospel-based teaching. This includes a number of types of instruction: he must teach the ignorant, urge the idle to progress, comfort the fainthearted, rebuke offenders, and refute false doctrine. In exercising this role the faithful pastor will be constant in prayer.

(2) Administering the sacraments. This is a subsection of the ministry of the word, since the sacraments are a proclamation of the gospel in visible form.

The Presbyterian confessions distinguish between ministers ordained to preach and the laity. By contrast the 1689 Baptist Confession takes a more egalitarian view: pastors and elders are not necessarily the only preachers in a congregation, and other men called to preach must also be allowed to exercise their gifts.

WRONG VIEWS OF THE MINISTRY

The confessions reject three erroneous approaches to Christian ministry.

(1) The priesthood. Christ abolished the ancient priesthood, and is now the only priest. Eldership and priesthood are very different things: all believers are priests, but some are called to be ministers of the word.

(2) False prophets. This term refers to men who abandon the pure gospel and preach heresy.

(3) Visionaries. This refers to pastors who have denied the need for the preaching of the word. They expect God to speak directly. They

conclude that there is no need for preparation. The thoughts given to them in the moment are God's word for the occasion. The confessions insist that true preaching will always be anchored in Scripture.

CHURCH DISCIPLINE

The confessions follow the pattern spelt out by the Lord in Matthew 18:15–17. Discipline must be exercised in loving, brotherly tenderness; the aim is that the erring Christian amends his ways. Excommunication, when necessary, must take a form appropriate to the nature of the offence. Sometimes a temporary ban from the Lord's Table may suffice. In more extreme cases the offender may need to be barred from participation in all aspects of church life. The aim is always restoration as the offender repents. The purpose is "the removal of sin from the sinner, not the removal of sinners from the church."[21]

The confessions consider who may be candidates for church discipline. The Genevan Confession refers to those who hold God's word in contempt and take no account of exhortation. Its list of sins requiring discipline, clearly alludes to the ten commandments: it is God's law which defines sin. It insists that the sin must be "manifest," because church discipline must never be exercised on the basis of mere suspicion or hearsay. Williamson adds the point that the issue in church discipline is not so much the notoriety of the sin committed as the persistence in it and the refusal to repent.[22]

Modern Confessions of Faith

In general the modern confessions follow closely the teaching of the earlier documents. They certainly do not attempt to be innovative. The Indian confession has just one phrase on the subject of the church in its article dealing with the duties of Christians, one of which is to unite in church fellowship. William Stewart makes a helpful comment on the phrase:

> This article of our confession reminds us that the heart of our Christian duty lies in the fact that we are not our own. To be redeemed in Christ is not to be set apart for a kind of lonely isolation. Others are also redeemed and to be "in him" is to be

21. Williamson, *Westminster*, 238.
22. Williamson, *Westminster*, 239.

> brought into fellowship with them. Therefore it is in the Christian fellowship that love is given which meets an answering love, and we are built up together into a great harmony, the harmony which begins to show what God meant men to be like.[23]

Stewart's point is that in the church we see the inauguration of the new, restored humanity. That is why the Indian confession is so keen to insist that participation in Church fellowship is a matter of duty.

The Chinese confession clarifies the doctrine of the universal church by specifying that, in addition to the saints already in glory, it includes "all churches of orthodox faith currently existing in all parts of the earth." So-called churches which hold to heretical teachings are not being acknowledged as genuine parts of the universal church. The Chinese confession affirms the priesthood of all believers, defining this to mean that "all have the authority and responsibility to preach the gospel to the ends of the earth." It also rejects secular control of the church, as well as attempts by the church to use political power to facilitate growth, or involvement in activities which threaten the unity of the state and people.

The Indonesian confession is the fullest on this subject. It takes up three of the early church's terms, speaking of the church as holy, universal, and one. It rejects the idea of a state church, and insists that Christ alone is Head of the church. Its most interesting insight is seen in its comments on the holiness of the church, where we read: "the church is not holy because its members as such are holy, but because Jesus Christ, its Head, is holy. The church thus becomes holy because Christ has sanctified her."

Since God accepts the church's members as holy, there is no justification for "schisms based on the fact that there is still sin among the church members." The only valid reason for separation from a congregation is false teaching. This confession also lists the marks of the church, corresponding to those which we have already noted in connection with the Reformation confessions.

HISTORICAL ELABORATION

Here we shall do two things. First, we shall survey and synthesize the teaching on the church in the writings of the Apostolic Fathers, the earliest Christian theologians after the New Testament.[24] Then we shall look

---

23. W. Stewart, *Faith We Confess*, 37.

24. Barnabas, Clement, 2 Clement, Hermas, Ignatius, Polycarp, Church of Smyrna's

at *The New Directory for Baptist Churches*, written in 1894 by American pastor, Edward Hiscox.[25]

The Church in the Writings of the Apostolic Fathers

The doctrine of the church was a major theme in these writers, whose shared perspective was the relationship between church and world as one of fundamental antithesis. The church is an outpost of the world to come, sojourning in the present world. It is the only place in the world where salvation can be found. Membership of the church requires a radical break with the world. In the present world, the church must expect to suffer, as it shares in Christ's passion.

These works especially highlight two marks of the church. One is church unity—a vital necessity, sealed by frequency of meeting. A church is bound together by mutual love, and its unity is a reflection of the divine unity: a united church enjoys communion with God, but where division is found, God is not present. Unity is essential because the church is both an army and a body. However, church unity applies not only to the local congregation, but also to the universal church, where it is expressed mainly in prayer for the churches throughout the world, although it embraces all believers of both dispensations.

The second mark of the church emphasized by these writers is its holiness, which is also a reflection of the divine nature. Church members are expected to flee ungodliness and strive after holiness. Where holiness is contradicted by sin the Lord's name is blasphemed. One reason why holiness is important is that Christ will return for a church purified through its rejection of wickedness and hypocrisy.

Despite the stress on unity and holiness, the Apostolic Fathers were well aware that the reality often fell short of the ideal. Some of the churches addressed in these works had been afflicted by division, and others were marked by moral laxness. The church on earth is a mixed company, part truly the church, and part still really of this world. So as long as the church is in this world, it is anticipating its eschatological perfection, but also facing the constant challenge to overcome the jealousy which leads to disunity and the sin which corrupts holiness.

The Martyrdom of Polycarp, and the anonymous work, *The Didache*, In Lake (ed.), *passim*.

25. Hiscox, *New Directory, passim*.

Some of these writers emphasize the role of ministries within the church. The elders are both the focus of the church's unity and the men primarily responsible to exhort the church to holiness. Ignatius makes a distinction between the overseer and the elders, though this is not typical of that time. Itinerant preachers were common in those early days, and they were to be received, though with discernment. Tithes were to be used to support ministry, but where a church did not have a settled pastor, the tithes were to be used to help the poor. Preachers were to be respected, because where the Lord's name is proclaimed, he is himself present. Christ's obedience to his Father is the model for the church's loyalty to its leadership. But the overseer has responsibilities too: he must protect church unity, love all his people, pray diligently, be gentle with troublesome members, be sober, stand firm, take especial care of the needy, and arrange frequent gatherings. There is always a danger that the leadership might fail, by pandering to the wants of the congregation, or by teaching without meekness or with an eye to reward.

The issue of church discipline is raised, most especially by Polycarp. The starting point must be sorrow for the offender, leading to sincere prayer for his repentance. Discipline must be exercised with moderation: the offender must be viewed as a straying member, a casualty in the spiritual battle, not as an enemy, and the aim must be to call him back, recognizing that without him the body is incomplete.

The other main theme which we find in these writings is the pre-existence of the church. As God's holy elect, the church existed from eternity with the pre-incarnate Christ, independently of those who would in time become its members. All things were created for the sake of the church. When Christ appeared in the flesh, he brought that eternal spiritual church to earth with him. After his return to heaven, as the second creation of the last days, it began to be filled up with its children.

Edward Hiscox's *New Directory for Baptist Churches*

The publishers of the 1970 reprint, called this book "a genuine classic," rating it "the greatest work on Baptist church government ever written."

Hiscox defines a Christian Church as "a company of regenerate persons, baptized on a profession of faith in Christ." They have made a covenant commitment to unite "for worship, instruction, the observance of Christian ordinances, and for such service as the gospel requires." A regenerate membership is crucially important: just as the character of a building depends on the materials from which it is constructed, so the admission into the church of unsuitable materials (unregenerate members) will hasten decline and decay in life and doctrine.

Christ is the only Lord and Lawgiver for his churches. This means that churches cannot make laws for their own government; they must obey the statute book which they have been given, namely the New Testament. Local congregations are independent, though fellowship between churches is to be maintained. Hiscox argues for the church meeting as the ultimate seat of authority within a local church: all the members seek together to discern the will of Christ, albeit that the church delegates the responsibility for day-to-day leadership to its officers. Each local church has liberty to direct its own affairs, though this needs qualification: a church's liberty is limited by the laws of Christ, and freedom of conscience may not be violated; the rights of individual members may restrict what a church together decides.

Baptists reject the distinction between clergy and laity: all believers form a holy priesthood. Hiscox equates pastors and elders and insists that they must be chosen by the congregation. They are not dictators, but shepherds, who lead, feed, guide, and guard the flock; church members can only respond to a shepherd whom they have freely chosen.

A pastor's work has two aims: the winning of souls and the edification of saints. The chief means by which both purposes are fulfilled is the preaching of the word. This implies that preparation for such ministry is the major part of a pastor's work. Hiscox rightly notes that the faithful preaching of the word is the only thing that will draw and keep a congregation: thoughtful people will soon tire of tricks and gimmicks. Pastoral visitation is also important: the pastor must know and be known by the people if he is to benefit them spiritually.

Hiscox sees the deacon as the other office in the church. The deacon's role includes caring for sick and needy members, overseeing the church's temporal affairs, and helping and advising the elders.

Hiscox addresses the subject of church discipline. He admits that this word has an unpleasant sound, but reminds us that "discipline, in its larger sense, means training, cultivation, improvement." Nevertheless, there are, sadly, times when corrective discipline is necessary. The church on earth represents the kingdom of Christ: "unless law prevail in the kingdom and order be maintained, how shall the king be honored, the kingdom advanced, or the world blessed by its coming and triumph?"

The main objective of discipline is to remove evil from the church, which is best achieved by regaining the offender. Discipline must therefore be carried out in a spirit of gentleness and love. The biblical procedure laid down in Matthew 18:15–17 must be followed.

The *Directory* includes a section on Christian mission. The church is in the world with an evangelistic mandate. A local church should be looking out for those places near at hand which are destitute of gospel witness, and should take the gospel to them, but should also have the world in its sights. Every church has an obligation to aid in sending the gospel to the ends of the earth: "No church can hope for prosperity at home unless it strives to give the means of salvation to all men." Hiscox stresses the responsibility of pastors to impart this vision.

PRACTICAL APPLICATION

(1) We must never forget the importance of meeting together as the church. The Bible from start to finish emphasizes the vital centrality of the gathered assembly. We are warned in Hebrews 10:25 not to forsake "the assembling of ourselves together." Here we have a necessary caution for our times. The internet can be very useful for keeping in the loop church members who are permanently housebound or temporarily unwell. However, if a church member who is well enough to make the journey to the meeting place nonetheless stays at home to connect to the service online, that is a serious act of disobedience, which must be challenged. Churches ought not to allow such negligence to become a possibility.

(2) As the church, we must live as those called out of the world. The ways of the Lord are antithetical to the ways of the world. To become part of Christ's church is to make a radical break with the sinful world. We must cultivate a healthy fear of the Lord, actively pursue holiness and obedience, and so live genuinely under Christ's Lordship.

(3) Those of us called to be pastors must fulfil our ministry. We must ensure that the Word of God retains central place in church life. We must commit ourselves to study and preparation in order that we can effectively feed and edify the flock of God. We must teach sound doctrine, seek clarity on issues facing the church, and protect the church from error. We must also seek to be soul-winners, preaching the gospel faithfully. We must strive to preach in clear and simple language, aiming to do our hearers good, not to impress them with our eloquence. We

must not become dictators in our churches, and must not, by our mode of operation, convey a false, priestly view of the ministry. We are called to be examples to the flock.

(4) We must aim to develop a family atmosphere in the local church, characterized by love, leading to unity. At times this may demand tough honesty, if love and unity are under threat. But challenges must not come across as the expression of arrogance. We must respect the liberty of our brothers and sisters: unity does not mean uniformity: there must be space for variety in a church family. The varied gifts of the members must be encouraged, so that the church as a whole benefits from the diversity of grace amongst its people. Those in need must be cared for. We must remember that fellowship in Christ bridges the generation gap: the teenage believer and the elderly believer are one in a unique way, unknown outside of Christ. We must do all that we can to cultivate the reality of this oneness in our churches.

(5) Care is necessary in assessing applicants for membership. To equate "church" and "elect" means that a significant evidence of election, except in very exceptional circumstances, will be a hearty commitment to the church. "If we are not faithfully participating in the life of a faithful local church, we are not really living as Christians."[26] We should not subject membership candidates to too gruelling an interrogation, but must make a full and honest assessment of their spiritual condition: we must ensure that we do not admit unconverted people, who may well cause chaos in the church later. Baptism should be a requirement for membership.

(6) There are, sadly, times when church discipline is inescapable, but it must be administered with care. It must be carried out in line with the pattern spelt out by the Lord. Gossip must be ruled out. A spirit of gentleness and love should prevail, in order to recover the offender as speedily as possible.

(7) We should develop relationships with other churches. The oneness of the global Christian community in its vast diversity is a glorious reality. A local church must not become isolated from the wider body. Our meeting is only a tiny part of the whole worldwide people of God across the centuries, and we all need each other. We need to receive the witness of the entire church across the world and throughout history.

26. Williamson, *Heidelberg*, 100–101.

Because the communion of saints stretches back through time, we also read the works of our predecessors.

The starting-point for this is the cultivation of fellowship with other churches local to us, even those whose theological position and practices may be different from ours. This does not validate an ecumenism which tolerates heresy in the name of love. Unity can only be on the basis of truth. However, where the Word of God is central, where the gospel is faithfully preached, where the Lord is genuinely adored, then we are one in him, and we accept one another as brothers and sisters in Christ, our minor differences of outlook, understanding, practice, and culture, notwithstanding.

From my years of serving in the Far East, I have come to learn that, far more significant than the cultural diversity within the global church, is the unity that we share within a new Christian culture which transcends every cultural tradition on the international stage. That unifying Christian culture is something which we must value and cherish with great joy and thankfulness. To cohere with the trans-generational and international Christian culture is far more important than local and temporal cultural relevance.

(8) Mission and evangelism must be a priority. Every church should be seeking to win souls for Christ, and every local church should have a global vision, supporting world mission in whatever ways are realistic. Children should be targeted in the church's outreach, both children growing up within the church family—the offspring or adopted children of believing parents—and those whose families are complete outsiders.

(9) Be ready for persecution. It has frequently been the church's calling to suffer persecution. Jesus warns us, his followers, "in the world you will have tribulation," but immediately adds, "but be of good cheer; I have overcome the world" (John 16:33). We should not be surprised if we have to suffer for the sake of our Savior, but let's not provoke persecution unnecessarily through our own foolishness.

(10) We must pray for God's blessing. We ought to be expecting growth. In difficult days we must hold on to God's promise that he will gather in his elect from the ends of the earth. However, we must always remember that it is Jesus who is the builder of his church: we are just his under-shepherds, so our confidence must be in him, not in our own gifts and abilities. This leads us to pray with urgency, to cry out for the power of the Holy Spirit in our ministries. Without him we can do nothing.

14

The Doctrine of Worship, Preaching, and the Sacraments

IN THIS CHAPTER OUR concern is a set of doctrines subsidiary to that of the church. How are we to understand the church's worship, those occasions when the church assembles to praise the Lord, to hear his word, and to celebrate the sacraments?

BIBLICAL FOUNDATION

Old Testament

We shall take two sample passages to illustrate the Old Testament material relevant to this theme.

2 Chronicles 29:20–36

We read here of a great assembly which took place in Jerusalem following Hezekiah's reform of the temple and its worship. The assembly begins with the offering of sacrifices: atonement is made for the people. The offerings are accompanied by "the song of the LORD" (verse 27), led by the prescribed musical instruments (verse 25). Verse 28 informs us that "all the assembly worshipped." There were no mere spectators. The connotation of the word translated "worshipped" (*šāḥâ*), which appears twice more in the next two verses, is to bow down before a superior, acknowledging one's own lowliness and shame. This assumption of a posture of humility is emphasized by the observation repeated in verses 29 and 30 that the people bowed as they worshipped.

Verse 30 informs us that the songs sung were from the Book of Psalms, and that the entire atmosphere was one of gladness. Further sacrifices and offerings then follow, expressing "a willing heart" (verse 31). Verse 36 reiterates the note of joy.

This event reminds us that in our church assemblies the sacrifice of the cross should always be at the forefront of our thoughts: our united worship is a response to what our Savior has done for us. Worship includes music and song, and takes place in an atmosphere of humble reverence and joyful gratitude.

Psalm 22:22–31

Many of the Psalms are relevant to the theme of this chapter. We shall use this one as an example, because the word "assembly" comes twice (verses 22 and 25), as does the word "worship" (verses 27 and 29).

Jesus quoted the opening words of this Psalm as he hung on the cross (Matt 27:46; Mark 15:34). The first three sections depict different aspects of his suffering, but in the middle of each section we hear the words, "But you" (verses 3, 9, and 19). The second part of each section explains why Jesus did not cave in to utter despair. We may summarize as follows: (1) Jesus was forsaken by God, and yet was consoled by the character of God [verses 1–5]; (2) Jesus was rejected by people, yet was reassured by God's past faithfulness [verses 6–11]; (3) Jesus was in intense pain, but was confident of God's future salvation [verses 12–21].

Then follows our passage, and here the tone is totally different. God has heard his servant's cry, and the Psalm closes on a note of victory. In verse 22 (cf. verse 25) Jesus is in the midst of the assembly, made up of his brothers. That is our standing! There he praises the LORD, and leads his people in praise. Praise entails glorifying him and fearing him. Even though we are unworthy, as the name "Jacob" affirms, we have been changed by God's grace into "Israel," those on whose behalf God has prevailed (verse 23). And the grand motivation for our praise is that God "has not despised nor abhorred the affliction of the afflicted." Rather, he has raised his afflicted Son from the dead, and exalted him "to his right hand *to be* Prince and Savior" (Acts 5:31). The note of praise and worship permeates the remaining verses of the Psalm. The church's praise is a response to the satisfaction which we find in Christ (verse 26), and leads to the proclamation of his righteousness (verses 30–31).

New Testament

We shall look at four relevant passages from the New Testament

Acts 2:41–42

Here we get a brief glimpse of the activities of the church at Jerusalem, the only Christian congregation in the world at that time. The means by which new converts were admitted to the church was baptism. Despite the different views on baptism, we should all agree that an unbaptized church member is a contradiction in terms.

That first church engaged in four regular activities, and the record stands as a model for the practice of all churches since.

(1) The apostles' doctrine. Back then the apostles themselves were the teachers of the doctrine. They are no longer with us, but a true church must be founded on the apostolic teaching recorded in the New Testament. A vital element in the work of the church is to teach believers from the word, so that they may have a sound and mature grasp of the truth.

(2) Fellowship. The Greek word is *koinōnia*, which speaks of joint participation in something shared in common. A true church is one in which the members share their life. They do not merely meet at meetings, but feel that they belong together and so enjoy being together. This is so because they are united in Christ and the gospel by the Holy Spirit. We get an insight from verses 44–45 into what this meant in practice for the Jerusalem church. They "had all things in common (*koinos*)," and used their resources to help those in need.

(3) The breaking of bread. This is one of the Bible's terms for the service of remembrance. The regular breaking of bread emphasized the centrality to the church's existence of the death of Christ as the means of his people's righteousness. Verse 46 implies that the earliest church celebrated this remembrance in homes, perhaps alongside a meal.

(4) The prayers. This refers to gatherings for prayer. The word translated "prayers," *proseuchē*, highlights petitionary or intercessory prayer, reminding us that such is a vital element in church life.

1 Corinthians 11:23–26

The instructions regarding the Lord's Supper originated with the Lord himself. In these verses Paul cites, in summary form, Jesus' words at the last supper, the Passover meal. This commemorated the death of the lamb in the place of Israel, the LORD's firstborn. In celebrating the Lord's Supper we acknowledge with immense gratitude that "Christ our Passover" (1 Cor 5:7) died instead of us so that we live eternally.

Paul twice uses the word "remembrance," translating *anamnēsis* (verses 24 and 25). The word has occurred in Luke's account of the last supper (Luke 22:19). The prefix, *ana-*, means "upwards."[1] To remember the Lord around his table is more than a mere memory exercise: it is to be led upwards into deepened fellowship with him.

In verse 26 the apostle emphasizes the proclamatory power of the Lord's Supper. God achieves and sustains his saving work in his people's hearts through the preaching of his word. The word spoken audibly appeals via the hearing to the mind. In the Lord's Supper the word enacted symbolically appeals to our other senses—to sight as we see the elements on the table, to smell as the fragrance of bread and wine fills the air, to touch as we handle the bread and the cup, to taste as we place them in our mouths. This serves for the believer's assurance as God's word is received in such a vivid form, and also has evangelistic power if unbelievers are observing.

The final words of verse 26 indicate that the Lord's Supper is only for the present life. However, they also remind us that in the Supper, not only do we look back to the cross, we also look on in anticipation to the Lord's return, when we shall feast with him at the heavenly banquet.[2]

1 Timothy 2

This chapter concerns aspects of church practice. In the first two verses, using four different words, the apostle emphasizes the vital place of

1. Thayer, *Lexicon*, 35.
2. This section is a summary of Bayes, *Apostles' Creed*, 187–97.

prayer in church life. Prayer is to be offered for all people, including those who form the world's governments. The motivation in praying for them is that there might be an environment conducive to gospel work.

Verse 8 highlights a crucial principle to do with prayer: "the men" are to pray. This is not to exclude women (cf. 1 Cor 11:5), but the men are to take the lead. "The men," with the definite article, clearly means all the men. Paul does not say "some men," or even "men" in an imprecise sense. A Christian man who does not lead in prayer at the church prayer meeting is acting in disobedience to the Lord. All the men should pray first, and then the women may follow.

In the same verse Paul also speaks about posture in prayer: "lifting up holy hands." When Jesus ascended to heaven, he did so with his hands lifted to bless the disciples (Luke 24:50–51). This symbolized the fact that he would be permanently blessing his people from heaven. Prayer with lifted hands, reproducing his departing posture, represents the blessing which he is constantly pronouncing on his church. Our prayers in church gatherings take place within the atmosphere of the blessing of our ascended Lord, and call that blessing down upon his people.

But lifted hands must be holy hands. A man cherishing sinful thoughts and vices will not be able to lead God's people in prayer effectively. The phrase "without wrath and doubting" probably defines what "holy" means in this particular context. Christian men must guard their hearts and seek before God a sweetness of spirit and a confidence in his truth and power. If we pray with bitterness in our hearts or scepticism in our minds, we shall undermine the impact of our prayers.

Having addressed the men, the apostle instructs women to dress modestly, and then verses 11 and 12 forbid women to be teachers of men or to be in a position of authority over men; rather they are to "learn in silence with all submission," and "to be in silence." Women may certainly teach other women and children (cf. Titus 2:3–5). What is ruled out is a teaching ministry at gatherings of the whole church.

The word "silence" translates *hēsuchia*. It does not prohibit women from saying anything at all; it has to do with attitude. Women may pray and prophesy (1 Cor 11:5) without flouting this instruction. The word "submission" (*hupotagē*) defines this quiet spirit: a woman places herself willingly under authority. She will not take the initiative, but will follow the men raised up by God to exercise authority in the church.

Two matters of principle underly these practical arrangements. The first is God's creation order. God made Adam first (verse 13), so setting him in the position of leader. This predates the fall. Male headship is not God's response to sin, but part of the created order of things. The second reason has to do with the order of events at the fall. In verse 14 the apostle picks up Eve's own admission to the LORD, "The serpent deceived me" (Gen 3:13). The woman was taken in by the serpent's lies; but she "did not deceive the man, but persuaded him."[3] This in no way exonerates him, but, as Ann Bowman explains:

> Paul's point is that this role reversal that caused such devastation at the beginning must not be repeated in the church. The woman must not be the one who leads the man in obedience to her. Thus when the teaching of the Word of God in the assembly occurs, a qualified male elder should fill the role of teacher.[4]

1 Peter 3:18–22

Peter refers here to Noah's ark, "in which a few, that is, eight souls, were saved through water" (verse 20). Then in verse 21 he writes,

> There is also an antitype which now saves us—baptism (not the removal of the filth of the flesh, but the answer of a good conscience toward God, through the resurrection of Jesus Christ.

The ark was a picture, and the corresponding reality is seen in baptism. The eight in the ark were saved through water, as the water enabled the ark to float above the devastation of the judgment of the flood. In a similar way, our salvation comes to us through the waters of baptism.

We have to be careful to understand this correctly. Peter is not saying that we are saved merely by getting wet in the baptismal water. That is why he adds the qualifying phrase, "not the removal of the filth of the flesh." The eight souls were brought safely through the water only because they were inside the ark. Outside, the water was deadly. So we are saved by the water of baptism only as we are found in Christ. That is the significance of the reference to "a good conscience." But who can possibly have a good conscience—we are all sinners. Hebrews 9:14 says that Christ's blood cleanses our conscience, and that is what Peter is talking about in verse 18, where he says that "Christ also suffered once for sins, the just for the unjust, that he might bring us to God."

3. Bengel, *Gnomon*, Vol. 4, 254.
4. Bowman, "Women in Ministry," 206.

Because Christ suffered in our place, we have been brought to God, cleansed, perfected, rendered righteous in his holy sight, our conscience forever cleared, our guilt and shame cancelled once for all. Peter continues by pointing out that, having been "put to death in the flesh," Jesus was "made alive by the Spirit." In raising Jesus from the dead, God gave his resounding endorsement to all that his Son had achieved on the cross. So in the event of baptism we make our personal affirmation: he died for me, he rose again for me. We identify with him in his death and resurrection, our old life dead and buried as we are immersed in the water, out of which we rise again to new life in him. Baptism symbolizes our conviction that "he did it for me," and seals our commitment to die to sin and to live for him. It is in that sense that we are saved through baptism.

DOCTRINAL FORMULATION

The Early Creeds

There is just one relevant phrase in the Nicene Creed, when it says, "I acknowledge one baptism for the remission of sins." The phrase "one baptism" is taken from Ephesians 4:5, where it occurs in a list which also includes the terms, one body, one Spirit, one hope, one Lord, one faith, one God and Father (verses 4–6). The list is introduced by the exhortation in verse 3 "to keep the unity of the Spirit in the bond of peace." Because there is only one Holy Spirit who has brought into being the one body of the one Lord Jesus Christ, the only Son of the one God and Father, there is also only one saving faith leading to the one eternal hope. All this is signalled by the one baptism.

The insistence on the oneness of baptism arises from an issue faced by the early church, namely whether those who had been baptized in separatist groups, such as the Donatists, should be re-baptized if they returned to the one church. The conclusion was that they should not: baptism is unrepeatable; its efficacy derives from Christ, not from the human agent who baptizes, nor the context in which it takes place.

The phrase "for the remission of sins" is also scriptural: preaching on the Day of Pentecost, Peter said "Repent and let every one of you be baptized in the name of Jesus Christ for the remissions of sins" (Acts 2:38). However, the bare act of baptism cannot confer forgiveness. Without true repentance, baptism is meaningless. The fourth-century creed composed by Epiphanius, spoke of "one baptism of repentance," emphasizing the necessity of a genuine personal response to the gospel.[5]

The Reformation Confessions

We shall divide our consideration of the confessions into three sections, mirroring the title of this chapter. There is a huge amount of material in the confessions relevant to this chapter. This reflects the fact that, to a large degree, it was in these areas that the medieval church was most in need of reformation. The church's doctrinal errors had a knock-on effect which severely distorted its application of biblical practice, most especially as regards the sacraments, though to some extent in the field of worship more generally.

Worship

The reformers insisted that attendance at meetings for worship is a believer's duty; it is part of the commitment of church membership.

THE FORM OF WORSHIP

The confessions teach that pure and acceptable worship follows the pattern prescribed in Scripture and rejects all human inventions.

There has been some diversity in the understanding of what this entails, with two main approaches. The first teaches that anything not explicitly forbidden in Scripture is allowable, the second that only what Scripture explicitly commands is permissible. The first is known as the "normative principle," the second as the "regulative principle." The first denotes that Scripture provides norms which lay out a framework for worship, the second that Scripture regulates worship in its totality.

In general, the reformers saw worship practices not clearly contrary to Scripture as matters of Christian liberty. Scripture establishes the basic order for worship, but does not contain a complete prescription for every detail. It is a matter of common-sense observation that cultural differences may lead to diversity in worship. The 1689 Baptist Confession maintains this balance: it says that the Lord gives each local church "all

---

5. Epiphanius, "Ancoratus," 38.

the power and authority which is in any way required for them to carry on the order of worship . . . which he has instituted."

Weekly worship

The confessions support the normal practice of using the Lord's Day for a church's main worship gatherings. There is, however, a difference of emphasis between different confessions. The Westminster Confession, for example, sees the Lord's Day as the Christian Sabbath; meeting on that day is therefore a matter of binding biblical principle. By contrast, the Second Helvetic Confession represents the merely pragmatic argument that the churches should, where possible, perpetuate the example set by the early church of meeting on the first day of the week. It does not see the Lord's Day as the new Sabbath; rather the Sabbath has been abolished.

The debate between these two positions continues. It is a subject where we must each be persuaded in our own minds, and accept one another with our different outlooks. It need not become a divisive issue. The Second Helvetic Confession is right that the Lord's Day is preserved for the sake of "worship and love." If controversy over the day of worship reflects a lack of love, then our priorities are wrong.

Christian festivals

The confessions were unanimous in their rejection of the commemoration of the feast days of the "saints." At the Westminster Assembly all acknowledgement of festivals, including Christmas and Easter, was rejected as a Catholic innovation.[6] The Second Helvetic Confession, however, approved the specific celebration of the Lord's birth, circumcision, passion, resurrection, and ascension, and the outpouring of the Spirit at Pentecost. However, it said that whether or not a church celebrates these events is a matter of Christian liberty.

---

6. Westminster Assembly, "Directory for Publick Worship," 394.

THE CONTENT OF WORSHIP

The confessions list six ingredients of biblically regulated worship. (1) Prayer. Intercessory prayer is especially commended, specifically for governments, for those in authority in every sphere of life, for pastors, for the needs of the churches, and for those who are suffering. (2) Thanksgiving. (3) The reading of the Scriptures. (4) Preaching. Assemblies for Christian worship are primarily gatherings in which God's inspired word is brought to bear on the lives which people are living and on the challenges of the day. (5) Singing. There is, perhaps, surprisingly little reference to this subject in the confessions. The Second Helvetic Confession takes the view that singing is not essential, and if it takes place it must be in moderation. The Westminster Confession advocated the use of the Psalms in Christian worship, believing that God should be praised in the words which he himself had inspired. (6) Provision for those in need. Both the Heidelberg Catechism and the Second Helvetic Confession include this as an element in worship. This ties practical love for other people into worship. What validates our worship is its outflow in care for the needy.

THE LANGUAGE OF WORSHIP

The confessions insist that worship must be conducted in the common language of the people. They rejected the Catholic use of Latin for worship. By the sixteenth century, this was a dead language. It was the language of scholarship, but was unknown to the common people.

This requirement reflects the Reformation conviction that the gospel is a universal message. Every single language group on earth must be enabled to worship God in its own language.

Preaching

The ministry of the word is the central ingredient in Christian worship, and the chief role of pastors in particular.

THE VITAL NEED FOR THE HOLY SPIRIT IN PREACHING

One thing on which the confessions are clear is that preaching needs to be urgent. Although it has an instructional aspect, it must never be merely educational. Preaching is more than just the exposition of Scripture, far more than the teaching of the Bible. In the preaching of the word, the things announced are actually being offered by God to the hearers. Whenever preaching takes place the church must cry out to God to release the power of the Spirit mightily. This does not only mean that the preacher must be aided by the Spirit, but also that the hearts of the hearers must be moved by his power.

CONGREGATIONAL RESPONSIBILITY IN THE PREACHING OF THE WORD

Although the greatest responsibility for the faithful preaching of the word lies with the preacher, the rest of the people have a responsibility too: they must hear true preachers as the voice of God himself. Each hearer must listen carefully, actively, making personal application to his own conscience, determined to act upon what he hears. Preaching is a two-way thing: the hearers' response makes an impact on the preacher.

The Sacraments

The Baptist confessions prefer the term "Ordinances." This emphasizes that they were ordained by Christ himself. However, Samuel Waldron finds no intrinsic objection to the use of the word "sacrament," as long as it is not understood in the superstitious sense that there is an efficacy in the mere use of the ordinances, independently of the faith of the recipient.[7] We shall consider first the Reformation understanding of the sacraments in general, and then focus on each particular sacrament.

THE THEOLOGY OF THE SACRAMENTS

There are two sacraments

The confessions stress that baptism and the Lord's Supper are the only sacraments. The Roman Catholic church claimed that there were seven sacraments—the other five being confirmation, penance, ordination, marriage and extreme unction. The Reformers admitted that ordination

---

7. Waldron, *Modern Exposition*, 422.

and marriage, though not sacramental, were profitable things. The other three, however, were rejected as merely human inventions.

The sacraments are "signs"

The sacraments point beyond themselves. They are outward, visible symbols, pointing to that which is inward and invisible. They are like signposts, directing us to God's saving work in Christ. The word "shadows" is also used. The sacraments are not the substantial reality: that is found in Christ alone. They are like his shadow falling upon this world, giving us a faint outline of what he has done. They are symbolic, and so we cannot be saved merely by participation in the sacraments, but only by that which they symbolize.

The sacraments are "seals"

This is the most common term used to denote the fact that sacraments are more than mere signs or symbols. The word "seal" appears in conjunction with the word "sign" in Romans 4:11. A seal serves for confirmation and authentication. Participation by faith in the sacraments results in the reinforcement of the believer's assurance. What is confirmed is not just the faith which the church confesses, but the personal faith of the participant. As participation takes place the Holy Spirit seals to the participant his or her personal interest in the gospel promise in Christ.

In this connection the sacraments are sometimes referred to as "mystical symbols." They are more than bare symbols which achieve nothing: they truly foster our mystical union with Christ. There is no automatic efficacy or power in the sacraments themselves, but their use does make a real spiritual impact when they are received by faith. By the power of the Holy Spirit, the Lord Jesus Christ is genuinely present in the sacraments and our faith in him is strengthened, our union with him is deepened, our salvation is confirmed to our hearts.

The reason why Christ gave the sacraments

In giving us the sacraments, the Lord makes a concession to our weakness. His word proclaims to us the gospel, and the sacraments are added as a confirmation of its truth. God knows our humanity and its infirmities. If we had to rely on hearing alone, we would miss so much. Through the sacramental symbols God directs his word in vivid form to all our senses, and so compensates for our proneness to be forgetful.

Participation in the sacraments as a pledge of allegiance

Robert Shaw points out that the term "sacrament" was borrowed from Roman military usage, where it meant the oath by which a soldier bound himself to be faithful to his general, and not to become a deserter.[8] In a similar way, in the sacramental ordinances we enlist in the service of Christ, the captain of our salvation. We engage to follow him wherever he leads, we pledge ourselves never to become deserters, and our separation from the sinful world is underlined.

Errors regarding the sacraments which must be rejected

The confessions mention three main types of error.

(1) The Roman Catholic view. Catholicism ties what the sacraments signify so closely to the sign that it concludes that all who receive the sign also receive what is signified, regardless of what kind of lives they are living or whether they have genuine faith in Jesus Christ.

(2) The "Zwinglian" view. This teaches that the sacraments are nothing more than mere symbols. They are memorials of what Christ has done, but they have no spiritual efficacy. Their use is a matter of obedience, but they are not means of grace in the power of the Spirit. Although this view has become linked with the name of Zwingli, it is not clear from his own writings that this is actually what he believed.

(3) The enthusiastic view. This entails the rejection of the sacraments altogether on the grounds that they are superfluous, because we are already enjoying the reality which they symbolize.

---

8. Shaw, *Confession*, 279.

Baptism

Eligible candidates for baptism

Most of the Reformation confessions were paedobaptist, though they restricted baptism to the children of at least one believer. They based this on Genesis 17, where the LORD commits himself to be God to Abraham and his descendants, and commands that the children receive the covenant sign.

By contrast, the Baptist confessions insist that baptism is only for those who profess repentance, faith and obedience.

Significantly, the paedobaptist confessions can seem embarrassed and apologetic about their own teaching, as if they are aware that their statements are illogical. So the French Confession says this of baptism: "although it is a sacrament of faith and penitence, yet as God receives little children into the Church with their fathers, we say, upon the authority of Jesus Christ, that the children of believing parents should be baptized." That sounds like a tacit recognition that you would not expect such a conclusion to follow from the premise!

The Genevan Catechism devotes eight consecutive questions to a discussion of this difficulty. It accepts the biblical view that baptism is for those who have exercised faith and repentance, who have been forgiven, who feel the power of the indwelling Spirit, and whose way of life commends the reality of their profession. This inevitably raises the question, "how comes it that we baptize infants?" The answer reads, "it is not necessary that faith and repentance should always precede baptism," and claims that it is sufficient that baptized infants should exhibit these realities once they have grown up.

This argument is clearly weak, and so the next question asks whether reason can demonstrate that this is not an absurd position to maintain. It is fascinating that the catechism resorts to reason rather than Scripture: its compilers were clearly aware that they could offer no biblical defense. Their "rational" answer first asserts the parallel with circumcision, assuming that the promises are the same under both administrations of the covenant of grace. However, this does not yet prove that the sign of the covenant should still be applied to infants. Here again the catechism bases its answer not on Scripture, but on "due pondering" of the issue, the key being that in Christ God's grace is more, not less, abundant than previously, whereas to deny baptism to infants would lessen God's mercy. The children of Christian parents, being heirs of the blessing promised to the seed of believers, are therefore baptized, the terms of their baptism being that, having grown up, they acknowledge its reality and produce its fruit. These arguments overlook one decisive distinction between circumcision and infant baptism: whereas circumcision left its permanent mark in the flesh, a baptized infant retains no memory of the event, and receives no lasting mark to confirm its having occurred.

The weakness of this argument is obvious, and the setting of terms which can only be fulfilled subsequently is patently absurd. It seems that this was clear even to the composers of the catechism. In an earlier question they had already faced up to the problem that the baptized children of believers do not invariably follow in their parents' footsteps. The explanation given is that God, in pledging his mercy to believers and their children, did not thereby bind himself never under any circumstances to reject the offspring of a believer, but that when he does so, he tempers his judgment with mercy to prove that his promise is not vain. That reads as an admission of defeat! If God even once fails to keep a covenant promise, then he is not a trustworthy God, and the claims made for the covenant are spurious and empty.

David Wright fears that the Westminster Confession comes perilously close to teaching baptismal regeneration. He notes the Westminster Assembly's confusion: its participants sensed (rightly) that the New Testament teaches "faith-baptism," and yet were unable to break free from the constraints of a situation in which, under medieval Catholicism, infant baptism had become the norm.[9]

A text often used in defense of paedobaptism is 1 Corinthians 7:14: "the unbelieving husband is sanctified by the wife, and the unbelieving wife is sanctified by the husband; otherwise your children would be unclean, but now they are holy."

Paedobaptist commentators usually read this as a reference to covenantal holiness. Albert Barnes (himself a paedobaptist), however, recognizes that such an interpretation has to be read into the text and is not its obvious meaning. He argues that "holy" and "unholy" are simply the equivalents in New Testament times to the modern terms "legitimate" and "illegitimate." For a newly converted spouse to walk out of a

---

9. D. F. Wright, "Baptism," 168–74.

marriage would imply that the marriage ought never to have taken place, and therefore that the offspring are illegitimate children.[10]

Another reading has been proposed by both David Kingdon and Tom Wright. They see this text as a simple declaration that the children of a believer are "within the sphere of God's love and the power of the gospel."[11]

The appropriate method of baptism

The 1604 edition of the Anglican Catechism defines the outward sign of baptism as "water, wherein the person baptized is dipped, or sprinkled with it." Anglicanism originally regarded infant baptism by immersion as the norm, with sprinkling as an occasional provision for the case of a sickly child.[12] However, in the course of time, sprinkling (or sometimes pouring) displaced immersion as the usual mode of baptism.

By contrast, Baptists have insisted that immersion is the proper method of baptism. The 1689 Confession says: "Immersion—the dipping of the person in water—is necessary to the due administration of this ordinance." The 1644 Confession elaborates on this point: "The way and manner of the dispensing of this ordinance the Scripture holds out to be dipping or plunging the whole body under water: it being a sign, must answer the thing signified."

The things signified in baptism

On this point Baptists and paedobaptists are in general agreement, a fact which again exposes the inconsistencies in the infant Baptist position. The passage just quoted from the 1644 Baptist Confession continues by mentioning three things which are signified in baptism. Some confessions add a fourth.

(1) Cleansing from sin. The believer's whole soul is washed clean in the blood of Christ. It follows that the thorough soaking of the entire body in the water is necessary, otherwise the picture would fail to do justice to the reality.

---

10. Barnes, *New Testament*, Vol. 5, 117–18.

11. N. T. Wright, *1 Corinthians*, 84; cf. Kingdon, *Children of Abraham*, 90.

12. I learned this from a lecture delivered by Anglican minister, Alec Motyer.

(2) Identification with Christ. In baptism, the candidate affirms his participation in Christ's death, burial, and resurrection. This again underlines the importance of immersion: no other method can do justice to the reference to being "buried with him in baptism" (Col 2:12; cf. Rom 6:4). Baptism signified the putting off of the old man and the putting on of the new. This exchange is true judicially: in God's sight we stand justified, righteous, new creatures in Christ. It is also true morally and progressively: in baptism we signify our intention to mortify sin and to give ourselves up to walk in newness of life by the power of the Holy Spirit.

(3) Future resurrection from the dead. There is an eschatological element to baptism: we look towards the day when the power of the risen Christ will transform our mortal bodies and impart to them eternal life. This hope is as certain as the fact that the body is immersed in the baptismal water and then brought up again.

(4) Regeneration, adoption, and sanctification. Baptism is an initiatory ordinance: it speaks of the beginnings of the Christian life, of being born again, adopted into the family of God, and set apart from the world. The Belgic Confession puts it like this: baptism "witnesses to us that God, being our gracious Father, will be our God forever."

The main "direction of movement" in baptism

There is a tendency in Baptist circles to speak about baptism in terms of the candidate witnessing to his faith. This reflects a misunderstanding of the deepest significance of the ordinance. It suggests that the main direction of movement is from the baptized person to his fellow believers and even to the unconverted world.

The confessions saw the main direction of movement differently: it was from God to the baptismal candidate. The word "witness" may still be used, but, as the French Confession puts it, baptism is "a lasting witness that Jesus Christ will always be our justification and sanctification." In other words, baptism is the Lord's testimony to us. A major purpose of the ordinance, therefore, is to give assurance to the person baptized of God's gracious acceptance of him in Christ. Baptism is a source of comfort as it emphasizes God's favor, renewing the baptized person in the conviction that God is favorable to him personally.

While a felt faith is certainly something to be prized, a danger arises if we over-emphasize felt experience: feelings and emotions can fluctuate.

However, the specific event of baptism is a constant, undeniable fact. Here we see God's kindness: he does not force us to rely on our feelings alone. In our baptism he proclaims that he really does love us forever.

Baptism as the gateway into the church

To describe baptism in this way is to agree with the confessions that baptism is the sacrament of our admission into the body of Christ on earth. Some Baptist churches have been lax about this. Professing believers have been admitted into membership without baptism. The baneful consequences of this practice have become apparent. A professing believer who will not be baptized is probably not genuine. The biblical command to be baptized upon repentance (Acts 2:38; 10:48) is absolute: it is the first step in discipleship. A professing believer who falls at the first hurdle is exposed as spurious.

Baptism as an obligation

It follows from what has been said that baptism may never be treated as optional. It is an absolute obligation immediately upon profession of faith in the Lord Jesus Christ. To reject or neglect baptism is sin.

However, we must not go to the extreme of tying salvation so tightly to baptism as to imply that it is impossible to be saved without baptism. The thief on the cross was never baptized. Occasionally, there may be circumstances which make baptism impossible. However, this must never be allowed as an excuse for those for whom there are no obstacles.

The Lord's Supper

The Lord's Supper and the church

Whereas baptism is the sacrament of initiation into the church, the Lord's Supper is the sacrament of preservation within the church. Participation is limited to those who are already incorporated into the household of faith.

The confessions insist that the Lord's Supper may only take place within the assembly of God's people. Private communion is inadmissible.

This need not mean that those who are housebound, or unable to get to meetings of the assembly because of illness, are excluded from the Lord's table. There are two ways in which they may be involved without falling into the trap of privatizing communion. (1) The church may go to such people. Home communion services are not intrinsically wrong, provided that they do not involve merely the pastor and the sick person. If a representative group from the congregation is involved, this legitimates the practice. (2) An early church practice might be reinstated. This involved the deacons taking the elements out to the housebound while the Lord's Supper was being celebrated in the congregation.

Admission to the Lord's Supper

The confessions have two things to say about this.

THERE IS A DUTY OF SELF-EXAMINATION

Before attending the Lord's Supper, every believer must examine his faith, his holiness, and his duty towards his neighbor. This involves asking himself three questions. (1) Am I truly trusting in Christ alone for salvation, and placing no confidence in my own works? (2) Am I striving to obey God's law, not as an attempt to earn his favor, but as the expression of grateful love in response to the favor which he has already shown me in Christ? (3) Am I maintaining the unity of the body, and striving for peace with all people, seeking to serve others as I am able?

The Heidelberg Catechism offers some wise advice. It says that the Supper is

> for those who are truly sorrowful for their sins, and yet trust that these are forgiven them for the sake of Christ; and that their remaining infirmities are covered by his passion and death; and who also earnestly desire to have their faith more and more strengthened, and their lives more holy.

This guards against the perfectionist attitude which makes church members with a sensitive conscience feel disqualified from taking the bread and wine.

The confessions assumed that attendance at the table could never be a merely voluntary matter. The elders are to keep watch over the flock, and to intervene in the case of those whose confession of faith lacks credibility or whose way of life lacks the fruits of true repentance.

The significance of the Lord's Supper

The sacramental symbolism is obvious. Like the bread, Christ's body was broken; like the poured-out wine, his blood was shed for us. The Lord's Supper keeps the remembrance of those key facts perpetually fresh in the church's consciousness.

However, the Lord's Supper is not a bare recollection of a far-off historical event. It is also an occasion of testimony and assurance. It seals to believers the benefits of Christ's sacrifice. As such, it is more than just a general message to the church as a whole. It also brings to every believing participant individually the reaffirmation that he was personally saved through the death of Christ. At those times when a believer is struggling, his faith weak and in danger of wavering, participation in the Supper is a source of renewed strength.

Spiritual nourishment in the Lord's Supper

This is probably the main thing which the reformers stressed in their extensive discussions of this sacrament. They understood it as a genuine feasting on the body and blood of Christ himself.

Just as bread and wine feed the body, so the body and blood of Christ are food and drink for the soul. In the sacrament Christ does indeed feed and nourish us with his flesh and blood, and so the sacrament seals to us our continuing growth in him. The frequent repetition of the sacrament serves our continual spiritual progress towards the goal of eternal life. The confessions comment on the method by which this takes place. The physical elements of bread and wine serve our spiritual nourishment as they show us that Christ's body and blood are our food and drink. In the bread and the cup Christ's body and blood are represented outwardly and symbolically. Simultaneously, his body and blood are communicated to us inwardly and substantially.

The confessions are careful to distinguish this from the Roman Catholic view that in the mere participation in the sacrament grace is conferred automatically, and from its doctrine of transubstantiation, which teaches that the bread and wine actually change into Christ's body and blood, so that taking the elements equates with feeding on him.

In offering a contrasting explanation of how grace is conferred through the sacrament, the confessions admit that mystery is involved. We are dealing with a heavenly reality which exceeds the measure of our senses. However, three things are mentioned: (1) the communication of Christ's body and blood in the sacrament comes to those who have grace; (2) what is represented by the bread and the wine Christ works by the Spirit; (3) it is by faith that we receive the heavenly bread signified in the sacramental bread.

Grace, the Spirit, and faith are the vital ingredients. Grace and the Spirit are given to those who believe. From the human side, faith alone makes the supper effectual. The unbeliever who partakes of the bread and wine receives only the outward elements, without the spiritual substance, and eats and drinks judgment upon himself.

The Belgic Confession puts it like this: "this feast is a spiritual table, at which Christ communicates himself with all his benefits to us, and gives us there to enjoy both himself and the merits of his suffering and death."

The Second Helvetic Confession helpfully compares the presence of Christ in the Supper, even though his body is seated in heaven at the Father's right hand, to the effectual presence of the sun on earth, even though its actual position is the sky. It also distinguishes three types of eating—physical (the taking of the material food and cup), spiritual (believing on Christ and so partaking of the benefits of his death), and sacramental (receiving the thing signified alongside the sign).

The distinction between spiritual and sacramental eating underlines a point sometimes made in the confessions: it is not only when participating in the sacrament that believers feed spiritually on Christ. By faith, we may feast spiritually on Christ's body and blood every moment of our lives. The sacramental eating in which we participate from time-to-time seals to us the efficacy of Christ on which we are relying constantly. That is why the 1689 Baptist Confession is happy to follow the wording of Westminster and call the Supper a pledge of the believer's communion with Christ. Because of our union with him, we enjoy communion, or fellowship, with him, not only at the "communion service," but always, the service confirming and sustaining that communion.

The Lord's Supper and the fellowship of believers

The confessions echo the New Testament emphasis that the Lord's Supper is the focus of the unity of the church and the mutual love of its members. It represents the life which we all share in common, because all have received it from Christ. Robert Shaw expounds this point well, demonstrating that it transcends the local body of believers:

> All true saints are members of one body, and in the holy supper they have communion, not merely with those who sit along with them at the same table, but "with all that in every place call upon the name of Jesus Christ," their common Lord . . . . This ordinance is very expressive of the communion of the saints, and has a powerful tendency to cherish it. They meet together at the same table, as brethren and children of the same family, to partake of the same spiritual feast.[13]

Errors about the Lord's Supper which must be rejected

Many of the Roman Catholic errors which formed the background to the Reformation revolved around the Lord's Supper. The reformers saw the Roman mass as idolatrous, because the teaching of transubstantiation led to the elements being regarded as the divine Christ himself. To uplift the bread for adoration was therefore the offering of worship to an object which was not God.

Moreover, the doctrine of the mass undermined the sufficiency of Christ's once-for-all sacrifice on the cross. The celebration was itself seen as sacrificial and propitiatory. This rendered it a blasphemous ritual. The idea that the celebrant was a priest was an insult to Christ, because he alone is the High Priest of his new covenant people, and there can be no other mediator.

Because the Catholic Church saw the body of Christ as physically present in the broken bread, it taught that participation in the sacrament automatically entailed participation in Christ. Against this, the reformers

13. Shaw, *Confession*, 295.

insisted on the necessity of faith and the work of the Holy Spirit for participation in Christ to be a reality.

Modern Confessions of Faith

The Chinese confession does not address the specific subjects which make up the content of this chapter. The other two modern confessions have significant things to say. We shall look at each of them in turn.

Confession of Faith of the United Church of Northern India

The observation of the sacraments is listed as a Christian duty. It is placed second in the list of duties after unity in fellowship. This is surely significant. There is a danger, especially in those churches where the Lord's Supper is held separately from the main services, that it becomes regarded as an option, as superfluous to genuine requirements. I well remember as a youngster in the church where I grew up, every time a communion service was to follow the main service of worship, observing, with some bewilderment, something of a mass exodus of professing Christians who, for some reason, did not think the ensuing celebration of the Lord's Supper was for them. By listing observation of the sacraments as a priority in the list of Christian duties, this confession guards against that tendency to treat the table with contempt. Other duties, related to our current theme, required of all believers are: "to continue in prayer, to keep holy the Lord's Day, to meet together for his worship, to wait upon the preaching of his word, to give as God may prosper them."

The phrase "wait upon the preaching" is an interesting one. No doubt the term is an intentional echo of the Scriptures, where waiting on the Lord is mentioned a number of times (e.g., Pss 25:5; 27:14; 37:9, 34; 52:9). In all but one instance the words "wait on" translate the Hebrew term *qāwâ*. It has the sense of tarrying with hopeful expectation.[14] By using the term in the present context the Indian confession emphasizes the fact that preaching is not something that we can expect to be rushed, and that we should listen with the expectation that God will actually achieve something in our lives through his preached word. The following amplification of the term "waiting" has been offered:

14. Schibler, "*qwh*," 892.

> Waiting with steadfast endurance is a great expression of
> faith . . . . Waiting involves the very essence of a person's being,
> his soul. Those who wait in true faith are renewed in strength so
> that they can continue to serve the Lord.[15]

It is through preaching as a means of grace that that strength for service
is renewed week by week.

In his exposition of the Indian confession, William Stewart comments on "the practice of public worship." The gathering of believers is an occasion of great joy, "especially on the joyful "Lord's Day" on which the Savior had risen—to express their thanksgiving to God in acts and words of praise." He points out that "there are depths in his love which to the end of our days we shall hardly have begun to sound. In the practice of worship we learn something of these." Moreover, God himself "is at the center when we meet for worship; this is the place where our Lord has especially promised his presence."[16]

Confession of Faith of the Huria Kristen Batak Protestant

This Indonesian document confesses "only two sacraments ordered by the Lord Jesus." It explicitly refutes the Roman Catholic claim that there are seven sacraments. The purpose of the sacraments is to impart invisible grace through visible signs. The invisible grace referred to is defined as "the remission of sin, redemption, life and glory," and is received by faith. That final comment intentionally guards against the misconception that the mere participation in sacramental symbolism is sufficient of itself as a means of grace. The idea that the mass is a sacrifice is rejected as "not based on the Word of God."

This confession affirms that certain church festivals are to be celebrated, namely "the birth, the death, the resurrection and ascension of the Lord Jesus and the feast of the pouring out of the Holy Spirit." A word of caution is then added: "everyone should remember that no one can win remission of sins even by observation of all these festivals."

Sunday "has been celebrated by the Christians since the very beginning of the church." This confession offers three reasons why the Lord's Day is to be kept holy: it is "the day of the Lord (on which God began creation), the day of the resurrection of the Lord Jesus, and the day of

---

15. Hartley, "qāwâ," 1994.0.
16. W. Stewart, *Faith We Confess*, 38–39.

the outpouring of the Holy Spirit." It is interesting to note the link with creation. The puritans had traced the origin of the Sabbath requirement to Genesis 2,[17] but this confession validates the alteration of the day of worship from the seventh to the first day of the week by moving backwards, in the light of the new creation initiated in the gospel events, from the finished work of creation to its inception.

At two points a Baptist must take exception to this confession's position. It claims that infants should be baptized, "since through baptism they are taken up into the communion of those for whom Christ died," and it asserts that "it is not necessary to baptize by immersion."

HISTORICAL ELABORATION

This section will fall into four parts. (1) In 1667 John Owen wrote a catechism for Independent Churches. Its first eighteen questions address the subject of worship. We first look at that section of this work.[18] (2) Then we shall glance briefly at the Westminster Assembly's *Directory for the Public Worship of God*, written in 1645. (3) Next, we return to Edward Hiscox's *New Directory for Baptist Churches* to hear his defense of believer's baptism by immersion. (4) Finally, we shall examine Robert Letham's arguments against the Baptist position in his *Systematic Theology*, and offer a reply.

John Owen: *A Brief Instruction in the Worship of God*

Owen starts with the duty of worshipping God in the way that he has appointed. He sees the recognition of this duty as inbuilt into human nature. However, because of the ignorance of our fallen nature, we need the revelation of God's word to know what are the appropriate ways of worship. Some people, it is true, take the view that we may worship as seems right in our own eyes. Owen concedes that there are things which the Lord has left to the judgment of prudence, such as the times and places of meeting; these things must be arranged to ensure that nothing can hinder the edification of the church. However, the observation of Christ's positive instructions is a matter of binding obligation.

---

17. Beeke & Jones, *Puritan Theology*, 653–60.
18. Owen, "Worship," 447–79.

Moreover, we are forbidden to add anything to what God has prescribed. It is true that, with the coming of Christ, the requirements for worship were altered. During the Old Testament age worship directed God's people towards the expectation of his coming. With his coming the final stage of the revelation of God's will was initiated. With the fulfilment of the promises in Christ's life and death, the pointers towards it were no longer necessary: worship now rests on what is already accomplished. Hence there is no basis for any further alterations to the institutions of worship.

Owen demonstrates the absurdity of making innovations in worship. The book of Hebrews emphasizes Christ's superiority to Moses, which entitled him to institute a perfected form of worship, beyond that given under the law. To make modifications to the prescribed form of worship today would amount to the preposterous claim to be superior to Christ.

Owen considers the argument that some rites not explicitly commanded in Scripture may nonetheless help worshippers to express their devotion, and add decency, order and beauty to the worship. He replies that acceptable devotion can only be the fruit of faith; outward rites without a biblical warrant can, at most, excite carnal emotions. Furthermore, worship derives its comeliness and beauty solely from its relation to Christ, and from the enabling work of the Holy Spirit. Any supposed glory in outward ceremonies demeans worship, since it diverts attention from the gospel. Orderliness in worship is defined by its adherence to the rules laid down in God's word. Adornments of human invention are in truth corruptions. Owen admits that it was impossible for every possible human invention to be explicitly forbidden by Scripture. However, God prohibits any additions at all.

The converse of not introducing human innovations in worship is twofold: (1) we must omit nothing that Christ has commanded; (2) we fulfil our obligations in the manner that he has prescribed.

This means that we should not simply follow the practices of others; every church and every member must diligently search the Scriptures to ensure that we are fully acquainted with Christ's will.

Owen goes on to consider our main aims in observing the gospel institutions. His answer falls into four parts. I shall save till last that aim to which Owen gives the longest treatment.

We aim to verify our subjection to Christ as Lord

A profession of faith is verified by obedience to our Lord's commands. Part of that obedience involves worshipping according to his own institution.

We aim to build ourselves up in our most holy faith

In instructing us to worship, God is inviting us into communion with himself in Christ, and through that communion his grace is increased in us as he testifies to his love and goodwill towards us.

We aim to confirm our mutual love as believers

We worship as the one family of the one Father, participating together in the one Spirit, by whom we are all baptized into the one body. By the joint celebration of the ordinances of worship we together profess the one faith, love, and hope, and so grow up together into the one head, and testify to the loving union which binds us together.

We aim to sanctify God's name

This is our greatest duty. Unless we worship so that his name is hallowed, whatever we do is an abomination to him. Owen suggests five ways in which we respect God's holiness as we worship according to his pattern: (1) we honor his authority, which is not the case if we respect formality, custom, or human precepts; (2) we recognize his promised presence, and so worship with proper reverence; (3) we receive the promises of his grace as we worship in a due manner by faith; (4) we honor God as we find a delight in gospel worship; (5) when we face opposition, or have to battle with weariness, God is glorified by our perseverance in worship, and in faith and love.

On the fourth point, Owen adds a telling comment: this delight, he says,

> consists not in any carnal self-pleasing, or satisfaction in the outward modes or manner of the performance of divine worship; but it is a holy, soul-refreshing contemplation on the will, wisdom, grace, and condescension of God, in that he is pleased,

of his own sovereign mere will and grace, so to manifest him-self unto such poor sinful creatures as we are, so to condescend unto our weakness, so to communicate himself unto us, so to excite and draw forth our souls unto himself, and to give us such pledges of his gracious intercourse with us by Jesus Christ. By the contemplation of these things is the soul drawn forth to delight in God.

Owen warns us that to come to worship with any other purpose in mind than those which God has appointed is to dishonor him and to deceive ourselves. He takes up the Bible's pleasant analogy which represents God as married to his people, as a husband who is jealous for our loyalty. When we worship him in line with his own precepts, we discharge our duty as the bride of Christ, but to neglect worship, or to profane it by additions of our own, is spiritual disloyalty to the covenant.

Having laid down these vital principles which undergird the church's worship, Owen lists the elements of worship which God has commanded. They are prayer, singing, preaching the word, and adminis-tration of the sacraments of baptism and the Lord's supper.

"The Directory for the Publick Worship of God"

This work has been described as "the archetype of truly reformed worship."[19] It was written against the background of dissatisfaction with the Anglican *Book of Common Prayer*. Its list of the elements of biblically directed worship is similar to Owen's. It contains one additional ingredi-ent—the public reading of Scripture, advocating the reading of a passage from each Testament at every service of worship, and the reading of the entire Bible over a period of time.

This document has an instructive introductory section, entitled *Of the assembling of the congregation, and their behavior in the publick worship of God*. It reminds church members of the duty of worship, of the sin of absence through negligence, and of the need to prepare their hearts prior to the gathering. On arrival, people must avoid irreverence. Once worship has begun they must concentrate, not reading anything other than the passage being heard. Private whispering is forbidden, as are smiling or waving to other members of the congregation, or gaz-ing around. Worship must not be seen as an opportunity for a snooze.

19. Webster, *Religious Thought*, 28.

Participants must not distract others in any way, nor hinder themselves from the service of God. It is recognized that unavoidable circumstances may occasionally result in a late arrival. Latecomers must immediately compose themselves and join in reverently with the part of the worship taking place at that moment.

Edward Hiscox on Baptism

Like all Baptists, Hiscox insists that only those who have exercised and professed saving faith in Christ are entitled to be baptized. As the outward sign of an inward grace, it can have no significance for those who have not been born again by the Spirit.

For those who have been born again, baptism is a binding obligation. It is the first step in discipleship, the initial act of submission to the authority of the Lord. It is essential to obedience. Hiscox reckons that the refusal to obey Christ's command to be baptized is evidence that a person has not truly been born again.

From the fact that baptism is the first duty of the believer after exercising saving faith in Christ, it follows that only those who have been baptized may be admitted to church membership. Baptism stands at the entrance to the church, and displays the unity of the faith and the fellowship of God's people: in the one baptism they profess the one faith in the one Lord.

Hiscox also provides ample evidence that baptism must be by immersion. As a sign, the form of baptism must express its meaning, namely the candidate's identification with Christ in his death and resurrection. If immersion is replaced by some other form, then this symbolic significance is lost, and what takes place is not a genuine baptism. Moreover, there was no example of any other form before AD 250, and even after that, immersion remained the norm for 1300 years, until the Roman Catholic Church abandoned it. Eastern Orthodoxy, however, has never departed from the practice, and Greek dictionaries invariably define *baptizō* as "to immerse."

Unlike many Reformed theologians, Hiscox does not limit the right of administering baptism to ordained pastors. Although, this will normally be the case, baptism is equally valid if administered by any church member appointed for that service.

There is one aspect of Hiscox's teaching on baptism which, in my judgment, ought not to be endorsed. Hiscox affirms, correctly, that believer's baptism is unrepeatable. However, he cites the case of someone who has been baptized, but it subsequently becomes apparent that this person was not truly saved. He suggests that, in such a case, when the person is truly converted, baptism may be repeated. He claims that this would not really be rebaptism, since the earlier baptism was found to be invalid, and therefore not a true baptism at all.

However, I think of Pat, a lady in a congregation which I served at one time. She had the kind of personality which is always looking for some new spiritual experience. Every time such an experience occurred, she assumed that this was her real conversion, and that on the previous occasions she had merely supposed that she had been born again. On one such occasion she asked me to baptize her, having come to the conclusion that at her previous immersion she had merely got wet, that it wasn't her true baptism. I disagreed, so she went to another church and asked the pastor there to baptize her, which he did.

What Hiscox says here leaves the door open for those who temporarily lack assurance to be baptized again and again. He seems to overstress the human side of exercising saving faith. We need to remember that the exercise of faith is the fruit of a prior work of God's grace. In many cases, a believer may not be totally sure at what point in God's gracious process of working in the heart he was actually born again and savingly believed.

But baptism points us first of all to God's work of incorporating us into Christ in his death and resurrection—and he never makes a mistake, he never has to repeat the saving work. It follows that believer's baptism is always unrepeatable. No doubt the ideal and the norm is that we first believe and then are baptized. However, if, occasionally, the order becomes confused, that does not invalidate the baptism. God know his own works, and he will bring to completion every good work which he has begun, as Philippians 1:6 assures us.

A Reply to Robert Letham

Robert Letham's *Systematic Theology* is a magnificent work. However, his assessment of the Baptist position requires a response.

Letham defends the view that the new covenant is made with believers and their children, on the basis of the corporate context in which Scripture sets individuals. He claims that Baptists, believing the new covenant to be made with the believer only, highlight individual responsibility. This, however, is incorrect. Two points may be made.

(1) The Baptist position assumes the election of a people in Christ: baptism is not an individualistic matter. Like the Westminster Confession, so the 1689 Baptist Confession defines the universal church as "the whole number of the elect," and affirms that a people was given to Christ to be his seed. The Baptist position is no less corporate than that of the paedobaptists.

(2) Baptists affirm the priority of God's electing grace in enabling individual response. The assertion that Baptists condition covenantal grace on the individual response is not true. Again, like Westminster, the 1689 Confession recognizes that God requires faith in order that people may be saved, but then adds that he promises "to give unto all those that are ordained unto eternal life, his Holy Spirit, to make them willing and able to believe." Letham misrepresents the position when he contrasts the basic Baptist paradigm that faith precedes baptism with the paedobaptist understanding that grace is prior to faith. The Baptist equally accepts that latter truth.

Furthermore, Letham claims that the New Testament teaches that baptism precedes faith, an order which Baptists reverse. However, his claim is not defensible. In every passage where faith and baptism are mentioned together, the order is invariably faith first, then baptism (Mark 16:16; Acts 8:12–13, 36–37; 16:31–33; 18:8; 19:1–5; Eph 4:5; Col 2:12).

Moreover, Letham's inaccurate accusation that Baptists make individual response normative, rather than the prevenient grace of God, is actually true of the paedobaptist position. Believers' children do not always embrace their parents' faith. How is God then the God of believers and their children? Has he not broken his covenant promise? What becomes of his faithfulness? The only way out of this dilemma is to take exactly the position wrongly ascribed to Baptists—to make personal response the decisive reality.

Letham refers to the "repeated and unrestricted references to households" in the New Testament. This is, however, an exaggeration. In the thirty-year period covered by the book of Acts and the letters of Paul we hear only of six households being saved and baptized. Letham assumes that the household baptisms mentioned included infants: this, however, is mere speculation.

Other New Testament evidence which Letham offers in support of paedobaptism is not compelling. He refers to Acts 2:39, "the promise is to you and to your children," but fails to notice how the verse continues: "and to all who afar off." Does this then require indiscriminate baptism? But the verse finishes, "as many as the Lord our God will call," a phrase which qualifies both the preceding categories. This text says nothing to undermine the Baptist conviction that the counterpart in the new covenant of the children of the covenant people is not those born into a believing family, but those newly born again.

Letham also suggests that whereas paedobaptists stress the continuity between the old and new covenants, Baptists emphasize the discontinuity. This, however, is debatable. The 1689 Confession is clear that there has only ever been one covenant of grace, revealed first to Adam, then "by farther steps," until the completion of its "full discovery" in the New Testament. Continuity does not mean that nothing changes at all, as, indeed, Letham acknowledges.

Some of Letham's arguments in defense of the paedobaptist position raise questions. He notes the connection between circumcision and baptism made in Colossians 2:11–13, but goes beyond the text in inferring infant baptism. Circumcision here symbolizes new life in Christ. There is no mention of children, as in the Old Testament references to the covenant. Letham's claim that the children addressed in Colossians 3:20 and Ephesians 6:1–4 are being "considered 'in the Lord,'" seems to overlook the real possibility of conversion taking place during childhood.

As with all paedobaptist arguments, Letham's comments point logically to the Baptist position. He emphasizes the connection in the New Testament between baptism and regeneration, faith, cleansing from sin, reception of the Holy Spirit, and union with Christ, and depicts baptism as marking the start of the Christian life. Such a definition does not seem consistent with the practice of paedobaptism. Moreover, Letham rejects paedocommunion on the grounds that the means of grace may become means of judgment if wrongly used; he argues therefore that it is essential that the participants be penitent sinners. It seems inconsistent to apply this to the Lord's Supper but not to baptism. Letham rightly states that in the New Testament baptism was administered when a person could first be considered a Christian, but goes on to make the dubious claim that, in the case of an infant born in a Christian home, this is at birth.

He points out that there is no New Testament record of a child born in a believing home not being baptized until later. The absence of such a statement comes as no surprise at all to a Baptist: the issue did not even arise in those days.

Having said all that, there are points where a Baptist will wholeheartedly endorse Letham's comments. He correctly says that baptism is not merely symbolic: it does accomplish something in the life of the believer. It really is a means of grace.

PRACTICAL APPLICATION

(1) We must maintain a proper attitude in worship. We must always approach God in lowly humility, remembering his fearful greatness, his awesome glory, his dazzling holiness. Our proper place is to bow low before him, in heart at least, whether or not we bow literally and bodily. At the same time, as the church, we must be a joyful people, as we celebrate the finished atonement, a free salvation, total forgiveness, and a sure and certain hope.

(2) We must ensure that our form of worship corresponds to Scripture. The church must be subject to Christ, and must therefore be governed in all things by God's Word. The pattern is laid down there for much of the church's life and activities, including its worship.

In Old Testament times, the LORD indicated which instruments were acceptable for use in worship. Only three regular instruments were allowed—the harp, the lyre, and the cymbal—with the addition of the trumpet when a burnt sacrifice was being offered (e.g., 1 Chr 15:16). Peter Masters rightly observes:

> We realize that the church of Jesus Christ is not under the rules
> of the Old Testament, and their regulations for worship do not
> bind us today. However the *general principles* of caution in the
> use of instruments taught then by God still apply.[20]

The whole of our worship must be governed and directed by Scripture. Worship must contain the biblical ingredients, including Scripture reading, vocal praise, intercession, and the preaching of the word.

---

20. Masters, *Worship*, 44 (italics original).

We must also maintain the biblical gender role distinctions in worship and teaching. Men must not neglect to take the lead, and women may not intrude themselves into areas which the Bible forbids.

(3) We must make sure that the Scripture dictates the contents of church life. It is not our worship only which must be shaped by Scripture but everything that we do as the people of God. We must avoid organizing activities which are a mere distraction or encumbrance. Biblical ministry, spiritual fellowship, the sacraments, and prayer—these must always be the chief elements in a church's program.

(4) The language of the people should be used. Those responsible for leading the flock in worship, or bringing them to the throne of grace in prayer, must take care to speak in an idiom which everyone can understand. Those who minister to God's people must be simple without becoming simplistic, contemporary without becoming crude. Our language must always be decent, becoming, and never less than spiritual, but not so academic that half the congregation has no idea what we mean.

(5) Those called to minister the word must devote themselves to the word. This applies both to appointed pastors, and to those who exercise a preaching or teaching ministry from time-to-time. It is the word of God which must be proclaimed in the church, and therefore those responsible for its proclamation must be familiar with it, and growing in their own understanding. It is important to study the word daily, to prepare the word thoroughly, and to preach the word enthusiastically.

(6) We must remember the importance of the work of the Holy Spirit in preaching. However enthusiastic the preacher may be, without the presence, help, and power of the Spirit, the preaching will not achieve a thing. The preacher and the church must therefore together pray fervently for the outpouring of the Spirit's power upon the preaching of the word.

(7) We must never neglect participation in church life. It is a sad reality that some people absent themselves from gathered worship for no valid reason. This lack of commitment to the body reflects a commitment to Christ which is, at best, half-hearted. Part of our faithfulness to the congregation to which we belong is that we are present at its regular gatherings, unless prevented by some extraordinary circumstance.

(8) Christ and the cross must be central to church life. The cross must be at the forefront of our praise. We must make sure that our ministry is always grace-shaped, not legalistic, and that all our service is an expression of gratitude for God's mercy towards us in Jesus Christ. By his grace,

we must avoid falling into the trap of thinking that our service contributes either to our own salvation or to the power of his grace at work.

Because Christ and the cross are central to church life, regular participation in the Lord's Supper is one of the duties to which believers are called, and this duty must not be shirked. We must remember, and put into practice, the three words in which the confessions sum up the right reception of the Lord's Supper: humility, reverence, and thanksgiving.

15

The Doctrine of Angels and Demons

THERE ARE SOME BIBLICAL references to the Angel of the LORD which speak of God the Son making an appearance in human form prior to his incarnation as a human being, though it is often a matter of personal judgment whether a particular example has this meaning. I shall not comment on those texts, where, in my judgment, that is the meaning, as this is really an aspect of Christology. Our concern here is the angelic beings whom God created in the beginning, both those who remained faithful, and those that fell with the devil and became known as demons.

BIBLICAL FOUNDATION

We shall separate from each other those texts relevant respectively to angels and demons, and deal with each in turn.

Angels

Hebrews 1:5–7 and 13–14 is a useful starting-point for the biblical teaching about angels. Found in the New Testament, but containing five quotations from the Old, the passage helpfully bridges the two, and also highlights the major functions which the angels fulfil. They serve two main purposes: they are worshippers (verse 6), and servants (verses 7, 14), and it is specifically "those who will inherit salvation" that they are commissioned to serve. References to these two tasks recur throughout Scripture.

The description in verse 7 of the angels as "spirits" and "a flame of fire" serves to emphasize the speedy delight with which they fulfil their mission—with "wind-like velocity" and "burning devotion."[1]

Initially, we shall organize our consideration of relevant scriptural material under the two headings derived from this passage. Then we shall mention some special Old Testament angelic titles. Next, we shall note one aspect of Christ's teaching about angels, before observing some fresh New Testament light on Old Testament teaching.

The Angels as Worshippers of God

In Hebrews 1:6 the angels are directed to worship God the Son. The writer quotes verbatim part of the Septuagint version of Deuteronomy 32:43, which also closely resembles some words from Psalm 97:7. Although the Hebrew text uses the word *ᵉlōhîm*, which is duly translated "gods" in the New King James Version, the Septuagint translators understood the word to refer not to false gods, but to angels. Their rationale was the recognition that false gods do not actually exist, whereas angelic spirits do. The object of angelic worship is the LORD, but with the coming of Christ, a new dimension appears. Christ is himself a legitimate object of the angels' worship within the context of worship of the triune God. We note three other texts relevant to the angels' role as worshippers.

PSALM 103:20–21

David begins and ends this Psalm with an exhortation to his own soul to bless the LORD. Just before he concludes, he extends that exhortation to God's entire creation, at the head of which are the hosts of angels. Verse 20 gives us something of a definition of the angels: they are beings "who excel in strength," and who hear and obey God's word.

It is appropriate that the angels should be called upon to lead creation in praise: being so strong, they "can render more acceptable praise than can ever come from human lips."[2] An observation frequently made

---

1. Fausset, "Hebrews," 1001.
2. Barnes, *Old Testament*, Psalms, Vol. 3, 80.

by commentators is that the praise of the angels ought to rouse us, God's creatures of a lower order, to comparable praise.

REVELATION 5:11–12

Angelic praise is directed specifically to God the Son. The countless hosts of angels worship him as the Lamb of God who was slain. His sacrifice qualifies him to receive the loudest praise.

REVELATION 7:11–12

The angelic worship recorded here is prompted by the praise of the innumerable, international multitude of saved sinners before the throne, who gratefully acknowledge that their salvation is the work of God alone, through Jesus Christ the Lamb of God. Although salvation is foreign to the angels' personal experience, they are, nonetheless, able to add their "Amen" to the church's worship. Even as onlookers, they can admire the divine wisdom and power which has achieved the transformation of such a large company of sinners.

The Angels as Servants of God's People

This is the dominant note in the Bible as regards angelic activity. They perform five main functions. We shall look at one example of each from each Testament, plus, where applicable, examples of Christ as himself the recipient of angelic ministry.

ANGELS ARE GOD'S MESSENGERS

Genesis 19 opens with the arrival in Sodom of "two angels." The Hebrew term is *mal'āk*, meaning a representative or messenger. This is its first occurrence, other than references in Genesis 16 to the Angel of the LORD.

The opening words of chapter 19 equate the angels with the two men who appeared to Abraham, along with the LORD himself, in the previous chapter. When angels appear to human beings they usually appear in human form. An angel's true identity may become clear to the recipient of his message in the course of the encounter, but not at the outset. There is no indication that Lot ever became aware that he was conversing with angels. He calls them men (verse 8), as do the citizens of Sodom (verse 5); the narrative refers to them as men in verses 10 and 12, to "angels" in verse 15, before reverting to the word "men" in verse 16. The angels are bearers of the message from the LORD which will result in Lot's preservation when Sodom and Gomorrah are destroyed.

Angels served as messengers to God's people at two key points in New Testament history—at Christ's birth and at his resurrection. During the period when he entered the world, angels appeared to Zechariah, Mary, Joseph, and the shepherds.

The angel who appeared to Zechariah and to Mary is one of only two angels whose names we know. "Gabriel" means "God's mighty one." It is an apt depiction of any angel. Angels have all the God-given might that they need to complete whatever task the Lord entrusts them with.

The other angel whose name we know is Michael, mentioned three times in Daniel, once in Revelation, and also in Jude 9, where he is identified as "the archangel." His name means "Who is like God?" It is an assertion of the absolute uniqueness of the Creator

There is no evidence that Gabriel appeared to Mary in any other than a human form. It is what he says that troubles her, not his appearance (Luke 1:29). It is true that Zechariah was troubled when he saw him (Luke 1:12). However, this does not prove that the angel's appearance was unusual. Rather, it was the sudden appearance from nowhere, within the temple, where no-one other than the officiating priest was allowed to be at that moment, which alarmed Zechariah: this must be an emissary from God, whatever he may have looked like.

At the other end of Jesus' earthly experience, angels were the first messengers of the resurrection. It may seem from the account in Matthew 28:3 that our comment about angelic appearance needs to be qualified: this angel appeared "like lightning" with "clothing as white as snow." However, the parallel verse in Mark 16:5 speaks of "a young man clothed in a long white robe." The lightning to which Matthew refers is not the glory of the angel. This angel in human form reflects the glory of God. The same had been true when the angel brought the shepherds the message of a Savior's birth. "An angel of the Lord stood before them, and the glory of the Lord shone around them, and they were greatly afraid" (Luke 2:9). It was not the glory of the angel, but the Lord's glory which blazed out of heaven! That was what terrified the shepherds.

ANGELS MEDIATE GOD'S GUIDANCE

In Genesis 24 Abraham delegates his servant to seek a bride for Isaac his son. He must not find a Canaanite woman, but must travel to Abraham's homeland. His servant is anxious: a suitable woman might be unwilling to uproot; so Abraham encourages him in these words: "the LORD God of heaven . . . will send his angel before you, and you shall take a wife for my son from there" (verse 7).

Later, having met Rebekah, the servant paraphrases Abraham's words in his testimony to her household like this: "he said to me, 'The LORD . . . will send his angel with you and prosper your way; and you shall take a wife for my son from my family and from my father's house'" (verse 40).

The servant voices his perception of the general outcome when the Lord interposes an angelic guide: God's people's way is then prosperous. No angelic appearance is recorded here. God is working in the background through unseen angelic agency.

Having learned of Mary's pregnancy, and as he ponders his options, Joseph is addressed by an angel during his sleep (Matt 1:20–21). He is given an explanation of the situation, and clear instructions as to what he must do.

He receives further angelic guidance a couple of years later when Herod plots to destroy the Christ-child: "an angel of the Lord appeared to Joseph in a dream, saying, 'Arise, take the young child and his mother, flee to Egypt, and stay there until I bring you word'" (Matt 2:13).

As promised, "when Herod was dead, behold, an angel of the Lord appeared in a dream to Joseph in Egypt" and gave him leave to take the family back home (Matt 2:19–20).

ANGELS BRING GOD'S ENCOURAGEMENT

In Genesis 32:1–2 Jacob is returning home after twenty years away. He is aware of the potential danger that awaits him: he will soon meet his brother Esau for the first time since he secured their father's blessing through an act of trickery. The last time that Jacob had seen Esau, his brother was seething with murderous rage towards him. In this moment of fear and peril, Jacob is visited by God's angels.

The wording implies that it was a considerable number of angels who met him. He names the venue where this vision of angels took place

"Mahanaim," meaning "two camps." This could refer to the camps of God and of Jacob, but Calvin makes the attractive suggestion that the angels are themselves distributed between two camps, thus surrounding Jacob, in line with the promise of Psalm 34:7, "The angel of the LORD encamps all around those who fear him, and delivers them."

Calvin sees a twofold purpose in this vision of angels: the Lord intended, first, to alleviate Jacob's fear about the immediate future, and second, to fix in his mind the memory of this deliverance, and so to give him hope for the long-term future.[3]

In Acts 27:22 and 25 Paul twice seeks to encourage his fellow-travelers on the voyage towards Rome. The word rendered "take heart" is *euthumeō*. It is in the present tense, and so has the sense of maintaining a good spirit. A bit later Paul exhorts the ship's company, who have not eaten for two weeks, to take food. He sets the example. Verse 36 reads: "Then they were all encouraged [which is the related word *euthumos*] and also took food themselves."

Paul was able to be an encourager because, as verses 23 and 24 indicate, he himself had received encouragement from an angel sent by God, urging him not to be afraid. The implication is that Paul had been fearful. Earlier (verse 10) he had spoken, not as directed by the Lord, but out of his own perception, voicing his fear that the entire company were facing death by drowning. Having been corrected by this angelic visitation, he is able to become a minister of encouragement to the rest of those on board.

We know of two occasions on which the Lord Jesus himself received angelic encouragement. Both Matthew and Mark speak of the angels who "ministered to him" during and after his temptation at the start of his ministry (Matt 4:11; Mark 1:13), while Luke inserts in the middle of his account of Jesus' struggle in Gethsemane at the end of his ministry these words in Luke 22:43: "then an angel appeared to him from heaven, strengthening him."

ANGELS ARE AGENTS OF GOD'S PROTECTION AND DELIVERANCE

King Darius has spent a sleepless night, having succumbed to the deception of his officers and allowed Daniel to be thrown into the lions' den. He rises at dawn, and hurries to the den. In the conversation which

---

3. Calvin, *Genesis*, Vol. 2, 185.

ensues, Daniel is able to give this information to the king in Daniel 6:22: "My God sent his angel and shut the lions' mouths, so that they have not hurt me, because I was found innocent before him; and also, O king, I have done no wrong before you."

In Acts 12 Peter has been imprisoned by King Herod. The night before the very day when Herod intended to execute the apostle, Peter is rescued by an angel (verses 7–11). He visits the church before going into hiding temporarily.

We have referred already to Matthew 2:13 in connection with the angel's guidance given to Joseph. The instruction to flee with the family to Egypt was primarily, of course, for the protection of the Christ child.

ANGELS USHER THE SOULS OF BELIEVERS TO GLORY

In Luke 16:22 we hear of the beggar who "died, and was carried by the angels to Abraham's bosom." Here we find an angelic service unique to the New Testament. When believers die, Christ sends "special messengers to fetch them to himself . . . . Saints shall be brought home, not only safely, but honorably."[4] Calvin calls it "a happiness more desirable than all the kingdoms of the world"[5] to be escorted to heaven by angels.

Special Angelic Titles

There are two specific titles which we must consider.

CHERUBIM

This word occurs once in the New Testament (Heb 9:5), but numbered amongst the things of which "we cannot now speak in detail." Substantially, therefore, it is an Old Testament term. We meet it first in Genesis 3:24, where, having driven Adam out, the LORD God "placed cherubim at the east of the garden of Eden, and a flaming sword which turned every way, to guard the way to the tree of life." This is, indeed, the first mention of angelic beings in Scripture. Their task is to prevent sinful human beings from accessing the tree of life. God's intention is to avert the disaster

4. Henry, *New Testament,* Vol. 3, 391.
5. Calvin, *Evangelists,* Vol. 2, 186.

that the human race might attain eternal life prematurely, before sin has been dealt with.

Scofield claims that "the cherubim have to do with the holiness of God as outraged by sin."[6] However, I am not sure that this is right. Throughout Scripture God's characteristic mercy defines the role of the cherubim. They figure most prominently in the tabernacle and temple, which were liberally and lavishly decorated with figures of cherubim.

Their most significant location was on the mercy seat above the ark of the covenant, and the placing of the cherubim at the gate of Eden anticipates the mercy seat: it was an act of mercy on God's part that Adam could not attain to endless life in his fallen state.

In Exodus 25:22 God says of the mercy seat, "there I will meet with you, and I will speak with you from above the mercy seat, from between the two cherubim which *are* on the ark of the testimony." Despite human sin, God establishes a way by which he may continue to have fellowship with his people. The presence of cherubim in Genesis 3 signifies that the relationship is not destroyed. B. H. Carroll writes eloquently on this point, describing it as "the intervention of grace:"

> having expelled man from the garden, God established a throne of grace and furnished the means to recover from the death which had been pronounced. There was the mercy scat and there were the Cherubim . . . , and whoever worshiped God after man sinned must come to the mercy seat to worship and he must approach God through a sacrifice. In no other way than through an atonement could one attain to the tree of life. All passages that refer to the Cherubim connect them with grace and the mercy seat, not as ministers of divine vengeance, but as symbols of divine mercy.[7]

SERAPHIM

This angelic title occurs only in Isaiah 6. It is used just twice (verses 2 and 6). We learn that the seraphim stand above the throne of God, "in the position of servants . . . waiting on a seated master."[8] They worship the thrice-holy LORD as they survey his worldwide glory.

---

6. Scofield, *Reference Bible*, 840.
7. Carroll, *Interpretation*, 121–22.
8. Motyer, *Isaiah*, 76.

A seraph has six wings. He uses two to cover his face, signifying his noble reticence in the presence of the God of glory; the word "seraphim" means "burning ones," "yet they hide their faces from the greater burning glory of the Lord,"[9] by which even angels are dazzled. Another two wings cover a seraph's feet, representing his refusal to make his own decisions about where to go, and with the remaining two he flies in order to carry out God's orders at top speed. In verse 6 we see the execution of this task of instant obedience. A seraph flies to the prophet to communicate the assurance of sin purged and guilt cancelled. What glorious comfort it brings to the children of God to realize that the angels are poised above all else to serve them with the gift of assurance of salvation.

Christ's Teaching about Angels

Jesus spoke several times of the role of angels at his second coming. He will return along with the angels (Matt 16:27; 25:31). He links their presence with glory, both his own, and that of his Father. It is not that the presence of the angels will enhance Christ's glory, but rather that their formation of his royal train will underline his own intrinsic glory.

The angels will then serve as harvesters: Jesus explains that, at the end of the age, the angels will be assigned the task of gathering together all those destined for eternal punishment, and consigning them to their fate (Matt 13:41–42). Elsewhere, he indicates that it will also be their duty to "gather together his elect from the four winds, from one end of heaven to the other" (Matt 24:31). The angelic responsibility at the end will therefore be threefold: they will gather both sets of people, separate them from one another, and conduct each set to its appointed place.

The Angels' Involvement at the Giving of the Law

The New Testament sheds fresh light on this key Old Testament event. When God gave the law on Mount Sinai, angels played a part.

This information is given by three separate New Testament authors. As Stephen addresses the Jewish council, he accuses them like this in Acts 7:53: you "have received the law by the direction of angels and have not kept it." In Galatians 3:19 Paul says that the law "*was* appointed through

---

9. Grogan, "Isaiah," 55.

angels by the hand of a mediator." Finally, the writer to the Hebrews describes the law as "the word spoken through angels" (Heb 2:2).

Each writer is making a different, but supplementary, point. Stephen is stressing the law's majesty: the presence of angels verifies that it truly is a word from the LORD. Paul's point is that the law, given indirectly through angels, is subordinate to the covenant with Abraham, given directly by God himself. The writer to the Hebrews highlights the superiority of the gospel message, spoken not by angels, but by the Son.

Demons

We shall look at the Old and New Testaments separately at this point.

Old Testament

The Hebrew word *šēdîm*, translated "demons" in Deuteronomy 32:17 and Psalm 106:37, occurs only in those two texts. Its root is the verb *šûd*, which appears just once—in Psalm 91:6, where it is rendered "lays waste." That emphasizes the basic idea of the demonic: demons bring devastation, destruction, ruin.

The Septuagint uses the Greek word *daimonion* in all three of those texts, and also introduces it in several others, including Psalm 96:5. There the Hebrew refers to "the gods of the peoples" as "idols;" the Septuagint reads, "the gods of the peoples are demons." The Old Testament recognizes that false gods, though truly non-entities, are nonetheless expressions of demonic spirits, and that behind all idolatrous religion stands demonic power. This fact is brought out also in Deuteronomy 32:16–17.

Psalm 106:37 reads: "they even sacrificed their sons and their daughters to demons." Grudem notes that this discloses "the purpose of Satan to destroy all the good works of God." He comments: "Worship of demons will regularly lead to immoral and self-destructive practices."[10]

The most notable Old Testament experiences of demonic involvement concern King Saul. 1 Samuel 16:14–16 refers to "a distressing spirit from the LORD," which "troubled" Saul. Saul's servants suggest that they "seek out a man *who is* a skilful player on the harp." Their hope is that, when the distressing spirit is upon Saul, the music will bring some improvement to Saul's condition.

10. Grudem, *Systematic Theology*, 417.

Saul acquiesces with this suggestion, and David is brought to the palace. Verse 23 informs us that "whenever the spirit from God was upon Saul," David would play the harp, and "Saul would become refreshed and well, and the distressing spirit would depart from him."

It is a matter of debate whether the spirit involved here is the Spirit of God deputed to impose judgment, or whether it is a demon. Personally, I incline towards the latter option. What is then clear is that even demons cannot act independently of God's permission, and that he may sometimes choose to use them as channels of his judgment. Both Matthew Poole and Matthew Henry observe that the music had no direct impact on the demon itself: it was the demon's access to Saul's mind which was temporarily blocked as the music lifted his spirit.[11]

In 1 Samuel 28 we read of Saul's visit to the medium at Endor. Verse 3 sets the background by noting that "Saul had put the mediums and the spiritists out of the land." In doing this he had acted in line with the stipulations of Leviticus 20:27: "A man or a woman who is a medium, or who has familiar sprits, shall surely be put to death." Now, however, in his desperation, because "when Saul inquired of the LORD, the LORD did not answer him" (verse 6), Saul locates a medium, disguises himself, goes to her house, and instructs her, "Please conduct a séance for me, and bring up for me the one I shall name to you" (verse 8).

The woman scents a trap, but Saul reassures her. He asks her to bring up from the dead the spirit of Samuel. The woman obliges, and at this point suddenly recognizes Saul, and is gripped by fear. He reassures her again and asks what she can see. The conversation continues:

> The woman said to Saul, "I saw a spirit ascending out of the earth." So he said to her, "What *is* his form?" And she said, "An old man is coming up, and he *is* covered with a mantle." And Saul perceived that it *was* Samuel, and he stooped with his face to the ground and bowed down.

The words "Saul perceived that it was Samuel" must be read as a statement of his mental condition, because, as Matthew Henry observes, it is absurd to imagine that a good soul would come back at the beck of an evil spirit.[12] A demon is impersonating Samuel, but Saul is not in a fit

---

11. Poole, *Annotations*, 673; Henry, *Whole Bible*, 306.
12. Henry, *Whole Bible*, 321.

state of mind to tell the difference. Matthew Poole explains the devil's purpose in this pretense as the ensnaring of Saul.[13]

It is significant that Saul did not see the spirit. He was totally dependent on the woman's description. We might wonder whether she actually saw anything herself, or was she being deceptive? The demonic words were the significant thing, not the alleged appearance.

This fact tallies with the regular biblical distinction between the false messages which stem from the evil one, and the truth encapsulated in the word of God. Two passages are worth citing.

In Isaiah 8:19–20, we read this:

> When they say to you, "Seek those who are mediums and wizards, who whisper and mutter," should not a people seek their God? *Should they seek* the dead on behalf of the living? To the law and to the testimony! If they do not speak according to this word, *it is* because *there is* no light in them.

The twin terms "whisper" (*ṣāpap*) and "mutter" (*hāgâ*) convey the idea that the words derived from demonic influence are as empty as the tuneless noise of a startled bird, and as unsubstantial as the indistinct growling of a contented animal.[14] By contrast, the teaching (*tôrâ*) and the testimony (*te'ûdâ*) of God's words are sound and substantial instruction.

Deuteronomy 18:10–15 also forbids listening to demon-inspired chatter. Here the contrast is with Christ himself. The words of verse 15 are fulfilled in him (Acts 3:22; 7:37). He is the prophet, the source of God's true word.

New Testament

The New Testament echoes the Old Testament teaching that false gods are demonic: "the things which the Gentiles sacrifice they sacrifice to demons and not to God" (1 Cor 10:20). It also notes that demons are angels who fell into sin (2 Pet 2:4; Jude 6), and that demonic activity is widespread in the world, as Ephesians 2:2 brings out with its reference to "the prince of the power of the air, the spirit who now works in the sons of disobedience."

In connection with the work of Christ demonic activity rose to a new level. Perhaps the explanation is that taking possession of people

---

13. Poole, *Annotations*, 706.
14. Cf. Hartley, "ṣāpap," 1957.0; Wolf, "hāgâ," 467.0.

was the nearest that the devil could achieve to mimicking the incarnation of the Son of God. In the gospels, in addition to passing references to the casting out of demons, there are several more detailed accounts of Jesus' encounters with the devil and his demons. We shall analyze the teaching of the gospels by reference to five such incidents, noting where applicable the parallel accounts.

MATTHEW 4:1–11; LUKE 4:1–13

We have here the account of Jesus' temptation by the devil in the wilderness. Before his ministry commenced the devil did his best to prevent Jesus from fulfilling his God-given mission. He attacked Jesus in his weakness—when he was hungry. Although the human nature which Jesus assumed was not a fallen human nature, it was nevertheless vulnerable to the effects of human fallenness, of which hunger was one. In Deuteronomy 32:24 to be "wasted with hunger" is one of the disasters which God threatens to heap upon his provocative people. The devil first tries to lure Jesus into asserting his innocence in a self-serving way. In the other two temptations the devil's aim is to destroy Jesus, both spiritually and physically. However, through the power of God's word, Jesus overcomes the devil, and he has to depart for a time.

MARK 1:23–27; LUKE 4:33–36

We hear next of Jesus' encounter in the synagogue with "a man who had a spirit of an unclean demon," to quote Luke's wording. The main thing of note is that the demons were well aware of who Jesus was. This demon says, "I know who you are—the holy one of God." Where the Jewish religious leaders failed to recognize him as their Messiah, the demonic world was under no illusions. They were well aware that the ultimate purpose of his coming was their own destruction. That was why they became so active in opposition to him.

MATTHEW 8:28–34; MARK 5:1–20; LUKE 8:26–39

The incident at Gadara supplies the most detailed account of Jesus' dealings with demons. Matthew speaks of two men, but Mark and Luke write in the singular: perhaps one of the men was more severely affected than the other, and he becomes their focus.

The demon-possessed men are "fierce." Mark speaks of super-human strength, and of a noisy disposition. He also tells how self-harm had become normal practice in this demonic experience. Living amongst the tombs speaks of how they have been brought into the realm of death. Luke tells how the man with whom he is concerned would often make for the desert and would walk around naked. Demons have turned him against human company and human etiquette.

The demons indicate their recognition of who Jesus is, and of the fate that awaits them, namely torment in the "abyss," to use Luke's word.

After Jesus' intervention, Mark and Luke tell us that the man was found "in his right mind," indicating that it is primarily upon the human mind that demonic power operates. Mark's account reaches its climax in the reference to the compassion which Jesus had on the man in delivering him from this demonic destruction.

It is an interesting question why the demons wanted to enter the pigs and why Jesus granted this request. Calvin alludes to the view that it represents the demonic intent to destroy the whole of God's creation, but prefers to see it as motivated by the desire to cause the local people to curse God for the loss of their livelihood. Jesus' consent is a test of the people's character.[15]

On observing that Jesus' power is vastly superior to that of the demonic world, the people were "seized with great fear," as Luke puts it.

MATTHEW 17:14–18; MARK 9:17–27; LUKE 9:37–43

This demon inflicts multiple injuries on its victim, who suffers from epileptic convulsions and from dumbness, apart from periodic inarticulate outcries. Constantly the helpless lad comes perilously close to destruction.

According to Luke, the upshot of Jesus' healing is the amazement of the crowd at the divine majesty. The word rendered "amazed" is *ekplessō*, which has connotations of terror, as a tremendous power is displayed.

---

15. Calvin, *Evangelists*, Vol. 1, 433.

The opening verse in each account highlights the simple fact that Jesus totally reverses the work of the demonic powers. However, the main thing here is the refusal of the Jewish authorities to endorse the work of Christ, attributing his success to the chief of the demons, designated Beelzebul, whom Jesus identifies with Satan. Both names carry significance.

"Beelzebul" was a title invented by the Jews to represent their scorn for the devil. It means "lord of filth" or "lord of dung." This may be intended as a reference to the filth of idolatry, or may merely be a term of contempt.[16] "Satan" means "enemy," and signifies his opposition primarily to God, but also to God's people.

Jesus' main point is made in verse 28 of Matthew's account (verse 20 in Luke): his victory over demons is evidence that the kingdom of God has come. Jesus is the stronger one, who overcomes the devil and plunders his goods.

DOCTRINAL FORMULATION

The Early Creeds

There is just one relevant phrase in the creeds. It occurs in the Nicene creed, where God is described as "the Maker of all things, visible and invisible." These words acknowledge that there is an invisible world containing invisible beings, namely the angels. In his sermon on the creed Augustine referred to the invisible things in heaven, and listed thrones, dominions, principalities, powers, archangels, and angels.

But the creed's words also imply God's sovereignty, by virtue of his rights as Creator, over all invisible things without exception. This includes the devil and those angels who sinned and became demons. The devil is denied by this phrase to have such power as can rival the sovereign rule of God alone.

The Reformation Confessions

On this subject the confessions have more to say about the devil than the angels! We may summarize their teaching under nine headings.

---

16. Thayer, *Lexicon*, 100; Bietenhard, "Satan," 469.

The invisible spiritual beings were created by God

Alongside human beings, angels are the most excellent of all God's creatures, as the Westminster Larger Catechism explains: "God created all the angel spirits, immortal, holy, excelling in knowledge, mighty in power, to execute his commandments, and to praise his name." All the spiritual beings were created good.

Some angels continued in their created state of goodness

These angels were said to be preserved by grace, and so established in the state of goodness forever. The good angels are described as God's servants and messengers. Their service is willing and faithful. To quote the Westminster Larger Catechism again, the angels in heaven submit to God's will with "humility, cheerfulness, faithfulness, diligence, zeal, sincerity, and constancy."

Although the confessions do not enlarge on this, they define angelic service as including four things: glorifying God, promoting the salvation of the elect, serving the elect, and administering God's power, mercy, and justice.

Some angels fell into perdition

These are known as devils or evil spirits. They fell of their own free will, yet only by the permission of God's providence. They are "reserved in chains of darkness unto the judgment of the great day," as the Irish Articles word it, echoing 2 Peter 2:4. Their position is irrecoverable.

Even evil spirits are included within God's providence

Their first fall was limited, and was ordered for God's own glory. Even now, the French Confession explains, God "has wonderful means of so making use of devils that he can turn to good the evil which they do;" yet at the same time, he "restrains the devils."

Evil spirits are the instigators of sin and deception

Demonic spirits have no time for anything good at all. They are, therefore, always attempting to spread evil in actions and ideas. It was through the devil's suggestion that the human race fell from honor and became enslaved to him. Satan used the serpent as his instrument, and became the author of death, since sin led to death.

The work of the devil continues in human life. By nature, we are all under his dominion. Our sinful souls are given over to serve the devil. He pricks the lusts of unbelievers, causing them to pursue them keenly.

The devil's main work is deception and lying. In the light of Saul's encounter with the medium of Endor, the Second Helvetic Confession defines apparitions which appear as if they are the souls of the dead as one form of devilish deceit. We should probably add that ghosts and haunted houses are really demonic impersonations.

Evil spirits oppose God's true church

Both the church as a united entity and each member individually come under attack from evil spirits, who often use the false church as their weapon. Satan wants to ruin the church, if only he could. In becoming Christians we are transferred out of his kingdom, set free from his dominion and tyranny. However, Satan does not let his former slaves go easily. That is why the Christian life is one of constant battle.

False doctrine and false worship are inspired by the devil

The Scottish Confession saw the "doctrine of devils" as intended to draw us away from the pure voice of God. Similarly, the French Confession defined false worship as a Satanic device to lead people astray from "the right way of worship."

In terms of doctrinal error, it was false teaching in the area of Christology which the confessions saw as especially devilish. They recognized that the devil's strategy always involves a head-on collision with the Savior of the world. As regards false worship, their main concern was the teaching on the mass as a sacrifice, which was described by the Genevan Confession as "a reprobate and diabolical ordinance," which involved undermining the completed work of Christ. Just as the Bible characterized idol-worship as the worship of demons, so, in seeing the mass as effectively idolatrous, the confessions inevitably saw it as demonic.

In a sense the confessions are seeing false doctrine (especially christological) and false worship (especially the mass) as continuous with the devil's attempts to destroy Jesus during his earthly life.

Jesus destroys the work of the devil

The Scottish Confession refers to the promise, fulfilled in Christ Jesus, that the seed of the woman would destroy the devil's works. The conversion of sinners and their preservation in grace to the end is the first instalment of that victory.

False doctrine regarding angels is rejected

Two areas of false doctrine in particular are highlighted: that of the Sadducees, who, akin to contemporary materialist philosophies, denied the existence of the spirit world, and that of the Manichees, who taught that the devils had a separate origin from God's creation and are, therefore, a genuine rival power to God.

Modern Confessions of Faith

The Indian confession echoes the creedal statement which notes that God created all things, including invisible things, while emphasizing that God is distinct from all other spirits. The Chinese confession contains just one passing reference to this whole subject, noting that "angels will blow the horn" when Jesus comes again.

The Indonesian confession has the most to say on this subject. It alludes to Hebrews 1:14 in describing the angels whom God created to serve him as "ministering spirits sent by God to help those who are heirs of salvation." This confession also refers in three different contexts to the devil and to evil spirits. In connection with the doctrine of God it refutes the expectation that blessing may come from "the spirits of the grandfathers," and also rejects "lucky days, fortune-telling, and reading fate in the lines of one's hands." The first sentence in the articles regarding sin reads, "The Devil is the source of sin," but the article on the sacraments includes amongst the benefits granted to the believer by means of baptism "redemption from death and the Devil."

HISTORICAL ELABORATION

The most comprehensive patristic work on angels was *The Celestial Hierarchies*, written by the sixth-century theologian known as Pseudo-Dionysius the Areopagite.[17] That will be our starting-point in this section. Next, we shall turn to Dutchman Herman Bavinck. Karl Barth regrets that "we have almost completely forgotten that we are surrounded by the angels;"[18] he notes that after Dionysius until the early twentieth century significant attention was given to the subject by only five systematic theologians,[19] of whom Bavinck was one. Thirdly, I believe that it is necessary to consider whether there is angelic and demonic activity in a secular society, such as the contemporary west. We shall consider the matter of demonic involvement first, in order to end on a positive note as we recount one uplifting experience of a possible angelic encounter in recent times.

Pseudo-Dionysius: *The Celestial Hierarchies*

As the title implies, Dionysius assumed that the angels were arranged in ranks and orders. He saw the relation between time and eternity in terms of a great "chain" of being, with the angels at the top,[20] but themselves ordered into three main categories, with three types of angel in each rank. The task of each order is to communicate the divine perfections to those below them.

The highest order includes seraphim, cherubim, and thrones. The title "seraphim" speaks of glowing exuberance, which fires the ranks below them. Cherubim possess the power of knowing God and contemplating his beauty; in turn they impart wisdom to the lower ranks. The thrones are untainted by anything base as they ascend to the heights and then manifest God to their inferiors.

---

17. Pseudo-Dionysius, "Celestial Hierarchies," *passim*.
18. Barth, *Church Dogmatics, Vol. 2*, 648.
19. Barth, *Church Dogmatics, Vol. 3*, 5.
20. Pelikan, *Eastern Christendom*, 115.

The middle rank is dominions, virtues, and powers. These angelic beings are purified by the divine illuminations bestowed on them through the first order in the hierarchy. The name "dominions" signifies the elevated aspiration to true lordship, which lifts those below to give themselves to the true authority which is God. Virtues mount upwards to be fashioned after the divine perfection, and cause true virtue to flow on to those below them. The power possessed by the powers is intellectual; they lead those below to God who is the supreme Power and the source of all power.

The lowest rank consists of principalities, archangels, and angels. The title "principalities" speaks of Godlike authority; their role is to lead others in princely fashion. The archangels mediate and interpret to the lowest order the revelations passed down to them from above. The angels are the bridge between the angelic hierarchies and the visible, earthly world.

This is entirely speculative, and cannot be defended from Scripture. Dionysius has simply lifted from the biblical text various titles allotted to angels and allocated them to the different rankings in a completely arbitrary way. Strangely, the only title which has any hierarchical overtones at all, *archangel* (meaning chief angel) appears not at the top, but as the lowest ranking but one.

Herman Bavinck: *Heaven: The Spiritual World*[21]

This is the title of chapter 9 of Volume 2 of Bavinck's *Reformed Dogmatics*. Like Barth, Bavinck regrets the deficiency of Reformed theology on this subject, because "the angels are of extraordinary significance for the kingdom of God and its history," since God, in his working in the sphere of grace, chooses to use their ministry. However, our knowledge of angels is not subjective: Christian experience does not include communion with the world of angels. It is only from revelation that we know about angels.

Bavinck affirms that the diverse terms used in the Bible to refer to angels imply that there are distinct kinds of angel, that the angelic world is rich in variety. Their number is very large, and the assumption is that they are ordered in ranks, though Scripture gives little information on this subject. Nonetheless, there is a unity in the angelic world: all the angels are created, spiritual, rational, and moral beings.

21. Bavinck, *Dogmatics, Vol. 2*, 443–72

These qualities indicate a similarity between the angels and human beings; however, the differences are great. The human race is made in God's image, angels are not, even though various traits belonging to the image are found in them. The human race is entrusted with dominion over the earth, whereas angels are merely servants in God's creation. Whereas a human being is a combination of soul and body, angels are complete as spirits. They are not, therefore, bound to each other, as human beings are, by ties of blood and by a union of essence and nature. We speak of "humanity," but there is no such thing as "angelity." Consequently, when some angels fell, not all did.

While angels are mightier in intellect and power, human experience is psychologically deeper and mentally richer. Human beings have rich relationships to God, the world, and one another. Angels know God's power, wisdom, goodness, holiness, and majesty, but God's richest attributes (the depths of his compassion) are known only to humans.

The angels' relation to Christ is different. All things (including the angels) were created by the Son of God. Christ is certainly the mediator of the reconciliation of all created things, but the angels are not themselves the objects of grace as human beings are. They are only witnesses at that point, though they are part of the total wrecked creation which is restored in Christ.

Bavinck distinguishes between the ordinary and the extraordinary ministry of angels. Their ordinary ministry from creation is to praise God, while their extraordinary role, beginning after the fall, involves guarding Eden, conveying revelations, administering blessing and punishment: it has become their task to accompany the history of redemption at cardinal points. Consequently, they are active in the church, and for the interests of the church, and their service is now exercised especially in the realm of grace: for example, they rejoice when sinners are converted, they protect believers, they are present in the worship of the church, and they usher believers to heaven.

Bavinck considers whether there are such things as "guardian angels." He recognizes that the book of Daniel portrays the war between the kingdoms of God and Satan as being waged in heaven as well as on earth, but rejects the idea of individual guardianship.

He highlights the danger of veneration of angels. This is clearly forbidden in Scripture. We honor angels in the same way as we honor the civil authorities, but we do not offer them such homage as belongs exclusively to God.

Bavinck finds in the doctrine of angels a source of consolation and encouragement. It assures us that we are not alone in our spiritual struggle: there is a better world, for which we feel both nostalgia and anticipation. In revelation the world of angels has come down to us; in Christ the church rises up to greet that world: "we shall be like the angels, and daily see the face of our Father, who is in heaven."

Angels and Demons and the Secular West

Possible Demonic Activity

In the modern, secular west it is very easy to assume that the demonic, while perhaps still relevant in other cultures where false religion abounds, is not a phenomenon which we are seeing here. I would suggest, however, that this is because we have developed an unduly limited concept of demonic activity. We noted earlier how demons regularly attack people's minds. It seems to me that the typical western anti-supernatural mindset is therefore demonically inspired. The current transgender ideology is, I suspect, a most emphatic symptom of this demonic manipulation of the western mind, and we need to understand it as such in order to counter it effectively.

As far as I have been able to discover, there is not yet a great deal of material available exploring the connection between this contemporary cultural movement and the power of the demonic. However, two contributions, both from people associated with the apologetic ministry, *Answers in Genesis*, are particularly helpful.

Terry Mortensen: *Are Demons Active Today?*

This article[22] considers the issue of the demonic in contemporary western society in general terms. Starting with the observation that Jesus and the apostles often encountered demonic activity, the author then asks, "Why isn't this happening today? Or is it?" He mentions how missionaries working in places where false religion or witchcraft are prevalent do see comparable things, and then notes how the anti-supernatural mentality in our culture may prevent us from recognizing demonic activity,

---

22. Mortensen, "Demons," *passim.*

because it takes different forms in such a setting. He suggests that the rejection of the supernatural is itself an expression of demonic deception.

Mortensen points out that, ever since the Garden of Eden, the questioning of God's authority has always had a demonic origin, and that the devil continues to blind the minds of unbelievers.

HEIDI ST. JOHN: *TRANSGENDERISM AND DEMONIC POSSESSION: IS IT REAL?*

This contribution is available both as a podcast and as a video.[23] The author starts by stressing the fact that the transgender movement "is absolutely demonic in nature," and that standing against it is part of the spiritual battle in which the church is engaged. She sees that categorization as far more significant than referring to it merely as a cultural battle. Transgenderism, ultimately, is a demonic attack against God as the Creator, because it opposes the truth that God created human beings male and female in his own image, even though that truth is backed up by science.

Heidi St. John acknowledges that Satan, the father of lies, will always oppose what God does by seeking to counterfeit it, and that the transgender movement is the supreme example of this in our culture right now. She finds the primary evidence of the demonic nature of transgenderism in its wicked attack on children.

Referring to the evidence from the times of Jesus and the apostles that demons, though spiritual beings, can take possession of physical bodies, she suggests that

> we are seeing a demonic possession of unparalleled proportions in the United States right now and around the world through the transgender movement, this normalization of what we know to be wrong.

Whether it would be right to classify every case of gender dysphoria or transitioning as demon possession I personally would question, but I certainly agree that the movement as a whole is demonically inspired.

---

23. St. John, *Transgenderism and Demonic Possession*," *passim.*

A Possible Modern Encounter with an Angel

No doubt Bavinck's claim that we only know of angelic ministry by revelation is broadly right. However, perhaps he goes too far in saying categorically that angels no longer appear to us. Here is a first-hand account of an experience which I heard recounted while I was in my teens by David Shafik, the leader of the youth work at the church in London where I grew up. I have never forgotten it:

> One very wet and cloudy day in February 1963, I was driving back from a building site to my office. At a certain point the road ran close to an escarpment high above a Gliding Club some 150 feet below. The road was very straight: one could see for a long way in both directions completely unhindered. I drove on to the grass verge, and faced the aerodrome below. It was a marvelous, breath-taking view across the valley to the hills in the far distance. I ate my lunch and prepared to leave.
>
> I was around twenty feet from the edge and could easily turn round, drive slowly back to the road, and be on my way. The grass was fairly long and very wet but, to my surprise, as I started, the wheels began to spin. I slipped nearer to the edge of the escarpment. I stopped to assess the situation and decided to reverse back to more level ground. Unfortunately, there was no grip and, although in reverse, the car moved forward. I stopped revving, turned off the engine, and re-assessed the situation. If I tried any more the car would continue slipping on down and over the edge of the cliff taking me with it. What I really needed was someone in front of the car to push backward whilst I was in reverse gear so that I could get back to a flatter surface nearer the road.
>
> There was no-one else about—it was so cold and wet and windy. I got out of the car, walked a few steps back towards the road and in the distance I saw a middle-aged man on a bicycle. What he was doing in that location on such a cold and wet day I had no idea! However, I waited for him to get to me, waved him down, and explained the situation. He immediately agreed to help, got off his bicycle, and came across. In a few seconds with me in reverse and him pushing the front, I gained traction, and within a few yards was safe. I got out of the car to thank him, but he was nowhere to be seen. During the time taken he would have needed to move at the speed of light in order to mount up and cycle on down the road and vanish into the distance. But already he was nowhere to be seen.

I can never say for certain of course, but I do think that the "man" was an angel sent by the Lord at a moment of extreme need.[24]

PRACTICAL APPLICATION

(1) We must follow the angelic lead in worship. The angels' primary ministry is that of worshippers. As such, they are our example. They are the worship-leaders for the whole of creation, and our joyful duty is to follow their lead. We must never lose our sense of wonder that the angels escort God into the presence of the worshipping assembly, that they are present as we worship. When we contemplate the fervor with which the angelic hosts celebrate the glory of God, we should raise our hearts and voices with enthusiasm as we imitate their example. Eventually the time will come when all the redeemed and all the angels will be together in glory worshipping God for all eternity. Such a prospect beckons us onwards, and fills our lives with joyful praise.

Part of the angels' worship involves the celebration of salvation. In this respect, should we not be even more fervent in praise than they are? After all, we are the recipients of salvation; they are mere observers. We should be captivated and motivated to praise God by the truth that our experience of his grace goes far deeper than anything that the angels can ever know.

(2) We should give thanks for the unseen service of the angels. As Hebrews 1:14 informs us, the angels are "ministering spirits sent forth to minister for those who will inherit salvation." Even though we may not always be aware of the service which the angels are rendering on our behalf, we have God's word for it that they are busy for our sake. We should be genuinely grateful to God that this is so. It represents the intense care which God takes for the protection of his people, that he even uses unseen angels. Here is a reason indeed for deep thankfulness.

There is a vivid illustration of the ministry of the angels in 2 Kings 6:16–17. The Syrian army was trying to attack Israel. Repeatedly God revealed to Elisha where the Syrians would strike. Elisha would warn the King of Israel, and repeatedly the Israelite army was able to catch the Syrians out. The King of Syria learned that Elisha was the problem, and so

---

24. David Shafik, from a personal email dated 6th September, 2020. With grateful thanks for his permission to recount this incident.

sent a great army of horses and chariots to capture Elisha. Elisha's servant panicked, but Elisha gave him a word of assurance: "those who *are* with us *are* more than those who *are* with them." He then prayed that God would show him how safe he was, and "the LORD opened the eyes of the young man, and he saw. And behold, the mountain *was* full of horses and chariots of fire all around Elisha."

Although we may not understand all the forms of service which the angels perform, we know enough to be truly thankful. We are defended by a numerous invisible guard. Angels are the carriers of mercy, the bringers of assurance, and for these helps we must glorify God.

Moreover, it is an angelic duty to usher the souls of believers into heaven. This truth should fill our souls with the sweetest of comfort. Our loved ones who have died in the Lord, are safe, and when our own time comes to depart this life, we shall have nothing to worry about.

(3) We must follow the angelic lead in service. The angels, we learned, serve speedily with passionate devotion. As such, their example challenges us if ever we become sluggish and half-hearted in our walk with the Lord. May we be given the grace to imitate the angels' example in this respect too.

(4) We must never underestimate the power of the demonic world. In the devil we are up against a real foe, accompanied as he is by all his angels—those celestial beings who rebelled with him. Their constant aim is to frustrate gospel success, and to impede our growth in grace. We need to be constantly prayerful that the Lord will enable us to stand firm against the devil's wiles, remembering always that, of ourselves, we are weak and vulnerable in this battle.

We must beware of ever dabbling in the occult. We must take a firm stand against such things as "trick or treat," never giving the slightest impression that anything with its roots in witchcraft and the demonic can ever become harmless.

(5) Neither must we overestimate the power of the demonic world. The devil's capabilities must not be exaggerated. He can never be a successful rival to the Lord Jesus Christ. "For this purpose the Son of God was manifested, that he might destroy the works of the devil" (1 John 3:8). Satan is a defeated foe, and we may press on with the assurance that he cannot prevail against the people of God. There is no need for us to be gripped by fear of the unseen demonic world. In fact, we may rejoice that the demons are completely limited and restricted by God's permission,

and should find great comfort in the truth of God's sovereignty, even over the devil.

(6) We praise God for Christ's victory over Satan. It follows from what we have just said that the Lord is to be perpetually praised that Christ has won the ultimate battle. He conquered the devil at every point in his ministry on earth and still drives home that conquest through his present ministry in heaven. He deserves the praise for this guaranteed victory.

(7) We must pray for those who serve demons by worshipping idols. As Satan tries to retain them in his clutches, we must pray that the power of the gospel may be seen and felt in their lives. The Bible defines idol-worship as demonic. Those involved in the worship of false gods lay themselves open to demonic influence. We must pray for their liberation, and share with them the good news of a Savior who is the master of deliverance.

In this connection, we remind ourselves that the more sophisticated idolatry of the modern atheistic, materialistic world is no less devil-inspired than the traditional idolatry which bows down to man-made images, or which intentionally offers worship to the things which God has made, such as the sun. In prayer for the godless world in which so many live today, we still do battle with Satan.

We see demonic influence also in the prevalence of the so-called "multi-faith" approach, which regards biblical Christianity as on a par with all the other religions of the world. We must pray for a breakthrough of the exclusive claim of Christ alone as Savior of the world, against all devilish schemes to water down this truth.

(8) We pray for those in the grip of demonic power. Demonic deceit is seen also in the way in which some people find themselves helplessly enslaved by immoral practices, perverse worldviews, or self-destructive tendencies, for example. These victims of Satan's malice need our prayers. We must also pray for divine wisdom to know how best to witness to them, to minister to their needs, and to lead them, by God's grace, to freedom.

(9) We must pray for pastoral discernment. Those of us involved in pastoral ministry need wisdom and God-given insight into the needs of the people with whom we are called to work. It is not the case that every sinner is "demonized." If we misread a situation, and try to deal with it as an example of direct demonic involvement when it is not, we may do more harm than good. In our limited understanding, we must pray earnestly for the ability to make a correct assessment of every situation.

(10) We must ensure that we are regularly hearing God's true word. In a world where the false voices of error, prompted by the devil and his evil hordes, clamor to be heard, we must devote ourselves to the daily reading of God's word, to the regular hearing of the truth preached to our souls. Only a firm grip on the truth will keep us safe as we negotiate our way through a world under the sway of Satan.

16

The Doctrine of the Last Things

AN ALTERNATIVE TERM FOR this subject is "eschatology," based on the Greek words *eschatos* and *logos*, meaning the study of the end.

In my view, there is no "correct" Reformed eschatology. In some of the areas where biblical believers have come to different conclusions—most obviously, probably, on the issue of the millennium—Reformed scholars also have embraced various views, premillennial, amillennial, or postmillennial. We must certainly never make a person's millennial viewpoint a touchstone for his orthodoxy.

Of course, on most of the elements of eschatology all Bible-believing Christians are at one. The return of Christ, the resurrection of the dead, the final judgment, the eternal glory of the redeemed—on these essentials there is universal agreement. In areas where there are differences, we all need humility. The areas of difference are not the most vital ingredients of a biblical systematic eschatology.

BIBLICAL FOUNDATION

We find eschatology, strictly defined, in the New Testament. The hope to which the Old Testament primarily looked forward was the first coming of Christ. As the first instalment of the last things, this was an eschatological event. However, our present concern is the ultimate future, and it is in the New Testament that we find clearer information regarding this subject. Old Testament prophecy tends to conflate Christ's two comings: from its vantage point it was not possible to discern the time lapse between these two peaks in the divine purpose. We may compare the prophetic perspective with our experience of looking across a huge sweep of countryside to a mountain range in the distance: two summits may appear to be quite close together; we cannot tell that they are separated by a long valley until we get much closer.

The New Testament contains a wealth of eschatological teaching. We shall select just six representative passages.

Matthew 24:3–14

In response to a question from his disciples, Jesus gives them some clear eschatological teaching, The question is one which always fascinates believers: "what *will be* the sign of your coming, and of the end of the age?" This question presupposes two things.

First, there will be an end to the age of time as we know it. The word translated "end" (*sunteleia*) speaks of a conclusion when everything comes together. It reminds us that the present world is disorderly and chaotic because of sin, but at the end everything will fall neatly into place.

Second, the close of the age will be simultaneous with the second coming of Jesus. The word rendered "coming" is *parousia*. It speaks of one person being alongside another. It is a lovely, gentle description of the Lord's return. It depicts Jesus arriving at the side of his people and remaining with them so that they live from then on in his presence.

The belief that this age would reach a climactic conclusion had already been impressed upon the disciples by the Lord in his teaching. He referred to "the end of the age" three times in Matthew 13 (verses 39, 40, 49). Again, they were already aware of this future coming of Jesus because of his own teaching. Although Jesus never used the noun *parousia*, he had referred to his coming in glory in other terms. For example, in Matthew 16:27 he says, "the Son of Man will come in the glory of his Father with his angels."

The Lord begins his answer to the disciples' question, in verses 4–12, by highlighting things which are not signs of the end—the growth of false religion with its deceptions, war, famine, and earthquakes (representative of natural disasters in general), and persecution and consequent backsliding. In verse 6 Jesus says that when these things take place "the end is not yet," and in verse 8 he calls them "the beginning of sorrows." Such phenomena are normal throughout the period between the two comings of Christ. Their occurrence can never be a sign that the end is drawing near.

In verse 13 Jesus redirects the disciples' focus. Precisely when the end will come is not the important thing. Looking for signs of the end is not a valid pastime. What matters is that we should endure to the end, that we should still be holding fast to faith in Christ when the end does come. Enduring to the end therefore includes the challenge to be enduring at every moment before the end comes.

In verse 14 Jesus mentions the only sign of the end that there is, namely, the worldwide proclamation of the gospel. The second coming will take place only after the gospel has been preached to every nation. This reminds us that, until the end, the church has an ongoing task of evangelistic enterprise into all the world. We are to worry more about getting the job done than about prying into God's secret calendar for the date of the end.

Romans 11:25–27

We hear now of God's future purpose for Israel, namely that all Israel shall be saved. This appears to mean that before the end there will be, through the preaching of the gospel accompanied by a powerful work of revival on the part of the Holy Spirit, a great turning back to the Lord on the part of the Jewish people. They will recognize the Lord Jesus as their Messiah, and put their trust in him. This will apply not only to those Jews resident in the land of Israel, but also to the Jewish diaspora throughout the world. Some people read this to mean not necessarily that every individual Israelite of that final generation will be converted, but just the overwhelming majority. However, the word "all" does at least hold out the prospect that there will be no exceptions at all.

That we are talking here about salvation in the sense of true spiritual renovation is clear from the Old Testament quotation which follows. It entails the banishment of ungodliness and the taking away of sins.

To be fair, we must note that not all interpreters read this passage in the way suggested here. Stuart Olyott, for example, argues that Paul is referring to the spiritual Israel, the elect of every nation, and declaring that God will not fail to gather in all his elect,[1] while Hendriksen interprets the

---

1. Olyott, *Gospel*, 96–107.

verse to refer specifically and only to the elect within Israel.[2] The problem with these readings is that the word "Israel" in verse 26 suddenly acquires a meaning different from every occurrence in Romans up until that point. Moreover, it becomes something of an anti-climax to the argument, for there was never any doubt that God will save all his elect. However, the fact that that includes "all Israel" of the final generation is a staggering additional truth, calculated to evoke wonder, worship, and humility.

1 Corinthians 15:12–58

In the church at Corinth there were some people who denied the resurrection of the dead. Paul writes this passage in response to this error. These people may have been influenced either by Sadducean teaching, or by the emphasis in Geek philosophy on the immortality of the soul leading to a disembodied spiritual afterlife. It seems that they did not deny the resurrection of Christ, and Paul starts by highlighting the inconsistency in denying the resurrection in general, while still confessing that Jesus was raised from the dead. His one resurrection is sufficient to verify that the dead are raised. Indeed, as the "firstfruits," his resurrection guarantees the general resurrection, which, as verse 23 notes, will take place when Jesus returns, heralding the end. At the end Jesus will secure his victory over all his enemies, and "the last enemy *that* will be destroyed is death" (verse 26). It is resurrection which achieves the destruction of death.

The point of verse 29 seems simply to be that it is a general human assumption that the dead will be raised. It is a belief ingrained in the human personality. Human life can only take place authentically in a body: that is how God created us. The body is not an inferior, dispensable part of our make-up. It is a vital, integral element of our humanity.

At verse 35, Paul begins to tell us what the resurrection body will be like. He makes some introductory remarks, in which he stresses that there are differences between different kinds of body, and then, from verse 42, outlines some of the differences between the bodies we know now and our resurrection bodies. Resurrection entails transformation. The believer will not return in a body identical to the one in which he died.

Our present bodies are marked by four characteristics: (1) "corruption" (*phthora*), emphasizing our physical mortality, experienced

2. Hendriksen, *Romans*, 381–82.

via the ageing process though which our faculties gradually decay; (2) "dishonor" (*atimia*), a word with moral connotations [cf. Rom 1:26]: the body is the primary source of temptation to all varieties of immorality; (3) "weakness" (*astheneia*), implying that physical strength is sapped by disease, that the body is exposed to danger and is easily damaged; (4) "natural" (*psychikos*), "concerned with this life only."[3]

The resurrection body will be the opposite of all that. Four contrasting characteristics are highlighted: (1) "incorruption" (*aphthora*), the exact reverse of the present reality, referring to its immortality; (2) "glory" (*doxa*), the exalted splendor of a body which has been remade morally; (3) "power" (*dunamis*), a body with all expressions of weakness resulting from the fall eliminated, every ability restored, a body re-empowered for untainted service for the Lord; (4) "spiritual" (*pneumatikos*), renewed by the Spirit of God, a body unfettered by annoying limitations.

With reference to that final point, the following observation has been made:

> that by "spiritual" here Paul means completely non-material is incompatible with the whole context, which discusses the differing organizations of material substance. The spiritual body is an imperishable, yet utterly real body—one of a different order and having different functions from the earthly body . . . —a body glorified with eternal life.[4]

Such a transformation is essential because "flesh and blood cannot inherit the kingdom of God" (verse 50), and so this corruptible and mortal body must put on incorruptible immortality (verse 53).

The main point of verses 46–49 is that our resurrection bodies will be in the image of Christ's heavenly body. Moreover, the transformation will affect all believers, even those still alive when Christ returns (verse 51): even the final generation, alive at the return of Christ must go through a process of transformation akin to resurrection without first passing through death. The transformation will be so complete, the difference between mortal and immortal life so total, that it will be as huge a change as if they had actually died and risen again. It will take place instantaneously, and will be the last thing to happen in this present history (verse 52), as "death is swallowed up in victory" (verse 54). The Old

---

3. Liddell & Scott, *Lexicon*, 798.
4. Mare, "1 Corinthians," 290.

Testament passage referred to in those words is Isaiah 25:8, which reads, "He will swallow up death forever."

The word translated "swallowed up" is *katapinō*. More literally it means "swallowed down." It is an image borrowed from having a drink. A drink is swallowed down, and it is gone. The victory of resurrection will drink death up, swallow it down, devour it completely. The victory over death will be endlessly secure: never again will there be any possibility of a reversal of this victory. By the resurrection death will cease to exist, it will have no further reality, it will be completely devoured.

All this leads up to the conclusion in verse 58, which assures us that we are not wasting our lives if we spend them serving the Lord.

1 Thessalonians 4:13—5:11

This has been described as "one of the classic New Testament passages on the Lord's return."[5] It seems that some in the church at Thessalonica were under the misapprehension that fellow believers, who had died would miss out when the Lord returned. Paul writes to reassure them and to strengthen their hope. He affirms that God will raise from the dead Christians who have died, that they will return along with Jesus, and that believers alive at the second coming "will by no means precede those who are asleep." The word rendered "precede" is *phthanō*. Although its literal meaning is to arrive ahead, the apostle may be using it here in a metaphorical sense: the last generation of believers will have no advantage over those of previous generations.

In verses 16–17 he outlines the order of events at the Lord's return. First, the Lord will descend from heaven, and this will be accompanied by three great noises: the Lord's own shout (probably the summons to believers who have died to rise, akin to his call to Lazarus in John 11:43), an archangel's voice, and the trumpet blast.

The trumpet blast served seven key functions in Scripture. It was (1) a summons to gather (Exod 19:13), (2) an announcement of God's presence (Exod 19:16), (3) the start of the celebration of liberty in the Year of Jubilee (Lev 25:9), (4) a proclamation of victory (Josh 6:5), (5) a declaration of kingship (2 Sam 15:10), (6) the alarm for war (Jer 4:19), and (7) a warning of danger (Ezek 33:3–5).

5. R. L. Thomas, "1 & 2 Thessalonians," 275.

Perhaps this final trumpet will be the culminating blast for all of them: (1) it will summon believers, dead and alive, to assemble to Jesus in the air; (2) it will alert the world to the presence of God the Son; (3) it will inaugurate the era of everlasting liberty; (4) it will proclaim Christ's final victory over all that opposes the gospel; (5) it will declare that Jesus is truly and finally King of kings and Lord of lords; (6) it will inform a world at war with God that he now declares war on sin in the final judgment; (7) it will warn the unbelieving world that the final chance for repentance has arrived.

Next the resurrection of the believing dead will take place, and then living believers will be caught up with them to meet the Lord in the air. This meeting place is significant in view of the description in Ephesians 2:2 of Satan as "the prince of the power of the air." The meeting will take place at the heart of Satan's kingdom, symbolizing its overthrow. From then on Christ and his people will be eternally inseparable.

When Jerome translated the Bible into Latin he chose the verb *rapio* to render *arpazō*, translated by the phrase "caught up" in verse 17. This Latin word is the basis for the technical term, "the rapture of the saints." It has become a matter of debate whether this is a secret rapture prior to the Lord's final coming, or whether it refers to what takes place at the Lord's final return. Once again, we need to take care not to create disunity in the body of Christ because of differences of opinion on this subject.

The opening verses of chapter 5 remind us that we do not know the timing of these events. The day "so comes as a thief in the night"—unannounced. There will be no signs to alert us when the day of the Lord's coming is approaching. Its coming will be sudden (*aiphnidios*, unexpected, unforeseen), when everything is plodding on as normal. In the course of history disasters often strike suddenly, reversing a seemingly smooth course of events. Such occasions are previews of this final day, and are challenges to be ready.

Paul assures us that this day will not overtake believers by surprise since we are expecting it. However, our ignorance of the date is a challenge to "watch and be sober". We watch (*grēgoreō*) by being alert to anything which could hinder our spiritual progress, and we are sober (*nēphō*) in that we take a serious approach to life, knowing the eternal consequences of what we do.

2 Peter 3:3–15

Peter addresses the issue of those who scoff at the idea that Jesus will come again. Their argument is that nothing in this world ever changes. In response, Peter insists that the second coming of Christ will definitely take place, that judgment will ensue, and that out of the ashes of the old order will arise new heavens and a new earth.

So why the delay in the fulfilment of the promise that Christ will return? Peter's reply is first of all explanatory. God's timescale is very different from ours. A period of twenty centuries for us is equivalent to just a couple of days from God's standpoint. So God is not being slow concerning his promise.

But Peter then emphasizes the Lord's motivation in the apparent delay, from our perspective, of the coming day of the Lord. It has to do with his patience. Peter refers to this first in verse 9. The Lord puts up with a sinful, unbelieving world, restraining his anger against sin, for a very long time. The reason is that he is "not willing that any should perish but that all should come to repentance." No one can ever say, "God did not give me a chance to be saved." He gives everyone chances repeatedly. In verse 15 Peter presses home the evangelistic challenge of this eschatological postponement: "consider *that* the longsuffering of our Lord *is* salvation." God's patience is a powerful incentive for the unbeliever to seek his salvation.

Revelation 20:1–15

There are four main views of these verses. They may be summarized as follows.

(1) Historic Premillennialism. Jesus will return before the thousand-year reign on earth, and his thousand-year reign will happen before the final, eternal state begins.

(2) Amillennialism. There will be no literal reign of Christ on earth; this passage is symbolic of the present age, which will be followed directly by the eternal state when Jesus returns.

(3) Postmillennialism. Jesus will return after the thousand-year reign; this passage tells us that he will reign on earth through the preaching of the gospel: before the end there will be a worldwide revival which will totally Christianize the entire world.

(4) Dispensationalism. As in Historic Premillennialism, Jesus will return before the thousand-year reign; however, there are two different schemes of salvation, one for the church, and another for Israel: during Christ's thousand-year reign on earth Israel will be the leading earthly empire, while the church will be in heaven, and will take no part in what happens on earth.

I have held three of these views in the course of my Christian life. I was brought up in a dispensationalist church, and initially I simply assumed that that was the biblical teaching. However, as a student I came across the historic pre-millennial position, and found it more convincing than the dispensationalism of my upbringing. Some years later, while reading Charles Hodge, I came to find the postmillennial outlook compelling, and that has been my position ever since. I have never been persuaded by amillennialism, primarily because it seems inconsistent with the teaching of the book of Revelation as a whole. We read in Revelation 20:3 that the devil "should deceive the nations no more until the thousand years were finished." This contrasts with three references earlier in the book to the nations being deceived (Rev 12:9; 13:14; 18:23). I fail to see, therefore how those contexts can be referring to the same period of time as chapter 20, as Hendriksen, for example, claims.[6]

That said, a believer's view on the millennium may never be used as a test of orthodoxy. It would be sinful to dismiss other believers because they hold a different view from our own. Each of us needs to hold our millennial position with humility, with the thought, "I could be wrong."

Whether the thousand years is to be understood literally is an open question. Most of the numbers in the book of Revelation are symbolic, so it would not be surprising if this one is too. One thousand is a well-rounded number, symbolizing that the millennium will last for precisely the right duration, however long that may turn out to be. It may also contrast with the three and a half years of suffering depicted in chapter 11, which "would be a mere blink of an eye compared to the long and glorious rule of God that would ensue."[7]

A word is in order about the structure of this passage. It seems to me that verses 1–4a are a summary, and that verses 4b–15 then elaborate and fill in the details. The summary runs like this: first, Satan is bound for a thousand years so that there is no more deception (verses 1–3a); next,

6. Hendriksen, *More than Conquerors*, loc. 369.
7. White, *Millennial Expectation, passim.*

he is released after the thousand years for a little while (verse 3b); finally, judgment takes place (verse 4a).

The details then follow.

First, during the thousand years that Satan is bound, the saints, living as a result of the first resurrection (probably a reference to the spiritual resurrection from death to life at regeneration[8]), reign with Christ, and all those who have participated in the first resurrection will avoid the second death, which is defined in verse 14 as the eternal death which follows the final judgment (verses 4b–6, amplifying verses 1–3a).

Then Satan is released, the nations are deceived again, Satan's battle with God resumes, centering in his attack on the church, but God intervenes, finalizing his victory, and the devil is dispatched to his final doom (verses 7–10, amplifying verse 3b).

Finally, the great white throne is set up, and the resurrection of unbelievers for condemnation takes place, followed by the final judgment (verses 11–15, amplifying verse 4a).

One intriguing question raised by this chapter is this: why is Satan released at the end of the thousand years? Perhaps the reason is that it serves to make obvious the incorrigibility of the sinful human heart. Apart from regenerating grace, we never will submit to God. Even after a thousand years of peace and joy, still the moment the devil reappears on the scene, the nations fall for his deception.

That underlines for us as believers that, as we pass from time into eternity, uppermost in our minds can only be the thought that I am here only because of God's grace in Christ, because left to myself I instinctively rebel against God. It follows that eternity will involve magnifying a magnificent God for his magnificent grace, and admiring a marvelous Savior with wonder and awe for such a glorious and undeserved salvation!

DOCTRINAL FORMULATION

The Early Creeds

Eschatological comments appear in three of the creeds of the early church: the Apostles' Creed, the Nicene Creed, and the Athanasian Creed. There are five main themes.

---

8. So, e.g., Bavinck, *Dogmatics, Vol. 4*, 681; Still, *Vision of Glory*, 135–36; Wilcock, *Heaven Opened*, 192.

Jesus will come

All three of these creeds make this statement, to which the Nicene Creed adds the word "again." It also describes Jesus' coming again as being "with glory." The Apostles' and Athanasian Creeds both note that the coming will be from heaven.

He will judge the living and the dead

Kelly notes that this is a standard phrase borrowed from the New Testament, where it is found three times (Acts 10:42, 2 Tim 4:1, and 1 Pet 4:5).[9]

His kingdom shall never end

This phrase, found in the Nicene Creed, again echoes scriptural material. A similar statement is found in Luke 1:33, which alludes to Isaiah 9:7.

Kelly points out that this was a particularly important statement in the mid-fourth century, when Marcellus of Ancyra taught that the being of Son of God was limited to the time of the incarnation, and that after the consummation the Son will disappear as a distinct being with an identifiable existence, becoming integrated into the Father, who will then be all-in-all. This will be a return, he claimed, to the pre-incarnate situation.[10] By saying that the kingdom of Christ is endless, the early church was insisting that the Son of God is an eternal distinct person within the Godhead, whose personal existence will continue into all eternity.

The dead will be raised

The Nicene Creed refers to the resurrection of the dead. The Apostles' Creed speaks more specifically of the resurrection of the body. The Athanasian goes into more detail by saying that at Christ's coming people will rise again with their bodies and give account for their works. The most important thing here is the reference to the body.

This phrase may be linked with the preceding clause in both the Apostles' and Nicene creeds, concerning the forgiveness of sins. That clause relates the redemption accomplished by Christ to man's spiritual

---

9. J. N. D. Kelly, *Creeds*, 152.
10. J. N. D. Kelly, *Creeds*, 338.

nature. The resurrection of the body relates redemption to the material nature. The two phrases together stress that redemption embraces the whole of human personality, not merely some aspect of it.

Very early on the primitive church had to contend with those who construed salvation in entirely spiritual terms. The result of such an emphasis was that the immortality of the soul was put forward as the ultimate goal of the work of Christ. The orthodox church had to fight against this immaterial, spiritualistic view, and therefore insisted on the bodily resurrection of the believer. During the second century, Polycarp suspected that the rejection of resurrection was motivated by the desire to deny the doctrine of judgment.[11] Irenaeus observed that the denial of resurrection was also linked with the view that material things are essentially evil.[12] This led to an understanding of salvation as rising above, and becoming free from, all contact with anything material. By contrast, the early church saw the resurrection of the body as one part of the total renovation of God's entire creation.

Everlasting life will follow

This is affirmed briefly by the Apostles' and Nicene creeds. The Athanasian Creed elaborates: it says that the good (that is, believers) will receive eternal life, and the evil will experience eternal fire.

Kelly sees a pastoral function in the reference to everlasting life at the end of the creeds. To stop with the resurrection of the dead could imply that resurrected believers will die again like Lazarus. The mention of life everlasting adds the point that the resurrection of believers is modelled on Christ's resurrection as described in Romans 6:9: "Christ, having been raised from the dead, dies no more. Death no longer has dominion over him." Eternal life is, therefore, the full significance of the resurrection of the body.

Kelly refers to two fourth-century writers. He observes that Cyril of Jerusalem clarifies the truth that everlasting life is more than mere endless continuance of life; it means real, true life—the very life which is found in God himself. Similarly, Nicetas notes that everlasting life is the life of eternally blessed quality with Christ in heaven. Kelly then cites Thomas Aquinas to this effect: "the first truth about eternal life is that a

11. Polycarp, "Philippians," 7.
12. Irenaeus, "Against All Heresies," 1.22.1.

man there finds union with God, who is the reward and end of all our labors, and crowns all our desires."[13] Kelly also aptly sums up the spiritual emotions behind the creeds, speaking of the "excited anticipation, eager and at the same time apprehensive, of the Savior's second coming," knowing that he would come to exercise the final judgment.[14]

The Reformation Confessions

I shall here try to synthesize the various points made by different confessions in the order of their expected occurrence in the future.

The coming of God's kingdom in the course of history

The Westminster Larger Catechism understands the petition "your kingdom come" as a prayer for the progress of the gospel throughout the world. Two particular expectations stand out: the calling of the Jews, and the bringing in of the fullness of the Gentiles (Rom 11:25–26). Iain Murray demonstrates how it was their eschatological vision which led to the great missionary enterprise on the part of Reformed churches, especially towards the Jews.[15]

The Reformers and their early successors were not all in agreement on eschatology. While many had a postmillennial outlook, the Second Helvetic Confession dismisses as "dreams" the idea "that there will be a golden age on earth before the Day of Judgment, and that the pious, having subdued all their godless enemies, will possess all the kingdoms of the earth."

Death and the intermediate state

Since the Christian hope centers around the expectation of the Lord's return and the resurrection of the dead, an important question arises: what happens in the meantime to those who have died?

---

13. J. N. D. Kelly, *Creeds*, 388.
14. J. N. D. Kelly, *Creeds*, 152.
15. I. H. Murray, *Puritan Hope, passim.*

THE DEATH OF THE BODY

The Westminster Confession says that "the bodies of men after death return to dust and see corruption." This applies to all people, believers and unbelievers alike, although the Westminster Larger Catechism points out that, even in dying, believers are delivered from the sting and curse of death in a way that unbelievers are not. For the unbeliever death remains the punishment for sin. However, for the believer, "death is not the proper punishment of sin, but the termination of all sin and sorrow, and an entrance into life eternal."[16]

In answer to the question, "why is there no difference between believers and unbelievers as far as physical death is concerned?" G. I. Williamson answers: "It has pleased God to delay the physical benefits of Christ's redemption until the end of time." He suggests that the purpose of this is that no one is encouraged to be a Christian merely for the sake of liberation from physical difficulties, such as sickness, suffering, and death. Also, death, like sickness and suffering, is a means of sanctification:

> it causes us to remember our frame, that we are dust. It helps to wean us from the pride of life and the love of this present world. It encourages us to cast ourselves more and more upon God and to cry out to him for deliverance.[17]

THE INTERMEDIATE STATE OF THE SOUL

Physical death may be defined as the separation of body and soul. Although this comes to all people, the condition of the soul after death is very different in the case of the believer and the unbeliever.

The intermediate state for the believer

At death, the soul of the believer is made perfect in righteousness, and is received immediately into heaven, "there to enjoy unspeakable comforts," to quote the Irish Articles. These include the experience of peace and rest, and deliverance from fear, torment, and temptation.

However, the best comfort of all is deeper communion with Christ, described by the Westminster Confession as to "behold the face of God

16. Shaw, *Confession*, 315.

17. Williamson, *Westminster*, 252–53.

in light and glory." Not even death can separate the believer from God's love in Christ, as Romans 8:38–39 assures us. Nonetheless, the souls of believers after death are "waiting for the full redemption of their bodies." The intermediate state is certainly not the final state. When we think about the future hope for the believer, we must keep our focus on the Lord's return and the final consummation of God's eternal purpose, which will include our complete glory. Our full redemption is not a disembodied state in heaven, but a redeemed body in the new heaven and the new earth.

However, that the souls of departed saints do immediately enjoy heavenly glory is clear from Philippians 1:21 and 23: "to me, to live *is* Christ, and to die *is* gain . . . . to depart and be with Christ, *which is* far better."

The intermediate state for the unbeliever

The unbeliever is said to be cast immediately into hell, where the experience is one of inexpressible anguish, torment, pain, and utter darkness.

The contrast between the intermediate states for believer and unbeliever is that for the believer the grave is like a bed, for the unbeliever it is like a prison.

TEACHINGS REJECTED

The confessions explicitly reject two teachings.

Purgatory

The Westminster Confession comments that "besides these two places for souls separated from their bodies [heaven and hell], the Scripture acknowledges none." Purgatory is mentioned by name and rejected in the Irish Articles and in the French Confession, which describes it as "an illusion" proceeding from Satan.

Williamson points out that the idea of purgatory is not only contrary to Scripture, but also undermines the sufficiency of the work of Christ. It is claimed to be a place

> where those "who die in the state of grace but are guilty of venial
> sin, or have not fully satisfied for the temporal punishment due

to their sins," go to receive that punishment and to make that satisfaction.

However, this conflicts with the teaching of Hebrews 10:14, which affirms that Christ, by one offering, has forever perfected his people.[18]

Soul sleep

This is the idea that after death neither believers nor unbelievers are conscious of anything until the resurrection. While rejecting this idea, Williamson speculates that the believer after death may have a consciousness of time that is different from what we experience on earth, one "that is no longer circumscribed by our present temporal boundaries."[19]

The expectation of the rise of Antichrist

Most of the confessions identified Antichrist with the Pope, and some seemed to expect a time when Roman Catholicism would conquer the world. Just before the Lord's return, says the Second Helvetic Confession, wickedness will be at its greatest in the world, and "the Antichrist, having corrupted true religion, will fill up all things with superstition and impiety and will cruelly lay waste the Church."

The return of the Lord

The confessions point out that the same Christ will return from heaven. They are emphasizing that the one who will come will not be a stranger, but one already well known to his people in the spiritual experience of his friendship. He will come bodily and visibly, on the clouds of heaven, with glory and majesty, the clouds indeed being God's "shekinah" glory.

Three things in particular are stressed regarding the second coming.

It will occur at the appointed time

The Belgic Confession calls this "the time appointed by the Lord," and notes that it "is unknown to all creatures." This reminds us that, in the

18. Williamson, *Westminster*, 254.
19. Williamson, *Westminster*, 256.

plan of God, the end was fixed from the beginning. The reassuring implication is that this world and its history is not haphazard or chaotic. God
will not be making a snap decision on a whim. Everything is orderly.

It will result in the destruction of Antichrist

In the context of the Reformers' time, this probably meant that, with the
coming of Christ, Roman Catholicism would be exposed for the sham
that it really is.

It will be Christ's vindication

The Westminster Larger Catechism includes the question, "How is Christ
to be exalted in his coming again to judge the world?" It is worth quoting
in full the splendid answer:

> Christ is to be exalted in his coming again to judge the world,
> in that he, who was unjustly judged and condemned by wicked
> men, shall come again at the last day in great power, and in the
> full manifestation of his own glory, and of his Father's, with all
> his holy angels, with a shout, with the voice of the archangel, and
> with the trumpet of God, to judge the world in righteousness.

The main point here is the contrast between Jesus' wicked and unjust
condemnation on the cross, and now his manifest power and glory.

The resurrection of the dead

The confessions teach the general resurrection of all the dead at the time
of the Lord's second coming. Resurrection entails the reunion of soul
and body, and that forever. These will be the same bodies in which we
formerly lived, although, as the Westminster Confession emphasizes,
they will now have "different qualities."

The resurrection will be accomplished by God's mighty power, by the
power of Christ, by the Spirit of God, and by virtue of Christ's resurrection
as the head of his people. The Scottish Confession expresses this vividly:

> there shall be given to every man and woman resurrection of
> the flesh; for the sea shall give her dead, the earth those that
> therein be enclosed; yes, the Eternal, our God, shall stretch out

his hand upon the dust, and the dead shall arise incorruptible, and that in the substance of the self-same flesh that every man now bears.

Noting the term "self-same," used also by the Westminster Confession, Shaw comments that "the very term *resurrection* implies that the same bodies shall be raised that fell by death; for if God should form new bodies and unite them to departed souls, it would not be a resurrection, but a new creation."[20]

Similarly, Williamson observes that, though the nature of the resurrection is a great mystery, the resurrection body being radically different from what it was before, nevertheless there will be a continuity between the identity of the body laid in the grave and the body raised up at the last day: "it will not be a 'new body' created out of nothing as a habitation for the soul. It will be the 'old body' made into a 'new body.'"[21]

Some people have characterized such teaching as bizarre. There is a traditional Yorkshire song designed to convey an amusing message. Written in the local dialect, it is very repetitive. I have rendered it into normal English without the repetitions, to capture the main point:

> Where have you been since I saw you?
> On Ilkley Moor without a hat on.
> You're bound to catch your death of cold!
> Then we shall have to bury you.
> Then worms will come and eat you up.
> Then ducks will come and eat the worms.
> Then we shall go and eat the ducks.
> Then we shall all have eaten you!

It is certainly true that the physical particles of mortal bodies are constantly being recycled. Does this make it impossible for God to perform a general resurrection? Is he bewildered by the question, into which body should which particle go?

We certainly do have to admit that there is mystery here. But then we acknowledge that although it is beyond our understanding, it is not beyond God's capability to achieve the resurrection of the dead. As Paul asked the assembly at Caesarea, "Why should it be thought incredible by you that God raises the dead?" (Acts 26:8).

---

20. Shaw, *Confession*, 320–21.
21. Williamson, *Westminster*, 256–57.

Indeed, the resurrection is more than merely the reconstitution of physical particles. It is the renovation of the entire human person, not excluding the physical element, but including also our emotions, intellect, will, and so on—all restored to perfect harmony.

For the redeemed, our resurrection bodies will be glorified in incorruptibility, power, spirituality (1 Cor 15:42–44). However, the greatest glory will be to be conformed to Christ's glorious body.

The transformation of the living

The confessions recognize that for the final generation of believers, those Christians still living when Christ returns, there will not be death and resurrection, but still "we shall all be changed" (1 Cor 15:51). In effect that generation will experience the realities of resurrection without having to suffer death first. Perhaps we get a glimpse of this in the cases of Enoch (Gen 5:24) and Elijah (2 Kgs 2:11). This experience of "change" for the living will be instantaneous, "in the twinkling of an eye" (1 Cor 15:52)—words quoted by some of the confessions.

The rapture of the saints

Although the confessions were written prior to the emergence in the 1830s of the notion of a secret rapture, they acknowledged the teaching of 1 Thessalonians 4:17: the dead will be raised, the living changed, and then "all the faithful will be caught up to meet Christ in the air, so that then they may enter with him into the blessed dwelling-places to live forever."

Jesus will judge the living and the dead

This is the final judgment, both of men, and of angels. Everyone who has ever lived will have to appear. The judgement will be conducted in perfect righteousness. It will be personal, involving examination of the conscience. The Belgic Confession includes this sobering reflection: all people "shall give an account of every idle word they have spoken, which the world only counts amusement and jest; and then the secrets and hypocrisy of men shall be disclosed." The purpose of the day of judgment will be the manifestation of God's glory in both his mercy and his judgment.

This leads us to consider the different outcomes of the final judgment for unbelievers and believers.

FOR UNBELIEVERS

The outcome of the judgment for unbelievers is summed up the in the grim phrase, "the pains of hell forever." The Puritan writer, Thomas Vincent, distinguishes between "the punishment of sense"—the actual experience of pain, and "the punishment of loss," namely eternal banishment from the comfortable presence of God.[22]

Although this terminology is Vincent's, the two themes recur in the confessions. The phrase "eternal torment" appears frequently. Torment affects both body and soul, but cannot be described. There is never a moment's respite. Hell is pictured as a dungeon full of total darkness, where fire and worms constantly burn and devour. Hell was prepared for the devil and his angels, and part of its pain for human beings is to have to share their presence, with no prospect of ever being rescued. When we realize that in the presence of God there is fullness of joy (Ps 16:11), that fellowship with God is the true criterion of human happiness, then the loss of that favorable presence is the greatest possible catastrophe. This ought to stir up our evangelistic passion.

Today there are some who deny that hell is forever. There is nothing new about this. The Second Helvetic Confession had to reject the teaching "that there would be an end to punishments. For the Lord has plainly declared: 'Their fire is not quenched, and their worm does not die.'"

FOR BELIEVERS

The confessions speak of believers' glory, honor, immortality, joy, and blessedness—and all to the highest possible degree, indeed to a height which is beyond our present capacity to imagine. The believer's full deliverance from death will be achieved. Every tear will be wiped away in the enjoyment of the Lord's refreshing presence and in everlasting participation in his praise. The ultimate magnificence of the eternal state will be that we shall enter into a communion with Christ which, in intimacy, goes far beyond what is attainable now, even for the most spiritually attuned soul. In defining the full enjoyment of God which believers will experience in

---

22. Vincent, *Shorter Catechism*, 66–67.

the world to come, Vincent includes the following statement: "they shall have both a full persuasion and sense of God's love unto them, and perfect love in their hearts towards him."[23] What a wonderful prospect!

The renovation of creation

The eschatological hope is not restricted to believing human beings: the whole of God's creation will be renewed and restored. It is good to be reminded of this, as it is a point which we can be prone to overlook.

The Belgic Confession says that God "will burn this old world, in fire and flame, in order to cleanse it." It is noteworthy that God's purpose is not defined as the destruction of the old creation. His plan is not to consume it and reduce it to ashes. Rather, it is to be cleansed. God will finally purge out of creation everything sinful and evil; all the effects of the curse will be cancelled. What will remain is God's creation restored to its pristine goodness as at the beginning.

The Scottish Confession describes the Lord's return as "the time of refreshing and restitution of all things." The eternal kingdom is larger than the church or believers only. It speaks of God's everlasting rule over his entire universe made new.

The appropriate response to the doctrine of the last things

The Belgic Confession describes the consideration of judgment as something "horrible and dreadful to wicked and evil people." The implication is that this ought to lead the ungodly to repentance. However, the confessions are far more concerned with the response of the believer to eschatological truth. The response described is threefold.

COMFORT

This word appears in many of the confessions. They acknowledge that life in this world is often one of trial and adversity. However, to know that there will be an end to all such experiences, that we will be on the victory side, and that there is eternal glory to come, is a source of incalculable consolation. From it we derive encouragement to press on through this vale of tears.

23. Vincent, *Shorter Catechism*, 108.

The thought that Christ is coming puts a bridle on our lusts. It helps to deter us from sin. It prompts us to shake off worldly and fleshly attitudes and aspirations. It enables us to avoid complacency and carnal security. The doctrine of the last things keeps us on our toes, so that we do pursue that "holiness, without which no one will see the Lord" (Heb 12:14).

WATCHFULNESS

The very fact that the date and time of the second coming of Christ are unknown calls for a response. The day and hour are hidden from everyone "that all may watch and pray, and be ever ready for the coming of the Lord."

Modern Confessions of Faith

The three confessions which we have been using have much in common. All of them teach that the Lord Jesus Christ shall come again a second time on the final day. Two things will then ensue: the dead will be raised, and all people without exception will appear before the judgment seat of Christ.

The different outcomes of the judgment for unbelievers and believers are detailed, albeit that the wording varies between the three confessions. As regards unbelievers, the Indian confession speaks of their condemnation, and says that they "shall suffer the punishment due to their sins." The Indonesian confession states that unbelievers "will go to everlasting torment," while the Chinese confession reads: "All those names not written in the book of life shall be cast into the lake of fire." For believers, by contrast, the outcome of the judgment is glory and everlasting life with God.

Two of the confessions (the Indonesian and the Chinese) make the point that we do not know when Christ's second coming will take place. The Indonesian confession words it in terms of the impossibility of computing the time, while the Chinese confession acknowledges that only God the Father knows the date of Jesus' return, "but," it insists, "we firmly believe that Christ will come again."

Having detailed these strands common to these confessions, there are elements of each one which merit specific mention.

Confession of Faith of the United Church of Northern India

In his commentary on this confession, William Stewart makes one cautionary point, and endorses two particular emphases of the document.

His cautionary point relates to the confessional statements that at the judgment all people "shall receive according to the deeds done in this present life whether good or bad," and that believers "shall be openly acquitted." His concern is that this should not be misread to mean that we can earn acquittal by doing good; this was certainly not the intention of the compilers of the confession. Noting our constant failures, Stewart rightly says that our only hope for the day of judgment is found in the cross of our Lord Jesus Christ.

His first endorsement of the wording of the confession concerns the description of the fate of the lost. He applauds its reserved tone. It refers to the punishment due to their sins, but it does not enlarge on what this will involve. Stewart regrets the way that Christians have sometimes given lurid descriptions of everlasting torture, which go way beyond what the Bible tells us. This confession's brevity is more appropriate.

Stewart's second endorsement relates to the clause, "those who have believed in Christ and obeyed him shall be openly acquitted and received into glory." He commends the inclusion of the word "obeyed:" "our act of faith, if real, is no mere matter of words." Obedience is the evidence that a profession of faith in Christ is not just empty talk, "but the expression of a life truly committed to him."[24]

Confession of Faith of the Huria Kristen Batak Protestant

The Indonesian confession specifies that Jesus "will come again to this earth." It has just spoken of his descent into hell and then his ascension into heaven, but it wants to underline the point that the Lord has not abandoned this world in which he lived out his incarnate life. His return will be most definitely to this same earth. In the same context, and in speaking of the final judgment, this confession takes up the biblical language that Jesus Christ will judge the living and the dead.

In a later section it connects this universal judgement with the truth that "Jesus Christ is the Lord of the living and the dead," an echo of Romans 14:9. Not even death can remove a human person out of the sphere

---

24. W. Stewart, *Faith We Confess*, 42–44.

of Christ's Lordship, and it is his universal Lordship which provides the basis for his universal judgment.

Following on from this comment, the confession makes a salutary point: "When we thus remember the dead, then we remind ourselves of our own death." The fact is that all people are destined to die and then to face the judgment. When we grieve because of the death of a loved one, or when we hear of multiple deaths in the tragedies of life, these are occasions for pausing, for reflecting upon our own mortality. To skip through life as if we face no danger is the attitude of a fool. Wisdom calls upon us to face up to reality: I shall not be here for ever; one day my turn to die will come. This, the confession affirms, enables us to renew our hope in God, and to "strengthen our hearts in our struggle in this life."

However, as a later chapter adds, "the sure destination of those who believe will be the side of God in eternity." These words portray this uncertain life in which the threat of death constantly hangs over us as a journey whose end is secure. Moreover, we shall find our final resting place at God's side—the most blessed location conceivable.

This confession rejects four errors related to the doctrine of the last things. Two of them are rejected by Reformed confessions of faith in general: the notion of purgatory, and the practice of praying to the saints and venerating their relics. The other two have a more local significance: the teaching that the souls of the dead have some influence on those who are still alive, and that the soul of a dead person remains in the grave.

These are allusions to traditional beliefs of the Batak people, who understood that, after death, a person's "death-soul" remains in the grave until the corpse has decomposed, and then continues to live near his previous house, and can contact his family in both positive and negative ways, becoming a guardian spirit, or, if dissatisfied with their behavior, bringing misfortune.[25]

This confession ends by stressing the solemnity of the doctrine of the last things: "We confirm with emphasis: his coming will be unexpected. Therefore, let us always be ready, as he has warned us."

Confession of Faith of House Churches in China

The Chinese confession is heavily influenced by Dispensationalism. It gives a detailed account of the events surrounding the second coming,

---

25. Sibeth, *Batak*, 67, 76.

based on 1 Thessalonians 4:13–18 and the book of Revelation. This account separates the resurrection of those who are saved from that of the unbelieving world. Significantly, it says, "No one knows the specific dates of the second coming of Christ," the plural indicating acceptance of the theory of a two-stage coming, in which the rapture of the saints is separated from the Lord's final coming as judge. The confession claims that it is possible to know some signs of the second coming, but does not specify what these are.

This confession assumes a literal millennium following Christ's initial return, but it explicitly leaves open the question whether the return of the Lord will take place before or after the tribulation.

A very forthright statement is made of opposition "to the teaching that Christ has come the second time in his incarnated form." The comment is added: "All who claim that Christ has already come the second time should be declared heretics." An introduction to the confession observes that the church leaders involved in drawing up the document wanted their confession specifically to refute some of the heretical teachings prevailing in China at the time. One of those is then detailed as follows:

> that Christ has already come the second time, and he has done so in an incarnated form in the person of a Chinese woman called Ms. Deng in Zhengzhou, Henan; this is the teaching of "Oriental Lightning."[26]

I have already outlined the teaching of this sect, also known as "Eastern Lightning."

This confession understands the doctrine of the last things to have practical consequences:

> As believers wait for the Second Coming of Christ, they should be diligent doing the work of the Lord, preach the Word of life, shine for the Lord on earth, and bear abundant fruit in word, deed, faith, love, and holiness . . . . The responsibility of Christians is to be alert and be prepared to welcome the Second Coming of Christ.

---

26. Aikman, *Beijing Factor*, 296.

HISTORICAL ELABORATION

In this section I want to survey the four main millennial theories which have emerged in the course of church history. I shall comment in each case on two proponents from different periods.

Historic Premillennialism

Justin Martyr

Justin, who lived during the second century, will serve as our example of what was a fairly widely held understanding in the first four centuries of the Christian era. Justin is questioned by Trypho, a Jew, as to whether he admits that Jerusalem will be rebuilt, and whether he expects Christian believers, along with the patriarchs, the prophets, as well as the rest of the pre-Christian Jewish believers and proselytes, there to be made joyful with Christ. In response, while acknowledging that many true Christians amongst his contemporaries did not hold to this position, Justin affirms his personal view that there will be a resurrection of the believing dead, followed by a thousand years in a rebuilt, adorned, and enlarged, Jerusalem.

Justin quotes in full the prophecy of a new heaven and new earth from Isaiah 65:17–25, interpreting it to predict, albeit obscurely, this thousand-year period. Isaiah depicts it as a time of joy and gladness, longevity, security, fruitfulness, and justice, a time of peace under the Lord's blessing. Justin refers also to the book of Revelation as teaching that believers in Christ would dwell for a thousand years in Jerusalem prior to the general resurrection and judgment of all people.[27]

George Eldon Ladd

Ladd, writing about 50 years ago, understood Revelation 20 to teach a temporal kingdom of Christ, preceded by the binding of Satan so that the nations are no longer deceived, and by the resurrection of all the saints who have died in the course of history, and the transformation of those still alive as Christ returns to earth. They will then reign with Christ for a thousand years. This will be a time of unparalleled righteousness. Evil

27. Justin Martyr, "Trypho," 80–81.

will be restrained, social, political, and economic justice will prevail, and people will dwell together under Christ's government in peace and prosperity. At the end of that time Satan will be briefly released and will again entice the nations into rebellion. He will then be dispatched forever to the lake of fire, and the rest of the dead will be raised for judgment. Finally, the eternal kingdom, the new heaven and new earth, will come. Ladd relates Isaiah's prophecy to a different epoch than Justin.

Ladd sees the purpose of the millennial kingdom as twofold.

(1) It will be the time of the open manifestation of Christ's glory and sovereignty. Christ is reigning now, but in a way which is veiled and unrecognized by the world at large. The ultimate future will be the age of the Father's glory, when Christ will deliver the kingdom to his Father, and will take his place as subject to him (1 Cor 15:24–28). In between those two periods the millennial kingdom will be the time when Christ's enemies will be subdued and his reign universally acknowledged.

(2) It will demonstrate the justice of the final judgment. The release of Satan at the end of the millennium will result in the nations being deceived again, so revealing the incorrigible wickedness of the human heart. With the millennium as its backdrop, a period in which the social environment has been as nearly perfect as is possible, the righteousness of God's judgment on human rebellion will be totally vindicated.[28]

Amillennialism

Augustine

Augustine once held to the historic premillennial position. However, he changed his mind as a result of observing the carnality which had crept in to the description of the millennium. He re-read the book of Revelation and, having considered several possible meanings of the thousand-year reign of Christ, which he took to be a figurative description, concluded that it was symbolic of the entire period between his first and second comings.

This led him to understand the first resurrection, referred to in Revelation 20:5–6, to be not bodily, but spiritual, the resurrection of the soul from its death in sin, which is the forgiveness of sins and justification, that spiritual renewal whereby sinners are brought into the church. By

---

28. Ladd, *Theology*, 628–31.

contrast, the second resurrection, at the end of the thousand years, will be bodily, and will be a resurrection to judgment. All people shall have a part in the second resurrection, some being dismissed into the second death and others entering into eternal life. The first resurrection, however, pertains only to those destined for that eternal blessedness.

Revelation 20 opens with the binding of Satan, which also continues through the thousand years. Augustine understands this to mean that he is allowed no power to keep his hold on those who are to be freed from sin. He retains no ability to harm or seduce those of any nation who have experienced the first resurrection, those who are genuine believers.

During this thousand-year period the saints reign with Christ. Augustine identifies the church with the kingdom of heaven, and says that for believers to reign with Christ is to set their minds on things above and live in obedience to his word, and so to him as their King.

The purpose of Satan's loosing at the end of the thousand years Augustine sees as giving proof of the fortitude of the holy city, the church, on which Satan will briefly rage with all his force.[29]

Anthony Hoekema

Hoekema understands the opening verses of Revelation 20 as taking us back to the beginning of the New Testament era. The defeat of Satan, described in that chapter, began to take place with the first coming of Christ, and the millennial reign occurs before his second coming, since the final judgment, which follows the millennium, is invariably linked in Scripture with Christ's return. The thousand-year reign runs, therefore, from Christ's first coming until just before his second coming. Hoekema makes the point that, since Revelation is full of symbolic numbers, it is probable that the number 1000 is symbolic of length and completeness.

During this era Satan is bound, so that he can no longer deceive the nations. Hoekema sees a contrast with the Old Testament epoch during which Israel was the only recipient of God's revelation of the truth, the rest of the nations living then in Satanic deception. However, with the coming of Christ, the gospel commission extends to all nations, and Satan is unable to prevent its spread to the ends of the earth.

Hoekema sees a shift in Revelation 20:4 from earth (the concern in verses 1–3) to heaven, where he sees thrones occupied by the souls of

29. Augustine, *City*, 20.6–10.

those who have participated in the first resurrection. This Hoekema understands as referring to the intermediate state between death and physical resurrection, when the souls of deceased believers are with Christ in heaven. Their privilege is to share in Christ's reign over all things.

After the thousand years the rest of the dead are said to come to life again. In this context, Hoekema concludes, this is not a reference to the general resurrection, but to the consignment to the second death, the lake of fire, of the souls of unbelievers.[30]

Postmillennialism

Jonathan Edwards

This third eschatological viewpoint, though certainly represented in earlier centuries, became a dominant emphasis amongst the followers of Calvin during the seventeenth, eighteenth, and nineteenth centuries. Edwards was one notable representative of the position. He reads Revelation 20 as anticipating a destruction of Satan's kingdom, coincident with an advancement of the church on earth into a glorious state. He understands the thousand years as representative of a period of long continuance. This is the next great event revealed in prophecy.

Edwards expects this work to take place gradually by means of the preaching of the gospel, albeit fairly quickly. It will be a glorious work of God's Spirit, taking place as he is poured out in various nations successively for the revival of the Christian church across the world. Multitudes will be converted, and fresh vitality will mark the church.

Christ and his church will achieve a total victory, worldwide in its scope, over the fiercest opposition, resulting in the destruction of Satan's visible kingdom. This will mean the abolition of all forms of heresy in the church, and the overthrow of false religions. Now will follow a time of global spiritual harvest. It will be the principal time of the kingdom of heaven on earth, the glorious day of the gospel.

Those will be days when the light of knowledge abounds, when holiness shall prevail, an era of great joy. The world's governments will seek the glory of Christ. There will be universal peace, and the peoples will be knit together in love. Health and prosperity will characterize that age. The church will be united, and will be a true reflection of heaven.

---

30. Hoekema, *Bible and Future*, 227–38.

At the end of the thousand years, when Satan is released, there will be a short period of widespread apostasy. Darkness will descend, and wickedness will abound. The church will again face great opposition until Christ returns for the final judgment.[31]

Loraine Boettner

Since the twentieth century the so-called "postmillennial" position has been less specifically tied to the interpretation of Revelation 20, which tends to be read as symbolic of the entire church age. This means that much modern "postmillennialism" really amounts to amillennialism with a happy ending.

Boettner is an exception to this trend. He understands the millennium as a golden age of spiritual prosperity, a long period of righteousness and peace at the end of this present church age, during which the entire world is Christianized. More specifically, he anticipates an era of social, economic, political, and cultural uplift. Evil will be reduced to negligible proportions, and Christian principles will rule everywhere, as Satan will no longer be able to deceive the nations.

Boettner takes the thousand years to be a symbolic number, representing a time of indefinite length, a complete and perfect period. He conjectures that it may even be far longer than a literal thousand years.

The movement towards this time of glory on earth will be gradual, coming about through the worldwide preaching of the gospel and the ongoing work of the Holy Spirit, through which, eventually, the vast majority of people in every nation will be converted. Unlike Edwards, Boettner does not anticipate further specific outpourings of the Spirit. The millennium will be a spiritual kingdom in human hearts, the kingdom of grace attaining its full development, and fulfilling Christ's great commission promise. The binding of Satan which precedes the millennium (Rev 20:1–3) is again a gradual development over a considerable period of time.

At the close of the millennial age Christ will return to a converted world, a world conquered by the gospel. Boettner again differs from Edwards in that he does not expect a final apostasy immediately before the second coming. Perhaps the emphasis in Revelation 20:7–9 is the immediate defeat of the devil. Christ's coming will be followed by the

---

31. J. Edwards, "Work of Redemption," 604–11.

general resurrection, the final judgment, and the introduction of heaven and hell in their fullness.[32]

Dispensational Premillennialism

John Nelson Darby

This position originated in Darby's writings in the 1830s. He held that the present period of time will end suddenly with the first resurrection, that of dead believers, who, along with the saints living at the time, will be raptured to meet the Lord in the air. The church will depart from this world to be with its Lord in heaven.

After the rapture Antichrist will emerge as world ruler. The apostate church, left behind when true believers were raptured, will associate itself with Antichrist, and seduce the earth's inhabitants to acknowledge him. At the same time the Jews will return to their land and join in alliance with Antichrist. However, a small remnant from amongst the Jews will reject this alliance and render testimony to God.

Darby taught that for three and a half years the nation of Israel will flourish. However, the beast will then break his treaty with the Jews and put an end to the testimony rendered by the remnant, who will flee into the desert. At this point Satan will be cast out of heaven to earth and the great tribulation will begin, during which the Jews will be fiercely persecuted. After a further three and a half years Christ's public appearance along with the saints will take place.

Christ's coming will result in the destruction of Antichrist, the judgment of the professing church and the Gentile nations, and the binding of Satan. Darby believed that Israel would now recognize Jesus as Messiah and be re-established in the promised land. The millennial reign of Christ on earth will begin, from his throne in Jerusalem. This will be an era of happiness, peace, and uninterrupted blessing.

At the end of the thousand years Satan will be let loose to test the earth's inhabitants. He will deceive the nations and bring them against Jerusalem, but will not succeed. He will be cast into the lake of fire, and the unbelieving dead raised in the second resurrection to face judgment.[33]

---

32. Boettner, *Millennium*, 3–72.

33. W. Kelly, *Writings of Darby*, especially Vols. 2, 5, and 11 [Prophetic Nos. 1, 2, and 4], *passim.*

John MacArthur

MacArthur's eschatology is driven by the conviction that a faithful God must fulfil all his promises to Israel revealed in Old Testament prophecy. Christ's one-thousand-year reign on earth will be the time of this fulfilment.

The unannounced rapture of the saints will first occur, followed by the great tribulation. During this time the Jews will be converted. Christ will return, publicly and visibly, to earth. He will destroy the ungodly, Satan will be bound, and the millennial reign will ensue.

Israel will be restored to its land, and Christ will reign personally on earth from his capital city, Jerusalem. His reign will encompass the whole world, all nations, and all creation. His rule over the tribes of Israel will be delegated to the apostles, and the rest of the saints of both the Old and the New Testament eras, raised in the first resurrection, will come to earth in their glorified bodies and reign under Christ. The temple will be rebuilt and become the focal point for all peoples to come and worship the Messiah.

MacArthur includes amongst the qualities of the millennial age the renewal of earth's environment with the lifting of the curse, as well as the establishment of an epoch free from war, oppression, injustice, poverty, and illness. By contrast, this will be a time of righteousness, peace, and joy, marked by prosperity, health, and longevity. Christ himself will set the world's agenda, and so truth will prevail throughout society. Education, morality, economics, and all aspects of social life will reflect the mind of Christ. Every outbreak of sin will be swiftly and firmly judged.

MacArthur envisages exponential population growth, though not everyone born during the millennium will become a believer. At the end of the thousand years Satan will therefore be released to inspire a rebellion which will be quickly aborted. The final judgment will take place and the eternal state will be installed.[34]

PRACTICAL APPLICATION

In a sense, to draw out the practical implications of this doctrine is easy, in that the New Testament itself constantly makes it clear that eschatology is not revealed merely to satisfy our curiosity or to stimulate our

---

34. MacArthur, *Earthly Kingdom, passim.*

ingenuity, but because of the practical impact which it should have on our lives. We shall divide the application into two parts, considering first the evangelistic application, and then the application to believers.

Evangelistic Application

The doctrine of the last things may serve as the Lord's appeal to the unbeliever to get right with him and so be ready for the end of all things. For those of us involved in Christian ministry, the truths associated with the end times may be used to alert unbelievers to their danger and need. We can make four points of application in this connection.

(1) The unbeliever needs to be warned of the reality of hell. Jesus does so in Matthew 10:28: "fear him who is able to destroy both soul and body in hell." The word translated "destroy" (*apollumi*) does not speak of annihilation. It can mean "to fall into ruin."[35] Hell is everlasting existence as an utterly ruined parody of true humanness. Jesus presses home this warning in Mark 9:43–48. Five times he portrays hell as unquenchable fire, and says three times that in hell the "worm does not die," depicting torments which eat away at the personality of the condemned sinner without ever totally devouring him. In the light of this awful reality, Jesus calls for radical repentance. He urges a decisive break with absolutely anything which prevents uncompromised allegiance to him. To refuse to make the break, is to condemn oneself to unending torment.

(2) We must also face up to the fact that judgment is worse for those who have rejected the gospel than for those who have never heard it. In Matthew 10:15, as he sends out his disciples to minister in his name, he says of the places which reject their words, "it will be more tolerable for the land of Sodom and Gomorrah in the day of judgment than for that city" (cf. Matt 11:21–24). Sodom and Gomorrah were the most morally notorious cities of Old Testament times, but they never had the opportunity to hear the gospel, as the people of Jesus' own generation had. The final judgment will be more lenient for them than for those who rejected the personal coming of the Savior. In the same way today, to hear the gospel and reject is to be in a far worse position in the judgment than for those who have never been in a position to hear it at all. For those who have been privileged to hear the gospel, the fact of coming judgment is a warning of the need to repent.

35. Liddell & Scott, *Lexicon*, 88.

(3) The unbeliever needs to face up to the fact that it is pointless to forfeit one's soul for the sake of present gain. This is what the Lord Jesus says in Matthew 16:26: "what profit is it to a man if he gains the whole world and loses his own soul?" We could become the richest people the world has ever known, but if we miss out on eternal life, what benefit will our possessions be to us? We cannot enjoy the world in hell. Jesus goes on in the next verse to remind us that he is going to come again, and that he will repay each of us, not according to what we own, or what we have achieved, or what power and influence we have had, but according to what we have done. If we have no works worth rewarding, even though we may have gained all that there is to gain in the way of things, we face total loss.

(4) Eschatological truth warns us not to leave it too late to believe the gospel. That was the message of the story of the rich man and Lazarus which Jesus told in Luke 16:19–31. For the rich man, a godless unbeliever, death is followed by torment, which is exacerbated by the fact that he can see the saints at peace, enjoying their place amongst God's covenant people. He first asks for some relief for his anguish to be sent from heaven, only to hear that no passage between heaven and hell is possible, because "a great gulf" separates the two. The point is that our destiny is sealed with finality during our earthly lifetime. It is too late to reconsider things once death has taken us.

Application to Believers

(1) We may find joy in the truth of the heavenly reward. In the context of a world where Christians face opposition and persecution, the certainty of the ultimate victory is a source of great joy, even in the midst of earthly pains. Having spoken of the sufferings of his disciples for his sake, Jesus urges them to "leap for joy" (Luke 6:22–23). He is not minimizing the severity of an experience of trial. However, he challenges us not to allow ostracism, misrepresentation, false accusation to lead us to despondency, but rather to find exuberant joy in the certainty of a great reward in heaven. The greatness of the reward makes the trials of today pale away into insignificance.

(2) We must examine our priorities in life. In the light of the eternal future, Jesus challenges us in Matthew 6:19–20 not to live for the things of this earth, where nothing lasts. By contrast, heavenly treasure is never

vulnerable. Don Carson defines "treasures in heaven" as "whatever is of good and eternal significance that comes out of what is done on earth."[36] Those words remind us that whatever we do on earth does have eternal significance. We must therefore examine our priorities, and ensure that we are doing on earth those things which will count in heaven, and not just living for the accumulation of material wealth. Paul also ranks the "eternal weight of glory" far beyond the transient things of sight (2 Cor 4:17–18). We must allow the eschatological hope to define our priorities.

(3) We must endure to the end. We saw how Jesus warns us against trying to read the signs of the times, and then says, "he who endures to the end will be saved." Our task is to hold on to faith in Christ until the day of glory dawns. The word which Jesus used, translated "end" is *telos*. It is connected with the idea of attaining a goal. It does not mean merely a full stop, but rather the ultimate realization of all our hopes. When we truly live in the light of the eschatological glory, we shall find the strength to persevere through the hardships of this present life.

(4) We must live a life of service. The assurance of the heavenly reward is a powerful encouragement to serve our fellow believers, even in the most ordinary of ways. Jesus offers us this incentive in Matthew 10:42: "whoever gives one of these little ones only a cup of cold *water* in the name of a disciple, assuredly, I say to you, he shall by no means lose his reward." Sometimes small acts of service can be harder than more difficult challenges. Those secret, unseen, little acts of kindness bring us no glory now. But when we know that the tiniest kindnesses performed for Jesus' sake will be rewarded in eternity, there is a great impetus to self-forgetful service.

(5) We should be constantly vigilant. Three times in Mark 13:34–37 the Lord exhorts his followers to "watch," translating the word *grēgoreō*, which may be defined as "take heed, lest through remission and indolence some destructive calamity suddenly overtake."[37] Walter Wessel comments, "Jesus' call for vigilance pervades this paragraph."[38] We must not be caught napping when he returns. We must be alert to possible hindrances to our spiritual progress, and, with Paul, should be able to say, "I myself always strive to have a conscience without offence toward God and men" (Acts 24:16). The word rendered "strive" (*askeō*) implies

36. D. A. Carson, "Matthew," 177.

37. Thayer, *Lexicon*, 122.

38. Wessel, "Mark," 752.

that maintaining a clear conscience can be a laborious effort. Constant vigilance is vital.

(6) We may find comfort in the face of life's difficulties, and of our own mortality, because we know that the end will be glorious. This is the import of Jesus' words to his disciples in John 14:1–3. He says, "let not your hearts be troubled," and then assures them of a glorious future. The word translated "troubled" (*tarassō*) speaks of a sense of agitation, of emotions in commotion. It may come to expression in constant restlessness and a spirit of anxious fear.[39] Such a response to life's challenges and uncertainties is wholly inappropriate in a follower of the Lord Jesus Christ, because, whatever we may have to pass through on the way, we know that we are heading for our Father's house, where our place is prepared by our Savior, who has promised to come again to take us to himself.

---

39. Thayer, *Lexicon*, 615.

Bibliography

à Brakel, Wilhelmus. *The Christian's Reasonable Service.* Vol. 1 (1700). Grand Rapids: Reformation Heritage, 1992 reprint.

Aikman, David. *The Beijing Factor.* Oxford: Monarch, 2005.

Alexander, Joseph Addison. *The Earlier Prophecies of Isaiah.* New York: Wiley & Putnam, 1846.

———. *The Psalms Translated and Explained.* Edinburgh: Elliot & Thin, 1864.

Allen, Leslie C. *Psalms 101–150.* Dallas: Word, 1983.

Allen, Ronald B. "*āṣab.*" In *Theological Wordbook of the Old Testament,* edited by Gleason L. Archer et al., 1666. Chicago: Moody, 1980.

Andrews, Edgar H. *Free in Christ.* Darlington: EP, 1996.

Anon. "The Didache." In *The Apostolic Fathers, Vol. 1,* edited by Kirsopp Lake, 308–33. London: Heinemann, 1912.

Anselm. *Cur Deus Homo?* (1098). London: Griffith, Farran, Okeden, & Welsh, 1889 reprint.

Appéré, Guy. *The Mystery of Christ.* Welwyn: EP, 1984.

Aquinas, Thomas. *Summa Theologica, Vol. 1.* Albany: Ages, 1997.

Athanasius. "Festal Letter No. 39." In *The Nicene and Post-Nicene Fathers,* edited by Philip Schaff. Albany: Ages, 1997. Second Series, Vol. 4, 1288–90.

Augustine. *The City of God* (426). New York: Modern Library, 1950 reprint.

———. "The Confessions." In Schaff, ed., *Nicene and Post-Nicene Fathers,* First Series, Vol. 1, 76–384.

———. "The Creed: A Sermon to the Catechumens." In Schaff, ed., *Nicene and Post-Nicene Fathers,* First Series. Vol. 3, 689–701.

———. "The Enchiridion, or On Faith, Hope, and Love." In Schaff, ed., *Nicene and Post-Nicene Fathers,* First Series. Vol. 3, 453–543.

———. "The Harmony of the Gospels." In Schaff, ed., *Nicene and Post-Nicene Fathers,* First Series. Vol. 6, 161–499.

————. "Lectures or Tractates on the Gospel According to St. John." In Schaff, ed., *Nicene and Post-Nicene Fathers*, First Series. Vol. 7, 11–909.

————. "On the Trinity." In Schaff, ed., *Nicene and Post-Nicene Fathers*, First Series. Vol. 3, 28–441.

————. "Reply to Faustus the Manichaean." In Schaff, ed., *Nicene and Post-Nicene Fathers*, First Series. Vol. 4, 277–646.

————. "Sermons on Selected Lessons of the New Testament." In Schaff, ed., *Nicene and Post-Nicene Fathers*, First Series. Vol. 6, 512–1181.

————. "A Treatise on the Merits and Forgiveness of Sins and on the Baptism of Infants." In Schaff, ed., *Nicene and Post-Nicene Fathers*, First Series. Vol. 5, 143–286.

————. "Treatise on Rebuke and Grace." In Schaff, ed., *Nicene and Post-Nicene Fathers*, First Series. Vol. 5, 1123–70.

Baldwin, Joyce G. "*gemō.*" In *The New International Dictionary of New Testament Theology Vol. 1*, edited by Colin Brown, 742–43. Exeter: Paternoster, 1975.

Barnabas. "Epistle." In Lake, ed., Vol. 1, 341–409.

Barnes, Albert. *Notes on the Old Testament* (1838). Grand Rapids: Baker, 1950 reprint.

————. *A Popular Family Commentary on the New Testament*. London: Blackie, 1886.

Barth, Karl. *Church Dogmatics, Vol. 2, Part 1*. London: T. & T. Clark, 1957.

————. *Church Dogmatics, Vol. 3, Part 2*. London: T. & T. Clark, 1960.

Basil. "Letter 140: To the Church of Antioch." In Schaff, ed., *Nicene and Post-Nicene Fathers*, Second Series. Vol. 8, 489–90.

————. "On the Holy Spirit." In Schaff, ed., *Nicene and Post-Nicene Fathers*, Second Series. Vol. 8, 119–207.

Bauder, Wolfgang. "*paraptōma.*" In *The New International Dictionary of New Testament Theology, Vol. 3*, edited by Colin Brown, 585–86. Exeter: Paternoster, 1978.

Baugus, Bruce. *Christological Confusion and China's Reforming Churches*. www.reformation21.org/blogs/christological-confusion-china.php, Parts 1–12.

Bavinck, Herman. *The Doctrine of God* (1951). Edinburgh: Banner of Truth, 1977 reprint.

————. *Reformed Dogmatics, Vol. 2: God and Creation*. Grand Rapids: Baker, 2004.

————. *Reformed Dogmatics, Vol.4: Holy Spirit, Church, and New Creation*. Grand Rapids: Baker, 2008.

Bayes, Jonathan F. *The Apostles' Creed: Truth with Passion*. Eugene, OR: Wipf and Stock, 2010.

————. "Propitiation for the World." *New Focus*, Vol. 2, No. 1 (June–July 1997) 12–16.

————. *Revival: the New Testament expectation*. Eugene, OR: Resource Publications, 2016.

————. *The Threefold Division of the Law*. Newcastle upon Tyne: Christian Institute, 2005.

————. *The Weakness of the Law*. Carlisle: Paternoster, 2000.

Beckwith, Roger T. "Canon of the Old Testament." In *The Illustrated Bible Dictionary*, edited by J. D. Douglas et al., Part 1, 235–38. Leicester: IVP, 1980.

Beeke, Joel R., and Mark Jones. *A Puritan Theology*. Grand Rapids: RHB, 2012.

Beeke, Joel R., and Paul M. Smalley. *Reformed Systematic Theology, Vol. 3: Spirit and Salvation*. Wheaton: Crossway, 2021.

Belleville, Linda L. *2 Corinthians*. Leicester: IVP, 1996.

Bengel, John Albert. *Gnomon of the New Testament*. Edinburgh: T. & T. Clark, 1858.

Berkhof, Louis. *Systematic Theology* (1941). Edinburgh: Banner of Truth, 1958 reprint.

Berkouwer, G. C. *Divine Election*. Grand Rapids: Eerdmans, 1960.

———. *Faith and Justification*. Grand Rapids: Eerdmans, 1954.

———. *General Revelation*. Grand Rapids: Eerdmans, 1955.

———. *Man: the Image of God*. Grand Rapids: Eerdmans, 1962.

Bernard of Clairvaux. "Sermons on the Song of Songs." In *Saint Bernard of Clairvaux Collection*, 1678–2543. Dallas: Aeterna, 2014.

Beyer, Brian E. "*nb*." In *New International Dictionary of Old Testament Theology and Exegesis*, edited by Willem A. VanGemeren. Vol. 3, 15–16. Grand Rapids: Zondervan, 1997.

Bietenhard, Hans. "Satan." In Brown, ed., Vol. 3, 468–72.

Bird, Michael F., and Preston M. Sprinkle, eds. *The Faith of Jesus Christ*. Peabody: Hendrickson, 2009.

Blum, Edwin A. "1 & 2 Peter." In *The Expositor's Bible Commentary, Vol. 12*, edited by Frank E. Gaebelein, 207–89. Grand Rapids: Zondervan, 1981.

Boettner, Loraine. *The Millennium*. Philipsburg: Presbyterian and Reformed, 1957.

———. *The Reformed Doctrine of Predestination*. Phillipsburg: Presbyterian & Reformed, 1932.

Boice, James Montgomery. "Galatians." In *The Expositor's Bible Commentary, Vol. 10*, edited by Frank E. Gaebelein, 409–508. Grand Rapids: Zondervan, 1976.

———. "The Sovereignty of God." In *To Glorify and Enjoy God*, edited by John L. Carson and David W. Hall, 197–209. Edinburgh: Banner of Truth, 1994.

———. *Standing on the Rock*. Grand Rapids: Baker, 1994.

Boston, Thomas. *Human Nature in its Fourfold State* (1720). London: Banner of Truth, 1964 reprint.

Bousset, Wilhelm. *Kyrios Christos* (1913). Nashville: Abingdon, 1970 reprint.

Bowling, Andrew. "*ṭôb*." In Archer et al., eds., 793.

Bowman, Ann L. "Women in Ministry: An Exegetical Study of 1 Timothy 2:11–15." *Bibliotheca Sacra* Vol. 149, No. 594 (April–June, 1992) 193–213.

Brandt, Gareth. "A Radical Christology for a Radical Youth Ministry." *Direction*, Vol. 31, No. 1 (Spring, 2002) 26–34.

Bray, Gerald, ed. *Ancient Christian Commentary on Scripture. New Testament, Vol. 6: Romans*. Downers Grove: IVP, 1998.

———. *Ancient Christian Commentary on Scripture. New Testament, Vol. 11: James, 1—2 Peter, 1—3 John, Jude*. Downers Grove: IVP, 2000.

———. *God Has Spoken: a History of Christian Theology*. Nottingham: Apollos, 2014.

Brock, Cory C., and N. Gray Sutanto. *Neo-Calvinism: A Theological Introduction*. Bellingham: Lexham, 2022.

Brooks, Philips. "The Eternal Humanity." In *A Treasury of Great Preaching, Vol. 6: Spurgeon to Meyer, 1834–1929*, edited by Clyde E. Fant and William M. Pinson, 153–61. Dallas: Word, 1995.

Brown, Francis, et al. *Hebrew and English Lexicon of the Old Testament*. Oxford: Clarendon, 1906.

Bruce, F. F. *1 & 2 Thessalonians*. Dallas: Word, 1982.

Budd, Philip J. *Numbers*. Dallas: Word, 1984.

Butterworth, Mike. "*rḥm*." In VanGemeren, ed., Vol. 3, 1093–95.

Calvin, John. *Commentaries on the Catholic Epistles* (1551). Grand Rapids: Baker, 1979 reprint.

———. *Commentaries on the Epistles of Paul the Apostle to the Philippians, Colossians, and Thessalonians*. Grand Rapids: Baker, 1979 reprint.

————. *Commentaries on the Epistles to Timothy, Titus, and Philemon* (1556). Grand Rapids: Baker, 1979 reprint.

————. *Commentaries on the First Book of Moses called Genesis* (1563). Grand Rapids: Baker, 1979 reprint.

————. *Commentaries on the Four Last Books of Moses arranged in the form of a Harmony* (1563). Grand Rapids: Baker, 1979 reprint.

————. *Commentary on a Harmony of the Evangelists* (1558). Grand Rapids: Baker, 1979 reprint.

————. *Commentaries on the Twelve Minor Prophets, Vol. 4* (1559). Grand Rapids: Baker, 1979 reprint.

————. *Institutes of the Christian Religion* (1536). MacDill: MacDonald reprint, n.d.

Campbell, Ted A. *Christian Confessions*. Louisville: Westminster John Knox, 1996.

Campbell Morgan, G. *Notes on the Psalms*. London: Walter, 1946.

Candlish, Robert S. *A Commentary on 1 John* (1866). London: Banner of Truth, 1973 reprint.

Canons of the Synod held in the City of Laodicea, The. In Schaff, ed., *Nicene and Post-Nicene Fathers*, Second Series, Vol. 14, 265–338.

Carpenter, Eugene, and Emile Nicole. "*gzr*." In VanGemeren, ed., Vol. 1, 847–48.

Carroll, B. H. *An Interpretation of the English Bible, Vol. 1: Genesis* (1913). Grand Rapids: Baker, 1948 reprint.

Carson, D. A. "Matthew." In *The Expositor's Bible Commentary, Vol. 8*, edited by Frank E. Gaebelein, 1–599. Grand Rapids: Zondervan, 1984.

Carson, Herbert M. *The Epistles of Paul to the Colossians and Philemon: An Introduction and Commentary*. Leicester: IVP, 1963.

Cassuto, Umberto. *A Commentary on the Book of Genesis 1–11, Vol. 1*. Jerusalem: Magnes, 1961.

Chalke, Steve. "Crosspurposes." *Christianity* (September, 2004) 44–48.

Chalke Steve, and Alan Mann. *The Lost Message of Jesus*. Grand Rapids: Zondervan, 2003.

Chantry, Walter J. *God's Righteous Kingdom*. Edinburgh: Banner of Truth, 1980.

Childs, Brevard S. *Exodus*. London: SCM, 1974.

Christensen, Duane L. *Deuteronomy 1:1—21:9*. Dallas; Word, 1991.

Chrysostom, John. "Homilies on the Epistle of St. Paul the Apostle to the Romans." In Schaff, ed., *Nicene and Post-Nicene Fathers*, First Series, Vol. 11, 566–1016.

————. "Homilies on the First Epistle of St. Paul the Apostle to the Corinthians." In Schaff, ed., *Nicene and Post-Nicene Fathers*, First Series, Vol. 12, 18–599.

————. "Homilies on the Gospel According to St. Matthew." In Schaff, ed., *Nicene and Post-Nicene Fathers*, First Series, Vol. 10, 31–1113.

Church of Smyrna. "The Martyrdom of Polycarp." In *The Apostolic Fathers, Vol. 2*, edited by Kirsopp Lake, 312–45. London: Heinemann, 1913.

Clarke, Adam. *Commentary on the Bible* (1831). Albany: Ages, 1997 reprint.

Clement of Alexandria. "Paedagogos." In *The Ante-Nicene Fathers*, edited by Alexander Roberts and James Donaldson, Vol. 2, 400–580. Albany: Ages, 1997.

————. "Stromata." In Roberts and Donaldson, eds., Vol. 2, 584–1153.

Clement of Rome. "The First Epistle to the Corinthians." In Lake, ed., Vol. 1, 8–121.

2 Clement. "Epistle to the Corinthians." In Lake, ed., Vol. 1, 128–63.

Coenen, Lothar. "Church, Synagogue." In Brown, ed., Vol. 1, 291–305.

Cohen, Boaz. *Law and Tradition in Judaism*. New York: JTSA, 1959.

Conn, Harvie M. *Contemporary World Theology*. Philadelphia: Presbyterian & Reformed, 1973.

Coppes, Leonard J. "'*ānâ*." In Archer, et al., eds., 1650.

―――. "*nûaḥ*." In Archer et al., eds., 1323.

―――. "*rāḥam*." In Archer et al., eds., 2146.

Cosgrove, Charles H. "Justification in Paul: A Linguistic and Theological Reflection." *Journal of Biblical Literature*, Vol. 106, No. 4 (December, 1987) 653–70.

Cotterell, Peter. *Mission and Meaninglessness*. London: SPCK, 1990.

Council of Ephesus. "Decree of the Council Against Nestorius." In Schaff, ed., *Nicene and Post-Nicene Fathers*, Second Series, Vol. 14, 441–42.

Cover, George. *How to be Born Again*. http://misslink.org/born.html.

Cranfield, C. E. B. *The Apostles' Creed*. London: Continuum, 2004.

―――. *The Epistle to the Romans*, Vol. 1. Edinburgh: T. & T. Clark, 1975.

Craven, William. "The Testimony of Christ to the Old Testament." In *The Fundamentals*, edited by R. A. Torrey, 59–68. Grand Rapids: Kregel, 1958 reprint [revised 1990].

Culver, Robert D., "*šāpaṭ*," In Archer, et al., eds., 2443

Cunningham, William. *Historical Theology* (1882). Edmonton: Still Waters, 1991 reprint.

Cyprian. "On the Advantage of Patience." In Roberts and Donaldson, eds., Vol. 5, 989–1004.

Dabney, Robert Louis. *Systematic Theology* (1871). Edinburgh: Banner of Truth, 1985 reprint.

Davies, John A. "Toward a Biblical Theology of the Environment." *Reformed Perspectives Magazine Online*, Vol. 1, Nos. 15 and 16 (June, 1999). http://reformedperspectives. org/magazine/article.asp/link/http:%5E%5Ereformedperspectives. org%5Earticles%5Ejoh_davies%5EPT.Davies.Environment.1.html/at/ Toward%20a%20Biblical%20Theology%20of%20the%20Environment,%20 part%201; and http://reformedperspectives.org/magazine/article.asp/link/ http:%5E%5Ereformedperspectives.org%5Earticles%5Ejoh_davies%5EPT. Davies.Environment.2.html/at/Toward%20a%20Biblical%20Theology%20of%20 ᵗʰe%20Environment,%20part%202).

DeYoung, Kevin. *The Hole in our Holiness: Filling the Gap between Gospel Passion and the Pursuit of Holiness*. Wheaton: Crossway, 2012.

Dodd, C. H. *The Bible and the Greeks*. London: Hodder & Stoughton, 1935.

du Toit, Andrie B. "Canon: New Testament." In *The Oxford Companion to the Bible*, edited by Bruce M. Metzger and Michael D. Coogan, 102–4. Oxford University Press, 1993.

Dunn, James D. G. *Romans 1—8*. Dallas: Word, 1988.

―――. *The Theology of Paul the Apostle*. Grand Rapids: Eerdmans, 1998.

Durham, John I. *Exodus*. Dallas: Word, 1987.

Eaton, Michael. *How to Live a Godly Life*. Tonbridge: Sovereign World, 1993.

Edwards, Brian. *Can we Pray for Revival?* Darlington: EP, 2001.

Edwards, Jonathan. "A History of the Work of Redemption" (1739). In *The Works of Jonathan Edwards* [1834], edited by Edward Hickman, Vol. 1, 532–619. Edinburgh: Banner of Truth, 1974 reprint.

Eichrodt, Walther. *Theology of the Old Testament, Vol. 1*. Philadelphia: Westminster, 1961.

Ellison, H. L. *Ezekiel: the Man and his Message*. Exeter: Paternoster, 1967.

Ellul, Jacques. *The Judgment of Jonah*. Grand Rapids: Eerdmans, 1971.

Elowsky, Joel C. ed. *Ancient Christian Commentary on Scripture, New Testament, Vol. 4a: John 1—10.* Downers Grove: IVP, 2006.

Enns, Peter. "*ḥōq.*" In VanGemeren, ed., Vol. 2, 250–51.

———. "Law of God." In VanGemeren, ed., Vol. 4, 893–900.

Epiphanius. "Ancoratus, chs. 119–20." In *The Creeds of Christendom, Vol. 2: The Greek and Latin Creeds,* edited by Philip Schaff, 32–38. New York: Harper & Brothers, 1877.

———. "Interpretation of the Gospels." In *Ancient Christian Commentary on Scripture, New Testament, Vol. 1b: Matthew 14—28,* edited by Manlio Simonetti. Downers Grove: IVP, 2002.

Esser, Hans-Helmut. "*stoicheia.*" In *The New International Dictionary of New Testament Theology, Vol. 2,* edited by Colin Brown, 451–53. Carlisle: Paternoster, 1976.

Eusebius. "Church History." In Schaff, ed., *Nicene and Post-Nicene Fathers,* Second Series, Vol. 1, 151–512.

Farthing, John L. "Zanchi, Jerome *(1516–1590).*" In *Dictionary of Major Biblical Interpreters,* edited by Donald K. McKim, 1076–80. Downers Grove: IVP, 2007.

Fausset, Andrew Robert. "The Epistle of Paul the Apostle to the Hebrews." In Robert Jamieson, et al., *Commentary,* 985–1179. Albany: Ages, 1997 reprint.

Feinberg, Charles L. "Jeremiah." In *The Expositor's Bible Commentary, Vol. 6,* edited by Frank E. Gaebelein, 355–691. Grand Rapids: Zondervan, 1986.

Fesko, John V. "Girolamo Zanchi on Union with Christ and the Final Judgment." *Perichoresis,* Vol. 18, Issue 1 (March 2020) 41–56.

———. "Union with Christ." In *Reformation Theology: A Systematic Summary,* edited by Matthew Barrett, 423–50. Wheaton: Crossway, 2017.

Finney, Charles Grandison. *Regeneration.* https://www.gospeltruth.net/1849–51Penny_Pulpit/491121pp_regeneration.htm.

———. *Systematic Theology* (1878). Albany: Ages, 1997 reprint.

———. *Views of Sanctification.* Toronto: Willard, 1877.

Fisher, George Park. *History of Christian Doctrine.* Edinburgh: T. & T. Clark, 1896.

Flavel, John. *The Mystery of Providence* (1678). Edinburgh: Banner of Truth, 1963 reprint.

Gilchrist, Paul R. "*yāʿaṣ,*" In Archer et al., eds., 887.

Gill, John. *An Exposition of the Old and New Testament.* London: Mathews & Leigh, 1809.

Godet, Frédéric Louis. *Commentary on St. Paul's Epistle to the Romans, Vol. 2.* Edinburgh: T. & T. Clark, 1882.

Goldberg, Louis. "*pātâ.*" In Archer et al., eds., 1853.

Gordon, Robert P. "*ṭôb.*" In VanGemeren, ed., Vol. 2, 353–57.

Gordon, Sam. *Five Marks of a Gospel Church: 1 Thessalonians Made Simple.* Kilmarnock: CYP, 2018.

Grant, Robert M. *Gods and the One God.* London: SPCK, 1986.

Gray, James M. "The Inspiration of the Bible—Definition, Extent and Proof." In Torrey, ed., 137–58.

Greenlee, J. Harold. *A Concise Exegetical Grammar of New Testament Greek.* Grand Rapids: Eerdmans, 1963.

Gregory of Nyssa. "On the Making of Man." In Schaff, ed., *Nicene and Post-Nicene Fathers,* Second Series, Vol. 5, 747–830.

Grogan, Geoffrey W. "Isaiah." In Gaebelein, ed., Vol. 6, 3–354.

Grudem, Wayne. *Systematic Theology.* Leicester: IVP, 1994.

Hamilton, Victor P. "*dāmâ.*" In Archer et al., eds., 437.

———. "*nś,*" In VanGemeren, ed., Vol. 3, 160–63.

Hannah, John D. *1, 2 and 3 John: Redemption's Certainty.* Fearn: Christian Focus, 2016.

Harris, Murray J. "2 Corinthians." In Gaebelein, ed., Vol. 10, 299–406.

Harris, R. Laird. "*ḥsd.*" In Archer et al., eds., 698.

———. "*kāpar.*" In Archer et al., eds., 1023.

———. "Leviticus." In *The Expositor's Bible Commentary, Vol. 2*, edited by Frank E. Gaebelein, 499–654. Grand Rapids: Zondervan, 1990.

Harrison, Everett F. "Romans." In Gaebelein, ed., Vol. 10, 1–171.

Hartley, John E. "*ḥšb.*" In VanGemeren, ed., Vol. 2, 303–10.

———. *Leviticus.* Dallas: Word, 1992.

———. "*qāwâ.*" In Archer et al., eds., 1994.

———. "*ṣāpap.*" In Archer et al., eds., 1957.

Hasker, William, et al. *The Openness of God.* Downers Grove: IVP, 1994.

Hendriksen, William. *Colossians and Philemon.* Edinburgh: Banner of Truth, 1971.

———. *Ephesians.* Edinburgh: Banner of Truth, 1967.

———. *More than Conquerors.* Grand Rapids: Baker, 1967.

———. *Romans, Vol. 2: Chapters 9–16.* Edinburgh: Banner of Truth, 1981.

Hendry, George S. "Christology." In *A Dictionary of Christian Theology*, edited by Alan. Richardson, 51–64. London: SCM, 1969.

Henry, Matthew. *Commentary on the Whole Bible in One Volume*, edited by Leslie F. Church. London: Marshall, Morgan and Scott, 1960.

———. *Exposition of the New Testament* (1706). London: Mackenzie, 1886 reprint.

Heppe, Heinrich. *Reformed Dogmatics* (1861). London: Wakeman Reprints, 1950.

Hermas. "The Shepherd," In Lake, ed., Vol. 2, 6–305.

Hesselink, I. John. *Calvin's First Catechism: A Commentary.* Louisville: Westminster John Knox Press, 1997.

Hiscox, Edward T. *The New Directory for Baptist Churches* (1894). Grand Rapids: Kregel, 1970 reprint.

Hodge, Archibald Alexander. *Outlines of Theology* (1879). Edinburgh: Banner of Truth, 1972 reprint.

Hodge, Charles. *A Commentary on 1 & 2 Corinthians* (1857, 1859). Edinburgh: Banner of Truth, 1974 reprint.

———. *A Commentary on the Epistle to the Ephesians.* New York: Carter, 1860.

———. *A Commentary on Romans* (1864). Edinburgh: Banner of Truth, 1972 reprint.

———. "Finney's Lectures on Systematic Theology." *Biblical Repertory and Princeton Review*, Vol. 19, No. 2 (April, 1847) 237–77.

———. *Systematic Theology.* London: Nelson, 1880.

Hodges, William Robert. "Voice of Grief in the Pre-funeral Wakes of Protestant Toba Batak." Ph.D. diss., University of California, 2009.

Hoekema, Anthony A. *The Bible and the Future.* Exeter: Paternoster, 1978.

Hopkins, Evan H. *The Law of Liberty in the Spiritual Life.* London: Marshall, Morgan & Scott, 1952.

Horton, Michael S. "Finney's Attacks on the Westminster Confession." In *The Westminster Confession into the 21st Century, Vol. 1*, edited by J. Ligon Duncan, 367–412. Fearn: Mentor, 2003.

Hughes, Philip Edgcumbe. *Paul's Second Epistle to the Corinthians.* Grand Rapids: Eerdmans, 1962.

Humphreys, Christmas. *Buddhism*. Harmondsworth: Penguin, 1951.

Ignatius. "The Epistles." In Lake, ed., Vol. 1, 172–301.

Irenaeus. "Against All Heresies." In Roberts and Donaldson, eds., Vol. 1, 620–156.

Jackson, Blomfield. "Preface to The Book of Saint Basil on the Spirit." In Schaff, ed., *Nicene and Post-Nicene Fathers*, Second Series, Vol. 8, 4–118.

Jones, Hywel R. *Only One Way*. Bromley: Day One, 1996.

Josephus, Flavius. "Antiquities of the Jews." In *The Works of Flavius Josephus*, edited by William Whiston, 23–442. London: Milner & Sowerby, 1866.

Justin Martyr. "Dialogue with Trypho." In Roberts and Donaldson, eds., Vol. 1, 359–529.

Kaiser, Walter C. "*ʿābad*." In Archer et al., eds., 1553.

———. "*sālaḥ*." In Archer, et al., eds., 1505.

Kalland, Earl S. "*bārar*." In Archer et al., eds., 288.

———. "Deuteronomy." In *The Expositor's Bible Commentary, Vol. 3*, edited by Frank E. Gaebelein, 1–235. Grand Rapids: Zondervan, 1990.

Kantzer, Kenneth S. "The Miracle of Christmas." *Christianity Today*, Vol. 28, No. 18 (December 14, 1984) 14–15.

Kelly, J. N. D. *Early Christian Creeds*. Harlow: Longman, 1972.

———. *Early Christian Doctrines*. London: A. & C. Black, 1977.

Kelly, William, ed. *The Collected Writings of John Nelson Darby*. Kingston: Stow Hill, 1962.

Kendall, R. T. *Calvin and English Calvinism to 1649*. Oxford: University Press, 1979.

———. *Once Saved, Always Saved*. Carlisle: Paternoster, 1983.

Keown, Gerald L., et al. *Jeremiah 26—52*. Dallas: Word, 1995.

King, Guy H. *The Fellowship: An Expositional Study of 1 John*. London: Marshall, Morgan & Scott, 1954.

Kingdon, David. *Children of Abraham*. Worthing: Carey, 1973.

Kitamori, Kazoh. *Theology of the Pain of God*. London: SCM, 1966.

Kline, Meredith G. "Genesis." In *The New Bible Commentary Revised*, edited by Donald Guthrie and J. Alec Motyer, 79–114. Leicester: IVP, 1970.

Konkel, A. H. "*dmh*." In VanGemeren, ed., Vol. 1, 967–70.

Lactantius. "On the Anger of God." In Roberts and Donaldson, eds., Vol. 7, 539–84.

Ladd, George Eldon. *A Theology of the New Testament*. Guildford: Lutterworth, 1974.

Lampe, G. W. H. "Christian Theology in the Patristic Period." In *A History of Christian Doctrine*, edited by Hubert Cunliffe-Jones, 21–180. Edinburgh: T. & T. Clark, 1978.

Lang, George H. *The Epistle to the Hebrews* (1951). Haysville: Schoettle, 1985 reprint.

Law, Henry. *Daily Prayer and Praise: The Book of Psalms Arranged for Private and Family Use* (1878). Edinburgh: Banner of Truth, 2000 reprint.

Leith, John H. *Basic Christian Doctrine*. Louisville: Westminster John Knox Press, 1993.

Leith, John H., ed. *Creeds of the Churches*. Louisville: Westminster John Knox Press, 1982.

Leo the Great. "Letter 28: To Flavian Commonly Called 'The Tome.'" In Schaff, ed., *Nicene and Post-Nicene Fathers*, Second Series, Vol. 12, 95–103.

Letham, Robert. *The Holy Trinity*. Phillipsburg: Presbyterian & Reformed, 2019.

———. *Systematic Theology*. Wheaton: Crossway, 2019.

Leupold, Herbert C. *Exposition of Genesis*. Columbus: Wartburg, 1942.

Liddell, Henry George, and Robert Scott. *Greek-English Lexicon, Abridged*. Oxford: Clarendon, 1940.

Liefeld, Walter L. "Luke." In Gaebelein, ed., Vol. 8, 795–1059.

Lietzmann, Hans. *Apollinarius von Laodicea und seine Schule*. Tübingen: Mohr, 1904.

Lincoln, Andrew T. *Ephesians*. Dallas: Word, 1990.

Linder, Robert D. "Rome Responds." In *A Lion Handbook: The History of Christianity*, edited by Tim Dowley, 404–22. Berkhamsted: Lion, 1977.

Lindsell, Harold. *The Battle for the Bible*. Grand Rapids: Zondervan, 1976.

Lloyd-Jones, D. Martyn. *Romans—An Exposition of Chapter 5: Assurance*. Edinburgh: Banner of Truth, 1971.

Longenecker, Richard N. "Acts," In *The Expositor's Bible Commentary, Vol. 9*, edited by Frank E. Gaebelein, 205–573. Grand Rapids: Zondervan, 1990.

Luther, Martin. *Lectures on Romans* (1515). Philadelphia: Westminster, 1961 reprint.

MacArthur, John F. *The Coming Earthly Kingdom of the Lord Jesus Christ*, Parts 1—4. https://www.gty.org/library/sermons-library/66-73/the-coming-earthly-kingdom-of-the-lord-jesus-christ-part-1; https://www.gty.org/library/sermons-library/66-74/the-coming-earthly-kingdom-of-the-lord-jesus-christ-part-2; https://www.gty.org/library/sermons-library/66-75/the-coming-earthly-kingdom-of-the-lord-jesus-christ-part-3; and https://www.gty.org/library/sermons-library/66-76/the-coming-earthly-kingdom-of-the-lord-jesus-christ-part-4.

———. *The Gospel According to Jesus*. Grand Rapids: Zondervan, 2008.

Machen, J. Gresham. *God Transcendent*. Edinburgh: Banner of Truth, 1949.

Macleod, Donald. *Behold Your God*. Fearn: CFP, 1990.

———. *A Faith to Live by*. Fearn: Mentor, 1998.

Mare, W. Harold. "1 Corinthians." In Gaebelein, ed., Vol. 10, 173–297.

Marsden, George M. *Jonathan Edwards: A Life*. New Haven: Yale University Press, 2004.

Marshall, I. Howard. *The Epistles of John*. Grand Rapids: Eerdmans, 1978.

Martin, Ralph P. *Colossians and Philemon*. London: Oliphants, 1978.

Masters, Peter. *The Baptist Confession of Faith 1689, Updated with Notes*. London: Wakeman, 1981.

———. *Physicians of Souls*. London: Wakeman, 2002.

———. *Worship or Entertainment?* London: Wakeman, 2020.

Maue, Dieter. "Three Languages on one Leaf." *Bulletin of SOAS*, Vol. 71, No. 1 (February 2008) 59–73.

McComiskey, Thomas E. "*ānaš.*" In Archer et al., eds., 135.

McLoughlin, William G. *Introduction* to "C.G. Finney, *Lectures on Revivals of Religion* (1835)." Cambridge: Harvard University Press, 1960 reprint.

Michaels, J. Ramsey. *1 Peter*. Dallas: Word, 1988.

Moo, Douglas J. *The NIV Application Commentary: Romans*. Grand Rapids: Zondervan, 2000.

Moore, Michael S. "Azazel." In VanGemeren, ed., Vol. 4, 421–22.

Morris, John. *The Young Earth*. Colorado Springs: Master Books, 1994.

Morris, Leon. *The First and Second Epistles to the Thessalonians*. Grand Rapids: Eerdmans, 1959.

———. *The Gospel According to John*. London: Marshall, Morgan & Scott, 1971.

———. "The Meaning of *hilastērion* in Romans iii.25." *New Testament Studies*, Vol. 2, No. 1 (September, 1955) 33–43.

Mortensen, Terry. "Are Demons Active Today?" *Answers Magazine*, edited by Mike Matthews, Vol. 8, No. 1 (January–March 2013) 77.

Motyer, J. Alec. *The Prophecy of Isaiah*. Leicester: IVP, 1993.

Moule, Handley C. G. *Colossian Studies*. London: Hodder & Stoughton, 1903.

Moulton, Harold K. *The Analytical Greek Lexicon Revised*. Grand Rapids: Zondervan, 1978.

Mounce, William D. *Pastoral Epistles*. Nashville: Nelson, 2000.

Müller, Dietrich. "Will, Purpose." In Brown, ed., Vol. 3, 1015–23.

Mundle, Wilhelm. "Hear, Obey." In Brown, ed., Vol. 2, 172–80.

Munhall, L. W. "Inspiration." In Torrey, ed., 159–72.

Murray, Iain H. *The Puritan Hope*. Edinburgh: Banner of Truth, 1971.

———, *Revival and Revivalism*. Edinburgh: Banner of Truth, 1994.

Murray, John. *Collected Writings. 2: Systematic Theology*. Edinburgh: Banner of Truth, 1977.

———. *Redemption Accomplished and Applied* (1955). London: Banner of Truth, 1961 reprint.

O'Brien, Peter T. *Colossians, Philemon*. Dallas: Word, 1982.

O'Grady, Joan. *Heresy*. Shaftesbury: Element, 1985.

Olivier, J. P. J. "*slḥ*." In VanGemeren, ed., Vol. 3, 259–64.

Olyott, Stuart. *The Gospel as It Really Is: Romans Simply Explained*. Welwyn: EP, 1979.

———. *Ministering Like the Master*. Edinburgh: Banner of Truth, 2003.

Oosthuizen, G. C. *Theological Discussions and Confessional Developments in the Churches of Africa and Asia*. Franeker: Wever, 1958.

Origen. "De Principiis." In Roberts and Donaldson, eds., Vol. 4, 456–1337.

Oswalt, John N. "*bārak*." In Archer et al., eds., 285.

Owen, John. "A Brief Instruction in the Worship of God and Discipline of the Churches of the New Testament" (1667). In *The Works of John Owen, Vol. 15*, edited by William H. Goold, 445–530. London: Banner of Truth, 1966 reprint.

———. "A Discourse Concerning the Holy Spirit" (1674). In *The Works of John Owen, Vol. 3*, edited by William H. Goold. London: Banner of Truth, 1965 reprint.

Packer, James I. *I Want to be a Christian*. Eastbourne: Kingsway, 1977.

———. *What did the Cross Achieve? The Logic of Penal Substitution*. Leicester: TSF, 1974.

Palmer, Edwin H. *The Holy Spirit*. Phillipsburg: Presbyterian & Reformed, 1964.

Pannenberg, Wolfhart. *The Apostles' Creed in the Light of Today's Questions*. London: SCM, 1972.

Parker, Samuel. *A Defence and Continuation of The Ecclesiastical Politie*. London: Martyn, 1671.

———. *A Discourse of Ecclesiastical Politie*. London: Martyn, 1669.

Parker, Thomas H. L. "Providence." In *Baker's Dictionary of Theology*, edited by Everett F. Harrison, 426–27. Grand Rapids: Baker, 1960.

Passantino, Robert, and Gretchen Passantino. *The Gates of Hell*. Answers in Action, 2003. http://www.answers.org/bible/gatesofhell.html.

Payne, J. Barton. "*āqab*." In Archer et al., eds., 1676.

———. "*rûaḥ*." In Archer, et al., eds., 2131.

Pelikan, Jaroslav. *The Spirit of Eastern Christendom*. Chicago: University of Chicago Press, 1974.

Philip, James. *Union with Christ*. St. Andrews: IVF. 1973.

Pierson, Arthur T. "The Testimony of the Organic Unity of the Bible to its Inspiration." In Torrey, ed., 195–204.

Pink, Arthur W. "The Doctrine of Reconciliation." *Studies in the Scriptures*, Vol. 23, No. 3 (March, 1944) to Vol. 25, No. 12 (December, 1946).

———. *Eternal Security.* https://pstrknghtblog.files.wordpress.com/2010/01/eternal-security-by-aw-pink.pdf.

———. *Gleanings in Genesis.* Chicago: Moody, 1922.

Pinnock, Clark. *Most Moved Mover.* Grand Rapids: Baker, 2001.

———. "Open Theism: What is this? A new teaching—and with authority!" *Ashland Theological Journal,* Vol. 34 (2002) 39–53.

———. "The Role of the Spirit in Creation." *Asbury Theological Journal,* Vol. 52, No. 1 (Spring, 1997) 47–54.

Piper, John. *Desiring God.* Leicester: IVP, 1986.

———. *The Future of Justification.* Wheaton: Crossway, 2007.

———. *The Pleasures of God.* Manila: CGM, 1991.

Platt, David. "What I Really Think About the 'Sinner's Prayer,' Conversion, Mission, and Deception." *Christianity Today* (June 28, 2012). https://www.christianitytoday.com/ct/2012/juneweb-only/david-platt-sinners-prayer.html

Pocock, J. G. A., et al. *The Varieties of British Political Thought, 1500–1800.* Cambridge: University Press, 1993.

Polycarp. "Epistle to the Philippians." In Lake, ed., Vol. 1, 282–301.

Poole, Matthew. *Annotations upon the Holy Bible, Vol. 1.* Edinburgh: Turnbull, 1800 reprint.

———. *A Commentary on the Holy Bible, Vol. 3: Matthew to Revelation* (1685). Edinburgh: Banner of Truth, 1963 reprint.

Prestige, G. Leonard. *Fathers and Heretics.* London: SPCK, 1940.

Pridgeon, Charles H. *Is Hell Eternal? Or Will God's Plan Fail?* Pittsburgh: Evangelization Society of Pittsburgh Bible Institute, 1920.

Procksch, Otto. *Die Genesis Übersetzt und Erklärt.* Leipzig: Deicherische Verlagsbuchhandlung, 1924.

Pseudo-Dionysius the Areopagite. "The Celestial Hierarchies," In *The Works of Dionysius the Areopagite,* edited by John Parker, Part 2, 1–66. London: Parker, 1899.

Reisinger, John. *Tablets of Stone.* Southbridge: Crowne, 1989.

Reymond, Robert. *A New Systematic Theology of the Christian Faith.* Nashville: Nelson, 1998.

Ridderbos, Herman. *Paul: An Outline of his Theology.* London: SPCK, 1975.

Roberts, Maurice J. "The Free Offer of the Gospel." *Banner of Truth,* Issue 503–4 (August-September, 2005) 39–46.

Robertson, O. Palmer. "The Holy Spirit in the Westminster Confession of Faith." In Duncan, ed., 57–99.

Rohl, David. *A Test of Time.* London: Century, 1995.

Rufinus. "A Commentary on the Apostles' Creed." In Schaff, ed., *Nicene and Post-Nicene Fathers,* Second Series, Vol. 3, 1095–1136.

Sailhamer, John H. "Genesis." In Gaebelein, ed., Vol. 2, 1–284.

Sanders, John, and Christopher A. Hall. "Does God know your Next Move?" *Christianity Today* (May 21, 2001) 38–45, (June 7, 2001) 50–56.

Schaeffer, Francis A. *Pollution and the Death of Man: The Christian View of Ecology.* London: Hodder & Stoughton, 1970.

Schibler, David. "*qwh.*" In VanGemeren, ed., Vol. 3, 892–96.

Schönweiss, Hans. "*deomai.*" In Brown, ed., Vol. 2, 860–61.

Schultz, Carl. "'*ûd.*" In Archer et al., eds., 1576.

Scofield, Cyrus I. *The Scofield Reference Bible*. New York: Oxford University Press, 1917.

Scott, Jack B. "*'lh*." In Archer et al., eds., 93.

Scott, James M. "Adoption," In *Dictionary of Paul and his Letters*, edited by Gerald F. Hawthorne et al., 15–18. Leicester: IVP, 1993.

Seebass, Horst. "Righteousness, Justification." In Brown, ed., Vol. 3, 352–56.

Seiss, Joseph. *Holy Types; or The Gospel in Leviticus*. Austin: WORDsearch, 2007.

Sen, K. M. *Hinduism*. Harmondsworth: Penguin, 1961.

Shaw, Robert. *An Exposition of the Confession of Faith* (1845). Lochcarron: CFP, 1980 reprint.

Shedd, William G. T. *Calvinism: Pure and Mixed* (1893). Edinburgh: Banner of Truth, 1986 reprint.

Sibeth, Achim. *The Batak*. London: Thames and Hudson, 1991.

Silvius, John E. "Christian Stewardship of the Environment." *Creation Social Science and Humanities Society Quarterly Journal*, Vol. 10, No. 3 (Spring, 1988) 24–27.

Simpson, E. K. *Commentary on the Epistle to the Ephesians*. Grand Rapids: Eerdmans, 1957.

Smick, Elmer B. "Job." In *The Expositor's Bible Commentary*, *Vol. 4*, edited by Frank E. Gaebelein, 841–1060. Grand Rapids: Zondervan, 1990.

Socrates Scholasticus. "Ecclesiastical History." In Schaff, ed., *Nicene and Post-Nicene Fathers*, Second Series, Vol. 2, 39–396.

Spurgeon, Charles Haddon. "The Simplicity and Sublimity of Salvation." *Metropolitan Tabernacle Pulpit, Vol. 38,* Sermon 2259 (March 6, 1890).

———. *The Treasury of the New Testament*. London: Marshall, Morgan & Scott, 1934.

Stewart, Alexander. *Creeds and Churches*. London: Hodder & Stoughton, 1916.

Stewart, William. *The Faith We Confess: A Short Exposition of the Confession of Faith of the United Church of Northern India*. Madras: CLS, 1960.

Stigers, Harold G. "*ṣādeq*." In Archer et al., eds., 1879.

Still, William. *A Vision of Glory*. Glasgow: Gray, 1987.

St. John, Heidi. *Transgenderism and Demonic Possession: Is It Real?* http://heidistjohn. com/blog/podcasts/transgenderism-demonic-possession-real; and https://www. youtube.com/watch?v=7BZmnCIZDhw)

Talley, David. "*ḥpṣ*." In VanGemeren, ed., Vol. 2, 231–34.

Tenney, Merrill C. "John." In Gaebelein, ed., Vol. 9, 1–203.

Tertullian. "Exhortation to Chastity." In Roberts and Donaldson, eds., Vol. 4, 100–117.

———. "Prescription Against Heretics." In Roberts and Donaldson, eds., Vol. 3, 436–80.

Thayer, Joseph Henry. *A Greek-English Lexicon of the New Testament*. Edinburgh: T. & T. Clark, 1901.

Thomas, Derek W. H. *How the Gospel Brings Us All the Way Home*. Sanford: Ligonier, 2011.

Thomas, Robert L. "1 & 2 Thessalonians." In *The Expositor's Bible Commentary, Vol. 11*, edited by Frank E. Gaebelein, 227–337. Grand Rapids: Zondervan, 1990.

Thong, Chan Kei. *Faith of our Fathers: God in Ancient China*. Shanghai: Orient Publishing Center, 2006.

Theophilos. "To Autolycus." In Roberts and Donaldson, eds., Vol. 2, 159–235.

Toom, Tarmo. *Classical Trinitarian Theology*. New York: T. & T. Clark, 2007.

Tregelles, Samuel P., ed. *Gesenius's Hebrew and Chaldee Lexicon to the Old Testament Scriptures*. London: Bagster, 1857.

Trumper, Timothy J. R. "A Fresh Exposition of Adoption: I. An Outline," *Scottish Bulletin of Evangelical Theology*, Vol. 23, No. 1 (Spring, 2005) 60–80.

———. "A Fresh Exposition of Adoption: II. Some Implications," *Scottish Bulletin of Evangelical Theology*, Vol. 23, No. 2 (Autumn, 2005) 194–215.

———. "The Metaphorical Import of Adoption: A Plea for Realisation. I: The Adoption Metaphor in Biblical Usage." *Scottish Bulletin of Evangelical Theology*, Vol. 14, No. 2 (Autumn, 1996) 129–45.

———. "From Slaves to Sons," *Foundations*, No. 55 (Spring, 2006) 17–19.

Tsumura, David T. "*rāqiyaʿ*." In VanGemeren, ed., Vol. 3, 1198.

Turretin, Francis. *Institutes of Elenctic Theology, Vol. 2* (1682). Phillipsburg: Presbyterian & Reformed, 1994 reprint.

Unmack, Robert V. "Abide, Abiding." In Harrison, ed., 15–16.

VanGemeren, Willem A. "Psalms." In *The Expositor's Bible Commentary, Vol. 5*, edited by Frank E. Gaebelein, 3–880. Grand Rapids: Zondervan, 1991.

Van Groningen, Gerard. "*ābar*." In Archer et al., eds., 1556.

Van Pelt, Miles V., and Walter C. Kaiser. "*ml*." In VanGemeren, ed., Vol. 2, 939–41.

Vaughan, Curtis. "Colossians." In Gaebelein, ed., Vol. 11, 161–226.

Vincent, Thomas. *The Shorter Catechism Explained from Scripture* (1674). Edinburgh: Banner of Truth, 1980 reprint.

Waldron, Samuel E. *A Modern Exposition of the 1689 Baptist Confession of Faith.* Darlington: EP, 2013.

Wall, Robert W. *Colossians and Philemon.* Downers Grove: IVP, 1993.

Wallace, Daniel B. *Greek Grammar Beyond the Basics.* Grand Rapids: Zondervan, 1996.

Warfield, Benjamin B. "The Biblical Doctrine of the Trinity," In Warfield, *Biblical and Theological Studies*, 22–59. Philadelphia: Presbyterian & Reformed, 1952.

———. *Biblical Doctrines* (1929). Edinburgh: Banner of Truth, 1988 reprint.

———. *Entire Sanctification.* http://articles.ochristian.com/article12927.shtml.

———. *The Person and Work of Christ.* Philadelphia: Presbyterian & Reformed, 1950.

———. *The Plan of Salvation.* https://www.monergism.com/thethreshold/sdg/warfield/warfield_plan.html.

———. *Studies in Perfectionism.* Phillipsburg: Presbyterian & Reformed, 1958.

———. *Studies in Tertullian and Augustine* (1930). Westport: Greenwood, 1970 reprint.

Watts, Isaac. *The Glory of Christ as God-Man.* Boston: West, 1795.

Watts, John D. W. *Isaiah 1—33.* Dallas: Word, 1985.

Wax, Trevin. 'Faith in Christ' or 'Faithfulness of Christ.' https://blogs.thegospelcoalition.org/trevinwax/2011/05/23/faith-in-christ-or-faithfulness-of-christ/.

Webb, William J. *Slaves, Women & Homosexuals: Exploring the Hermeneutics of Cultural Analysis.* Downers Grove: IVP, 2001.

Webster, Peter Jonathan. "The Relationship between Religious Thought and the Theory and Practice of Church Music in England, 1603–c.1640." Ph.D. thesis, University of Sheffield, 2001.

Wells, Tom. *A Vision for Missions.* Edinburgh: Banner of Truth, 1985.

Wenham, Gordon J. *Genesis 1—15.* Dallas: Word, 1987.

Wesley, John. *Explanatory Notes upon the New Testament* (1754). London: Epworth, 1941 reprint.

———. *A Plain Account of Christian Perfection* (1767). London: Epworth, 1968 reprint.

Wessel, Walter W. "Mark." In Gaebelein, ed., Vol. 8, 601–793.

Westcott, Brooke Foss. *The Gospel According to St. John.* London: Murray, 1887.

Westminster Assembly. "The Directory for the Publick Worship of God" (1645) In *The Westminster Confession of Faith*, 369–94. Glasgow: Free Presbyterian Publications, 1985 reprint.

Whale, John Seldon. *Victor and Victim*. Cambridge: CUP, 1960.

White, L. Michael. *Christian Millennial Expectation Through the Centuries*. https:// www.pbs.org/wgbh/pages/frontline/shows/apocalypse/readings/white.html.

Wilcock, Michael. *I Saw Heaven Opened*. London: IVP, 1975.

Williams, Gary J. "Penal Substitution: A Response to Recent Criticisms." In *The Atonement Debate: Papers from the London Symposium on the Theology of Atonement*, edited by Derek Tidball et al., 172–90. Grand Rapids: Zondervan, 2008.

Williams, Tyler F. "*pqd.*" In VanGemeren, ed., Vol. 3, 657–63.

———. "*ṣwh.*" In VanGemeren, ed., Vol. 3, 776–80.

Williamson, G. I. *The Heidelberg Catechism: A Study Guide*. Phillipsburg: Presbyterian and Reformed, 1993.

———. *The Westminster Confession of Faith for Study Classes*. Philadelphia: Presbyterian & Reformed, 1964.

Wiseman, Donald J. "*yāšār.*" In Archer, et al., eds., 930.

Wolf, Herbert. "*hāgâ.*" In Archer et al., eds., 467.

Wood, Leon J. "*ḥāpēṣ.*" In Archer et al., eds., 712.

———. "*ḥāšab.*" In Archer et al., eds., 767.

Wright, David F. "Baptism at the Westminster Assembly." In Duncan, ed., 161–85.

Wright, J. Stafford. "Ecclesiastes." In Gaebelein, ed., Vol. 5, 1135–97.

Wright, N. T. *Justification: God's Plan and Paul's Vision*. London: SPCK, 2009.

———. *Paul for Everyone: 1 Corinthians*. London: SPCK, 2004.

———. *Paul for Everyone: Romans*. London: SPCK, 2004.

Yamauchi, Edwin. "*ḥānan.*" In Archer et al., eds., 694.

Youngblood, Ronald F. "1 and 2 Samuel." In Gaebelein, ed., Vol. 3, 551–1104.

———. *The Book of Genesis: An Introductory Commentary*. Grand Rapids: Baker, 1991.

Zanchi, Girolamo. *Confession of Christian Religion* (1586). Cambridge: Legat, 1599 reprint.

Zeng Shao Kai. *The Ghost of Apollinaris in Chinese Churches Today*. https://www.tapatalk. com/groups/rti/the-ghost-of-apollinaris-in-chinese-churches-today-t2097.html.

www.ingramcontent.com/pod-product-compliance
Ingram Content Group UK Ltd.
Pitfield, Milton Keynes, MK11 3LW, UK
UKHW030040181224
452508UK00004BA/5